NEW MERMAIDS

General editors:
William C. Carroll, Boston University
Brian Gibbons, University of Münster
Tiffany Stern, University of Oxford

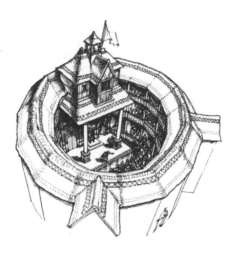

Reconstruction of an Elizabethan theatre
by C. Walter Hodges

NEW MERMAIDS

NEW MERMAIDS

WOMEN ON THE EARLY MODERN STAGE

A WOMAN KILLED WITH KINDNESS
THE TAMER TAMED
THE DUCHESS OF MALFI
THE WITCH OF EDMONTON

Introduction by Emma Smith

methuen | drama

LONDON · NEW YORK · OXFORD · NEW DELHI · SYDNEY

METHUEN DRAMA
Bloomsbury Publishing Plc
50 Bedford Square, London, WC1B 3DP, UK
1385 Broadway, New York, NY 10018, USA
29 Earlsfort Terrace, Dublin 2, Ireland

BLOOMSBURY, METHUEN DRAMA and the Methuen Drama logo are
trademarks of Bloomsbury Publishing Plc

First published in Great Britain 2014
Reprinted 2019, 2020, 2021

A catalogue record for this book is available from the British Library.

A catalog record for this book is available from the Library of Congress.

ISBN: PB: 978-1-4081-8231-4
ePDF: 978-1-4081-8232-1
eBook: 978-1-4081-8233-8

Series: Play Anthologies

Typeset by Country Setting, Kingsdown, Kent CT14 8ES
Printed and bound in Great Britain

To find out more about our authors and books visit www.bloomsbury.com
and sign up for our newsletters.

CONTENTS

ACKNOWLEDGEMENTS

This anthology brings together the texts and commentaries from individual plays in the current New Mermaids series, originally edited by Frances E. Dolan (*A Woman Killed with Kindness*), Lucy Munro (*The Tamer Tamed*), Brian Gibbons (*The Duchess of Malfi*) and Arthur F. Kinney (*The Witch of Edmonton*). The introduction to this anthology offers an overview of the four plays and their significance to the portrayal of women in the early modern theatre. The 'Notes on the Texts' are taken from the original single editions and placed at the end of the collection.

INTRODUCTION

Early Modern Women

In his account of his visit to London in 1599 from his native Switzerland, Thomas Platter quoted approvingly the proverb that 'England is a woman's paradise'. He elaborated: 'the women-folk of England, who have mostly blue-grey eyes and are fair and pretty, have far more liberty than in other lands, and know just how to make good use of it', citing their unusual freedom to 'frequent taverns or ale-houses for enjoyment'. A highlight of Platter's visit was a trip to the Globe theatre, where he 'witnessed an excellent performance of the first Emperor Julius Caesar with a cast of some fifteen people; when the play was over, they danced very marvelously and gracefully together as is their wont, two dressed as men and two as women'.[1]

Platter's experiences excerpted here draw on three distinct ideas of women: the generalised cultural category of 'woman' found in proverbial literature, which we might call 'the ideology of gender'; real women going about their business in London's streets, shops and alehouses, if indeed Platter the tourist could accurately report or interpret them ('empirical women'); and the performance of actors dressed 'as women' ('stage women'). The connection – and in some cases the disconnection – between these three concepts is a fraught and a suggestive one for students of early modern theatre, and most especially for those dramas, including the plays collected here, that have at their core questions about women's conduct and character.

There was no shortage of material from the early modern period concerned with the ideology of gender. The expanding print market was flooded with conduct literature and sermons instructing women in appropriate behaviour. Suzanne Hull condensed their main arguments into the title of her landmark study of books for women in the period 1475–1640, *Chaste, Silent & Obedient*.[2] But assessing this material requires care: what is it evidence of? Firstly, gender is always a relational concept, which requires us to understand ideas of masculinity as well as femininity. Reading conduct literature solely for its commentary on female behaviour is only half the story: there are reciprocal, although not identical, obligations on male conduct. William Gouge's *Of Domestical*

---

1 Clare Williams (trans.), *Thomas Platter's Travels in England, 1599* (London: Jonathan Cape, 1937), pp. 182–3; p. 170; p. 166.

2 Suzanne Hull, *Chaste, Silent & Obedient: English Books for Women, 1475–1640* (San Marino, CA: Huntington Library, 1982).

Duties (1622), for example, sets out 'common-mutual duties betwixt man and wife', and even as he asserts that 'it is given by nature that he should govern, she obey', he also acknowledges that 'all his actions wherein he hath to do with his wife must be seasoned with love'. Gouge articulates what is sometimes known as 'companionate marriage', a new Protestant understanding of a more mutual, but still not equal, relation within marriage, in which 'a wife is the most proper object of love: nor friend, nor child, nor parent ought so to be loved as a wife'.[3]

Certainly we can see that the emphasis in conduct literature on female behaviour suggests that this is of contemporary cultural concern, particularly to men (the repertoire of the theatre might also tell us this). But this emphasis certainly does not prove that women internalised these instructions, nor that these prescriptions describe actual behaviours. Conduct literature by definition prescribes rather than describes conduct. The analogy with contemporary conduct literature is a helpful one: historians of the future would be misled if they interpreted our own culture's preoccupation with healthy living as a sign that the early twenty-first century was the era of the health freak: as we all know, it is precisely because our behaviour is so far from ideal that the ideal needs to be so insistently promulgated. Like proverbs, then, conduct literature operates within the realm of gender ideology rather than practice: it is revealing about cultural concerns, but cannot be read as a description of women's actual behaviour. Indeed, adverse reactions from women and men in his parish in the theatre district of Blackfriars meant that Gouge had to apologise and amend some of his suggestions in the second edition of his conduct book, so 'that I might not ever by judged (as some have censured me) *an hater of women*': the book thus acknowledges that gender ideology is an ongoing and heterogeneous debate rather than fixed monolithic precept.[4]

A second source for thinking about women's role in early modern society attempts to draw from specific historical examples a sense of what was possible for women at the time. Often, this is engagingly far from the conduct-book ideal. Witness 'Captain Dorothy' Dawson, who led a number of married middle-aged women in anti-enclosure protests in Yorkshire; Anne Young, who sued her violent husband for separation at the London consistory court; Mary Frith, arraigned for dressing in male clothing; or the nameless women licensed as searchers of bodies during periods of plague in London.[5] Court records show women speaking,

---

3 William Gouge, *Of Domestical Duties* (London: 1622), title-page; p. 270; pp. 350–1.

4 William Gouge, *Of Domestical Duties* (London: 1634), p. 4.

5 Laura Gowing, *Gender Relations in Early Modern England* (Harlow: Pearson Education, 2012), pp. 150–1; pp. 127–9; p. 136.

often boldly; works in print and in manuscript show them writing, across a range of genres. Although average literacy levels were lower for women than for men, many upper-class women were highly educated: the Countess of Bridgewater owned a library of over two hundred books filled with works by Shakespeare, Jonson, Spenser, and Sidney, with sermons and religious literature alongside titles on astronomy and politics.[6] Clearly these are all differently exceptional women – orthodox female lives tend to remain unrecorded – but they make us pause at over-generalisations. Social and marital status, region, education and temperament probably differentiated early modern women more than their sex united them (modern feminism has also had to come to terms with this in its own contemporary politics). Local investigations and attention to textual and contextual specifics are needed here. Simply identifying both the impoverished old woman Elizabeth Sawyer and the aristocratic widow the Duchess of Malfi as female characters does not get us very far.

This example pre-empts the final question: how might these complex and highly differential ideas about and experiences of women relate to the early modern theatre? The theatre is, after all, a distinctly masculine sphere during this period. All actors in the public theatres were male; all playwrights, so far as we know, were male; and even audiences for the plays seem to have been male-dominated. We have no direct accounts from women of attending the theatre, so, for example, there is no female perspective on the Venetian ambassador's breathless report of being 'amongst a bevy of young women' at the Fortune theatre where a 'very elegant dame, but in a mask' performed an exciting display peeling off three layers of gloves.[7]

Representations of women on the stage (like many other aspects of early modern drama) draw as much – or perhaps more – from literature as from life: they are never simply mimetic, but always fictionalised interventions into gender debates. Writing to his friend Dudley Carleton in 1620, John Chamberlain reported that 'our pulpits ring continually of the insolence and impudence of women, and to help the matter forward the players have likewise taken them to task'.[8] But in the theatre, these debates were also negotiated via various extant and emerging generic and plot archetypes. The title-page of *The Witch of Edmonton* is transparent about this, describing the play as 'a known true story composed into a tragicomedy by diverse well-esteemed poets': real events are shaped into a

---

6 Heidi Brayman Hackel, *Reading Material in Early Modern England: Print, Gender, and Literacy* (Cambridge: Cambridge University Press, 2005), pp. 260–81.

7 Andrew Gurr, *Playgoing in Shakespeare's London* (Cambridge: Cambridge University Press, 1987), p. 231.

8 Quoted in Gurr, p. 243.

specific genre. Further, it is clear, the genre of comedy offers different possibilities for female agency than does tragedy: this tells us less about women as a category and more about how the available plotlines might work. To ask questions, therefore, about the representation of women in these plays is simultaneously to ask questions about their dramaturgy. And the means of production in the theatre, the impersonation of femininity by male actors, is also highly significant. Available women's roles do not suggest that playwrights anticipated any lack of ability in these performers, and English spectators of mixed-sex theatre elsewhere in Europe were not particularly impressed: George Sandys, visiting the theatre in Sicily in 1610, saw there that 'the parts of women are acted by women, and too naturally passionated'.[9] Our assumption that women playing women's roles would always be more compelling than transvestite performance does not seem to have been shared by early modern theatregoers.

A theatre in which gender was itself a performance was particularly well suited to the thematic exploration of gender roles, as both characters and actors put on and take off different behavioural possibilities in different contexts. In its identification of gender as performative – what you do – rather than essential – what you are – the theatre offered to early modern culture a range of improvisatory characterisations and inter-ventions into debates about the proper conduct of men and women. But the theatre was commercially successful because it was entertaining rather than didactic: these plays capitalise on the perennial appetite for stories about sexual transgression, and create a fantasy space in which the gendered behaviour of fictional men and women can be observed and enjoyed free from the need for moral judgement.

Thomas Heywood, *A Woman Killed with Kindness*

Written and first performed by Queen Anne's Men in 1603.
Printed in 1607.

> Just what did Heywood really think about the death of Anne? Whose side is he on: hers or her husband's? It's a truly ambivalent ending. It's just genius. So modern. (Katie Mitchell, director of the 2011 National Theatre production)[10]

Thomas Heywood's play *A Woman Killed with Kindness* can be read as part of a cluster of works concerned with crime and passion set in

---

9 George Sandys, *A Relation of a Journey begun An.Dom 1610* (London, 1615), pp. 245–6.
10 Katie Mitchell, *Metro*, 31 July 2011.

.middling or gentry households, often based on salaciously moralised 'true stories' circulating in pamphlet form, and known collectively as 'domestic tragedy'. Although this play does not appear to have a historical source, nevertheless, the detail of the domestic setting is crucial. It is a play full of household props, as the lengthy stage direction opening Scene VIII exemplifies; lovers flirt during an intense game of cards; the stage direction 'Enter Frankford as it were brushing the crumbs from his clothes with a napkin, and newly risen from supper' (stage direction at VIII.20) constructs the offstage space as another room in the house, anticipating the later invocation of the 'polluted bedchamber' (XIII.14) to which Anne and Wendoll withdraw in his absence. The 'blemish of my house' (XIII.119) is what the householder Frankford most fears – and Mountford echoes this in his 'blur our house that never yet was stained' (XIV.128) – while Anne's banishment from the domestic sphere appropriate to the wife is the equivalent, and foretaste, of her death.

The story of Anne Frankford's dalliance with Wendoll and her husband's response to the discovery of her infidelity is interwoven with the decline of Sir Charles Mountford, ruined after his intemperate murder of Acton's servants during a quarrel about hawking. Acton – Anne's brother – attempts to blackmail Mountford into prostituting his sister Susan in order to prevent him calling in his ruinous debts. Susan's preserved virginity, Anne's compromised chastity and Mountford's financial security are all metaphorically connected in this drama of emotional and fiscal profligacy. The disarray of the Frankford household, choreographed in the frantic movement of figures in nightgowns in Scene XIII, is juxtaposed with the following stage direction, 'Enter Sir Charles, gentlemanlike, and his sister, gentlewomanlike' (Scene XIV, opening stage direction). The play's monetary and sexual economies are inseparable, in a world which monetises chastity just as it prostitutes capital: 'my dear sister, whose chaste honour / I prize above a million. Here – nay, take her; / She's worth your money' (XIV.107–9).

At the outset, the marriage of Anne and Frankford seems to embody the companionate ideal. At their wedding celebration Mountford celebrates the 'equality / In this fair combination' (I.66–7). The intervention of Wendoll as a third party in the marriage interrupts this union, since he is attractive to both husband and wife. For Frankford he is 'a good companion' whom he has 'preferred . . . to a second place / In my opinion, and my best regard' (IV.30–4), thus interposing him in between the married couple. Anne's response is more difficult to assess, since she has no soliloquies or asides to the audience in which we might hear her authentic feelings, only the injunction to women in the audience, 'you that have yet kept / Your holy matrimonial vow unstained, / Make me your instance' (XIII.142–4). When Wendoll expresses his desire for her she appears passive: 'What shall I say? / My soul is wandering, and hath lost her way' (VI.148–9), but the inarticulate moan 'O Master Wendoll, O' (VI.150) that follows may catch her own desire more clearly. Wendoll's own tortured struggle with the morality of his wishes cannot name adultery, preferring the evasive 'such a thought' or 'the deed' (VI.2). He and Anne seem trapped in the headlights of sudden, unsought but irresistible passion. Blame is surprisingly fugitive: Anne's immediate and self-abnegating acceptance of her shame, and Wendoll's post-coital torment and his adoption of the role of the cursed Cain, substitute the agony of individual shame for external judgement.

A Woman Killed with Kindness shares with other plays of the turn of the seventeenth century an interest in the humours – those physiological elements understood to determine character and behaviour – and in particular with the interplay of excess and restraint. Passion is destructive, from Mountford's 'heat of blood' (III.49) which, 'killing both of Sir Francis his men' (stage direction III.41), 'removes me from myself' (III.50), to Wendoll's fierce recognition that 'some fury pricks me on' (VI.98). That Anne's death should be the excess of self-discipline – 'She hath plainly starved herself' (XVII.34) – is the play's final attempt to compensate for the humoral failures of its passionate plot.

John Fletcher, *The Tamer Tamed*

Written and performed c. 1609–11, perhaps by the King's Men. First printed in 1647.

> *The Tamer Tamed* is the play that all women should see, especially those who have a problem with [Shakespeare's *The Taming of*] *The Shrew*. In fact there are morals for both sexes to take on board in this play. (Steve Orme, reviewing Gregory Doran's RSC production, 2003)[11]

John Fletcher, who collaborated with Shakespeare on the co-authored *Two Noble Kinsmen* and *All is True*, engaged with his senior Kings' Men colleague in a different conversation with *The Woman's Prize, or The Tamer Tamed*. Written as a sequel, homage, and riposte to Shakespeare's own *The Taming of the Shrew* (although the necessary information about what has happened in the past is provided and audiences do not need to

---

11 British Theatre Guide, www.britishtheatreguide.info/reviews/tamertamed-rev

know this earlier play), *The Tamer Tamed* reintroduces Shakespeare's Petruchio, now widowed and about to remarry the apparently meek Maria. After the wedding, the tables are turned on the bridegroom: Maria and her women friends barricade the bedchamber and negotiate their terms. In the end, Maria's triumph over her husband is complete – even his faked death does not fool her – and from this position she and Petruchio agree a mutual, and more orthodox, basis for their future relationship. 'I have tamed ye', concedes Maria, 'And now am vowed your servant' (V.iv.45–6). It is precisely Maria's new feistiness that attracts Petruchio, as he reveals in the series of asides at the beginning of Act IV, and the play's understanding of aggressively witty repartee as a form of sexual foreplay gives it a screwball quality, akin to classic Hollywood comedies such as *Bringing up Baby* or *His Girl Friday*.

Fletcher's play draws extensively on the popular cultural trope of the 'shrew', the disobedient woman who defies male authority, particularly through her abusive speech. 'The noise at London Bridge is nothing near her', replies Sophocles to Petruchio's wary question 'She doth not talk, I hope' (I.iii.84, 82). It is a play dominated, quantitatively and qualitatively, by women. II.v is exceptional in the early modern theatre in requiring five speaking parts for women plus a further three women on stage: the use of the upper stage also puts the major female characters in a spatial position of power. Throughout, the play is fascinated by the behaviour appropriate to women – and it deftly enjoys the dramatic potential of transgressive femininity (after all, who would want to see a play about those 'chaste, silent and obedient' paragons?). The struggle over who wears the breeches – the metonym for male authority – is a running joke in the play, and one which resonates differently in an all-male theatre, where costume and gesture are the only available signifiers of femininity. The women in the play 'Dance with their coats tucked up to their bare breeches' (II.v.40), and sing that 'For the good of the commonweal / The women shall wear the breeches' (II.v.52–3), and the nightmarish memory of Petruchio's first wife has him 'hiding his breeches out of fear her ghost / Should walk and wear 'em yet' (I.i.35–6).

It is tempting, while anachronistic, to think about this apparently permissive dramatisation of powerful women in terms of modern feminism. In the modern theatre, the play has tended to be performed in repertoire with Shakespeare's *The Taming of the Shrew*, as the female rejoinder which balances out the notorious gender politics of Shakespeare's original by offering a riposte to the earlier play (such paired narratives are common in shrew literature, as in, for example, Chaucer's *Canterbury Tales*). Whether Fletcher's play endorses or satirises the women's aspirations, and whether it offers radical roles for women or trades on old stereotypes, is, however, moot. Reading the paper of the women's demands, Petruchio's response, 'As I expected: liberty and clothes' (II.v.137) – the best laugh in a 'one-joke play', as the theatre critic Michael Billington put it[12] – neutralises Maria's wifely resistance into a readily available narrative of women's trivial consumerism: 'New coaches', 'Hangings', 'jewels for her private use' and French lessons all feature as girly must-haves (II.v.141–5), and the 'liberty' here seems to be merely the freedom to go shopping. But Maria also wants to commission epic wall-decorations 'of the civil wars of France' (III.ii.107), and articulates the ideal of equal marriage as the union of equal persons: 'take two small drops of water, equal weighed' (III.ii.150). Act IV opens with Petruchio and Jacques ruefully surveying the damage to the house and its furnishings during the skirmish, identifying men with the conventionally female sphere of the home and the women with house-breaking rather than house-keeping. The women also use their advantage to negotiate Livia's marriage to her preferred suitor Roland, rather than the elderly pantaloon Moroso, suggesting a broader sense of female agency. What is most powerful about Fletcher's dramaturgy is its sense of collective female action, particularly in the play's central scenes. Often romantic comedy shows the friendship of its female characters severed by rivalry or jealousy: Fletcher instead depicts a powerful sorority. He even allows 'Colonel Bianca' (I.iii.70), who imagines herself an Aeneas seeking a new land 'Where, like a race of noble Amazons, / We'll root ourselves and to our endless glory / Live and despise base men' (II.i.37–9), that most unusual outcome for a woman in a comedy – remaining unmarried.

John Webster, *The Duchess of Malfi*

Written and performed by the King's Men at Blackfriars, 1614.
First published 1623.

> Womanly. Mother. Lusty. Reckless. Courageous. Honourable. Autocratic. Wilful. Democratic. Deceiving. Beautiful. Cunning. Dazzling. Wise. A healthy set of contradictions, but you see how hard it is to avoid value judgements? Try again. Italian. Dark eyed (I've got that bit anyway). Flared nostrils. Thoroughbred horse. Active not pensive. Hot blood. Dark, from the same crucible as her brother. (Actor Harriet Walter, on preparing her role as the Duchess)[13]

12 Michael Billington, *The Guardian*, 11 April 2003, review of Gregory Doran's production for the Royal Shakespeare Company.

John Webster's *The Duchess of Malfi* tells the story of the eponymous Duchess, a widow who marries her steward Antonio in secret and against the express wishes of her strongly controlling brothers, Ferdinand and the Cardinal, that she will not take another husband. Ferdinand's spy Bosola, planted in the Duchess's household, betrays the couple, leading to the Duchess's murder, and an increasingly confused sequence of deaths at the play's conclusion. Webster's plot is based on a historical story given a strongly moralistic gloss in its English retellings. Thomas Beard's *The Theatre of Gods Judgements* (1597) lists it under the heading 'of whoredomes committed under colour of marriage', suggesting that the Cardinal is an agent of God's justice.[14] In William Painter's *The Palace of Pleasure*, the blame is placed on the Duchess – for being a lusty widow who 'waxed very weary of lying alone' – and on Antonio, who has ambitiously transgressed his proper social position: 'we ought never to climb higher than our force permitteth, nor yet surmount the bounds of duty, and less suffer ourselves to be haled fondly forth with desire of brutal sensuality'.[15]

Webster's play certainly does not perpetuate this moralising, but nor does it completely recast the play's central couple as heroic. The Duchess herself is presented ambivalently, tricking Antonio into marriage while remaining at an anonymous distance from the audience and defined by the rank of her first, noble husband. On the other hand, though, there are many more sympathetic aspects to her presentation: the intimacy of the domestic scene in which the couple and the Duchess's servant Cariola joke together, for example, and the immense stoicism of her death. She refuses to be broken by the lunatic pageant arranged by Ferdinand: 'I am Duchess of Malfi still' (IV.ii.130) – and her last words remember her children in touching detail: 'look thou giv'st my little boy / Some syrup for his cold' (IV.ii.190–1). The very different death of Cariola, begging for mercy, seems designed to emphasise the Duchess's self-possession and grace. In the theatre, the scene of the Duchess's murder cannot possibly produce Painter's moral that her lusty behaviour deserved such a punishment. As one of the play's commendatory verses, published before the text of the play in the quarto of 1623, asks, 'whoe'er saw this Duchess live and die / That could get off under a bleeding eye?' The play's inconsistent attitudes to the Duchess may suggest its own struggle with what she represents, and with the impossibility of reconciling her own aspiration to self-governance with the patriarchal world in which she, and her

---

13 Martin White, *Renaissance Drama in Action: An Introduction to Aspects of Theatre Practice and Performance* (London: Routledge, 1998), p. 89.

14 Thomas Beard, *The Theatre of Gods Judgements* (London, 1597), pp. 321–3.

15 William Painter, *The Second Tome of the Palace of Pleasure* (London, 1567), p. 173; p. 194.

Jacobean audience, largely live. Audiences then, as now, probably reacted diversely: the real-life parallel of Arbella Stuart, a cousin of King James, who married a lower-status man against the King's command, is instructive. As Sara Jayne Steen has shown, indulgent sympathy for the romance of this couple's story in some quarters was matched by condemnation elsewhere, and the same may well have been true about attitudes to the Duchess's behaviour.[16]

Perhaps, then, we can see the play's own hiccups and plot inconsistencies less as a failure of Websterian craftsmanship and more as a document of contemporary cultural uncertainty. With the laughter in the theatre when Delio, hearing news of the Duchess's exponentially growing family, remarks 'Methinks 'twas yesterday' (III.i.8), the play seems to enjoy a metatheatrical joke about its own potentially ludicrously elastic timescale. But the Duchess's excessive fertility is not just comic in terms of raising a laugh, it is comic generically: if tragedy is the genre associated with death and destruction, comedy is associated with rebirth, with spring, with new futures. Through this outbreak of children in the middle of the play, the Duchess, and the tragedy that bears her name, seem to be trying to elude the narrative logic of the story in which they find themselves – making a last-ditch attempt to recuperate the story as comedy rather than tragedy. The children are indeed incongruous, though not primarily because the timescale is all compressed but because they belong to another, incompatible genre.

Theatrical self-consciousness is a feature of the play's conclusion. Bosola, the marginal intelligencer who is the play's dominant character, is a curious admixture: part the manipulative amorality of Shakespeare's Iago; part the bleak metaphysical intelligence of John Donne. At the play's conclusion, Bosola is asked how Antonio died. 'In a mist', replies the fatally wounded Bosola. 'I know not how; / Such a mistake as I have often seen / In a play' (V.v.93–5). Bosola's understanding of himself as an actor who does not understand, or need to understand, the role in which he finds himself, may have an affinity with the theatre practice whereby actors had their own lines and their cues (rather than access to the whole text). But his admission seems to cast the play in an absurdist frame in its conclusion. Bosola's characteristic ability to stand outside situations – to comment on them from the sidelines, to remain aloof from their sentimental connotations, to present himself as a gun for hire – is here turned sceptically on the play itself. He may thus embody the play's ultimate ambivalence to the story it tells, and his sudden repentance of

16 Sara Jayne Steen, 'The Crime of Marriage: Arbella Stuart and *The Duchess of Malfi*', *The Sixteenth Century Journal* 22 (1991), pp. 61–76.

his work with the Duchess's brothers stands in for the play's own squeamishness about the inevitable end of the moralising story it has chosen to retell.

Thomas Dekker, John Ford and William Rowley, *The Witch of Edmonton*

Written and performed by Prince Charles' Men in 1621.
First published in 1658.

> In the case of Elizabeth, we're not entirely sure what crimes she is responsible for, or the extent to which the townspeople turn her into the vengeful harpy she becomes. Guilt, it seems, is a gray zone in Edmonton. (Review of Jesse Berger's 2011 Production for the Red Bull Theater, New York)[17]

The source for Dekker, Ford and Rowley's play *The Witch of Edmonton* is a pamphlet written by Henry Goodcole, the visitor of Newgate prison, published shortly after the execution of Elizabeth Sawyer as a witch at Tyburn in 1621, and it forms part of an excitable range of topical publications about the trial. The play's title clearly capitalises on contemporary interest, slightly misleadingly, since Sawyer's part is the minor one. The dominant plot is that of reluctant bigamist Frank Thorney, who is secretly married to a fellow servant Winifred, but coerced into a second marriage to Susan, whose substantial dowry can save his father from ruin. Elizabeth Sawyer's plot has a comic, burlesque tone. The character of Dog, her familiar, is a compelling figure on stage, and her interactions with the rustic Cuddy and his morris dancing friends seem to construct her as the comedy subplot to the anxious melodrama of Thorney's marriages. But Elizabeth Sawyer and Frank are alike in one crucial respect: each is forced into aberrant behaviour by the pressures of social expectation, in a play preoccupied with the intersection between individual responsibility and social pressures. Frank finds himself victim of a situation in which he cannot do the right thing: he must either abandon Winifred or his father's hopes; similarly, Sawyer's choices – to be a witch or to be called a witch – are no choice at all. When the devil-dog 'rubs' Frank (stage direction, III.iii.14), prompting and shaping his inchoate plan to murder Susan, it is hard to know whether he should be understood as a manifestation of Frank's unconscious desires or an external image of evil, and whether the crime is human or diabolic in origin. Since the dog operates independently of Elizabeth Sawyer it seems as if she is acted

17 Ben Brantley, *New York Times*, 4 February 2011.

upon, rather than acting: her agency is to inhabit the role that has been forced on her by the community: 'Some call me witch . . . This they enforce upon me. And in part / Make me to credit it' (II.i.8–15). The dog preys on her while she is 'cursing' (II.i.120) and wishing revenge on her neighbours – the encounter in the play chosen for the illustration on the first printed edition of 1658 – and thus confirms the perverse allegiance between the diabolic and the community: both want to claim Elizabeth Sawyer as a witch, and so she has little choice but to accede.

Edmonton, a small village to the north-east of early modern London, is a realised rural community. It may be that the play's title is more important in its emphasis on place than on witchcraft: Sawyer may come to serve as the focus for communal discontents but she is hardly their originator – the head of this closely realised and stratified society, Sir Arthur Clarington, is engaged in an adulterous relationship with his servant Winifred for which he undergoes only mild punishment. Rural life is difficult and financially precarious: the Thorney family troubles are echoed in the farmers' worries about their livestock, and witchcraft provides a ready excuse for small but crucial mishaps and problems, such as the burning thatch or Anne Radcliffe's mental health. This representation of rural life was constructed for an urban audience who may well have believed themselves sophisticates (and the play had a performance at court at the end of December 1621). The play deftly has it both ways on the contemporary debate about witchcraft. In presenting Elizabeth Sawyer's witchcraft as the construct of a superstitious community, the play subscribes to the learned scepticism which was beginning to understand the accusation of witchcraft as social or physiological, rather than demonic. But in its deployment of the panoply of witchcraft tropes including the blood bargain, the play can also indulge its audience in the theatrical enjoyment of scenes of possession and diabolically inspired evil – a dramatic fashion dubbed by Diane Purkiss the 'Jacobean witch-vogue'. Both witch-accusers and the witch are constructed as 'crude, unlearned, ugly, illiterate, irrational, and deeply unfashionable'.[18] This is a deeply human vision of the cultural work of supernatural belief in a small community. At the end of the play there is some forgiveness for what has passed, as the execution of Sawyer makes her into Edmonton's final scapegoat, and allows Frank to be readmitted into the community where 'Harms past may be lamented, not redressed' (V.iii.170).

---

18 Diane Purkiss, *The Witch in History: Early Modern and Twentieth-Century Representations* (London: Routledge, 1996), p. 199; p. 232.

Reading the Plays Today

A woman who takes on the role of witch placed on her by her community; a woman sexually drawn towards a house guest and thus to the destruction of her domestic life; a woman who revisits a dramatic narrative of patriarchal control while barricaded with a troop of female accomplices in her honeymoon suite; a woman who marries against family strictures and suffers the consequences: written over two decades, these four plays attest to the lively range of representations of women in the Jacobean theatre. They share an interest in women as dramatic agents but cast this agency in quite different terms. From the psychology of communal alienation for Elizabeth Sawyer, to the struggle against the didacticism of the source for *The Duchess of Malfi*, and from the tension of Fletcher's (and Maria's) rewriting of Shakespeare's gender politics to Heywood's depiction of Anne and Susan as contrasting wives, these plays make it impossible to uphold a monolithic idea of early modern gender. And further, all these plays – particularly *The Duchess of Malfi* – have enjoyed modern stage success. While they capture aspects of early seventeenth-century ideological struggles, therefore, the ambiguities of their social worlds map on to continuing questions of gender, representation, and agency, and their theatrical confidence confirms their ongoing vitality.

FURTHER READING

Texts

For excellent introductions to the themes of the plays and to questions of textual transmission, the individual New Mermaids editions are highly recommended: Lucy Munro's *The Tamer Tamed* (2010), Brian Gibbons's *The Duchess of Malfi* (2001), Frances Dolan's *A Woman Killed with Kindness* (2012), and Arthur F. Kinney's *The Witch of Edmonton* (1998).

Women and Early Modern Culture

Kate Aughterson (ed.), *Renaissance Woman: Constructions of Femininity in England* (Routledge: London, 1995)

Alison Findlay, *A Feminist Perspective on Renaissance Drama* (Oxford: Blackwell, 1999)

Laura Gowing, *Gender Relations in Early Modern England* (Harlow: Pearson Education, 2012)

Karen Newman, *Fashioning Femininity and English Renaissance Drama* (Chicago: University of Chicago Press, 1991)

A Woman Killed With Kindness

Allison P. Hobgood, *Passionate Playgoing in Early Modern England* (forthcoming, Cambridge University Press, 2014)

Jennifer Panek, 'Punishing Adultery in *A Woman Killed With Kindness*', *Studies in English Literature* 34 (1994), 358–78

Catherine Richardson, 'Properties of Domestic Life: The table in Heywood's *A Woman Killed With Kindness*', Jonathan Gil Harris and Natasha Korda (eds), *Staged Properties in Early Modern English Drama* (Cambridge: Cambridge University Press, 2002), 129–52

The Tamer Tamed

Celia Daileader, *Eroticism on the Renaissance Stage: Transcendence, Desire, and the Limits of the Visible* (Cambridge: Cambridge University Press, 1998)

Karen Kettnich, '*The Tamer Tamed*: a Dramaturg's Perspective', *Shakespeare* 7 (2011), 361–8

Molly Easo Smith, 'John Fletcher's Response to the Gender Debate: *The Woman's Prize* and *The Taming of the Shrew*', *Papers on Language & Literature*, 31 (1995), 38–60

The Duchess of Malfi

Dympna Callaghan, '*The Duchess of Malfi* and early modern widows', Garrett A. Sullivan, Patrick Cheney and Andrew Hadfield (eds), *Early Modern English Drama: A Critical Companion* (Oxford: Oxford University Press, 2005)

Judith Haber, '*The Duchess of Malfi*: Tragedy and gender', Emma Smith and Garrett A. Sullivan (eds), *The Cambridge Companion to English Renaissance Tragedy* (Cambridge: Cambridge University Press, 2010), 236–48

Christina Luckyj (ed), *The Duchess of Malfi: A Critical Guide* (New York: Continuum, 2011)

The Witch of Edmonton

Roberta Barker, '"An Honest Dog Yet": Performing *The Witch of Edmonton*', *Early Theatre: A Journal Associated with the Records of Early English Drama*, 12 (2009), 263–82

Anthony B. Dawson, 'Witchcraft/Bigamy: Cultural Conflict in *The Witch of Edmonton*', *Renaissance Drama* 20 (1989), 77–98

David Nicol, 'Interrogating the Devil: Social and demonic pressure in *The Witch of Edmonton*', *Comparative Drama* 38 (2004), 425–46

ABBREVIATIONS

Baskervill C. R. Baskervill, V. V. Heltzel, and A. H. Nethercot, eds, *Elizabethan and Stuart Plays* (New York, 1934)

Bates K. L. Bates, ed., *A Woman Killed with Kindness and The Fair Maid of the West* (Boston, 1917)

Bentley G. E. Bentley, *The Jacobean and Caroline Stage* (Oxford, 1941–68)

Bowers Fredson Bowers, ed., *The Dramatic Works of Thomas Dekker*, vol. 3 (Cambridge, 1958)

Brown John Russell Brown, ed., *The Duchess of Malfi*, Revels Plays (London, 1964)

Chappell W. Chappell, ed., rev. H. E. Wooldridge, *Old English Popular Music* (London, 1893)

Daileader Celia R. Daileader and Gary Taylor, eds, *The Tamer*
and Taylor *Tamed, or The Woman's Prize*, Revels Student Editions (Manchester, 2006)

Dent R. W. Dent, *Proverbial Language in English Drama Exclusive of Shakespeare, 1495–1616: An Index* (Berkeley, 1984)

Dodsley James Dodsley, ed., *Select Collection of Old Plays*, vol. 4 (London, 1744)

Forker Charles Forker, *The Skull beneath the Skin* (Carbondale, 1995)

Genest John Genest, *Some Account of the English Stage, from the Restoration in 1660 to 1830*, 10 vols (Bath, 1832)

Harris Anthony Harris, *Night's Black Agents: Witchcraft and Magic in Seventeenth-Century English Drama* (Manchester, 1980)

Hoy Cyrus Hoy, *Introductions, Notes, and Commentaries to Texts in the Dramatic Works of Thomas Dekker* (Cambridge, 1980)

Livingston Meg Powers Livingston, ed., *The Woman's Prize by John Fletcher*, Malone Society Reprints, vol. 172 (Manchester, 2008 for 2007)

Lopez Jeremy Lopez, *Theatrical Convention and Audience Response in Early Modern Drama* (Cambridge, 2003)

Lucas F. L. Lucas, ed., *The Complete Works of John Webster* (London, 1927)

Luckyj Christina Luckyj, ed., *The Duchess of Malfi: A Critical Guide* (New York, 2011)

Marcus Leah Marcus, ed., *The Duchess of Malfi*, Arden Early Modern Drama (London, 2009)

Mason	John Monck Mason, *Comments on the Plays of Beaumont and Fletcher* (London, 1798)
MLR	*Modern Language Review*
Montaigne	Michel de Montaigne, *The essayes or morall, politike and millitarie discourses*, trans. J. Florio (1603)
N&Q	*Notes and Queries*
NCW	*The Works of John Webster*, ed. David Carnegie, D. C. Gunby and Antony Hammond (Cambridge, 1995)
Norton	*English Renaissance Drama: A Norton Anthology*, ed. David Bevington *et al.* (New York, 2002)
OED	*Oxford English Dictionary*
Orlin	Lena Cowen Orlin, *Private Matters and Public Culture in Post-Reformation England* (Ithaca, 1994)
Pliny	(Caius Plinius secundus,) *The historie of the world*, trans. P. Holland (1601)
RES	*Review of English Studies*
Sidney, *Works*	*The Complete Works of Sir Philip Sidney*, ed. A. Feuillerat (Cambridge, 1912–26)
Sugden	Edward Holdsworth Sugden, *A Topographical Dictionary to the Works of Shakespeare and His Fellow Dramatists* (London, 1925)
Thomas	Keith Thomas, *Religion and the Decline of Magic* (Harmondsworth, 1978, 1988)
Tilley	M. P. Tilley, *A Dictionary of the Proverbs in England in the Sixteenth and Seventeenth Centuries* (Ann Arbor, 1950)
Van Fossen	R. W. Van Fossen, ed., *A Woman Killed with Kindness*, Revels Plays (London, 1961)
Verity	A. W. Verity, ed., *Thomas Heywood* (London, 1888)
Wiggin	Pauline G. Wiggin, *An Inquiry into the Authorship of the Middleton-Rowley Plays* (Boston, 1897)
Williams	Gordon Williams, *A Dictionary of Sexual Language and Imagery in Shakespearean and Stuart Literature*, 4 vols (London, 1994)

A
WOMAN
KILDE
with Kindneſſe.

Written by Tho: Heywood.

LONDON
Printed by William Iaggard dwelling in Barbican, and
are to be ſold in Paules Church-yard.
by Iohn Hodgets. 1607.

[DRAMATIS PERSONAE

JOHN FRANKFORD
ANNE FRANKFORD, *his wife, sister of Sir Francis Acton*
WENDOLL, *friend of Frankford*
SIR CHARLES MOUNTFORD
SUSAN MOUNTFORD, *his sister*   5
SIR FRANCIS ACTON
CRANWELL, *friend of Frankford*
MALBY, *friend of Sir Francis*
OLD MOUNTFORD, *uncle of Sir Charles*
TYDY, *cousin of Sir Charles*   10
SANDY, *former friend of Sir Charles*
RODER, *former tenant of Sir Charles*
SHAFTON, *false friend of Sir Charles*
NICK, *servant of Frankford*
JENKIN, *servant of Frankford*   15
SPIGGOT, *Frankford's butler*
SISLY MILK-PAIL, *servingwoman to Frankford*
ROGER BRICKBAT }
JACK SLIME } *country fellows, Frankford's farm servants*
JOAN MINIVER }   20
JANE TRUBKIN } *country wenches, Frankford's farm servants*
ISBEL MOTLEY }
SHERIFF
KEEPER
SERGEANT   25
MUSICIANS, HUNTSMEN, FALCONERS, SERVINGMEN,
SERVING WOMEN, CARTERS, COACHMAN, FRANKFORD'S
CHILDREN, OFFICERS]

THE PROLOGUE

I come but like a harbinger, being sent
To tell you what these preparations mean:
Look for no glorious state, our muse is bent
Upon a barren subject, a bare scene.
We could afford this twig a timber tree,   5
Whose strength might boldly on your favours build;
Our russet, tissue; drone, a honey-bee;
Our barren plot, a large and spacious field;
Our coarse fare, banquets; our thin water, wine;
Our brook, a sea; our bat's eyes, eagle's sight;   10
Our poet's dull and earthy muse, divine;
Our ravens, doves; our crow's black feathers, white.
    But gentle thoughts when they may give the foil,
    Save them that yield, and spare where they may spoil.

1–14   Cf. Shakespeare's Prologue to *Henry V*.
   1   *like* Q1 (as Q3).
   5   *afford* put forward, present.
   7   *Our russet, tissue* i.e. that our plain clothes were fine.
  13   *gentle* of gentlemen, and women. A reflection upon the implied social status and
       breeding of the audience.
       give the foil bring about the overthrow or defeat. The term comes from wrestling
       (*OED*), where it signifies something less than a *fall*.
  14   *spoil* destroy.

[SCENE I]

Enter MASTER JOHN FRANKFORD, SIR FRANCIS ACTON,
MISTRESS ANNE FRANKFORD, SIR CHARLES MOUNTFORD,
MASTER MALBY, MASTER WENDOLL, *and* MASTER CRANWELL

SIR FRANCIS
  Some music there! None lead the bride a dance?
SIR CHARLES
  Yes, would she dance 'The Shaking of the Sheets'.
  But that's the dance her husband means to lead her.
WENDOLL
  That's not the dance that every man must dance
  According to the ballad.
SIR FRANCIS   Music ho!   5
  By your leave, sister – by your husband's leave
  I should have said – the hand that but this day
  Was given you in the church, I'll borrow. Sound,
  This marriage music hoists me from the ground.
FRANKFORD
  Aye, you may caper, you are light and free.   10
  Marriage hath yoked my heels, pray then pardon me.
SIR FRANCIS
  I'll have you dance too, brother.
SIR CHARLES   Master Frankford,
  You are a happy man, sir, and much joy
  Succeed your marriage mirth. You have a wife
  So qualified, and with such ornaments   15
  Both of the mind and body. First, her birth
  Is noble, and her education such

---

2 *'The Shaking of the Sheets'* a popular ballad tune, here referred to with a bawdy *double
   entendre*. In the ballad the dance is that of the dying (see Wendoll's remark in l. 4),
   which in its turn strikes an appropriately ominous note in the play, anticipating
   Frankford's 'a cold grave must be our nuptial bed' (Scene XVII, 123).

5 *According to the ballad* See the note on l. 2. The relevant lines from the ballad are 'Can
   you dance the shaking of the sheets, / A dance that every man must do?' See
   Chappell, I, 228.
   Music ho! For the thematic significance of music in the play see Cecile W. Cary, '"Go
   Break Thus Lute": Music in Heywood's *A Woman Killed with Kindness*', *Huntington
   Library Quarterly*, 37 (1974), pp. 111–22.

11 *pray then pardon me* Q1 (pray pardon me Q3).

As might become the daughter of a prince,
Her own tongue speaks all tongues, and her own hand
Can teach all strings to speak in their best grace,   20
From the shrill treble, to the hoarsest base.
To end her many praises in one word,
She's beauty and perfection's eldest daughter,
Only found by yours, though many a heart hath sought her.

FRANKFORD

But that I know your virtues and chaste thoughts,   25
I should be jealous of your praise, Sir Charles.

CRANWELL

He speaks no more than you approve.

MALBY

Nor flatters he that gives to her her due.

ANNE

I would your praise could find a fitter theme
Than my imperfect beauty to speak on;   30
Such as they be, if they my husband please,
They suffice me now I am married.
His sweet content is like a flattering glass,
To make my face seem fairer to mine eye,
But the least wrinkle from his stormy brow,   35
Will blast the roses in my cheeks that grow.

SIR FRANCIS

A perfect wife already, meek and patient.
How strangely the word 'husband' fits your mouth,
Not married three hours since, sister. Tis good;
You that begin betimes thus, must needs prove   40
Pliant and duteous in your husband's love.
Godamercies, brother, wrought her to it already?
'Sweet husband,' and a courtesy the first day?
Mark this, mark this, you that are bachelors,
And never took the grace of honest man,   45
Mark this against you marry, this one phrase:

---

21   *shrill* Q1 (shrill'st Q3).
27   *approve* show to be true (by marrying her).
36   *blast* wither, blight, shrivel.
42   *Godamercies* Q1 (Gramercies Q3).
43   *courtesy* curtsy, a gesture of submission.
45   *took the grace of honest man* i.e. married, became husband.
46   *against* 'in anticipation of the time when' (Van Fossen).

'In a good time that man both wins and woos
That takes his wife down in her wedding shoes.'

FRANKFORD

Your sister takes not after you, Sir Francis.
All his wild blood your father spent on you;   50
He got her in his age when he grew civil.
All his mad tricks were to his land entailed,
And you are heir to all. Your sister, she
Hath to her dower her mother's modesty.

SIR CHARLES

Lord sir, in what a happy state live you;   55
This morning, which to many seems a burden
Too heavy to bear, is unto you a pleasure.
This lady is no clog, as many are.
She doth become you like a well-made suit
In which the tailor hath used all his art,   60
Not like a thick coat of unseasoned frieze,
Forced on your back in summer. She's no chain
To tie your neck, and curb you to the yoke,
But she's a chain of gold to adorn your neck.
You both adore each other, and your hands   65
Methinks are matches. There's equality
In this fair combination; you are both scholars,
Both young, both being descended nobly:
There's music in this sympathy; it carries
Consort and expectation of much joy,   70

---

48   *takes . . . shoes* asserts superiority over her from the first day of their marriage. The
      phrase appears to be proverbial, though not in *Tilley* or the *Oxford Dictionary of
      Proverbs*. Van Fossen cites an instance in Dekker.
50   *spent on you* used engendering you, and therefore bequeathed you. Sir Francis's
      actions in the play would tend to confirm that he has inherited his father's rashness,
      as here suggested by Frankford.
51   *civil* decent, sober, responsible.
52   *to his land entailed* bestowed inseparably with the land; who inherited the one,
      inherited the other.
54   *dower* dowry.
58   *clog* an impediment attached to the heels or necks of prisoners to prevent escape, a
      block of wood, here used figuratively.
61   *unseasoned frieze* a thick coarse woollen cloth, worn out of season.
63   *curb* Q3 (curbs Q1).
65   *adore* Q1 (adorne Q3).
69   *sympathy* harmony, concord.
70   *Consort* accord, agreement, concurrence.

Which God bestow on you, from this first day
Until your dissolution – that's for aye.

SIR FRANCIS

We keep you here too long, good brother Frankford.
Into the hall! Away, go cheer your guests!
What, bride and bridegroom both withdrawn at once?   75
If you be missed, the guests will doubt their welcome
And charge you with unkindness!

FRANKFORD   To prevent it,
I'll leave you here, to see the dance within.

ANNE

And so will I.

SIR FRANCIS   To part you it were sin.

                    [*Exeunt* FRANKFORD *and* ANNE]

Now gallants, while the town musicians   80
Finger their frets within, and the mad lads
And country lasses, every mother's child
With nose-gays and bride-laces in their hats,
Dance all their country measures, rounds and jigs,
What shall we do? Hark, they are all on the hoigh;   85
They toil like mill-horses, and turn as round,
Marry, not on the toe. Ay, and they caper,
But without cutting. You shall see tomorrow
The hall floor pecked and dinted like a millstone,
Made with their high shoes; though their skill be small,   90
Yet they tread heavy where their hobnails fall.

SIR CHARLES

Well, leave them to their sports. Sir Francis Acton,
I'll make a match with you: meet me tomorrow
At Chevy Chase, I'll fly my hawk with yours.

SIR FRANCIS

For what? for what?

---

83 *bride-laces* laces of gold silk formerly used to tie nosegays in the hats of wedding
    guests. 'A nosegay bound with laces in his hat, bridelaces, sir' cited in *OED* from
    Porter's *Angry Woman of Abingdon* (1599).
85 *on the hoigh* eager, excited.
86 *turn as round* the horse driving a mill turned only by plodding round in a circle.
88 *cutting OED* records that to cut in dancing was to 'spring from the ground, and while
    in the air to twiddle the feet one in front of the other alternatively, with great
    rapidity.' The first instance of this sense is given from Florio in 1603.
93 *me* Q1 (*omitted* Q3).
94 *Chevy Chase* the place-name is apparently derived from the ballad of that name,
    which gives an account of a famous border skirmish.

SIR CHARLES	Why, for a hundred pound.	95

SIR FRANCIS
Pawn me some gold of that.

SIR CHARLES   Here are ten angels,
I'll make them good a hundred pound tomorrow
Upon my hawk's wing.

SIR FRANCIS   'Tis a match, 'tis done.
Another hundred pound upon your dogs,
Dare you Sir Charles?

SIR CHARLES   I dare. Were I sure to lose,   100
I durst do more than that: here's my hand,
The first course for a hundred pound.

SIR FRANCIS   A match.

WENDOLL
Ten angels on Sir Francis Acton's hawk;
As much upon his dogs.

CRANWELL
I am for Sir Charles Mountford, I have seen   105
His hawk and dog both tried. What, clap you hands?
Or is't no bargain?

WENDOLL   Yes, and stake them down,
Were they five hundred they were all my own.

SIR FRANCIS
Be stirring early with the lark tomorrow.
I'll rise into my saddle ere the sun   110
Rise from his bed.

SIR CHARLES   If there you miss me, say
I am no gentleman: I'll hold my day.

SIR FRANCIS
It holds on all sides. Come, tonight let's dance;
Early tomorrow let's prepare to ride.
We had need be three hours up before the bride.   115

                                        [*Exeunt*]

---

96   *Pawn* deposit as security for the wager, pledge.
       angels a gold coin.
102   *course* race or competition between two hounds after game.
106   *clap* shake (to seal the wager).
107   *stake them down* deposit as a pledge in the wager.
112   *hold my day* keep my appointment.

[SCENE II]

Enter NICK *and* JENKIN, JACK SLIME, ROGER BRICKBAT
with COUNTRY WENCHES [*including* SISLY MILK-PAIL],
and TWO *or* THREE MUSICIANS

JENKIN

Come Nick, take you Joan Miniver to trace withall; Jack Slime,
traverse you with Sisly Milk-pail. I will take Jane Trubkin, and
Roger Brickbat shall have Isbel Motley, and now that they are
busy in the parlour, come, strike up, we'll have a crash here in the
yard.   5

NICK

My humour is not compendious: dancing I possess not, though
I can foot it; yet since I am fallen into the hands of Sisly Milk-
pail, I assent.

JACK SLIME

Truly Nick, though we were never brought up like serving
courtiers, yet we have been brought up with serving creatures, ay   10
and God's creatures too, for we have been brought up to serve
sheep, oxen, horses and hogs, and such like. And though we be
but country fellows, it may be in the way of dancing, we can do
the horse-trick as well as servingmen.

 0.3   s.d. TWO *or* THREE MUSICIANS An evidence of authorial foul papers as copy for Q1,
     since such vagueness would not normally be characteristic of any manuscript used
     in the playhouse.

  1   *trace* dance.

  2   *traverse* 'to march up and down, or to move the feet with proportion, as in dancing'
     Bullokar, *An English Expositor* (1616).

  4   *crash* a bout of revelry, amusement.

  6   *humour* temperament.
     compendious presumably an error for 'comprehensive'.

  8   *assent* Q1 (consent Q3).

9–10 *like serving courtiers* i.e. like gentlemen.

 10   *with serving creatures* to feed and tend the livestock, playing alliteratively on
     creature/courtier.

 12   *horses and hogs* Q1 (Horses, Hogges Q3).

13–14 *country fellows . . . horse-trick* It is difficult to ignore the possibility of unconscious
     bawdry here, or indeed a deliberate play on words. The term *servant* was a courtly
     term for a lover, and has also (in addition to the sense of *domestic attendant*) a
     frankly sexual application. There is also a likely pun on horse/whores. The passage
     as a whole is a defence of the farm labourers against the more 'courtly' household
     servants.

ROGER BRICKBAT

    Ay, and the cross-point too.   15

JENKIN

    O Slime, O Brickbat! Do not you know that comparisons are
    odious? Now we are odious ourselves too, therefore there are no
    comparisons to be made betwixt us.

NICK

    I am sudden and not superfluous;
    I am quarrelsome, and not seditious;   20
    I am peaceable, and not contentious;
    I am brief, and not compendious.
    Slime, foot it quickly. If the music overcome not my melancholy
    I shall quarrel, and if they suddenly do not strike up, I shall pre-
    sently strike thee down.   25

JENKIN

    No quarrelling for God's sake: truly, if you do, I shall set a knave
    between you.

JACK SLIME

    I come to dance, not to quarrel. Come, what shall it be? 'Rogero'?

JENKIN

    'Rogero'? No, we will dance 'The Beginning of the World'.

SISLY

    I love no dance so well as 'John, Come Kiss Me Now'.   30

---

15   *cross-point* a dance step, but also with bawdy possibilities.
17   *odious* presumably he means 'we too are servants, inferiors', but with a play on
     odorous, glancing at the intimacy of Slime with his sheep, oxen, horses and hogs.
19   *sudden* peremptory, prompt.
     superfluous inclined to do more than is necessary.
20   *seditious* turbulent, causing trouble.
22   *compendious* Nick would appear to be carried away by the flow of his own rhetoric.
     This word of course means 'brief' with the sense of economical, succinct, concise.
     How he might conceive of it as a demerit is not clear. See above (line 6) where his
     misunderstanding of the word is again assumed.
23   *Slime, foot it* Q1 (*Slime.* Foot it Q3 – as though it were a new speech attributed to
     Slime) The confusion in Q3 comes from the setting of Q1 which sets lines 19–22 as
     verse, and then begins a prose line with this phrase. Q1 does not however indent
     Slime as is its practice with speech-heads.
28   Q1 reads *'Slime.* I come . . . ' without an indented speech-head; perhaps the speech
     makes one very full line.
     'Rogero' A popular tune.
29   *'The Beginning of the World'* An alternative name for 'Sellenger's Round', another
     popular tune.
30   *'John . . . Now'* Another popular tune of the day.

NICK

I, that have ere now deserved a cushion, call for 'The Cushion Dance'.

ROGER BRICKBAT

For my part, I like nothing so well as 'Tom Tyler'.

JENKIN

No, we'll have 'The Hunting of the Fox'.

JACK SLIME

'The Hay', 'The Hay', there's nothing like 'The Hay'.   35

NICK

I have said, I do say, and I will say again –

JENKIN

Every man agree to have it as Nick says.

ALL

Content.

NICK

It hath been, it now is, and it shall be –

SISLY

What Master Nichlas, what?   40

NICK

'Put on Your Smock a Monday'.

JENKIN

So the dance will come cleanly off. Come, for God's sake agree of something! If you like not that, put it to the musicians or let me speak for all, and we'll have 'Sellenger's Round'.

ALL

That! that! that!   45

NICK

No, I am resolved thus it shall be,
First take hands, then take you to your heels.

31–2 'The Cushion Dance' This dance is described in *The Dancing Master* (1703).

33 ROGER Q3 (Rogero Q1).

   'Tom Tyler' Again a tune, possibly 'Tom Tinker'.

34 'The Hunting of the Fox' A tune so far unidentified.

35 'The Hay' Described in C.J. Sharp's *Country Dance Book* II, 41–8, this was a physical and noisy country dance.

36 *I have ... again* Q1 (It hath bene, it now is, and it shall be Q3).

41 'Put on Your Smock a Monday' A popular tune, also known as 'Pretty Nancy'. Given in *Chappell*, I, 234.

   Smock a woman's undergarment, a shift or chemise.

44 'Sellenger's Round' Name of another popular tune. See *Chappell*, I, 256.

JENKIN

Why, would you have us run away?

NICK

No, but I would have you shake your heels. Music, strike up!

They dance. NICK, *dancing, speaks stately and scurvily,*
the rest after the country fashion

JENKIN

Hey, lively my lasses, here's a turn for thee.   50

Exeunt

[SCENE III]

Wind horns. Enter SIR CHARLES, SIR FRANCIS, MALBY,
CRANWELL, WENDOLL, FALCONERS, *and* HUNTSMEN

SIR CHARLES

So! well cast off. Aloft, aloft! well flown!
O now she takes her at the souse, and strikes her
Down to the earth, like a swift thunderclap.

WENDOLL

She hath struck ten angels out of my way.

SIR FRANCIS

A hundred pound from me.

SIR CHARLES   What, falconer!   5

FALCONER

At hand, sir.

SIR CHARLES

Now she hath seized the fowl, and 'gins to plume her,

---

49   s.d. *scurvily* rudely, discourteously.

0.1   s.d. *Wind* sound, blow.
0.2   *FALCONERS* ed. (Falconer Q1, Q3).
2   *at the souse* as the prey was rising from the ground.
2–3   These lines are punctuated as prose in both quartos, without initial capitalisation
      in line 3.
7–8   As prose in Q3.

Rebeck her not, rather stand still and check her.
So! seize her gets, her jesses, and her bells.
Away!   10

SIR FRANCIS

My hawk killed too.

SIR CHARLES   Ay, but 'twas at the querre,
Not at the mount, like mine.

SIR FRANCIS   Judgement, my masters!

CRANWELL

Yours missed her at the ferre.

WENDOLL

Ay, but our merlin first hath plumed the fowl,
And twice renewed her from the river too.   15
Her bells, Sir Francis, had not both one weight,
Nor was one semitune above the other.
Methinks these Milan bells do sound too full,
And spoil the mounting of your hawk.

SIR CHARLES   'Tis lost.

SIR FRANCIS

I grant it not. Mine likewise seized a fowl   20
Within her talents, and you saw her paws

---

  8   *Rebeck* beckon back, recall. This is the only example of this meaning cited in the
        OED.
        check Bates' emendation, adopted by Van Fossen, to the word 'cherk' makes good
        sense. *OED*, citing *The Book of St Albans*, gives for 'cherk' or 'chirk' the meaning 'to
        incite by "chirking"' or making a birdlike sound with the lips. Such a reading would
        supply the necessary contrast with the sense of 'rebeck'.
  9   *gets, her jesses and her bells* The jesses were usually leather straps attached to the
        hawk's legs, as were the bells. 'Gets' are almost certainly the same as jesses, since they
        etymologically derive from the same source. They are so defined by the *OED*, giving
        this passage as the sole instance.
11–12 *the querre . . . mount* i.e. before the prey rose from the ground, not as it was rising.
        (See Van Fossen and Bates for a correction of the *OED* definition of 'querre'.)
  13 *ferre* An obscure falconry term indicating one side or the other of a river. *The Book
        of St Albans* distinguishes between the 'fer Jutty' (the far side) and the 'Jutty ferry' (the
        near side). Such a distinction hardly clarifies the present usage.
  14 *merlin* a species of falcon, 'one of the smallest, but one of the boldest, of European
        birds of prey' (*OED*).
        hath Q1 (had Q3).
  15 *renewed* drove out by attack.
  17 *one semitune above the other* a hawk's bells, according to *The Book of St Albans*, ought
        to be so pitched.
  18 *Milan* the metal work of this city was famous.

Full of the feathers; both her petty singles
And her long singles gripped her more than other;
The terrials of her legs were stained with blood –
Not of the fowl only she did discomfit   25
Some of her feathers, but she brake away!
Come, come, your hawk is but a rifler.

SIR CHARLES   How?

SIR FRANCIS

Ay, and your dogs are trindle-tails and curs.

SIR CHARLES

You stir my blood!
You keep not a good hound in all your kennel,   30
Nor one good hawk upon your perch.

SIR FRANCIS   How, knight?

SIR CHARLES

So, knight? You will not swagger, sir?

SIR FRANCIS

Why, say I did?

SIR CHARLES

Why sir, I say you would gain as much by swaggering
As you have got by wagers on your dogs.   35
You will come short in all things.

SIR FRANCIS   Not in this!
Now I'll strike home!

SIR CHARLES   Thou shalt to thy long home.
Or I will want my will!

22–3   *petty . . . long singles* short and long claws of the hawk.
  24   *terrials* OED thinks this an error for some term in falconry, most likely 'terrets', rings
       enabling the jesses to be attached to the leash
24–6   *with blood . . . away* i.e. our hawk drew blood, not just feathers, but the prey escaped.
27–31 *Come, come . . . perch* See K. M. Sturgess, 'The Early Quartos of Heywood's *A woman
       killed with kindness*', in *The Library* (fifth series), vol. XXV, 2 (1970), pp. 93–104,
       together with the discussion in the Note on the Text, pp. 547–9. Sturgess attributes
       line 27 to Sir Charles, enabling him otherwise to follow Q1 in speech ascriptions,
       arguing that the 1617 edition made an unsuccessful attempt to correct the slip in Q1,
       thereby showing its dependence on the 1607 text, as well as setting more textual
       difficulties. For a detailed discussion resisting Sturgess see pp. 546–50.
  27   *rifler* a hawk that fails to take the prey cleanly, but seizes only feathers (*The Book of
       St Albans*).
  28   *trindle-tails* dogs with curly tails, low-bred dogs.
  30   *a* Q1 (one Q3).
  32   *swagger* quarrel, bluster, be insolent.
34–6   Printed as prose in the quartos.
  37   *long home* grave (proverbial, from the Bible).

SIR FRANCIS
All they that love Sir Francis follow me.
SIR CHARLES
All that affect Sir Charles draw on my part.   40
CRANWELL
On this side heaves my hand.
WENDOL   Here goes my heart.
They divide themselves

SIR CHARLES, CRANWELL, FALCONER, *and* HUNTSMAN
fight against SIR FRANCIS, WENDOLL, *his* FALCONER,
and HUNTSMAN, *and* SIR CHARLES *hath the better, and
beats them away, killing both of* SIR FRANCIS *his men.*

[*Exeunt all except* SIR CHARLES]

SIR CHARLES
My God! what have I done? what have I done?
My rage hath plunged into a sea of blood
In which my soul lies drowned, poor innocent
For whom we are to answer. Well, 'tis done,   45
And I remain the victor. A great conquest,
When I would give this right hand, nay, this head,
To breathe in them new life whom I have slain.
Forgive me God, 'twas in the heat of blood,
And anger quite removes me from myself: 50
It was not I, but rage, did this vile murder;
Yet I, and not my rage, must answer it.
Sir Francis Acton, he is fled the field,
With him all those that did partake his quarrel,
And I am left alone, with sorrow dumb,   55
And in my height of conquest, overcome.

Enter SUSAN

41   s.d. *killing both* Q3 (*killing one* Q1). See Note on the Text, p. 545.
      s.d. *men* Q3 (*huntsmen* Q1). One of those he kills is the Falconer.
44   *innocent* Q1 (innocents Q3). The Q3 variant implies that the innocents are those he
      has killed; the word might just as easily apply to his soul, for whom he has to answer
      on the Judgement Day, and about whose drowning he is after all expressing concern
      before any remorse about the literal death of Sir Francis's men.
56   s.d. SUSAN Q3 (*Iane* Q1). See the Note on the Text, p. 545.
57   SUSAN ed. (*om.* Qq.). See Note on the Text, pp. 547–8.
      among Q1 (mong Q3).

SUSAN

O God, my brother wounded among the dead!
Unhappy jest that in such earnest ends.
The rumour of this fear stretched to my ears,
And I am come to know if you be wounded.   60

SIR CHARLES

O sister, sister, wounded at the heart.

SUSAN

My God forbid!

SIR CHARLES

In doing that thing which he forbade,
I am wounded, sister.

SUSAN   I hope not at the heart.

SIR CHARLES

Yes, at the heart.

SUSAN   O God! a surgeon there!   65

SIR CHARLES

Call me a surgeon, sister, for my soul;
The sin of murder it hath pierced my heart,
And made a wide wound there, but for these scratches,
They are nothing, nothing.

SUSAN   Charles, what have you done?
Sir Francis hath great friends, and will pursue you   70
Unto the utmost danger of the law.

SIR CHARLES

My conscience is become my enemy,
And will pursue me more than Acton can.

SUSAN

O fly, sweet brother.

SIR CHARLES   Shall I fly from thee?
What, Sue, art weary of my company?   75

SUSAN

Fly from your foe.

SIR CHARLES   You, sister, are my friend,
And flying you, I shall pursue my end.

58   *jest* Q1 (iests Q3).
59   *rumour of this fear* news of this feared happening.
      stretched to reached.
71   *Unto . . . the law* to the full extent of the punishments decreed by law.
72   *my* Q1 (mine Q3).
75   *What, Sue* ed. (What *Iane* Q1; Why *Sue* Q3).

SUSAN

> Your company is as my eyeball dear;
> Being far from you, no comfort can be near:
> Yet fly to save your life. What would I care   80
> To spend my future age in black despair,
> So you were safe? And yet to live one week
> Without my brother Charles, through every cheek
> My streaming tears would downwards run so rank
> Till they could set on either side a bank,   85
> And in the midst a channel; so my face
> For two salt water brooks shall still find place.

SIR CHARLES

> Thou shalt not weep so much, for I will stay
> In spite of danger's teeth. I'll live with thee,
> Or I'll not live at all. I will not sell   90
> My country, and my father's patrimony,
> No, thy sweet sight, for a vain hope of life.

Enter SHERIFF *with* OFFICERS

SHERIFF

> Sir Charles, I am made the unwilling instrument
> Of your attach and apprehension.
> I am sorry that the blood of innocent men   95
> Should be of you exacted. It was told me
> That you were guarded with a troop of friends,
> And therefore I come armed.

SIR CHARLES   O Master Sheriff,

> I came into the field with many friends,
> But see, they all have left me; only one   100
> Clings to my sad misfortune, my dear sister.
> I know you for an honest gentleman;
> I yield my weapons and submit to you.
> Convey me where you please.

SHERIFF   To prison then,

> To answer for the lives of these dead men.   105

SUSAN

> O God! O God!

88   *shalt* Q1 (shall Q3).
94   *attach* arrest.
96   *exacted* Q1 (enacted Q3). 'Exacted' here means shed or spilled.
98   *I come armed* Q1 (came thus arm'd Q3).
99   *many* Q3 (man Q1).

SIR CHARLES   Sweet sister, every strain
   Of sorrow from your heart augments my pain;
   Your grief abounds and hits against my breast.
SHERIFF
   Sir, will you go?
SIR CHARLES   Even where it likes you best.

                                        [*Exeunt*]

[SCENE IV]

Enter MASTER FRANKFORD *in a study*

FRANKFORD
   How happy am I amongst other men
   That in my mean estate embrace content.
   I am a gentleman, and by my birth
   Companion with a king; a king's no more.
   I am possessed of many fair revenues,   5
   Sufficient to maintain a gentleman.
   Touching my mind, I am studied in all arts;
   The riches of my thoughts and of my time
   Have been a good proficient. But the chief
   Of all the sweet felicities on earth,   10
   I have a fair, a chaste, and loving wife,
   Perfection all, all truth, all ornament.
   If man on earth may truly happy be,
   Of these at once possessed, sure I am he.

Enter NICK

108   *abounds* overflows.

   0   s.d. *in a study* i.e. deep in thought.
   2   *mean* modest.
   4   *Companion ... no more* Frankford uses a similar expression at VI.39, again expressing
       pride in his social rank, 'companion with the best and chiefest / In Yorkshire'.
   9   *Have been ... proficient* have made profitable use, or have been one who has made
       good use.
   12 *all ornament* composed of qualities conferring beauty, grace, or honour.
   14 *at once* simultaneously, at the same time.

NICK

Sir, there's a gentleman attends without to speak with you.

FRANKFORD   15

On horseback?

NICK

Ay, on horseback.

FRANKFORD

Entreat him to alight; I will attend him.

Knowest thou him, Nick?

NICK   I know him; his name's Wendoll.

It seems he comes in haste. His horse is booted

Up to the flank in mire, himself all spotted   20

And stained with plashing. Sure he rid in fear

Or for a wager; horse and man both sweat.

I ne'er saw two in such a smoking heat.

FRANKFORD

Entreat him in. About it instantly.

                                                        [*Exit* NICK]   25

This Wendoll I have noted, and his carriage

Hath pleased me much. By observation

I have noted many good deserts in him:

He's affable, and seen in many things,

Discourses well, a good companion,

And though of small means, yet a gentleman   30

Of a good house, somewhat pressed by want.

I have preferred him to a second place

In my opinion, and my best regard.

Enter WENDOLL, ANNE, *and* NICK

ANNE

O Master Frankford, Master Wendoll here

Brings you the strangest news that ere you heard.   35

FRANKFORD

What news, sweet wife? What news good Master Wendoll?

17   *Ay* I Q1 (Yes Q3).
18   *I will* Q1 (and ile Q3).
19   *I know him* Q1 (Know him Q3)
22   *plashing* splashing.
26   *carriage* conduct.
29   *seen* (well) versed.
33   *preferred* promoted.
34   s.d. ANNE *Mistress Frankford* Q3 (*Maister Frankford* Q1).

WENDOLL

    You knew the march made 'twixt Sir Francis Acton and

    Sir Charles Mountford?

FRANKFORD   True, with their hounds and hawks.

WENDOLL

    The matches were both played.

FRANKFORD   Ha! and which won?

WENDOLL   40

    Sir Francis, your wife's brother, had the worst,

    And lost the wager.

FRANKFORD   Why, the worse his chance.

    Perhaps the fortune of some other day

    Will change his luck.

ANNE   O, but you hear not all.

    Sir Francis lost, and yet was loth to yield.

    In brief, the two knights grew to difference,   45

    From words to blows, and so to banding sides,

    Where valorous Sir Charles slew in his spleen

    Two of your brother's men: his falconer

    And his good huntsman, whom he loved so well.

    More men were wounded, no more slain outright.   50

FRANKFORD

    Now, trust me, I am sorry for the knight.

    But is my brother safe?

WENDOLL   All whole and sound,

    His body not being blemished with one wound.

    But poor Sir Charles is to the prison led,

    To answer at th'assize for them that's dead.   55

FRANKFORD

    I thank your pains, sir. Had the news been better

    Your will was to have brought it, Master Wendoll.

    Sir Charles will find hard friends; his case is heinous,

    And will be most severely censured on.

---

40   *both* There is no indication that both matches were played, unless that with the
       hounds preceded the fatal match with hawks (see Scene III).

44   *ANNE* Q1, Q3. It was Baskervill who plausibly reassigned this speech to Wendoll on
       the strength of the reference to 'your brother' in line 49, but Anne might as well be
       retelling what Wendoll has just told her off-stage.

46   *In brief* Q1 (At length Q3).

57–8   *Had the news . . . it* i.e. you would have brought us more pleasing news had you any
       choice in the matter.

59   *find hard friends* find support difficult to come by.

I am sorry for him. Sir, a word with you.   60
I know you, sir, to be a gentleman
In all things, your possibilities but mean.
Please you to use my table and my purse,
They are yours.

WENDOLL   O Lord, sir, I shall never deserve it!

FRANKFORD   65

O sir, disparage not your worth too much.
You are full of quality and fair desert.
Choose of my men which shall attend on you,
And he is yours. I will allow you, sir,
Your man, your gelding, and your table,
All at my own charge. Be my companion.   70

WENDOLL

Master Frankford, I have oft been bound to you
By many favours; this exceeds them all
That I shall never merit your least favour.
But when your last remembrance I forget,
Heaven at my soul exact that weighty debt.   75

FRANKFORD

There needs no protestation, for I know you
Virtuous, and therefore grateful. Prithee Nan,
Use him with all thy loving'st courtesy.

ANNE

As far as modesty may well extend,
It is my duty to receive your friend.   80

FRANKFORD

To dinner, come sir; from this present day,
Welcome to me forever. Come away!

          [*Exeunt* FRANKFORD, ANNE *and* WENDOLL]

NICK

I do not like this fellow by no means:
I never see him but my heart still earns.

---

63   *possibilities* Q1 (possibility Q3).
68   *on you* Q1 (you sir Q3).
70   *table* board, meals.
75   *your last remembrance* i.e. this latest kindness.
80   *As far . . . extend* Perhaps Anne's reservation here indicates her own anticipation of
     the moral difficulty to come.
84   *not* Q1 (nor Q1).
85   *earns* grieves (Van Fossen), but the word also means 'curdles' (*OED* v^2) and the
     sense of 'turns sour' figuratively seems appropriate here.

Zounds, I could fight with him, yet know not why.   85
The Devil and he are all one in my eye.

Enter JENKIN

JENKIN

O Nick, what gentleman is that comes to lie at our house? My
master allows him one to wait on him, and I believe it will fall to
thy lot.

NICK   90

I love my master, by these hilts I do,
But rather than I'll ever come to serve him,
I'll turn away my master.

Enter SISLY

SISLY

Nicklas, where are you Nicklas? You must come in, Nicklas, and
help the young gentleman off with his boots.

NICK   95

If I pluck off his boots, I'll eat the spurs,
And they shall stick fast in my throat like burrs.   *Exit* NICK

SISLY

Then Jenkin, come you?

JENKIN

'Tis no boot for me to deny it. My master hath given me a coat
here, but he takes pains himself to brush it once or twice a day
with a holly-wand.   100

SISLY

Come, come, make haste, that you may wash your hands again,
and help to serve in dinner.

---

86   *Zounds* God's wounds.
87   *my* Q1 (mine Q3).
      Q3 gives an exit for Nick here.
88   *that* Q1 (that that Q3).
91   *hilts* i.e. of his dagger.
92   *him* i.e. Wendoll.
95   *young* Q1 (*omitted* Q3).
99   *'Tis* Q1 (Nay 'tis Q3).
      boot avail (also a pun).
      coat i.e. the servant's livery.
100–1   *to brush . . . holly-wand* i.e. to give me a beating.

JENKIN

[*To audience*] You may see, my masters, though it be afternoon
with you, 'tis but early days with us, for we have not dined yet.
Stay but a little, I'll but go in and help to bear up the first course   105
and come to you again presently.

Exeunt JENKIN *and* SISLY

[SCENE V]

Enter MALBY *and* CRANWELL

MALBY

This is the sessions day. Pray, can you tell me
How young Sir Charles hath sped? Is he acquit,
Or must he try the law's strict penalty?

CRANWELL

He's cleared of all, spite of his enemies,
Whose earnest labours was to take his life.
But in this suit of pardon he hath spent   5
All the revenues that his father left him,
And he is now turned a plain countryman,
Reformed in all things. See, sir, here he comes.

Enter SIR CHARLES *and his* KEEPER

KEEPER

Discharge your fees and you are then at freedom.

104–5   *afternoon . . . yet* Plays were performed in the afternoon, though the action of the play
has only reached noon, the usual dinner hour. The willingness to draw attention to
the discrepancy says something about the Elizabethan conventions of theatrical
realism.

107   *presently* A break in the action, an act division or perhaps a brief interval, seems to
be implied here. In that case, the word would mean 'shortly' rather than its normal
17th-century sense of 'immediately'. There is a break in time between the events of
this scene and those of the next, which are quickly located in time by the opening
sentence.

3   *try* endure, suffer.
8   *a plain countryman* i.e. he is no longer a landlord.
9   *Reformed* changed, transformed.
s.d. CHARLES Q3 (Francis Q1).

SIR CHARLES   10
    Here, Master Keeper, take the poor remainder
    Of all the wealth I have. My heavy foes
    Have made my purse light, but, alas, to me
    'Tis wealth enough that you have set me free.
MALBY
    God give you joy of your delivery;
    I am glad to see you abroad, Sir Charles.   15
SIR CHARLES
    The poorest knight in England, Master Malby;
    My life hath cost me all the patrimony
    My father left his son. Well, God forgive them
    That are the authors of my penury.

                                                       20

                  Enter SHAFTON

SHAFTON
    Sir Charles, a hand, a hand – at liberty!
    Now by the faith I owe, I am glad to see it.
    What want you? Wherein may I pleasure you?
SIR CHARLES
    O me! O most unhappy gentleman!
    I am not worthy to have friends stirred up
    Whose hands may help me in this plunge of want.   25
    I would I were in heaven to inherit there
    Th'immortal birthright which my Saviour keeps,
    And by no unthrift can be bought and sold;
    For here on earth, what pleasures should we trust?
SHAFTON   30
    To rid you from these contemplations
    Three hundred pounds you shall receive of me –
    Nay, five for fail. Come sir, the sight of gold
    Is the most sweet receipt for melancholy,
    And will revive your spirits. You shall hold law

---

16   *abroad* out of confinement, at liberty
18   *the* Q1 (my Q3).
21   s.d. *SHAFTON* Q1 (speech-head omitted in Q3). See Note on the Text, p. 548.
22   *owe* own, profess.
26   *plunge of want* crisis of poverty.
28   *immortal birthright* the promise of eternal life.
29   *unthrift* spendthrift.
33   *for fail* in order to be sure.
34   *receipt* recipe, antidote.

With your proud adversaries. Tush, let Frank Acton   35
Wage with knighthoodlike expense with me,
And he will sink, he will. Nay, good Sir Charles,
Applaud your fortune, and your fair escape
From all these perils.
SIR CHARLES   O sir, they have undone me!
Two thousand and five hundred pound a year   40
My father at his death possessed me of,
All which the envious Acton made me spend.
And notwithstanding all this large expense,
I had much ado to gain my liberty;
And I have now only a house of pleasure,   45
With some five hundred pounds, reserved
Both to maintain me and my loving sister.
SHAFTON
          [*Aside*] That must I have; it lies convenient for me.
If I can fasten but one finger on him,
With my full hand I'll grip him to the heart.   50
'Tis not for love I proffered him this coin,
But for my gain and pleasure.
          [*To* SIR CHARLES]   Come, Sir Charles,
I know you have need of money; take my offer.
SIR CHARLES
Sir, I accept it, and remain indebted,
Even to the best of my unable power.   55
Come, gentlemen, and see it tendered down.

          Exeunt

---

37   *Wage with knighthoodlike* Q1 (Wage his Knight-hood-like Q3).
46   *now only* Q1 (only now Q3).
      house of pleasure a house used for recreation or pleasure, a summer-house.
56   *unable* feeble.
57   *tendered down* paid according to legal form (something more contractual than the *OED*'s simple 'laid down in payment' seems implied here).

[SCENE VI]

Enter WENDOLL, *melancholy*

WENDOLL

I am a villain if I apprehend
But such a thought; then, to attempt the deed –
Slave, thou art damned without redemption.
I'll drive away this passion with a song.
A song! Ha, ha! A song, as if, fond man,
Thy eyes could swim in laughter when thy soul   5
Lies drenched and drowned in red tears of blood.
I'll pray, and see if God within my heart
Plant better thoughts. Why, prayers are meditations,
And when I meditate – O God forgive me –
It is on her divine perfections.   10
I will forget her; I will arm myself
Not to entertain a thought of love to her;
And when I come by chance into her presence,
I'll hale these balls until my eye-strings crack,
From being pulled and drawn to look that way.   15

Enter over the stage FRANKFORD, ANNE, *and* NICK

O God! O God! with what a violence
I am hurried to my own destruction.
There goest thou, the most perfect'st man
That ever England bred a gentleman;
And shall I wrong his bed? Thou God of thunder,   20
Stay, in thy thoughts of vengeance and of wrath,
Thy great, almighty and all-judging hand
From speedy execution on a villain,
A villain, and a traitor to his friend.

     25

Enter JENKIN [*unobserved by* WENDOLL]

---

1   WENDOLL Q1 (*omitted* Q3) See the Note on the Text, p. 548.
       apprehend think, conceive, formulate.
5   *fond* foolish.
15   *balls* eyeballs.
18   *my* Q1 (mine Q3).
19   *perfect'st* Q1 (perfect's Q3).

27

JENKIN

Did your worship call?

WENDOLL

[*Unhearing*] He doth maintain me; he allows me largely
Money to spend –

JENKIN

[*Aside*] By my faith, so do not you me; I cannot get a cross of
you.

WENDOLL   30

My gelding and my man.

JENKIN

[*Aside*] That's Sorrel and I.

WENDOLL

This kindness grows of no alliance 'twixt us.

JENKIN

[*Aside*] Nor is my service of any great acquaintance.

WENDOLL

I never bound him to me by desert;
Of a mere stranger, a poor gentleman,   35
A man by whom in no kind he could gain,
He hath placed me in the height of all his thoughts,
Made me companion with the best and chiefest
In Yorkshire. He cannot eat without me,
Nor laugh without me; I am to his body   40
As necessary as his digestion,
And equally do make him whole or sick.
And shall I wrong this man? Base man! Ingrate!
Hast thou the power straight with thy gory hands
To rip thy image from his bleeding heart?   45
To scratch thy name from out the holy book
Of his remembrance, and to wound his name
That holds thy name so dear, or rend his heart
To whom thy heart was joined and knit together?

27   *largely* generously.
29   *cross* a coin (bearing the mark of a cross).
34   *of any great acquaintance* i.e. because I have known Wendoll for a particularly long
      time. (Wendoll's word 'kindness' is matched by Jenkin's 'service', and 'alliance' by
      'acquaintance', in parodic deflation.)
35   *me* Q3 (be Q1).
36   *mere* entire, complete.
38   *He hath . . . thoughts* Q1 (And he hath plac'd me in his highest thoughts Q3).
50   *joined and knit* Q1 (knit and ioyn'd Q3).

And yet I must. Then, Wendoll, be content.   50
Thus villains, when they would, cannot repent.

JENKIN

[*Aside*] What a strange humour is my new master in. Pray God
he be not mad. If he should be so, I should never have any mind
to serve him in Bedlam. It may be he is mad for missing of me.

WENDOLL   55

[*Seeing* JENKIN] What, Jenkin? Where's your mistress?

JENKIN

Is your worship married?

WENDOLL

Why dost thou ask?

JENKIN

Because you are my master, and if I have a mistress, I would be
glad, like a good servant, to do my duty to her.

WENDOLL   60

I mean where's Mistress Frankford?

JENKIN

Marry, sir, her husband is riding out of town, and she went very
lovingly to bring him on his way to horse. Do you see, sir, here
she comes, [*Aside*] and here I go.

WENDOLL

Vanish.

                                                      Exit JENKIN   65

                        Enter ANNE

ANNE

You are well met, sir. Now in troth my husband
Before he took horse had a great desire
To speak with you. We sought about the house,
Hallowed into the fields, sent every way,
But could not meet you. Therefore he enjoined me
To do unto you his most kind commends.   70
Nay, more; he wills you as you prize his love,
Or hold in estimation his kind friendship,
To make bold in his absence and command

---

55   *Bedlam* the famous London asylum for the insane.
61   *where's Mistress* Q1 (Mistris Q3).
69   *Hallowed* Q1 (Hollow'd Q3).
71   *kind* Q3 (kinds Q1).
      commends compliments.

29

Even as himself were present in the house,
For you must keep his table, use his servants,   75
And be a present Frankford in his absence.

WENDOLL

I thank him for his love.
[*Aside*] Give me a name, you whose infectious tongues
Are tipped with gall and poison; as you would
Think on a man that had your father slain,   80
Murdered thy children, made your wives base strumpets,
So call me. Call me so? Print in my face
The most stigmatic title of a villain,
For hatching treason to so true a friend.

ANNE   85

Sir, you are much beholding to my husband.
You are a man most dear in his regard.

WENDOLL

I am bound unto your husband and you too.
[*Aside*] I will not speak to wrong a gentleman
Of that good estimation, my kind friend.
I will not! Zounds, I will not! I may choose,   90
And I will choose! Shall I be so misled?
Or shall I purchase to my father's crest
The motto of a villain? If I say
I will not do it, what thing can enforce me?
Who can compel me? What sad destiny   95
Hath such command upon my yielding thoughts?
I will not! Ha! some fury pricks me on;
The swift fates drag me at their chariot wheel,
And hurry me to mischief. Speak I must –
Injure myself, wrong her, deceive his trust.   100

ANNE

Are you not well, sir, that you seem thus troubled?

---

76   *keep* preside over, take care of, take charge of, maintain.
82   *thy* Q1 (your Q3).
83   *Call . . . Print* i.e. Not only do I deserve to be called by such a name, but to have it
      printed in my face.
84   *stigmatic* infamous, severely condemnatory.
91   *Zounds* God's wounds.
93–4 *crest . . . villain* The crest and motto were the heraldic marks of gentility; the word
      'villain' revives in a pun its etymological relation to 'villein' = feudal serf.
96   *Who* Q1 (What Q3).   *sad* causing sorrow, distressing.
102   *you seem* Q1 (ye seeme Q3).

There is sedition in your countenance!
WENDOLL
   And in my heart, fair angel, chaste and wise.
   I love you – start not, speak not, answer not.
   I love you – nay, let me speak the rest.   105
   Bid me to swear, and I will call to record
   The host of heaven.
ANNE   The host of heaven forbid
   Wendoll should hatch such a disloyal thought.
WENDOLL
   Such is my fate; to this suit I was born:
   To wear rich pleasure's crown, or fortune's scorn.   110
ANNE
   My husband loves you.
WENDOLL   I know it.
ANNE   He esteems you
   Even as his brain, his eye-ball, or his heart.
WENDOLL
   I have tried it.
ANNE
   His purse is your exchequer, and his table
   Doth freely serve you.   115
WENDOLL   So I have found it.
ANNE
   O with what face of brass, what brow of steel,
   Can you unblushing speak this to the face
   Of the espoused wife of so dear a friend?
   It is my husband that maintains your state;
   Will you dishonour him? I am his wife   120
   That in your power hath left his whole affairs;
   It is to me you speak?
WENDOLL   O speak no more,
   For more than this I know and have recorded
   Within the red-leaved table of my heart.
   Fair, and of all beloved, I was not fearful   125
   Bluntly to give my life into your hand,

103   *sedition* internal strife or tumult.
106   *me* Q3 (we Q1).
114   *tried* put to the proof.
115   *your* Q3 (you Q1)
125   *table* notebook.

And at one hazard all my earthly means.
Go, tell your husband; he will turn me off,
And I am then undone. I care not, I –
'Twas for your sake. Perchance in rage he'll kill me.   130
I care not – 'twas for you. Say I incur
The general name of villain through the world,
Of traitor to my friend – I care not, I.
Beggary, shame, death, scandal, and reproach,
For you I'll hazard all – what care I?   135
For you I'll live, and in your love I'll die.

ANNE
You move me, sir, to passion and to pity.
The love I bear my husband is as precious
As my soul's health.

WENDOLL   I love your husband too,
And for his love I will engage my life.   140
Mistake me not, the augmentation
Of my sincere affection borne to you
Doth no whit lessen my regard of him.
I will be secret, lady, close as night,
And not the light of one small glorious star   145
Shall shine here in my forehead to bewray
That act of night.

ANNE   What shall I say?
My soul is wandering, and hath lost her way.
O Master Wendoll, O.

WENDOLL   Sigh not, sweet saint,
For every sigh you breathe draws from my heart   150
A drop of blood.

ANNE   I ne'er offended yet.
My fault, I fear, will in my brow be writ.
Women that fall not quite bereft of grace

128   *at one hazard* at once put at risk.
136   *what care* Q1 (why what care Q3).
137   *live* Q1 (loue Q3).
145   *close* secretive.
147   *bewray* betray, expose, reveal.
148   *act of night* i.e. adultery.
151–2 *every sigh . . . blood* An exploitation of the popular belief that a sigh cost one's heart
       a drop of blood. (Van Fossen cites Donne's use in the song 'Sweetest love I do not
       go': 'When thou sigh'st, thou sigh'st not winde, / But sigh'st my soule away.')
153   *my* Q3 (*omitted* Q).

Have their offences noted in their face.
I blush and am ashamed. O Master Wendoll,   155
Pray God I be not born to curse your tongue
That hath enchanted me. This maze I am in
I fear will prove the labyrinth of sin.

Enter NICK [*unnoticed by* ANNE *and* WENDOLL]

WENDOLL
The path of pleasure, and the gate to bliss,
Which on your lips I knock at with a kiss.   160
                                    [*Kisses* ANNE]

NICK
[*Aside*] I'll kill the rogue.

WENDOLL
Your husband is from home, your bed's no blab –
Nay, look not down and blush.
                              Exeunt ANNE *and* WENDOLL
NICK   Zounds, I'll stab.
Ay, Nick, was it thy chance to come just in the nick.
I love my master, and I hate that slave;   165
I love my mistress, but these tricks I like not.
My master shall not pocket up this wrong;
I'll eat my fingers first. What sayest thou metal?
                              [*Drawing his dagger*]
Does not the rascal Wendoll go on legs
That thou must cut off? Hath he not hamstrings   170
That thou must hough? Nay metal, thou shalt stand
To all I say. I'll henceforth turn a spy,
And watch them in their close conveyances.
I never looked for better of that rascal
Since he came miching first into our house.   175
It is that Satan hath corrupted her,

158 *maze* a pun (a) state of bewilderment (b) labyrinth (in line 159).
163 *blab* tell-tale.
164 *Zounds* God's wounds.
165 *in the nick* at the critical moment (punning on his name).
168 *pocket up* submit to, endure meekly or in ignorance.
170 *the* Q1 (that Q3).
172 *hough* cut (the tendons behind the knee), disable.
     shalt Q1 (shall Q3).
174 *close conveyances* secret communications.
176 *miching* skulking, pretending poverty.

For she was fair and chaste. I'll have an eye
In all their gestures. Thus I think of them:
If they proceed as they have done before,
Wendoll's a knave, my mistress is a etcetera.   *Exit*   180

[SCENE VII]

Enter SIR CHARLES *and* SUSAN

SIR CHARLES
Sister, you see we are driven to hard shift
To keep this poor house we have left unsold.
I am now enforced to follow husbandry,
And you to milk. And do we not live well?
Well, I thank God.
SUSAN   O brother, here's a change
Since old Sir Charles died in our father's house.   5
SIR CHARLES
All things on earth thus change, some up, some down;
Content's a kingdom, and I wear that crown.

Enter SHAFTON *with a* SERGEANT

SHAFTON
Good morrow, good morrow, Sir Charles. What, with your sister,
Plying your husbandry? Sergeant, stand off.
You have a pretty house here, and a garden   10
And goodly ground about it. Since it lies
So near a lordship that I lately bought,
I would fain buy it of you. I will give you –

179   *gestures* actions, deeds.
181   *etcetera* Q1 (— — Q3).

  1   *hard shift* difficult expedients.
  3   *husbandry* i.e. farming.
  9   SHAFTON Q1 (*omitted* Q3). See Note on the Text, p. 548.
       morrow, good morrow Q1 (morrow, morrow Q3).
 10   *Sergeant* a legal officer charged with the arrest of offenders and summoning persons
       before court.
 13   *lordship* estate, domain (land belonging to a lord).

SIR CHARLES

    O pardon me, this house successively
    Hath 'longed to me and my progenitors   15
    Three hundred year. My great-great-grandfather,
    He in whom first our gentle style began,
    Dwelt here, and in this ground increased this mole-hill
    Unto that mountain which my father left me.
    Where he the first of all our house began,   20
    I now the last will end and keep this house,
    This virgin title never yet deflowered
    By any unthrift of the Mountford's line.
    In brief, I will not sell it for more gold
    Than you could hide or pave the ground withal.   25

SHAFTON

    Ha, ha! a proud mind and a beggar's purse.
    Where's my three hundred pounds, beside the use?
    I have brought it to an execution
    By course of law. What? Is my money ready?

SIR CHARLES   30

    An execution, sir, and never tell me
    You put my bond in suit? You deal extremely.

SHAFTON

    Sell me the land and I'll acquit you straight.

SIR CHARLES

    Alas, alas! Tis all trouble hath left me
    To cherish me and my poor sister's life.
    If this were sold our means should then be quite   35
    Razed from the bead-roll of gentility.

16   *'longed* belonged.
17   *year* Q1 (yeeres Q3).
18   *gentle style* status of gentility.
23   *title* legal right to possession.
28   *beside* Q1 (besides Q3).
        use interest.
29   *an* Q1 (*omitted* Q3).
        execution legal seizure of goods or person of a defaulting debtor.
30   *money* Q1 (monies Q3).
32   *put . . . in suit* set the law in motion concerning my bond.
        extremely with a very great degree of severity.
35   *cherish* support, foster.
36   *means* Q1, Q3 (names *Dodsley's emendation*).
37   *Razed* erased.
        bead-roll list.

You see what hard shift we have made to keep it
Allied still to our own name. This palm you see
Labour hath glowed within; her silver brow,
That never tasted a rough winter's blast   40
Without a mask or fan, doth with a grace
Defy cold winter and his storms outface.

SUSAN

Sir, we feed sparing and we labour hard,
We lie uneasy, to reserve to us
And our succession this small plot of ground.   45

SIR CHARLES

I have so bent my thoughts to husbandry
That I protest I scarcely can remember
What a new fashion is, how silk or satin
Feels in my hand. Why, pride is grown to us
A mere, mere stranger. I have quite forgot   50
The names of all that ever waited on me;
I cannot name ye any of my hounds,
Once from whose echoing mouths I heard all the music
That e'er my heart desired. What should I say?
To keep this place I have changed myself away.   55

SHAFTON

Arrest him at my suit. Actions and actions
Shall keep thee in perpetual bondage fast.
Nay, more, I'll sue thee by a late appeal,
And call thy former life in question.
The keeper is my friend; thou shalt have irons   60
And usage such as I'll deny to dogs. Away with him!

---

40   *glowed* Sturgess proposed that Heywood wrote 'gald', that it was misread by the 1607
     compositor as 'gloud' (= gloved), and subsequently changed to 'glow'd' by the
     compositor of 1617. See K. M. Sturgess, 'The Early Quartos of Heywood's *A woman
     killed with kindness*', in *The Library* (fifth series), vol. XXV, 2 (1970), pp. 93–104, and
     Note on the Text, pp. 549–50.

42   *mask or fan* i.e. as protections against the weather, the effects of which on the
     complexion were not then valued by the upper or wealthier classes.

45   *uneasy* uncomfortably.
     reserve preserve.

51   *mere* absolute, complete.

54   *the* Q1 (*omitted* Q3).

57   *actions* i.e. legal actions.

58   *perpetual* Q1 (continuall Q3).

59   *late appeal* i.e. revived charge (of killing Sir Francis's men).

SIR CHARLES
    You are too timorous, but trouble is my master
    And I will serve him truly. My kind sister,
    Thy tears are of no force to mollify
    This flinty man. Go to my father's brother,   65
    My kinsmen and allies, entreat them from me
    To ransom me from this injurious man
    That seeks my ruin.
SHAFTON   Come, irons, irons, away!
    I'll see thee lodged far from the sight of day.

                  Exeunt [SHAFTON *and* SERGEANT   70
                  with SIR CHARLES *in irons*]

      Enter SIR FRANCIS *and* MALBY
    [*unseen by* SUSAN *and not noticing her*]

SUSAN
    My heart's so hardened with the frost of grief
    Death cannot pierce it through. Tyrant too fell!
    So lead the fiends condemned souls to hell.
SIR FRANCIS
    Again to prison! Malby, hast thou seen
    A poor slave better tortured? Shall we hear
    The music of his voice cry from the grate   75
    'Meat for the Lord's sake'? No, no, yet I am not
    Throughly revenged. They say he hath a pretty wench
    Unto his sister: shall I, in mercy sake
    To him and to his kindred, bribe the fool
    To shame herself by lewd dishonest lust.   80
    I'll proffer largely, but the deed being done
    I'll smile to see her base confusion.

---

63   *You* Q1 (Ye Q3).
     timorous fearful of my resistance, or possibly the sense 'dreadful, terrible' favoured
     by Van Fossen.
69   *irons, irons, away* Q1 (irons, irons; come away Q3).
70   s.d. *Enter . . .* This entrance appears after Susan's speech (ll. 71–3) in Q3.
72   *fell* cruel, ruthless.
76   *grate* prison bars.
77   *Lord's sake* Q3 (Lord sake Q1).
79   *Unto* Q1 (To Q3).
     mercy Q1 (my mercy Q3).
81   *dishonest* dishonourable, unchaste.
82   *largely* generously.

MALBY

    Methinks, Sir Francis, you are full revenged
    For greater wrongs than he can proffer you.
    See where the poor sad gentlewoman stands.   85

SIR FRANCIS

    Ha, ha! Now I will flout her poverty,
    Deride her fortunes, scoff her base estate.
    My very soul the name of Mountford hates.
    But stay, my heart, O what a look did fly
    To strike my soul through with thy piercing eye.   90
    I am enchanted, all my spirits are fled,
    And with one glance my envious spleen struck dead.

SUSAN

    [*Seeing them*] Acton, that seeks our blood!   *Runs away*

SIR FRANCIS   O chaste and fair!

MALBY

    Sir Francis, why Sir Francis? Zounds, in a trance?
    Sir Francis, what cheer man? Come, come, how is't?   95

SIR FRANCIS

    Was she not fair? Or else this judging eye
    Cannot distinguish beauty.

MALBY   She was fair.

SIR FRANCIS

    She was an angel in a mortal's shape,
    And ne'er descended from old Mountford's line.
    But soft, soft, let me call my wits together.   100
    A poor, poor wench, to my great adversary
    Sister, whose very souls denounce stern war
    One against other? How now, Frank, turned fool
    Or madman, whether? By no! master of
    My perfect senses and directest wits.   105
    Then why should I be in this violent humour
    Of passion and of love, and with a person
    So different every way, and so opposed

---

    87   *I will* Q1 (will I Q3).
    89   *hates* Q1 (hate Q3).
    90   *O what* ed. (or what Q1, Q3).
    94   *s.d. Runs* Q3 (Run Q1).
    95   *Zounds* God's wounds (*omitted* Q3).
    103   *denounce* declare, announce.
    104   *One* Q1 (Each Q3).
    106   *directest* most straightforward, unambiguous.

In all contractions and still warring actions?
Fie, fie, how I dispute against my soul.   110
Come, come, I'll gain her, or in her fair quest
Purchase my soul free and immortal rest.

Exeunt

[SCENE VIII]

Enter THREE *or* FOUR SERVINGMEN [*including* NICK *and*
SPIGGOT *the Butler*], *one with a voider and a wooden knife
to take away all, another the salt and bread, another
the table-cloth and napkins, another the carpet.*
JENKIN *with two lights after them*

JENKIN

So, march in order and retire in battle 'ray. My master and the
guests have supped already, all's taken away. Here now spread
for the servingmen in the hall. Butler, it belongs to your office.

SPIGGOT

I know it, Jenkin. What do you call the gentleman that supped
there tonight?

JENKIN   5

Who, my master?

SPIGGOT

No, no, Master Wendoll, he is a daily guest. I mean the gentleman
that came but this afternoon.

JENKIN

His name is Master Cranwell. God's light, hark within there! My
master calls to lay more billets on the fire. Come, come! Lord,
how we that are in office here in the house are troubled. One   10

110   *contractions* counteractions (not in *OED* in this sense).

0.1   s.d. THREE *or* FOUR Q1, Q3. This reading suggests the authorial foul papers that lie
       behind the first edition. No theatrical document would allow itself this measure of
       imprecision.

0.3   s.d. *away all* Q1 (away Q3).
   1   *'ray* Q1 (array Q3).
   4   *do you* Q1 (de'ye Q3).
   7   s.p. SPIGGOT ed. (*But* Q1; *Wen* Q3).
  10   *billets* thick pieces of wood.   *on* Q1 (vppon Q3).

spread the carpet in the parlour and stand ready to snuff the
lights; the rest be ready to prepare their stomachs. More lights in
the hall there! Come Nicklas.

[*Exeunt all but* NICK]

NICK

I cannot eat, but had I Wendoll's heart
I would eat that; the rogue grows impudent.   15
O I have seen such vile notorious tricks,
Ready to make my eyes dart from my head.
I'll tell my master, by this air I will;
Fall what may fall, I'll tell him. Here he comes.

Enter FRANKFORD *as it were brushing the crumbs from his clothes*   20
with a napkin, and newly risen from supper

FRANKFORD

Nicklas, what make you here? Why are not you
At supper in the hall there with your fellows.

NICK

Master, I stayed your rising from the board
To speak with you.

FRANKFORD   Be brief then, gentle Nicklas,
My wife and guests attend me in the parlour.
Why dost thou pause? Now Nicklas, you want money,   25
And unthrift-like would eat into your wages
Ere you have earned it. Here's, sir, half-a-crown,
Play the good husband and away to supper.

NICK

[*Aside*] By this hand, an honourable gentleman! I will not see
him wronged. Sir, I have served you long. You entertained me   30
seven years before your beard. You knew me, sir, before you knew
my mistress.

12   *spread the carpet* i.e. on the table, rather than the floor.
20   s.d. *and* Q1 (as Q3).
22   *there with* Q1 (among Q3).
23   *stayed* waited until.
25   *attend* await.
26   *want* lack.
27   *unthrift-like* spendthriftlike.
28   *Here's, sir* Q1 (heere sirs Q3).
29   *Play the good husband* i.e. manage the money well, be thrifty (but ironically
     exploiting the play on the word 'husband').
31   *entertained* retained in service, employed.

FRANKFORD
    What of this, good Nicklas?
NICK
    I never was a make-bate or a knave.
    I have no fault but one – I am given to quarrel,   35
    But not with women. I will tell you, master,
    That which will make your heart leap from your breast,
    Your hair to startle from your head, your ears to tingle.
FRANKFORD
    What preparation's this to dismal news?
NICK   40
    'Sblood sir, I love you better than your wife.
    I'll make it good.
FRANKFORD
    Thou art a knave, and I have much ado
    With wonted patience to contain my rage
    And not to break thy pate! Thou art a knave;
    I'll turn you with your base comparisons   45
    Out of my doors.
NICK
    Do, do.
    There's not room for Wendoll and me too
    Both in one house. O master, master,
    That Wendoll is a villain.   50
FRANKFORD
    Ay, saucy!   [FRANKFORD *strikes him*]
NICK
    Strike, strike, do strike, yet hear me. I am no fool,
    I know a villain when I see him act
    Deeds of a villain. Master, master, that base slave
    Enjoys my mistress and dishonours you.   55
FRANKFORD
    Thou hast killed me with a weapon whose sharpened point
    Hath pricked quite through and through my shivering heart.

35   *make-bate* mischief-maker, breeder of quarrels.
41   *'Sblood* i.e. God's blood.
42   *I'll make . . . good* i.e. I'll justify my words. Perhaps, as Van Fossen suggests, Frankford
      threatens to strike him for his impudence.
43   *Thou art* Q1 (Y'are Q3).
56   *Enjoys* i.e. sexually.
57   *sharpened* Q1 (sharp Q3).

Drops of cold sweat sit dangling on my hairs
Like morning's dew upon the golden flowers,
And I am plunged into a strange agony.   60
What didst thou say? If any word that touched
His credit or her reputation,
It is as hard to enter my belief
As Dives into heaven.

NICK   65

I can gain nothing. They are two
That never wronged me. I knew before
'Twas but a thankless office, and perhaps
As much as my service or my life is worth.
All this I know, but this and more,
More by a thousand dangers could not hire me   70
To smother such a heinous wrong from you.
I saw, and I have said.

FRANKFORD

[*Aside*] 'Tis probable. Though blunt, yet he is honest.
Though I durst pawn my life, and on their faith
Hazard the dear salvation of my soul,   75
Yet in my trust I may be too secure.
May this be true? O may it, can it be?
Is it by any wonder possible?
Man, woman, what thing mortal may we trust,
When friends and bosom wives prove so unjust?   80
[*To* NICK] What instance hast thou of this strange report?

NICK

Eyes, eyes.

FRANKFORD

Thy eyes may be deceived I tell thee,
For should an angel from the heavens drop down
And preach this to me that thyself hast told,   85
He should have much ado to win belief,
In both their loves I am so confident.

---

61   *a strange agony* Q1 (strange agonies Q3).
63   *credit* good name, honour.
65   *Dives* popular name for a rich man. The reference is to the parable in *Luke* xvi.
69   *as my* Q1 (as is my Q3).
80   *may* Q1 (can Q3).
81   *unjust* faithless, dishonest.
82   *instance* evidence.
83   *Eyes, eyes* Q1 (Eyes master, eyes Q3).

NICK

Shall I discourse the same by circumstance?

FRANKFORD

No more; to supper, and command your fellows
To attend us and the strangers. Not a word,   90
I charge thee on thy life; be secret then,
For I know nothing.

NICK

I am dumb. And now that I have eased my stomach,
I will go fill my stomach.   *Exit* NICK

FRANKFORD   95

Away, be gone.
She is well born, descended nobly,
Virtuous her education, her repute
Is in the general voice of all the country
Honest and fair, her carriage, her demeanour
In all her actions that concern the love   100
To me, her husband, modest, chaste, and godly.
Is all this seeming gold plain copper?
But he, that Judas that hath borne my purse,
And sold me for a sin – O God, O God,
Shall I put up these wrongs? No, shall I trust   105
The bare report of this suspicious groom
Before the double gilt, the well hatch ore
Of their two hearts? No, I will loose these thoughts.
Distraction I will banish from my brow,
And from my looks exile sad discontent.   110
Their wonted favours in my tongue shall flow.

---

91   *strangers* guests, visitors.
94   *eased my stomach* 'got it off my mind', rid myself of what stifled my appetite.
104   *Judas that hath borne my purse* Christ's betrayer was by John's account reputed to
      have held the money-bag (*John* xiii, 29). This is the first of two allusions Frankford
      makes to Wendoll as Judas (and by implication to himself as betrayed Christ). The
      other occurs at XIII.76–8.
106   *put up* submit to, endure, suffer quietly.
107   *groom* serving-man.
108   *the double gilt, the well hatch ore* The richness of 'double gilt' is intended to contrast
      with the poverty of Nick's 'bare report' (previous line), but also there is the inevitable
      pun on 'double gilt'. 'To hatch' is to inlay with gold or silver. Verity proposed the
      emendation of the quarto readings to 'well-hatched', which makes good sense. The
      phrase persists in the suggestion that gilded and decorated superficiality is at the
      same time being consciously preferred and subconsciously exposed by Frankford
      through Heywood's puns (hatched o'er = covered over?).

Till I know all, I'll nothing seem to know.
Lights and a table there! Wife, Master Wendoll and gentle Master
Cranwell –

Enter ANNE, WENDOLL, CRANWELL, NICK *and* JENKIN   115
with cards, carpet, stools and other necessaries

FRANKFORD

O you are a stranger, Master Cranwell, you,
And often baulk my house; faith, you are a churl.
Now we have supped, a table, and to cards.

JENKIN

A pair of cards, Nicklas, and a carpet to cover the table. Where's
Sisly with her counters and her box? Candles and candlesticks
there! Fie, we have such a household of serving creatures! Unless   120
it be Nick and I, there's not one amongst them all can say boo to
a goose. Well said, Nick.

They spread a carpet, set down lights and cards

ANNE

Come, Master Frankford, who shall take my part?

FRANKFORD

Marry, that will I, sweet wife.

WENDOLL   125

No, by my faith, sir, when you are together I sit out; it must be
Mistress Frankford and I, or else it is no match.

FRANKFORD

I do not like that match.

NICK

[*Aside*] You have no reason, marry, knowing all.

---

115   s.d. *carpet* Q1 (Carpets Q3).
      s.d. *other necessaries* a further instance of authorial papers, hardly tolerable in the
      playhouse.
116   *O you are a stranger, Master Cranwell, you,* Q1 (O master Cranwel, you are are [sic]
      a stranger heere Q3).
117   *baulk* avoid or pass by.
119   *pair* pack.
      carpet . . . table This was the usual practice of the age. See above, line 115 s.d.
120   *counters and her box* i.e. to score the game.
122–3 *can say boo to a goose* are capable of the simplest task (proverbial).
123   *Well said, Nick* well done. There is a temptation to propose this as a speech by Nick,
      perhaps garbled in the printer's copy for Q1.
126   *faith, sir* Q1 (Faith Q3).
127   *match* This word here and in the following line takes us back to the 'matches' of the
      opening scenes. In both there is a double meaning.

FRANKFORD

    'Tis no great matter neither. Come, Master Cranwell, shall you

    and I take them up?   130

CRANWELL

    At your pleasure, sir.

FRANKFORD

    I must look to you, Master Wendoll, for you will be playing false

    – nay, so will my wife too.

NICK

    [*Aside*] Ay, I will be sworn she will.

ANNE   135

    Let them that are taken playing false forfeit the set.

FRANKFORD

    Content. It shall go hard but I'll take you.

CRANWELL

    Gentlemen, what shall our game be?

WENDOLL

    Master Frankford, you play best at Noddy.

FRANKFORD

    You shall not find it so; indeed you shall not.

ANNE   140

    I can play at nothing so well as Double Ruff.

FRANKFORD

    If Master Wendoll and my wife be together, there's no playing

    against them at double hand.

NICK

    I can tell you, sir, the game that Master Wendoll is best at.

WENDOLL

    What game is that, Nick?

NICK   145

    Marry, sir, Knave Out of Doors.

---

133   *playing false* (a) at cards (b) deceiving me with my wife.

135   *Ay, I* Q1 (I Q3).

137   *take you* detect you, find you out.

139   *Noddy* (a) a card game (b) fool, the cuckold.

141   *Double Ruff* (a) another card game, like whist (b) with 'double' in the sense of

    'deceitful, with duplicity', and 'excitement, passion' as the sense of 'ruff'.

143   *double hand* i.e. (a) when they are partners in a card game (b) at duplicity.

146   *Knave Out of Doors* another card game, and another play on words, in this instance

    'knave' meaning 'rascal'.

WENDOLL

She and I will take you at Lodam.

ANNE

Husband, shall we play at Saint?

FRANKFORD

[*Aside*] My saint's turned devil. [*To them*] No, we'll none of
Saint. You're best at New Cut, wife; you'll play at that.

WENDOLL   150

If you play at New Cut, I'm soonest hitter of any here, for a
wager.

FRANKFORD

[*Aside*] Tis me they play on; well, you may draw out.
For all your cunning, 'twill be to your shame.
I'll teach you at your New Cut, a new game.
[*To them*] Come, come.   155

CRANWELL

If you cannot agree upon the game, to Post and Pair.

WENDOLL

We shall be soonest pairs, and my good host,
When he comes late home, he must kiss the post.

FRANKFORD

Whoever wins, it shall be to thy cost.

CRANWELL   160

Faith, let it be Vide-ruff, and let's make honours.

---

147   *Lodam* a game of cards, in one form called 'losing loadum', in which the loser won
       the game (*OED*). The paradoxical nature of the game is presumably part of the
       double entendre. Van Fossen also draws attention to Florio's etymology (*OED*) in
       which he derives the name from the Italian *carica l'asino*, 'load the ass', likewise
       appropriate to the play on meanings in this passage.

148   *Saint* the name of this game derives from 'cent', one hundred points being required
       for a win. The anglicised title of course contributes to the series of *double entendres*,
       as the following lines indicate.

150   *New Cut* another 'old card game' (*OED*), this time with a bawdy allusion.

151   *hitter* scorer, but again with a bawdy allusion in view of the sense of 'cut'.

153   *draw out* i.e. both their cards and their play on him.

157   *Post and Pair* a game with three cards each (hence the analogy with their triangular
       relationship).

159   *post* i.e. the doorpost or gatepost; *to kiss the post* means 'to be disappointed, shut
       out, excluded'.

161   *Vide-ruff* the game of ruff again (see line 141), but in some variant that involves
       vying or backing the trump. There is also the double sense of competing for the
       lady, here (as above) representing Anne, who presumably wears one.
       honours in cards the four highest trumps (ace, king, queen and knave).

FRANKFORD

If you make honours, one thing let me crave,

Honour the King and Queen; except the knave.

WENDOLL

Well, as you please for that. Lift who shall deal.

ANNE

The least in sight. What are you, Master Wendoll?

WENDOLL   165

[*Cutting the cards*] I am a knave.

NICK

[*Aside*] I'll swear it.

ANNE

I a queen.

FRANKFORD

[*Aside*] A quean thou should'st say.

[*To them*]   Well, the cards are mine.

They are the grossest pair that e'er I felt.

ANNE   170

Shuffle, I'll cut. [*Aside*] Would I had never dealt.

                                    [FRANKFORD *deals the cards*]

FRANKFORD

I have lost my dealing.

WENDOLL

Sir, the fault's in me.

This queen I have more than my own, you see.

Give me the stock.

                                    [WENDOLL *deals*]

163   *King and Queen . . . knave* In the *double entendre* that persists through this episode,
       these cards signify Frankford, Anne and Wendoll.
       except exclude.
164   *Lift* cut.
       deal a sexual *double entendre*, picked up in the following line by Anne, meaning 'have
       intercourse'.
165   *least in sight* i.e. the player drawing the lowest card will be dealer, but Wendoll is in
       social terms 'the least' and likewise a sexual 'dealer'.
168   *a queen* Q1 (am Queene Q3).
169   *quean* harlot.
170   *grossest pair* crudest pack (of cards), but also an allusion to the moral turpitude of
       Anne and Wendoll.
       felt (a) handled (b) tested (morally).
171   *dealt* i.e. sexually.
174   *my own* Q1 (mine owne Q3).

FRANKFORD   My mind's not on my game.
  [*Aside*] Many a deal I have lost, the more's your shame.   175
  [*To him*] You have served me a bad trick, Master Wendoll.
WENDOLL
  Sir, you must take your lot. To end this strife,
  I know I have dealt better with your wife.
FRANKFORD
  Thou hast dealt falsely then.
ANNE
  What's trumps?   180
WENDOLL
  Hearts. Partner, I rub.
FRANKFORD
  [*Aside*] Thou robb'st me of my soul, of her chaste love;
  In thy false dealing, thou hast robbed my heart.
  Booty you play; I like a loser stand,
  Having no heart, or here, or in my hand.   185
  [*To them*] I will give o'er the set; I am not well.
  Come, who will hold my cards?
ANNE
  Not well, sweet Master Frankford?
  Alas, what ail you? 'Tis some sudden qualm.
WENDOLL
  How long have you been so, Master Frankford?   190
FRANKFORD
  Sir, I was lusty, and I had my health,
  But I grew ill when you began to deal.
  Take hence this table.

          Enter SERVANTS *to remove table, cards, etc.*

                    Gentle Master Cranwell,
  You are welcome; see your chamber at your pleasure.
  I am sorry that this megrim takes me so,   195

177 *trick* (a) hand of cards (b) deceit.
181 *rub* to take all the cards of one suit (*OED* v¹). Also possibly 'annoy, irritate'.
184 *Booty* i.e. falsely in league against me. To play booty meant to play badly with the
     intention of losing the game, hence falsely betraying and victimising one player.
189 *qualm* feeling of illness or sickness, but also with the (unintended, but more
     accurate) sense of 'sickening fear, sinking or faintness of heart'.
191 *lusty* full of healthy vigour.
192 *deal* again, with a double sense, see above ll. 164, 176.
195 *megrim* migraine.

I cannot sit and bear you company.
Jenkin, some lights, and show him to his chamber.

ANNE

A nightgown for my husband, quickly there.

Enter SERVANT *with nightgown, and exit*

It is some rheum or cold.

WENDOLL

Now, in good faith, this illness you have got   200
By sitting late without your gown.

FRANKFORD

I know it, Master Wendoll.
Go, go to bed, lest you complain like me.
Wife, prethee wife, into my bed-chamber.
The night is raw and cold and rheumatic.   205
Leave me my gown and light; I'll walk away my fit.

WENDOLL

Sweet sir, good night.   [*Exit* WENDOLL]

FRANKFORD

Myself, good night.

ANNE

Shall I attend you, husband?

FRANKFORD

No gentle wife, thou'lt catch cold in thy head.   210
Prethee begone, sweet; I'll make haste to bed.

ANNE

No sleep will fasten on mine eyes, you know,
Until you come.   *Exit* ANNE

FRANKFORD   Sweet Nan, I prethee go.
[*To* NICK] I have bethought me. Get me by degrees
The keys of all my doors, which I will mould   215
In wax, and take their fair impression,
To have by them new keys. This being compassed,
At a set hour a letter shall be brought me,
And when they think they may securely play,

---

199   *rheum* cold in the head, catarrh.
205   *rheumatic* likely to cause catarrh, etc.
208   *Myself* i.e. my intimate friend.
210   *thou'lt catch cold* ed. (thout catcht cold Q1; thou't catch hold Q3) Van Fossen does
      not record the *hold* variant in Q3.

49

They are nearest to danger. Nick, I must rely   220
Upon thy trust and faithful secrecy.

NICK

Build on my faith.

FRANKFORD   To bed then, not to rest.
Care lodges in my brain, grief in my breast.

Exeunt

[SCENE IX]

Enter SUSAN, OLD MOUNTFORD, SANDY, RODER *and* TYDY

OLD MOUNTFORD

You say my nephew is in great distress –
Who brought it to him but his own lewd life?
I cannot spare a cross. I must confess
He was my brother's son – why, niece, what then?
This is no world in which to pity men.   5

SUSAN

I was not born a beggar; though his extremes
Enforce this language from me, I protest
No fortune of mine own could lead my tongue
To this base key. I do beseech you, uncle,
For the name's sake, for Christianity,   10
Nay, for God's sake, to pity his distress.
He is denied the freedom of the prison,
And in the hole is laid with men condemned.
Plenty he hath of nothing but of irons,
And it remains in you to free him thence.   15

OLD MOUNTFORD

Money I cannot spare. Men should take heed.
He lost my kindred when he fell to need.

220   *are nearest* Q1 (neerest are Q3).

  2   *lewd* wicked.   3 *cross* type of small coin.
  4   *my* Q3 (me Q1).
  8   *mine own* Q3 (mine Q1).
 10   *the name's sake* i.e. the family name or honour.
 13   *hole* dungeon, specifically one of the worst apartments of London's Counter prison,
       though the action of this play seems to be laid in Yorkshire.

Exit OLD MOUNTFORD

SUSAN

    Gold is but earth; thou earth enough shalt have
    When thou hast once took measure of thy grave.
    You know me, Master Sandy, and my suit.   20

SANDY

    I knew you, Lady, when the old man lived;
    I knew you ere your brother sold his land.
    Then you were Mistress Sue, tricked up in jewels;
    Then you sung well, played sweetly on the flute;
    But now I neither know you nor your suit.   [*Exit* SANDY]   25

SUSAN

    You, Master Roder, was my brother's tenant.
    Rent-free he placed you in that wealthy farm
    Of which you are possessed.

RODER   True, he did,

    And have I not there dwelt still for his sake?
    I have some business now, but without doubt   30
    They that have hurled him in will help him out.   *Exit* RODER

SUSAN

    Cold comfort still. What say you, cousin Tydy?

TYDY

    I say this comes of roisting, swaggering.
    Call me not cousin; each man for himself.
    Some men are born to mirth and some to sorrow.   35
    I am no cousin unto them that borrow.   *Exit* TYDY

SUSAN

    O Charity, why art thou fled to heaven,
    And left all things on this earth uneven?
    Their scoffing answers I will ne'er return,
    But to myself his grief in silence mourn.   40

Enter SIR FRANCIS *and* MALBY

SIR FRANCIS

    She is poor; I'll therefore tempt her with this gold.
    Go, Malby, in my name deliver it,
    And I will stay thy answer.

24   *flute* Q1 (Lute Q3).
32   *Cold comfort* i.e. discouraging; the phrase is proverbial.
33   *roisting* revelling.   38 *uneven* unequal, unjust.
39   *return* either (a) report (to Charles) or (b) reply to, respond to.
43   *stay* await.

MALBY

    Fair Mistress, as I understand, your grief

    Doth grow from want, so I have here in store   45

    A means to furnish you, a bag of gold

    Which to your hands I freely tender you.

SUSAN

    I thank you, heavens; I thank you, gentle sir!

    God make me able to requite this favour.

MALBY

    This gold Sir Francis Acton sends by me,   50

    And prays you [*Whispers to her*]

SUSAN

    Acton! O God, that name I am born to curse.

    Hence bawd! hence broker! See, I spurn his gold;

    My honour never shall for gain be sold.

SIR FRANCIS

    Stay, lady, stay!

SUSAN   From you I'll posting hie,   55

    Even as the doves from feathered eagles fly.   *Exit* SUSAN

SIR FRANCIS

    She hates my name, my face; how should I woo?

    I am disgraced in everything I do.

    The more she hates me and disdains my love,

    The more I am wrapped in admiration   60

    Of her divine and chaste perfections.

    Woo her with gifts I cannot, for all gifts

    Sent in my name she spurns. With looks I cannot,

    For she abhors my sight. Nor yet with letters,

    For none she will receive. How then, how then?   65

    Well I will fasten such a kindness on her

    As shall o'ercome her hate and conquer it.

    Sir Charles, her brother lies in execution

    For a great sum of money, and besides,

---

44   *MALBY* Q1 (*Fran.* Q3).

45   *in store* in plentiful supply.

51   *prays you* Q3 (prayes you &c Q1) The *etcetera* has been taken to indicate stage business, in this case a whispered proposition. The instance of its use at Scene VI line 181 is different.

55   *posting* in haste, hurriedly.

68   *in execution* seized under legal enforcement, legally imprisoned.

The appeal is sued still for my huntsmen's death,   70
Which only I have power to reverse.
In her I'll bury all my hate of him.
Go seek the keeper, Malby, bring me to him.
To save his body, I his debts will pay;
To save his life, I his appeal will stay.   75

Exeunt SIR FRANCIS *and* MALBY

[SCENE X]

Enter SIR CHARLES *in prison, with irons, his feet bare,*
his garments all ragged and torn

SIR CHARLES

Of all on the earth's face most miserable,
Breathe in the hellish dungeon thy laments.
Thus like a slave ragged, like a felon gyved,
That hurls thee headlong to this base estate.
O unkind uncle! O my friends ingrate!   5
Unthankful kinsmen! Mountfords all too base!
To let thy name lie fettered in disgrace!
A thousand deaths here in this grave I die:
Fear, hunger, sorrow, cold – all threat my death,
And join together to deprive my breath.   10
But that which most torments me, my dear sister
Hath left to visit me, and from my friends
Hath brought no hopeful answer; therefore I
Divine they will not help my misery.
If it be so, shame, scandal and contempt   15
Attend their covetous thoughts, need make their graves.

70   *appeal is sued still* i.e. he is still being pursued legally through the courts.
      huntsmen's Q1 (Huntsmans Q1).
73   *me to him* Q1 (him to me Q3).

0   s.d. *feet* Q3 (*face* Q1).
2   *the* Q1 (this Q3).
3   *gyved* shackled.
5   *unkind* (a) unnatural or cruel (b) denying kinship.
      ingrate ungrateful.
7   *lie* Q1 (be Q3).

Usurers they live, and may they die like slaves.

Enter KEEPER

KEEPER

Knight, be of comfort for I bring thee freedom
From all thy troubles.

SIR CHARLES   Then I am doomed to die.
Death is the end of all calamity.   20

KEEPER

Live! Your appeal is stayed, the execution
Of all your debts discharged, your creditors
Even to the utmost penny satisfied,
In sign whereof your shackles I knock off.
You are not left so much indebted to us   25
As for your fees; all is discharged, all paid.
Go freely to your house, or where you please.
After long miseries, embrace your ease.

SIR CHARLES

Thou grumblest out the sweetest music to me
That ever organ played. Is this a dream?   30
Or do my waking senses apprehend
The pleasing taste of these applausive news?
Slave that I was to wrong such honest friends,
My loving kinsmen and my near allies.
Tongue, I will bite thee for the scandal breath   35
Against such faithful kinsmen. They are all
Composed of pity and compassion,
Of melting charity, and of moving ruth.
That which I spake before was in my rage;
They are my friends, the mirrors of this age,   40
Bounteous and free. The noble Mountfords' race
Ne'er bred a covetous thought or humour base.

Enter SUSAN

SUSAN

I can no longer stay from visiting
My woeful brother. While I could I kept

21 *stayed* stopped.
32 *applausive* agreeable, acceptable.
38 *ruth* compassion.
40 *mirrors* i.e. models, exemplars.
42 *humour* temperament, disposition.

My hapless tidings from his hopeful ear.   45

SIR CHARLES
Sister, how much am I indebted to thee
And to thy travail.

SUSAN   What, at liberty?

SIR CHARLES
Thou seest I am, thanks to thy industry.
O unto which of all my courteous friends
Am I thus bound? My uncle Mountford? He   50
Even of an infant loved me; was it he?
So did my cousin Tydy; was it he?
So Master Roder, Master Sandy too;
Which of all these did this high kindness do?

SUSAN
Charles, can you mock me in your poverty,   55
Knowing your friends deride your misery.
Now I protest I stand so much amazed
To see your bonds free and your irons knocked off
That I am rapt into a maze of wonder,
The rather for I know not by what means   60
This happiness hath chanced.

SIR CHARLES   Why, by my uncle,
My cousins, and my friends; who else, I pray,
Would take upon them all my debts to pay?

SUSAN
O brother, they are men all of flint,
Pictures of marble, and as void of pity   65
As chased bears. I begged, I sued, I kneeled,
Laid open all your griefs and miseries,
Which they derided. More than that, denied us
A part in their alliance, but in pride
Said that our kindred with our plenty died.   70

SIR CHARLES
Drudges too much! What, did they? O known evil,
Rich fly the poor, as good men shun the Devil.
Whence should my freedom come; of whom alive,

45   *hapless* unhappy, unfortunate (note the play on 'hopeful' later in the line).
47   *travail* trouble, exertion.
65   *Pictures of marble* i.e. statues.
66   *chased* hunted, or possibly tormented (as in bear-baiting).
69   *alliance* kinship.
71   *Drudges* slaves, servile creatures.

Saving of those, have I deserved so well?
Guess, sister, call to mind, remember me. 75
These I have raised, these follow the world's guise,
Whom, rich in honour, they in woe despise.

SUSAN
My wits have lost themselves. Let's ask the keeper.

SIR CHARLES
Gaoler!

KEEPER
At hand, sir. 80

SIR CHARLES
Of courtesy resolve me one demand:
What was he took the burden of my debts
From off my back, stayed my appeal to death,
Discharged my fees, and brought me liberty?

KEEPER
A courteous knight, one called Sir Francis Acton. 85

SUSAN
Acton!

SIR CHARLES
Ha! Acton! O me, more distressed in this
Than all my troubles. Hale me back,
Double my irons, and my sparing meals
Put into halves, and lodge me in a dungeon 90
More deep, more dark, more cold, more comfortless.
By Acton freed! Not all thy manacles
Could fetter so my heels as this one word
Hath thralled my heart, and it must now lie bound
In more strict prison than thy stony gaol. 95
I am not free; I go but under bail.

KEEPER
My charge is done, sir, now I have my fees.
As we get little, we will nothing leese.   *Exit* KEEPER

---

76   *these* Q1 (they Q3).
77   *Whom ... despise* an elliptical construction variously interpreted in its detail, but the
      general sense is not in doubt: 'they despise you in misfortune, though you may be
      rich in honour.'
85   *one* Q1 (and Q3).
86   SUSAN *Acton!* Q1 (*omitted* Q3).
92   *Acton* Q3 (action Q1).
94   *thralled* brought into subjection, held captive.
98   *leese* lose, be deprived of.

SIR CHARLES

    By Acton freed, my dangerous opposite,
    Why? to what end? or what occasion? Ha!   100
    Let me forget the name of enemy,
    And with indifference balance this high favour. Ha!

SUSAN

    [*Aside*] His love to me, upon my soul 'tis so,
    That is the root from whence these strange things grow.

SIR CHARLES

    Had this proceeded from my father, he   105
    That by the law of nature is most bound
    In offices of love, it had deserved
    My best employment to requite that grace.
    Had it proceeded from my friends, or him,
    From them this action had deserved my life,   110
    And from a stranger more, because from such
    There is less execution of good deeds.
    But he, nor father, nor ally, nor friend,
    More than a stranger, both remote in blood
    And in his heart opposed my enemy,   115
    That this high bounty should proceed from him!
    O there I lose myself. What should I say?
    What think? what do, his bounty to repay?

SUSAN

    You wonder, I am sure, whence this strange kindness
    Proceeds in Acton. I will tell you, brother.   120
    He dotes on me, and oft hath sent me gifts,
    Letters, and tokens: I refused them all.

SIR CHARLES

    I have enough. Though poor, my heart is set
    In one rich gift to pay back all my debt.

                        Exeunt SIR CHARLES *and* SUSAN

---

  99   *opposite* enemy, adversary.
 100 *occasion* opportunity of taking advantage or attacking, i.e. 'What hold does it give
       him over me?'
 102 *indifference* impartiality.
       balance weigh.
 108 *employment* endeavours.
 109 *him* i.e. from my father.
 112 *execution* performance.
 119 *strange kindness* The phrase is paradoxical in a way closely related to the central
       paradox of the play.

[SCENE XI]

Enter FRANKFORD *and* NICK, *with keys, and a letter in his hand*

FRANKFORD
This is the night, and I must play the touch
To try two seeming angels. Where's my keys?

NICK
They are made according to your mould in wax.
I bade the smith be secret, gave him money,
And there they are. The letter, sir.   5

FRANKFORD
True, take it; there it is.
And when thou seest me in my pleasant'st vein
Ready to sit to supper, bring it me.

NICK
I'll do't, make no more question but I'll do't.   *Exit* NICK

Enter ANNE, CRANWELL, WENDOLL *and* JENKIN

ANNE
Sirrah, 'tis six o'clock already struck.   10
Go bid them spread the cloth and serve in supper.

JENKIN
It shall be done forsooth, mistress. Where is Spiggot the butler to
give us out salt and trenchers?   [*Exit* JENKIN]

WENDOLL
We that have been ahunting all the day
Come with prepared stomachs, Master Frankford.   15
We wished you at our sport.

---

    0   s.d. *with keys, and a letter in his hand* Q1, Q3. It is not entirely clear who has the
        letter; lines 5–6 suggest that it is Frankford who carries it on to the stage. But the
        alternative is not at all impossible, so I have left the text as it stands in the quartos.
    1   *and* Q1 (that Q3).
        the touch Q1 (my part Q3).
  1–2   *touch . . . angels* i.e. metaphorically test the worth of two apparently current coins by
        using a touchstone. There is of course a pun on 'angels'.
    5   *there* Q1 (heere Q3).
        The letter, sir. Q3 (*Erroneously given as a separate speech by Nick in* Q1).
    7   *pleasant'st* ed. (pleasantst Q1; pleasants Q3).
   13   *out* Q1 (our Q3).
        trenchers plates.
   15   *with prepared stomachs* i.e. with good appetites.

FRANKFORD

    My heart was with you, and my mind was on you.
    Fie, Master Cranwell, you are still thus sad.
    A stool, a stool! Where's Jenkin, and where's Nick?
    'Tis supper time at least an hour ago.   20
    What's the best news abroad?

WENDOLL   I know none good.

FRANKFORD

    [*Aside*] But I know too much bad.

> *Enter* SPIGGOT *and* JENKIN *with a tablecloth,*
> *bread, trenchers, and salt* [, *then exeunt*]

CRANWELL

    Methinks, sir, you might have that interest
    In your wife's brother to be more remiss
    In this hard dealing against poor Sir Charles,   25
    Who, as I hear, lies in York Castle, needy
    And in great want.

FRANKFORD

    Did not more weighty business of my own
    Hold me away, I would have laboured peace
    Betwixt them with all care; indeed I would, sir.   30

ANNE

    I'll write unto my brother earnestly
    In that behalf.

WENDOLL   A charitable deed,
    And will beget the good opinion
    Of all your friends that love you, Mistress Frankford.

FRANKFORD

    That's you for one; I know you love Sir Charles   35
    [*Aside*] And my wife too well.

WENDOLL   He deserves the love
    Of all true gentlemen. Be yourselves judge.

FRANKFORD

    But supper, ho! Now as thou lovest me, Wendoll,
    Which I am sure thou dost, be merry, pleasant,

---

23   *interest* Q3 (intrest Q1) i.e. influence (over or with).
24   *more remiss* less strict, more lenient.
25   *this* Q1 (his Q3).
       dealing conduct, behaviour.
28   *my* Q1 (mine Q3).
34   *Mistress* Q3 (Master Q1).

And frolic it tonight. Sweet Master Cranwell,   40
Do you the like. Wife, I protest my heart
Was ne'er more bent on sweet alacrity.
Where be those lazy knaves to serve in supper?

Enter NICK

NICK
Sir, here's a letter.
FRANKFORD
Whence comes it? and who brought it?   45
NICK
A stripling that below attends your answer,
And as he tells me it is sent from York.
FRANKFORD
Have him into the cellar; let him taste
A cup of our March beer. Go, make him drink.   [*Reads*]
NICK
I'll make him drunk, if he be a Trojan.   [*Exit*]   50
FRANKFORD
My boots and spurs! Where's Jenkin? God forgive me,
How I neglect my business. Wife, look here,
I have a matter to be tried tomorrow
By eight o'clock, and my attorney writes me
I must be there betimes with evidence,   55
Or it will go against me. Where's my boots?

Enter JENKIN *with boots and spurs*

ANNE
I hope your business craves no such dispatch
That you must ride tonight.
WENDOLL [*Aside*]   I hope it doth.

---

42   *alacrity* lively enjoyment.
44   *Sir, here's a letter* Q1 (Here's a letter sir Q3).
48–9 *Lineation* ed. (Have . . . cup / Of . . . drink Q1; *as prose* Q3).
50   *Trojan* the colloquial sense is 'a roisterer, one who leads a. dissolute life, a good
      fellow'. Following Bates, Van Fossen cites Heywood's use of the term in
      Philocothista (1635) for 'drunkard'.
51–2 *Lineation* Q1 (*as prose* Q3).
51   *Where's* Q3 (whetes Q1).
55   *betimes* early in the morning.

FRANKFORD

    God's me! No such dispatch?

    Jenkin, my boots. Where's Nick? Saddle my roan,   60

    And the grey dapple for himself.

                                [*Exit* JENKIN]

                        Content ye,

    It much concerns me. Gentle Master Cranwell

    And Master Wendoll, in my absence use

    The very ripest pleasure of my house.

WENDOLL

    Lord, Master Frankford, will you ride tonight?   65

    The ways are dangerous.

FRANKFORD   Therefore will I ride

    Appointed well, and so shall Nick, my man.

ANNE

    I'll call you up by five o'clock tomorrow.

FRANKFORD

    No, by my faith, wife, I'll not trust to that.

    Tis not such easy rising in a morning   70

    From one I love so dearly. No, by my faith,

    I shall not leave so sweet a bedfellow

    But with much pain. You have made me a sluggard

    Since I first knew you.

ANNE   Then if you needs will go

    This dangerous evening, Master Wendoll,   75

    Let me entreat you bear him company.

WENDOLL

    With all my heart, sweet mistress. My boots there!

FRANKFORD

    Fie, fie, that for my private business

    I should disease my friend, and be a trouble

    To the whole house. Nick!   80

                  [*Enter* NICK]

NICK

    Anon, sir.

---

59   *God's me* i.e. God save me.

61   *Content ye* Be assured.

66   *ways are dangerous* a reference to the footpads and highwaymen that constituted a threat to travellers in the period.

67   *Appointed well* well armed.

79   *disease* disturb, inconvenience.

FRANKFORD

Bring forth my gelding. [*Exit* NICK]
                         As you love me, sir,
Use no more words. A hand, good Master Cranwell.

CRANWELL

Sir, God be your good speed.

FRANKFORD

Goodnight, sweet Nan. Nay, nay, a kiss and part.   85
[*Aside*] Dissembling lips, you suit not with my heart.
                                        Exit FRANKFORD

WENDOLL

[*Aside*] How business, time and hours all gracious proves,
And are the furtherers to my new born love.
I am husband now in Master Frankford's place,
And must command the house. [*To* ANNE] My pleasure is   90
We will not sup abroad so publicly,
But in your private chamber, Mistress Frankford.

ANNE

[*To* WENDOLL] O sir, you are too public in your love,
And Master Frankford's wife –

CRANWELL   Might I crave favour,
I would entreat you I might see my chamber.   95
I am on the sudden grown exceeding ill,
And would be spared from supper.

WENDOLL   Light there, ho!
See you want nothing, sir, for if you do
You injure that good man, and wrong me too.

CRANWELL

I will make bold. Goodnight.   *Exit* CRANWELL

WENDOLL   How all conspire   100
To make our bosom sweet and full entire.
Come, Nan, I prithee let us sup within.

ANNE

O what a clog unto the soul is sin.

---

86 *suit not* do not match.
87 *proves* Q1 (proue Q3).
99 *injure* Q3 (injury Q1) The two forms were synonymous, though *c.* 1600 'injury' was
    supplanted as a verb by the current form. The compositors' preferences may simply
    record this process.
101 *bosom* desires (cf. *Measure for Measure* IV.iii.139 'You shall have your bosom on this
    fellow.') Van Fossen defines it as 'intimacy'.
103 *clog* impediment, encumbrance (see I.58 above).

We pale offenders are, still full of fear;
Every suspicious eye brings danger near,   105
When they whose clear heart from offence are free
Despise report, base scandals do outface,
And stand at mere defiance with disgrace.

WENDOLL

Fie, fie, you talk too like a puritan.

ANNE

You have tempted me to mischief, Master Wendoll.   110
I have done I know not what. Well, you plead custom;
That which for want of wit I granted erst
I now must yield through fear. Come, come, let's in.
Once o'er shoes, we are straight o'er head in sin.

WENDOLL

My jocund soul is joyful above measure;   115
I'll be profuse in Frankford's richest treasure.

Exeunt

[SCENE XII]

Enter SISLY, JENKIN *and* SPIGGOT

JENKIN

My mistress and Master Wendoll, my master, sup in her chamber
tonight. Sisly, you are preferred from being the cook to be

104   *pale* i.e. pale from fear, timorous.
106   *When* while, whereas.
107   *do* Q3 (to Q1).
109   *puritan* Q3 (Puritant Q1) Whether Q1's is a variant form or a variant spelling is not
      clear, though *OED* records it and suggests that it was formed by analogy with
      'protestant'.
111   *plead custom* i.e. that sin has acquired the force of right by habitual practice (an
      allusion to the legal force of custom).
112   *erst* first.

  0   s.d. *and* SPIGGOT ed. (and Butler Q3; Butler, and other Seruingmen Q1) Given the
      entry at line 16, and the nature of Jenkin's remarks, the entry of servingmen at this
      point seems unlikely. I have therefore followed Q3.
  2   *preferred* promoted.

chambermaid. Of all the loves betwixt thee and me, tell me what thou thinkest of this.

SISLY

Mum; there's an old proverb, 'When the cat's away, the mouse   5
may play'.

JENKIN

Now you talk of a cat, Sisly, I smell a rat.

SISLY

Good words, Jenkin, lest you be called to answer them.

JENKIN

Why, God make my mistress an honest woman – are not these
good words? Pray God my new master play not the knave with   10
my old master – is there any hurt in this? God send no villainy
intended, and if they do sup together, pray God they do not lie
together. God keep my mistress chaste, and make us all His
servants – what harm is there in all this? Nay, more: here is my
hand; thou shalt never have my heart unless thou say 'Amen'.   15

SISLY

Amen, I pray God, I say.

Enter SERVINGMEN

SERVINGMAN

My mistress sends that you should make less noise, to lock up the
doors, and see the household all got to bed. You, Jenkin, for this
night are made the porter, to see the gates shut in.

JENKIN

Thus, by little and little, I creep into office. Come, to kennel, my   20
masters, to kennel; 'tis eleven o'clock already.

SERVINGMAN

When you have locked the gates in, you must send up the keys
to my mistress.

SISLY

Quickly, for God's sake, Jenkin, for I must carry them. I am
neither pillow nor bolster, but I know more than both.   25

---

5   *Mum* be silent.
8   *Good words* i.e. be careful what you say.
13   *keep* Q1 (make Q3).
16   s.d *SERVINGMEN* Q1, Q3. See above. The stage business at this point requires only
     one servant, who comes on as a messenger, but the quartos agree on a plural. (This
     may, of course, be an instance of Q3's dependence on Q1.)
18   *this* Q3 (his Q1, *but with catchword reading* 'this').
20   *to kennel* i.e. as though they were a pack of hounds.

JENKIN

To bed, good Spiggot; to bed, good honest serving creatures, and
let us sleep as snug as pigs in pease-straw.

Exeunt

[SCENE XIII]

Enter FRANKFORD *and* NICK

FRANKFORD

Soft, soft. We have tied our geldings to a tree
Two flight shoot off, lest by their thundering hooves
They blab our coming back. Hearest thou no noise?

NICK

Hear? I hear nothing but the owl and you.

FRANKFORD

So; now my watch's hand points upon twelve,   5
And it is dead midnight. Where are my keys?

NICK

Here, sir.

FRANKFORD

This is the key that opes my outward gate;
This is the hall door; this my withdrawing chamber.
But this, that door that's bawd unto my shame,   10
Fountain and spring of all my bleeding thoughts,
Where the most hallowed order and true knot

27   *pease-straw* straw from the pea plant. The phrase 'as snug as pigs in pease-straw' is
      proverbial.

  1   *our* Q1 (*your* Q3).
1–3   *As prose in quartos.*
  2   *Two flight shoot* flight-shot arrows were specifically designed for distance competi-
      tions, so here, a distance twice the maximum range of bow and arrow.
  3   *blab* betray, reveal.
      back Q1 (*omitted* Q3).
  4   *Hear?* Q1 (*omitted* Q3).
  6   *dead* Q1 (*iust* Q3).
  9   *is* Q1 (*omitted* Q3).
      my Q1 (*the* Q3).
      withdrawing chamber a room to withdraw to, now a drawing room.

Of nuptial sanctity hath been profaned.
It leads to my polluted bedchamber,
Once my terrestial heaven, now my earth's hell,   15
The place where sins in all their ripeness dwell.
But I forget myself; now to my gate.

NICK

It must ope with far less noise than Cripplegate, or your plot's
dashed.

FRANKFORD

So, reach me my dark lantern to the rest.   20
Tread softly, softly.

NICK

I will walk on eggs this pace.

FRANKFORD

A general silence hath surprised the house,
And this is the last door. Astonishment,
Fear and amazement play against my heart,   25
Even as a madman beats upon a drum.
O keep my eyes, you heavens, before I enter,
From any sight that may transfix my soul.
Or if there be so black a spectacle,
O strike mine eyes stark blind; or if not so,   30
Lend me such patience to digest my grief
That I may keep this white and virgin hand
From any violent outrage or red murder.
And with that prayer I enter.   [*Exit* FRANKFORD]

NICK

[*Aside*] Here's a circumstance!   35
A man may be made cuckold in the time
That he's about it. And the case were mine,
As 'tis my master's, – 'sblood that he makes me swear –

---

18   *Cripplegate* one of the gates to the old city of London. If the play was performed at
the Red Bull theatre (as seems likely) this would be the gate through which spectators
passed en route to the playhouse.
20   *dark lantern* a lantern having an arrangement by which the light could be concealed.
22   *walk on eggs this pace* i.e. 'I'm treading so softly I could walk on eggs.'
23   *surprised* overtaken.
25   *play against* Q1 (beate vpon Q3).
35–8   *Lineation* Q1 (*as prose* Q3).
35   *circumstance* Q1 (circumstance indeed Q3).
36   *cuckold* Q1 (a Cuckold Q3).
37   *That* Q1 (*omitted* Q3)
    And if.

I would have placed his action, entered there.
I would, I would.   40

[*Enter* FRANKFORD]

FRANKFORD
O, O!
NICK
Master, 'sblood, master, master!
FRANKFORD
O me unhappy! I have found them lying
Close in each other's arms, and fast asleep.
But that I would not damn two precious souls   45
Bought with my Saviour's blood, and send them laden
With all their scarlet sins upon their backs
Unto a fearful judgement, their two lives
Had met upon my rapier.
NICK
'Sblood, master, have you left them sleeping still? 50
Let me go wake them.
FRANKFORD
Stay; let me pause awhile.
O God, O God, that it were possible
To undo things done, to call back yesterday;
That Time could turn up his swift sandy glass   55
To untell the days, and to redeem these hours.
Or that the sun
Could, rising from the west, draw his coach backward,
Take from the account of Time so many minutes,
Till he had all these seasons called again,   60
Those minutes and those actions done in them,
Even from her first offence, that I might take her
As spotless as an angel in my arms.
But O! I talk of things impossible,

---

39   *placed his action* It is unclear whether 'his' refers to Frankford or to Wendoll. The
     phrase could mean 'determined what Wendoll was doing' or 'established Frankford's
     case (against Wendoll)'.
44   *other's* Q1 (other Q3).
50–1 *Lineation* Q3 (*as prose* Q1).
50   *'Sblood master* Q1 (Master what Q3).
51   *them* Q1 (em Q3).
55   *sandy glass* i.e. an hourglass filled with sand.
56   *to untell* i.e. to count backwards in time.

And cast beyond the moon. God give me patience, 65
For I will in to wake them. *Exit* FRANKFORD

NICK

Here's patience perforce!
He needs must trot afoot that tires his horse.

Enter WENDOLL *running over the stage in a nightgown,*
[FRANKFORD] *after him with his sword drawn; the* MAID *in her*
smock stays his hand and clasps hold on him; he pauses awhile

FRANKFORD

I thank thee, maid. Thou like the angel's hand
Hath stayed me from a bloody sacrifice. 70
Go, villain, and my wrongs sit on thy soul
As heavy as this grief doth upon mine.
When thou recordest my many courtesies
And shalt compare them with thy treacherous heart,
Lay them together, weigh them equally, 75
'Twill be revenge enough. Go, to thy friend
A Judas. Pray, pray, lest I live to see
Thee Judas-like hanged on an elder tree.

Enter ANNE *in her smock, nightgown and night attire*

ANNE

O by what word, what title, or what name
Shall I entreat your pardon? Pardon! O 80
I am as far from hoping such sweet grace
As Lucifer from heaven. To call you husband!
O me most wretched, I have lost that name;
I am no more your wife.

NICK   'Sblood, sir, she sounds.

FRANKFORD

Spare thou thy tears, for I will weep for thee; 85
And keep thy countenance, for I'll blush for thee.

66   *to* Q1 (and Q3).
67   *perforce* of necessity. The phrase is proverbial.
69   *the* Q1 (an Q3).
69–70   *angel's hand ... sacrifice* The reference is to Abraham's proposed sacrifice of
      Issac, in *Genesis* xii, 11–12.
74   *shalt* Q1 (shall Q3).
78   *hanged on an elder tree* It was traditionally believed that the tree on which Judas
      hanged himself was an elder. See Note on VIII.104 above.
84   *sounds* i.e. swoons, faints.

Now I protest, I think 'tis I am tainted,
For I am most ashamed, and 'tis more hard
For me to look upon thy guilty face
Than on the sun's clear brow. What wouldst thou speak?   90

ANNE

I would I had no tongue, no ears, no eyes,
No apprehension, no capacity.
When do you spurn me like a dog? When tread me
Under your feet? When drag me by the hair?
Though I deserve a thousand thousandfold   95
More than you can inflict, yet, once my husband,
For womanhood – to which I am a shame
Though once an ornament – even for His sake
That hath redeemed our souls, mark not my face
Nor hack me with your sword, but let me go   100
Perfect and undeformed to my tomb.
I am not worthy that I should prevail
In the least suit, no, not to speak to you,
Nor look on you, nor to be in your presence.
Yet, as an abject, this one suit I crave;   105
This granted, I am ready for my grave.

FRANKFORD

My God with patience arm me! Rise, nay, rise,
And I'll debate with thee. Was it for want
Thou playedst the strumpet? Wast thou not supplied
With every pleasure, fashion, and new toy,   110
Nay, even beyond my calling?

ANNE   I was.

FRANKFORD

Was it then disability in me,
Or in thine eye seemed he a properer man?

---

90   *What . . . speak?* Q1 (*a separate line in* Q3).
94   *your feet* Q1 (feete Q3).
97   *a shame* ed. (ashamd Q1; asham'd Q3) Dodsley's suggested emendation supplies a
       grammatical parallel with 'ornament'.
105 *an abject* one who has been cast aside.
111 *beyond my calling* Van Fossen glosses calling as 'rank, station in life', with the
       implication, presumably, that he had over-indulged her whims. But the word also has
       the sense of 'duty, that which is morally or religiously required of one'. The
       distinction is an interesting one for readers scrutinising the Frankfords' relationship.
113 *properer* handsomer.

ANNE

O no.

FRANKFORD Did I not lodge thee in my bosom?
Wear thee here in my heart?

ANNE   You did.   115

FRANKFORD

I did indeed; witness my tears I did.
Go bring my infants hither.

[Exit MAID*]*

[Enter MAID *again with* TWO CHILDREN*]*

O Nan, O Nan,
If neither fear of shame, regard of honour,
The blemish of my house, nor my dear love
Could have withheld thee from so lewd a fact,   120
Yet for these infants, these young harmless souls,
On whose white brows thy shame is charactered,
And grows in greatness as they wax in years,
Look but on them, and melt away in tears.
Away with them, lest as her spotted body   125
Hath stained their names with stripe of bastardy.
So her adulterous breath may blast their spirits
With her infectious thoughts. Away with them!

[Exeunt MAID *with* CHILDREN*]*

ANNE

In this one life I die ten thousand deaths.

FRANKFORD

Stand up, stand up. I will do nothing rashly.   130

114–15 *Lineation* Q3 (Did I . . . thee / Here in my hart. Q1).
   114 *I not* Q1 (not I Q3).
         my Q3 (thy Q1).
   115 *here in* Q1 (in Q3)
   118 *neither* Q3 (either Q1)
   120 *fact* action, deed.
   122 *charactered* imprinted, written.
   123 *wax* grow.
   125 *spotted* morally stained.
   126 *stripe of bastardy* This example is cited by the *OED* as a figurative use of the *stripe*
         left by the rod of punishment, therefore a badge of shame, in this case of illegitimacy.
         Van Fossen draws attention to the heraldic use of the bend sinister to denote
         bastardy in arms.
   127 *blast* blight.

I will retire awhile into my study,
And thou shalt hear thy sentence presently.

Exit FRANKFORD

ANNE

'Tis welcome, be it death. O me, base strumpet,
That having such a husband, such sweet children,
Must enjoy neither. O to redeem my honour   135
I would have this hand cut off, these my breasts seared,
Be racked, strappadoed, put to any torment.
Nay, to whip but this scandal out, I would hazard
The rich and dear redemption of my soul.
He cannot be so base as to forgive me,   140
Nor I so shameless to accept his pardon.
O women, women, you that have yet kept
Your holy matrimonial vow unstained,
Make me your instance: when you tread awry,
Your sins like mine will on your conscience lie.   145

Enter SISLY, SPIGGOT, *all the* SERVINGMEN *and* JENKIN,
as newly come out of bed

ALL

O mistress, mistress, what have you done, mistress?
NICK

'Sblood, what a caterwauling keep you here.
JENKIN

O Lord, mistress, how comes this to pass? My master is run away
in his shirt, and never so much as called me to bring his clothes
after him.   150
ANNE

See what guilt is: here stand I in this place,
Ashamed to look my servants in the face.

132   *presently* immediately, in a very short space of time.
135   *my* Q1 (mine Q3).
136   *seared* i.e. with hot irons.
137   *strappadoed* a horrendous punishment or torture in which the arms were fastened
       behind the back and the victim hoisted by them into the air until he was his own
       height above the ground. He was then allowed to drop halfway down and his fall
       arrested with a jerk.
142   *have yet* Q1 (yet haue Q3).
144   *instance* example, lesson.
147   *'Sblood, what* Q1 (What Q3).
       caterwauling a noise like that of cats in heat.
149   *shirt* nightshirt.

Enter MASTER FRANKFORD *and* CRANWELL,
whom seeing she falls on her knees

FRANKFORD

My words are registered in heaven already;
With patience hear me. I'll not martyr thee,
Nor mark thee for a strumpet, but with usage   155
Of more humility torment thy soul,
And kill thee, even with kindness.

CRANWELL   Master Frankford –

FRANKFORD

Good Master Cranwell – woman, hear thy judgement:
Go, make thee ready in thy best attire,
Take with thee all thy gowns, all thy apparel;   160
Leave nothing that did ever call thee mistress,
Or by whose sight being left here in the house
I may remember such a woman by.
Choose thee a bed and hangings for a chamber;
Take with thee everything that hath thy mark,   165
And get thee to my manor seven mile off,
Where live. 'Tis thine; I freely give it thee.
My tenants by shall furnish thee with wains
To carry all thy stuff, within two hours,
No longer, will I limit thee my sight.   170
Choose which of all my servants thou likest best,
And they are thine to attend thee.

ANNE   A mild sentence.

FRANKFORD

But, as thou hopest for heaven, as thou believest
Thy name's recorded in the book of life,
I charge thee never after this sad day   175
To see me, or to meet me, or to send
By word, or writing, gift, or otherwise
To move me, by thyself, or by thy friends,
Nor challenge any part in my two children.

---

164   *a chamber* Q1 (thy chamber Q3).
165   *that* Q1 (which Q3)
168   *wains* wagons.
170   *will I limit thee my sight* i.e. will I permit you to remain within my sight.
174   *book of life* in the Bible the book containing the names of those who will inherit
          eternal life.

So farewell, Nan, for we will henceforth be   180
As we had never seen, ne'er more shall see.

ANNE

How full my heart is in my eyes appears.
What wants in words, I will supply in tears.

FRANKFORD

Come, take your coach, your stuff; all must along.
Servants and all make ready, all be gone.   185
It was thy hand cut two hearts out of one.

[*Exeunt*]

[SCENE XIV]

Enter SIR CHARLES, *gentlemanlike, and* [SUSAN] *his sister,*
gentlewomanlike

SUSAN

Brother, why have you tricked me like a bride?
Bought me this gay attire, these ornaments?
Forget you our estate, our poverty?

SIR CHARLES

Call me not brother, but imagine me
Some barbarous outlaw, or uncivil kerne,   5
For if thou shutt'st thy eye, and only hearest
The words that I shall utter, thou shalt judge me
Some staring ruffian, not thy brother Charles.
O Susan!

SUSAN

O brother, what doth this strange language mean?   10

SIR CHARLES

Dost love me, sister? Wouldst thou see me live
A bankrupt beggar in the world's disgrace,

182   *my eyes* Q1 (mine eies Q3).

1   *tricked* dressed, adorned, decked.
3   *estate* i.e. financial circumstances.
5   *uncivil kerne* uncivilised peasant or boor.
8   *staring* wild, frantic.
     ruffian Q3 (Ruffin Q1).

And die indebted to my enemies?
Wouldst thou behold me stand like a huge beam
In the world's eye, a byword and a scorn?   15
It lies in thee of these to acquit me free,
And all my debt I may outstrip by thee.

SUSAN

By me? Why I have nothing, nothing left;
I owe even for the clothes upon my back.
I am not worth –

SIR CHARLES   O sister, say not so.   20
It lies in you my downcast state to raise,
To make me stand on even points with the world.
Come, sister, you are rich! Indeed you are!
And in your power you have, without delay,
Acton's five hundred pound back to repay.   25

SUSAN

Till now I had thought you loved me, by mine honour,
Which I had kept as spotless as the moon.
I ne'er was mistress of that single doit
Which I reserved not to supply your wants,
And do you think that I would hoard from you?   30
Now, by my hopes in heaven, knew I the means
To buy you from the slavery of your debts,
Especially from Acton, whom I hate,
I would redeem it with my life or blood.

SIR CHARLES

I challenge it, and, kindred set apart,   35
Thus ruffianlike I lay seige to your heart:

---

13   *my* Q1 (mine Q3).
14–15   *beam / In the world's eye* i.e. in conspicuous disgrace. The allusion is to the well-
        known figure used in the Sermon on the Mount (*Matthew*, vii.3) of the mote and
        the beam.
15   *byword* object of scorn and contempt.
20   *worth* – ed. (worth, &c Q1; worth Q3) The ampersand in Q1 seems here to indicate
        interruption. (Cf. the use of the etcetera at VI.181 and IX.51 note).
22   *even points* equal terms.
26   *you loved* Q1 (y'had lou'd Q3).
        mine Q1 (my Q3).
27   *had* Q1 (haue Q3).
28   *doit* originally a Dutch coin of very slight value, it came to stand as the type of a
        small amount.
30   *do you* Q1 (de'ye Q3).
36   *your* Q1 (thy Q3).

What do I owe to Acton?

SUSAN
Why, some five hundred pounds, toward which I swear
In all the world I have not one denier.

SIR CHARLES
It will not prove so, sister. Now resolve me: 40
What do you think – and speak your conscience –
Would Acton give might he enjoy your bed?

SUSAN
He would not shrink to spend a thousand pound
To give the Mountford's name so deep a wound.

SIR CHARLES
A thousand pound! I but five hundred owe;   45
Grant him your bed, he's paid with interest so.

SUSAN
O brother!

SIR CHARLES   O sister! Only this one way,
With that rich jewel, you my debts may pay.
In speaking this my cold heart shakes with shame,
Nor do I woo you in a brother's name,   50
But in a stranger's. Shall I die in debt
To Acton, my grand foe, and you still wear
The precious jewel that he holds so dear?

SUSAN
My honour I esteem as dear and precious
As my redemption.

SIR CHARLES   I esteem you, sister,   55
As dear for so dear prizing it.

SUSAN   Will Charles
Have me cut off my hands, and send them Acton?
Rip up my breast, and with my bleeding heart
Present him as a token.

SIR CHARLES   Neither, sister,
But hear me in my strange assertion: 60

38   *toward which I swear* Q1 (*separate line* Q3).
39   *denier* like *doit* (above l. 28) used as the type of a very small sum of money, originally
     a small French coin worth one twelfth of a sou.
41   *conscience* i.e. what you know inwardly (without the moral sense of the present-day
     meaning).
55–6 *I esteem . . . sister, / As . . . it.* Q1 (I esteem . . . deare, / For so prizing it. Q3).
59   *token* present, keepsake.
     sister Q3 (Iane Q1).

Thy honour and my soul are equal in my regard,
Nor will thy brother Charles survive thy shame.
His kindness like a burden hath surcharged me,
And under his good deeds I stooping go,
Not with an upright soul. Had I remained   65
In prison still, there doubtless I had died.
Then unto him that freed me from that prison
Still do I owe that life. What moved my foe
To enfranchise me? 'Twas, sister, for your love.
With full five hundred pounds he bought your love,   70
And shall he not enjoy it? Shall the weight
Of all this heavy burden lean on me,
And will not you bear part? You did partake
The joy of my release; will you not stand
In joint bond bound to satisfy the debt?   75
Shall I be only charged?

SUSAN   But that I know
These arguments come from an honoured mind,
As in your most extremity of need,
Scorning to stand in debt to one you hate,
Nay, rather would engage your unstained honour   80
Than to be held ingrate, I should condemn you.
I see your resolution and assent;
So Charles will have me, and I am content.

SIR CHARLES
For this I tricked you up.

SUSAN   But here's a knife,
To save mine honour, shall slice out my life.   85

SIR CHARLES
I know thou pleasest me a thousand times
More in that resolution than thy grant.
[*Aside*] Observe her love; to soothe them in my suit
Her honour she will hazard, though not lose.
To bring me out of debt, her rigorous hand   90
Will pierce her heart. O wonder, that will choose
Rather than stain her blood, her life to lose.

---

63   *surcharged* overburdened, overloaded.
69   *enfranchise* free, release from gaol.
80   *engage* expose to risk, compromise.
87   *that* Q1 (thy Q3).
88   *to soothe them in my suit* to appease those who are pursuing me.
     them in Q1 (it to Q3).

[*To her*] Come, you sad sister to a woeful brother,
This is the gate. I'll bear him such a present,
Such an acquittance for the knight to seal,   95
As will amaze his senses, and surprise
With admiration all his fantasies.

Enter ACTON *and* MALBY

SUSAN
Before his unchaste thoughts shall seize on me
'Tis here shall my imprisoned soul set free.
SIR FRANCIS
How! Mountford with his sister hand in hand!   100
What miracle's afoot?
MALBY   It is a sight
Begets in me much admiration.
SIR CHARLES
Stand not amazed to see me thus attended.
Acton, I owe thee money, and being unable
To bring thee the full sum in ready coin,   105
Lo! for thy more assurance here's a pawn,
My sister, my dear sister, whose chaste honour
I prize above a million. Here, nay, take her;
She's worth your money, man; do not forsake her.
SIR FRANCIS
[*Aside*] I would he were in earnest.   110
SUSAN
Impute it not to my immodesty.
My brother being rich in nothing else
But in his interest that he hath in me,
According to his poverty hath brought you
Me, all his store, whom howsoe'er you prize   115
As forfeit to your hand, he values highly,
And would not sell but to acquit your debt
For any emperor's ransom.
SIR FRANCIS[*Aside*]   Stern heart, relent;

---

95 *acquittance ... to seal* document discharging the debt for Sir Francis to sign with his
    seal.
97 *admiration* astonishment, wonder.
99 *'Tis here* i.e. the knife which will release her.
106 *pawn* i.e. a pledge of security for the debt (*see* I.96).
113 *interest* a pun on the emotional and financial senses of the word.

Thy former cruelty at length repent.
Was ever known in any former age   120
Such honourable wrested courtesy?
Lands, honours, lives, and all the world forgo
Rather than stand engaged to such a foe.

SIR CHARLES

Acton, she is too poor to be thy bride,
And I too much opposed to be thy brother.   125
There, take her to thee; if thou hast the heart
To seize her as a rape or lustful prey,
To blur our house that never yet was stained,
To murder her that never meant thee harm,
To kill me now whom once thou savedst from death,   130
Do them at once on her; all these rely
And perish with her spotted chastity.

SIR FRANCIS

You overcome me in your love, Sir Charles.
I cannot be so cruel to a lady
I love so dearly. Since you have not spared   135
To engage your reputation to the world,
Your sister's honour which you prize so dear,
Nay, all the comforts which you hold on earth,
To grow out of my debt, being your foe,
Your honoured thoughts, lo, thus I recompence: 140
Your metamorphised foe receives your gift
In satisfaction of all former wrongs.
This jewel I will wear here in my heart,
And where before I thought her for her wants
Too base to be my bride, to end all strife   145
I seal you my dear brother, her my wife.

---

121 *wrested* strained, distorted.
122 *lives* Q1 (life Q3).
127 *lustful prey* victim of your lust.
128 *blur* blemish, defile.
131 *at once* i.e. in one action, since all of these consequences depend upon how you treat
     her.
     rely i.e. rely upon, depend upon.
138 *comforts* Q1 (comfort Q3).
139 *To grow out of* i.e. in order to grow out of, to disburden yourself.
144 *her wants* i.e. her poverty and lack of status.
146 *seal* It may be noted that Acton here and in his use of the word 'jewel' above (line 143)
     now echoes the language employed earlier by Sir Charles (see line 95 and 47–53).

SUSAN

> You still exceed us. I will yield to fate
> And learn to love where I till now did hate.

SIR CHARLES

> With that enchantment you have charmed my soul,
> And made me rich even in those very words.   150
> I pay no debt but am indebted more;
> Rich in your love I never can be poor.

SIR FRANCIS

> All's mine is yours; we are alike in state.
> Let's knit in love what was opposed in hate.
> Come, for our nuptials we will straight provide,   155
> Blest only in our brother and fair bride.

Exeunt

[SCENE XV]

Enter CRANWELL, FRANKFORD *and* NICK

CRANWELL

> Why do you search each room about your house,
> Now that you have dispatched your wife away?

FRANKFORD

> O sir, to see that nothing may be left
> That ever was my wife's. I loved her dearly,
> And when I do but think of her unkindness,   5
> My thoughts are all in hell, to avoid which torment,
> I would not have a bodkin or a cuff,
> A bracelet, necklace, or rebato wire,

150–2   *And made . . . poor* This passage signals the completion of one of the thematic discussions carried forward by the play, that of the value and significance of wealth as source of honour. The mismatch is resolved by love, whereas even moments before they were still perceiving one another's action in terms of 'exceed' (147) and 'overcome' (133). Now Sir Francis can observe 'we are alike in state'.

153   *All's* Q3 (Alas Q1).

156   *Blest only* i.e. without (the blessing of) a dowry.

7   *bodkin* a long pin used to fasten up the hair.
        cuff i.e. an ornamental cuff.

8   *rebato wire* collar made of wire to support a ruff in the dress of the period.

Nor anything that ever was called hers
Left me, by which I might remember her. 10
Seek round about.

NICK

'Sblood, master, here's her lute flung in a corner.

FRANKFORD

Her lute! O God, upon this instrument
Her fingers have run quick division,
Sweeter than that which now divides our hearts. 15
These frets have made me pleasant, that have now
Frets of my heartstrings made. O Master Cranwell,
Oft hath she made this melancholy wood,
Now mute and dumb for her disastrous chance,
Speak sweetly many a note, sound many a strain 20
To her own ravishing voice, which being well strung,
What pleasant strange airs have they jointly sung.
Post with it after her. Now nothing's left;
Of her and hers I am at once bereft.

NICK

I'll ride and overtake her, do my message, 25
And come back again. [*Exit* NICK]

CRANWELL   Meantime, sir, if you please,
I'll to Sir Francis Acton and inform him
Of what hath passed betwixt you and his sister.

FRANKFORD

Do as you please. How ill am I bestead
To be a widower ere my wife be dead. 30

[*Exeunt* FRANKFORD *and* CRANWELL]

---

  9   *called* Q3 (*omitted* Q1).
 14   *run* Q1 (ran Q3).
       division a melodic passage in music, a run, rapidly executed.
 16   *frets* a pun on the senses (a) divisions of the fingerboard of the lute, and (b) fretting
       sores, cankers.
       pleasant merry, jocular.
 19   *chance* fortune.
 21   *being well strung* i.e. presumably her voice.
 22   *strange* exceptional, wonderful.
 29   *bestead* situated, circumstanced.

[SCENE XVI]

Enter ANNE, *with* JENKIN, *her maid* SISLY, *her* COACHMAN,
and THREE CARTERS

ANNE

Bid my coach stay. Why should I ride in state,
Being hurled so low down by the hand of fate?
A seat like to my fortunes let me have,
Earth for my chair, and for my bed a grave.

JENKIN

Comfort, good mistress; you have watered your coach with tears   5
already. You have but two mile now to go to your manor. A man
cannot say by my old Master Frankford as he may say by me,
that he wants manors, for he hath three or four, of which this is
one that we are going to.

SISLY

Good mistress, be of good cheer. Sorrow you see hurts you, but   10
helps you not. We all mourn to see you so sad.

CARTER

Mistress, I spy one of my landlord's men
Come riding post. 'Tis like he brings some news.

ANNE

Comes he from Master Frankford, he is welcome,
So are his news, because they come from him.   15

Enter NICK

NICK

There.   [*Gives her the lute*]

ANNE

I know the lute. Oft have I sung to thee;
We both are out of tune, both out of time.

---

   8   *manors* a pun, of course, on 'manners'.
   9   *to* Q1 (to now Q3).
  12   *spy one* Q1 (see some Q3).
  13   *post* in haste.
  15   *are* Q1 (is Q3).
  17   *I know the lute* Q1, Q3. The conjectured reading, 'I know thee, lute,' proposed by
      G.B. Johnston in *N.&Q.*, cciii (1958), pp. 525–6, should be mentioned. It is possible,
      but unnecessary.
  18   *out of tune, both out of time* i.e. are both instruments of discord and disharmony.

NICK

    [*Aside*] Would that had been the worst instrument that e'er you
    played on. [*To her*] My master commends him to ye; there's all   20
    he can find that was ever yours. He hath nothing left that ever
    you could lay claim to, but his own heart, and he could afford
    you that. All that I have to deliver you is this. He prays you to
    forget him, and so he bids you farewell.

ANNE

    I thank him. He is kind and ever was.   25
    All you that have true feeling of my grief,
    That know my loss, and have relenting hearts,
    Gird me about, and help me with your tears
    To wash my spotted sins. My lute shall groan;
    It cannot weep, but shall lament my moan.   [*She plays*]   30

              Enter WENDOLL

WENDOLL

    Pursued with horror of a guilty soul,
    And with the sharp scourge of repentance lashed,
    I fly from my own shadow. O my stars!
    What have my parents in their lives deserved
    That you should lay this penance on their son?   35
    When I but think of Master Frankford's love,
    And lay it to my treason, or compare
    My murdering him for his relieving me,
    It strikes a terror like a lightning's flash
    To scorch my blood up. Thus I like the owl,   40
    Ashamed of day, live in these shadowy woods
    Afraid of every leaf or murmuring blast,
    Yet longing to receive some perfect knowledge
    How he hath dealt with her. [*Sees* ANNE] O my sad fate!
    Here, and so far from home, and thus attended!   45

---

19   *the worst instrument* i.e. with the implication of another, sexual instrument.
20   *to* Q1 (vnto Q3).
22   *lay claim to* Q3 (claim to lay Q1).
28   *Gird me about* gather round me.
31   WENDOLL Q1 (*omitted* Q3) See Note on the Text, p. 548.
33   *my own* Q1 (mine owne Q3).
35   *their* Q1 (your Q3).
37   *lay it to* i.e. in comparison.
43   *perfect* certain, reliable.

O God, I have divorced the truest turtles
That ever lived together, and being divided
In several places, make their several moan;
She in the fields laments, and he at home.
So poets write that Orpheus made the trees   50
And stones to dance to his melodious harp,
Meaning the rustic and the barbarous hinds,
That had no understanding part in them;
So she from these rude carters tears extracts,
Making their flinty hearts with grief to rise   55
And draw down rivers from their rocky eyes.

ANNE

[*To* NICK] If you return unto your master say –
Though not from me, for I am all unworthy
To blast his name so with a strumpet's tongue –
That you have seen me weep, wish myself dead –   60
Nay, you may say too, for my vow is past,
Last night you saw me eat and drink my last.
This to your master you may say and swear,
For it is writ in heaven and decreed here.

NICK

I'll say you wept; I'll swear you made me sad.   65
Why, how now, eyes? What now? What's here to do?
I am gone, or I shall straight turn baby too.

WENDOLL

[*Aside*] I cannot weep; my heart is all on fire.
Cursed be the fruits of my unchaste desire.

ANNE

Go break this lute upon my coach's wheel,   70
As the last music that I e'er shall make –

---

46   *truest turtles* The fidelity of the turtle dove to its mate was proverbial. See *Tilley*,
     T.624.
48   *several* separate.
50   *Orpheus* Legendary Greek poet who could move even inanimate things by his music.
     Wendoll's interpretation of Orpheus' mythical power was familiar enough in the
     Renaissance.
52   *hinds* rustics, boors.
56   *down* Q3 (*omitted* Q1).
57   *your* Q1 (my Q3).
59   *blast* wither.
     so Q1 (*omitted* Q1).
70   *upon* Q3 (*omitted* Q1).

Not as my husband's gift, but my farewell
To all earth's joy; and so your master tell.

NICK

If I can for crying.

WENDOLL [*Aside*]   Grief, have done,
Or like a madman I shall frantic run.   75

ANNE

You have beheld the woefullest wretch on earth,
A woman made of tears. Would you had words
To express but what you see; my inward grief
No tongue can utter. Yet, unto your power
You may describe my sorrow, and disclose   80
To thy sad master my abundant woes.

NICK

I'll do your commendations.

ANNE   O no!
I dare not so presume, nor to my children;
I am disclaimed in both; alas, I am.
O never teach them when they come to speak   85
To name the name of mother. Chide their tongue
If they by chance light on that hated word;
Tell them 'tis naught, for when that word they name,
Poor pretty souls, they harp on their own shame.

WENDOLL

[*Aside*] To recompense her wrongs, what canst thou do?   90
Thou hast made her husbandless and childless too.

ANNE

I have no more to say. Speak not for me,
Yet you may tell your master what you see.

NICK

I'll do it.   *Exit* NICK

WENDOLL

[*Aside*] I'll speak to her, and comfort her in grief.   95
O, but her wound cannot be cured with words.
No matter though, I'll do my best good will,
To work a cure on her whom I did kill.

---

79   *unto your power* as far as you are able.
82   *do your commendations* present your remembrances, greetings
88   *naught* presumably a pun (a) nothing (b) wicked, bad.
        word Q3 (wotd Q1).

ANNE

So, now unto my coach, then to my home,
So to my deathbed, for from this sad hour   100
I never will nor eat, nor drink, nor taste
Of any cates that may preserve my life.
I never will nor smile, nor sleep, nor rest,
But when my tears have washed my black soul white,
Sweet Saviour, to Thy hands I yield my sprite.   105

WENDOLL

[*To her*] O Mistress Frankford!

ANNE   O for God's sake fly!

The Devil doth come to tempt me ere I die.
My coach! This sin that with an angel's face
Courted mine honour till he sought my wrack,
In my repentant eyes seems ugly black.   110

> *Exeunt all* [*except* WENDOLL *and* JENKIN],
> *the* CARTERS *whistling*

JENKIN

What, my young master that fled in his shirt? How come you by
your clothes again? You have made our house in a sweet pickle,
have you not, think you? What, shall I serve you still, or cleave to
the old house?

WENDOLL

Hence, slave! Away with thy unseasoned mirth.   115
Unless thou canst shed tears, and sigh, and howl,
Curse thy sad fortunes, and exclaim on fate,
Thou art not for my turn.

JENKIN

Marry, and you will not, another will. Farewell and be hanged.

---

102   *cates* victuals, food.
105   *sprite* spirit.
109   *Courted* Q1 (Coniur'd Q3).
       wrack ruin, downfall.
110   *eyes* Q1 (eye Q3).
       s.d. *the* CARTERS *whistling* Van Fossen observes that carters were famous for their
       whistling, but this hardly seems the appropriate moment for a tune. Perhaps they are
       rather stirring their beasts to action again.
113   *have you* Q1 (ha'ye Q3).
115   *unseasoned* untimely, unseasonable.
117   *exclaim on* blame, make an outcry against.
118   *for my turn* suitable for my purposes or requirements.
119   *Marry* Originally an oath invoking the Virgin Mary, here merely an interjection.
       and if.

Would you had never come to have kept this coil within our   120
doors. We shall ha' you run away like a sprite again.

[Exit JENKIN]

WENDOLL

She's gone to death; I live to want and woe,
Her life, her sins, and all upon my head.
And I must now go wander like a Cain
In foreign countries and remoted climes,   125
Where the report of my ingratitude
Cannot be heard. I'll over first to France,
And so to Germany, and Italy,
Where, when I have recovered, and by travel
Gotten those perfect tongues, and that these rumours   130
May in their height abate, I will return.
And I divine, however now dejected,
My worth and parts being by some great man praised,
At my return I may in court be raised.

Exit WENDOLL

[SCENE XVII]

Enter SIR FRANCIS, SIR CHARLES, CRANWELL,
MALBY *and* SUSAN

SIR FRANCIS

Brother, and now my wife, I think these troubles
Fall on my head by justice of the heavens,
For being so strict to you in your extremities,
But we are now atoned. I would my sister
Could with like happiness o'ercome her griefs,   5
As we have ours.

---

120   *coil* confusion, disturbance.
121   *sprite* spirit, ghost.
124   *Cain* Biblical character condemned to wander the earth in punishment for the
       murder of his brother, Abel. See *Genesis* iv, 8–14.
125   *remoted* remote.
130   *Gotten those perfect tongues* learned those languages perfectly.

  4   *atoned* reconciled, set at one.

SUSAN

    You tell us, Master Cranwell, wonderous things

    Touching the patience of that gentleman.

    With what strange virtue he demeans his grief.

CRANWELL

    I told you what I was witness of.   10

    It was my fortune to lodge there that night.

SIR FRANCIS

    O that same villain Wendoll! 'Twas his tongue

    That did corrupt her; she was of herself

    Chaste and devoted well. Is this the house?

CRANWELL

    Yes, sir, I take it here your sister lies.   15

SIR FRANCIS

    My brother Frankford showed too mild a spirit

    In the revenge of such a loathed crime.

    Less than he did, no man of spirit could do.

    I am so far from blaming his revenge

    That I commend it. Had it been my case   20

    Their souls at once had from their breasts been freed.

    Death to such deeds of shame is the due meed.

Enter JENKIN *and* SISLY

JENKIN

    O my mistress, my mistress, my poor mistress!

SISLY

    Alas that ever I was born! What shall I do for my poor mistress?

SIR CHARLES

    Why, what of her?   25

JENKIN

    O Lord, sir, she no sooner heard that her brother and his friends

    were come to see how she did, but she for very shame of her

---

    9   *demeans* manages, governs.

  14   *devoted well* very faithful.

  22   *meed* recompense, reward, desert.

          s.d. *and* SISLY Q1 (*omitted* Q3).

  23   *my mistress* Q1 (mistris Q3).

26–9   *Lineation as prose* Q3 (*as verse* Q1).

  26   *his* Q1 (hir Q3).

guilty conscience fell into a swoon, and we had much ado to get
life into her.

SUSAN

Alas that she should bear so hard a fate;   30
Pity it is repentance comes too late.

SIR FRANCIS

Is she so weak in body?

JENKIN

O sir, I can assure you there's no help of life in her, for she will
take no sustenance. She hath plainly starved herself, and now
she is as lean as a lath. She ever looks for the good hour. Many   35
gentlemen and gentlewomen of the country are come to comfort
her.

Enter ANNE *in her bed*

MALBY

How fare you, Mistress Frankford?

ANNE

Sick, sick, O sick! Give me some air, I pray you.
Tell me, O tell me, where's Master Frankford?   40
Will not he deign to see me ere I die?

MALBY

Yes, Mistress Frankford; divers gentlemen,
Your loving neighbours, with that just request
Have moved and told him of your weak estate,
Who, though with much ado to get belief,   45

28   *a* Q1 (such a Q3).
      and Q1 (that Q3).
29   *into* Q1 (in Q3).
33–7 *Lineation as prose* Q3 (*as verse* Q1).
33   *help* Q1 (hope Q3).
34   *and* Q3 (that Q1).
35   *lath* a thin narrow strip of wood.
      good hour i.e. the hour of her death, when she will enter into the life hereafter.
37   s.d. *Enter* ANNE *in her bed* Precisely how such an entrance was accomplished is not
      quite clear, but it was by no means uncommon in the drama of the period. The bed
      may have been carried on to the stage or thrust out, or it may have been that she was
      simply 'discovered' by the drawing aside of a curtain over an inner, recessed stage.
      The conventional flexibility of the Jacobean stage as regards location is well
      exemplified by this scene.
39   *pray you* Q1 (pray Q3).
41   *he* Q1 (*omitted* Q3).
45   *though with much ado to get belief* i.e. though these neighbours had great difficulty
      in getting Frankford to believe them.

Examining of the general circumstance,
Seeing your sorrow and your penitence,
And hearing therewithal the great desire
You have to see him ere you left the world,
He gave to us his faith to follow us,   50
And sure he will be here immediately.

ANNE

You half revived me with those pleasing news.
Raise me a little higher in my bed.
Blush I not, brother Acton? Blush I not, Sir Charles?
Can you not read my fault writ in my cheek?   55
Is not my crime there? Tell me, gentlemen.

SIR CHARLES

Alas, good mistress, sickness hath not left you
Blood in your face enough to make you blush.

ANNE

Then sickness like a friend my fault would hide.
Is my husband come? My soul but tarries   60
His arrive and I am fit for heaven.

SIR FRANCIS

I came to chide you, but my words of hate
Are turned to pity and compassionate grief.
I came to rate you, but my brawls, you see,
Melt into tears, and I must weep by thee.   65
Here's Master Frankford now.

Enter FRANKFORD

FRANKFORD

Good morrow, brother; good morrow, gentlemen.
God, that hath laid this cross upon our heads,
Might, had He pleased, have made our cause of meeting

---

50 *faith* promise.
52 *half* Q1 (haue half Q3).
    those Q1 (the Q3).
54 *brother Acton* Q3 (maister Frankford Q1).
59 *Then . . . hide.* Q3 (*line attributed to Sir Charles* Q1).
61 *and* Q1 (then Q3).
62–6 SIR FRANCIS Q3 (*speech attributed to Sir Charles* Q1).
64 *rate* berate, reproach.
    brawls scoldings, quarrellings.
66 s.d. *Enter* FRANKFORD Q3 (*given before line 66 in* Q1).
67 *good morrow* Q1 (morrow Q3).

On a more fair and a more contented ground.   70
But He that made us, made us to this woe.

ANNE

And is he come? Methinks that voice I know.

FRANKFORD

How do you, woman?

ANNE

Well, Master Frankford, well; but shall be better,
I hope, within this hour. Will you vouchsafe,   75
Out of your grace and your humanity,
To take a spotted strumpet by the hand?

FRANKFORD

That hand once held my heart in faster bonds
Than now 'tis gripped by me. God pardon them
That made us first break hold.

ANNE   Amen, amen.   80
Out of my zeal to heaven, whither I am now bound,
I was so impudent to wish you here,
And once more beg your pardon. O good man
And father to my children, pardon me.
Pardon, O pardon me! My fault so heinous is   85
That if you in this world forgive it not,
Heaven will not clear it in the world to come.
Faintness hath so usurped upon my knees
That kneel I cannot; but on my heart's knees
My prostrate soul lies thrown down at your feet   90
To beg your gracious pardon. Pardon, O pardon me!

FRANKFORD

As freely from the low depth of my soul
As my Redeemer hath forgiven his death,
I pardon thee. I will shed tears for thee,
Pray with thee, and in mere pity   95

---

   70   *and a* Q1 (and Q3).
        more contented ground i.e. for happier reasons.
   71   *to this woe* i.e. that we might suffer this woe.
   74   *better* i e. in heaven.
   77   *spotted* morally blemished.
   78   *That* Q1 (This Q3).
   88   *usurped upon* taken possession of.
   92   *from the low depth of* i.e. from the bottom of.
95–6   *Lineation* Q1 (Pray with thee . . . estate, / Ile wish . . . Q3).
   95   *mere* complete, absolute.

Of thy weak state I'll wish to die with thee.

ALL

So do we all.

NICK

[*Aside*] So will not I!

I'll sigh and sob, but, by my faith, not die.

SIR FRANCIS

O Master Frankford, all the near alliance   100

I lose by her shall be supplied in thee.

You are my brother by the nearest way;

Her kindred hath fallen off, but yours doth stay.

FRANKFORD

Even as I hope for pardon at that day

When the Great Judge of Heaven in scarlet sits,   105

So be thou pardoned. Though thy rash offence

Divorced our bodies, thy repentant tears

Unite our souls.

SIR CHARLES   Then comfort, Mistress Frankford;

You see your husband hath forgiven your fall;

Then rouse your spirits and cheer your fainting soul.   110

SUSAN

How is it with you?

SIR CHARLES   How do you feel yourself?

ANNE

Not of this world.

FRANKFORD

I see you are not, and I weep to see it.

My wife, the mother to my pretty babes,

Both those lost names I do restore thee back,   115

And with this kiss I wed thee once again.

Though thou art wounded in thy honoured name,

And with that grief upon thy deathbed liest,

Honest in heart, upon my soul thou diest.

---

96 *state* Q1 (estate Q3).
100 *near alliance* close kinship.
103 *Her kindred hath fallen off* i.e. because she is about to die, she will no longer be my sister.
105 *in scarlet* i.e. in the robes of office of a judge.
111 *do you* Q1 (de'ye Q3).
117 *thy honoured name* your reputation.

ANNE

    Pardoned on earth, soul, thou in heaven art free.   120

    Once more thy wife dies thus embracing thee.

                                [ANNE *dies*]

FRANKFORD

    New married, and new widowed; O she's dead,

    And a cold grave must be our nuptial bed.

SIR CHARLES

    Sir, be of good comfort, and your heavy sorrow

    Part equally amongst us; storms divided   125

    Abate their force, and with less rage are guided.

CRANWELL

    Do, Master Frankford; he that hath least part

    Will find enough to drown one troubled heart.

SIR FRANCIS

    Peace be with thee, Nan. Brothers and gentlemen,

    All we that can plead interest in her grief,   130

    Bestow upon her body funeral tears.

    Brother, had you with threats and usage bad

    Punished her sin, the grief of her offence

    Had not with such true sorrow touched her heart.

FRANKFORD

    I see it had not; therefore on her grave   135

    I will bestow this funeral epitaph,

    Which on her marble tomb shall be engraved.

    In golden letters shall these words be filled:

    Here lies she whom her husband's kindness killed.

                         [*Exeunt*]

121   *Once more thy wife* i.e. having once more been restored to being your wife, (she dies ...)

An honest crew, disposed to be merry,
Came to a tavern by and called for wine.
The drawer brought it, smiling like a cherry,
And told them it was pleasant, neat, and fine.
    'Taste it,' quoth one. He did so. 'Fie!' quoth he,   5
    'This wine was good; now't runs too near the lee.'

Another sipped, to give the wine his due,
And said unto the rest it drunk too flat.
The third said it was old, the fourth too new.
'Nay,' quoth the fifth, 'the sharpness likes me not.'   10
    Thus, gentlemen, you see how in one hour
    The wine was new, old, flat, sharp, sweet, and sour.

Unto this wine we do allude our play,
Which some will judge too trivial, some too grave.
You, as our guests, we entertain this day   15
And bid you welcome to the best we have.
    Excuse us, then; good wine may be disgraced
    When every several mouth hath sundry taste.

THE TAMER TAMED

JOHN FLETCHER

The first page of the scribal manuscript of *The Tamer Tamed*, now owned by the Folger Shakespeare Library (MS J.b.3). Reproduced by permission of the Folger Shakespeare Library.

ACTUS PRIMUS
Scena jma.

Enter Moroso, Sophocles, Tranio, as from a
wedding.

Moroso	Heaven giue em ioy
Tran:	Amen.
Sopho.	Amen say I too.
	The puddings now ith'proofe, alas poore wench
	through what a myne of patience must thou worke
	ere thou knowst good houre more.
Tran:	'Tis too true, certaine.
	me thinks her father has dealt harshly with her,
	exceeding harshly, and not like a father,
	to match her to this dragon, I protest
	I pitty the poore gentlewoman.
Moro.	Me thincks now
	hee's not so terrible as people thinck him.
Sopho.	This old theefe flatters out of meere deuotion
	to please the father for his second daughter.
Tran.	But shall he haue her.
Soph.	Yes, when I haue Rome,
	and yet the father's for him.
Moro.	Ile assure ye
	I hold him a good man.
Soph.	Yes sure a wealthie,
	but whether a good womans man is doubtfull
Tra.	Would 'twere no worse.
Moro.	What though his other wife,
	out of her most abundant stubbornes,
	out of her dayly hue and cryes vpon him,
	for sure she was a rebell turn'd his temper.

[DRAMATIS PERSONAE

in order of appearance

MOROSO, *an elderly suitor to Livia*
SOPHOCLES, *friend of Petruchio*
TRANIO, *friend of Petruchio*
JAQUES, *servant of Petruchio*
ROLAND, *a young man, in love with Livia*   5
LIVIA, *daughter of Petronius and sister of Maria, in love with Roland*
BIANCA, *cousin of Maria and Livia*
MARIA, *daughter of Petronius, sister of Livia and second wife of Petruchio*
PETRUCHIO, *a famous shrew-tamer, husband of Maria*
PETRONIUS, *father of Maria and Livia*   10
PEDRO, *servant of Petruchio*
FIRST WENCH
SECOND WENCH
THIRD WENCH
CITY WIFE   15
COUNTRY WIFE
FIRST WATCHMAN
SECOND WATCHMAN
Petronius' SERVANT
Servants, Porters]   20

Neither F nor MS have a Dramatis Personae, but one is supplied in F2, headed 'The Persons
represented in the Play'. For names of some characters I have followed MS's spelling (i.e.
Petruchio rather than Petruccio, Bianca instead of F's Byancha).

  1   MOROSO described in F2 as '*an old rich doating Citizen, suitor to* Livia.'
  2, 3 SOPHOCLES . . . TRANIO '*Two Gentlemen, friends to* Petruchio.' (F2); in *The Taming
        of the Shrew* Tranio is Lucentio's personal attendant, but he appears to have risen
        in status.
  4, 11 JAQUES . . . PEDRO '*Two witty servants to* Petruchio.' (F2).
  5   ROLAND '*A young Gent. in love with* Livia.' (F2); Livia describes him as being 'under
        age', i.e. under twenty-one (I.iv.56).
  6   LIVIA '*Mistriss to* Rowland.' (F2).
  6, 8 LIVIA . . . MARIA '*The two masculine daughters of* Petronius.' (F2).
  7   BIANCA '*Their Cosin, and Commander in chief.*' (F2).
  8   MARIA '*A chaste witty Lady.*' (F2). Her name may have taken on new associations in
        the 1630s, when Henrietta Maria was queen.
  9   PETRUCHIO '*An* Italian *Gent. Husband to* Maria.' (F2.)
  10 PETRONIUS '*Father to* Maria *and* Livia.' (F2.)
  15, 16 CITY WIFE . . . COUNTRY WIFE '*To the relief of the Ladies, of which, two were drunk.*' (F2)

ACT I, SCENE i

Enter MOROSO, SOPHOCLES [*and*] TRANIO,
as from a wedding

MOROSO
  Heaven give 'em joy.
TRANIO   Amen.
SOPHOCLES   Amen say I too.
  The pudding's now i'th' proof. Alas, poor wench,
  Through what a mine of patience must thou work
  Ere thou know'st good hour more.
TRANIO   'Tis too true. Certain,
  Methinks her father has dealt harshly with her,   5
  Exceeding harshly, and not like a father,
  To match her to this dragon; I protest
  I pity the poor gentlewoman.
MOROSO   Methinks now
  He's not so terrible as people think him.
SOPHOCLES
  [*Aside to* TRANIO] This old thief flatters out of mere devotion   10
  To please the father for his second daughter.
TRANIO
  But shall he have her?

> *Act I, Scene i* ed. (ACTVS PRIMUS / Scaena i.^ma MS; *Actus Primus – Scæna Prima.*
> F.)
>
> 0   s.d. *Enter . . . wedding* MS (*Enter Moroso, Sophocles, and Tranio, with Rosemary, as
>   from a wedding* F).
>   *as from a wedding* The bunch of rosemary specified in F's stage direction was
>   conventional stage shorthand for a wedding.
> 1   *Heaven* MS (*God* F).
>   *Heaven . . . joy* a conventional expression of goodwill towards a married couple.
> 2   *pudding's . . . proof* a proverbial term ('the proof of the pudding is in the eating')
>   (Tilley P608).
>   *wench* an informal, affectionate term for a young woman.
> 3   *what . . . work* i.e. what an abundant supply of patience you must draw on ('mine'
>   and 'work' pun on the extraction of metal, coal, etc. from an excavation).
> 4   *Ere . . . more* i.e. before you enjoy any further happiness.
>   *Certain* Certainly.
> 5   *Methinks* It seems to me.
> 6   *Exceeding* Exceedingly.
> 10 *mere* (1) pure; (2) nothing short of.
>   *devotion* i.e. to Petronius, Maria's father.

SOPHOCLES   Yes, when I have Rome,
And yet the father's for him.
MOROSO   I'll assure ye
I hold him a good man.
SOPHOCLES   Yes, sure, a wealthy –
But whether a good woman's man is doubtful.   15
TRANIO
Would 'twere no worse.
MOROSO   What though his other wife,
Out of her most abundant stubbornness,
Out of her daily hue and cries upon him –
For sure she was a rebel – turned his temper
And forced him blow as high as she? Dost follow   20
He must retain that long-since-buried tempest
To this soft maid?
SOPHOCLES   I fear it.
TRANIO   So do I too,
And so far that if heaven had made me woman
And his wife that must be –
MOROSO   What would you do, sir?
TRANIO
I would learn to eat coals with an angry cat   25
And spit fire at him; I would – to prevent him –
Do all the ramping, roaring tricks a whore

12   *when I have Rome* i.e. never.
15   *a . . . man* i.e. a good man in his treatment of women.
16   *What* i.e. Even.
      his other wife i.e. Katherine, heroine of Shakespeare's *The Taming of the Shrew*; she
      is mentioned seven times in the play but is never referred to by name.
17   *stubbornness* MS (sobernesse F).
18   *hue and cries* outcry, shouting (originally refers to a call for the pursuit of a criminal).
19   *a rebel* i.e. against the authority of her husband.
20   *blow as high* rage as powerfully (Moroso puns on 'blow' in his reference to the
      'tempest' of Petruchio's rage in l. 21).
21   *retain* continue to use.
22   *soft* gentle, docile; quiet.
23   *heaven* MS (God F).
      me woman F (me a woman MS).
25   *to . . . cat* Fletcher uses a similar image in *Bonduca*, in which the First Daughter dec-
      lares that Roman women are 'cowards' and 'Eat coals like compell'd Cats'
      (IV.iv.116–17).
27   *ramping* violent, unrestrained (originally refers to an animal such as a lion standing
      on its hind legs in an aggressive pose, but often used to refer to a whore).
      roaring riotous.   *tricks* (1) crafty devices; (2) sexual acts.

Being drunk and tumbling ripe would tremble at.
There is no safety else, nor moral wisdom
To be a wife and his.
SOPHOCLES   So I should think too.   30
TRANIO
For yet the bare remembrance of his first wife
(I tell ye on my knowledge, and a truth too)
Will make him start in's sleep, and very often
Cry out for cudgels, cowl-staves, anything,
Hiding his breeches out of fear her ghost   35
Should walk and wear 'em yet. Since his first marriage,
He is no more the still Petruchio
Than I am Babylon.
SOPHOCLES   He's a good fellow,
And by my troth I love him, but to think
A fit match for this tender soul –   40
TRANIO
His very frown, if she but say her prayers
Louder than men talk treason, makes him tinder;

28   *tumbling* (1) falling or rolling about; (2) dancing with posturing, balancing, etc.;
      (3) having sexual intercourse.
      ripe in a fully developed manner.
31   *bare* mere, simple.
33   *in's* in his.
34   *cudgels* clubs.
      cowl-staves stout sticks used to carry tubs of water ('cowls') or other heavy items,
      often used as weapons and in shaming rituals which targeted hen-pecked
      husbands.
35   *Hiding his breeches* As in many early modern texts, a fight over who gets to wear the
      husband's breeches represents in miniature a wider struggle for domination.
37   *still* (1) quiet, meek, calm; (2) constant.
37–8 *still . . . Babylon* As Norton points out, Tranio's phrase recalls the metrical version
      of Psalm 37: 'By the still rivers of Babylon'.
38   *Babylon* i.e. the ruler of Babylon: refers either (1) to the former capital of the Chaldee
      Empire, the mystical city mentioned in the apocryphal New Testament book The
      Revelation of St John the Divine, or (2) to Rome.
39   *by my troth* MS (on my word F).
      by my troth truthfully; I declare.
40   *fit* suitable.
      match marriage partner, wife.
      this F (his MS).
      tender meek, gentle.
42   *Louder . . . treason* i.e. louder than a whisper.
      tinder i.e. liable to burst into flame.

The motion of a dial when he's testy
Is the same trouble to him as a waterwork.
She must do nothing of herself, not eat,   45
Sleep, say 'Sir, how do ye', make her ready, piss,
Unless he bid her.

SOPHOCLES   He will bury her,
Ten pounds to twenty shillings, within this three weeks.

TRANIO
I'll be your half.

Enter JAQUES

MOROSO   He loves her most extremely,
And so long 'twill be honeymoon. Now, Jaques,   50
You are a busy man I am sure.

JAQUES   Yes, certain;
This old sport must have eggs.

SOPHOCLES   Not yet this ten days.

JAQUES
Sweet gentlemen, with muscadel.

---

43   *dial* sundial, clock.
      testy irritable, short-tempered.
44   *waterwork* (1) system for raising and distributing water; (2) fountain.
46   *Sleep* MS (Drink F).
      make her ready dress herself.
      piss MS (unready F).
47   *bid* ask.
      bury her i.e. cause her death.
47–9 *He . . . half* Sophocles and Tranio do not necessarily seal a bet here (the language
      may be figurative rather than literal), but Fletcher echoes the last act of *The Taming
      of the Shrew*, in which the newly married men, Lucentio, Hortensio and Petruchio,
      bet on the behaviour of their wives.
48   *Ten . . . shillings* i.e. I bet you ten pounds to twenty shillings.
      this MS (these F).
49   *I'll . . . half* I'll be your partner (in the bet); I agree with you.
      s.d. *Enter* JAQUES MS (*Enter Jaques with a pot of Wine.* F).
50   *so* therefore.
      long . . . honeymoon i.e. their honeymoon period will last a long time.
      'twill it will.
52   *old* (1) ancient, primeval; (2) belonging to an old person (i.e. Petruchio); (3)
      decayed, stale.
      sport lovemaking.
      eggs eggs were thought to be aphrodisiacs.
      Not . . . days i.e. not for at least ten days.

TRANIO   That's right, sir.

MOROSO

This fellow broods his master. Speed ye, Jaques.

SOPHOCLES

We shall be for you presently.

JAQUES   Your worships   55
Shall have it rich and neat and, o' my conscience,
As welcome as our Lady Day. Ah, my old sir,
When shall we see your worship run at ring?
That hour a standing were worth money.

MOROSO   So, sir.

JAQUES

Upon my little honesty, your mistress,   60
If I have any speculation, must think
This single thrumming of a fiddle
Without a bow but even poor sport.

---

53   *muscadel* wine (usually white and sweet) made with Muscat grapes; Jaques refers
     to the belief that wine could assist sexual performance. In *The Taming of the Shrew*,
     Petruchio is said to drink copious amounts of muscadel during the (offstage)
     marriage to Katherine (III.ii.170–6).
54   *broods* cherishes, watches out for the good of.
     Speed ye 'God speed you' i.e. good luck to you.
55   *for* i.e. with.
     worships a title of honour, used to address people of high status.
56   *it* i.e. their entertainment.
     neat choice, skilfully prepared.
     o' on.
57   *Lady Day* 25 March, the feast of the Virgin Mary; often viewed as the start of
     spring.
     Ah ed. (a' MS; O F).
58   *run at ring* carry off the prize (in chivalric entertainments, a ring was hung from a
     post and riders competed to carry it off on their lances); there is also a pun on 'ring'
     as a symbol of marriage, and a *double-entendre* on ring = vagina.
59   *a* F (at MS).
     standing standing-place (i.e. on a stand or scaffold, so as to watch the
     entertainment).
     So An elliptical use of the word which may indicate either pleased approval or a
     desire for Jaques to move on to another topic.
60   *Upon my* i.e. I swear by (compare 'upon my faith').
61   *speculation* insight.
62–3 *This . . . bow* i.e. this display of impotence.
62   *thrumming* plucking, unskilful playing.
63   *but even* i.e. nothing but.

MOROSO   Y'are merry.

JAQUES

Would I were wise too. So heaven bless your worships.

                                                Exit [JAQUES]

TRANIO

The fellow tells you true.

SOPHOCLES   When is the day, man?   65

Come, come, you'd steal a marriage.

MOROSO   Nay, believe me,

But when her father pleases I am ready,

And all my friends shall know it.

TRANIO   Why not now?

One charge had served for both.

MOROSO

There's reason in't.

SOPHOCLES   Called Roland.

MOROSO   Will you walk?   70

They'll think we are lost. Come, gentlemen.

TRANIO   You have imped him.

SOPHOCLES

So will he never the wench, I hope.

TRANIO   I wish it.

                                                Exeunt

63–4   *merry . . . wise* echoes the proverb 'it is good to be merry and wise' (Tilley G324).
64   *heaven* MS (God F).
        s.d. *Exit* [JAQUES] ed. (Exit MS; *Exit Jaq.* F).
65   *tells you true* i.e. is telling you the truth.
66   *you'd* ed. (you'ld MS).
        you'd steal a marriage i.e. you intend to elope.
69   *charge* cost, expense; set of arrangements.
70   *There's . . . Roland* Moroso refers to Tranio's comment that a double wedding would halve the cost, but Sophocles takes 'in't' (in it) to refer either to the delay in Moroso's wedding to Livia because of a rival, 'Roland', or, perhaps, to Livia herself. *Will you walk* i.e. will you come along (Moroso tries to change the subject).
71   *imped him* MS (wip't him now F; whipped him now ed.)
        imped him clipped his wings (*OED*'s earliest citation is from 1657, but it was current as early as 1600). In the next line Sophocles puns on an alternative meaning, 'implanted'.

ACT I, SCENE ii

Enter ROLAND *and* LIVIA

ROLAND

Nay, Livia, if you'll go away tonight,
If your affections be not made of words –

LIVIA

I love you, and you know how dearly, Roland –
Is there none near us? – my affections ever
Have been your servants. With what superstition   5
I have ever sainted you –

ROLAND   Why, then take this way.

LIVIA

'Twill be a childish and less prosperous course
Than this that knows not care. Why should we do
Our honest and our hearty loves such wrong
To overrun our fortunes?

ROLAND   Then you flatter.   10

LIVIA

Alas, you know I cannot.

ROLAND   What hope's left else,

But flying, to enjoy ye?

LIVIA   None so far.

For let it be admitted we have time
And all things now in other expectation,
My father's bent against us; what but ruin   15

Act I, Scene ii ed. (Actus j.ᵐᵘˢ Scaena ij.ᵈᵃ MS; *Scæna secunda* F).

  1 *Nay* MS (Now F).
      if . . . away i.e. if you will elope with me.
  6 *sainted you* treated you like a saint, worshipped you.
  7 *prosperous* likely to be successful.
  8 *this* MS (his F).
      care trouble, anxiety.
  9 *honest* honourable, virtuous.
      hearty genuine, sincere.
 10 *overrun* trample under foot.
      you flatter i.e. you are only flattering me.
 12 *flying* fleeing, running away.
13–14 *we . . . expectation* i.e. time and everything else is stacked against us.
 15 *bent* inclined.

Can such a by-way bring us? If your fears
Would let you look with my eyes, I would show you,
And certain, how our staying here would win us
A course, though somewhat longer, yet far surer.

ROLAND
And then Moroso has ye.

LIVIA   No such matter.   20
For hold this certain: begging, stealing, whoring,
Selling – which is a sin unpardonable –
Of counterfeit cods, or musty English cracus,
Switches, or stones for th' toothache sooner finds me
Than that drawn fox Moroso.

ROLAND   But his money,   25
If wealth may win you –

LIVIA   If a hog may be
High priest among the Jews! His money, Roland?
O Love forgive me! What a faith hast thou?
Why, can his money kiss me?

ROLAND   Yes.

LIVIA   Behind,
Laid out upon a petticoat! Or grasp me   30

16   *by-way* detour, unfrequented path.
16–17 *If . . . eyes* i.e. if your fear would allow you to see things from my point of view.
18   *certain* assuredly.
19   *course* (1) path; (2) way of proceeding.
       surer less dangerous.
20   *No such matter* i.e. that's of no importance.
22   *which . . . unpardonable* Livia jokes that selling goods would be a greater sin than
       selling her body; her light tone contrasts with Roland's nervy anxiety.
23–4   *cods . . . toothache* The substances that Livia mentions are all either curative or
       cosmetic, suitable for the elderly Moroso.
23   *cods* perfumes (refers either to civet, or musk, a substance extracted from the anal
       pouch of animals of the civet genus, or to small bags containing it).
       cracus F (Crocus MS).
       cracus A kind of tobacco apparently named after Caracas but styled 'English'
       because of the settlers in Virginia in the 1610s who grew it. It was widely thought
       to have curative properties for venereal disease.
24   *Switches* Thin, flexible shoots cut from a tree, used in some early modern remedies.
       stones . . . toothache various kinds of natural and artificial stones were thought to
       cure toothache.
25   *drawn* disembowelled.
26–7   *If . . . Jews!* An impossibility. Jews, who do not eat pork, are assumed to avoid pigs
       altogether.
28   *Love* i.e. Cupid, the personification of love.

While I cry 'Oh, good, thank you'? O' my troth,
Thou mak'st me merry with thy fear! Or lie with me
As you may do? Alas, what fools you men are!
His mouldy money? Half a dozen riders
That cannot sit but stamped fast to their saddles?   35
No, Roland, no man shall make use of me;
My beauty was born free, and free I'll give it
To him that loves, not buys me. You yet doubt me.

ROLAND
I cannot say I doubt ye.

LIVIA   Go thy ways.
Thou art the prettiest, puling piece of passion!   40
Indeed I will not fail thee.

ROLAND   I had rather –

LIVIA
Prithee believe me, if I do not carry it
For both our goods –

ROLAND   But –

LIVIA   What but?

ROLAND   I would tell you –

LIVIA
I know all you can tell me; all's but this:
You would have me and lie with me. Is't not so?   45

ROLAND
Yes.

LIVIA   Why, you shall. Will that content you? Go.

ROLAND
I am very loath to go.

29–30   *Behind . . . petticoat* i.e. the only 'kiss' (or pleasure) his money can provide is in buying
me rich clothes; in context, Livia's exclamation may also suggest that Moroso's money
can kiss her arse.
   31   *O' my troth* On my faith (i.e. truly).
   32   *lie* have sex.
34–5   *Half . . . saddles* i.e. the riders stamped pictorially on the coins, who are as incapable
as Moroso himself of providing Livia with sexual pleasure (such coins were current
in Flanders, Holland and Scotland during the seventeenth century).
   39   *Go thy ways* Get along.
   40   *prettiest* most attractive; cleverest (said ironically or patronisingly).
        puling whining.
   41   *Indeed* MS (Yfaith F).
   42   *carry* manage.
   47   *loath* reluctant.

107

LIVIA   Now, o' my conscience
Thou art an honest fellow.

Enter BIANCA *and* MARIA

                         Here's my sister.
Go, prithee, go. This kiss, and credit me,   [*They kiss*]
Ere I am three nights older I am for thee.   50
You shall hear what I do.
ROLAND   I had rather feel it.
LIVIA
Farewell.
ROLAND   Farewell.   *Exit* ROLAND
LIVIA   Alas, poor fool, how it looks!
It would e'en hang itself should I but cross it.
For pure love to the matter, I must hatch it.
                    [*She hangs back, contemplating*]
BIANCA
Nay, never look for merry hour, Maria,   55
If now ye make it not; let not your blushes,
Your modesty and tenderness of spirit
Make you continual anvil to his anger.
Believe me, since his first wife set him going,
Nothing can bind his rage. Take your own counsel,   60
You shall not say that I persuaded you.
But if you suffer him –
MARIA   Stay, shall I do it?

47   *o' my conscience* i.e. truly.
50   *Ere* Before.
51   *I . . . it* Roland recovers himself enough to join in with Livia's sexual innuendo.
      I . . . it. MS (*om.* F). This line is apparently censored in F.
52   *it* used in patronising baby-talk.
53   *cross* thwart, contradict.
54   *to the matter* to the point, to the thing intended.
      hatch contrive.
55   *merry* happy.
56   *If . . . not* i.e. if you don't take this action.
58   *anvil to* i.e. target of.
59   *his first wife* i.e. Katherine.
60   *Take your own counsel* i.e. make up your own mind.
62   *But . . . him* – F (*om.* MS): the scribe apparently omitted this half-line accidentally.
      suffer tolerate.
      Stay i.e. give me time to consider.

BIANCA

Have you a stomach to it?

MARIA   I never showed it.

BIANCA

'Twill show the rarer and the stranger in you,

But do not say I urged you.

MARIA   I'll do it.   65

Like Curtius, to redeem my country have I

Leaped into this gulf of marriage;

Farewell all poor thoughts but spite and anger,

Till I have wrought a miracle upon him.

BIANCA

This is brave now, if you continue it,   70

But your own will lead you.

MARIA

Adieu all tenderness! I dare continue:

Maids that are made of fears and modest blushes,

View me and love example.

I am no more the gentle, tame Maria;   75

Mistake me not, I have a new soul in me

Made of a north wind, nothing but tempest,

And like a tempest shall it make all ruins

---

63   *a stomach to* 'an appetite for', the courage for ('stomach' can also mean 'malice' or 'spite').

64   *rarer* more worthy, more unexpected.

      stranger MS (stronger F).

65   *I'll do it.* MS (I am perfect F).

66-7 *Like . . . marriage* In his *History of Rome* (VII. 6) the Roman historian Livy tells the story of a chasm which opened in the middle of the Forum and which, according to an oracle, could only be closed if 'the chief strength of the Roman people' was put into it. The soldier Marcus Curtius, realising that this referred to Rome's soldiers, mounted his horse and leaped it, whereupon the hole closed. Maria compares marriage with the chasm and herself with Curtius; her 'country' consists of other women.

67   *into* F (in MS).

      marriage MS (marriage, and Ile do it F).

69-74 *upon . . . example* MS (Now cosen F).

70-1 ed. (This . . . now, / If . . . you. MS).

70   *brave* splendid; courageous; worthy.

72   *Adieu* Farewell.

73   *made* F (mayds MS).

75   *tame* docile, submissive.

77   *north wind* supposed to be particularly fierce.

Till I have run my will out.

BIANCA [*Seeing* LIVIA]   Here is your sister.

MARIA

Here is the brave old man's love.

BIANCA   That loves the young man.   80

MARIA

Aye, and hold thee there, wench: what a grief o' the heart is't,

When Paphos' revels should uprouse old Night,

To sweat against a cork, to lie and tell

The clock o' th' lungs, to rise sport-starved –

LIVIA   Dear sister,

Where have you been, you talk thus?

MARIA   Why, at church,   85

Where I am tied to talk thus: I am a wife now.

LIVIA

It seems so, and a modest.

MARIA   Y'are an ass.

When thou art married once, thy modesty

Will never buy thee pins.

LIVIA   Bless me!

MARIA   From what?

79–80   *Till . . . Here* MS (Till I have run my will out. / *Bya.* This is brave now, / If you
        continue it; but your own will lead you. / *Mar.* Adieu all tendernesse, I dare
        continue; / Maides that are made of feares and modest blushes, / View me, and love
        example. / *Bya.* Here F).
   79   *will* desire, longing.
   80   *brave* fine, worthy (said ironically).
 81–9   ed. (Aye . . . wench, / What . . . revels / Should . . . cork, / To . . . start'd / Dear . . . thus?
        / Why . . . thus; / I . . . modest. / Y'are . . . once / Thy . . . pins. MS).
   81   *Aye* ed. (I MS, F).
        hold thee there i.e. stay with that topic for a moment.
   82   *Paphos' revels* i.e. the entertainments/sexual pleasures of Venus, to whom the
        Cypriot city Paphos was dedicated.
        revels MS (Rebels F).
        should . . . Night i.e. should have the power to arouse even Moroso.
        Night (1) a personification of the night, which should be illumined by the revels of
        Paphos; (2) the aged Moroso.
   83   *cork* i.e. a dry, impotent penis.
 83–4   *to . . . lungs* i.e. to tell the time by the regular breathing/snoring of Moroso.
   84   *rise* get up.
        sport-starved sexually frustrated.
        starved F (starv'd) (start'd MS).
   86   *tied* bound, obliged.
   87   *modest* chaste, virtuous (said ironically).
 88–9   *When . . . pins* i.e. when you are married your modesty will be worth nothing.

BIANCA

    From such a tame fool as our cousin Livia.   90

LIVIA

    You are not mad?

MARIA

    Yes, wench, and so must you be – mark me, Livia –

    Or none of our acquaintance, or indeed fit for our sex.

    Pardon me, yellow Hymen, that I mean

    Thy offerings to protract, and to keep   95

    Fasting my valiant bridegroom.

LIVIA   Whither will this woman?

BIANCA

    You may perceive her end.

LIVIA   Or rather fear it.

MARIA

    Dare you be partner in't?

LIVIA   Leave it, Maria,

    I fear I have marked too much. For goodness leave it;

    Divest you with obedient hands: to bed.   100

MARIA

    To bed? No, Livia, there be comets hang

    Prodigious over that yet. There is a fellow

    Must yet before I know that heat – ne'er start, wench –

---

91   *mad* (1) insane (as Livia intends it); (2) angry (as Maria interprets it).

92–3   *Yes . . . sex* MS (Yes wench, and so must you be, / Or none of our acquaintance, marke me *Livia*. / Or indeed fit for our sex: Tis bed time. F).

92   *mark me* pay attention to me.

93   *fit for* i.e. properly qualified to be a member of.

94   *Hymen* god of marriage in Roman mythology, often portrayed with yellow hair or as wearing yellow.

95   *protract* postpone.

96   *Fasting* Hungry (i.e. without sex).
        Whither . . . woman i.e. where is this woman going? (The remark might be directed at Bianca, but it might be a more general question, or be aimed at the audience.)

97   *end* purpose, aim.

99   *marked* observed.   *too* F (to MS).

100   *Divest you* Undress yourself (can also mean 'strip yourself of your rights').

101   *be* MS (are F).
        comets ominous signs (comets were thought to be bad omens).

102   *Prodigious* Portentously, ominously.
        There is MS (there's F).
        a fellow i.e. Petruchio.

103   *that heat* i.e. sexual pleasure.
        ne'er start, wench Livia apparently flinches at Maria's words.

Be made a man, for yet he is a monster;
Here must his head be, Livia.
LIVIA   Never hope it.   105
'Tis with a sieve to scoop the ocean, as
To tame Petruchio.
MARIA   Stay. Lucina, hear me:
Never unlock the treasure of my womb
For human fruit to make it capable,
Nor never with thy secret hand make brief   110
A woman's labour to me, if I do
Give way unto my married husband's will,
Or be a wife in anything but hopes.
Till I have made him easy as a child,
And tame as fear. He shall not win a smile   115
Or a pleased look from this austerity,
Though it would pull another jointure from him
And make him every day another man.
And when I kiss him, till I have my will,
May I be barren of delights, and know   120
Only what pleasure is in dreams and guesses.
LIVIA

A strange exordium!
BIANCA   All the several wrongs
Done by imperious husbands to their wives
These thousand years and upward strengthen thee!

---

105   *Here . . . be* Maria may gesture at herself, to indicate that she aims to seize
       domination in her relationship with Petruchio (the marital relationship was often
       compared to a body, with the husband as the head), or she may mime placing her
       foot on Petruchio's head, recalling Katherine's declaration at the end of *The Taming
       of the Shrew* that the wives should 'place your hands below your husband's foot'
       (V.ii.178).
106   *'Tis . . . ocean* i.e. it is as easy as draining the ocean with a sieve: a proverbial phrase
       (Tilley W111).
       'Tis with MS (Tis as easie F).
107   *Lucina* Roman goddess of childbirth.
109   *human* ed. (humane MS).
111   *woman's* (mothers F).
       labour (1) work; (2) childbirth.
116   *austerity* self-restraint, abstinence.
117   *jointure* marriage settlement (usually the money or lands intended to provide for a
       widow after her husband's death).
121   *pleasure is* MS (pleasures are F).
122   *exordium* beginning (especially the introductory part of a treatise).
       several various.

Thou hast a brave cause.

MARIA   And I'll do it bravely,   125
Or may I knit my life out ever after.

LIVIA
In what part of the world got she this spirit?
Yet, pray, Maria, look before you truly.
Besides the disobedience of a wife,
Which you will find a heavy imputation,   130
Which yet I cannot think your own, it shows
So distant from your sweetness –

MARIA   'Tis, I swear.

LIVIA
Weigh but the person, and the hopes you have
To work this desperate cure.

MARIA   A weaker subject
Would shame the end I aim at. Disobedience?   135
You talk too tamely! By the faith I have
In mine own noble will, that childish woman
That lives a prisoner to her husband's pleasure
Has lost her making and becomes a beast
Created for his use, not fellowship.   140

LIVIA
His first wife said as much.

MARIA   She was a fool,
And took a scurvy course; let her be named
'Mongst those that wish for things but dare not do 'em.

---

126   *may . . . after* i.e. may I spend my life engaging in mundane and traditionally
       feminine activities.
127   *In . . . spirit* Livia's remark may be directed at Bianca, at the audience, or as a general
       rhetorical question.
128   *look before you* i.e. look into your future, look at what you're doing.
129   *the . . . wife* i.e. the accusation of being a disobedient wife.
130   *imputation* accusation.
131   *shows* appears.
133   *Weigh* Consider.
       hopes i.e. chance.
134   *desperate* reckless, risky.
139   *her making* i.e. the reason why she was created.
140   *Created . . . fellowship* According to Biblical narrative Eve was created to be Adam's
       companion, whereas everything else was created for his use (Genesis 1.1–2).
142   *scurvy* contemptible.
143   *'Mongst* amongst.

I have a new dance for him, and a mad one.

LIVIA

Are you of this faith?

BIANCA   Yes, truly, and will die in't.   145

LIVIA

Why then, let's all wear breeches!

BIANCA   That's a good wench!

Now thou com'st near the nature of a woman.

Hang those tame-hearted eyases, that no sooner

See the lure out, and hear their husbands' hallow,

But cry like kites upon 'em; the free haggard –   150

---

144 *dance* game, course of action.
     and a mad one MS (*om.* F).
     mad frantic, outrageous, chaotic.

145 *faith* belief.

146 *let's . . . breeches* i.e. let's all usurp male authority (said ironically).
     BIANCA MS (*Mar.* F).
     That's . . . wench MS (*om.* F).

146–58 *That's . . . again* Editors have usually conflated MS and F, keeping MS's attribution
     of 'That's a good wench!' to Bianca and using F's speech prefix for the remainder
     of the speech. This is perhaps in part because Livia addresses the speaker of this
     speech as 'sister' in l. 158, and Bianca is Livia's cousin. However, Bianca refers to
     Livia as 'sister' at II.i.29, 31, and there is no overwhelming reason to adjust MS's
     attribution here, especially as the speech's rhetoric is in tune with Bianca's style
     elsewhere.

148–58 *Hang . . . again* This speech adopts the language of Petruchio's statement of intent
     in *The Taming of the Shrew*, IV.i.176–84: 'My falcon now is sharp and passing
     empty, / And till she stoop she must not be full-gorg'd, / For then she never looks
     upon her lure. / Another way I have to man my haggard, / To make her come and
     know her keeper's call, / That is, to watch her, as we watch these kites / That bate
     and beat and will not be obedient'; however, it turns the image of taming into one
     of untamed freedom.

148 *those* MS (these F).
     eyases young hawks taken from the nest for training; imperfectly trained hawks.

149 *lure* a tool used by falconers in training birds of prey, usually made up of a bunch
     of feathers swung on a long cord or thong.
     hallow MS (holla F; holler ed.)
     hallow loud shout or cry (especially associated with hunting).

150 *cry* call in supplication, submit.
     kites birds of prey, often characterised as greedy scavengers (the word is frequently
     used as an insult).
     haggard a wild, adult female hawk (proverbially proud and difficult to tame: see
     Tilley T298, 'In time all haggard hawks will stoop to lure'). This is a key term in *The
     Taming of the Shrew*, used in Petruchio's soliloquy in Act IV (IV.i.181), and by
     Hortensio in his declaration that he will marry a wealthy widow 'which hath as
     long lov'd me / As I have lov'd this proud disdainful haggard' (IV.ii.38–9), the
     'haggard' here being Bianca.

Which is that woman that has wing, and knows it,
Spirit and plume – will make a hundred checks
To show her freedom, sail in every air
And look out every pleasure, not regarding
Lure nor quarry, till her pitch command   155
What she desires, making her foundered keeper
Be glad to fling out trains, and golden ones,
To take her down again.

LIVIA   You are learned, sister.
Yet I say still, take heed.

MARIA   A witty saying.
I'll tell thee, Livia, had this fellow tired   160
As many wives as horses under him,
With spurring of their patience, had he got
A patent with an office to reclaim us,
Confirmed by parliament, had he the malice
And subtlety of devils, or of us,   165
Or anything that's worse than both –

LIVIA
Hey, hey, boys; this is excellent!

MARIA   Or could he
Cast his wives new again, like bells, to make 'em
Sound to his will, or had the fearful name
Of the first breaker of wild women, yet –   170

---

151 *has* MS (hath F).
152 *Spirit* (1) the movement of the wind; (2) courage, vitality; (3) temperament.
     plume feathers (also refers figuratively to a mark of distinction or honour, deriving
     from the ornamental feathers worn on helmets).
     checks pursuits of game other than her target.
155 *quarry* prey.
     pitch the height that a bird of prey reaches before it swoops down onto its prey.
156 *foundered* disabled, helpless.
157 *trains* enticements: refers specifically to a live bird attached to a line, used to entice a
     young hawk during training.
158 *take her down* (1) persuade the hawk to return to him; (2) persuade her to sleep with
     him.
159 *take heed* be careful.
162 *spurring* (1) urging with the use of a spur; (2) testing, trying.
163 *us* i.e. women.
167 *Hey, hey, boys* A sarcastic encouragement: 'boy' can mean 'rogue' or 'ruffian', but it is
     infrequently used of women. Livia suggests that Maria's language is unfeminine.
     excellent honourable, praiseworthy (said sarcastically).
169 *Sound to his will* i.e. ring when and how he pleased.
170 *breaker* tamer (as in the 'breaking' of a horse).

Yet would I undertake this man, thus single,
And spite of all the freedom he has reached to,
Turn him, and bend him as I list, and mould him
Into a babe again, that aged women
Wanting both teeth and spleen may master him.   175

BIANCA
Thou wilt be chronicled.

MARIA   That's all I aim at.

LIVIA
I must confess I do with all my heart
Hate an imperious husband, and in time
Might be so wrought upon.

BIANCA   To make him cuckold –

MARIA
If he deserve it?

LIVIA   Then I'll leave you, ladies.   180

BIANCA
Thou hast not so much noble anger in thee.

MARIA
Go sleep, go sleep. What we intend to do
Lies not for such starved souls as thou hast, Livia.

LIVIA
Good night.
The bridegroom will be with you presently.   185

MARIA
That's more than you know.

LIVIA   If ye work upon him
As you have promised, ye may give example
Which no doubt will be followed.

171   *single* alone, unaided.
172   *reached to* clutched at; arrived at, attained.
173   *Turn* Shape, fashion; divert, deflect.
        bend him make him submit, make him tractable.
        list like.
175   *spleen* courage, ill-humour, passion.
176   *chronicled* i.e. recorded in the history books.
179   *wrought upon* persuaded.
        cuckold the husband of an unfaithful wife.
183   *starved* pinched, shabby.
186   *work* prevail.
187   *you* MS (ye F).
188–90   ed. (Which . . . followed. / So. / Good . . . further; / If . . . harm. MS).

MARIA	So.
BIANCA	Good night.

We'll trouble you no further;
If you intend no good, pray do no harm.   190

LIVIA

None but pray for ye.   *Exit* LIVIA

MARIA   Now, Bianca –

BIANCA   Cheer, wench?

MARIA

Those wits we have, let's wind 'em to the height.
My rest is up, wench, and I pull for that
Will make me ever famous; they that lay
Foundations are half-builders, all men say.   195

Enter JAQUES

JAQUES

My master, forsooth –

MARIA

Oh, how does thy master? Prithee commend me to him.

JAQUES

How's this? My master stays, forsooth –

MARIA

Why, let him stay. Who hinders him, forsooth?

JAQUES

[*Aside*] The revel's ended now. [*To* MARIA] To visit you.   200

MARIA

I am not sick.

JAQUES

I mean, to see his chamber, forsooth –

BIANCA *Good night . . . further* / *If . . . harm* MS (*By.* Good night: we'l trouble you
no further. / *Mar.* If you intend no good, pray doe no harm. F).

191   *Now . . . wench* F swaps the order of Maria and Bianca's speeches.
       Cheer i.e. what cheer: how are you (alternatively, 'Cheer, wench!': be of good cheer,
       take heart).

193   *My rest is up* i.e. I have staked everything (a 'rest' is a stake in a card game).
       pull draw a card: gamble.

196   *forsooth* truly.

198   *How's this?* This might be delivered as an aside, and is treated as such by Daileader
       and Taylor.   *stays* is waiting.

200   *The . . . now* i.e. the party's over now.

202   *his chamber* Jaques is actually referring to Maria's bedchamber in her father's
       house, as his comment at l. 206 makes clear, but Maria pretends that he is referring
       to Petruchio's own bedchamber.

MARIA

Am I his groom? Where lay he last night, forsooth?

JAQUES

In the low matted parlour.

MARIA

There lies his way, by the long gallery.   205

JAQUES

I mean your chamber; you are very merry, Mistress.

MARIA

'Tis a good sign I am sound-hearted, Jaques.
But if you will know where I lie, follow me,
And what thou see'st deliver to thy master.

BIANCA

Do, gentle Jaques.   *Exeunt* MARIA *and* BIAN[CA]

JAQUES   Ha! Is the wind in that door?   210
By'r Lady, we shall have foul weather then!
I do not like the shuffling of these women;
They are mad beasts when they knock their heads.
I have observed 'em all this day, their whispers
One in another's ear, their signs, and pinches,   215
And breaking often into violent laughters,
As if the end they purposed were their own.
Call you these weddings? Sure, this is knavery,
A very rank and dainty knavery,
Marvellous finely carried, that's the comfort.   220

203   *groom* man-servant (who would help Petruchio to bed).
204   *low* (1) on a lower story; (2) low-ceilinged (can also mean humble or inferior).
       matted laid with matting.
       parlour chamber, bedchamber.
205   *gallery* corridor.
207   *sound-hearted* healthy.
210   *Is . . . door* i.e. is that the way things are heading (a proverbial phrase [Tilley W419]).
211   *By'r Lady* By our Lady (i.e. the Virgin Mary): a mild oath.
212   *shuffling* shifty behaviour (also refers to the shuffling of a pack of cards, continuing
       Maria's metaphor of ll. 193–4).
213   *knock their heads* i.e. put their heads together, confer amongst themselves.
       heads MS (heads together F).
217   *As . . . own* i.e. as if they had an aim of their own.
218   *knavery* trickery; dishonest conduct.
       knavery MS (a knavery F).
219   *rank* MS (trick F).
       rank (1) proud, rebellious; (2) loathsome, rotten.
       dainty (1) delicate; (2) excellent (said sarcastically).
220   *carried* i.e. carried off.

What would these women do in ways of honour
That are such masters this way? Well, my sir
Has been as good at finding out these toys
As any living; if he lose it now
At his own peril be it. I must follow.   *Exit*   225

[ACT I, SCENE iii]

Enter SERVANTS (*with lights*), PETRUCHIO, PETRONIUS
MOROSO, TRANIO [*and*] SOPHOCLES

PETRUCHIO
  You that are married, gentlemen, have at ye
  For a round wager now.
SOPHOCLES   Of this night's stage?
PETRUCHIO
  Yes.
SOPHOCLES
  I am your first man:
  A pair of gloves of twenty shillings.
PETRUCHIO   Done.

221–2   *What . . . way* i.e. what honourable things could they do if they're so good at
        wickedness.
  222   *my sir* i.e. my master.
  223   *toys* (1) tricks, whims, pieces of nonsense; (2) frivolous people, playthings.

        [*Act I, Scene iii*] ed. (*Scena tertia* F).
    0   s.d. *with lights* Illusionistic lighting was not conventionally used on the early
        modern stage, so the servants carry lanterns to indicate that the scene takes place
        after dark.
    1   *have at ye* (I) challenge you.
        have MS (home F).
    2   *round* substantial.
  2–6   *For . . . bets* Petruchio encourages the other men to make bets on his sexual
        performance on his wedding night.
    2   *night's* F (nights) (night MS).
        stage (1) section of a journey; (2) sexual bout (Williams, 3: 1302).
    4   *your first man* i.e. the first man to make a bet.
  4–6   ed. (I . . . shillings / Done . . . bets MS).
    5   *twenty shillings* This sum would have the spending power of around £100 at the
        time of writing (2009).

Who takes me up else? I am for all bets.

MOROSO

Faith, lusty Lawrence, were but my night now,
Old as I am, I would make you clap on spurs
But I would reach you, and bring you to
Your trot too. I would, gallant.   10

PETRUCHIO

Well said, good will. But where's the stuff, boy? Ha?
Old Father Time, your hourglass is empty.

PETRONIUS

See how these boys despise us! Well son, well,
This pride will have a fall.

PETRUCHIO   Upon your daughter.
But I shall rise again, if there be truth   15
In eggs and buttered parsnips.

PETRONIUS

Will you to bed, son, and leave talking?
Tomorrow morning we shall have you look,

---

6   *else* MS (next F).
       else otherwise.
7   *Faith* MS (Well F).
       Faith A mild oath.
       lusty Lawrence Lancastrian hero of a lost ballad, supposed to have fathered 17 children in one year (see Williams, 2: 833–4).
7–10   *Faith . . . too* Moroso boasts that, though old, he would be able to outdo Petruchio's sexual endeavours if this were his wedding night.
8   *clap on spurs* Moroso begins a line of horse imagery that runs throughout the scene.
10   *Your trot* F (you troth MS).
       gallant MS (Gallants F).
11–12   *where's . . . empty* Petruchio suggests that Moroso is physically incapable of fulfilling his sexual boast.
11   *will* a slang term for sexual appetite or for the penis (see Williams, 3: 1536–7).
       stuff MS (staffe F).
       stuff substance.
       boy Old men are often addressed disrespectfully as 'boy' in early modern texts.
12   *hourglass* (1) sandglass; (2) scrotum.
12–13   F has two extra lines for Tranio between these speeches: See Appendix 1, Passage A.
13   *Well son, well* MS (Will you to bed sonne? F).
       son i.e. son-in-law (sons-in-law were often addressed simply as 'son').
14   *pride will have a fall* a proverbial phrase (Tilley P581).
16   *eggs . . . parsnips* aphrodisiacs. Williams (2: 757) notes that eggs were proverbially connected with Lancashire, home of the 'lusty Lawrence' mentioned by Moroso in l. 7.
17   *leave* stop.

For all your great words, like St George at Kingston,
Running a-footback from the furious dragon   20
That with her angry tail belabours him
For being lazy.
SOPHOCLES   His warlike lance
Bent like a crossbow lath, alas the while.
TRANIO
His courage quenched, and so far quenched –
PETRUCHIO   'Tis well, sir.
TRANIO
That any privy saint, even small St Davy,   25
May lash him with a leek.
PETRUCHIO
What then?
SOPHOCLES
   ""Fly, fly", quoth then the fearful dwarf,
   "Here is no place for living man.""

19–22   *St George . . . lazy* May refer either to an inn sign at Kingston upon Thames (a
        village around ten miles south-west of the City of London), or to a routine in a
        morris dance: Petronius casts Petruchio as humbled and sexually humiliated St
        George to Maria's unsatisfied dragon.
20   *a-footback* i.e. on foot ('footback' is a parody of 'horseback').
21   *tail* (1) the dragon's tail; (2) a slang term for the female genitals.
        belabours thrashes.
22–3   *His . . . while* MS (*om.* F): these lines may have been censored in F.
22   *lance* (1) the weapon carried by a knight; (2) a phallic image.
23   *lath* the bending part of a cross-bow.
        alas the while an expression of sorrow.
24   *courage* (1) bravery; (2) sexual capacity.
25   *privy* (1) private, reserved for a particular group of people; (2) native; (3) secret;
        (4) a 'saint of the privy', i.e. a penis.
        small short (Welsh people were stereotypically supposed to be short): also in this
        context suggests a lack of sexual potency.
        St Davy St David, patron saint of Wales.
25–6   *That . . . leek* MS (*om.* F). In F Petruchio's speech becomes "'Tis well Sir. / What
        then?'; the lines have probably been censored.
        That . . . leek i.e. that Petruchio will be reduced to sexual incapacity; compare
        Edward Sharpham, *Cupid's Whirligig* (London, 1607), in which a woman is
        recommended to marry an old man 'because thou maiest sleep quiet & not be
        troubled a nights', to which she responds that she would rather 'marrie a Saint
        Dauis Leeke' (sig. L1v).
26   *leek* a national symbol of Wales.
28   *dwarf* like the reference to 'small' in l. 25 suggests sexual incapacity.
28–9   *Fly . . . man* A slight misquotation of Spenser's *The Faerie Queene*, 1.I.xiii.8–9, 'Fly
        fly (quoth then / The fearefull Dwarfe:) this is no place for living men', referring to
        the den of Error; it maintains the mock-chivalric tone.

PETRUCHIO

Well, my masters, if I do sink under my business,　　　　　30
As I find 'tis very possible, I am not the first
That has miscarried so, that's my comfort.
What may be done without impeach or waste

Enter JAQUES

I can and will do. How now? Is my fair bride a-bed?

JAQUES

No, truly, sir.　　　　　35

PETRONIUS

Not a-bed yet?
Body o' me, we'll up and rifle her!
Here's a coil with a maidenhead; 'tis not entailed,
Is it?

PETRUCHIO

If it be, I'll try all the law i' th' land,　　　　　40
But I'll cut it off. Let's up, let's up, come.

JAQUES

That you cannot neither.

PETRUCHIO

Why?

JAQUES

Unless you'll drop through the chimney like a daw,
Or force a breach i'th' windows.　　　　　45

30　*my masters* a polite mode of address, like 'sirs'.
　　business task, (sexual) affairs.
33　*impeach* impediment; injury, damage; accusation.
　　waste (1) useless expenditure; (2) wasting of the body through (venereal) disease.
　　s.d. F places this after 'I can and will do.' (l. 34).
34　*and* F (or MS).
36–7　ed. (Not . . . her MS).
37　*Body o' me* body of me: an oath.
　　o' F (a MS); further instances have been silently modified.
　　rifle despoil, plunder (with sexual innuendo).
38　*coil with* fuss about.　　*maidenhead* state or condition of being a virgin.
　　entailed settled so that it cannot be bestowed on someone else (an entail controls
　　who can inherit an estate).
39　*Is it* F (is yet MS).
41　*it* i.e. the maidenhead and/or the entail.
　　off F (of MS).
44　*daw* jackdaw (a small member of the crow family).
45　*windows* F (windores MS).

You may untile the house, 'tis possible.

PETRUCHIO

What dost thou mean?

JAQUES

A moral, sir. The ballad will express it:
[*Sings*] '*The wind and the rain,*
            Has turned you back again,   50
            Ye cannot be lodged there.'
The truth is, all the doors are barricadoed,
Not a cat-hole but holds a murder in't;
She's victualled for this month.

PETRUCHIO   Art thou not drunk?

SOPHOCLES

He's drunk, he's drunk; come, come, let's up.

JAQUES   Yes, yes,   55
I am drunk; ye may go up, ye may, gentlemen,
But take heed to your heads. I say no more.

SOPHOCLES

I'll try that.   *Exit* SOPHOCLES

PETRONIUS

How dost thou say; the door fast locked, fellow?

JAQUES

Yes, truly, sir: 'tis locked and guarded too,   60
And two as desperate tongues planted behind it
As are yet battered.

45–6   ed. (or . . . the / house . . . possible MS).
  46   *untile the house* i.e. strip all of the tiles off in order to get access through the roof.
49–54   ed. (the . . . againe / ye . . . is / All . . . cat-hole / but . . . victuall'd / for . . . month
       MS).
49–51   *The . . . there* A snatch from an Elizabethan ballad of refusal usually known as 'Go
       From my Window', which is quoted in a number of early seventeenth-century plays.
  52   *barricadoed* blocked off with barricades.
  53   *cat-hole* a hole large enough to let a cat through.
       murder MS (murd'rer F).
  54   *victualled* supplied with provisions (as if preparing for siege).
       thou not MS (not thou F).
55–6   ed. (Hee's . . . vp. / Yes . . . may / gentlemen MS).
  59   *fast* securely.
60–6   ed. (Yes . . . desperate / toungues . . . vpon / their . . . composition; / I'le . . . and /
       bullets . . . them MS).
  60   *too* F (to MS).
61–6   *desperate . . . them* Throughout this speech Jaques compares the women's tongues
       with weapons.
  62   *are* MS (ere F; e'er ed.)

They stand upon their honours, and will not give up
without strange composition, I'll assure you; marching
away with their pieces cocked and bullets in their 65
mouths will not satisfy them.

PETRUCHIO

How's this? How's this? They are? Is there another with her?

JAQUES

Yes, marry, is there, and an engineer.

MOROSO

Who's that, for Love's sake?

JAQUES

Colonel Bianca. She commands the works: Spinola's but 70
a ditcher to her. There's a half moon – I am a poor
man, but if you'd give me leave, sir, I'll venture a year's
wages – draw all your force before it, and mount your
ablest piece of battery, you shall not enter in't these three
nights yet. 75

Enter SOPHO[CLES]

PETRUCHIO

I should laugh at that, good Jaques.

SOPHOCLES

Beat back again! She's fortified forever.

---

64 *composition* agreement for ceasing hostilities; terms of surrender.
65 *with . . . cocked* with their guns ready to be fired (with heavy sexual innuendo on
   'pieces' and 'cocked').
67 ed. (How's . . . are; / Is . . . her? MS).
68 *marry* a common oath (a corruption of 'by [the Virgin] Mary').
   engineer designer of military works for attack or defence.
69 *Love's* MS (loues) (Heavens F; [God's] ed.)
   Love's i.e. Cupid, the god of love; the oath 'for Love's sake' is funny coming from
   Moroso, and emendation to F's 'Heavens' or editors' 'God's' is not strictly necessary.
70 *works* i.e. the military defence works.
   Spinola Don Ambrogio Spinola Doria, 1st Marquis of the Balbases (1569–1630): an
   Italian general who fought for Spain and was in charge of the Spanish forces which
   besieged Ostend in 1603–4.
71 *half moon* a defensive fortification in the shape of a half moon.
   am a MS (am but a F).
72 *you'd* ed. (you'l'd MS; you'll F).
   sir MS (*om.* F).
74 *piece of battery* siege-gun ('piece' is often used as slang for genitals). Maintaining
   the innuendo of this exchange, Jaques imagines the house and its defences as a
   woman, and the invading force of the men as a sexual aggressor.

JAQUES
    Am I drunk now, sir?
SOPHOCLES
    He that dares most, go up now and be cooled.
    I have 'scaped a pretty scouring.   80
PETRUCHIO
    What, are they mad? Have we another Bedlam?
    She doth not talk, I hope.
SOPHOCLES
    Oh, terribly, extremely, fearfully!
    The noise at London Bridge is nothing near her.
PETRUCHIO
    How got she tongue?
SOPHOCLES   As you got tail; she was born to't.   85
PETRUCHIO
    Locked out o' doors, and on my wedding night?
    Nay, an I suffer this I may go graze!
    Come, gentlemen, I'll batter. Are these virtues?
SOPHOCLES
    Do, and be beaten off with shame, as I was.
    I went up, came to the door, knocked, nobody answered,   90
    Knocked louder, yet heard nothing, would have broke in
    By force; when suddenly a waterwork
    Flew from the window with such a violence

    79   *cooled* F (cool'd) (cold MS).
    80   *pretty* (1) crafty; (2) considerable; (3) splendid (said ironically).
         scouring (1) cleaning, especially with a jet or stream of water; (2) beating (also has
         military connotations, referring to enemy forces overrunning a country).
    81   *Bedlam* An early mental asylum, the Hospital of St Mary of Bethlehem, situated
         outside Bishopsgate, on the edge of the City of London, and used as a by-word for
         insanity.
    82   *She doth* MS (They doe F) (F's version stresses the solidarity between the women,
         whereas MS focuses on the Petruchio/Maria relationship).
    83   *extremely, fearfully!* MS (extreamly fearfull F).
    83-4 ed. (Oh . . . noyse / At . . . her MS).
    84   *London Bridge* Until 1750 the only bridge crossing the Thames, London Bridge was
         lined with two rows of shops, and was a notoriously bustling location.
    85   *tongue* i.e. the ability to speak.
         tail a penis (and, by extension, male authority).
    87   *an* if (and MS).   *I may go graze* i.e. I might as well be put out to pasture.
    91   *heard* F (hard MS).
    91-2 ed. (knock'd . . . haue / broke . . . worke. MS).
    92   *waterwork* cascade; system for distributing water (or, in this case, urine).
    93   *window* F (windore MS).   *such a* MS (such F).

That had I not ducked quickly like a friar
Cætera quis nescit?   95
The chamber's nothing but a mere Ostend:
In every window pewter cannons mounted;
You'll quickly find with what they are charged, sir.

PETRUCHIO

Why then, tantara for us.

SOPHOCLES

And all the lower works lined sure with small shot,   100
Long tongues with firelocks that at twelve score blank
Hit to the heart. Now, an' you dare go up –

Enter MARIA *and* BIANCA (*above*)

MOROSO

The window opens. Beat a parley first.
I am so much amazed my very hair stands.

94   *ducked . . . friar* Friars were commonly supposed to duck or bow in an obsequious
        fashion.
94–5   ed. (one line MS; prose in F).
95   *Caetera quis nescit?* Who does not know the rest? (a quotation from Ovid's *Elegies*,
        I.v.25, recycled in a number of early modern texts).
96   *Ostend* A city in West Flanders which was besieged by the Spanish between 1601
        and 1604, when General Spinoza finally breached its defences.
97   *window* F (windore MS).
        pewter canons i.e. chamber-pots.
99   *tantara* an imitation of the sound of a military flourish (and therefore a declaration
        of intent from Petruchio).
100   *works* fortifications.
        small shot musket bullets, as opposed to cannon-balls.
101   *tongues* i.e. things that protrude like tongues, such as gun barrels.
        firelocks gunlocks in which sparks are produced to ignite the gunpowder and fire
        the gun.
        twelve score blank i.e. at a range of 240 feet.
102   *an'* ed. (and MS).
        an' if.
        dare F (deare MS).
102   s.d. *above* The appearance of Maria and Bianca in the playhouse balcony recalls the
        staging of siege sequences in a number of early modern plays: see, for instance, the
        siege of Harfleur in Shakespeare's *Henry V* (III.iii).
103   *window* F (windore MS).
        Beat a parley Summon a truce (usually by beating a drum or sounding a trumpet).
104   *my . . . stands* i.e. my hair stands on end.
        stands F (stand MS).

PETRONIUS

    Why, how now, daughter? What, entrenched?   105

MARIA

    A little guarded for my safety, sir.

PETRUCHIO

    For your safety, sweetheart? Why, who offends you?

    I come not to use violence.

MARIA   I think

    You cannot, sir; I am better fortified.

PETRUCHIO

    I know your end, you would fain reprieve your maidenhead   110

    a night or two.

MARIA

    Yes,

    Or ten, or twenty, sir, or say a hundred;

    Or, indeed, till I list lie with you.

SOPHOCLES

    That's a shrewd saying! From this present hour   115

    I will never believe a silent woman;

    When they break out they are bonfires.

PETRONIUS

    Till you list lie with him? Why, who are you, madam?

BIANCA

    That trim gentleman's wife, sir.

PETRUCHIO

    Cry ye mercy, do ye command too?   120

---

  105   *entrenched* fortified.

108–9   ed. (I . . . violence. / I . . . fortified MS).

  110   *would fain* desire to.

  113   *sir* MS (*om.* F).

  114   *list* wish to.

  115   *shrewd* malicious, vile; punning on 'shrew' (an abusive or scolding woman).

           present hour F (houre MS).

  116   *will never* MS (never will F).

           a silent woman Alludes to the narrative of Ben Jonson's *Epicoene, or The Silent Woman*, a play written shortly before *The Tamer Tamed*.

  118   *you* Fathers would normally address their daughters with the informal 'thou' pronoun rather than the formal 'you'; Petronius's use of 'you' is in keeping with his addressing Maria as 'madam' and suggests his emotional distance from her.

  119   *trim* excellent, fine; neat, spruce (probably said ironically, especially if Petruchio is somewhat dishevelled at this point).

  120   *Cry ye mercy* I beg your pardon.

MARIA

Yes, marry, doth she, and in chief.

BIANCA

I do command, and you shall go without –
I mean your wife – for this night.

MARIA

And for the next too, wench, and so as't follows.

PETRONIUS

Thou wilt not; wilt 'a?

MARIA   Yes indeed, dear father,   125
And till he seals to what I shall set down,
For anything I know, forever.

SOPHOCLES

By'r Lady, these are bug's words.

TRANIO

You hear her, sir; she can talk, heaven be thanked!

PETRUCHIO

I would I heard it not.   130

SOPHOCLES

I find that all the pity bestowed upon this woman
Makes but an anagram of an ill wife,
For she was never virtuous.

124   *as't* as it.
125   *Thou* Petronius's increasing rage is suggested by his movement from addressing
      Maria with the polite or formal 'you', to the informal or abusive 'thou'.
      wilt 'a will you.
126   *seals to* ratifies (originally refers to the wax seals fixed to an agreement or contract).
      seals MS (seales) (seale F).
128   *By'r Lady* MS (Indeed F).
      By'r Lady By our Lady: a mild oath (our Lady: the Virgin Mary).
      bug's words words intended to intimidate, recalling Petruchio's 'Tush, tush, fear
      boys with bugs' in Shakespeare's *Taming of the Shrew* (I.ii.211).
129   *You . . . thanked!* Tranio's relaxed, sardonic reaction to the women's actions
      contrasts strongly with the other men's reactions, and foreshadows his alliance
      with Bianca later in the play.
      hear her MS (heare F).   *heaven* MS (God F).
130   *not* MS (not sir F).
132   *an anagram . . . wife* Daileader and Taylor point out that 'an ill wife' is an anagram
      of 'a fine will', but it is possible that an alternative early modern meaning for
      'anagram', transposition or mutation, is meant here: compare John Donne's *Elegy
      IV*, in which it is said of an ugly woman, 'Though all her parts be not in th' usual
      place, / She hath yet an anagram of a good face' (John Carey, ed., *John Donne: The
      Major Works* [Oxford, 2000], p. 17, ll. 15–16). In either case, Sophocles suggests
      that the former pity that the men felt for Maria has deceived them as to her true
      nature, or that their sympathy has spoiled her.

PETRUCHIO
    You'll let me in, I hope, for all this jesting?
MARIA
    Hope still, sir.
PETRONIUS You will come down, I am sure.   135
MARIA
    I am sure I will not.
PETRONIUS   I'll fetch you then.
BIANCA
    The power of the whole county cannot, sir,
    Unless we please to yield, which yet I think
    We shall not. Charge when you please, you shall
    Hear quickly from us.   140
MOROSO
    Heaven bless me from a chicken of thy hatching!
PETRUCHIO
    Prithee, Maria, tell me what's the reason,
    And do it freely, you deal thus strangely with me?
    You were not forced to marry; your consent
    Went equally with mine, if not before it.   145
    I hope you do not doubt I want that mettle
    A man should have to keep a woman waking;
    I would be sorry to be such a saint yet.
    My person, as it is not excellent,
    So 'tis not old, or lame, or weak with physic, 150
    But well enough to please an honest woman
    That keeps her house, and loves her husband.
MARIA   'Tis so.

138 *please* have the desire.
141 *Heaven bless me* MS (Bless me F; [God] bless me ed.)
   bless protect.
   hatching! MS (hatching, / 'Is this wiving?' F).
   Heaven . . . hatching i.e. preserve me from having a wife like this, preserve me from
   marrying a sister of yours.
142 *Prithee* (I) pray thee: please.
143 *deal* behave.
146 *mettle* sexual vigour.
147 *keep . . . waking* a cliché referring to a man's sexual endurance.
   waking awake.
149 *person* body, physical appearance.
150 *or . . . . or* MS (nor . . . nor F).
   physic medicine (by implication for venereal disease).
151 *honest* honourable, chaste.

PETRUCHIO

My means and my conditions are no shamers
Of him that owns them – all the world knows that –
And my friends no reliers on my fortunes. 155

MARIA

All this I believe and none of all these parcels
I dare except against. Nay, more, so far
I am from making these the ends I aim at –
These idle outward things, these woman's fears –
That were I yet unmarried, free to choose 160
Through all the tribes of man, I'd take Petruchio
In's shirt, with one ten groats to pay the priest,
Before the best man living, or the ablest
That e'er leaped out of Lancashire, and they
Are right ones. 165

PETRONIUS

Why do you play the fool, then, and stand prating
Out of the window like a broken miller?

PETRUCHIO

If you will have me credit you, Maria,

153 *means* resources (especially financial).
conditions circumstances.
154 *owns them* MS (owes 'em F).
155 *friends* family; companions (friends in the modern sense).
156 *parcels* items, points.
157 *except against* object to.
158 *ends* issues.
159 *idle* foolish, trivial.
161 *I'd* ed. (I would MS; I'ld F.)
162 *shirt* an undergarment for the upper part of the body, worn next to the skin and usually made of washable material such as linen, calico or silk; the shirt is often emblematic of male sexuality.
with . . . priest groats were worth 4 pence, so Maria imagines that 40 pence would be the minimum sum necessary to get married.
164–5 *That . . . ones* Lancashire was a by-word for sexual capacity, and Lancashire men had a reputation for athletic ability; in mentioning Lancashire Maria picks up Moroso's reference to 'lusty Lawrence' in l. 7.
165 *right* sound, healthy; sexually capable, lusty.
166–7 *stand . . . miller* Petronius perhaps has in mind a miller who shouts out of his window rather than allow his creditors to enter the mill to talk to him: in this case, the image would put Maria in the position of the debtor refusing to pay what is owed. Millers were proverbially dishonest (see Tilley M954–9). Another interpretation would draw on the tradition that millers were extremely deaf, due to the noisy environment in which they worked.
167 *broken* ruined; bankrupt.

Come down, and let your love confirm it.

MARIA   Stay there, sir,

That bargain's yet to make.

BIANCA   Play sure, wench;   170

The pack's in thine own hand.

SOPHOCLES   Let me die lousy

If these two wenches be not brewing knavery

To stock a kingdom.

PETRUCHIO   'Death, this is a riddle:

'I love ye, and I love ye not.'

MARIA   It is so,

And till your own experience do untie it   175

This distance I must keep.

PETRUCHIO   If you talk more

I am angry, very angry.

MARIA

I am glad on't, and I will talk.

PETRUCHIO   Prithee peace.

Let me not think thou art mad. I tell thee, woman,

If thou go'st forward, I am still Petruchio.   180

MARIA

And I am worse, a woman that can fear

---

168   *credit* believe.
170–1   ed. (that . . . make. / Play . . . hand. MS.)
171   *pack* i.e. the pack of cards: Bianca continues the line of references to gambling begun at the start of the scene, but reconceives Maria as someone who gambles on her own behalf rather than something on which bets are placed.
      Let me die lousy a statement along the same lines as 'I'll be damned . . . '
      lousy infested with lice.
172   *wenches* young women, hussies (Sophocles uses the word negatively, in contrast with Maria and Bianca).
172–3   *knavery . . . stock* i.e. enough trickery or dishonest behaviour to supply the entire nation ('knavery' perhaps also relates back to 'pack' in l. 171).
173   *'Death* MS (Why F).
      'Death a blasphemous oath, meaning 'by God's death' (many early modern oaths refer to Christ's crucifixion).
174–5   ed. (I . . . not. / It . . . it MS).
178   *peace* be quiet.
179   *thou . . . thee* This is the first time that Petruchio addresses Maria with the familiar 'thou' pronoun, suggesting his increasing anger towards her.
181   *can* F (*om.* MS).
181–2   F (And . . . woman / that . . . fame MS).

Neither Petruchio Furius, nor his fame,
Nor anything that tends to our allegiance.
There's a short method for ye: now you know me.

PETRUCHIO
If you can carry't so, 'tis very well.   185

BIANCA
No, you shall carry it, sir.

PETRUCHIO   Peace, gentle low-bell.

PETRONIUS
Use no more words, but come down instantly;
I charge thee by the duty of a child.

PETRUCHIO
Prithee come, Maria, I forgive all.

MARIA
Stay there. [*To* PETRONIUS] That duty that you charge me by   190
(If you consider truly what you say)
Is now another man's, you gave't away
I' th' church, if you remember, to my husband,
So all you can exact now is no more
But only a due reverence to your person,   195
Which thus I pay. Your blessing, and I am gone
To bed for this night.

PETRONIUS   This is monstrous!
That blessing that St Dunstan gave the devil

---

182   *Petruchio Furius* A mocking title: 'Furius' is derived from the Latin term *furor*, often
       used to refer to a kind of heroic fury or madness exhibited by the eponymous
       heroes of Seneca's classical tragedy *Hercules Furens* and Ariosto's Renaissance epic
       Orlando Furioso. Maria parodies Petruchio's invocation of his own heroic
       reputation by sardonically comparing him to these maddened heroes.
184   *method* set of rules.
185   *carry't so* succeed in this behaviour, pull this off.
186   *carry it* put up with it (with sexual innuendo).
       low-bell a small bell, especially a cow-bell or a sheep-bell.
188   *charge* command.
190–7 *That . . . night* Maria refers to the common belief that on her marriage a woman's
       primary allegiance transferred from her father to her husband; compare Cordelia's
       statement to Lear in the first scene of Shakespeare's *King Lear* (I.i.90–8).
196   *Which thus I pay* Maria may curtsey to Petronius at this point, punning on 'rever-
       ence', which means both respect and curtsey.
       Your blessing i.e. give me your blessing.
198–200 *That . . . nose* According to folklore, the devil came to St Dunstan in the shape of a
       beautiful young woman, but the saint saw through the deception and caught the
       devil by the nose with a pair of blacksmiths' tongs. The comparison suggests that
       Maria's outward appearance similarly conceals a devilish interior.

If I were near thee I would give thee –
Pull thee down by the nose.

BIANCA   Saints should not rave, sir;   200
A little rhubarb now were excellent.

PETRUCHIO
Then, by that duty you owe to me, Maria,
Open the door and be obedient.
I am quiet yet.

MARIA
I do confess that duty, make your best on't.   205

PETRUCHIO
Why, give me leave, I will.

BIANCA   Sir, there's no learning
An old stiff jade to trot: you know the moral.

MARIA
Yet as I take it, sir, I owe no more
Than you owe back again.

PETRUCHIO   You will not article?
All I owe, presently, let me but up, I'll pay.   210

MARIA
Y'are too hot, and such prove jades at length.

---

199   — F (, MS; , whore ed.)
201   *rhubarb* used as a laxative: purging the body was thought to improve physical and
          mental health.
202   *duty you owe* Petruchio refers to the general assumption that the wife should obey
          the husband, but over the following lines the words 'duty', 'owe' and 'pay' take on
          sexual significance; especially relevant here is the idea that the wife's duties
          included submitting to the sexual attentions of her husband.
203–4 ed. (one line MS).
205   *make . . . on't* i.e. do your best with it.
          on't F (out MS).
206   *Why . . . will* i.e. if you will let me in, I will show you what I can do.
          learning teaching.
206–7 *there's . . . moral* Bianca refers to a proverb similar to 'you can't teach an old dog
          new tricks'; the statement might refer to Maria or (more likely) to Petruchio.
207   *stiff* inflexible (with a *double entendre* on 'erect').
          jade a contemptuous term for a worn-out horse.
208–9 *I . . . again* As elsewhere in the play, Maria implicitly asserts her equal right to sexual
          pleasure.
209   *article* negotiate.
211   *too* F (to MS).
          hot eager; sexually excited.
          prove . . . length i.e. eventually wear themselves out.

You do confess a duty or respect
To me from you again, that's very near
Or full the same with mine?

PETRUCHIO
    Yes.   215

MARIA
Then by that duty, or respect, or what
You please to have it, go to bed and leave me,
And trouble me no longer with your fooling,
For know I am not for you.

PETRUCHIO   Well, what remedy?

PETRONIUS
A fine smart cudgel. Oh, that I were near thee!   220

BIANCA
If you had teeth now, what a case were we in.

MOROSO
These are the most authentic rebels next
Tyrone I ever read of.

MARIA
A week hence, or a fortnight, as you bear ye,
And as I find my will observed, I may   225
With intercession of some friends be brought
Maybe to kiss you, and so quarterly
To pay a little rent by composition.
You understand me?

212–14   ed. (you ... againe / that's ... mine? MS).
   214   *full the same* equal.
   219   *Well, what remedy?* This line might be a general declaration of despair, or be aimed specifically at the other men on stage.
   220   *smart* able to inflict pain.
   221   *what ... in* i.e. how much trouble would we be in.
              case condition, state of affairs.
222–3   ed. (These ... Tyrone / I ... of. MS).
   222   *authentic* genuine.
              next apart from.
   223   *Tyrone* Aodh Mór Ó Néill (known to the English as Hugh O'Neill), second Earl of Tyrone, leader of the Irish rebels during the Nine Years' War (1594–1603), and a consistent opponent of the English crown until his death in 1616; he was much talked of in London in 1610, a fact which helps to date the play's composition.
   224   *as you bear ye* i.e. if you behave yourself.
   226   *intercession* entreaty.
   228   *pay ... rent* i.e. engage in sexual activity other than kissing.
              composition mutual arrangement.

SOPHOCLES   Thou boy, thou!

PETRUCHIO   Well,

There are more maids than Maudlin. That's my comfort.   230

MARIA

Yes, and more men than Michael.

PETRUCHIO   I must not

To bed with this stomach and no meat, lady.

MARIA

Feed where you will, so it be sound and wholesome,

Else live at livery, for I'll none with ye.

BIANCA

You had best back one of the dairy maids;   235

They'll carry, but take heed to your girths,

You'll get a bruise else.

PETRUCHIO

Now, if thou wouldst come down and tender me

All the delights due to a marriage bed,

Study such kisses as would melt a man,   240

And turn thyself into a thousand figures

To add new flames unto me, I would stand

---

229   *boy* rogue, ruffian (rarely used of women, and suggests that Sophocles views Maria's behaviour as unwomanly).

229–30   ed. (you . . . me? / Thow . . . thou. / Well . . . Maudlin. / that's . . . comfort. MS).

230   *more . . . Maudlin* i.e. there are other women available to me, a proverbial phrase (Tilley M39); 'Maudlin' is a corruption of 'Magdalene'.

231–2   ed. (Yes . . . Michaell. / I . . . stomach / and . . . Lady. MS).

231   *more . . . Michael* i.e. there are other men available to me.

232   *stomach* (1) appetite; (2) sexual desire/frustration.

       meat (1) food; (2) woman (as sexual object).

233   *so* so long as, provided that.

       sound and wholesome i.e. good for you; free of (venereal) disease.

234   *live at livery* i.e. sleep with prostitutes; the word 'livery' was also used of the husbands of unfaithful women: compare John Marston, *The Dutch Courtesan*: ''Tis not in fashion to call things by their right names. Is a great merchant a cuckold? You must say he is one of the livery' (I.ii.102–3). Literally, the word refers to horses kept and stabled for an absent owner, continuing the line of equine imagery.

235   *back* mount, ride (often used of horses).

236   *carry* i.e. bear up during sexual intercourse (to 'carry' is a slang term for having sex).

       girths belts or bands securing a horse's saddle.

236–7   *take . . . else* i.e. be careful that you don't fall off.

238   *tender* offer.

240   *Study* devise.

241   *figures* (1) shapes, forms; (2) postures; (3) roles; (4) figures of speech (i.e. erotic dialogue).

242   *flames* refers to the metaphorical heat of sexual desire.

Thus heavy, thus regardless, thus despising
Thee, and thy best allurings. All the beauty
That's laid upon your bodies – mark me well,   245
For without doubt your minds are miserable;
You have no masks for them – all this rare beauty,
Lay but the painter and the silkworm by,
The doctor with his diets, and the tailor,
You appear like flayed cats, not so handsome.   250

MARIA

And we appear like her that sent us hither,
That only excellent and beauteous Nature,
Truly ourselves, for men to wonder at,
But too divine to handle. We are gold
In our own natures pure, but when we suffer   255
The husband's stamp upon us, then allays,
And base ones, of you men are mingled with us,
And make us blush like copper.

PETRUCHIO   Then, and never
Till then, are women to be spoken of,
For till that time you have no souls, I take it.   260

243   *heavy* serious; sluggish.   *regardless* indifferent.
244   *allurings* attempts at seduction.
247   *masks* F (maskes) (markes MS).
        masks Women of high social status often wore masks in public to preserve their
        complexions and their modesty.
248   *painter* i.e. the person who applies cosmetics.
        silkworm i.e. the means of producing rich silken clothes.
249   *diets* prescribed courses of food, intended to improve the health (often used to
        refer to cures for venereal disease: see Williams, 1: 385–6).
250   *You* MS (And you F).
        flayed cats cats' fur was used in clothing; 'cat' is also a slang term for a prostitute, so
        a 'flayed cat' would be a prostitute without her clothes and accessories.
254   *too* F (for MS).
254–8   *We . . . copper* Maria compares women with the pure metals that are adulterated
        and disfigured in the production of coins, medals and other objects; the word
        'stamp' (or 'impression') is often used in the context of a woman losing her
        virginity, or more generally to refer to the authority of men over women. Maria
        reformulates the image at III.ii.159–62, when she talks about the 'stamp' that the
        wife makes on the husband.
256   *allays* inferior metals mixed with ones of higher value.
257   *base* inferior, unworthy.
258–60 *Then . . . it* Petruchio argues that until they are married and under male authority
        women have no souls; the phrase 'women have no souls' was proverbial (Tilley
        W709), and the issue was debated (with varying degrees of seriousness) among
        theologians and other commentators.

Good night. Come, gentlemen, I'll fast for this night,
But by this hand – Well, I shall come up yet?

MARIA

No.

PETRUCHIO

There will I watch thee like a withered Jewry.
Thou shalt neither have meat, fire, nor candle,   265
Nor anything that's easy. Do you rebel so soon?
Yet take mercy.

BIANCA

Put up your pipes. To bed, sir. I'll assure you
A month's siege will not shake us.

MOROSO

Well said, colonel.   270

MARIA

To bed, to bed, Petruchio! Good night, gentlemen,
You'll make my father sick with sitting up.
Here you shall find us any time these ten days,
Unless we may march off with our contentment.

PETRUCHIO

I'll hang first.

---

262   *by this hand* – A declaration along the same lines as 'I swear', but Petruchio may
      wave his fist at Maria before reconsidering and making one last appeal to her.
      Alternatively, the line may also suggest that he will have to masturbate rather than
      sleeping with his wife.

264   *like . . . Jewry* Probably refers to a Jewish ghetto such as the one in Venice, which
      was locked and guarded at night; Daileader and Taylor also suggest an allusion to
      the Roman siege of Jerusalem, during which thousands of the inhabitants starved
      to death (this reference might therefore echo the allusions to the siege of Ostend in
      ll. 70 and 96). MS's 'Iewry' could also, however, be modernised as 'jury'.
      Jewry MS (Iewry) (Jewry F; Jury F2).
      withered decayed, reduced to poverty.

265–6 *Thou . . . easy* Petruchio threatens to replicate his treatment of Katherine in *The
      Taming of the Shrew*.
      anything that's easy i.e. anything that might make them comfortable.

267   *take mercy* Petruchio probably means 'throw yourself on my mercy' rather than
      'take mercy on me'.

268   *Put . . . pipes* stop what you are doing; be quiet: a proverbial phrase (Tilley P345).

269   *shake* disturb; dislodge.

272   *You'll . . . up* i.e. because he is old and not used to staying up late.
      sitting F (setting MS).

274   *off* F (of MS).
      contentment i.e. the thing that will make us content.

MARIA   And I'll quarter if I do not.   275
I'll make you know and fear a wife, Petruchio;
There lies my cause.
You have been famous for a woman-tamer,
And bear the feared name of a brave wife-breaker;
A woman now shall take these honours off   280
And tame you.
Nay, never look so big, she shall, believe me,
And I am she. What think ye? Good night to all,
You shall find sentinels.

BIANCA   If ye dare sally.
                          Exeunt [MARIA and BIANCA] *above*

PETRONIUS
The devil's in 'em, even the very devil,   285
The downright devil.

PETRUCHIO
I'll devil 'em; by these ten bones, I will.
I'll bring it to the old proverb: 'no sport, no pie'.
'Death, taken down i'th' top of all my speed!

---

275   *quarter* be cut into four parts (the treatment of a criminal after hanging); take up
       quarters (i.e. stay where I am); give quarters (i.e. lodging) to soldiers.
       if I do not i.e. if I do not get my 'contentment'.
275–84 *And . . . sentinels* The lineation of this speech is hard to establish. MS and F both
       include short lines (MS: 'for a woman Tamer'; F: 'There my cause lies'); I have
       placed the short lines at points where Maria might slow down, allowing the
       gathered men time to react to her statement before she moves on.
277   *lies my cause* MS (my cause lies F).
277–8 F (there . . . famous / for . . . Tamer, MS).
281–4 ed. (and . . . bigg, / she . . . yee? / good . . . Sentinels. / If . . . sallye MS).
282   *big* mighty, self-important.
284   *You* MS (ye F).
       sally attack.
286   *The downright devil* Definitely the devil.
287   *devil 'em* i.e. act like the devil towards them.
       ten bones i.e. two fists, consisting of ten knuckles (Petruchio may clench his fists as
       he speaks).
287–93 ed. (as prose MS).
288   *no . . . pie* This proverbial phrase (Tilley S777) probably derives from hunting or
       angling: without the chase, the hunter/angler does not get to consume his prey; it
       is used here with strong sexual innuendo.
       sport entertainment, recreational activity (in the early modern period, refers to
       hunting or angling).
       pie (1) the pie in which the hunted prey would be cooked; (2) a bold or
       impertinent person.
289   *'Death* MS (— F).

This is fine dancing, gentlemen. Stick to me. 290
You see our freeholds touched, and by this light
We will beleaguer 'em, and either starve 'em out
Or make 'em recreant.

PETRONIUS

I'll see all passages stopped but these about 'em;
If the good women of the town dare succour 'em 295
We shall have wars indeed.

SOPHOCLES

I'll stand *perdu* upon 'em.

MOROSO

My regiment shall lie before.

JAQUES

I think so: 'tis grown too old to stand.

PETRUCHIO

Let's in, and each provide him to his tackle; 300
We'll fire 'em out, or make 'em take their pardons,
Hear what I say on their bare knees, I vow.
Am I Petruchio, feared and spoken of?
And on my wedding night am I thus jaded?

Exeunt

290   *fine dancing* i.e. a great game (said ironically); 'dancing' was also a slang term for
      sexual intercourse.
291   *You . . . touched* i.e. our control over our possessions is threatened.
      freeholds lands or estates held permanently, which the owner can dispose of at will.
      by this light an oath (originally 'by God's light'): in this context the sense is similar
      to 'I swear'.
292   *beleaguer* besiege.
293   *make 'em recreant* make them accept their defeat.
294   *passages* passageways within the house; roads, routes; passing by of people.
      these MS (those F).
295   *good women* a polite form of address used ironically.
      succour support; help; relieve.
297   *perdu* sentinel, on guard (usually refers to extremely hazardous military
      situations).
299   *I . . . stand* Jaques picks up the *double entendre* of Moroso's line, and assumes that
      his 'regiment' is his penis.
      too F (to MS).
300   ed. (Let's . . . each / prouide . . . tackle MS).
      tackle equipment (with *double entendre*).
301   *fire* drive (with or without the use of fire).
302   *I vow* MS (— F; [Od's precious!] ed.)
304   *jaded* (1) treated like a worn-out horse; (2) treated as one would be by a vicious or
      bad-tempered horse; (3) (by extension) fooled, mistreated.

[ACT I, SCENE iv]

Enter ROLAND *at one door,* PEDRO *hastily at the other*

ROLAND
Now, Pedro!

PEDRO   Very busy, Master Roland –

ROLAND
What haste, man?

PEDRO   I beseech you pardon me,
I am not my own man.

ROLAND   Thou art not mad?

PEDRO
No, but believe me, as hasty.

ROLAND   The cause, good Pedro?

PEDRO
There be a thousand, sir. You are not married.   5

ROLAND
Not yet.

PEDRO   Keep yourself quiet then.

ROLAND   Why?

PEDRO   You'll find
A fiddle that never will be tuned else.
From all such women deliver me.   *Exit* PEDRO

ROLAND
What ails the fellow, trow? Jaques?

[*Act I, Scene iv*] ed. (*Scæna quarta* F).

0   s.d. *Enter . . . other* MS (*Enter Roland, and Pedro, at severall doores* F).

2   *What haste* i.e. why are you in such a hurry.
     beseech beg.

2–3   F (I . . . man. MS).

3   *I . . . man* i.e. I am under someone else's orders.
     my MS (mine F).

5   *You . . . married* F finishes this sentence with a question mark, and either might be
     adopted in performance.

6–8   ed. (Not yet. / Keepe . . . then. / Why? / You'l . . . else / from . . . me. MS).

6   *Keep . . . quiet* i.e. keep yourself in that untroubled state.

7   *fiddle . . . tuned* refers either to raucous speech or to unlicensed sexual behaviour.
     fiddle (1) violin; (2) vagina; (3) woman (compare III.iii.122).

8   *such* MS (om. F).
     From . . . me MS (from all women – – – F; From all such women God deliver me.
     ed.; From all such women, [Lord] deliver me! ed.)

9   *trow* truly; do you think.

Enter [JAQUES]

JAQUES   Your friend, sir,
But very full of business.

ROLAND   Nothing but business!   10
Prithee, thy reason; is there any dying?

JAQUES
I would there were, sir.

ROLAND   But thy business?

JAQUES
I'll tell you in a word: I am sent to lay
An imposition upon souse and puddings,
Pasties and penny custards, that the women   15
May not relieve yon rebels. Fare you well, sir.

ROLAND
How does thy mistress?

JAQUES   Like a resty jade;
She's spoiled for riding.   *Exit* [JAQUES]

ROLAND   What a devil ail they?
Custards and penny pasties, fools and fiddles?

Enter SOPHO[CLES]

---

9   s.d. *Enter* [JAQUES] F (*Enter Jaques*) (MS places the word '*Enter*' in the margin,
      between the speech prefixes '*Roland*' and '*Iaques*', with a line connecting '*Enter*' and
      '*Jaques*').

9–10 F (your . . . business. MS).

10   *full of business* i.e. busy.

11   *thy* MS (the F).

12   *But thy business?* i.e. what are you doing? What is keeping you busy?

14   *souse* parts of a pig, such as the ears and feet, pickled for preparation and
      preservation.
      puddings (1) sausages (especially black-pudding, etc.); (2) boiled, steamed or
      baked dishes (in this period sweet or savoury).

15   *Pasties* meat pies, enclosed with pastry and cooked without a dish.
      custards (1) custard in the modern sense; (2) an open pie similar to a quiche.

16   *yon* F (you' MS).

17   *thy* MS (my F).
      resty stubborn, uncontrollable.

18   *She's . . . riding* suggests either that Maria's temperament has been spoiled, or that
      she is no longer chaste enough to merit Petruchio's sexual attentions.
      s.d. *Exit* [JAQUES] F (*Exit Iaques*) (Exit MS).
      What . . . they i.e. what the devil is wrong with them.

19   *Enter* SOPHOCLES F places the stage direction at l. 18.

What's this to th' purpose? Oh, well met!   20

SOPHOCLES   Now, Roland,
I cannot stay to talk long –

ROLAND   What's the matter?
Here's stirring, but to what end? Whither go you?

SOPHOCLES
To view the works.

ROLAND   What works?

SOPHOCLES   The women's trenches.

ROLAND
Trenches? Are such to see?

SOPHOCLES   I do not jest, sir.

ROLAND
I cannot understand you.

SOPHOCLES   Do not you hear   25
In what a state of quarrel the new bride
Stands with her husband?

ROLAND
Let him stand with her, and there's an end.

SOPHOCLES
It should be, but by'r Lady
She holds him out at pike's end, and defies him,   30
And now is fortified. Such a regiment of rutters
Never defied men braver. I am sent
To view their preparation.

ROLAND   This is news
Stranger than armies in the air! You saw not
My gentle mistress?

SOPHOCLES   Yes, and meditating   35
Upon some secret business; when she had found it

---

20   *What's . . . purpose* i.e. what does this have to do with anything.
      well met a greeting to a friend encountered by chance.
20–1 F (What's . . . met. / Now . . . long. / What's . . . matter? MS).
22   *stirring* a commotion.
28   *Let . . . end* i.e. let them sleep together and that'll be the end of that.
30   *pike's end* i.e. the end of her lance or his penis.
31   *rutters* (1) cavalry soldiers; (2) promiscuous women (to 'rut' is to have sex); (3)
      swindlers.
34   *armies in the air* The appearance of armies in the air (probably caused by meteoro-
      logical conditions) was thought to have presaged disastrous events such as the
      destruction of the Temple at Jerusalem.

She leaped for joy, and laughed, and straight retired
To shun Moroso.
ROLAND   This may be for me.
SOPHOCLES
Will you along?
ROLAND   No.
SOPHOCLES   Farewell.   *Exit* SOPHOCLES
ROLAND   Fare you well, sir.
What should her musing mean, and what her joy in't,   40
If not for my advantage? Stay. May not
That bobtail jade Moroso, with his gold,
His gewgaws, and the hope she has to send him
Quickly to dust, excite this?

Enter LIVIA *and* MOROSO (*as unseen by her*)

                                        Here she comes,
And yonder walks the stallion to discover.   45
Yet I'll salute her. Save you, beauteous mistress.
LIVIA
[*Aside*] The fox is kennelled for me. [*To* ROLAND] Save you, sir.

---

37   *straight* immediately.
38   *This . . . me* i.e. this may be on my account.
39   *Farewell* F (Farewell you well MS).
        Fare you well, sir MS (Farewell sir F).
41   *Stay* MS (stay ye F).
        Stay i.e. hold on a moment.
42   *bobtail jade* (1) horse with its tail cropped; (2) impotent old man.
43   *gewgaws* ornaments, baubles (MS's 'gew-gaudes' is an alternative early modern
        spelling).
43–4   *the . . . dust* i.e. her expectation that he would die quickly.
44   s.d. *Enter . . . her*) MS (*Enter Livia at one doore, and Moroso at another harkning.* F);
        MS places the direction in the margins of ll. 43–4; F places it in the margins of ll.
        41–8.
45   *stallion* i.e. stud (Roland's fears have transformed Moroso from a worn-out nag to
        a prize stallion in the space of three lines.)
        discover eavesdrop.
46   *salute* greet.
47   *fox* refers to Moroso, as in I.ii.25.
        kennelled lurking.
        Save you i.e. God save you: a common greeting.
        Save you, sir Livia deliberately adopts a formal tone, so as to deceive Moroso about
        her feelings for Roland.

ROLAND
Why do you look so strange?
LIVIA
I use to look, sir, without examination.
MOROSO
[*Aside*] I thank thee for that word.   50
ROLAND
Belike then the object discontents you?
LIVIA
Yes it does.
ROLAND
Is't come to this? You know me, do you not?
LIVIA
Yes, as I may know many by repentance.
ROLAND
Why do you break your faith?
LIVIA   I'll tell you that too: 55
You are under age, and no band holds upon you.
MOROSO
Gramercy for that, wench.
LIVIA
Sue out your understanding,
And get more hair to cover your bare knuckle –

---

48   *strange* aloof, distant.
49   *use* am accustomed.
     without examination i.e. without being questioned about it.
50   *I thank thee* MS (Twenty Spur-Royals F).
51   *Belike . . . you* ed. (then / the . . . you? MS, F).
     Belike Perhaps.
54   *by repentance* to my sorrow.
56   *under age* i.e. under twenty-one, and therefore legally a minor, unable to sign a
     binding contract.
     band (1) obligation, bond, pledge; (2) chain; (3) power, binding force.
57   *Gramercy . . . wench* MS (Excellent wench F; [God-'a-mercy] for that, wench! ed.)
     Gramercy I thank you.
58   *Sue out* Request a court to grant you.
59   *And . . . knuckle* The ability to grow hair, especially on the face, was a key marker of
     adult masculinity in early modern England.
     knuckle F (knockle MS [an alternative early modern spelling]; noddle conj. Mason
     [p. 299]).
     knuckle sometimes used to refer to the fist in early modern texts; alternatively, Livia
     may gesture dismissively at Roland's hairless chin.

For boys were made for nothing but dry kisses –   60
And, if you can, more manners.

MOROSO   Better still.

LIVIA

And then if I want Spanish gloves, or stockings,
A ten-pound waistcoat, or a nag to hunt on,
It may be I shall grace you to accept 'em.

ROLAND

Farewell. And when I credit woman more,   65
May I to Smithfield, and there buy a jade –
And know him to be so – that breaks my neck.

LIVIA

Because I have known you, I'll be thus kind to you:
Farewell, and be a man, and I'll provide for you –
Because I see y'are desperate – some staid chambermaid   70
That may relieve your youth with wholesome doctrine.

MOROSO

[*Coming forward*] Ha, wench!

LIVIA   Ha, chicken?

She gives MOROSO *a box o' th' ear and exit*[*s*]

MOROSO   Is't come to this?

[*To* ROLAND]   Save you.

---

60   *dry* i.e. impotent.
61   *more manners* i.e. better social skills, more polished ways of behaving.
62   *Spanish gloves* notoriously expensive, and often perfumed.
63   *waistcoat* a short garment worn on the upper part of the body, often very elaborate
       and expensive.
       nag horse, especially an old or inferior one.
64   *grace you to accept* i.e. favour you by accepting.
66   *Smithfield* a famous London market specialising in the sale of livestock and horses.
67   *breaks* F (breake MS).
68   *known* been intimate with.
69   *for you* MS (you F).
70   *staid* sedate.
72   *Ha, wench* MS (She's mine from all the world: ha wench? F).
       ed. (Ha wench! / Ha chicken? / Is't . . . this, / Saue you. MS).
       chicken Used by Fletcher in several other plays as a term of endearment, so Livia
       may apply it ironically. Alternatively, the term can refer to someone as defenceless
       as a chicken, to a coward, or, as Daileader and Taylor note, Livia may be suggesting
       that Moroso is as wrinkled and loose-skinned as a plucked chicken.
       s.d. *She . . . exit*[*s*] MS (*gives him a box o'th eare and Ex.* F).
       Is't . . . you MS (How's this? I do not love these favours: save you. F).

145

ROLAND

The devil take you!   [*Wrings him by the nose*]

MOROSO

Oh!

ROLAND

There's a love token for you. Thank me now.   *Exit* [ROLAND]   75

MOROSO

I'll think on some of you, and if I live

My nose alone shall not be played withal.   *Exit*

73   *you* MS (thee F).
      s.d. *Wrings . . . nose* F (*wrings him hyth' nose*).
75   *Thank* F (thuck MS).
      s.d. *Exit* [ROLAND] ed. (Exit MS).
76   *you* MS (ye F).
77   *My . . . withal* (1) my nose will not be the only part of me that is played with; (2) my nose will not be the only thing that is treated like this.

ACT II, SCENE i

Enter LIVIA

LIVIA

Now if I can get in but handsomely,
Father, I shall deceive you, and this night;
For all your private plotting, I'll no wedlock.
I have shifted sail, and find my sister's safety
A sure retirement. Pray to heaven that Roland   5
Believe not too far what I said to him,
For yond' old fox-case forced me, that's my fear.
Stay, let me see, this quarter fierce Petruchio
Keeps with his Myrmidons. I must be sudden.
If he seize on me, I can look for nothing   10
But martial law. To this place have I 'scaped him.
Above there!

Enter MARIA *and* BIANCA *(above)*

Act II, Scene i ed. (ACTVS II.ᵘˢ Scaena j.ᵐᵃ MS; *Actus secundus. Scæna prima* F) F
includes a short additional scene here, consisting of an exchange between
Petronius and Moroso: see Appendix 1, Passage B.

0   s.d. *Enter* LIVIA MS (*Enter Livia alone* F).
1   *get in but* MS (but get in F).
    handsomely skilfully, carefully, elegantly.
3   *private* secret, confidential.
    wedlock marriage.
4   *shifted sail* changed direction.
    find F (finde) (finds MS).
5   *sure* secure.
    retirement retreat, place of safety.
6   *Believe not* MS (Do not beleeve F).
    too F (to MS).
7   *yond'* MS (yo'nd) (y'on F).
    yond' yonder: that.
    fox-case fox-skin (i.e. Moroso).
8   *quarter* part of the house, rooms (often refers to military barracks).
9   *with his Myrmidons* i.e. with his forces (In classical mythology, the Myrmidons
    were Thessalian troops brought by the Greek hero Achilles to the siege of Troy.)
    sudden quick.
11 *martial law* i.e. a trial under military law or authority, or under measures taken for
    the suppression of a rebellion, when normal laws are suspended.
    'scaped escaped.

MARIA	*Qui va la?*	
LIVIA	A friend.	
BIANCA	Who are you?	

LIVIA
Look out and know.

MARIA   Alas, poor wench, who sent thee?
What weak fool made thy tongue his orator?
I know you come to parley.

LIVIA   Y'are deceived.   15
Urged by the goodness of your cause, I come
To do as you do.

MARIA   Y'are too weak, too foolish,
To cheat us with your smoothness; do not we know
Thou hast been kept up tame?

LIVIA
Believe me.

MARIA   No. Prithee good Livia,   20
Utter thy eloquence somewhere else.

BIANCA   Good cousin,
Put up your pipes; we are not for your palate.
Alas, we know who sent you.

LIVIA   O' my faith –

BIANCA
Stay there. You must not think your faith, or troth,
Or by your maidenhead, or such Sunday oaths   25
Sworn after evensong, can inveigle us
To loose our handfast. Did their wisdoms think
That sent you hither we would be so foolish
To entertain our gentle sister Sinon,

12 *Qui va la?* Who goes there? (French).
15 *parley* negotiate (i.e. on behalf of Petruchio and the other men).
17 *too . . . too* F (to . . . too MS).
18 *smoothness* smooth-talking, simulated friendliness.
19 *tame* docile, submissive.
22 *we . . . palate* we are not to your taste.
23 *O'* F A (MS).   *faith* MS (word F).
24 *faith, or troth* MS (word F).
25 *Sunday oaths* i.e. mild oaths (the kinds of oaths that might be made on a Sunday, the day of religious observance).
26 *evensong* a church service held just before sunset.
27 *handfast* covenant, partnership.
29 *Sinon* The legendary betrayer of the city of Troy in classical mythology, who persuaded the Trojans to allow the wooden horse into the city.

And give her credit, while the wooden jade   30
Petruchio stole upon us? No, good sister,
Go home, and tell the merry Greeks that sent you,
Ilium shall burn, and I, as did Aeneas,
Will on my back, spite of the Myrmidons
Carry this warlike lady, and through seas   35
Unknown and unbelieved seek out a land
Where, like a race of noble Amazons,
We'll root ourselves and to our endless glory
Live and despise base men.
LIVIA   I'll second ye.
BIANCA
How long have you been thus?
LIVIA   That's all one, cousin;   40
I stand for freedom now.
BIANCA   Take heed of lying,
For by this light, if we do credit you
And find you tripping, his infliction
That killed the Prince of Orange will be sport
To what we purpose.

30   *credit* belief, trust.
     wooden jade Rather than comparing Petruchio with one of the Greek heroes, Bianca compares him with the wooden horse itself; 'jade' is a derogatory term for a horse, and 'wooden' also means stupid or worthless.
32   *merry Greeks* a proverbial phrase (Tilley M901).
33   *Ilium* Troy.
     Aeneas Trojan hero who escaped from the burning Troy carrying his father, Anchises, on his back.
34   *spite* i.e. in spite.
     of F (off MS).
36   *unbelieved* incredible, unbelievable.
37   *Amazons* A legendary race of women who lived without men.
38   *root* establish.
39   *base* contemptible, unworthy.
     second support, accompany.
40   *That's all one* i.e. that's as maybe, that doesn't matter.
42   *credit* trust.
43   *tripping* sinning.
43–4   *his . . . Orange* William of Orange, Prince of Nassau and military commander of the United Provinces (known as 'William the Silent'), who led the Dutch revolt against Spanish rule in the Netherlands. He was shot and fatally wounded on 10 July 1584 by Balthazar Gérard; Gérard was hung, drawn and quartered, the usual punishment for treason in this period.
44   *sport* entertainment, fun.
45   *purpose* intend.

LIVIA   Let me feel the heaviest.   45

MARIA

Swear by thy sweetheart, Roland (for by your maidenhead
I fear 'twill be too late to swear) you mean
Nothing but fair and safe, and honourable
To us and to our cause.

LIVIA   I swear.

BIANCA   Stay yet.

Swear as you hate Moroso, that's the surest,   50
And as you have a Christian fear to find him
Worse than a poor dried Jack, full of more aches
Than autumn has, more knavery, and usury,
And foolery, and brokery than Dogs' Ditch;
As you do constantly believe he's nothing   55
But an old empty bag with a grey beard,
And that beard such a bobtail that it looks
Worse than a mare's tail eaten off with flies;
As you acknowledge, that young handsome wench
That lies by such a bilbo blade, that bends   60

46-7 *for . . . swear* i.e. it's too late to swear on your virginity (which you've probably lost).
47   *too* F (to MS).
47–8 *you . . . safe* i.e. you mean to behave in a virtuous, trustworthy and honourable manner.
49   *our cause* MS (your selfe F).
50   *surest* most binding.
50–68 Bianca structures her speech around the repetition of 'as you', a rhetorical technique known as anaphora.
      Christian MS (certaine F).
51   *Christian* decent, becoming of a Christian.
52   *dried Jack* dried hake, a cheap variety of fish (also known as poor Jack or poor John).
54   *brokery* (1) the selling of second hand goods, especially clothes; (2) trafficking, underhand dealing.
      Dogs' Ditch A joking reference to Houndsditch, a street running along the outside of the city wall, where many of the houses were occupied by dealers in second-hand clothes.
56   *bag* money-bag.
57   *bobtail* the cropped (bobbed) tail of a horse.
58   *off with* F (with MS).
      flies ed. (fillyes MS, F).
60–1 *lies . . . hilts* i.e. that sleeps with such an impotent man (Bianca compares the thrusts of a sword during a fencing match with the efforts of Moroso in bed.)
60   *bilbo* a kind of sword with a particularly flexible blade, as the following line suggests.

With every pass he makes to th' hilts, most miserable,
A dry-nurse to his coughs, a fewterer
To such a nasty fellow, a robbed thing
Of all delights youth looks for, and, to end,
One cast away on coarse beef, born to brush   65
That everlasting cassock that has worn
As many servants out as the northeast passage
Hath consumed sailors. If ye swear this truly,
Without the reservation of a gown,
Or any meritorious petticoat,   70
'Tis like we shall believe you.
LIVIA   I do swear it.
MARIA
Stay yet a little. Came this wholesome motion –
Deal truly, sister – from your own opinion,
Or some suggestion of the foe?
LIVIA   Ne'er fear me,
For by that little faith I have in husbands,   75
And the great zeal I bear your cause, I come
Full of that liberty you stand for, sister.

61   *pass* lunge, thrust (a term from fencing).
      to th' hilts i.e. up to the hilt (handle) of the sword.
62   *dry-nurse* a woman who takes care of a child but does not feed it herself.
      fewterer attendant (originally refers to a keeper of greyhounds).
63   *nasty* contemptible, repellent; lewd.
      robbed MS (rob'd).
      robbed thing i.e. thing robbed.
65   *coarse beef* often mentioned as inexpensive or low status food in early modern texts.
65–8 *to . . . sailors* i.e. to make the same piece of clothing last an unfeasibly long time.
66   *cassock* a long coat, often associated with sailors, but also with usurers.
67   *servants* i.e. the servants responsible for looking after Moroso's clothes.
67–8 *as . . . sailors* Henry Hudson undertook voyages in search of a northeast sea-route from
      the Atlantic Ocean to the Pacific Ocean in 1607, 1608 and 1609, and a voyage in search
      of a northwest passage in 1610–11; this reference has been used as evidence to date the
      play's composition.
68   *this* MS (and F).
69–70 *Without . . . petticoat* Livia must not keep back any gifts that Moroso has given her; she
      must vow that she hates everything about him.
69   *reservation* keeping back.
70   *meritorious* (1) merited, deserved; (2) earned through prostitution.
72   *wholesome* salutary, morally beneficial.
73   *Deal* Behave, act.
      truly honourably, sincerely.
76   *zeal* enthusiasm, passionate adherence.

MARIA
>If we believe, and you prove recreant, Livia,
>Think what a maim you give the noble cause
>We now stand up for; think what women shall,   80
>A hundred year hence, speak thee, when examples
>Are looked for, and so great ones, whose relations,
>Spoke as we do 'em, wench, shall make new customs.

BIANCA
>If ye be false, repent, go home, and pray,
>And to the serious women of the city   85
>Confess yourself; bring not a sin so heinous
>To load thy soul to this place. Mark me, Livia,
>If thou be'st double, and betray'st our honours,
>And we fall in our purpose, get thee where
>There is no women living, nor no hope   90
>There ever shall be.

MARIA   If a mother's daughter
>That ever heard the name of stubborn husband
>Find thee, and know thy sin –

BIANCA   Nay, if old age,
>One that has worn away the name of woman
>And no more left to know her by but railing,   95
>No teeth, nor eyes, no legs but wooden ones,
>Come but i' th' windward of thee – for sure she'll smell thee,
>Thou'lt be so rank – she'll ride thee like a nightmare,

78   *recreant* cowardly, ready to surrender.
79   *maim* injury.
81   *speak thee* i.e. talk about you.
82   *relations* stories.
83   *Spoke . . . 'em* i.e. described as they happened.
      customs habits, fashions.
86–7 *so . . . soul* i.e. so atrocious as to be a burden on your soul.
87   *Mark me* Pay attention to me.
88   *double* deceitful, treacherous.
89   *fall* MS (fail F).
      fall are overthrown.
90   *is no women* MS, F. Although it is incorrect in Present-Day English, in Early
      Modern English words can sometimes have a plural form with a singular sense.
93   *old age* i.e. an old woman.
95   *railing* ranting, persistent complaining.
97   *i' th'* F (i'th) ('ath MS).
98   *Thou'lt* F (Th' root MS).
      ride . . . nightmare Nightmares were imagined as spirits that sat on or rode the
      dreamer.

And say her prayers backward to undo thee;
She'll curse thy meat and drink, and when thou marriest   100
Clap a sound spell forever on thy pleasures.

MARIA

Children of five year old, like little fairies,
Will pinch thee into motley. All that ever
Shall live and hear of thee – I mean all women –
Will like so many Furies shake their keys   105
And toss their flaming distaffs o'er their heads
Crying 'Revenge!' Take heed, 'tis hideous;
Oh, 'tis a fearful office! If thou hadst –
Though thou be'st perfect now – when thou cam'st first
A false imagination, get thee gone   110
And, as my learned cousin said, repent.
This place is sought by soundness.

LIVIA   So I seek it,
Or let me be a most despised example.

MARIA

I do believe thee. Be thou worthy of it.
You come not empty?

LIVIA   No. Here's cakes, and cold meat,   115
And tripe of proof; behold, here's wine and beer.

---

99   *say . . . backward* Superstition held that one could summon the devil by saying one's
      prayers backwards.

102–3 *like . . . pinch* In English folklore fairies were said to pinch viciously mortals who
      disturbed them.

103   *motley* cloth woven from threads of two or more colours. Coarse motley looked
      dark or mottled, as Maria imagines that Livia's skin will look.

105   *Furies* Avenging female deities in classical mythology, especially noted for punish-
      ing after death those who had committed sins against their families.

106   *distaffs* cleft sticks used in spinning. Maria domesticates the Furies, who were
      usually represented carrying torches and whips.

108   *office* duty, service.

109   *perfect* pure, blameless.
      first MS (hither F).

110   *false* (1) deceitful, treacherous; (2) counterfeited.
      imagination (1) scheme, stratagem; (2) thought.

112   *soundness* (1) constancy, freedom from weakness; (2) religious/political orthodoxy.

115   *empty* empty-handed.

115–16 *Here's . . . beer* In the 2003 RSC production Livia had the food and drink concealed
      under her cloak.

116   *tripe* a kind of offal: the first or second stomach of a ruminant such as a cow.
      proof proven quality.

Be sudden, I shall be surprised else.

MARIA

Meet at the low parlour door; there lies a close way.
What fond obedience ye have living in you,
Or duty to a man, before you enter   120
Fling it away; 'twill but defile our offerings.

BIANCA

Be wary as you come.

LIVIA   I warrant ye.

Exeunt

[ACT II, SCENE ii]

Enter ROLAND *at one door,* TRANIO *at the other*

TRANIO

Now, Roland –

ROLAND   How do you?

TRANIO   How dost thou, man?
Thou look'st ill!

ROLAND   Yes. Pray you tell me, Tranio,

117   *sudden* quick.
       surprised attacked, taken captive.
       else otherwise.
118   *close* (1) secret; (2) narrow.
       way passageway, doorway; route.
119   *fond* foolish.
121   *'twill* it will.
       defile our offerings i.e. violate the sanctity of our rites.
122   *wary* cautious, careful.
123   *I warrant ye* i.e. of course, I assure you (that I will).

[*Act II, Scene ii*] ed. (*Scæna Tertia . . . Scæna quarta* F). In F the short scene between
the three Country Wenches (II.iv in MS) appears here and is repeated later in the act,
in the position where it is found in MS; in F2 it appears only in the earlier position.
The later position is clearly correct, as Petruchio and the other men would other
wise be required to enter having only just exited, something which almost never
occurs in early modern drama.

0   s.d. *Enter . . . other* MS (*Enter Rowland and Tranio at severall doores* F).
2   *ill* (1) sick, disordered in mind or body; (2) hostile, aggressive.
2   *you* MS (can you F).

Who knew the devil first?

TRANIO   A woman.

ROLAND   So.

Were they not well acquainted?

TRANIO   Maybe so,

For they had certain dialogues together.   5

ROLAND

He sold her fruit, I take it.

TRANIO   Yes, and cheese

That choked all mankind after.

ROLAND   Canst thou tell me

Whether that woman ever had a faith

After she had eaten?

TRANIO   That's a great school question.

ROLAND

No, 'tis no question, for believe me, Tranio,   10

That cold fruit after eating bred naught in her

But windy promises and colic vows

That broke out both ways. Thou hast heard, I am sure,

Of Aesculapius, a far-famed surgeon,

One that could set together quartered traitors   15

And make 'em honest men?

TRANIO   How dost thou, Roland?

3–7   *Who . . . after* Refers to the Biblical story of the Fall from the Garden of Eden (Genesis 3), in which Eve is supposed to have yielded to the temptation of the serpent and to have eaten fruit from the forbidden tree on his invitation.

3–4   ed. (Who . . . first? / A woman. / So . . . acquainted? MS).
      So . . . acquainted MS (Thou has heard I am sure of E*sculapius.* / So were they not well acquainted? F).

6–7   *cheese . . . choked* Cheese was often eaten with fruit at the end of a meal; its texture was thought to cause choking.

8   *ever had a faith* i.e. was capable of being faithful.

9   *great* MS (*om.* F).
      school question i.e. an issue discussed by scholars (known as 'schoolmen').

10   ed. (No, / 'tis . . . Tranio MS).

12   *windy* (1) worthless, empty; (2) inflated, exaggerated, long-winded.
      colic severe attacks of stomach pain, here used figuratively to mean 'bloated' or 'violent'.

13   *both ways* i.e. in belching and flatulence.

14   *Aesculapius* The god of medicine in classical mythology, whose skills extended to bringing the dead back to life.

15   *quartered traitors* i.e. executed traitors (see I.iii.275 n.)

ROLAND

 Let him but take, if he dare do a cure
 Shall get him fame indeed, a faithless woman –
 There will be credit for him; that will speak him –
 A broken woman, Tranio, a base woman,   20
 And if he can cure such a wrack of honour,
 Let him come here and practise.

TRANIO   Now, for heaven's sake,
 What ail'st thou, Roland?

ROLAND   I am ridden, Tranio,
 And spur-galled to the life of patience –
 Heaven keep my wits together! – by a thing   25
 Our worst thoughts are too noble for: a woman.

TRANIO

 Your mistress has a little frowned, it may be.

ROLAND

 She was my mistress.

TRANIO   Is she not?

ROLAND   No, Tranio,
 She has done me such disgrace, so spitefully,
 So like a woman bent to my undoing,   30
 That henceforth a good horse shall be my mistress,
 A good sword, a book! And if you see her,
 Tell her, I do beseech you, ever for love's sake –
 Our old love and our friendship –

TRANIO   I will, Roland.

---

19 *that will speak him* i.e. proclaim his talents.
20 *broken* ruined.
  base without morals.
21 *wrack* MS (rack) (wreck ed.)
  wrack (1) destruction, ruin, downfall; (2) remnant, wreck.
22 *heaven's* MS (heauens) (honours F).
23 *What . . . thou* i.e. what is wrong with you.
  What MS (Why what F).
24 *spur-galled* wounded and/or irritated by a rider's spurs.
30 *bent* intent.
32 *a book* MS (or a Booke F).
33 *ever* MS (even F).
34 *Our . . . friendship* MS has a gap which would fit around 6–7 lines of text after this
  line; F moves the line to after l. 35.
34–5 ed. (friendship, / [6-line gap here] / I . . . Roland. / She . . . sooner / count . . . her,
  MS).

ROLAND

    She may sooner count the good I have thought her,   35
    Shed one true tear, mean one hour constantly,
    Be old and honest, married and a maid,
    Than make me see her more, or more believe her,
    And now I have met a messenger. Farewell, sir.

                          Exit [ROLAND]

TRANIO

    Alas, poor Roland, I will do it for thee.   40
    This is that dog Moroso, but I hope
    To see him cold i' th' mouth ere he joy her.
    I'll watch this young man; desperate thoughts may seize him,
    And if my purse or counsel can, I'll ease him.

                          Exit

[ACT II, SCENE iii]

Enter PETRUCHIO, PETRONIUS, SOPHOCLES [*and*] MOROSO

PETRUCHIO

    For look you, gentlemen, say that I grant her,
    Out of my free and liberal love, a pardon,
    Which you and all men else know she deserves not –
    Teneatis, amici – can all the world leave laughing?

36   *true* genuine.
37   *honest* chaste.
38   *her* F (here MS).
39   *a messenger* i.e. Tranio.
      s.d. *Exit* [ROLAND] ed. (Exit MS).
42   *cold i' th' mouth* dead; a proverbial phrase (Dent M1260.1).
43   *ere he joy her* i.e. before he enjoys her.
      joy MS (enjoy F).

    [*Act II, Scene iii*] ed. (*Scæna quinta* F).
2   *free* generous, magnanimous; unrestrained.
    liberal abundant, generous.
4   *Teneatis, amici* 'Understand, friends' (Latin). Petruchio quotes from a famous phrase
      in the Roman poet Horace's *Ars Poetica*, verse 5: 'Risum teneatis, amici?' ('Would
      you keep from laughing, friends?'), translating it freely in the rest of the line.
      leave cease, desist from.

PETRONIUS
  I think not.
PETRUCHIO   No, by this hand, they cannot.   5
  For, pray consider, have you ever read,
  Or heard of, or can any man imagine
  So stiff a tomboy, of so set a malice
  And such a brazen resolution
  As this young crab-tree? And then answer me –   10
  And mark but this too, friends, without a cause,
  Not a foul word come 'cross her, not a fear
  She justly can take hold on! And do you think
  I must sleep out my anger, and endure it?
  Sew pillows to her ease and lull her mischief?   15
  Give me a spindle first! No, no, my masters,
  Were she as fair as Nell of Greece, and housewife
  As good as the wise sailor's wife, and young still,
  Never above fifteen, and those tricks to it,
  She should ride the wild mare once a week, she should,   20
  Believe me friends she should; I would tabor her
  Till all the legions that are crept into her
  Flew out with fire i' th' tails.

5   *by this hand* MS (by — F).
     by this hand a mild oath.
8   *stiff* resolute, stubborn.
     set immovable, obstinate.
9   *brazen* shameless.
10 *crab-tree* a bad-tempered person (crab-apples are notoriously sour).
12 *'cross* across.
16 *Give . . . first!* i.e. reduce me to the status of a woman. Petruchio may have in mind
     the legend that the classical hero Hercules was set to work spinning by Omphale,
     Queen of Lydia, to whom he was enslaved for a year.
17 *Nell of Greece* The legendarily beautiful Helen of Troy, over whom the Greeks and
     Trojans fought the Trojan War.
18 *the . . . wife* Penelope, wife of Odysseus (Ulysses in Roman mythology), fended off
     suitors during her husband's twenty-year absence in the Trojan War by vowing not
     to choose any of them until she had woven or sewed an object (in one version her
     father-in-law's shroud) which she unpicked each night.
19 *those* MS (these F).
20 *ride the wild mare* Riding the wild mare was a game played at Christmas and other
     festivals, in which a 'rider' was required to do various tricks or tasks while sitting
     cross-legged on a pole hung horizontally above the floor; in the later seventeenth
     century it was also used to refer to a wooden frame on which soldiers were made to
     ride as a punishment.
21–3 *I . . . tails* i.e. I would beat the wickedness (the 'legions' of devils) out of her.
21 *tabor* beat (a tabor is a small drum).

SOPHOCLES   Methinks you err now,
And to me seems a little sufferance
Were a far sooner cure.
PETRUCHIO   Yes, I can suffer   25
Where I see promises of peace and 'mendment.
MOROSO
Give her a few conditions.
PETRUCHIO   I'll be hanged first.
PETRONIUS
Give her a crab-tree cudgel.
PETRUCHIO   So I will,
And after it a flock-bed for her bones,
And hard eggs till they brace her like a drum   30
She shall be pampered with.
She shall not know a stool in ten months, gentlemen.
SOPHOCLES
This must not be.

Enter JAQUES

JAQUES   Arm, arm, out with your weapons,
For all the women in the Kingdom's on ye!
They swarm like wasps, and nothing can destroy 'em   35
But stopping of their hive, and smothering of 'em.

---

24   *And* MS (For F).
       seems it seems that.
       sufferance patience.
25   *sooner* MS (surer F).
26   *'mendment* amendment: improvement.
28   *crab-tree cudgel* (1) a cudgel made from a crab-apple tree; (2) a cudgel appropriate
       for use against a bad-tempered, crabby woman.
29   *flock-bed* a bed with a mattress stuffed with flock (coarse tufts of cotton or wool
       and off-cuts of cloth), which would be particularly uncomfortable for someone
       who had just been beaten.
30–2 *hard . . . gentlemen* Petruchio imagines force-feeding Maria with eggs, which would
       make her constipated.
31   *pampered* fed, crammed.
       with MS (with — F) Although the sentence is grammatically complete, half a line
       is apparently missing here, as F's dash suggests. Daileader and Taylor assume that
       it has been censored, and fill it out with '[a shit-hole stopper]'; an alternative would
       be an oath such as 'by all the world', 'by all that's sacred', or a combination of oaths,
       such as 'marry, by this light'.

Enter PEDRO

PEDRO

Stand to your guard, sir, all the evils extant
Are broke upon us like a cloud of thunder!
There are more women marching hitherward
In rescue of my mistress than e'er turned tail   40
At Stourbridge Fair; and, I believe, as fiery.

JAQUES

The forlorn hope's led by a tanner's wife,
I know her by her hide – a desperate woman;
She flayed her husband in her youth, and made
Reins of his hide to ride the parish. Her placket   45
Looks like the straits of Gibraltar, still wider
Down to the gulf; all sun-burned Barbary
Lies in her breech. Take 'em all together,
They are a genealogy of jennets, gotten
And born thus by the boisterous breath of husbands.   50
They serve sure and are swift to catch occasion –

37   *evils* MS (devils F).
40   *turned tail* (1) ran away; (2) turned in opposition or defiance; (3) made themselves
       sexually available ('tail' is slang for the female genitalia and for the train on a dress).
41   *Stourbridge Fair* A long-established fair held on Stourbridge Common, Cambridge.
       fiery fierce, eager.
42   *The . . . led* i.e. the front line of the troops is led.
       a tanner's wife the wife of a man who makes his living by tanning animal hides to
       make leather.
45–8 *Her . . . breech* MS (*om.* F). The passage has apparently been censored in F.
45   *placket* an opening or slit in a woman's skirt or underskirt, often (as here) a
       euphemism for the female genitals.
46   *the straits of Gibraltar* a narrow channel separating Spain from Morocco.
47   *gulf* (1) 'long land-locked portions of sea opening through a strait' (*OED*) (2) the
       depths of the ocean; (3) something which devours, a voracious appetite; (4) vagina.
       Barbary countries along the north coast of Africa.
48   *breech* (1) buttocks; (2) breeches (trousers ending just below the knee).
49   *jennets* small Spanish horses (the term is often used to refer to women in a sexual
       context).
49–50 *gotten . . . husbands* The jennet's ability to gallop quickly seems to have bred a
       legend that the mares were impregnated by the wind.
51–2 *occasion . . . forelocks* a proverbial image: occasion or opportunity is often
       personified as a bald woman (or sometimes a man) with a long lock of hair that
       could be grabbed as s/he passed.
51   *serve* (1) provide sexual service; (2) fulfil their purpose.
       sure reliably.

I mean their foes or husbands – by the forelocks,
And there they hang like favours. Cry they can,
But more for noble spite than fear; and crying,
Like the old giants that were foes to heaven,   55
They heave ye stool on stool, and fling many pot-lids
Like massy rocks, dart ladles, toasting-irons
And tongs like thunderbolts till, overlaid,
They fall beneath the weight, yet still aspiring
At those imperious cod's-heads that would tame 'em.   60
There's ne'er a one of these, the worst, and weakest –
Choose where you will – but dare attempt the raising,
Against the sovereign peace of Puritans,
A maypole or a morris, maugre mainly
Their zeals and dudgen daggers, and – yet more –   65
Dares plant a stand of battering ale against 'em,
And drink 'em out o' th' parish.

---

52   *forelocks* MS, F (fore-locks) (forelock ed.)

53   *favours* gifts given to lovers, tokens given to a medieval knight by a lady.

55   *the . . . heaven* Refers to the classical legend of the Giants, the children of Gaia (Mother Earth) conceived from the blood of her husband Uranus when he was castrated by Cronus – and their rebellion against Zeus and the other Olympian gods.

56   *heave ye* In Early Modern English a pronoun could appear straight after the verb, without a preposition: in Present-Day English this might read 'heave upon you'.
     on i.e. after.
     many MS (manie) (main F).

57   *massy* massive.
     dart throw, shoot.
     toasting-irons MS (tosting irons) (tossing Irons F).
     toasting-irons iron implements used for toasting food in a fire.

58   *overlaid* overwhelmed.

59   *the weight* i.e. the weight of the opposing forces.

60   *cod's-heads* MS, F (Godheads F2).
     cod's-heads blockheads, punning on 'godheads'.
     would i.e. attempt to.

61–2   *ne'er a one . . . but* i.e. not one . . . who will not.

62   *raising* i.e. raising of.

63   *Against . . . Puritans* Puritans (radical Protestants who sought reform to the Church of England) were stereotypically depicted as opposed to popular festivities such as maypoles and morris dances.

64   *maugre* in spite of, notwithstanding.

65   *zeals* enthusiasm, fervour.
     dudgen (1) contemptible; (2) ordinary, homely.

66   *stand* military term referring to a standing in ambush or cover, or a group of soldiers halting to give battle.
     battering attacking.
     ale Puritans were stereotypically opposed to drinking alcohol.

PEDRO

There's one first brought in the bears, against the canons
Of two church-wardens, made it good, and fought 'em –
And in the churchyard, after evensong. 70

JAQUES

Another, to her everlasting fame, erected
Two alehouses of ease, the quarter sessions
Running against her roundly; in which business
Two of the disannullers lost their nightcaps,
A third stood excommunicate by the cudgel. 75
The constable, to her eternal glory,
Drunk hard, and was converted, and she victor.

SOPHOCLES

Lo ye, fierce Petruchio,
This comes of your impatience.

PETRUCHIO   Come, to council.

SOPHOCLES

Now ye must grant conditions, or the kingdom 80
Will have no other talk but this.

PETRONIUS   Away then,
And let's advise the best.

SOPHOCLES [*To* MOROSO]   Why do you tremble?

68–70   ed. (There's . . . against / the . . . good / and . . . song MS).
68   *brought . . . bears* i.e. set up a bear-baiting (a popular sport in rural and urban areas,
in which dogs were set to fight against a bear).
canons rules, decrees.
69   *made it good* justified it, proved it to be allowable.
fought 'em i.e. set them fighting.
70   *And . . . evensong* MS (*om.* F).
72   *alehouses of ease* Alehouses were one of the least socially exclusive kinds of public
house, selling beer and ale, and sometimes food and lodging; Jaques' 'alehouses of
ease' may refer to alehouses or, by extension, to brothels.
quarter sessions courts with limited criminal and civil jurisdiction held four times
a year before local justices of the peace.
73   *Running . . . roundly* i.e. taking harsh action against her.
business affair.
74   *disannullers* (would-be) abolitionists.
75   *stood . . . cudgel* i.e. was forbidden entry on the threat of a beating.
76   *constable* local law-enforcement officer.
77   *she victor* i.e. the alehouse woman won.
78–9   F moves Sophocles' speech to after l. 67, and inserts a seven-line speech here for
Pedro: see Appendix 1, Passage C.
78   *Lo ye* Look you; Mind this.
81   *talk* gossip.

MOROSO
    Have I lived thus long to be knocked o' th' head
    With half a washing-beetle? Pray be wise, sir.
PETRUCHIO
    Come.
    Something I'll do, but what it is I know not.   85
SOPHOCLES
    To council then, and let's avoid these follies.
    Guard all the doors, or we shall not have a cloak left.

Exeunt

[ACT II, SCENE iv]

Enter three COUNTRY WENCHES *at several doors*

FIRST WENCH
    How goes your business, girls?
SECOND WENCH   Afoot and fair.
THIRD WENCH
    If fortune favour us. Away to your strengths;
    We are discovered else.

83   *washing-beetle* an implement used in washing, with a heavy head and a handle.
85   *Something . . . not* Recalls the maddened Lear's statement in Shakespeare's *King Lear*: 'I will do such things – / What they are yet I know not, but they shall be / The terrors of the earth!' (II.ii.472–3).
84–5 ed. (Come . . . doe, / but . . . not MS).
86   *avoid* put an end to.
      these MS (their F).
87   *we . . . left* i.e. we will be reduced to nothing.

    [*Act II, Scene iv*] ed.
0   s.d. *Enter . . . doors* MS (*Enter three mayds, at severall doors* F).
1   FIRST WENCH ed. (I MS) and at l. 4.
    your MS (*the* F).
    SECOND WENCH ed. (II MS) and at l. 5.
    Afoot on the move, in progress.   *fair* i.e. going nicely, proceeding well.
2–4 *Away . . . Begone* MS (away to your strength, / The Country forces are arriv'd; be gon we are discovered else. F).
2   THIRD WENCH ed. (III MS) and at l. 6.
    strengths MS (strength F).
    strengths (1) defensive works, fortifications; (2) strong positions; (3) troops.

FIRST WENCH
The country forces are arrived. Begone!
SECOND WENCH
Arm and be valiant. Think of our cause.   5
THIRD WENCH
Our justice! Aye, aye, aye, 'tis sufficient.

Exeunt

[ACT II, SCENE v]

Enter PETRONIUS, PETRUCHIO, MOROSO,
SOPHOCLES [*and*] TRANIO
PETRONIUS
I am indifferent, though I must confess
I had rather see her carted.
TRANIO
No more of that, sir.
SOPHOCLES
Are ye resolved to give her fair conditions?
'Twill be the safest way.
PETRUCHIO   I am distracted;   5
Would I had run my head into a halter
When I first wooed her; if I offer peace
She'll urge her own conditions, there's the devil.
SOPHOCLES
Why, say she do?
PETRUCHIO   Say I am made an ass, then;

5–6   *Arm . . . sufficient* MS (1. Arme, and be valiant. / 2. Think of our cause. / 3. Our
      justice. / 1. Tis sufficient. F).
  6   *Aye . . . aye* ed. (I: I: I: MS).

      [*Act II, Scene v*] ed. (*Scena tertia* F).
  1   *indifferent* unbiased, impartial; not inclined to favour any option.
  2   *carted* carried in a cart, as a form of public humiliation (this was often a
      punishment for prostitutes or bawds).
  5   *distracted* (1) greatly troubled or perplexed; (2) driven out of my wits.
  6   *Would* i.e. I would rather.
      halter noose.
  9   *Why* F (They MS).

I know her aim. May I with reputation 10
(Answer me this) with safety of mine honour –
After the mighty manage of my first wife,
Which was indeed a Fury to this filly,
After my twelve-strong labours to reclaim her,
Which would have made Dom Hercules horn-mad, 15
And hid him in his hide – suffer this Cicely,
Ere she had warmed my sheets, ere grappled with me –
This pink, this painted foist, this cockle-boat –
To hang her fights out, and defy me, friends,
A well-known man-of-war? If this be equal 20
And I may suffer, say, and I have done.

PETRONIUS
I do not think you may.

TRANIO   You'll make it worse, sir.

SOPHOCLES
Pray hear me, good Petruchio. But even now
You were contented to give all conditions,

10   *with reputation* i.e. without losing my good name.
12   *manage* training, breaking (a term used of horses).
13   *to* i.e. in comparison to.
       filly female foal (continuing the equine imagery).
14   *twelve-strong labours* Alludes to the twelve labours undertaken by the classical hero
       Hercules as penance after he slew his wife, Megara, and their children in a fit of
       madness induced by the goddess Juno.
15   *Dom* MS (Don F).
       Dom Sir (a respectful title prefixed to a Portuguese man's forename).
       horn-mad mad with rage.
16   *hid . . . hide* The first of Hercules' labours was to kill the Nemean Lion, and he
       thereafter wore the lion's skin as a cloak.
       Cicely A name often associated with servants and other lower-class women; in the
       Induction to *The Taming of the Shrew* Christopher Sly is told that he 'would call out
       for Cicely Hacket', a woman that Sly identifies as 'the woman's maid of the house'
       (Ind.ii.93–4).
17   *Ere . . . me* i.e. before the marriage has even been consummated.
18   *pink* (1) small sailing boat or warship; (2) minnow; (3) whore.
       foist (1) small boat propelled by sails and oars; (2) small barge; (3) rogue, cheat.
       cockle-boat small boat (a variation, 'cock-boat', is used to refer to the genitals in
       sexual slang).
19   *fights* screens hung up during a naval battle to protect a vessel's crew.
20   *man-of-war* (1) fighting man; (2) vessel equipped for war.
       equal fair, just.
21   *suffer* (1) bear this injury; (2) tolerate this.
23   *even now* i.e. just now.

To try how far she would carry; 'tis a folly –   25
And you will find it so – to clap the curb on
Ere ye be sure it proves a natural wildness
And not a forced. Give her conditions,
For, on my life, this trick is put into her –

PETRONIUS
I should believe so too.

SOPHOCLES   And not her own.   30

TRANIO
You'll find it so.

SOPHOCLES   Then if she founder with you,
Clap spurs on, and in this you'll deal with temperance,
Avoid the hurry of the world –   *Music above*

TRANIO   And lose –

MOROSO
No honour, o' my life, sir.

PETRUCHIO   I will do it.

PETRONIUS
It seems they are very merry.

Enter JAQUES

PETRUCHIO   Why, long hold it.   35

MOROSO
Now, Jaques.

25   *how . . . carry* i.e. how far she would go.
26   *curb* chain or strap fastened to a horse's bit and passing under its lower jaw, used to
      control an unruly horse (used figuratively to refer to anything that curbs or restrains).
29   *on my life* a mild oath.
      this . . . her i.e. she has been put up to this trick.
      trick device, stratagem.
30   *too* F (to MS).
31   *founder* MS (flownder F).
      founder stumble violently, fall lame (Sophocles continues to imagine Maria as a
      horse being ridden by Petruchio).
32   *Clap* Put.
      temperance self-restraint, moderation.
33   *hurry* (1) haste; (2) agitation, commotion.
      s.d. MS. In F the direction appears in the margin of Tranio's speech.
35   *long* MS (God F; Heaven F2).
      hold continue.

JAQUES	They are i' th' flaunt, sir.
SOPHOCLES	Yes, we hear 'em.

JAQUES

They have got a stick of fiddles, and they firk it
In wondrous ways; the two grand capitanos
That brought the auxiliary regiments
Dance with their coats tucked up to their bare breeches   40
And bid the kingdom kiss 'em: that's the burden.
They have got metheglin and audacious ale
And talk like tyrants.   *Song*

PETRONIUS   How know'st thou?

JAQUES

I peeped in at a loose lansket.

TRANIO

Hark.   45

PETRONIUS

A song, pray you silence.

---

36   *i' th' flaunt* flaunting themselves.
37–8 *They . . . ways* The primary image is of the women dancing to the music that they
       have provided for themselves, but Jaques' description carries heavy sexual
       innuendo: here, as elsewhere in the play, the women's rebellion is shadowed by the
       men's fear that they may also be sexually independent.
37   *stick of fiddles* (1) a bunch of fiddles ('stick' being used as a collective noun); (2) a
       fiddle bow; (3) (as *OED* suggests) a fiddle player; (4) a bunch of dildos (Daileader
       and Taylor).
       firk it dance, frisk (with sexual innuendo).
38   *capitanos* captains.
39   *That* MS (They F).
       auxiliary supporting.
40   *coats* petticoats, skirts.
       breeches buttocks.
41   *the kingdom* MS (them F).
       burden refrain, chorus.
42   *metheglin* spiced mead.
       audacious inspiring boldness or impudence (this is *OED*'s only example).
43   s.d. *Song* The direction appears here in MS, and at l. 44 in F; these may be anti-
       cipatory directions indicating that the song is imminent, or an instruction for it to
       begin. Petronius' comment at l. 46 suggests that the song has already begun by this
       point, but that the lyric only becomes clear when the men fall silent.
44   *lansket* MS (latchet ed.)
       lansket This word appears nowhere else, and is usually glossed by editors as a shut-
       ter or the panel of a door; it is possible, however, that Daileader and Taylor's
       'latchet' (latch) is correct.
45   *Hark* Listen.

[WOMEN [*singing within*]
>> *A health for all this day*
>> *To the woman that bears the sway*
>> *And wears the breeches;*
>>> *Let it come, let it come.*   50

>> *Let this health be a seal,*
>> *For the good of the commonweal*
>> *The woman shall wear the breeches.*

>> *Let's drink then and laugh it,*
>> *And merrily, merrily quaff it,*   55
>> *And tipple, and tipple a round.*
>>> *Here's to thy fool*
>>> *And to my fool!*
>>> *Come, to all fools,*
>> *Though it cost us, wench, many a pound.*]   60

>> *Enter above* MARIA, BIANCA, a CITY WIFE,
>> a COUNTRY WIFE, *and* THREE WOMEN

MOROSO
>> They look out.

PETRUCHO   Good even, ladies.

MARIA   God you good even, sir.

47–60   *A . . . pound* F2 (*om.* MS, F) F2 adds the lyrics of a number of songs omitted from the first folio, including this one, which is placed after the direction 'SONG' at the bottom of p. 106, after line 44. Songs often seem to have been transcribed onto loose sheets of paper which may have circulated separately from the main playbook; it is therefore not unusual for songs to be omitted from printed play-texts. Since F2 was not published until 1679, this song could have been incorporated into the play at any time and it may not be the song included when the play was first performed. It has, however, been successfully performed in recent revivals such as that of the RSC in 2003.

48   *sway* command.

52   *commonweal* (1) body politic, community, state; (2) republic or democratic state.

54   *laugh it* i.e. laugh. In early modern English 'it' could be used as the object of a verb that would otherwise be intransitive (see also 'quaff it' in the next line).

55   *quaff it* i.e. drink copiously.

56   *tipple* drink, booze.

57–8   *thy fool . . . my fool* probably refers to the women's husbands.

60   s.d. *Enter . . .* WOMEN MS (*All the women above.* F; *All the Women above. / Citizens and Countrey / women.* F2).

>> s.d. THREE WOMEN These are probably the Country Wenches who appeared in II.iv.

PETRUCHIO
How have you slept tonight?
MARIA   Exceeding well, sir.
PETRUCHIO
Did you not wish me with you?
MARIA   No, believe me,
I never thought upon you.
COUNTRY WIFE   Is that he?
BIANCA
Yes.
COUNTRY WIFE   Sir –
SOPHOCLES [*To the men*] She has drunk hard, mark her hood.
COUNTRY WIFE   You are –   65
SOPHOCLES
Learnedly drunk, I'll hang else. Let her utter.
COUNTRY WIFE
And I must tell you, *viva voce*, friend,
A very foolish fellow –
TRANIO   There's an ale figure.
PETRUCHIO
I thank you, Susan Brotes.
CITY WIFE   Forward, sister!
COUNTRY WIFE
You have espoused here a hearty woman,   70

61   *God* ed. (Good MS, F).
      God . . . even A common expression meaning 'God give you a good evening'; MS
      and F's 'good you good ev'n' is probably a mistake or a bowdlerisation, although it
      is found elsewhere.
63–4 ed. (Did . . . you? / No . . . you. MS).
64   COUNTRY WIFE ed. (Country MS) and throughout this scene (Country/Coun. w. MS).
      mark pay attention to, look at.
65   *hood* i.e. her head-dress or cap (the Country Wife's hood is probably askew).
66   *Learnedly* i.e. profoundly.
      utter speak.
67   *viva voce* i.e. 'in plain speech', aloud.
68   *ale figure* i.e. a piece of rhetoric inspired by drink.
69   *Susan Brotes* Appears to be a semi-legendary figure: there is a reference to her in a
      marginal note in James Strong's *Joanereidos: or, Feminine Valour Eminently
      Discovered in Western Women* (London, 1645): 'See Mrs *Susan Brotus de Margar*'
      (sig. E2r).
      sister comrade; used by Christians to refer to other Christians, and often associated
      with Puritans.
69   CITY WIFE ed. (Citty MS) and throughout this scene (Citty/Citie/Citty w. MS).
70–1 ed. (You . . . couragious MS).

    Comely and courageous –

PETRUCHIO   Well I have so.

COUNTRY WIFE

    And to the comfort of distressed damsels,

    Women outworn in wedlock, and such vessels,

    This woman has defied you.

PETRUCHIO   It should seem so.

COUNTRY WIFE

    And why?

PETRUCHIO Yes, can you tell?

COUNTRY WIFE   For thirteen causes.   75

PETRUCHIO

    Pray, by your patience, mistress –

CITY WIFE   Forward, sister!

PETRUCHIO

    Do you mean to treat of all this?

CITY WIFE   Who shall let her?

PETRONIUS

    Do you hear, velvet hood, we come not now

    To hear your doctrine.

COUNTRY WIFE   For the first, I take it,

    It doth divide itself in seven branches –   80

PETRUCHIO

    Hark you, good Maria,

    Have you got a catechiser here?

---

71   *Comely* MS (A comely F).
       Comely (1) Pretty; (2) Decent, decorous.
       Well (1) Happily, advantageously; (2) Indeed, certainly; (3) Clearly; (4) Kindly, generously.

73   *vessels* individuals: 'vessel' is used figuratively to refer to individuals regarded as receptacles for something; women were proverbially described as 'the weaker vessel'.

76   *Pray* i.e. I pray you: please (Petruchio addresses the Country Wife with exaggerated politeness).

77   *treat . . . this* i.e. (1) carry out all the negotiations; (2) discuss all of these issues (i.e. the 'thirteen causes' of l. 75).
       this MS (these F).   *shall* F (sall MS).
       let hinder.

78   *velvet hood* associated with prosperous city women.

79   *doctrine* instruction, preaching, learning.

80   *in* MS (into F).
       branches sections, lines of thought or argument.

82   *catechiser* instructor in religious doctrine.

TRANIO   Good zeal!

SOPHOCLES

Good three-piled predication, will you peace,
And hear the cause we come for?

COUNTRY WIFE   Yes, bobtails,

We know the cause you came for:
[*Indicating* MARIA]   here's the cause.   85
But never hope to carry her, never dream
Or flatter your opinions with a thought
Of base repentance in her.

CITY WIFE   Give me sack.

By this, and next, strong ale –

COUNTRY WIFE   Swear forward, sister!

CITY WIFE

By all that's cordial in this place, we'll bury   90
Our bones, fames, tongues, our triumphs, and e'en all
That ever yet was chronicled of woman,
But this brave wench, this excellent despiser,
This bane of dull obedience, shall inherit
Her liberal will, and march off with conditions   95
Noble and worth herself.

COUNTRY WIFE   She shall, Tom Tylers,

82   *zeal* (1) fervour; (2) intention; (3) zealot.
83   *three-piled* refers to high-quality velvet (the 'pile' is the raised surface of the fabric).
     predication sermon, oration (Sophocles imagines her as a personification of
     preaching).
     will . . . peace i.e. will you be quiet.
84   *bobtails* rogues, curs (originally refers to dogs or horses with cropped tails, and so
     may suggest the men's powerlessness in the situation).
85   *the cause* i.e. Maria.
86   *carry her* (1) bear her away; (2) have sex with her.
88   *sack* white wine from Spain, usually dry and sweetened with sugar.
89   *Swear forward* i.e. continue swearing.
90   *cordial* (1) cheering, reviving (used of food, drink and medicine); (2) an alcoholic
     beverage.
91   *e'en* MS (eu'n) (then F; *om.* F2).
93   *despiser* someone who despises or scorns.
94   *bane* destroyer, nemesis.
95   *Her* MS (hir) (His F).
     liberal (1) bountiful, open-hearted; (2) unrestrained, indecorous.
     off F (of MS).
96   *Tom Tylers* i.e. would-be shrew-tamers. Tom Tyler is the hero of a sixteenth-century
     farce, *Tom Tyler and his Wife*, which focuses on Tom's unsuccessful attempts to sub-
     due Strife, his wife, and includes situations in which Strife and her female friends
     discuss ways of disciplining their husbands and sing raucous songs.

And brave ones too. My hood shall make a hearse-cloth
And I lie under it like Joan of Gaunt
Ere I go less; my distaff stuck up by me
For the eternal trophy of my conquests,   100
And loud fame at my head with two main bottles
Shall fill to all the world the glorious fall
Of old Don Gillian.
CITY WIFE   Yet a little further:
We have taken arms in rescue of this lady
Most just and noble. If ye beat us off   105
Without conditions, and we recreant,
Use us as we deserve, and first degrade us
Of all our ancient chambering; next that,
The symbols of our secrecy, silk stockings;
Hew off our heels; our petticoats of arms   110
Tear off our bodies; and our bodkins break
Over our coward heads.

---

97   *hearse-cloth* funeral pall: a cloth covering the coffin or bier.
98   *Joan of Gaunt* Plays on the name of John of Gaunt, Duke of Lancaster and uncle of
     King Richard II, who had a claim to the Castilian crown through his second wife,
     Constance of Castile; it may also be relevant that Gaunt had a daughter named
     Joan.
101 *two* F (too MS).
     main F (manie MS).
     main great.
102 *fill* raise a glass, toast.
103 *Don* MS (Dame ed.)
     Don Gillian like 'Joan of Gaunt' mixes up the genders, and also mixes class signi-
     fiers: 'Don' is a Spanish term of respect for a high-born man, while the name Gillian
     is often associated with lower-class women.
106 *recreant* surrender (MS originally read 'recant', which has been corrected; F also
     reads 'recant').
107 *Use* Treat.
108 *ancient* i.e. long-established.
     chambering (1) furnishing of a room; (2) luxury; (3) lascivious behaviour, sexual
     licence.
107–12 *first . . . heads* As Daileader and Taylor note, this parodies the ceremony with which
        a man's knighthood was removed: his spurs were hacked off, his coat-of-arms was
        removed, and his sword was broken over his head. The crimes for which knight-
        hood was revoked were treason, running away during a battle, and heresy.
110 *off* ed. (of MS, F).
111 *off* ed. (of MS, F).
     bodies MS, F (bod'ces ed.)
     bodkins (1) pins used for fastening up the hair; (2) small pointed instruments used
     for piercing holes in cloth; (2) daggers.

COUNTRY WIFE   And ever after,
To make the tainture most notorious,
At all our crests, *videlicet* our plackets,
Let laces hang, and we return again   115
Into our former titles, dairy maids.

PETRUCHIO

No more wars, puissant ladies. Show conditions
And freely I accept 'em.

MARIA   Call in Livia;
She is in the treaty too.

MOROSO   How, Livia?

Enter LIVIA *above*

MARIA

[*To* MOROSO] Heard you that, sir?   120
[*To* PETRUCHIO, *throwing down a paper*]
There's the conditions for you, pray peruse 'em.

PETRONIUS

Yes, there she is; 't had been no right rebellion
Had she held off. [*To* MOROSO] What think you, man?

MOROSO   Nay, nothing,
I have enough o' th' prospect, o' my conscience;
The world's end and the goodness of a woman   125
Will come together.

PETRONIUS   Are you there, sweet lady?

LIVIA

Cry you mercy, sir, I saw you not. Your blessing.

PETRONIUS

Yes, when I bless a jade that stumbles with me.
[*To* PETRUCHIO] How are the articles?

---

113   *tainture* (1) attainder: the legal consequences of a conviction for treason or felony;
       (2) dishonour, stain.
114   *crests* helmets.
       videlicet that is to say, namely.
       plackets slits in a skirt or underskirt giving access to a pocket or purse.
115   *Let laces hang* i.e. let them hang open (possibly suggesting sexual availability).
117   *puissant* powerful, mighty.
121   *you* MS (ye F).
122   *right* real, true.
125-6 *The . . . together* i.e. it is impossible to find a good woman.

LIVIA [*To* MOROSO]   This is for you, sir,
  And I shall think upon't.
MOROSO   You have used me finely.   130
LIVIA
  There is no other use of thee now extant
  But to be hung up, cassock, cap, and all,
  For some strange monster at apothecaries'.
PETRONIUS
  I hear you, whore.
LIVIA   It must be his, then,
  For need will then compel me.
CITY WIFE   Blessing on thee!   135
PETRONIUS
  There's no talking to 'em. [*To* PETRUCHIO] How are they, sir?
PETRUCHIO
  [*Reading*] As I expected: liberty and clothes
  When and in what way she will, continual monies,
  Company, and all the house at her dispose.
  No tongue to say, 'Why is this?', or 'Whither will it?'   140
  New coaches and some buildings she appoints here,
  Hangings, and hunting horses, and for plate
  And jewels for her private use, I take it,
  Two thousand pounds in present. Then, for music,

---

129   *This . . . sir* Livia probably throws Moroso a paper here, but she might also make a
       rude gesture at him.
130   *finely* (1) splendidly (said ironically); (2) cleverly, skilfully.
131   *extant* in existence, in fashion.
133   *For . . . apothecaries'* Apothecaries' shops sold medicinal drugs but were also
       renowned for the display of exotic artefacts such as stuffed animals.
134   *then* MS (then sir F).
134–5 *It . . . me.* i.e. I would only be a whore if I was married to him (either because she
       would be 'sold' by her father and thus prostituted, or because she would have no
       choice but to be unfaithful to Moroso).
135–6 F adds another speech for Livia between the City Wife and Petronius's speeches,
       and another joke at Moroso's expense. See Appendix 1, Passage D.
136   F (There's . . . em; / How . . . Sir? MS).
137   *Reading* ed. (*Reads* F: in right hand margin).
139   *dispose* disposal, management.
141   *appoints* sets out, stipulates.   *here* i.e. in the list of conditions.
142   *Hangings* tapestries or other drapery hung on the walls.
       plate tableware (especially vessels, etc., made of gold or silver).
144   *Two thousand pounds* This sum would have the spending power of around £195,760
       at the time of writing (2009); there may be an added irony here in the fact that in
       The Taming of the Shrew a needy Petruchio makes his money by marrying Katherine.

And women to read French –
PETRONIUS   This must not be.   145
PETRUCHIO
And at the latter end, a clause put in
That Livia shall by no man be importuned
This whole month yet to marry.
PETRONIUS   This is monstrous!
PETRUCHIO
This shall be done. I'll humour her a while;
If nothing but repentance and undoing   150
Can win her love, I'll make a shift for one.
SOPHOCLES
When ye are once a-bed, all these conditions
Lie under your own seal.
MARIA   Do ye like 'em?
PETRUCHIO   Yes,
And by that faith I gave ye 'fore the priest
I'll ratify 'em.
COUNTRY WIFE Stay, what pledges?
MARIA   No,   155
I'll take that oath, but have a care ye keep it.
CITY WIFE
''Tis not now as when Andrea lived.'
COUNTRY WIFE
[*To* PETRUCHIO] If ye do juggle,
Or alter but a letter of this creed
We have set down, the self-same persecution –   160

144   *in present* (1) immediately; (2) as a gift.
145   *read* teach.
145–57 In the manuscript this section appears on a smaller leaf which has been pasted in,
          apparently because the scribe mistakenly omitted it as he was transcribing the text.
          See Livingston, p. ix.
147   *importuned* urged, compelled.
149   *her* i.e. Maria.
150   *undoing* destruction, ruin.
151   *make . . . one* i.e. do my best, this once.
152–3 *all . . . seal* i.e. it is up to you whether you ratify them (with heavy sexual innuendo).
154   *faith* pledge, promise (i.e. the marriage oath).
157   *''Tis . . . lived'* A quotation from Thomas Kyd's popular play *The Spanish Tragedy*
          (III.xiv.111), meaning (in this context) things aren't what they used to be.
158   *juggle* i.e. attempt to cheat or deceive us.
159   *this creed* MS (these Articles F).   *creed* doctrine, formula of belief.
160   *the self-same* i.e. identical.

MARIA
Mistrust him not.
PETRUCHIO   By all my honesty –
MARIA
Enough, I yield.
PETRONIUS [*Looking at the paper*]
                         What's this inserted here?
SOPHOCLES
That the two valiant women that command here
Shall have a supper made 'em, and a large one,
And liberal entertainment without grudging,   165
And pay for all their soldiers.
PETRUCHIO   That shall be too.
And if a tun of wine will serve to pay 'em,
They shall have justice. I ordain ye all
Paymasters, gentlemen.
TRANIO   Then we shall have sport, boys.
MARIA
We'll meet ye in the parlour.
PETRUCHIO [*To* PETRONIUS]   Never look sad, sir,   170
For I will do it.
SOPHOCLES   There's no danger in't.
PETRUCHIO
For Livia's article, you shall observe it;
I have tied myself.
PETRONIUS   I will.
PETRUCHIO   Along then. Now,
Either I break, or this stiff plant must bow.

                                             Exeunt

162   ed. (Enough . . . yield. / What's this / inserted here? MS).
163   *the . . . women* i.e. the Country Wife and the City Wife.
167   *tun* barrel.
169   *Paymasters* officials responsible for issuing pay and settling debts.
      sport entertainment, fun (with sexual innuendo).
170–1 ed. (Wee'l . . . parlor. / Neuer . . . it MS).
172   *For* as for.
      article clause, stipulation.
173   *tied* bound, obligated.
174   *this stiff plant* (1) Maria (who must be defeated if Petruchio is not to be broken);
      (2) Petruchio's penis (i.e. he must either emasculate himself temporarily, or be
      defeated completely).
      bow bend.

ACT III, SCENE i

Enter ROLAND *and* TRANIO

TRANIO
Come, ye shall take my counsel.
ROLAND   I shall hang first.
  I'll no more love, that's certain; 'tis a bane –
  Next that they poison rats with – the most mortal.
  No, I thank heaven I have got my sleep again
  And now begin to write sense; I can walk ye   5
  A long hour in my chamber, like a man,
  And think of something that may better me,
  Some serious point of learning, or my state.
  No more 'Aye-me!'s, and mistresses, Tranio,
  Come near my brain. I'll tell thee, had the devil   10
  But any essence in him of a man,
  And could be brought to love, and love a woman,
  'Twould make his head ache worser than his horns do,
  And firk him with a fire he never felt yet;
  Would make him dance. I'll tell thee there is nothing   15
  (It may be thy case, Tranio, therefore hear me)
  Under the sun – reckon the mass of follies
  Crept into th' world with man – so desperate,
  So mad, so senseless, poor and base, so wretched,
  Roguey, and scurvy –

Act III, Scene i ed. (ACTVS III. Scaena j.^ma MS; *Actus tertius, Scæna prima.* F).
0   s.d. *Enter . . .* TRANIO MS (*Enter Tranio, and Rowland.* F).
1   *counsel* advice.
2   *bane* poison.
3   *mortal* deadly.
8   *point* detail, issue, subject.
    state (1) property or possessions; (2) state of (spiritual) existence.
9   *mistresses* MS (miseries F; *misereris* ed.)
14   *firk* drive, whip.
15   *Would* That would.
16   *It . . . case* i.e. you may be in the same situation.
17   *reckon* (1) count up; (2) consider.
18   *desperate* irretrievably wicked; extremely reckless or violent.
20   *Roguey* rascally, disreputable.
    scurvy worthless, contemptible, discourteous.

TRANIO	Whither wilt thou, Roland?	20

ROLAND
　As to be in love.

TRANIO　　　　　　And why, for heaven's sake?

ROLAND
　And why for heaven's sake? Dost thou not conceive me?

TRANIO
　No, by my troth.

ROLAND　　　　Pray, then, and heartily,
　For fear thou fall into 't. I'll tell thee why, too –
　For I have hope to save thee – when thou lov'st　　　　25
　And first begin'st to worship the calf with the white face,
　Imprimis, thou hast lost thy gentry,
　And like a prentice flung away thy freedom;
　Forthwith thou art a slave.

TRANIO　　　　　　That's a new doctrine.

ROLAND
　Next, thou art no more a man.

TRANIO　　　　　　What, then?

ROLAND　　　　　　　　　A frippery.　　　30
　Nothing but braided hair, and penny riband,
　Glove, garter, ring, rose, or at the best a swabber.
　If thou canst love so near to keep thy making,
　Yet thou wilt lose thy language.

TRANIO　　　　　　Why?

ROLAND　　　　　　Oh, Tranio,

20　*Whither wilt thou* i.e. where are you going with this; what's the point.
21　*heaven's* MS (vertue F; [God's] ed.)
22　*heaven's* MS (vertues F; [God's] ed.)
　　conceive understand.
26　*calf . . . face* MS (gilt calfe F; gilt calf / With the white face ed.)
　　calf . . . face a proverbial term (Tilley C19) used by Fletcher elsewhere as an endearment for an attractive woman.
27　*Imprimis* In the first place (Latin): commonly used to introduce a list of items, as in an inventory or a will.
　　lost thy gentry i.e. lost the status of a gentleman.
29　*Forthwith* Immediately.
30　*a man* MS (man F).
　　What, then i.e. what have I become, then.
　　frippery gaudy piece of clothing.
31　*riband* ribbon.
32　*at the best* MS (at best F).
　　swabber mop (specifically one used for cleaning ovens).
33　*making* character, true nature.

Those things in love ne'er talk as we do!

TRANIO   No?   35

ROLAND

No, without doubt, they sigh and shake the head
And sometimes whistle dolefully.

TRANIO   No tongue?

ROLAND

Yes, Tranio, but no truth in't, nor no reason,
And when they cant, for 'tis a kind of canting,
You shall hear – if you reach to understand 'em,   40
Which you must be a fool first, or you cannot –
Such gibberish, such 'Believe me, I protest, sweet',
And 'Oh, dear heavens, in which such constellations
Reigns at the births of lovers, this is too well',
And 'Deign me, lady, deign me, I beseech ye,   45
Your poor unworthy lump', and then she licks him.

TRANIO

Oh, pox on't! This is nothing.

ROLAND   Thou hast hit it.
Then talks she ten times worse, and wries, and wriggles
As though she had the itch – and so it may be.

TRANIO

Of what religion are they?

ROLAND   Good old Catholics;   50
They deal by intercession all. They keep
A kind of household gods called chambermaids,

39   *cant* (1) beg; (2) speak jargon (especially associated with thieves and beggars).
40   *You* MS (Ye F).
      reach attempt.
43–4 *constellations / Reigns* See II.i.90 n.
45   *Deign me* Condescend to accept me.
46   *licks him* i.e. licks him into shape (draws on the idea that baby bears were born
      shapeless, and were licked into shape by their mothers).
47   *Oh, pox* MS (O pox) (A — F).
      pox on't a plague on it (an expletive).
      nothing i.e. nothing of any significance.
      Thou hast hit it i.e. you're right (Roland misunderstands Tranio's 'nothing' as refer-
      ring to the women he is criticizing).
48   *wries* writhes.
49   *itch* scabies, a skin disease often confused (as here) with syphilis.
50–7 *Of . . . ended* MS (*om.* F). This passage appears to have been censored in F.
51   *intercession* i.e. the intervention of the saints, a belief rejected by Protestants.
52   *household gods* Draws on the Roman belief in *Lares* and *Penates*, who were thought to
      protect the household, and whose images were kept in the central room of the house.

Which being prayed to, and their offerings brought –
Which are in gold, yet some observe the old law
And give 'em flesh – *probatum est*, you shall have   55
As good love for your money, and as tidy,
As ere you turned your leg o'er, and that ended –

TRANIO

Why, thou art grown a strange discoverer!

ROLAND

Of mine own follies, Tranio.

TRANIO   Wilt thou, Roland,
Certain ne'er love again?

ROLAND   I think so, certain,   60
And if I be not dead drunk, I shall keep it.

TRANIO

Tell me but this, what dost thou think of woman?

ROLAND

Why, as I think of fiddles: they delight me
Till their strings break.

TRANIO   What strings?

ROLAND   Their modesties,
Faiths, vows and maidenheads, for they are like kits: 65
They have but four strings to 'em.

TRANIO   What wilt thou
Give me for ten pounds now, when thou next lov'st
And the same woman still?

ROLAND   Give me the money;
A hundred, an' my bond for't.

TRANIO   But, pray hear me,
I'll work all means I can to reconcile ye.   70

ROLAND

Do, do, give me the money.

TRANIO [*Giving him ten pounds*] There.

---

55   *flesh* (1) meat; (2) blood sacrifice; (3) sex objects.
      probatum est it has been proved (Latin).
56   *tidy* (1) attractive, healthy; (2) excellent, satisfactory.
57   *turned . . . o'er* i.e. mounted.
58   *discoverer* informer, spy.
62   *woman* MS (women F).
65   *kits* small fiddles, often used by dancing masters.
67   *Give* i.e. bet.
69   *an'* MS (an) (and F).
70   *work all means* i.e. try every method.

ROLAND   Work, Tranio.

TRANIO

You shall go sometimes where she is.

ROLAND   Yes, straight.

This is the first good I e'er got by woman.

TRANIO

You would think it strange, now, if another beauty,

As good as hers, say better –

ROLAND   Well.

TRANIO   Conceive me,   75

This is no point o' th' wager –

ROLAND   That's all one.

TRANIO

Love ye as much or more than she now hates ye.

ROLAND

'Tis a good hearing, let 'em love. Ten pound more

I never love that woman.

TRANIO [*Giving him another ten pounds*]

                                  There it is,

And so a hundred if ye lose.

ROLAND   'Tis done.   80

Have ye another to put in?

TRANIO   No more, sir.

ROLAND

I am very sorry. Now will I erect

A new game, and go hate for th' bell; I am sure

I am in excellent case to win.

TRANIO   I must have leave

To tell ye, and tell truth too, what she is,   85

71   *Work* i.e. get to work, do your worst.
72   *straight* i.e. straight away.
76   *This . . . wager* i.e. this isn't part of our bet.
     one i.e. one and the same.
77   *she now* MS (now she F).
78   *'Tis a good hearing* i.e. that's good news, that's a good rumour.
     Ten pound more i.e. I'll bet you ten pounds more.
81   *No more* MS (No, no F).
82   *erect* i.e. set up.
83   *hate for th' bell* i.e. win first prize in a competition to hate women.
     bell first prize.
84   *case* position.
     leave permission.
85   *too* F (to MS).

And what she suffers for you.

ROLAND   Ten pounds more
I never believe ye.

TRANIO   No, sir, I am stinted.

ROLAND
Well, take your best way then.

TRANIO   Let's walk. I am glad
Your sullen fever's off.

ROLAND   Shalt see me, Tranio,
A monstrous merry man. Now, let's to the wedding,   90
And as we go tell me the general hurry
Of these mad wenches, and their works.

TRANIO   I will.

ROLAND
And do thy worst.

TRANIO   Something I'll do.

ROLAND   Do, Tranio.

Exeunt

[ACT III, SCENE ii]

Enter PEDRO *and* JAQUES

PEDRO
A pair of stocks bestride 'em! Are they gone?

JAQUES
Yes, they are gone, and all the pans i' th' town
Beating before 'em. What strange admonitions

---

86 *what* MS (*how* F).
87 *stinted* finished.
88 *take . . . way* (1) do your best; (2) make the best of it.
89 *sullen* sulky; gloomy, melancholy.
    Shalt i.e. you will.
91 *hurry* commotion.
92 *works* (1) deeds; (2) defensive works.

    [*Act III, Scene ii*] ed. (*Scœna Secunda.* F).
1   *A . . . 'em* i.e. may they end up in the stocks (with sexual innuendo on 'bestride').
2–3 *all . . . 'em* The women at the head of the crowd are apparently beating pans as they
     march.
3   *admonitions* warnings.

They gave my master and how fearfully
They threatened if he broke 'em!

PEDRO   O' my conscience,   5
H'as found his full match now.

JAQUES   That I believe too.

PEDRO
How did she entertain him?

JAQUES   She looked on him –

PEDRO
But scurvily?

JAQUES   Faith, with no great affection
That I saw; and I heard some say he kissed her,
But 'twas upon a treaty, and some copies   10
Say but her cheek.

PEDRO   Faith, Jaques, what wouldst thou give
For such a wife now?

JAQUES   Full as many prayers
As the most zealous puritan conceives –
Out of the meditation of fat veal,
Or birds of prey, crammed capons – against players,   . 15
And to as good a tune too, but against her,
That heaven would bless me from her. Mark it, Pedro,
If this house be not turned within this fortnight
With the foundation upward, I'll be carted.
My comfort is yet that these Amorites   20
That came to back her cause, those heathen whores,

6   *H'as* He has.
      full absolute.
      too F (to MS).
7   *she* i.e. Maria.
8   *scurvily* sourly.
      Faith MS (*om.* F).
9   *he kissed her* F (she kist him MS). MS's version does not tally with 'but her cheek'
      in l. 11.
10   *copies* reports.
12–15 *Full . . . players* Jaques says that he would pray as hard as a hypocritical puritan does
      against the theatre (the puritan condemns playing as sinful but nonetheless
      commits the sin of gluttony).
16   *tune* i.e. a hymn tune.
19   *carted* See II.v.2 n.
20   *these* MS (those F).
      Amorites ancient heathens (refers to the tribes described in the Bible as inhabiting
      Canaan before the Israelites).

Had their hoods hallowed with sack.

PEDRO

How devilish drunk they were!

JAQUES

And how they tumbled, Pedro! Did'st mark
The country cavaliero?

PEDRO   Out upon her!   25

How she turned down the bragget!

JAQUES   Aye, that sunk her.

PEDRO

That drink was well put to her. What a somersault,
When the chair fell, she fetched, with her heels upward –

JAQUES

And what a piece of landscape she discovered.

PEDRO

Did'st mark her when her hood fell in the posset?   30

JAQUES

Yes, and there rid, like a Dutch hoy. The tumbrel,
When she had got her ballast –

PEDRO   That I saw too.

JAQUES

How fain she would have drawn on Sophocles

---

22   *hallowed* blessed. Jaques ironically compares the showering of the women with
     wine with the baptism ceremony.
24   *Did'st mark* MS (didst thou mark F).
25   *cavaliero* cavalier: knight; gallant.
26   *turned down* drank. *OED*'s earliest citation dates from 1760–72, but Fletcher also
     gives the expression this sense in *The Island Princess*, II.iv.42–3: 'I would very faine
     turne downe this liquor'.
     bragget a drink made from honey and ale fermented together.
     Aye (I MS).
27   *somersault* ed. (Summersett MS; sober salt F).
29   *landscape* (1) natural scenery; (2) painting representing natural scenery; (3) view,
     prospect (Jaques is actually talking about the display of the woman's buttocks
     and/or genitals).
     discovered revealed.
30   *posset* drink made from hot milk curdled with ale, wine or other liquid.
31   *Dutch hoy* small sailing vessel.
     tumbrel flat-bottomed barge, by extension refers to drunkards, who are loaded
     with drink.
32   *ballast* ed. (ballasse MS: an early modern alternative spelling).
     ballast stability, steadiness.
33   *drawn on* enticed.

To come aboard, and how she simpered it!

PEDRO

I warrant her she has been a worthy striker.   35

JAQUES

I' th' heat of summer there had been some hope on't,
For then old women are cool cellars.

PEDRO   Hang her.

JAQUES

She offered him a Harry-groat, and belched out,
Her stomach being blown with ale, such courtship,
Upon my life, has giv'n him twenty stools since.   40
Believe my calculation: these old women,
When they are tippled, and a little heated,
Are like new wheels; they'll roar you all the town o'er
Till they be greased.

PEDRO   The city cinquepace,
Dame Toast-and-Butter, had her bob too.

JAQUES   Yes,   45

But she was sullen drunk, and given to filching.
I see her offer at a spoon – My master!

34   *come aboard* i.e. to kiss and/or have sex with her.
      simpered it i.e. simpered.
35   *striker* sexual partner, whore.
36   *on't* of it.
36–7 *I' . . . cellars* Jaques suggests that Sophocles might have been tempted to sleep with
      the Country Wife during the summer, as having sex with an old woman cools one
      down ('cellar' was seventeenth-century slang for the vagina).
37   *For . . . cellars* MS (*om*. F). This line may have been censored from F.
38   *Harry-groat* i.e. a groat from the time of Henry VIII (appropriately, for an old
      woman).
40   *stools* bowel-movements.
41   *calculation* prediction, especially one made by astrologers.
42   *tippled* drunk.
      heated excited.
43   *roar* (1) run noisily (like a creaking wheel); (2) behave in a riotous manner.
44   *greased* Refers to the application of grease on a new wheel, but also carries sexual
      innuendo; 'greased' is also a euphemism for bribery (*OED*'s earliest example is
      from 1693, but it was in use in the 1590s).
      cinquepace a lively dance, fashionable in the sixteenth century. As Taylor and Daileader
      note, it may be used here as a term for a 'fast' woman.
45   *Toast-and-Butter* A slang term for a pampered citizen.
      bob sexual encounter.
46   *filching* stealing.
47   *see* MS, F (saw ed.); 'saw' is grammatically correct, but 'see' could work in per-
      formance.

I do not like his look; I fear h'as fasted,
For all this preparation. Let's steal by him.

Exeunt [JAQUES *and* PEDRO]

Enter PETRUCHIO [*and*] SOPHOCLES

SOPHOCLES
Not let you touch her all this night?
PETRUCHIO   Not touch her.   50
SOPHOCLES
Where was your courage?
PETRUCHIO   Where was her obedience?
Never poor man was shamed so; never rascal
That keeps a stud of whores was used so basely.
SOPHOCLES
Pray tell me one thing truly, do you love her?
PETRUCHIO
I would I did not; upon that condition   55
I had passed thee half my land.
SOPHOCLES   It may be, then,
Her modesty required a little violence.
Some women love to struggle.
[PETRUCHIO]   She had it,
And so much that I sweat for't. So I did,
But to no end – I wash an Ethiop.   60
She swore my force might weary her, but win her
I never could, nor should, till she consented.

---

48   *look* expression.
      fasted i.e. gone without sex.
49   *Enter . . .* SOPHOCLES MS (*Scena tertia.* F; 3.3. ed.) Other editions begin a new
      scene here, but the effect may be funnier if Jaques and Pedro briefly share the stage
      with Petruchio and Sophocles; MS has no scene division.
53   *stud* collection, establishment for breeding (used of horses).
54   *Pray* MS (Pray you F).
55   *would* wish, would rather.
55–6 *upon . . . land* i.e. I would give you half my land if you could stop me loving her.
58   [PETRUCHIO] F (*Petru.*) (Petro MS).
      it i.e. violence.
59   *for't* for it.
60   *to no end* i.e. with no effect.
      I . . . Ethiop A proverbial term for an impossible task (Tilley E186), premised on the
      impossibility of washing a black person's skin white.
      wash MS (washt F; washed ed.)

And I might take her body prisoner,
But for her mind or appetite –
SOPHOCLES   'Tis strange.
This woman is the first I ever read of   65
Refused a warranted occasion,
And standing on so fair terms.
PETRUCHIO   I shall 'quite her.
SOPHOCLES
Used you no more art?
PETRUCHIO   Yes, I swore unto her,
And by no little ones, if presently,
Without more disputation of the matter,   70
She grew not nearer to me, and dispatched me
Out of the pain I was – for I was nettled –
And willingly, and eagerly, and sweetly,
I would to her chambermaid, and in her hearing
Begin her such a hunt's up.
SOPHOCLES   Then she startled?   75
PETRUCHIO
No more than I do now; marry, she answered,
If I were so disposed she could not help it,
But there was one called Jaques, a poor butler,
One that might well content a single woman.

66   *warranted* approved, allowed.
      occasion i.e. sexual opportunity.
67   *standing . . . terms* i.e. offered in such an advantageous manner (that is, in the
      physique and/or sexual prowess of Petruchio).
      'quite requite, retaliate against.
68   *art* skill, cunning.
      unto MS (to F).
69   *by . . . ones* i.e. on no trivial subjects. Petruchio probably means that he swore
      blasphemous oaths such as 'Sdeath' or 'God's wounds', rather than more trivial oaths
      such as 'by my faith', scorned by Bianca as 'Sunday oaths' in II.i.25.
70   *of* MS (on F).
72   *pain* (1) emotional anguish; (2) physical discomfort (caused by sexual frustration).
      I was i.e. I was in.
      nettled provoked, irritated.
75   *hunt's up* A song played to wake hunters in the morning; it might also be addressed
      to newly married couples and was therefore a euphemism for sex (see Williams 2:
      699–700).
      startled MS (started F).
      startled (1) wavered; (2) moved swiftly.
78   *butler* servant in charge of the wine cellar (MS uses the common early modern
      spelling 'botler').

SOPHOCLES
    And he should tilt her?

PETRUCHIO   To that sense. And last,   80
    She bade me yet these six months look for nothing,
    Nor strive to purchase it, but fair goodnight,
    And so good morrow, and a kiss or two
    To close my stomach, for her vow had sealed it,
    And she would keep it constant.

SOPHOCLES   Stay, stay,   85
    Was she so when you wooed her?

PETRUCHIO   Nothing, Sophocles,
    More kindly eager; I was oft afraid
    She had been light and easy, she would shower
    Her kisses so upon me.

SOPHOCLES   Then I fear
    Another spoke is i' th' wheel.

PETRUCHIO   Now thou hast found me;   90
    There gnaws my devil, Sophocles. O Patience
    Preserve me, that I make her not example
    By some unworthy way, as flaying her,
    Boiling, or making verjuice, drying her –

SOPHOCLES
    I hear her.

PETRUCHIO   Mark her, then, and see the heir   95

---

80   *tilt* A common euphemism for having sex: the literal sense is to thrust with a
        weapon.
        sense effect.
81   *months* MS (nights F).
        look for expect.
82   *purchase* arrange, obtain.
84   *close* satisfy.
        stomach sexual frustration.
        sealed confirmed.
85   *Stay, stay* MS (Stay ye, stay ye F; Stay ye, stay ed.)
        Stay Wait (i.e. wait a minute).
87   *kindly* MS (keenely F).
        kindly (1) readily; (2) affectionately; (3) naturally.
88   *light and easy* i.e. sexually promiscuous, lustful.
90   *Another . . . wheel* i.e. another man is involved.
        thou . . . me i.e. you follow me, you have the right idea.
91   *There . . . devil* i.e. that is what's eating away at me.
92   *make . . . example* I do not make an example of her.
94   *verjuice* A sour-tasting liquor used in cooking and medicine, usually made from the
        juice of unripe grapes or crab-apples.

Of spite and prodigality; she has studied
A way to beggar's both, and, by this hand,
She shall be, if I live, a doxy.

MARIA [*appears*] *at the door, and* SERVANTS

SOPHOCLES   Fie, sir!

MARIA

[*To* SERVANTS] I do not like that dressing; 'tis too poor.
Let me have six gold laces, broad and massy,   100
And betwixt every lace a rich embroidery;
Line the gown through with plush, perfumed, and purfle
All the sleeves down with pearls.

PETRUCHIO [*Aside to* SOPHOCLES] What think you, Sophocles?
In what point stands my state now?

MARIA   For those hangings,
Let 'em be carried where I gave appointment,   105
They are too base for my use, and bespeak
New pieces of the civil wars of France;
Let 'em be large and lively, and all silk-work,
The borders gold.

96   *prodigality* irresponsible and wasteful behaviour.
97   *beggar's* beggar us.
     by this hand Petruchio repeats one of his favourite oaths.
98   *doxy* a slang term for the unmarried partner of a beggar, also used to refer to
     prostitutes.
     s.d. *and* SERVANTS MS (*and Servant and woman* F).
99   [*To* SERVANTS] Maria may address the servants as a group, or different sections of
     her speeches here may be addressed to individual servants. F's stage direction
     requires two actors, suggesting that ll. 99–103, 104–9 and 110–12 would be add-
     ressed to the 'woman' and ll. 112–18 and 121–3 to the 'servant'.
     dressing decoration (on clothing).
100 *laces* ornamental braid, often sewn onto a bodice or doublet.
     massy heavy, solid (often used of precious metals).
102 *plush* rich (and expensive) fabric with a texture similar to velvet.
     purfle decorate, trim.
104 *In what point* i.e. what is the position of.
     state estate, financial wellbeing.
     For As for.
105 *where I gave appointment* i.e. where I ordered.
106 *base* inferior, shoddy.
     bespeak commission, order.
107 *pieces* i.e. tapestries.

SOPHOCLES   Aye, marry, sir, this cuts it.

MARIA

That fourteen yards of satin give my woman.   110
I do not like the colour; 'tis too civil.
There's too much silk i' th' lace too. Tell the Dutchman
That brought the mares, he must with all speed send me
Another suit of horses and, by all means,
Ten cast of hawks for th' river. I much care not   115
What price they bear, so they be sound and flying.
For the next winter I am for the country
And mean to take my pleasure. Where's the horseman?

PETRUCHIO [*Aside to* SOPHOCLES]

She means to ride a great horse.

SOPHOCLES   With a side-saddle?

PETRUCHIO

Yes, and she'll run a-tilt within this twelve month.   120

MARIA

Tomorrow I'll begin to learn, but pray, sir,
Have a great care he be an easy doer,
'Twill spoil a scholar else.

SOPHOCLES [*Aside to* PETRUCHIO] An easy doer,

109   *Aye* (I MS).
     cuts F (cutte MS).
     cuts hurts, damages.
     it i.e. Petruchio's estate.
111   *too* F (to MS).
     civil like that of a citizen (as opposed to a gentlewoman or lady).
112   *There's . . . too* Laces consisted of thread with wire (of gold, silver, copper, etc)
     wound around it; Maria complains that too much silk is visible through the
     precious metal.
114   *suit* set.
115   *cast* pairs (two hawks would be cast off at the same time).
116   *so* so long as.
     sound healthy.
     flying rapid.
117   *for* i.e. intending to go to.
119   *great horse* warhorse, charger (thought inappropriate for women).
120   *run a-tilt* take part in tournaments (probably also carries sexual innuendo: either
     Maria will be promiscuous, or she will insist in being the dominant partner during
     sex).
121   *to learn* i.e. to ride, but in context the statement may be read as an unconscious
     response to Petruchio's last line.
122   *an easy doer* a gentle ride (but with a sexual pun on 'do', which Sophocles picks up
     in l. 123).

Did you hear that?

PETRUCHIO   Yes, I shall meet her morals
Ere it be long, I fear not.

[*Exeunt* SERVANTS]

MARIA [*To* PETRUCHIO *and* SOPHOCLES]
                    Oh, good morrow.   125

SOPHOCLES
Good morrow, lady. How is't now?

MARIA   Faith, sickly,
This house stands in an ill air –

PETRUCHIO [*Aside*]   Yet more charges!

MARIA
Subject to rots and rheums. Out on't, 'tis nothing
But a tiled fog.

PETRUCHIO   What think you of the lodge, then?

MARIA
I like the seat, but 'tis too little. Sophocles,   130
Let me have your opinion; thou hast judgement.

PETRUCHIO
[*Aside*] 'Tis very well.

MARIA   What if I pluck it down,
And build a square upon it with two courts
Still rising from the entrance?

PETRUCHIO [*Aside*]   And i' th' midst,
A college for your young scolds.

123–4   F (*An . . . that?* / *Yes* MS).
   124   *meet her morals* i.e. sink to her level.
   127   [*Aside*] This line and Petruchio's following speeches (ll. 132, 134–5 and the first half
         of ll.138–9) might be said aloud, as hostile interruptions during Maria's speech, but
         they seem more likely to be asides, delivered either to self or to Sophocles.
   128   *rots* (1) rotting of the fabric of the house; (2) the rot, a liver disease in sheep fed on
         moist pasture-land; (3) diseases more generally, including venereal disease.
         rheums conditions caused by an excess of moisture, especially colds, catarrh and
         rheumatic pains.
         Out on't Curses upon it.
   129   *lodge* a smaller building in the grounds of an estate, often occupied by a game-
         keeper or gardener.
   130   *seat* position, location.
   131   *your* MS (*thy* F).
   133   *build* ed. (*built* MS, F).
         courts courtyards.
134–5   F (*And . . . scoldes* / *&* MS).
   135   *your young* MS (*yong* F).
         A . . . scolds i.e. a training-place for disobedient wives.

191

MARIA   And to the southward   135
   Take in a garden of some twenty acres,
   And cast it of the Italian fashion, hanging.
PETRUCHIO [*Aside*] And you could cast yourself so too.
   [*To* MARIA]   Pray, lady,
   Will not this cost much money?
MARIA   Some five thousand,
   Say six. I'll have it battled too.
PETRUCHIO   And gilt? Maria,   140
   This is a fearful course you take; pray think on't.
   You are a woman now, a wife, and his
   That must in honesty look for
   Some due obedience from you.
MARIA   That bare word
   Shall cost you many a pound more. Build upon't,   145
   Tell me of due obedience. What's a husband?
   What are we married for? To carry sumpters?
   Are we not one piece with you, and as worthy
   Our own intentions as you yours?
PETRUCHIO   Pray hear me.
MARIA
   Take two small drops of water, equal weighed;   150
   Tell me which is the heaviest, and which ought
   First to descend in duty.
PETRUCHIO   ·   You mistake me.
   I urge not service from you, nor obedience
   In way of duty, but of love and credit;
   All I expect is but a noble care   155

---

137   *hanging* i.e. appearing to hang, by being situated on a steep slope or on top of a
      wall.
138   *And . . . too* i.e. I wish you could hang yourself.
139   *five thousand* £5000 would be worth around £489,400 at time of writing (2009).
140   *six* £6000 would be worth around £587,280 in 2009.
      battled decorated with battlements.
141   *on't* i.e. about it.
143   *honesty* MS (honesty, and justice F).
144   *due* rightful, appropriate.
147   *sumpters* packs or saddle-bags.
148   *one piece* (1) equal; (2) alludes to the Biblical narrative in which Eve is created from
      Adam's rib (Genesis 2.18–25); (3) refers to the idea that the husband and wife
      became 'one flesh' on marriage.
150   *equal weighed* i.e. of equal weight.
154   *credit* (1) reputation, personal honour; (2) trust.

Of what I have brought you, and of what I am,
And what our name may be.

MARIA   That's in my making.

PETRUCHIO
'Tis true, it is so.

MARIA   Yes it is, Petruchio,
For there was never man without our moulding,
Without our stamp upon him, and our justice,   160
Left anything three ages after him
Good, and his own.

SOPHOCLES   Good lady, understand him.

MARIA
I do too much, good Sophocles. He's one
Of a most spiteful self-condition,
Never at peace with anything but age,   165
That has no teeth left to return his anger.
A bravery dwells in his blood yet of abusing
His first good wife; he's sooner fire than powder,
And sooner mischief.

PETRUCHIO   If I be so sudden,
Do not you fear me?

MARIA   No, nor yet care for you;   170
And if it may be lawful, I defy you.

PETRUCHIO
Does this become you now?

MARIA   It shall become me.

PETRUCHIO
Thou disobedient, weak, vainglorious woman,
Were I but half so wilful as thou spiteful,
I should now drag thee to thy duty.

MARIA   Drag me?   175

---

157   *name* family name, reputation.
161   *Left* i.e. who left.
      ages generations.
163   *too* F (to MS).
      good MS (sweet F).
164   *self-condition* character.
165   *age* i.e. old people.
167   *bravery* bravado, swaggering.
168   *sooner . . . powder* quicker to take fire than gunpowder.
169   *sudden* impetuous.
173   *vainglorious* vain, boastful.

PETRUCHIO

But I am friends again. Take all your pleasure.

MARIA

Now you perceive him, Sophocles.

PETRUCHIO   I love thee

Above thy vanity, thou faithless creature.

MARIA

[*To* SOPHOCLES] Would I had been so happy when I married

But to have met an honest man like thee,   180

For I am sure thou art good, I know thou art honest,

A handsome, hurtless man, a loving man,

Though never a penny with him; and those eyes,

That face, and that true heart. Wear this for my sake.

[*She gives him a ring*]

And when thou thinkst upon me, pity me.   185

I am cast away.   *Exit* MARIA

SOPHOCLES   Why, how now, man?

PETRUCHIO   Pray leave me,

And follow your advices.

SOPHOCLES   The man's jealous!

PETRUCHIO

I shall find a time ere it be long to ask you

One or two foolish questions.

SOPHOCLES   I shall answer

As well as I am able when you call me.   190

[*Aside*] If she mean true, 'tis but a little killing,

And if I do not venture it, rots take me.

[*To* PETRUCHIO] Farewell, sir.   *Exit* SOPHOCLES

---

176   *friends* F (friend MS).
       Take all your pleasure i.e. do as you please.
       your Petruchio's use of the formal 'you' signals his attempt to control his temper,
       but in his next speech he quickly switches back to 'thou'.
179   *happy* fortunate.
182   *hurtless* harmless.
183   *never . . . him* i.e. not rich.
187   *follow your advices* i.e. do as you please.
       The . . . jealous! This line might be delivered as an aside.
191   *'tis . . . killing* i.e. I'm only risking my life (said ironically).
       but only.
192   *it, rots take me* MS (its —).
       rots . . . me an oath similar in effect and force to 'I'll be damned' ('rots' here refers
       to venereal disease).

PETRUCHIO   Pray, farewell. Is there no keeping
A wife to one man's use? No wintering
This cattle without straying? 'Tis hard dealing,   195
Very hard dealing, gentlemen, strange dealing.
Now, in the name of madness, what star reigned,
What dog-star, bull- or bear-star, when I married
This second wife, this whirlwind that takes all
Within her compass? Was I not well warned   200
(I thought I had, and I believe I know it)
And beaten to repentance in the days
Of my first doting? Had I not wife enough
To turn my tools to? Did I want vexation
Or any special care to kill my heart?   205
Had I not every morning a rare breakfast
Mixed with a learned lecture of ill language
Louder than Tom o' Lincoln, and at dinner
A diet of the same dish? Was there evening
That e'er passed over us without 'Thou knave',   210
Or 'Thou whore' for digestion? Had I ever

194   *wintering* keeping over winter.
195   *This* MS (These F).
      This cattle See II.i.90 n.
      without straying without it straying.
      hard dealing a rough deal, harsh treatment.
196   *gentlemen* i.e. the gentleman in the audience, some of whom may have been sitting
      on stools on the stage if *The Tamer Tamed* was performed in an indoor playhouse.
197–8 *what . . . star* i.e. what were the (fateful) astrological conditions (the 'dog-star' is
      Sirius in the constellation Canis Major, associated with the stifling 'dog-days' of
      August, which are in turn associated with madness; the 'bull' and 'bear' refer to the
      constellations of Taurus and Ursa Major).
200   *compass* reach.
201   *had* had been.
203   *doting* infatuation.
204   *turn . . . to* get to work on (with sexual innuendo).
      tools MS (love F).
      to ed. (too MS).
      want lack.
205   *care* hardship.
206   *rare* F (reare MS).
      rare exceptional.
208   *Tom o' Lincoln* Probably refers to the famous bell in Lincoln cathedral, which was
      re-cast in December 1610 and hung on 27 January 1611; the original Tom o'
      Lincoln is a romance hero who appears in early modern fiction and drama.

A pull at this same poor sport men run mad for,
But like a cur I was fain to show my teeth first,
And almost worry her? And did heaven forgive me,
And take this serpent from me, and am I   215
Keeping tame devils now again? My heart aches.
Something I must do speedily. I'll die
If I can handsomely, for that's the way
To make a rascal of her. I am sick,
And I'll go very near it, but I'll perish.   *Exit* 220

[ACT III, SCENE iii]

Enter LIVIA, BIANCA, ROLAND [*and*] TRANIO

LIVIA
Then I must be content, sir, with my fortune.
ROLAND
And I with mine.
LIVIA   I did not think a look,
Or a poor word or two, could have displanted
Such a fixed constancy, and for your end too.
ROLAND
Come, come, I know your courses. There's your gewgaws,   5
Your rings, and bracelets, and the purse you gave me;

---

212   *pull* attempt.
        sport entertainment, sexual play.
        run i.e. go.
213   *cur* bad-tempered dog.
        fain eager.
214   *worry* attack (often used of a dog or wolf).
215   *serpent* Disruptive women are often compared to snakes in early modern texts, due
        to a conflation of the Biblical Eve with the serpent that was said to have tempted
        her (Genesis 3.1–6).
218   *can* can do it.
219   *make . . . her* i.e. to get the better of her.
220   *I'll perish* (1) I'll die; (2) I'll be damned; (3) I'll sink, I'll be shipwrecked; (4) I'll be
        ruined.

        [*Act III, Scene iii*] ed. (*Scæna Quarta.* F).
  4   *for your end* i.e. for your benefit.

The money's spent in entertaining you
At plays and cherry gardens.   [*He gives her the tokens*]
LIVIA   There's your chain too.
                              [*She gives him the chain*]
But if you'll give me leave, I'll wear the hair still;
I would yet remember you.
BIANCA   Give his love, wench,   10
The young man has employment for't.
TRANIO   Fie, Roland!
ROLAND
You cannot fie me out a hundred pound
With this pure plot. [*Aside*] Yet let me never see day more
If something do not struggle strangely in me.
BIANCA
Young man, let me talk with you.
ROLAND   Well, young woman?   15
BIANCA
This was your mistress once?
ROLAND   Yes.
BIANCA   Are ye honest?
I see you are young and handsome.
ROLAND   I am honest.
BIANCA
Why, that's well said. And there's no doubt your judgement
Is good enough, and strong enough, to tell you
Who are your foes and friends. Why did you leave her?   20
ROLAND
She made a puppy of me.
BIANCA   Be that granted,
She must do so sometimes, and oftentimes,

7–8   F (*the . . . playes* / & MS).
   8   *too* F (to MS).
   9   *the hair* i.e. a lock of Roland's hair, kept in a locket.
  10   *Give his love* i.e. give him back his love, so that he can become entangled with
       another woman.
       his MS (him his F).
       love MS, F (lock ed.)
  11   *Fie* An expression of reproach or disgust.
  13   *pure* MS (poore F).
       pure guileless, obvious.
       let . . . more A mild oath (comparable with 'I'll be blowed').
  15   *woman* F (man MS).
  21   *puppy* fool (often used of young men).

Love were too serious else.

ROLAND   A witty woman.

BIANCA

   Had ye loved me –

ROLAND   I would I had.

BIANCA   And dearly,

   And I had loved you so – you may love worse, sir,   25
   But that is not material.

ROLAND [*Aside*]   I shall lose.

BIANCA

   Some time or other, for variety,
   I should have called ye fool, or boy, or bid ye
   Play with the pages, but have loved you still
   Out of all question, and extremely too.   30
   You are a man made to be loved.

ROLAND [*Aside*]   This woman
   Either abuses me, or loves me dearly.

BIANCA

   I'll tell you one thing. If I were to choose
   A husband to my own mind, I should think
   One of your mother's making would content me,   35
   For o' my conscience she gets good ones.

ROLAND   Lady,
   I'll leave you to your commendations.
   [*Aside*] I am in again; the devil take their tongues!

                                          [*He goes to leave*]

BIANCA

   You shall not go.

ROLAND   I will. [*To* LIVIA] Yet thus far, Livia,
   Your sorrow may induce me to forgive ye,   40
   But never love again. [*Aside*] If I stay longer,

---

23   *else* otherwise.
26   *material* important, relevant.
     lose i.e. lose the bet.
32   *abuses* (1) insults; (2) deceives.
     dearly MS (deadly F).
34   *to my own mind* according to my own tastes.
     my MS (mine F).
36   *gets* MS (makes F).
     gets begets.
38   *in* i.e. in trouble, in too deep.

I have lost two hundred pound.   [*He goes to leave*]

LIVIA   Good, sir, but thus much –

TRANIO

Turn if thou be'st a man.

LIVIA   But one kiss of ye,

One parting kiss, and I am gone too.

ROLAND   Come.   [*They kiss*]

[*Aside*] I shall kiss fifty pound away at this clap!   45

[*To* LIVIA] We'll have one more, and then farewell. [*They kiss*]

LIVIA   Farewell, sir.

BIANCA

Well, go thy ways. Thou bear'st a kind heart with thee.

TRANIO

H'as made a stand.

BIANCA   A noble, brave young fellow

Worthy a wench indeed.

ROLAND   I will – I will not –   *Exit* ROLAND

TRANIO

Is gone, but shot again. Play you but your part   50

And I will keep my promise. Forty angels

In fair gold, lady. Wipe your eyes; he's yours

If I have any wit.

LIVIA   I'll pay the forfeit.

BIANCA

Come, then, let's see your sister, how she fares now

After her skirmish; and be sure Moroso   55

Be kept in good hand. Then all's perfect, Livia.

                                    Exeunt

---

42   *two hundred pound* i.e. because he would be in love with Livia and have another
     woman in love with him (see III.i.66–80).

44   *too* F (to MS).

45   *at this clap* in one blow, at once.

46   *sir* MS (*om*. F).

50   *shot again* i.e. with Cupid's arrow.

51   *angels* gold coins worth around 10 shillings which had an image of the archangel
     Michael on them; forty angels would have been worth around £20 (equivalent to
     around £1,957.60 in 2009).

52   *Wipe* F (to wipe MS).

53   *I'll pay the forfeit* i.e. I'll willingly lose the forty angels (to Tranio, if he succeeds).

55   *skirmish* Continues the use of military language in connection with Maria's
     activities.

[ACT III, SCENE iv]

Enter PEDRO *and* JAQUES

PEDRO
Oh, Jaques, Jaques, what becomes of us?
Oh, my sweet master!
JAQUES   Run for a physician
And a whole peck of 'pothecaries, Pedro:
He will die, 'diddle diddle, die' if they come not quickly;
And bring all empirics straight, and mountebanks   5
Skilful in lungs and livers; raise the neighbours,
And all the aqua-vitae bottles extant;
And oh, the parson, Pedro, oh, the parson!
A little of his comfort, never so little –
Twenty to one you find him at the Bush: 10
There's the best ale.
PEDRO   I fly.   *Exit* PEDRO

Enter MARIA [*and*] SERVANTS
carrying out household stuff and trunks

[*Act III, Scene iv*] ed. (*Scena quinta*. F).
0   s.d. *Enter . . .* JAQUES MS. (*Enter Jaques and Pedro* F).
3   *peck* considerable number, crowd.
    'pothecaries apothecaries.
4   *die . . . die* Incorporates a common refrain from popular songs, similar to the 'dilly
    dilly' found in 'Lavender's Blue'.
5–6 *empirics . . . Skilful* MS (people that are skilfull F).
5   *empirics* (1) physicians who base their diagnosis on personal observation; (2)
    quack-doctors.
    straight straightaway.
    mountebanks travelling medics (often considered charlatans) who sold medicines
    and remedies.
7   *aqua-vitae* spirits used as restoratives (e.g. brandy).
8   *And . . . parson!* Jaques is apparently overcome with emotion and can barely bring
    himself to mention the parson, who would administer the last rites to a dying man.
10 *Bush* i.e. a pub called the Bush.
11 *fly* flee, make haste.
11 s.d. *Enter . . . trunks* MS (*Enter Maria, and Servants*. F).
    household stuff utensils, linens, goods, etc. belonging to the household (Maria is
    clearing out everything portable.)

MARIA [*To* SERVANTS]   Out with the trunks, ho!
[*To* JAQUES] Why are you idle, sirrah? Up to the chamber,
And take the hangings down, and see the linen
Packed up and sent away within this half hour.
What, are the carts come yet? Some honest body   15
Help down the chests of plate, and some the wardrobe.
Alas, we are undone else!
JAQUES   Pray, forsooth,
And I beseech you, tell me, is 'a dead yet?
MARIA
No, but is drawing on. [*To* SERVANTS] Out with the armour!
JAQUES
Then I'll go see him.
MARIA   Thou art undone then, fellow;   20
No man that has been near him come near me.

> *Enter* SOPHOCLES, PETRONIUS, LIVIA,
> BIANCA [*and*] TRANIO

SOPHOCLES
Why, how now, lady, what means this?
PETRONIUS   Now, daughter,
How does my son?
MARIA [*To* SERVANTS] Save all ye can, for heaven's sake!
LIVIA
Be of good comfort, sister.
MARIA   Oh, my casket!
PETRONIUS
How does thy husband, woman?
MARIA   Get you gone   25
If you have a care to save your lives! The sickness –

16   *wardrobe* clothing.
18   *you* MS (ye F).
19   *drawing on* i.e. getting close.
21   s.d. *Enter* . . . TRANIO MS (*Enter Sophocles, and Petronius.* F).
23   F inserts a stage direction, '*Enter Livia, Byancha, and Tranio*' here.
24   *casket* small box, often expensively decorated, used for storing prized objects such
       as jewels and letters.
26   *have a care* MS (mean F).
       sickness i.e. plague, which was endemic in Britain in the early seventeenth century,
       and which often led to the closure of London's playhouses: there was a prolonged
       outbreak in 1608–9, not long before the writing and first performance of *The
       Tamer Tamed*.

PETRONIUS
   Stand further off, I prithee!
MARIA   Is i' th' house, sir.
   My husband has it now, and raves extremely.
   Give some counsel, friends.
BIANCA   Why, lock the doors up,
   And send him in a woman to attend him!   30
MARIA
   I have bespoke two women, and the city
   Has sent a watch, I thank 'em; meat nor money
   He shall not want, nor prayers.
PETRONIUS   How long is't
   Since it first took him?

Enter the WATCHMEN

MARIA   But within this three hours.
   I am frighted from my wits, my friends. The watch!   35
   [*To* WATCHMEN] Pray do your office, lock the doors up fast,
   And patience be his angel.   *They lock the door*
TRANIO   This comes unlooked for.
MARIA
   I'll to the lodge; some that are kind, and love me,
   I know will visit me.
PETRUCHIO [*Within*]   Do you hear, my masters?
   You that lock the doors up?
PETRONIUS   'Tis his voice.   40
TRANIO
   Hold, and let's hear him.

---

    27   *off* F (of MS).
    28   *now, and* MS (now; / Alas he is infected, and F).
    29   *Give some* MS (Give me some F).
    31   *bespoke* ordered, arranged.
    32   *watch* guard.
          I thank 'em MS (by this time F).
 33–4   ed. (He . . . prayers. / How . . . him? / But F).
    35   *my friends. The watch!* MS (O here's the watch F).
    36   *fast* MS (friends F).
    37   *comes unlooked for* i.e. is unexpected.
    39   *Within* In MS the speech prefix is 'Petruchio w^{th}in'; F places a stage direction
          ('*Petruchio within*') in the right hand margin.
39–40   ed. (Doe . . . vp MS).
    40   *You* MS (Ho, you F).

PETRUCHIO   Will ye starve me here?
  Am I a traitor, or an heretic,
  Or am I grown infectious?
PETRONIUS   Pray, sir, pray –
PETRUCHIO
  I am as well as you are, goodman puppy!
MARIA
  Pray, have patience.   45
  [*Calling to* PETRUCHIO] You shall want nothing, sir.
PETRUCHIO   I want a cudgel
  And thee, thou wickedness!
PETRONIUS   He speaks well enough.
MARIA
  Had ever a strong heart, sir.
PETRUCHIO   Will ye hear me?
  First, be pleased
  To think I know ye all, and can distinguish   50
  Every man's several voice: you that spoke first
  I know my father-in-law; the other, Tranio;
  And I heard Sophocles; the last, pray mark me,
  Is my damned wife, Maria. Gentlemen,
  'Death, gentlemen, do you make a May-game on me?   55
  I tell you once again, I am as sound,
  As well, as wholesome, and as sensible
  As any of ye all. Let me out quickly
  Or, as I am a man, I'll beat the walls down,
  And the first thing I light upon shall pay for't.   60
PETRONIUS
  Fetch a doctor presently, and if
  He can do no good on him, he must to Bedlam.

---

44   *goodman* A respectful form of address for a man with a social status below that of
       gentleman, often used condescendingly.
48   *Had* He had.
48–9 F (Will . . . pleasd MS).
54   *Maria. Gentlemen* F omits 'Gentlemen' and adds at this point a short sequence in
       which the doctor arrives and attempts to diagnose Petruchio; the surrounding
       dialogue is also reworked: see Appendix 1, Passage E.
55   *'Death* MS (— F).   *you* MS (ye F).
       May-game i.e. a fool.   *on* of.
57   *sensible* sane.
61–2 ed. (Fetch . . . presently, / and . . . Bedlam MS).
62   *Bedlam* See I.iii.81 n.

PETRUCHIO

Will it please ye open?

TRANIO   His fit grows stronger still.

MARIA

Let's save ourselves. He's past all worldly cure.

PETRONIUS

[*To* WATCHMEN] Friends, do your office.   65
And what he wants – if money, love, or labour,
Or any way may win it, let him have it.
Farewell, and pray, my honest friends.

Exeunt [*all except the*] WATCHMEN

PETRUCHIO   Why, rascals!

Friends! Gentlemen! Thou beastly wife! Jaques!
None hear me? Who's at the door there?

FIRST WATCHMAN   Think, I pray, sir,   70

Whither ye are going, and prepare yourself.

SECOND WATCHMAN

These idle thoughts disturb ye. The good gentlewoman
Your wife has taken care you shall want nothing.

PETRUCHIO

The blessing of her grandam Eve light on her,
Nothing but thin fig-leaves to hide her knavery!   75
Shall I come out in quiet, answer me,
Or shall I charge a fowling piece, and make
Mine own way? Two of ye I cannot miss,
If I miss three. Ye come here to assault me.

FIRST WATCHMAN

There's onions roasting for your sore, sir.

---

64   ed. (Let's . . . all / worldly care. MS).   *ourselves* MS (ourselves, sir F).
68   s.d. *Exeunt . . .* WATCHMEN ed. (*Exeunt. / manent Watchmen.* MS).
71   FIRST WATCHMAN ed. (1. Watch MS) and at ll. 80, 83, 87.
72–3   F (These . . . ye, / The . . . care / You . . . nothing MS).
72   SECOND WATCHMAN ed. (2. Watch MS) and at l. 83
74–5   *The . . . knavery* MS (*om.* F). These lines may have been censored in F.
74   *grandam* grandmother.   *light* fall.
75   *Nothing . . . knavery* i.e. may she have nothing to conceal her wickedness. According
       to Biblical narrative, Adam and Eve first became aware of their nakedness after they
       succumbed to temptation and ate the fruit of the forbidden tree (Genesis 3.7).
76   *in quiet* quietly, peacefully.
77   *charge* load, prepare.
       fowling piece handgun, of the kind used to shoot wildfowl.
79   *If* Even if.
80   *onions* to make a poultice for Petruchio's supposed plague sores.

PETRUCHIO   People,   80
    I am as excellent well, I thank heaven for't,
    And have as good a stomach at this instant –
SECOND WATCHMAN
    That's an ill sign.
FIRST WATCHMAN Aye, he draws on; he's a dead man.
PETRUCHIO
    And sleep as soundly. Will ye look upon me?
FIRST WATCHMAN
    Do ye want pen and ink? While you have sense, sir,   85
    Settle your state.
PETRUCHIO   Sirs, I am as well as you are,
    Or any rascal living.
FIRST WATCHMAN   Would you were, sir.
PETRUCHIO
    Look to yourselves, and if ye love your lives,
    Open the door and fly me, for I shoot else:
    I swear I'll shoot, and presently, chain-bullets,   90
    And under four I will not kill.
SECOND WATCHMAN   Let's quit him.
    It may be 'tis a trick.
FIRST WATCHMAN
    The devil take the hindmost, I cry.

                                      Exeunt running

Enter PETRUCHIO *with a piece, and forces the door open*

80–1   *There's . . . People* MS (*om.* F).
  82   *stomach* appetite.
  83   *Aye* ed. (I MS, *om.* F).
  86   *Settle your state* i.e. make your will.   *as well* MS (wel, as F).
  88   *lives* F (lifes MS).
  89   *fly me* flee from me.
  90   *I swear* MS (— F; [God's light,] ed.)
        chain-bullets chain-shot: 'A kind of shot formed of two balls, or half-balls,
        connected by a chain', often used in naval warfare (*OED*).
  91   SECOND WATCHMAN ed. (2. Watch MS; *1 Watch* F).
        quit leave.
  92   *trick,* MS (trick: he's dangerous F).
  93   FIRST WATCHMAN ed. (1. Watch MS; *2 Watch* F).
        The . . . hindmost i.e. the devil will catch the last to leave: let's get out of here.
  93   s.d. *Enter . . . open* MS (*Enter Petruchio with a piece* F); in the RSC production of
        2003, Petruchio broke in by firing at the door.
        s.d. *piece* firearm.

PETRUCHIO
    Have among ye!
    The door shall open too; I'll have a fair shot!   95
    Are all gone? Tricks in my old days? Crackers
    Put now upon me? And by Lady Greensleeves?
    Am I grown so tame after all my triumphs?
    But that I should be thought mad if I railed
    As much as they deserve against these women,   100
    I would now rip up from the primitive cuckold
    All their arch-villainies, and all their doubts,
    Which are more than a hunted hare e'er thought on.
    When a man has the fairest and the sweetest
    Of all their sex and, as he thinks, the noblest,   105
    What has he then? And I'll speak modestly –
    He has a quartain ague, that shall shake
    All his estate to nothing, never cured,
    Nor never dying; h'as a ship to venture
    His fame and credit in, which if 'a man not   110
    With more continual labour than a galley
    To make her tithe, either she grows a tumbrel
    Not worth the cloth she wears, or springs more leaks
    Than all the fame of his posterity

94   *Have among ye* Watch out.
96   *Are all* MS (Are ye F).
       in my old days i.e. at my age.
       Crackers Lies.
97   *Lady Greensleeves* inconstant heroine of a popular song often attributed to Henry
       VIII (refers to Maria).
99   *railed* ranted.
101   *primitive cuckold* i.e. the first man whose wife cheated on him.
102   *doubts* MS (dobles F; doubles ed.)
       doubts (1) fears; (2) strongholds.
107   *quartain ague* a fever or sickness that recurs every four days.
109   *h'as* F (has MS); he has.
112   *tithe* i.e. to pay her the money owed to her (a tithe is a 10 per cent tax).
       grows a grows into a.
       tumbrel (1) a flat-bottomed boat or barge, and, by extension, a drunkard; (2) a
       dung-cart; (3) an instrument of punishment, often associated with the cucking
       stool used to discipline unruly wives.
113   *springs more leaks* i.e. engages in more incontinent sexual behaviour (continuing
       the nautical flavour of *tumbrel*).
114–15 *Than . . . again* i.e. than the good reputations of his children and descendents can
       conceal.
110   *'a* he.

Can ever stop again. Out on 'em, hedgehogs!   115
He that shall touch 'em has a thousand thorns
Runs through his fingers. If I were unmarried
I would do anything below repentance,
Any base dunghill slavery, be a hangman,
Ere I would be a husband. Oh, the thousand,   120
Thousand, ten thousand ways they have to kill us!
Some fall with too much stringing of the fiddles,
And those are fools; some that they are not suffered,
And those are maudlin lovers; some like scorpions
They poison with their tails, and those are martyrs;   125
Some die with doing good, those benefactors,
And leave 'em land to leap away; some few –
For those are rarest – they are said to kill
With kindness and fair usage, but what they are
My catalogue discovers not, only 'tis thought   130
They are buried in old walls with their heels upward.
I could rail twenty days together now.
I'll seek 'em out, and if I have not reason,
And very sensible, why this was done,
I'll go a-birding yet, and some shall smart for't.   *Exit*   135

115   *Can . . . hedgehogs* MS (Can ever stop againe: I could raile twenty daies; / Out on 'em
       hedge-hogs F).
       Out on 'em Curses on them.
       hedgehogs prickly beasts.
118   *below* short of.
119   *dunghill* a byword for inferior working conditions.
120   *Ere* Before.
122   *Some . . . fiddles* i.e. some are worn out by having to pleasure their wives sexually
       (compare I.iv.6–7).
       too F (to MS).
123   *not suffered* i.e. rejected.
125   *poison . . . tails* infect with venereal disease (*tail* is a slang term for the female genitals).
126   *die . . . good* i.e. die, leaving their wives as well-to-do widows.
127   *leap away* squander (possibly involving dancing or other forms of public display).
128   *those* F (these MS).
       they i.e. the women.
131   *They . . . upward* (1) refers to the supposed burial position of cowards; (2) refers to
       undignified sexual posture (Perhaps these husbands have to submit sexually in order
       to please their wives and win 'kindness and fair usage' from them.)
133   *'em* i.e. Maria, Petronius, Sophocles, *et al*.
134   *sensible* reasonable.
135   *a-birding* hunting for birds.
       some . . . for't i.e. someone will pay.

ACT IV, SCENE i

Enter PETRUCHIO, JAQUES *and* PEDRO

JAQUES
    And, as I told your worship, all the hangings,
    Brass, pewter-plate, even to the very pisspots.
PEDRO
    And that that hung for our defence, the armour,
    And the March beer was going too. Oh, Jaques,
    What a sad sight was that?
JAQUES   Even the two roundlets,   5
    The two that was our hope of muscadel –
    Better ne'er tongue tipped over – those two cannons
    To batter brawn withal at Christmas, sir,
    Even those two lovely twins, the enemy
    Had almost cut off clean.
PETRUCHIO   Go trim the house up,   10
    And put the things in order as they were.

                                    Exit JAQUES *and* PEDRO
    I shall find time for all this. Could I find her
    But constant any way, I had done my business:
    Were she a whore directly, or a scold,

Act IV, Scene i ed. (ACTVS IIII. Scæna j.^{ma} MS) F inserts an extra scene here, featuring discussion between Moroso and Petronius, and between Petronius and Bianca: see Appendix 1, Passage F.

2   *pisspots* MS (looking-glasses F).
     pisspots chamber-pots.
3   *that that* that which.
4   *March beer* strong beer, usually brewed in the spring.
     too F (to MS).
5   *roundlets* small casks, apparently holding muscadel wine.
7   *tipped* MS (tipt) (tript F).
     tipped made itself drunk (*OED* tip v.² 5).
     those MS (these F).
7–8 *cannons . . . withal* Jaques imagines the wine as artillery to be directed against the main part of the Christmas meal.
8   *brawn* the flesh of a boar or pig (probably here refers to roast boar).
9   *those* F (these MS).
10 *off* F (of MS).
     trim tidy.
13 *But . . . way* i.e. consistent in anything.
14 *directly* straightforwardly, completely.

An unthrift, or a woman made to hate me,   15
I had my wish and knew which way to rein her.
But while she shows all these, and all their losses,
A kind of linsey-wolsey mingled mischief
Not to be guessed at, and whether true or borrowed
Not certain neither – what a hap had I,   20

Enter MARIA

And what a tidy fortune, when my fate
Flung me upon this bear whelp? Here she comes.
Now, if she have a colour for this fault –
A cleanly one – upon my conscience,
I shall forgive her yet, and find a something   25
Certain I married for: her wit. I'll mark her.

MARIA

[*To herself*] Not let his wife come near him in his sickness?
Not come to comfort him, she that all laws
Of heaven and nations have ordained his second?
Is she refused? And two old paradoxes,   30
Pieces of five and fifty without faith,
Clapped in upon him? Has a little pet,
That all young wives must follow necessary,
Having their maidenheads –

15   *unthrift* spendthrift.
16   *rein her* rein her in (but there is probably an aural pun on 'reign': rule).
18   *linsey-woolsey* cloth made from a mixture of wool and flax, used metaphorically to mean a confused mixture.
20   *what a hap* what luck (said ironically).
     s.d. MS has entrance directions for Maria in both margins.
21   *tidy* excellent (also said ironically).
22   *bear whelp* baby bear: shapeless thing (compare III.i.46).
23   *colour* pretext, excuse.
     for . . . fault MS (for the fault is F).
24   *cleanly* (1) neat, elegant, clever; (2) virtuous, chaste.
     upon my conscience i.e. upon my word, truly.
26   *Certain* (1) not variable, unchanging; (2) trustworthy; (3) in particular.
29   *second* i.e. his second self, his supporter (compare the use of a 'second' in a duel).
30   *two* F (the two MS).
     paradoxes impossible or contradictory things (here old women who are irreligious).
32   *Clapped . . . upon* Imprisoned with.
     pet fit of peevishness, childish sulk.
34   *Having their maidenheads* Refers to a belief that virginity and sexual frustration could lead to irrational behaviour in women.

PETRUCHIO [*Aside*]   This is an axiom
    I never heard before.
MARIA   Or say rebellion,   35
    If we durst be so foul – which two fair words
    Alas would win us from in an hour, an instant,
    We are so easy – made him so forgetful
    Both of his reason, honesty and credit,
    As to deny his wife a visitation?   40
    His wife that, though she was a little foolish,
    Loved him (O Heaven, forgive her for't!), nay, doted,
    Nay, had run mad had she not married him.
PETRUCHIO
    [*Aside*] Though I do know this falser than the devil,
    I cannot choose but love it.
MARIA   What do I know   45
    But those that came to keep him might have killed him?
    In what case had I been then? I dare not
    Believe him such a base, debauched companion
    That one refusal of a tender maid
    Would make him feign this sickness out of need,   50
    And take a keeper to him of fourscore
    To play at billiards: one that mewed content
    And all her teeth together. Not to come near him!
PETRUCHIO
    [*Aside*] This woman would have made a most rare Jesuit.
    She can prevaricate on anything;   55

34 *axiom* rule, maxim.
36 *two* F (too MS). MS's 'too' might be retained (i.e. 'which, too, fair words').
37 *would win* MS (would is interlined) (win F).
38 *easy* pliable, docile.
46 *But* But that.
    came F (come MS).
47 *In . . . been* i.e. in how much trouble would I have been.
    what case MS (what a case F).
48 *companion* (1) fellow; (2) marriage partner.
52–3 *that . . . together* i.e. that lost the capacity for sexual pleasure when she lost her teeth.
52 *mewed* shut away.
53 *to come* MS (come F).
54 *rare* excellent.
    Jesuit member of the Society of Jesus, a Roman Catholic order. Jesuit priests were often associated with manipulative or hypocritical rhetoric in Protestant England.
55 *prevaricate* quibble, speak evasively or hypocritically.

There was not to be thought a way to save her,
In all imagination, beside this.

MARIA

His unkind meaning, which was worst of all,
In sending, heaven knows whither, all the plate,
And all the household stuff, had I not crossed it   60
By a great providence and my friends' assistance,
Which he will thank me one day for. Alas!
I could have watched as well as they, have served him
In any use better and willinger.
The law commands me do it, love commands me,   65
And my own duty charges me.

PETRUCHIO [*Aside*]   Heaven bless me!
And now I have said my prayers, I'll go to her.
[*To* MARIA] Are you a wife for any man?

MARIA   For you, sir,
If I were worse, I were better. That ye are well
(At least that ye appear so) I thank heaven.   70
Long may it hold! And that you are here, I am glad too.
But that you have abused me wretchedly,
And such a way that shames the name of husband,
Such a malicious, mangy way, so mingled
(Never look strangely on me, I dare tell you)   75
With breach of honesty, care, kindness, manners –

PETRUCHIO

Holla: ye kick too fast!

56   *to be thought* F (thought MS).
56–7 *There . . . this* i.e. a better excuse could not be devised.
58   *unkind* cruel, unnatural.
      meaning MS (dealing F).
59   *whither* MS (whether: an alternative early modern spelling). The scribe originally
      wrote 'away', but crossed it out and interlined 'whether'.
62   *Alas* F (*om.* MS).
63   *I . . . watched* i.e. I could carry out the duty of watching.
      watched F (watch'd) (watch MS).
65   *me do* MS (me to do F).
66   *Heaven* MS, F ([God] ed.)
69   *If . . . better* i.e. the worse a wife I was, the better I would be suited to you.
71   *hold* last.
      too F (to MS).
74   *mangy* contemptible.
76   *breach* F (breacth MS: originally read 'breath' and a 'c' has been inserted).
77   *Holla* Stop there.
      too F (to MS).

MARIA   Was I a stranger?
Or had I vowed perdition to your person?
Am I not married to you? Tell me that.

PETRUCHIO
I would I could not tell you.

MARIA   Is my presence,   80
The stock I come of, which is worshipful –
If I should say 'right worshipful' I lied not:
My grandsire was a knight –

PETRUCHIO   O' th' shire.

MARIA   A soldier,
Which none of all thy family e'er heard of,
But one conductor of thy name, a grazier   85
That ran away with pay. Or am I grown –
Because I have been a little peevish to you,
Only to try your temper – such a dog-leech
I could not be admitted to your presence?

PETRUCHIO
If I endure this, hang me.

MARIA   And two death's heads,   90
Two Harry-groats that had their faces worn,

---

77   *stranger* someone unconnected by family ties.
78   *perdition* utter ruin, damnation.
80–6 *Is . . . pay* Maria begins a sentence which should end with something like 'hateful
       to you', but she gets distracted by comparing her and Petruchio's family histories.
81   *stock* family.
       worshipful honourable, of a high status (used as a term of address to high-ranking
       people).
82   *right worshipful* of an extremely high status (often used as a form of address to
       knights).
83   *grandsire* grandfather.
       O' th' shire Of the country (i.e. a member of the rural gentry rather than someone
       knighted for their brave deeds in battle).
84   *e'er heard of* could boast about.
85   *conductor* (1) carrier; (2) leader (i.e. a leading member of Petruchio's family).
86   *ran* F (runne MS).
       with MS, F (wi'th' ed.)
       with pay with a thrashing (that is, he left his employment in harsh circumstances).
88   *such a dog-leech* i.e. such a poor doctor.
       dog-leech (1) vet who treats dogs; (2) quack doctor.
90   *death's heads* skulls (referring back to the old women who tended to Petruchio).
91–2 *Two . . . too* Maria compares the women to coins that are so old that the face of the
       monarch and even his name are in danger of being worn away.
       Harry-groats see III.ii.38.

Almost their names too –
PETRUCHIO   Now hear me,
   For I will stay no longer.
MARIA   This you shall.
   However you shall think to flatter me
   For this offence, which no submission   95
   Can ever mediate for, you'll find it so;
   Whatever ye shall do by intercession,
   What ye can offer, what your land can purchase,
   What all your friends or families can win
   Shall be but this: not to forswear your knowledge   100
   But ever to forbear it. Now your will, sir.
PETRUCHIO
   Thou art the subtlest woman, I think, living;
   I am sure the lewdest. Now be still, and mark me.
   Were I but any way addicted to the devil,
   I should now think I had met a playfellow   105
   To profit by, and that way the most learned
   That ever taught to murmur. Tell me, thou,
   Thou most poor, paltry, spiteful whore – Do you cry?
   I'll make you roar before I leave –
MARIA   Your pleasure.
PETRUCHIO
   Was it not sin enough, thou fruiterer   110
   Full of the fall thou eat'st, thou devil's broker,

92   *names too* MS (names away too F).
93   *This you shall* i.e. you will stay to hear this.
96   *mediate for* intercede for, make amends on behalf of.
100 *forswear* abandon, renounce.
     knowledge acquaintance, (sexual) intimacy.
101 *But . . . sir.* F (*om.* MS). The scribe apparently missed a line.
     forbear endure, tolerate.
     your will i.e. tell me what you want.
102 *subtlest* most crafty.
104 *but* i.e. in.   *addicted* devoted.
106 *that way* in that way, according to those standards.
107 *murmur* whisper, insinuate.
108 *paltry* worthless, petty.
109 *roar* The scribe originally wrote 'cry', then crossed it out.
110 *fruiterer* dealer in fruit (i.e. the fruit of the forbidden tree that Eve ate and gave to
     Adam in the Biblical narrative [Genesis 3.1–6]).
111 *fall* sin (refers to the fall from the Garden of Eden).
     broker agent, dealer (refers in particular to a dealer in second-hand goods).

Thou seminary of all sedition,
Thou sword of vengeance, with a thread hung o'er us,
Was it not sin enough, and wickedness
In full abundance, was it not vexation   115
At all points *cap-à-pie* – nay, I shall pinch ye
Thus like a rotten rascal – to abuse
The name of heaven, the tie of marriage,
The honour of thy friends, the expectation
Of all that thought thee virtuous, with rebellion,   120
Childish and base rebellion, but continue
After forgiveness too? And worse, your mischief,
And against him – setting the hope of heaven by,
And the dear reservation of his honour –
Nothing above ground could have won to hate thee?   125
Well, go thy ways.

MARIA   Yes.   [*She goes to leave*]
PETRUCHIO   You shall hear me out first.
What punishment mayst thou deserve, thou thing,
Thou idle thing of nothing, thou pulled primrose
That two hours after art a weed, and withered,
For this last flourish on me? Am I one   130
Selected out of all the husbands living
To be so ridden by a tit of ten pence?

112   *seminary* seed-plot; training place (especially used of colleges in which Roman Catholic priests were trained).
113   *Thou . . . us* In classical legend the flattering courtier Damocles swaps places with the tyrant Dionysius for a day, and at a banquet he is disconcerted to find that a sword is suspended over his head, hanging on a single horse-hair. The 'sword of Damocles' thus emblematises the constant fear and uncertainty that an autocratic ruler experiences. In Petruchio's imagination, Maria is herself the sword which might unpredictably fall on mankind.
116   *At all points* In every way.
       cap-à-pie from head to foot (derives from military terminology).
       pinch attack, bite.
121   *continue* MS (continuing F).
123–5 *against . . . thee* i.e. against the person who could never hate you, as long as it did not affect his honour and his hope of salvation and eternal life.
126   *go thy ways* go ahead; the term also means 'get along with you', or 'go away', which is the meaning that Maria takes.
128   *pulled* uprooted, plucked.
130   *flourish* display (especially used of the gestures made by fencers at the start of a match); linguistic display.
132   *tit* girl, hussy.
       of i.e. worth (Daileader and Taylor gloss 'tit of ten pence' as 'two-bit hussy').

Am I so blind and bed-rid? I was mad,
And had the plague, and no man must come near me;
I must be shut up, and my substance 'bezzled   135
And an old woman watch me –

MARIA   Well, sir, well,
You may glory in't.

PETRUCHIO
And when it comes to opening, 'tis my plot:
I must undo myself, forsooth. Dost hear me?
If I should beat thee now as much as may be,   140
Dost thou not well deserve it, o' thy conscience,
Dost thou not cry 'Come beat me'?

MARIA   I defy you,
And my last loving tears, farewell. The first stroke,
The very first you give me, if you dare strike –
Try me, and you shall find it so – forever,   145
Never to be recalled (I know you love me,
Mad till you have enjoyed me), do I turn
Utterly from you, and what man I meet first
That has a spirit to deserve a favour –

133 *bed-rid* confined to bed.
135 *substance* possessions.
  'bezzled embezzled.
136–7 *well . . . in't* Maria pretends that Petruchio is boasting about these things, not complaining about them.
137 *may* MS (may well F).
138 *opening* revealing all (perhaps also recalls the fact that Petruchio had to force his way out of the door in III.iv).
138–9 *'tis . . . myself* i.e. it is my own scheme to ruin myself (rather than Maria's).
140 *as may* MS (may F).
  as may be as could possibly be done.
141–2 F (do'st . . . me. / I . . . stroake MS).
141 *o'* on.
143–8 *The . . . you* Maria's syntax – which coveys her emotional disturbance – is confusing. If the digressions are removed, she says that if Petruchio strikes her she will reject him completely. This was a pivotal moment in the RSC production of 2003, in which the lines were condensed to: 'The first stroke, / The very first you give me, if you dare strike, / I do turn utterly from you. Try me / And you shall find it so, for ever, / Never to be recall'd' (*The Royal Shakespeare Company Production of The Tamer Tamed* [London, 2003], p. 72).
145 *Try me* Test me, try it out.
147 *Mad till* i.e. and will be mad until. *till* F (tell MS).
  do I MS (I doe F).
149 *That . . . favour* i.e. that has enough courage to deserve a (sexual) reward.
  has a MS (has but F).

Let him bear any shape, the worse the better –   150
Shall kill you, and enjoy me. What I have said
About your foolish sickness, ere you have me
As you would have me, you shall swear is certain,
And challenge any man that dares deny it,
And in all companies approve my actions.   155
And so farewell for this time.   *Exit* [MARIA]
PETRUCHIO   Grief go with thee!
If there be any witchcrafts, herbs, or potions,
Saying my prayers backwards, fiends or Furies,
That can again unlove me, I am a man.   *Exit*

[ACT IV, SCENE ii]

Enter BIANCA *and* TRANIO

TRANIO
Faith, mistress, you must do it.
BIANCA   Are the writings
Ready I told ye?
TRANIO   Yes, they are ready,
But to what use I know not.

---

150   *bear any shape* have any appearance.
152–3   *ere . . . me* i.e. before I will behave in the way you want.
153   *certain* true.
155   *approve* defend, appear to be in favour of.
156   *Exit* [MARIA] ed. (*Exit Mar.* F; Exit MS).
       Grief . . . thee i.e. may grief come to you (a mild oath; compare 'go and be hanged').
158   *Saying . . . backwards* Saying one's prayers backwards was thought to be a way of
       summoning devils.
       Furies MS (Fayries F).
       Furies avenging spirits: see II.i.105 n.
159   *can . . . me* i.e. that can make me not love Maria.
       a man MS (made F).
       I . . . man i.e. I will regain the status and authority of a man.

       [*Act IV, Scene ii*] ed. (*Scæna Secunda* F).
  1   *Faith* MS (*om.* F).
       writings documents.
  2   *I told ye* as I instructed you.   *ye* MS (you of F).
1–2   ed. (Faith . . . it. / Are . . . readie / I . . . ye? MS).

BIANCA   Y'are an ass,
You must have all things constered.
TRANIO   Yes, and pierced too,
Or I find a little pleasure.
BIANCA   Now you are knavish.   5
Go to, fetch Roland hither presently;
Your twenty pounds lies bleeding else. She is married
Within these twelve hours if we cross it not.
And see the papers of one size.
TRANIO   I have ye.
BIANCA
And for disposing of them –
TRANIO   If I fail ye,   10
Now I have found the way, use martial law
And cut my head off with a hand-saw.
BIANCA   Well, sir,
Petronius and Moroso I'll see sent for.
About your business, go.
TRANIO   I am gone.   *Exit* [TRANIO]
BIANCA   Ho, Livia!

Enter LIVIA

LIVIA
Who's that?
BIANCA   A friend of yours. Lord! How you look now   15

---

4   *constered* MS (constru'd F).
     constered construed, explained.
     pierced (1) broken down, made sense of; (2) sexually penetrated (Tranio picks up
     the aural pun on the first syllable of 'constered': 'con' is the French word for 'cunt',
     or the female genitals.)
     too F (to MS).
5   *a little* MS (little F).
     knavish rascally, rude.
6   *Go to* Hurry up.
8   *cross* prevent.
9   *see . . . size* make sure that the documents are the same size.
     I have ye i.e. now I understand you.
10   *disposing* managing.
     them MS ('em F).
11   *Now . . . way* i.e. now that I understand what we're doing.
14   s.d. *Exit* [TRANIO] ed. (*Exit Tranio* F, *Exit* MS).

    As if you had lost a carrack!
LIVIA   Oh, Bianca,
    I am the most undone, unhappy woman!
BIANCA
    Be quiet, wench. Thou shalt be done, and done,
    And done, and double done, or all shall split for't.
    No more of these mixed passions: they are mangy   20
    And ease thee of nothing but a little wind;
    An apple will do more. Thou fear'st Moroso?
LIVIA
    E'en as I fear the gallows.
BIANCA   Keep thee there still.
    And you love Roland? Say.
LIVIA   If I say not,
    I am sure I lie.
BIANCA   What wouldst thou give that woman,   25
    In spite of all his anger and thy fear,
    And all thy father's policy, that could
    Clap ye within these two nights quietly
    Into a bed together?
LIVIA   How?
BIANCA   Why, fairly,
    At half-sword: man and wife. Now the red blood comes;   30
    Aye, marry, now the matter's changed.
LIVIA   Bianca,
    Methinks you should not mock me.
BIANCA   Mock a pudding!

---

16   *carrack* large trading ship or galleon (both valuable and distressing to lose).
18   *done* i.e. the opposite of 'undone', with sexual innuendo ('do' often means 'to have sex' in early modern slang).
19   *all . . . for't* i.e. everyone will be ruined (a term often used in relation to shipwreck, continuing the nautical language of *carrack*).
20   *mixed* i.e. made up of a variety of emotions.
      mixed MS (minc'd F).
23   *E'en* Even; As much as.
      Keep . . . still i.e. keep that in mind, remember that.
27   *policy* cunning.
28   *Clap* Put.
30   *At half-sword* In close proximity, with only half a sword's length between them.
      Now . . . comes i.e. now you're blushing.
32   *Mock a pudding!* A derisive exclamation similar to 'pah!', perhaps meaning something like 'I might as well mock a pudding', though compare 'not worth a pudding', which means 'of little or no worth'.

I speak good honest English, and good meaning.

LIVIA

I should not be ungrateful to that woman.

BIANCA

I know thou wouldst not. Follow but my counsel   35
And if thou hast him not, despite of fortune,
Let me ne'er know a good night more. You must
Be very sick o' th' instant.

LIVIA   Well, what follows?

BIANCA

And in that sickness send for all your friends,
Your father, and your fever, old Moroso,   40
And Roland shall be there too.

LIVIA   What of this?

BIANCA

Do ye not twitter yet? Of this shall follow
That that shall make thy heart leap, and thy lips
Venture as many kisses as the merchants
Do dollars to the East Indies. You shall know all.   45
But first walk in and practise. Pray ye, be sick.

LIVIA

I do believe ye, and I am sick.

BIANCA   So,

To bed then, come. I'll send away your servants.
Post for your fool and father. And good fortune,
As we mean honestly, now strike an upshot!   50

Exeunt

37   *Let . . . more* i.e. let me never enjoy sex again.
38   *o' th' instant* instantly, suddenly.
40   *fever* i.e. the illness that afflicts you.
41   *too* F (to MS).
42   *Do . . . yet* i.e. aren't you trembling with anticipation yet? (alternatively, 'stop chattering', but the first sense is used by Fletcher elsewhere).
43   *That that* MS (That which F).
45   *dollars* English name for Spanish pesos, widely used in international trade.
46   *Pray ye* MS (pray F).
47   *So* MS (Doe F).
49   *Post* Send.
     your fool i.e. Moroso.
50   *strike an upshot* i.e. ensure a good result (an upshot is the last shot in an archery contest).

[ACT IV, SCENE iii]

Enter TRANIO *and* ROLAND

TRANIO
Nay, o' my conscience, I have lost my money.
But that's all one. I'll never more persuade ye;
I see you are resolute, and I commend ye.
ROLAND
But did she send for me?
TRANIO   Ye dare believe me.
ROLAND
I cannot tell. You have your ways for profit   5
Allowed ye, Tranio, as well as I
Have to avoid them.
TRANIO   No, I protest, sir,

Enter SERVANT

I deal directly with ye.
ROLAND [*To* SERVANT]   How now, fellow,
Whither post you so fast?
SERVANT   Oh, sir, my master –
Pray, did you see my master?
ROLAND   Why your master?   10
SERVANT
My pretty mistress Livia –
ROLAND   What of her?
SERVANT
Oh sir, his jewel –

[*Act IV, Scene iii*] ed. (*Scæna Tertia* F).
2   *that's all one* never mind.
5   *your* The scribe originally omitted this word, and it is interlined.
7   *avoid them* MS (avoid 'em feare F; avoid 'em F2; Have (to avoid 'em) fear ed.)
    protest MS (on my word F; [o' God's name] ed.)
    s.d. MS; F places the direction in the margin next to Tranio's half of l. 8.
9   *post* rush.
11–12   F changes the order of these lines, to give: '*Serv.* Sir his Jewell. / *Row.* With the gilded Button? / *Serv.* My pretty Mistresse *Livia*. / *Row.* What of her?'.

ROLAND   With the gilded button.

SERVANT

 Is fallen sick o' th' sudden.

ROLAND   How, o' th' sullens?

SERVANT

O' th' sudden, sir, I say, and very sick.

ROLAND

It seems she hath got the toothache with raw apples.   15

SERVANT

It seems you have got the headache. Fare ye well, sir.
You did not see my master?

ROLAND   Who told you so?

TRANIO

No, no, he did not see him.

Exit SERVANT

ROLAND   Farewell, bluebottle.

What should her sickness be?

TRANIO   For you, it may be.

ROLAND

Yes, when my brains are out I may believe it;   20
Never before, I am sure. Yet I may see her;
'Twill be a point of honesty.

TRANIO   It will so.

ROLAND

It may be not, too. You would fain be fing'ring
This odd sin-offering of two hundred, Tranio.
How daintily and cunningly you drive me   25
Up like a deer to the toil! Yet I may leap it,

12   *With . . . button* i.e. with a fake stone.
      button The scribe originally omitted this word, and it appears to be inserted in a
      different hand.
13   *o' th' sullens* i.e. in a sulk.
15   F (It . . . tooth-ache / with MS).
      toothache . . . apples i.e. either from the sour taste, or from the hardness, which
      might dislodge a rotten tooth (the phrase may refer – again – to the story of Eve).
18   s.d. F places the direction after Roland's 'Farewell, bluebottle'.
      bluebottle refers to the blue uniforms conventionally worn by servants.
20   *when . . . out* i.e. when I have lost my senses.
22   *point* issue.   *honesty* courtesy, decency.
24   *odd* MS (old F).
      sin-offering money offered in atonement of sin.
26   *toil* net (i.e. that set by a hunter).
      leap it leap over it.

And what's the woodman then?

TRANIO   A loser by ye.
Speak: will you go or not? To me 'tis equal.

ROLAND
Come, what goes less?

TRANIO   Nay, not a penny, Roland.

ROLAND
Shall I have liberty of conscience,   30
Which by interpretation is ten kisses?
Hang me if I affect her! Yet it may be
This whoreson manners will require a struggling
Of two and twenty, or, by'r Lady, thirty.

TRANIO
By'r Lady, I'll require my wager then,   35
For if you kiss so often, and no kindness,
I have lost my speculation. I'll allow ye –

ROLAND
Speak like a gamester now.

TRANIO   It may be, two.

ROLAND
Under a dozen, Tranio, there's no setting.
You shall have forty shillings; wink at small faults.   40
Say I take twenty; come, by all that's honest,
I do it but to vex her.

TRANIO   I'll no by-blows.
If you can love her, do; if ye can hate her,
Or any else that loves ye –

ROLAND   Prithee, Tranio.

28   *To . . . equal* i.e. it's all the same to me.
29   *Come . . . less* i.e. what odds will you give me; how about a smaller bet (Roland
       seems to understand ''tis equal' as meaning that the odds are even whether he will
       go to see Livia or not.)
32–4 *Yet . . . thirty* i.e. it is possible that this bastard manners will make me kiss her
       twenty two, or, indeed, thirty times.
33   *whoreson* bastard, son-of-a-bitch.
35   *require my wager* take back my bet.
36   *For . . . kindness* i.e. if you can kiss so many times and feel nothing for her.
38   *gamester* habitual gambler.
       two i.e. two kisses.
39   *there's . . . setting* i.e. bets are off.
40   *wink at* i.e. if you take no notice of.
41   *twenty* i.e. twenty kisses.
42   *I'll no by-blows* I'm taking no bets on the side.

TRANIO
    Why, farewell twenty pound; 'twill not undo me.   45
    You have my resolution.
ROLAND   And your money.
    Which, since you are so stubborn, if I forfeit
    Make me a Jack-a-Lent, and break my shins
    For untagged points and counters. I'll go with you,
    But if thou get'st a penny by the bargain –   50
    A parting kiss is lawful?
TRANIO   I allow it.
ROLAND
    Knock out my brains with apples. Yet a bargain?
TRANIO
    I tell you I'll no bargain. Win and wear it.
ROLAND
    Thou art the strangest fellow.
TRANIO   That's all one.
ROLAND
    Along, then. Twenty pound more, if thou dar'st,   55
    I give her not a good word.
TRANIO   Not a penny.

                          Exeunt

45   *undo* ruin, bankrupt.
46   *You . . . resolution* You know what I've decided.
47   *Which* F (wth MS).
48   *Jack-a-Lent* i.e. a target for anything to throw things at (a Jack-a-Lent was a human figure similar to an Aunt Sally, set up at Lent).
49   *untagged . . . counters* worthless items: laces with no metal ends or 'points', and counters used in place of currency.
51   *parting* farewell.
53   *I'll* i.e. I'll make.
     bargain MS (bargaines F).
     Win . . . it A proverbial term (Tilley W408) meaning 'enjoy it once you have it' (more often used in relation to the wooing of women, and so used ironically by Tranio here).
55   *Twenty pound more* i.e. I'll bet you a further twenty pounds.

[ACT IV, SCENE iv]

Enter PETRUCHIO, JAQUES [*and*] PEDRO

PETRUCHIO

Prithee entreat her come; I will not trouble her
Above a word or two.

Exit PEDRO

      Ere I endure
This life, and with a woman, and a vowed one
To all the mischiefs she can lay upon me,
I'll go to plough again, and eat leek-porridge;   5
Begging's a pleasure to't not to be numbered.
No, there be other countries, Jaques, for me,
And other people, yea, and other women,
If I have need – 'Here's money', 'There's your ware',
Which is fair dealing – and the sun, they say,   10
Shines as warm there as here. And till I have lost
Either myself or her, I care not whether,
Nor which first –

JAQUES   Will your worship hear me?

PETRUCHIO

And utterly outworn the memory
Of such a curse as this, none of my nation   15
Shall ever know me more.

JAQUES   Out, alas, sir,
What a strange way do you run!

PETRUCHIO   Any way,
So I outrun this rascal.

[*Act IV, Scene iv*] ed. (*Scæna Quarta* F).

3–4 *vowed . . . me* i.e. one who has vowed to do every mischievous thing she can to me.

5 *go . . . again* return to work as a ploughman (this may suggest that Petruchio is from a humble background: compare Maria's comments at IV.i.83–6); interestingly, 'again' is omitted in F2.
  leek-porridge a stereotypically humble meal.

6 *to't* to it: in comparison with it.
  not . . . numbered incalculable.

9 *ware* merchandise (i.e. sexual favours).

12 *whether* which.

16–17 F (Shall . . . more. / Out, . . . run! MS).

16 *Out* An exclamation indicating dismay.

JAQUES   Methinks, now,
   If your good worship could but have the patience –

PETRUCHIO
   The patience, why the patience?

JAQUES   Why, I'll tell you.   20
   Could you but have the patience –

PETRUCHIO   Well, the patience.

JAQUES
   To laugh at all she does, or when she rails
   To have a drum beaten o' th' top o' th' house
   To give neighbours warning of her larum,
   As I do when my wife rebels.

PETRUCHIO   Thy wife?   25
   Thy wife's a pigeon to her; a mere slumber.
   The dead of night's not stiller.

JAQUES   Nor an iron mill.

PETRUCHIO
   But thy wife is certain.

JAQUES   That's false doctrine –
   You never read yet of a certain woman.

PETRUCHIO
   Thou know'st her way.

JAQUES   I should do, I am sure;   30
   I have ridden it night and day this twenty year.

PETRUCHIO
   But mine is such a drench of balderdash,
   Such a strange-carded cunningness, the rainbow,
   When she hangs bent in heaven, sheds not her colours
   Quicker and more than this deceitful woman   35

---

18   *this rascal* i.e. Maria.
22–5   *To . . . rebels* Jaques recommends the traditional methods used to shame or punish
      an unruly wife.
24   *neighbours* MS (the neighbours F).
      larum (1) call to arms; (2) uproar.
26   *pigeon* (1) coward; (2) darling, sweetheart.
27   *Nor . . . mill* i.e. she is even noisier than an iron mill.
28   *certain* constant (in her behaviour), faithful.
29   *read yet* MS (read F).
30   *way* ways (Jaques understands it as 'the way into her' or 'her path').
32   *drench* potion (often forcibly given).
      balderdash mixture of liquids.
33   *strange-carded* strangely woven.

Enter PEDRO

Waves in her dyes of wickedness. [*To* PEDRO] What says she?

PEDRO
Nay, not a word, sir, but she pointed to me
As though she meant to follow. Pray, sir, bear it
Easy as you may. I need not teach your worship
The best man hath his crosses; we are all mortal –   40

PETRUCHIO
What ails the fellow?

PEDRO   And no doubt she may, sir –

PETRUCHIO
What may she, or what does she, or what is she?
Speak and be hanged!

PEDRO   She is mad, sir.

PETRUCHIO   Heaven continue it.

PEDRO
Amen, if it be his pleasure.

PETRUCHIO   How mad is she?

PEDRO
As mad as heart can wish, sir. She has dressed herself,   45
Saving your worship's reverence, just i' th' cut
Of one of those that multiply i' th' suburbs
For single money, and as dirtily.
If any speak to her, first she whistles,
And then begins her compass with her fingers,   50
And points to what she would have.

PETRUCHIO   What new way's this?

PEDRO
There came in Master Sophocles.

---

35   s.d. *Enter* F (Enter's MS). F places the direction in the margins of ll. 35–6.
36   *Waves* MS (Weaves F).
      dyes colours.
39   *Easy . . . may* i.e. with as much grace as you can.   *Easy* MS (Ev'n F).
      teach F (to teach MS).
40   *The . . . mortal* Clichés about the need to react positively to misfortune.
      man hath his MS (men have their F).
43   *Heaven* MS, F ([God] ed.)
44   *his* i.e. God's.
46   *Saving . . . reverence* i.e. begging your pardon, sir.
      cut fashion.
47–8 *one . . . money* i.e. cheap prostitutes.
50   *begins her compass* begins to draw a circle.

Enter SOPHOCLES

PETRUCHIO   And what
Did Master Sophocles when he came in?
Get my trunks ready. I'll be gone straight.

PEDRO
He's here to tell you –   55
[*To* JAQUES] She's horn-mad, Jaques.

                          [*Exit* JAQUES *and* PEDRO]
SOPHOCLES   Call ye this a woman?

PETRUCHIO
Yes, sir, she's a woman.

SOPHOCLES   Sir, I doubt it.

PETRUCHIO
I had thought you had made experience.

SOPHOCLES   Yes, I did so,
And almost with my life.

PETRUCHIO   You ride too fast, sir.

SOPHOCLES
Pray be not you mistaken. By this light,   60
Your wife is chaste and honest as a virgin
For anything I know. 'Tis true she gave me
A ring –

PETRUCHIO   For rutting.

SOPHOCLES   You are much deceived still.
I swear I never kissed her since, and now,
Coming in visitation like a friend,   65
I think she is mad, sir. Suddenly she started,
And snatched the ring away, and drew her knife out,

52–3   F (There . . . Sophocles. / And . . . in? MS).
   54   *ready* MS (ready sirha F; ready, sirrah ed.)
        straight straightaway.
   56   *horn-mad* stark mad, mad with rage (i.e. like a bull about to charge). The phrase is
        often used of cuckolds, but may here suggest that Pedro thinks that making
        Petruchio a cuckold has driven Maria mad.
        s.d. [*Exit* JAQUES *and* PEDRO] ed.
   57   *Sir, I* F (I MS).
   58   *made experience* i.e. tested it out (by having sex with Maria).
   59   *You . . . fast* i.e. you're going too far.
        ride MS (rid F).
   60   *light* MS (hand F).
   63   *rutting* fornicating (with an obscene pun on *ring* = vagina).
   64   *I swear* MS (Beleeve me F; ['Od's me] ed.)

To what intent I know not.

PETRUCHIO   Is this certain?

SOPHOCLES

As I am here, sir.

PETRUCHIO   I believe ye honest,

Enter MARIA

And pray continue so.

SOPHOCLES   She comes.

PETRUCHIO   Now, damsel,   70

What will your beauty do if I forsake you?

                                        [MARIA *gestures at him*]

Do you deal by signs and tokens? As I guess, then,

You'll walk abroad this summer, and catch captains,

Or hire a piece of holy ground i' th' suburbs,

And keep a nest of nuns.

SOPHOCLES   Oh, do not stir her!   75

You see in what a case she is.

PETRUCHIO   She is dogged,

And in a beastly case, I am sure. [*Aside*] I'll make her,

If she have any tongue, yet tattle. [*Aloud*] Sophocles,

Prithee observe this woman seriously,

And eye her well, and, when thou hast done, but tell me   80

(For thou hast understanding) in what case

My sense was when I chose this thing.

SOPHOCLES   I'll tell ye,

I have seen a sweeter.

PETRUCHIO   A hundred times cry 'Oysters!'

There's a poor beggar wench about Blackfriars

Runs on her breech, may be an empress to her.   85

72   *tokens* symbols.
73   *walk abroad* i.e. walk the streets.
75   *nest of nuns* brothel ('nun' is a slang term for a prostitute).
76   *case she is* i.e. what a state she's in.
       a case F (case MS).
       dogged malicious, spiteful.
81–2   *what . . . was* what was my mental state.
83   *A . . . 'Oysters'!* Petruchio compares Maria's dishevelled state with that of London's
       oyster sellers.
85   *Runs . . . breech* either (1) suffers from incontinence; or (2) runs around wearing
       unflattering breeches.
       to in comparison with.

SOPHOCLES
  Nay, now you are too bitter.
PETRUCHIO   Never a whit, sir.
  [*To* MARIA] I'll tell thee, woman, for now I have day to see thee,
  And all my wits about me, and I'll speak
  Not out of passion neither. Leave your mumping;
  I know y'are well enough. [*Aside*] Now would I give   90
  A million but to vex her. [*To* MARIA] When I chose thee
  To make a bedfellow, I took more trouble
  Than twenty terms can come to: such a cause,
  Of such a title, and so everlasting
  That Adam's genealogy may be ended   95
  Ere any law find thee. I took a leprosy;
  Nay, worse, the plague; nay, worse yet, a possession;
  And had the devil with thee, if not more.
  And yet worse, was a beast, and like a beast
  Had my reward, a jade to fling my fortunes.   100
  For who that had but reason to distinguish
  The light from darkness, wine from water, hunger
  From full satiety, and fox from fern-bush
  That would have married thee?
SOPHOCLES   She is not so ill.
PETRUCHIO
  She is worse than I dare think of. She's so lewd   105
  No court is strong enough to bear her cause.
  She hath neither manners, honesty, behaviour,
  Wifehood, nor womanhood, nor any moral

 86 *Never a whit* Not at all.
 87 *now . . . thee* i.e. now I can see you properly.
     day F (a day MS).
 88 *I'll* MS (Ile) (I F).
 89 *passion* anger.
     mumping grimacing, making faces.
 92 *took* took on.
 93· *terms* periods during which the law courts were in operation.
95–6 *Adam's . . . thee* i.e. the human race will come to an end before you are properly
     punished.
 98 *if not more* i.e. if not more than one, if not something worse.
100 *fling* fling off (like an unruly horse bucking).
103 *fox . . . fern-bush* to know a fox from a fern-bush is a proverbial phrase (Tilley
     F265).
104 *ill* bad.
106 *bear her cause* hear her case.
108 *womanhood* F (man-hood MS).

Can force me think she had a mother. No,
I do believe her steadfastly and know her   110
To be a woman-wolf by transmigration;
Her first form was a ferret's underground.
She kills the memories of men. [*Aside*] Not yet?

SOPHOCLES
Do you think she's sensible of this?

PETRUCHIO   I care not.
Be what she will, the pleasure I take in her   115
Thus I blow off; the care I took to love her,
Like this point, I untie, and thus I loose it;
The husband I am to her, thus I sever.
My vanity, farewell. [*To* MARIA] Yet, for you have been
So near me as to bear the name of wife,   120
My unquenched charity shall tell you thus much:
Though you deserve it well you shall not beg;
What I ordained your jointure, honestly
You shall have settled on you, and half my house.
The other half shall be employed in prayers –   125
That meritorious charge I'll be at also –
Yet to confirm ye a Christian. Your apparel,
And what belongs to build up such a folly,
Keep, I beseech ye; it infects our uses.
And now I am for travel.

MARIA   Now I love ye,   130
And, now I see ye are a man, I'll talk to ye,

---

110 *know* F (I know MS).
111 *transmigration* Refers to the (heretical) idea that souls might transfer after death
     from animals into humans, and *vice versa.*
113 *kills . . . men* i.e. blackens the reputation of mankind.
     Not yet i.e. aren't you reacting yet.
114 *sensible* aware.
116 *blow off* cast away.
     off F (of MS).
117 *this point* Petruchio unties a lace – probably at the neck of his shirt – as he speaks.
119 *for* because.
123 *ordained* arranged, planned.   *jointure* See I.ii.117 n.
124 *house* estate.
125 *employed* i.e. spent.
126 *be at* undertake.
127 *ye a* MS (you F; ye ed.)
129 *uses* habits, employment.
130 *for* prepared for, intending to undertake.

And I forgive your bitterness.

SOPHOCLES   How now, man?

PETRUCHIO

O Pliny, if thou wilt be ever famous
Make but this woman all thy wonders!

MARIA   Sure, sir,
You have hit upon a happy course, a blessed,   135
And what will make you virtuous.

PETRUCHIO   She'll ship me!

MARIA

A way of understanding I long wished for;
And now 'tis come, take heed you fly not back, sir.
Methinks you look a new man to me now,
A man of excellence, and now I see   140
Some great design set in ye. You may think now,
And so may most that know me, 'twere my part
Weakly to weep your loss, and to resist ye,
Nay, hang about your neck and, like a dotard,
Urge my strong tie upon ye. But I love ye,   145
And all the world shall know it, beyond woman,
And more prefer the honour of your country
(Which chiefly you are born for, and may perfect),
The uses you may make of other nations,
The ripening of your knowledge, conversation,   150
The full ability and strength of judgement,
Than any private love, or wanton kisses.
Go, worthy man, and bring home understanding.

SOPHOCLES

This were an excellent woman to breed schoolmen!

MARIA

For if the merchant through unknown sea plough   155

---

132   *forgive* MS (forget F).
133   *Pliny* Pliny the Elder (23–79 CE), whose *Natural History* includes numerous
       fantastic stories.
136   *ship me* i.e. put me on a ship (this might be delivered as an aside, or to Sophocles).
138   *take heed* take care.
143   *resist ye* i.e. to try to make you stay.
145   *Urge . . . ye* i.e. plead with you, reminding you of my status as your wife.
146   *beyond woman* i.e. beyond the ability of most women.
154   *schoolmen* scholars (because of her rhetorical abilities).
155   *sea* MS (Seas F).

To get his wealth, then, dear sir, what must you
To gather wisdom? Go, and go alone,
Only your noble mind for your companion.
And if a woman may win credit with you,
Go far – too far you cannot; still the farther,   160
The more experience finds you. And go sparing –
One meal a week will serve you, and one suit
Through all your travels, for, you'll find it certain,
The poorer and the baser ye appear,
The more you look through still.

PETRUCHIO   Dost hear her?
SOPHOCLES   Yes.   165
PETRUCHIO
What would this woman do, if she were suffered,
Upon a new religion?
SOPHOCLES   Make us pagans.
I wonder that she writes not.
MARIA   Then, when time
And fullness of occasion have new-made you,
And squared you from a sot into a senior,   170
Or, nearer, from a jade into a courser,
Come home an agèd man as did Ulysses,
And I your glad Penelope.–

156   *what must you* what must you do.
159   *if . . . you* i.e. if you will believe a woman.
161   *sparing* i.e. with little baggage or money.
165   *The . . . still* (1) the better you will see things as they truly are; (2) the more your true
        nature will shine through; (3) the more your poverty and baseness will be evident.
166   *suffered* allowed.
167   *Upon* i.e. in the creation of.
        religion MS (adventure F): F appears to have been censored at this point.
        pagans MS (nothing F).
168   *writes not* i.e. doesn't take up writing religious tracts.
169   *occasion* opportunity.
170   *sot* (1) fool; (2) drunkard.
        senior MS (Signour F); revered elder (also, possibly, 'signior', a nobleman or person
        of note).
171   *nearer* more likely.
        courser a swift racing horse.
172   *Ulysses* the Roman name for Odysseus, the crafty and well-travelled hero of Virgil's
        Odyssey, whose voyage home to Ithaca from the decade-long Trojan war also took
        ten years.
173   *Penelope* Ulysses's legendarily chaste and patient wife, who resisted numerous
        suitors during his twenty-year absence (also mentioned at II.iii.18).

PETRUCHIO   That must have
　　As many lovers as I languages,
　　And what she does with one in the day, i' th' night   175
　　Undo it with another.
MARIA   Much that way, sir.
　　For in your absence it must be my honour
　　To have temptations, and not little ones,
　　Daily and hourly offered me, and strongly –
　　That, that must make me spoken of hereafter –   180
　　Almost believed against me, to set off
　　The faith and loyalty of her that loves ye.
PETRUCHIO
　　What should I do?
SOPHOCLES   Why, by my troth, I would travel.
　　Did you not mean so?
PETRUCHIO   Alas, nothing less, man!
　　I did it but to try her. She's the devil,   185
　　And now I find it. She drives me. I must go.
　　[Calling to servants offstage]
　　Are my trunks down there? And my horses ready?
MARIA
　　Sir, for your house, and if you please to trust me
　　With those you leave behind –
PETRUCHIO [Calling]   Bring down the money!
MARIA
　　As I am able, and to my poor fortunes,   190
　　I'll govern as a widow. I shall long
　　To hear of your well-doing and your profit,
　　And when I hear not from you once a quarter
　　I'll wish you in the Indies, or Cataia;

175–6　*And . . . another* Refers to the story that in order to put off her suitors, Penelope
　　　　undid at night all the needlework that she had done during the day; in Petruchio's
　　　　version, Maria would 'undo' the work of one lover by having sex with another.
180　*That . . . hereafter* In F this line appears after l. 178.
　　　That i.e. people will talk about the strength of the temptation that Maria will be
　　　faced with.
181　*set off* highlight, show off.
183　*my troth* MS (my — F).
184　*you not* MS (not you F).　　*mean so* i.e. intend to do so.
185　*her* MS (sir F).
186　*it* MS (it, for).
189　*those* MS (that F).
194　*Indies* the West or East Indies.　　*Cataia* Cathay (an archaic name for China).

233

Those are the climates must make you.

PETRUCHIO [*Calling*]   How's the wind?   195

[*Aside*] She'll wish me out of the world anon.

MARIA   For France

'Tis very fair. Get ye abroad tonight, sir,

And lose no time; you know the tide stays no man.

I have cold meats ready for you.

PETRUCHIO   Fare thee well.

Thou hast fooled me out o' th' kingdom with a vengeance,   200

And thou canst fool me in again.

MARIA   Not I, sir.

I love you better. Take your time and pleasure.

I'll see you horsed.

PETRUCHIO   I think thou would see me hanged too,

Were I but half as willing.

MARIA   Anything

That you think well of, I dare look upon.   205

PETRUCHIO

You'll bear me to the land's end, Sophocles,

And other o' my friends, I hope?

MARIA   Ne'er doubt, sir.

Ye cannot want companions for your good.

I am sure you'll kiss me ere I go. I have business,

And stay long here I must not.

PETRUCHIO   Get thee going,   210

For if thou tarriest but another dialogue,

I'll kick thee to thy chamber.

MARIA   Fare you well, sir,

And bear yourself – I do beseech ye once more,

Since you have undertaken, doing wisely –

---

195   *climates* MS (climes F).
197   *'Tis* i.e. the wind is.   *abroad* MS (aboard F).
198   *the . . . man* a proverbial phrase (Tilley T323).
      stays waits for.
200   *fooled* tricked.
      out MS (*om.* F).
202   *better* i.e. better than to let you stay.
203   *would* MS (wouldst F).
206   *bear . . . end* accompany me to the shore.
209   *business* things to attend to.
211   *thou tarriest* you linger.
      another dialogue i.e. to speak any further.

Manly and worthily; 'tis for my credit. 215
And, for those flying fames here of your follies,
Your gambols, and ill-breeding of your youth –
For which I understand you take this travel,
Nothing should make me leave you else – I'll deal
So like a wife that loves your reputation, 220
And the most large addition of your credit,
That those shall die. If ye want lemon-water
Or anything to take the edge o' th' sea off,
Pray speak, and be provided.

PETRUCHIO   Now the devil,
That was your first good master, shower his blessing 225
Upon ye all, into whose custody –

MARIA

I do commit your reformation.
And so I leave you to your *stilo novo*.   *Exit* [MARIA]

PETRUCHIO

I will go; yet I will not. Once more, Sophocles,
I'll put her to the test.

SOPHOCLES   You had better go. 230

PETRUCHIO

I will go, then. Let's seek my father out,
And all my friends to see me fair aboard.
Then, women, if there be a storm at sea
Worse than your tongues can make, and waves more broken
Than your dissembling faiths are, let me feel 235
Nothing but tempests, till they crack my keel.

Exeunt

215   *credit* honour, reputation.
216   *flying fames* rumours.
217   *gambols* merrymaking.
221   *the . . . credit* i.e. the greatest improvement of your reputation.
222   *lemon-water* used to prevent or cure sea-sickness.
228   *stilo novo* (1) new style (Italian); (2) the 'new' Gregorian calendar used in
       continental Europe from 1582, which was ten days ahead of the 'old' Julian
       calendar used in Britain until 1752.
       s.d. *Exit* [MARIA] ed, (*Exit Maria* F, *Exit* MS).
229   *I . . . not* may suggest Petruchio's scheme in Act V, though he seems to abandon the
       idea here.
231   *father* father-in-law (i.e. Petronius).
232   *fair* safely.
233   *women* Petruchio may address women in the audience, as he addressed men at
       III.ii.196.
235   *dissembling* deceptive.

Enter PETRONIUS *and* BIANCA [*with four documents*]

BIANCA

    Now whether I deserve that blame you gave me,
    Let all the world discern it, sir.

PETRONIUS   If this motion –
    I mean, this fair repentance of my daughter –
    Spring from your good persuasion, as it seems so,
    I must confess I have spake too boldly of you,   5
    And I repent.

BIANCA   The first touch was her own,
    Taken, no doubt, from disobeying you;
    The second I put to her, when I told her
    How good and gentle yet, with free contrition,
    Again you might be purchased. Loving woman,   10
    She heard me, and, I thank her, thought me worthy
    Observing in this point. Yet all my counsel
    And comfort in this case could not so heal her
    But grief got his share too, and she sickened.

PETRONIUS

    I am sorry she's so ill, yet glad her sickness   15

Enter MOROSO

    Has got so good a ground.

Act V, Scene i (ed. Actus V. Scæna j.^{ma} MS; Actus Quintus, Scæna Prima. F).

  0 s.d. [*with four documents*] ed. (*with foure papers* F). These are the two copies of the
       formal renunciation that Livia and Roland have agreed to sign, and two copies of
       the marriage pre-contract that Bianca intends them to sign. Petronius is aware only
       of the first two.
  2 *discern it* MS (discern F).
      discern see.
      motion plan.
  5 *spake* MS (spoke F).
      spake spoken.
  6 *touch* i.e. touch of repentance.
 12 *Observing* Paying attention to, heeding.
 16 *ground* cause.

BIANCA
    Here comes Moroso.
PETRONIUS   Oh, you are very welcome!
    Now you shall know your happiness.
MOROSO   I am glad on't.
    What makes this lady here?
BIANCA   A dish for you, sir,
    You'll thank me for hereafter.
PETRONIUS   True. Moroso,   20
    Go get you in, and see your mistress.
BIANCA   She is sick, sir,
    But you may kiss her whole.
MOROSO   How?
BIANCA   Comfort her.
MOROSO
    Why am I sent for, sir?
PETRONIUS   Will you in and see?
BIANCA
    Maybe she needs confession.
MOROSO   By St Mary,
    She shall have absolution then, and penance,   25
    But not above her carriage.

                    Enter ROLAND *and* TRANIO

[PETRONIUS]   Will you in, fool?

                                            Exit MOROSO

BIANCA
    Here comes the other two.
PETRONIUS   Now, Tranio.
    [*To* ROLAND] Good e'en to you too, and y'are welcome.

19   *What . . . here* What is this lady doing here (Bianca takes 'makes' literally in her reply.)
22   *kiss her whole* i.e. kiss her back to health.
      How? What? (Moroso hears 'whole' as 'hole', and thinks that he is being told to kiss
      Livia's arse.)
26   *not . . . carriage* (1) not more than is appropriate; (2) not more than she can bear
      (there is possibly a sexual pun here).
      s.d. (*Enter . . .*) F places this at l. 27.
      s.p. [PETRONIUS] F (*om.* MS).
      Will MS (Get F).
27   *comes . . . two* See II.i.90 n.   *two* MS (too F).
28   *e'en* evening.
      too This word was omitted by the scribe, and is interlined.

237

ROLAND   Thank you.

PETRONIUS

I have a certain daughter.

ROLAND   Would you had, sir.

PETRONIUS

No doubt you know her well.

ROLAND   Nor never shall, sir.   30
She is a woman, and the ways into her
Are like the finding of a certain path
After a deep-fall'n snow.

PETRONIUS   Well, that's by th' by still.
This daughter that I tell you of is fall'n
A little crop-sick with the dangerous surfeit   35
She took of your affection.

ROLAND   Mine, sir?

PETRONIUS

I think it well you would see her.

ROLAND   If you please, sir,
I am not squeamish of my visitation.

PETRONIUS

But this I'll tell you: she is altered much;
You'll find her now another Livia.   40

ROLAND

I had enough o' th' old, sir.

PETRONIUS   No more fool
To look gay babies in your eyes, young Roland,
And hang about your pretty neck –

ROLAND   I am glad on't,
And thank my fates I have 'scaped such executions.

---

29   *Would you had* i.e. I wish that your daughter was certain (faithful, constant).
30   *Nor never shall* No, and never shall.
31   *into* MS (unto F).
32   *certain* safe, secure.
35   *crop-sick* suffering from an upset stomach.   *surfeit* overindulgence.
36–7 F adds some extra lines between Roland and Petronius's speeches: see Appendix 1,
      Passage G.
37   *it* MS ('twere F).
38   *of* about.
42   *To . . . eyes* i.e. to gaze happily into your eyes ('babies' are the miniature reflections
      seen in another person's pupils).
43   *your* F (you MS).
44   *executions* MS (execution F).
      executions performances, duties (with a pun on 'hanging').

PETRONIUS
    And buss you till you blush again.

ROLAND   That's hard, sir;   45
    She must kiss shamefully ere I blush at it.
    I was never so boyish. Well, what follows?

PETRONIUS
    She's mine now as I please to settle her,
    At my command, and where I please to plant her;
    Only she would take a kind farewell of ye,   50
    And give you back a wandering vow or two
    You left in pawn, and two or three slight oaths
    She lent you too, she looks for.

ROLAND   She shall have 'em
    With all my heart, sir, and if you like it better,
    A free release in writing.

PETRONIUS   That's the matter;   55
    And you from her. You shall have another, Roland,
    And then turn tail-to-tail, and peace be with you.

ROLAND
    Why, so be it. [*To* TRANIO] Your twenty pounds sweat, Tranio.

TRANIO
    'Twill not undo me, Roland; do your worst.

ROLAND
    Come, shall we see her, sir.

45   *buss* kiss.
      till F (tell MS).
      hard hard to do.
46   *shamefully* i.e. in a shameful manner.
47   *was never* MS (never was F).
48   *settle* place, direct.
50   *Only* But.
      kind MS (kind of F).
52   *in pawn* i.e. in payment of a debt.
      slight trifling, insubstantial.
55   *release* i.e. release from the vows (vows of marriage could sometimes be binding in
      early modern England, and Petronius is keen to make sure that Roland has no
      claim on Livia).
56   *her. You shall* F (her, you shall) (her shall MS).   *another* i.e. another woman.
57   *turn tail-to-tail* i.e. and then be sexually matched.
58   *Why* MS (*om.* F; [Faith] ed.)
      Your . . . sweat i.e. your money is in danger (at this point Roland is sure that he will
      be able to resist Livia).
      pounds sweat MS (pound sweats F).
60–2 (Come . . . Sir. / What . . . manly, / for . . . peeuish / Lett . . . talke, MS).

BIANCA   Whate'er she says   60
You must bear manly, for her sickness
Has made her somewhat peevish.
ROLAND   Let her talk
Till her tongue ache: I care not. By this hand,
Thou hast a handsome face, wench, and a body
Daintily mounted. [*Aside*] Now do I feel a hundred   65

> Enter LIVIA *sick, carried in a chair by* SERVANTS,
> [*with*] MOROSO *by her*

Running directly from me, as I pissed it.
BIANCA
[*To* SERVANTS] Pray bear her softly.
[*To* PETRONIUS]   The least hurry, sir,
Puts her to much impatience.
PETRONIUS   How is't, daughter?
LIVIA
Oh, sick, very sick – yet somewhat better
Because this good man has forgiven me.   70
[*To* SERVANTS] Pray set me higher. Oh, my head!
BIANCA [*Aside*]   Well done, wench!
LIVIA
Father, and all good people that shall hear me,
I have abused this man perniciously,

61   *manly* MS (manly *Rowland* F).
      manly in a manly fashion.
62   *peevish* MS (teatish F; pettish F2).
65   *a hundred* i.e. the hundred pounds that he would owe Tranio if he was to be loved
      by another woman (see III.i.74–80).
      s.d. *Enter . . . by her* MS (*Enter Livia discovered abed, and Moroso by her.* F). MS's
      stage direction is an indication that the version of the play represented by MS was
      performed in a playhouse which did not have a discovery space, or one large
      enough to fit a bed in it. F places the stage direction after l. 66; MS places it in the
      margins of ll. 65–7.
66   *Running* F (runningly MS). *as* as if.
67   *bear her* MS (draw 'em F).
68   *Puts . . . impatience* i.e. makes her irritable or restless.
69   *Oh . . . sick* MS (O very sick, very sick F).
69–70 *somewhat . . . Because* MS (somewhat / Better I hope; a little lightsommer, / Because
      F).
70   *this good man* i.e. Moroso.
73   *perniciously* F (perintiously MS).
      perniciously hurtfully.

Was never old man humbled so. I have scorned him
And called him nasty names; I have spit at him,   75
Flung candles' ends in his beard, and called him harrow
That must be drawn to all he does; contemned him,
For methought then he was a beastly fellow,
And gave it out his cassock was a barge-cloth
Pawned to his predecessor by a sculler,   80
The man yet extant. I gave him comfits
At a great christening once,
That spoiled his camlet breeches, and one night
I strewed the stairs with peas as he passed down,
And the good gentleman (woe worth me for't!)   85
E'en with this reverent head, this head of wisdom,
Told two-and-twenty stairs, good and true,
Missed not a step, and as we say, *verbatim*,
Fell to the bottom, broke his casting-bottle,
Lost a fair toad-stone of some eighteen shillings,   90
Jumbled his joints together, had two stools,
And was translated. All this villainy
Did I: I, Livia, I alone, untaught.

MOROSO
And I, unasked, forgive it.

74–6   ed. (Was ... so, / I ... names, / I ... him, / flung ... harrow MS).
76   *in his* MS (in's F).
       harrow a heavy timber or iron frame used to prepare arable land after ploughing.
77   *That ... does* Livia implies that Moroso would need help in the bedroom.
78   *fellow* MS (fellow. / (Oh God my side), a very beastly fellow: F).
79   *barge-cloth* a heavy cloth used to protect a barge.
80   *predecessor* ancestor.
       sculler someone who makes his living working sculls (rowing-boats).
81   *extant* MS (living F).
       comfits MS (purging-comfits F).
       comfits sweets usually made of preserved fruits, etc., cased in sugar.
83   *That ... breeches* i.e. Livia fed Moroso so many sweets that he became incontinent.
       camlet an expensive fabric, usually made with silk and angora hair.
85   *woe ... for't* i.e. may I be repaid with sadness for it.
86   *with this* MS (with his F).
87   *Told* Counted.
88   *verbatim* exactly, word-for-word.
90   *toad-stone* stone or similar object shaped like a toad, or thought to have been produced by one, thought to have medicinal properties.
       of worth.
91   *stools* bowel movements.
92   *translated* changed in form.

LIVIA   Where's Bianca?

BIANCA

Here, cousin.

LIVIA   Give me drink.

BIANCA   There.

LIVIA   Who's that?

MOROSO   Roland.   95

LIVIA

Oh, my dissembler. You and I must part.

Come nearer, sir.

ROLAND   I am sorry for your sickness.

LIVIA

Be sorry for yourself, sir. You have wronged me,

But I forgive ye. Are the papers ready?

BIANCA

I have 'em here. [*To* PETRONIUS] Wilt please you view 'em?

PETRONIUS   Yes.   100

LIVIA

Show 'em the young man too; I know he's willing

To shift his sails too, 'tis for his more advancement.

Alas! We might have beggared one another;

We are young both, and a world of children

Might have been left behind to curse our follies.   105

We had been undone, Bianca, had we married,

Undone forever. I confess I loved him,

I care not who shall know it, most entirely,

And once, upon my conscience, he loved me.

But farewell that – we must be wiser, cousin.   110

Love must not leave us to the world.

[*To* ROLAND]   Have ye done?

ROLAND

Yes, and am ready to subscribe.

LIVIA   Pray, stay, then.

---

  96   *dissembler* person who deceived me.
 101   *Show 'em* show them to.
 102   *shift his sails* (1) take another course; (2) find another lover.
        too F (to MS).
        more greater.
 111   *Love . . . world* i.e. love must not leave us at the mercy of the world's cruelties.
112–13 F (Yes . . . subscribe, / Pray . . . papers, / and . . . them, MS).
 112   *stay* wait (Livia needs to be able to handle the documents, so that she can exchange
        the renunciation for the marriage contract.)

Give me the papers, and let me peruse them,
And so much time as may afford a tear
At our last parting.

BIANCA   Pray retire and leave her;   115
I'll call you presently.

PETRONIUS   Come gentlemen;
The shower must fall.

ROLAND   Would I had never seen her.
                    Exeunt all but BIANC[A] *and* LIVIA

BIANCA
Thou hast done bravely, wench.

LIVIA   Pray heaven it prove so.

BIANCA
There are the other papers.   [*They switch the documents*]
                    When they come,
Begin you first, and let the rest subscribe   120
Hard by your side; give 'em as little light
As drapers do their wares.

LIVIA   Didst mark Moroso?
In what an agony he was, and how he cried most
When I abused him most?

BIANCA   That was but reason.

LIVIA
Oh, what a stinking thief it is!   125
Though I was but to counterfeit, he made me
Directly sick indeed. Thames Street to him

114   *afford* yield naturally.
116   *you* MS (ye F).
116–17 ed. (Come . . . fall. MS).
117   *shower* i.e. of tears.
118   *bravely* courageously, splendidly.
119   *the other papers* i.e. the two copies of the marriage contract.
120   *you* F (your MS).
121   *Hard* Close.
121–2 *give . . . wares* i.e. so that they cannot see what they are signing.
124   *That . . . reason* i.e. that was logical.
125   *it* i.e. Moroso (Livia again refers to one of the men in patronising baby-talk: see
      I.ii.52.)
      it is MS (is this? F).
126   *counterfeit* fake it.
127   *Directly* Instantly, absolutely.
      Thames Street an almost proverbially smelly street in the City of London.
      to him compared to him.

Is a mere pomander.

BIANCA

Let him be hanged.

LIVIA   Amen.

BIANCA   And sit you still,

And once more to our business.

LIVIA   Call 'em in,   130

And if there be a power that pities lovers,

Help now, and have my prayers.

Enter PETRONIUS, MOROSO, ROLAND [*and*] TRANIO

PETRONIUS   Is she ready?

BIANCA

She has done her lamentations. Pray go to her.

LIVIA

Roland, come near me, and, before you seal,

Give me your hand. Take it again. Now kiss me.   [*They kiss*] 135

This is the last acquaintance we must have.

I wish you ever happy. There's the paper.

ROLAND

Pray stay a little.

PETRONIUS   Let me never live more

But I do begin to pity this young fellow.

How heartily he weeps!

BIANCA [*To* ROLAND]   There's the pen and ink, sir.   140

---

128   *mere* absolute, veritable.

       pomander mixture of sweet-smelling substances, often in the shape of a ball, carried in a box or bag, in the hand or on a chain around the neck; used to protect the bearer against unpleasant smells.

129   *sit you still* i.e. stay in your chair.

       sit MS (lie F).

130   *our* MS (your F).

131   *power* supernatural power, god.

132   *have* MS (heare F).

133   F (She . . . lamentations, / pray . . . her. MS).

134   *seal* sign (with the implication that a wax seal will be attached to authenticate the document).

138   *Pray . . . little* i.e. don't leave me yet.

       Let . . . more A mild oath.

139   *But* i.e. if I do not.

140   *the pen* MS (Pen F).

LIVIA
    Even here, I pray you; 'tis a little emblem
    How near you have been to me.
ROLAND   There.   [*Signing*]
BIANCA [*To* PETRONIUS *and* MOROSO]   Your hands too,
    As witnesses.
PETRONIUS   By any means. [*He signs*] To th' book, son.
MOROSO
    With all my heart.   [*He signs*]
BIANCA [*To* ROLAND]   You must deliver it.
ROLAND   [*Giving* LIVIA *the document*]
    There, Livia, and a better love light on thee.   145
    I can no more.
BIANCA   To this you must be witness too.
PETRONIUS
    We will.
BIANCA [*To* LIVIA] Do you deliver it now.
LIVIA [*To* SERVANTS]   Pray set me up.
               [*Giving* ROLAND *the document*]
    There, Roland, all thy old love back, and may
    A new to come exceed mine, and be happy.
    I must no more.
ROLAND   Farewell.
LIVIA   A long farewell.
                     Exit ROLAND   150

BIANCA
    Leave her, by any means, till this wild passion
    Be off her head.

---

141   *emblem* symbol.
142   *near* intimate, dear.
143   ed. (By . . . means: / to . . . sonne, MS).
       By any means i.e. certainly.
       book official document.
       son Petronius addresses Moroso as if he was already his son-in-law.
144   *With . . . heart* i.e. gladly.
       deliver it hand it over (i.e. to Livia).
145   *light* fall.
146   *can* can do.
148   *all . . . back* i.e. in the renunciation, which supposedly symbolises the end of their
       love.
152   *Be . . . head* MS (Be off her head: draw all the Curtaines close F). This line again
       suggests that MS has been adapted for a stage without a discovery space.

A day hence you may see her. 'Twill be better;
She is now for little company.

PETRONIUS   Pray tend her;
I must to horse straight.
[*To* MOROSO]   You must needs along too,   155
To see my son aboard. Were but his wife
As fit for pity as this wench, I were happy.

BIANCA
Time must do that too. Farewell. [*To* MOROSO] Tomorrow
You shall receive a wife to 'quite your sorrow.

                                                    Exeunt

[ACT V, SCENE ii]

Enter JAQUES *and* PEDRO, [*and*] PORTERS
with a trunk and hampers

JAQUES
Bring 'em away, sirs.

PEDRO   Must the great trunk go too?

JAQUES
Yes, and the hampers. [*To* PORTERS] Nay, be speedy, masters,
He'll be at sea before us else.

PEDRO   Oh, Jaques,
What a most blessed turn hast thou!

JAQUES   I hope so.

PEDRO
To have the sea between thee and this woman!   5
Nothing can drown her tongue but a storm.

155   *along* i.e. go along.
156   *son* son-in-law (i.e. Petruchio).
157   *fit* suitable.
159   *'quite* requite, atone for.

      [*Act V, Scene ii*] ed. (*Scœna secunda.* F).
  0   s.d. *a trunk* MS (*Chest* F).
  1   *trunk* MS (*Trunks* F).
  4   *blessed turn* good luck (i.e. in going to sea with Petruchio, rather than staying with
      Maria).

JAQUES   By your leave,
  We'll get us up to Paris with all speed,
  For, on my word, as far as Amiens
  She'll carry blank. [*To* PORTERS] Away to Lyon Quay,
  And ship them presently; we'll follow ye.   10
PEDRO
  Now could I wish her in that trunk.
JAQUES   Heaven shield, man,
  I had rather have a bear in't.
PEDRO   Yes, I'll tell thee,
  For in the passage, if a tempest take you,
  As many do, and you lie beating for it,
  Then, if it pleased the Fates, I would have the master,   15
  Out of a careful providence, to cry
  'Lighten the ship of all hands, or we perish!'
  Then this for one, as best spared, should by all means
  Overboard instantly.
JAQUES   O' that condition,
  So we were certain to be rid of her,   20
  I would wish her with us; but believe me, Pedro,
  She would spoil the fishing on this coast forever,
  For none would keep her company but dogfish

---

  8   *word* MS (*soule* F).
      Amiens a city in northern France, between Calais and Paris.
  9   *carry blank* be within range (a 'blank' is the white spot in the middle of a target).
      Lyon Quay Located on Lower Thames Street, near to the Tower of London, from
      whence barges took passengers downriver to Gravesend and ships to the continent.
10   *them* MS ('*em* F).
11   *Heaven* MS (*God* F).
      shield i.e. protect us from it.
12   *thee* MS (*ye* F).
13   *passage* voyage.
      you MS (*ye* F).
14   *lie . . . it* i.e. are striving against contrary winds or currents (*OED*'s first citation
      dates from 1677, but examples can be traced in the early seventeenth century).
16   *careful* MS (*powerful* F).
17   *of all hands* (1) on all sides; (2) everyone.
18   *this* i.e. the trunk containing Maria.
19   *Overboard instantly* Be thrown overboard immediately.
      instantly MS (*presently* F).
20   *So* Provided that.
21   *me* The scribe omitted this word, and it has been interlined.
23   *dogfish* species of small shark.

As currish as herself, or porpoises,
Made to all fatal uses. The two Fish Streets, 25
Were she but once arrived among the whitings,
Would sing a woeful *miserere*, Pedro,
And mourn in Poor John, till her memory
Were cast ashore again with a strong sea-breach.
She would make god Neptune and his fire-fork, 30
And all his demigods and goddesses,
As weary of the Flemish channel, Pedro,
As ever boy was of the school. 'Tis certain
If she but meet him fair, and were well angered,
She would break his godhead.

PEDRO   Oh, her tongue! 35

JAQUES
Rather, her many tongues.

PEDRO   Or rather, strange tongues.

JAQUES
Her lying tongue –

PEDRO   Her lisping tongue –

JAQUES   Her long tongue –

PEDRO
Her lawless tongue –

JAQUES   Her loud tongue –

PEDRO   And her lickerish –

24   *currish* bad-tempered (like a hostile dog, or cur).
     porpoises associated with storms, and through to bring bad luck to sailors.
25   *The . . . Streets* i.e. the inhabitants of Old and New Fish Street in the City of
     London, where fish markets were held.
26   *among* MS (amongst F).
     whitings small fish, prized as good eating (and therefore likely to be sold in
     London's fish markets).
27   *miserere* MS (*misereri* F).
     miserere lament (originally refers to Psalm 51, which begins *Miserere mei Deus*:
     'Have mercy upon me, O God').
28   *Poor John* dried hake (see II.i.52 n.)
29   *ashore* MS (a shore) (o' shore F).
     sea-breach breaker, strong wave.
30   *fire-fork* trident.
32   *Flemish channel* section of the English channel separating England and Belgium.
34   *fair* according to the rules, without unfair advantage on either side.
35   *her tongue* MS (her tongue, her tongue F).
38   *lickerish* lustful.
39   *more* MS (other F).

JAQUES

Many more tongues, and many stranger tongues
Than ever Babel had to tell his ruins,   40
Were women raised withal, but never a true one.

Enter SOPHOCLES

SOPHOCLES

Home with your stuff again, the journey's ended.

JAQUES

What does your worship mean?

SOPHOCLES

Your master – Oh, Petruchio! Oh, poor fellows!

PEDRO

Oh, Jaques, Jaques!

SOPHOCLES   Oh! Your master's dead.   45
His body coming back. His wife – His devil –
The grief of her –

JAQUES   Has killed him!

SOPHOCLES   Killed him, killed him!

PEDRO

Is there no law to hang her?

SOPHOCLES   Get you in,
And let her know her misery. I dare not,
For fear impatience seize me, see her more;   50
I must away again. Bid her for wifehood,
For honesty, if she have any in her,
E'en to avoid the shame that follows her,
Cry if she can. Your weeping cannot mend it.
The body will be here within this hour, so tell her,   55
And all his friends to curse her. Farewell, fellows.

Exit [SOPHOCLES]

---

40   *Babel* Legendary city which is a by-word for a confused mixture of languages: in Biblical narrative its inhabitants presumptuously attempt to build a high tower and are punished by God, who gives them each a different tongue (Genesis 11.1–9).
       tell speak of.

41   *withal* with.

42   *stuff* i.e. the luggage.

47   *grief of her* MS (griefe of – her F).

48   *you* MS (ye F).

51   *for wifehood* i.e. on account of her status as a wife.

56   *Exit* [SOPHOCLES] ed. (*Exit Soph.* F; Exit MS).

PEDRO
  Oh, Jaques, Jaques!
JAQUES   Oh, my worthy master!
PEDRO
  Oh, my most beastly mistress! Hang her!
JAQUES   Split her!
PEDRO
  Drown her directly!
JAQUES   Starve her!
PEDRO   Stink upon her!
JAQUES
  Stone her to death! May all she eat be eggs,   60
  Till she run kicking-mad for men.
PEDRO   And he,
  That man that gives her remedy, pray heaven
  He may e'en *ipso facto* loose his fadings.
JAQUES
  Let's go discharge ourselves. And he that serves her
  Or speaks a good word of her, from this hour   65
  A Sedgeley curse light on him, which is, Pedro,
  The fiend ride through him booted and spurred,
  With a scythe at's back.

                                      [*Exeunt*]

58   *Split her* Cause her pain.
59   *directly* immediately.
      Stink MS, F ([shit] ed.)
      Stink upon her i.e. may she stink.
60   *eggs* thought to be aphrodisiacs: see I.i.52.
61   *run . . . for men* i.e. until she is so aroused that it drives her into a frenzy.
61–2 *And . . . heaven* F (one line MS).
62   *heaven* MS, F ([God] ed.)
63   *ipso facto* by that fact.
      fadings MS (longings F; faddings ed.)
      fadings i.e. virility (A 'fading' was apparently an Irish dance, and 'with a fading' was
      the chorus of a sexually explicit ballad.)
64   *discharge ourselves* resign our positions.
66   *Sedgeley* ed. (seagly MS).
      Sedgeley curse The curse, which Jaques quotes in ll. 67–8, is named after a town in
      Staffordshire, to the north of Birmingham.
68   *at's* at his.

[ACT V, SCENE iii]

Enter ROLAND, [*and*] TRANIO *stealing behind him*

ROLAND

What a dull ass was I to let her go thus!
Upon my life she loves me still. Well, paper,
Thou only monument of what I have had,
Thou all the love now left me, and now lost,
Let me yet kiss her hand, yet take my leave   5
Of what I must leave ever. Farewell, Livia!
Oh! Bitter words, I'll read ye once again,
And then forever study to forget ye.   [*Reads the paper*]
How's this? Let me look better on't. A contract!
I swear, a contract, sealed and ratified,   10
Her father's hand set to it, and Moroso's.
I do not dream, sure! Let me read again.
The same still; 'tis a contract!

TRANIO   'Tis so, Roland,

And, by the virtue of the same, you pay me
A hundred pound tomorrow.

ROLAND   Art sure, Tranio,   15

We are both alive now?

TRANIO   Wonder not: you have lost.

ROLAND

If this be true, I grant it.

TRANIO   'Tis most certain.

[*Act V, Scene iii*] ed. (*Scæna tertia* F).
2 *Well, paper* Roland addresses the document that Livia gave him.
5 *kiss her hand* kiss her handwriting, punning on the practice of kissing someone's
   hand when saying goodbye.
8 *study* strive.
10 *I swear* MS (— F; By Heaven ed.; [Good Lord,] ed.)
11 *hand* i.e. signature.
12 *sure* surely.
15 *A* MS (An F; Two ed.)
   A . . . pound i.e. the hundred pounds that Roland bet that he would not love Livia
   again (see III.i.66–71).
   Art are you.
16 *you* MS (ye F).

There's a ring for you too.   [*Gives him a ring*]
                You know it?

ROLAND   Yes.

TRANIO

  When shall I have my money?

ROLAND   Stay, stay.

  When shall I marry her?

TRANIO   Tonight.

ROLAND   Take heed now   20

  You do not trifle with me. If you do,
  You'll find more payment than your money comes to.
  Come, swear. I know I am a man, and find
  I may deceive myself. Swear faithfully,
  Swear me directly: am I Roland?

TRANIO   Yes.   25

ROLAND

  Am I awake?

TRANIO   You are.

ROLAND   Am I in health?

TRANIO

  As far as I conceive.

ROLAND   Was I with Livia?

TRANIO

  You were, and had this contract.

ROLAND   And shall I enjoy her?

TRANIO

  Yes, if you dare.

ROLAND   Swear to all this.

TRANIO   I will.

ROLAND

  As thou art honest, as thou hast a conscience,   30
  As that may wring thee if thou liest: all these
  To be no vision, but a truth, and serious?

TRANIO

  Then, by my honesty, and faith, and conscience,
  All this is certain.

19   *Stay, stay* MS (Stay ye, stay ye F; Stay ye, stay ed.)
26   *You* MS (Ye F).
29   *you* MS (ye F).
     this MS (these F).
31   *wring* vex.

ROLAND   Let's remove our places.
   Swear it again.
TRANIO   I swear 'tis true.   35
ROLAND
   I have lost then, and heaven knows I am glad on't!
   Let's go, and tell me all, and tell me how,
   For yet I am a pagan in it.
TRANIO   I have a priest too,
   And all shall come as even as two testers.

                                             Exeunt

[ACT V, SCENE iv]

   Enter PETRONIUS, SOPHOCLES, [*and*] MOROSO,
   [*with*] PETRUCHIO *in a coffin, carried by* SERVANTS

PETRONIUS
   Set down the body, and one call her out.
                         [*A* SERVANT *moves to the door*]

   Enter MARIA *in black,* [*with*] JAQUES [*and*] PEDRO

   You are welcome to the last cast of your fortunes.
   There lies your husband, there your loving husband,
   There he that was Petruchio, too good for ye;
   Your stubborn and unworthy way has killed him   5
   Ere he could reach the sea. If you can weep,

34 *remove our places* switch places.
35 *I swear* MS (By — 'tis true F; I sweare by Heaven ed.; I swear, by [God,] ed.)
36 *heaven* MS, F ([God] ed.)
38 *I . . . it* i.e. I don't believe it.
39 *testers* usually glossed as 'sixpences', but may refer to the canopies hung over a bed,
    also known as testers.

    [*Act V, Scene iv*] ed. (*Scæna Quarta* F).
0   s.d. *Enter . . .* SERVANTS MS (*Enter Petronius, Sophocles, Moroso, and Petruchio born
    in a Coffin* F).
1   s.d. *Enter . . .* PEDRO MS (*Enter Maria in blacke, and Jaques* F).
2   *cast* throw (as in a game of dice).
6   *Ere* Before.   *you* MS (ye F).

Now you have cause, begin, and after death
Do something yet to th' world, to think ye honest.
So many tears had saved him, shed in time,
And as they are – so a good mind go with 'em –   10
Yet they may move compassion.

MARIA   Pray you all hear me,
And judge me as I am, not as you covet,
For that would make me yet more miserable.
'Tis true, I have cause to grieve, a mighty cause,
And truly and unfainèdly I weep it.   15

SOPHOCLES
I see there's some good nature yet left in her.

MARIA
But what's the cause? Mistake me not, not this man
As he is dead I weep for – heaven defend it,
I never was so childish – but his life,
His poor, unmanly, wretched, foolish life,   20
Is that my full eyes pity; there's my mourning.

PETRONIUS
Dost thou not shame?

MARIA   I do, and even to water,
To think what this man was, to think how simple,
How far below a man, how far from reason,
From common understanding, and all gentry   25
While he was living here he walked amongst us.
He had a happy turn he died. I'll tell ye,
These are the wants I weep for, not his person;

---

  7   *you* MS (ye F).
  8   *to . . . honest* i.e. to make them think you are honest.
       honest chaste, honourable.
 10   *so . . . 'em* i.e. if the intentions behind them are good.
 11   *you* MS (ye F).
 12   *not . . . covet* i.e. not as you would want me to be.
 15   *unfainèdly* without deception.
17–18   *not . . . for* i.e. I do not weep because this man is dead.
 20   *poor* pitiable, insignificant.
       wretched, foolish ed. (wretched-foolish MS).
 21   *there's my mourning* i.e. that's the thing I'm mourning.
 22   *shame* i.e. feel shame.
       to water to the point of tears.
 23   *simple* foolish.
 25   *gentry* gentility.
 27   *happy turn* piece of good luck.
 28   *wants* things lacking.

. The memory of this man, had he lived
But two years longer, had begot more follies   30
Than wealthy autumn flies. But let him rest.
He was a fool, and farewell he, not pitied –
I mean, in way of life, or action –
By any understanding man that's honest,
But only in's posterity, which I   35
(Out of the fear his ruins might outlive him
In some bad issue) like a careful woman,
Like one indeed born only to preserve him,
Denied him means to raise.

PETRUCHIO *rises out of the coffin*

PETRUCHIO   Unbutton me!
I vow, I die indeed else. Oh, Maria!   40
Oh, my unhappiness, my misery!

PETRONIUS
[*To* MARIA] Go to him, whore. I swear, if he perish,
I'll see thee hanged myself.

PETRUCHIO   Why, why, Maria!

MARIA
I have done my worst, and have my end. Forgive me;
From this hour make me what you please. I have tamed ye,   45
And now am vowed your servant. Look not strangely,
Nor fear what I say to you. Dare you kiss me?
Thus I begin my new love.   [*They kiss*]

---

31   *Than . . . flies* i.e. than a mild autumn breeds flies.
32–9 *not . . . raise* Maria suggests that Petruchio will not be mourned by any wise and
      virtuous men, or even by his children, since she (sensibly in her view) denied him
      the opportunity to father any.
35   *in's* in his.
36   *ruins* bad behaviour.
37   *issue* offspring.
39   *Unbutton me* This may parody a line from the climax of Shakespeare's *King Lear*,
      where the dying king says 'Pray you, undo this button' (V.ii.285); in the 2003 RSC
      production, Petruchio emerged from the coffin attempting to undo a winding-
      sheet which was wrapped around his head.
40   *I vow* MS (— F; By Heaven ed.; [God wot] ed.)
42   *I swear* MS (— F; by Heaven ed.; [God's my judge] ed.)
44   *have my end* i.e. have finished, have achieved my aim.

PETRUCHIO   Once again?
MARIA
    With all my heart, sir.   [*They kiss*]
PETRUCHIO   Once again, Maria.   [*They kiss*]
    [*To the other men*] Oh, gentlemen, I know not where I am!   50
SOPHOCLES
    Get you to bed, then, there you'll quickly know, sir.
PETRUCHIO
    [*To* MARIA] Never no more your old tricks?
MARIA   Never, sir.
PETRUCHIO
    You shall not need, for, as I have a faith,
    No cause shall give occasion.
MARIA   As I am honest,
    And as I am a maid yet, all my life,   55
    From this hour, since you make so free profession,
    I dedicate in service to your pleasure.
SOPHOCLES
    Aye, marry, this goes roundly off!
PETRUCHIO   Go, Jaques;
    Get all the best meat may be bought for money,
    And let the hogshead's blood. I am born again!   60
    Well, little England, when I see a husband
    Of any other nation stern or jealous,
    I'll wish him but a woman of thy breeding,
    And if he have not butter to his bread

---

48   *again?* F (againe?) (again, MS; again. ed.) F's punctuation suggests that Petruchio
        is still hesitant about Maria's intentions, whereas a full stop indicates something
        closer to a command.
51   *Get . . . sir* The narrative has come full circle, with the men again urging Petruchio
        to get Maria into bed.
        you MS (ye F).
53   *as . . . faith* i.e. I vow on my religious faith.
54   *No . . . occasion* i.e. I will give you no reason to.
54–5 *As . . . yet* i.e. I vow on my honesty, and my status as a virgin.
56   *you* MS (ye F).
        free profession i.e. such a sincere promise.
58   *Aye* ed. (I MS, F).
        this . . . off i.e. this is a fitting conclusion.
60   *let . . . blood* i.e. let the beer-cask flow.
61   *little England* An affectionate reference to England, which was 'little' in comparison
        to the contemporary superpowers France and Spain.
64   *if . . . bread* i.e. if he does not get his just deserts.
        his MS (thy F).

Till his teeth bleed, I'll never trust my travel.   65

Enter ROLAND, LIVIA, BIANCA [*and*] TRANIO,
as from marriage

PETRONIUS
What have we here?
ROLAND   Another morris, sir,
That you must pipe too.
TRANIO   A poor married couple
Desire an offering, sir.
BIANCA [*To* PETRONIUS] Never frown at it;
You cannot mend it now. There's your own hand,
And yours, Moroso, to confirm the bargain.   70
            [*She shows them the documents*]

PETRONIUS
My hand?
MOROSO   Or mine?
BIANCA   You'll find it so.
PETRONIUS   A trick,
I swear, a trick!
BIANCA   Yes, sir, we tricked ye.
LIVIA [*To* PETRONIUS]   Father.
PETRONIUS
Hast thou lain with him? Speak.
LIVIA   Yes truly, sir.
PETRONIUS
And hast thou done the deed, boy?
ROLAND   I have done, sir,
That that will serve the turn, I think.

----

 65   *his* MS (*thy* F).
       travel might be modernised as 'travail' (hardship).
       s.d. *Enter . . . marriage* MS (*Enter Roland, Livia, Byancha, and Tranio* F). The stage
       direction probably indicates that they are carrying rosemary (see I.i.0.s.d. n.)
 66   *morris* morris dance.
 67   *must pipe* i.e. must play along with.
 68   *offering* i.e. a dowry for Livia.
71–2 *A . . . trick!* F (*A . . . trick*, MS).
 72   *I . . . trick!* MS (*By — a trick* F; *By Heaven* ed.; *By* [*God*] ed.)
 73   *Hast . . . him* It was much harder to contest a clandestine marriage if it had been
       consummated, as Petronius acknowledges in ll. 75–8.
 75   *serve the turn* i.e. do the trick.

PETRONIUS   A match, then.   75
　　I'll be the maker-up of this, Moroso.
　　There's now no remedy, you see; be willing,
　　For be or be not, he must have the wench.
MOROSO
　　Since I am overreached, let's in to dinner,
　　And if I can, I'll drink't away.
TRANIO   That's well said.   80
PETRONIUS
　　[*To* ROLAND] Well, sirrah, ye have played a trick. Look to't,
　　And let me be a grandsire within's twelvemonth,
　　Or, by this hand, I'll curtail half your fortunes.
ROLAND
　　There shall not want my labour, sir. [*To* TRANIO] Your money;
　　Here's one has undertaken.
TRANIO   Well, I'll trust her,   85
　　And glad I have so good a pawn.
ROLAND   I'll watch ye.
PETRUCHIO
　　Let's in, and drink of all hands, and be jovial.
　　I have my colt again, and now she carries,
　　And, gentlemen, whoever marries next,
　　Let him be sure he keep him to his text.   90

                                                              Exeunt

FINIS

75　　PETRONIUS MS (Petro.) (*Petru.* F).
76　　*maker-up* (1) peace-maker; (2) person who compensates or makes amends.
78　　*For . . . not* i.e. because if whether you're willing or not.
79　　*overreached* outsmarted.
81　　*Look to't* see to it.
82　　*within's* within this.
83　　*curtail* cut off.　　*fortunes* i.e. dowry, the money that Petronius will settle on Livia.
84　　*labour* effort, hard work (the emphasis may be on '*my* labour' as opposed to Livia's
　　　labour during childbirth).
84–5　*Your . . . undertaken* i.e. here's someone (Livia) who has agreed to pay your money.
86　　*so . . . ye* Tranio pretends to think that Roland is giving him Livia as security on his
　　　money, provoking Roland's reply, which is probably mock-jealous rather than genuine.
87　　*drink . . . hands* i.e. drinks for everyone.
88　　*colt* a young horse (usually male). The word is used to refer to inexperienced or
　　　lively people of either sex, and particularly those in need of training.
　　　carries i.e. is prepared to let me ride her.
90　　*keep . . . text* follow the rules (as established here).

APPENDIX I

LONGER ADDITIONAL PASSAGES

These passages do not appear in the manuscript of *The Tamer Tamed* but are to be found in both Folio texts. The majority relate to the Livia-Moroso-Roland plot and while they serve to deepen the characterisation of Moroso and Bianca they do not add materially to the narrative. Folio-only sections shorter than two lines can be found in the notes to the main text.

Passage A: Additional lines after I.iii.12

TRANIO
> A good tough train would break thee all to pieces;
> Thou hast not breath enough to say thy prayers.

Passage B: Opening of Act II

Enter PETRONIUS *and* MOROSO

PETRONIUS
> A box o' th' ear, do you say?

MOROSO   Yes, sure, a sound one,
> Beside my nose blown to my hand. If Cupid
> Shoot arrows of that weight, I'll swear devoutly
> H'as sued his livery, and is no more a boy.

PETRONIUS
> You gave her some ill language?

MOROSO   Not a word.   5

PETRONIUS
> Or might be you were fumbling?

MOROSO   Would I had, sir!

Passage A
> 1   *train* course of riding (used of horses).

Passage B
> 1   *sound* forceful.
> 2   *Beside . . . hand* i.e. as well as being wrung by the nose.
> 4   *sued his livery* i.e. finished his apprenticeship.
>   *and is* F2 (and F).
> 6   *might be* maybe.
>   *fumbling* attempting to grope her, making clumsy sexual advances.

I had been aforehand then. But to be baffled,
And have no feeling of the cause –
PETRONIUS   Be patient.
I have a medicine clapped to her back will cure her.
MOROSO
No, sure, it must be afore, sir.
PETRONIUS   O' my conscience,   10
When I got these two wenches (who till now
Ne'er showed their riding) I was drunk with bastard,
Whose nature is to form things like itself,
Heady and monstrous. Did she slight him too?
MOROSO
That's all my comfort. A mere hobby-horse   15
She made Childe Roland. 'Sfoot, she would not know him,
Not give him a free look, not reckon him
Among her thoughts, which I held more than wonder,
I having seen her within's three days kiss him
With such an appetite as though she would eat him.   20

7   *aforehand* prepared (with a pun on 'hand').
      baffled disgraced; foiled.
8   *feeling* understanding.
9   *I . . . her* Petronius suggests that being whipped would improve Livia's behaviour.
      clapped i.e. which if it is applied.
10   *No . . . afore* Moroso mistakenly thinks (or pretends to think) that Petronius is
      talking about sex, so he responds by saying that Livia must be approached from the
      front rather than be taken from behind.
11   *got* begot.
12   *Ne'er . . . riding* i.e. never revealed their true nature (as at I.iv.18, 'riding' can refer
      to sex, so Petronius may allude to his daughters' conception).
      bastard sweet Spanish wine.
14   *Heady* Violent, impetuous, passionate.
      slight disdain.
15   *hobby-horse* i.e. fool, buffoon (Refers to the popular figure of the hobby-horse in
      the morris dance, but in context suggests that Livia made Roland look like a mere
      simulation of a man.)
16   *Childe Roland* A legendary hero of folklore and ballads, also mentioned in
      Shakespeare's *King Lear* (III.iv.178–80).
      Childe In the ballad tradition 'child' is a title given to young noblemen; in early
      modern English it often refers to pages or attendants, or is used as an insult
      towards someone considered to be immature.
      'Sfoot a blasphemous oath (a contraction of 'by God's foot').
18   *held . . . wonder* i.e. found very strange.
19   *within's* within these.

PETRONIUS
There is some trick in this. How did he take it?

MOROSO
Ready to cry, he ran away.

PETRONIUS   I fear her.
And yet, I tell you, ever to my anger
She is as tame as innocency. It may be
This blow was but a favour.

MOROSO   I'll be sworn   25
'Twas well tied on, then.

PETRONIUS   Go to. Pray forget it.
I have bespoke a priest, and within's two hours
I'll have ye married. Will that please you?

MOROSO   Yes.

PETRONIUS
I'll see it done myself, and give the lady
Such a sound exhortation for this knavery,   30
I'll warrant you, shall make her smell this month on't.

MOROSO
Nay, good sir, be not violent.

PETRONIUS   Neither –

MOROSO   It may be
Out of her earnest love there grew a longing
(As you know women have such toys), in kindness
To give me a box o' th' ear or so.

PETRONIUS   It may be.   35

MOROSO
I reckon for the best still. This night, then,

22   *fear* distrust.
23   *to* in response to.
24   *innocency* innocence.
25   *favour* See II.iii.53 n.
26   *Go to* An exclamation expressing indignation or sorrow.
     to ed. (too F).
27   *bespoke* arranged for.
30   *exhortation* i.e. an earnest lecture about her behaviour (but the next lines suggest
     that Petronius actually has a beating in mind).
31   *smell . . . on't* i.e. the effects will last for a month ('smell' is used metaphorically).
     on't of it.
32–5   *It . . . so* Moroso suggests that Livia's love is so violent that it expresses itself in
     physical blows.
34   *toys* whims, fancies.
36   *reckon for the best* i.e. count on the best outcome.

I shall enjoy her?

PETRONIUS   You shall handsel her.

MOROSO

Old as I am, I'll give her one blow for't
Shall make her groan this twelvemonth.

PETRONIUS   Where's your jointure?

MOROSO

I have a jointure for her.

PETRONIUS   Have your counsel   40
Perused it yet?

MOROSO

No counsel but the night, and your sweet daughter,
Shall e'er peruse that jointure.

PETRONIUS   Very well, sir.

MOROSO

I'll no demurrers on't, nor no rejoinders.
The other's ready sealed.

PETRONIUS   Come, then, let's comfort   45
My son Petruchio. He's like little children
That lose their baubles, crying ripe.

MOROSO   Pray tell me,
Is this stern woman still upon the flaunt
Of bold defiance?

PETRONIUS   Still, and still she shall be
Till she be starved out. You shall see such justice   50
That women shall be glad after this tempest
To tie their husbands' shoes and walk their horses.

[MOROSO]

That were a merry world! Do you hear the rumour?

---

37   *handsel* (1) try, taste; (2) be the first to enjoy.
39   *groan* i.e. in childbirth.
       jointure See I.ii.117 n.
40   *jointure* i.e. sexual reward.   *counsel* lawyers.
44   *demurrers* objections (originally a legal term referring to a pleading which temporarily stops the action).
       rejoinders answers (originally refers to a defendant's answer to the plaintiff's replication in a legal case).
45   *other's* i.e. the other contract is.
47   *baubles* toys.
       crying ripe (1) crying copiously; (2) ready to cry.
48   *this stern woman* i.e. Maria.
       stern (1) grim, harsh; (2) merciless, cruel.
48–9 *upon . . . Of* i.e. displaying herself in.

They say the women are in insurrection,
And mean to make a –
PETRONIUS   They'll sooner   55
Draw upon walls, as we do. Let 'em, let 'em!
We'll ship 'em out in cuck-stools; there they'll sail,
As brave Columbus did, till they discover
The happy islands of obedience.
We stay too long. Come.
MOROSO   Now St George be with us.   60

          Exeunt

Passage C: Additional lines after II.iii.77

PEDRO
Then are they victualled with pies and puddings
(The trappings of good stomachs), noble ale
(The true defender), sausages – and smoked ones,
If need be, such as serve for pikes – and pork
(Better the Jews never hated); here and there   5
A bottle of metheglin, a stout Briton
That will stand to 'em. What else they want, they war for.

53   [*MOROSO*] F2 (*om.* F).
55   *to make a –* A two- or three-syllable word or phrase (probably obscene, or
      containing a blasphemous oath) seems to be missing here; Daileader and Taylor
      supply 'cunt-republic' (i.e. 'democratic nation of women' or 'country public').
55–6 *They'll . . . do* i.e. they're more likely to develop the ability to urinate standing up.
57   *cuck-stools* i.e. cucking stools, on which a disobedient woman might be dunked in
      a pond or river in order to shame or punish her.
57–9 *there . . . obedience* i.e. they'll be left at sea until they learn how to be obedient.
      Petronius may also allude to the legend that tribes of Amazons had been found by
      European explorers in South America.
59   *happy islands* Refers to the classical legend of the utopian 'Fortunate Isles' to be
      found somewhere in the Atlantic Ocean.
60   *St George* As in I.iii.19–22, the women are cast as the dangerous dragons to the men's
      Saint George.   *be with us* i.e. support us.

Passage C
1   *victualled* supplied.
2   *trappings* ornaments, decorations.
4   *pikes* pointed staffs, spears.
4–5 *pork . . . hated* See I.ii.26–7 n.
6   *metheglin* a spiced or medicated variety of mead associated particularly with Wales
      (and therefore Celtic or 'British').
7   *stand to 'em* i.e. stand up for them.

Passage D: Additional lines after II.v.135

LIVIA
He will undo me in mere pans of coals
To make him lusty.

Passage E: Replacing III.iv.55-63

[PETRUCHIO]
If any man misdoubt me for infected,
There is mine arm, let any man look on't.

Enter DOCTOR *and* APOTHECARY

DOCTOR
Save ye, gentlemen.
PETRONIUS   Oh, welcome, Doctor!
Ye come in happy time. Pray, your opinion;
What think you of his pulse?
DOCTOR   It beats with busiest,   5
And shows a general inflammation
Which is the symptom of a pestilent fever.
Take twenty ounces from him.
PETRUCHIO   Take a fool!
Take an ounce from mine arm and, Doctor Deuce-ace,

Passage D
    1   *undo* ruin financially.
         in i.e. in buying.
    1–2 *pans . . . lusty* i.e. to keep him warm and therefore sexually active.

Passage E.
    1   *misdoubt me for* fear that I am.
    2   s.d. APOTHECARY ed. (*Pothecary* F).
    3   *Save ye* i.e. God save you: a common greeting.
    4   *happy* good.
    5   *It . . . busiest* i.e. it beats as fast as any.
    8   *ounces* i.e. ounces of blood (the Doctor recommends bleeding Petruchio).
         from F2 (frow F).
         Take a fool i.e. like hell you will (Daileader and Taylor).
    9   *Deuce-ace* ed. (Deuz-ace F).
         Deuce-ace A bad throw in dice (turning up deuce [two] with one die and ace [one]
         with the other), often linked to bad luck or lack of social status, and therefore used
         as an insult.

I'll make a close-stool of your velvet costard.   10
'Death, gentlemen, do ye make a May-game on me?
I tell ye once again, I am as sound,
As well, as wholesome and as sensible
As any of ye all. Let me out quickly
Or, as I am a man, I'll beat the walls down,   15
And the first thing I light upon shall pay for't.

                    Exit DOCTOR *and* APOTHECARY

PETRONIUS

Nay, we'll go with you, Doctor.

MARIA   'Tis the safest.

I saw the tokens, sir.

PETRONIUS   Then there is but one way.

Passage F: Opening of Act IV

Enter MOROSO *and* PETRONIUS

MOROSO

That I do love her is without all question,
And most extremely, dearly, most exactly;
And that I would even now, this present Monday,
Before all others – maids, wives, women, widows,
Of what degree or calling – marry her,   5
As certain too. But to be made a whim-wham,

---

10   *close-stool* chamber-pot.
        velvet i.e. velvet-capped.
        costard head.
11   *'Death* MS (— F, F2).
        May-game i.e. a fool.
12   *sound* healthy.
13   *wholesome* healthy.
        sensible mentally sound.
16   *light* come, fall.
        for't for it.
        s.d. APOTHECARY ed. (*Pothecary* F).
18   *tokens* i.e. spots that were symptoms of the plague.

Passage F
  5   *degree* social status.
        calling profession, way of life.
  6   *As* Is as.
        whim-wham trifle.

A jib-crack, and a gentleman o' th' first house
For all my kindness to her –

PETRONIUS   How you take it!
Thou get a wench, thou get a dozen nightcaps.
Wouldst have her come and lick thee like a calf,   10
And blow thy nose, and buss thee?

MOROSO   Not so neither.

PETRONIUS
What wouldst thou have her do?

MOROSO   Do as she should do.
Put on a clean smock, and to church, and marry,
And then to bed, i' God's name. This is fair play,
And keeps the King's peace. Let her leave her bobs,   15
I have had too many of them, and her quillets;
She is as nimble that way as an eel,
But in the way she ought to me especially
A sow of lead is swifter.

PETRONIUS   Quote your griefs down.

MOROSO
Give fair quarter. I am old and crazy,   20
And subject to much fumbling, I confess it,
Yet something I would have that's warm to hatch me.
But understand me, I would have it so

---

7   *jib-crack* knick-knack, useless ornament.
    gentleman . . . house upstart (someone whose family ['house'] is not long-estab-
    lished).
9   *Thou . . . nightcaps* i.e. if you do manage to marry you're likely to be cuckolded a
    dozen times.
    a dozen F2 (dozen F).
11 *buss* kiss.
14 *i'* ed. (a F).
15 *the King's peace* i.e. good order.
    bobs tricks, mockery.
16 *quillets* specious arguments, quibbles.
17–19 *She . . . swifter* i.e. she is quick to insult me but is as heavy as lead when it comes to
    fulfilling her duty to me.
19 *sow* ingot.
    Quote . . . down i.e. make a mental note of the things done to you.
20 *Give fair quarter* i.e. make allowances.
    crazy frail, feeble.
21 *fumbling* nervous clumsiness; sexual impotence.
22 *something . . . me* Moroso imagines himself as an egg kept warm and brought to life
    by his new young wife.
23 *so* i.e. in such a manner.

I buy not more repentance in the bargain
Than the ware's worth I have. If you allow me   25
Worthy your son-in-law, and your allowance,
Do it a way of credit; let me show so,
And not be troubled in my visitations
With blows and bitterness, and downright railings,
As if we were to couple like two cats   30
With clawing and loud clamour.

PETRONIUS   Thou fond man,
Hast thou forgot the ballad 'Crabbèd age'?
Can May and January match together
And never a storm between 'em? Say she abuse thee,
Put case she do.

MOROSO   Well.

PETRONIUS   Nay, believe she does.   35

MOROSO

I do believe she does.

PETRONIUS   And devilishly;
Art thou a whit the worse?

MOROSO   That's not the matter.
I know, being old, 'tis fit I am abused.
I know 'tis handsome, and I know, moreover,
I am to love her for't.

25   *Than . . . have* i.e. than the goods are worth.
25–6   *allow . . . your* i.e. admit that I am worthy to be.
27   *it . . . credit* i.e. in a creditable fashion.
        show so appear worthy.
29   *downright* plain, absolute.
        railings rantings, abusive speech.
30   *couple* mate.
31   *and* F2 (add F).
        fond foolish.
32   *ballad 'Crabbèd age'* Refers to a song apparently first printed in a collection
        published under Shakespeare's name, *The Passionate Pilgrim* (1599). The speaker is
        a young woman and the first lines run: 'Crabbed age and youth cannot live
        together: / Youth is full of pleasance, age is full of care; / Youth like summer morn,
        age like winter weather; / Youth like summer brave, age like winter bare'.
33   *May and January* i.e. a young woman and an old man.
34   *Say* Suppose.
35   *Put case* Suppose.
37   *a whit the worse* i.e. at all worse off.
        That's not the matter i.e. that's not what I'm worried about.
38   *fit* appropriate.
39   *handsome* becoming, appropriate.

PETRONIUS   Now you come to me.   40
MOROSO
　　Nay, more than this, I find too, and find certain,
　　What gold I have, pearl, bracelets, rings, or ouches,
　　Or what she can desire – gowns, petticoats,
　　Waistcoats, embroidered stockings, scarves, cauls, feathers,
　　Hats, five-pound garters, muffs, masks, ruffs and ribbons –   45
　　I am to give her for't.
PETRONIUS   'Tis right, you are so.
MOROSO
　　But when I have done all this, and think it duty,
　　Is't requisite another bore my nostrils?
　　Riddle me that.
PETRONIUS   Go, get you gone, and dream
　　She's thine within these two days, for she is so.   50
　　The boy's beside the saddle. Get warm broths
　　And feed apace; think not of worldly business,
　　It cools the blood. Leave off your tricks, they are hateful,
　　And mere forerunners of the ancient measures.
　　Contrive your beard o' th' top cut like verdugo's;   55
　　It shows you would be wise. And burn your nightcap;
　　It looks like half a winding-sheet, and urges
　　From a young wench nothing but cold repentance.
　　You may eat onions so you'll not be lavish.

40　*Now . . . me* i.e. now you're getting the point.
42　*ouches* brooches.
44　*embroidered* ed. (Enbroydered F).
　　cauls caps, head-dresses.
45　*five-pound* i.e. costing five pounds (worth around £489.40 in 2009) and therefore costly.
　　ribbons ed. (Ribands F: an archaic form of 'ribbons').
48　*bore my nostrils* i.e. make me a cuckold.
49　*Riddle me that* i.e. explain that to me.
51　*The . . . saddle* i.e. everything is ready (the 'boy' is the attendant holding the head of the horse while it awaits its rider).
53　*tricks* mannerisms, physical ticks.
54　*mere . . . measures* i.e. even more outdated than the oldest dances.
55　*like verdugo's* Probably means 'in a Spanish style', but 'verdugo' means executioner in Spanish and in *The Alchemist* (1610) Jonson appears to use 'verdugoship' as a synonym for 'hangman' (III.iii.71); 'verdugo' appears as an insult in Beaumont and Fletcher's *The Scornful Lady* (II.i.127).
57　*winding-sheet* shroud.
59　*onions* Thought to invigorate sexually (see Williams, 2: 972).
　　so provided.

MOROSO

    I am glad of that.

PETRONIUS   They purge the blood, and quicken;   60

    But after 'em, conceive me, sweep your mouth,

    And where there wants a tooth, stick in a clove.

MOROSO

    Shall I hope once again? Say't.

PETRONIUS   You shall, sir.

    And you shall have your hope.

Enter BIANCA *and* TRANIO [*in conversation*]

MOROSO   Why, there's a match, then.

BIANCA

    You shall not find me wanting. Get you gone.   65

    Here's the old man; he'll think you are plotting else

    Something against his new son.

                         Exit TRANIO

MOROSO

    Fare ye well sir.   *Exit* MOROSO

BIANCA [*Sings*] *An' every buck had his doe,*

       An' every cuckold a bell at his toe,

       Oh, what sport should we have then, then, boys, then,   70

       Oh, what sport should we have then!

PETRONIUS

    [*Aside*] This is the spirit that inspires 'em all.

BIANCA

    [*Making to leave*] Give you good even.

PETRONIUS   A word with you, sweet lady.

BIANCA

    I am very hasty, sir.

---

  60   *quicken* enliven it.

  61   *conceive* believe, understand.

         sweep clean, wash out.

  62   *there wants a tooth* i.e. where a tooth is missing.

  63   *Say't* Say it (i.e. tell me).

  67   *son* i.e. Moroso, Petronius's intended son-in-law.

68–71   *An'... then!* This song is apparently original to *The Tamer Tamed*.

  68   *An'* ed. (And F).   *An'* If.

  69   *An'* ed. (And F).   *An'* If.

  72   *spirit* character, person of a particular disposition.

  73   *Give... even* See II.v.61 n.

  74   *very hasty* in a great hurry.

PETRONIUS   So you were ever.
BIANCA
    Well, what's your will?
PETRONIUS   Was not your skilful hand   75
    In this last stratagem? Were not your mischiefs
    Eking the matter on?
BIANCA   In's shutting up?
    Is that it?
PETRONIUS Yes.
BIANCA   I'll tell you.
PETRONIUS   Do.
BIANCA   And truly.
    Good old man, I do grieve exceeding much,
    I fear too much –
PETRONIUS   I am sorry for your heaviness.   80
    Belike you can repent, then?
BIANCA   There you are wide too.
    Not that the thing was done (conceive me rightly)
    Does any way molest me –
PETRONIUS   What, then, lady?
BIANCA
    But that I was not in't: there's my sorrow, there.
    Now you understand me. For I'll tell you,   85
    It was so sound a piece, and so well carried,
    And, if you mark the way, so handsomely,
    Of such a height, and excellence, and art,
    I have not known a braver. For, conceive me,
    When the gross fool her husband would be sick –   90

72   *you* F2 (your F).
77   *Eking* Urging.
      In's In his (i.e. Petruchio's).
80   *heaviness* sorrow.
81   *Belike* Perhaps.
      wide i.e. wide of the mark.
82   *the thing* i.e. the imprisonment of Petruchio.
      conceive me rightly understand me correctly.
83   *molest* trouble, grieve.
84   *in't* i.e. involved in it.
86   *piece* action, plot.   *carried* i.e. carried out.
87   *handsomely* skilfully.
88   *such a height* i.e. of such good quality.
89   *braver* more splendid.
90   *would be* i.e. would decide to be.

PETRONIUS
Pray, stay.
BIANCA   Nay, good, your patience! And no sense for't,
Then stepped your daughter in –
PETRONIUS   By your appointment.
BIANCA
I would it had, on that condition
I had but one half smock, I like it so well.
And, like an excellent cunning woman, cured me   95
One madness with another, which was rare,
And to our weak beliefs, a wonder.
PETRONIUS   Hang ye,
For, surely, if your husband look not to ye,
I know what will.
BIANCA   I humbly thank your worship.
And so I take my leave.   [*She goes to leave*]   100
PETRONIUS
You have a hand, I hear, too –
BIANCA   I have two, sir.
PETRONIUS
In my young daughter's business.
BIANCA   You will find there
A fitter hand than mine to reach her frets,

91   *your patience* i.e. be patient.
       And . . . for't i.e. and with no good reason for his sickness.
92   *By your appointment* i.e. as you arranged.
93–4   *I . . . smock* i.e. I would give almost everything I own to have been the organiser of
       this.
95   *cunning woman* female healer.
       cured me i.e. cured for me (see II.iii.56 n.)
96   *madness* i.e. mad plot.
       rare remarkable.
97   *wonder* miracle.
98   *your husband* This is the play's only reference to Bianca's husband, although it
       could refer to a hypothetical husband rather than a real one. It was omitted by the
       RSC in 2003, and the production strongly implied that the black-clad Bianca was
       a widow.
101   *I have two* Bianca pretends to take Petronius's 'hand' literally rather than
       figuratively.
103   *fitter hand* i.e. that of Roland, rather than Moroso.
       to . . . frets (1) to 'play' her sexually; (2) to deal with her moods.
       frets (1) rings or ridges on the fingerboard of a stringed instrument; (2) moods,
       peevishness.

And play down-diddle to her.

PETRONIUS   I shall watch ye.

BIANCA

Do.

PETRONIUS And I shall have justice.

BIANCA   Where?

PETRONIUS   That's all one.   105

I shall be with you at a turn henceforward.

BIANCA

Get you a posset too. And so good even, sir.

Exeunt

Passage G: Additional lines after V.i.36

PETRONIUS   Yes, sir,

Or rather, as it seems, repenting. And there

She lies within, debating on't.

ROLAND   Well, sir.

---

104 *down-diddle* A ballad refrain often used as a euphemism for sex (see Williams, 1: 411).

106 *I . . . henceforward* i.e. I shall soon be even with you.

107 *posset* See III.ii.30 n. Possets were often drunk before bed.
     even evening.

Passage G

2–3 ed. (Or . . . repenting / And . . . on't F).

APPENDIX 2

PROLOGUES AND EPILOGUES

A: 1633 (?) Prologue and Epilogue

Printed in the 1647 Folio, this prologue and epilogue were probably written for the 1633 revival, possibly by William Davenant, who wrote prologues and epilogues for other Fletcher plays revived by the King's Men in the 1630s.

PROLOGUE

Ladies to you, in whose defence and right
Fletcher's brave Muse prepared herself to fight
A battle without blood – 'twas well fought too;
The victory's yours, though got with much ado –
We do present this comedy, in which   5
A rivulet of pure wit flows, strong and rich
In fancy, language, and all parts that may
Add grace and ornament to a merry play,
Which this may prove. Yet not to go too far
In promises from this our female war,   10
We do entreat the angry men would not
Expect the mazes of a subtle plot,
Set speeches, high expressions, and, what's worse
In a true comedy, politic discourse.
The end we aim at is to make you sport,   15
Yet neither gall the city, nor the court.
Hear and observe his comic strain, and when

Prologue 1633

2   *Fletcher's . . . prepared* The use of Fletcher's name and of the past tense suggests that the prologue was written after the dramatist's death in 1625.

6   *rivulet* stream.

7   *fancy* imagination.

11–16   *We . . . court* The denial that there is political material or satire in a comedy is a conventional one, but its use here may reflect on the problems that the King's Men had with the censor.

12   *mazes* i.e. puzzling complexities.

13   *Set . . . expressions* i.e. elaborate rhetoric (thought inappropriate for comedy).

16   *gall* irritate.

17   *his* i.e. Fletcher's.

Y'are sick of melancholy, see't again.
'Tis no dear physic, since 'twill 'quite the cost,
Or his intentions, with our pains, are lost.   20

EPILOGUE

The tamer's tamed, but so as nor the men
Can find one just cause to complain of, when
They fitly do consider in their lives
They should not reign as tyrants o'er their wives;
Nor can the women from this precedent   5
Insult or triumph, it being aptly meant
To teach both sexes due equality
And, as they stand bound, to love mutually.
If this effect, arising from a cause
Well laid and grounded, may deserve applause,   10
We something more than hope our honest ends
Will keep the men, and women too, our friends.

B: 1660 Prologue and Epilogue

This prologue and epilogue were written by Thomas Jordan for a
performance of *The Tamer Tamed* at the Red Bull playhouse on 24
June 1660. This was not long after the dissolution of the so-called
Rump Parliament and the return of Charles II from exile, and the
uncertain political climate is a constant theme. Jordan, a playwright
and former actor, was strongly royalist in his sympathies, and his
prologue and epilogue are therefore hostile to those perceived as

18   *see't* see it.
19   *dear* expensive.
      physic medicine.
      'quite requite, repay.
20   *pains* efforts.

Epilogue 1633
      This epilogue was probably delivered by the actor playing Maria.
1–2   *so . . . Can* i.e. in such a manner that the men cannot.
3   *consider* consider that.
6   *Insult* boast contemptuously.
8   *stand bound* are required.
      mutually equally, reciprocally.
11   *something . . . hope* i.e. we are convinced.
      ends intentions, purposes.

political threats to the new regime. The prologue and epilogue
were printed in Jordan's *A Royal Arbour of Loyal Poesie* (London,
1663), pp. 20–1.

A Prologue to the Comedy called *The Tamer Tamed*,
June 24 1660.

Enter [PROLOGUE] *Reading of the Bill*

The Tamer Tamed? What do the players mean?
Shall we have Rump and rebel in the scene?
Juntos of safety with the righteous rabble
Of apron-peers, knights of Sir Arthur's table?
Shall Baxter, Hewson, Scott, and Fox be named?   5
These were our tamers, but I hope they're tamed,
For those were men who (in their holy rage)
Did things too horrid for a civil stage,

Prologue 1660

> *June 24 1660* The professional stage had been banned during the Commonwealth
> and Protectorate, but performances seem to have begun to be permitted again late
> in 1659.

0   s.d. *Bill* playbill (a poster advertising the play to be performed that day).

2   *Rump* Alludes to the Rump Parliament, the remnant of the 'Long Parliament' after
> those hostile to the execution of Charles I were ejected, which was dissolved by
> Cromwell in April 1653 but reinstated in May 1659. The Rump Parliament finally
> dissolved itself on 6 March 1660, prior to the return of Charles II, who arrived in
> London on 8 May.
> *rebel* Refers to those who took arms against Charles I in 1642.

3   *Juntos* factions, cliques (often used to refer to the Parliaments of the 1640s and
> 50s).

4   *apron-peers* workmen with pretensions to authority.
> *Sir Arthur's table* Parodies King Arthur's table, where his knights legendarily met,
> with reference to Sir Arthur Hesilrige (1601–61), a leading republican politician
> and member of the Rump Parliament, who was imprisoned in the Tower of
> London on Charles II's return and died there in April 1661.

5   *Baxter* Richard Baxter (1615–91), a leading Presbyterian minister, and author of *A
> Holy Commonwealth* (1659).
> *Hewson* John Hewson (*fl.* 1630–60), a leading soldier who was one of Charles I's
> judges at his 1649 trial and a signatory on the king's death warrant; he apparently
> fled to the continent on Charles II's return.
> *Scott* Thomas Scott (*d.* 1660), a leading republican politician who was a judge at
> Charles I's trial and signed his death warrant; he left England in April 1660 but was
> returned in July and was eventually executed on 17 October.
> *Fox* Probably refers to George Fox (1624–91), a leading Quaker and author of *Fifty-
> Nine Particulars for the Regulating [of] Things* (1659), who was jailed for five
> months after Charles II's return.

Unless our company should all comply
To leave good language and speak blasphemy.　　　　　10
This play, *The Tamer Tamed*, is Fletcher's wit,
A man that pleased all palates, therefore sit
And see the last scene out, pray do not run
Into confusion till the play be done.
Should strangers see you mix among us thus,　　　　　15
They would be apt to think you some of us.
Pray keep your seats, you do not sit in fear
As in the dangerous days of Oliver.
It is not now – in good time be it spoke –
'*Enter the Red-Coats*', '*Exit Hat and Cloak*'.　　　　　20
But such a prosperous change doth now attend ye,
That those who did affront ye shall defend ye.

The Epilogue, Spoken by the Tamer, a Woman.

With licence of my husband, I apply
Myself to this honoured society.
I fear I have offended the good laws
Of household government, and given cause
By my example (in this wild assay)　　　　　5
For some to put in practice what we play,

12　　*palates* tastes.
12–17　　*therefore . . . seats* Suggests that the Red Bull audience were likely to behave in a disruptive fashion.
15　　*strangers* foreigners.
16　　*of us* i.e. of the actors, because they are on the stage.
18　　*Oliver* Oliver Cromwell (1599–1658), Lord Protector of England 1653–8, another judge at Charles I's trial and signatory of the death warrant.
19　　*in good time* (1) luckily; (2) quickly; (3) indeed, to be sure.
20　　*Red-Coats* The New Model Army, established by Cromwell and Parliament in 1645, wore red coats, and these were retained by Charles II's army after the Restoration. *Hat and Cloak* i.e. civilised or civilian clothing.
22　　*those . . . ye* i.e. the red-coated soldiers.

Epilogue 1660
　　Spoken . . . Woman i.e. by the actor playing Maria (probably, at this point, a male actor).
1　　*With . . . husband* In contrast with the 1630s epilogue, which emphasises mutuality, Jordan attempts to reinstate Petruchio's authority over Maria.
3–8　　*I . . . mistake* The epilogue fears that women in the audience will take Maria's revolt seriously and will desire to challenge gender roles as a result.
5　　*assay* attempt.

And 'cause the breeches now come near the make
Of petticoats, may willingly mistake.
These are old quarrels, and no doubt came in
When Adam digged and Madam Eve did spin;   10
They're ne'er the honester for that. The crime
Of bold rebellion is older than time;
The breach of trust is old, the breach of laws,
Murder of kings: witness 'The Good Old Cause'.
But we exhibit to your approbation   15
Not the rebellion but the reformation.

C: 1757(?) Epilogue

This epilogue survives in Folger Shakespeare Library Manuscript
W.b.467, fols 5–6. It was apparently written for an adaptation of
The Tamer Tamed prepared by the actor-manager David Garrick
(1717–79) for Drury Lane in 1757, but may not have been
performed.

A Epilogue Designed for the Wedding-Night
Taken From Beaumont and Fletcher's *Tamer Tamed*,
to be Spoke by Mrs Clive

7–8   *breeches . . . petticoats* Refers to a Restoration fashion for voluminous 'petticoat'
      breeches, often trimmed with ribbons.
10   *When . . . spin* Alludes to the words supposedly uttered by the Lollard preacher
      John Ball during the Peasants' Revolt of 1381: 'When Adam delved and Eve span, /
      Who was then the gentleman?' The phrase had enormous currency during the
      Civil War, especially in radical sectarian thought, and Jordan is keen to discredit
      challenges to both gender and class roles.
11   *They're* i.e. the quarrels.
14   '*The . . . Cause*' Coined by soldiers in the New Model Army to describe the original
      political and religious aims of the republican forces, used by General John Lambert
      in April 1660 in his attempt to rally opposition to the Restoration.

Epilogue 1757
      Beaumont and Fletcher's In the eighteenth and nineteenth centuries plays by
      Fletcher and his collaborators were often indiscriminately referred to as being by
      'Beaumont and Fletcher'.
      Mrs Clive Catherine (Kitty) Clive (1711–85), one of the leading comic actresses of
      her day and one of Garrick's co-stars at Drury Lane. Genest (4: 483, 485) records
      that Hannah Mary Pritchard played Maria on 30 April and 2 May 1757, so it is
      possible that the casting changed after this epilogue was drafted.

The struggle past, domestic peace proclaimed,
Myself victorious, and my monster tamed,
I'm come, no suppliant, but resolved to know
Who dares pronounce himself the poet's foe.
A dreadful corps though I confess you are,   5
With all your engines of theatric war,
Yet lay them by, I'll take the boldest down,
Fight me but face-to-face, and one by one.
The critic swear, I'm told, should this play live,
That man would loose his grand prerogative.   10
The beaux put on an ill-becoming frown,
And – more unnatural – swear they'll knock him down.
What satisfaction can those things demand?
They are by nature ready tamed to hand;
If not, their wives were in a poor condition,   15
For beaux have nought to please us but submission.
Be wise for once, regard a female tutor,
And, as you are of neither sex, stand neuter.
The cits would damn, but dare not for their lives;
Few cits come here without their taming wives.   20
If any here this night are stole without 'em,
'Tis those our author says will surely rout him,
For boys who most are curbed, and kept in fear,
Are most unlucky when no master near;
So you who wear the bridle all the day   25
And slip it once a week to see a play,
Like truant boys around the house you roam,
And what in me you censure, bear at home.   *Bell rings*

2   *my monster* i.e. Petruchio.
3   *suppliant* humble petitioner.
5   *corps* body of men, division of an army.
6   *engines* (1) plots, stratagems; (2) military machinery.
    theatric theatrical.
9   *critic* i.e. critics.
10 *grand prerogative* i.e. his ability to control women.
11 *beaux* fops, dandies.
12 *And ... down* Eighteenth-century dandies were often assumed to be effeminate (see
    also ll. 17–18).
13 *those things* i.e. the beaux.
14 *tamed to hand* i.e. so tame that they will take food from the tamer's hand.
19 *cits* citizens.
22–4 *'Tis ... near* i.e. the citizens who are normally under their wives' thumbs will be the
    most likely (in the author's opinion) to behave in a disruptive fashion.

But hark, he rings – my summons to his bed.
I now no more this bullying hero dread;   30
No more he courts me with his former wooing,
Nor blusters now, but gently calls me to him.
I go, I freely now obey his will,
And by obeying, make him tamer still.
For all who know us this sure truth must own,   35
That women have more ways to tame than one.
Exert your power, protect the bard, ye fair!
The man who fights your cause, deserves your care.

D: 1760 Epilogue

This epilogue was written by the poet Richard Owen Cambridge (1717–1802), and was published in *The Works of Richard Owen Cambridge, Esq.* (London, 1803), pp. 314–15.

Epilogue Spoken at Drury-Lane Theatre, by Miss Pritchard,
in the Character of Maria in *The Tamer Tamed*: 1760

Well! Since I've thus succeeded in my plan,
And conquered this all-conquering tyrant, man,
To farther conquests still my soul aspires,
And all my bosom glows with martial fires.
Suppose a female regiment we raise;   5
We must – for men grow scarce-ish now-a-days,
Now every man of spirit is enlisted.
Why, ladies, these brave lads should be assisted.
The glorious scheme my flutt'ring heart bewitches,

30   *this bullying hero* i.e. Petruchio.
35   *sure* certain.
37   *bard* i.e. the author, against any attacks from the men in the audience.
      ye fair i.e. the women in the audience.

Epilogue 1760
      Miss Pritchard Hannah Mary Pritchard (1739–81), daughter of the more famous
      Hannah Pritchard, who made her debut with Garrick's company in October 1756
      when she played Juliet and her mother the Nurse. According to Genest (4: 483, 485,
      588) she played Maria on 30 April and 2 May 1757 and on 30 April 1760, the
      occasion for which this epilogue was apparently written.
  6   *now-a-days* i.e. during the Seven Years' War (1754–63) fought between Britain and
      France and their allies.

But hold – I've promised not to wear the breeches.   10
No matter: in this variegated army
We'll find some regimentals that shall charm ye.
If plumes and lace recruiting can persuade,
We'll try to show our taste in masquerade.
My feather here is fitted in a trice,   15
Then for the crest, the motto, and device
Death's head and bones! No – we'll have flames and darts!
In Latin mottos men may show their parts,
But ours shall be true English – like our hearts.
Our uniform we'll copy from the Greek,   20
The drapery and emblems true antique:
Minerva's aegis! And Diana's bow!
And thus equipped to India's coasts we'll go;
Temples of gold and diamond mines we'll rob,
And every month we'll make a new Nabob.   25
Amid this glorious scene of contributions,
Spoil, presents, hourly change and revolutions,
While high on stately elephants we ride,
Whose feet can trample European pride,
Think not our country we can e'er forget;   30
We'll plunder but to pay the nation's debt.
Then there's America – We'll soon dispatch it,
This tedious war, when we take up the hatchet.

11   *variegated* diverse.
12   *regimentals* uniforms.
14   *masquerade* i.e. in the fashion of a masquerade ball.
15   *feather* i.e. the feather that she wears in her hair.
17   *Death's head* i.e. a skull.
        flames and darts conventional attributes of the lover, referred to in many eighteenth-
        century texts (the flames of passion and Cupid's arrows or passionate glances).
22   *Minerva* Roman equivalent of Athena, the warlike goddess of wisdom.
        Diana Roman equivalent of Artemis, goddess of the moon, virginity and hunting.
        aegis shield.
25   *Nabob* (1) nawab: viceroy of a province under the Mughal empire; (2) British person
        who acquired a fortune in India.
29   *European* i.e. the continental European nations that the British were currently at
        war with.
30   *e'er* ever.
32   *Then there's America* Part of the Seven Years' War involved the so-called French and
        Indian War, fought between the British and the French and their Native American
        allies; it eventually resulted in the British conquest of Canada.

Heroes and soldiers Indian wiles may catch,
But in a woman they may meet their match.   35
To art, disguise, and stratagem no strangers,
We fear no hazard, nor once think of dangers ·
In our true character of female rangers.

34   *Indian* i.e. Native American.
38   *rangers* members of an armed group charged with protecting a particular part of a
     country (a term generally used in a North American context).

THE
TRAGEDY

OF THE DVTCHESSE
Of Malfy.

*As it was Presented priuatly, at the Black-
Friers; and publiquely at the Globe, By the
Kings Maiesties Seruants.*

The perfect and exact Coppy, with diuerse
things Printed, that the length of the Play would
not beare in the Presentment.

VVritten by *John Webster.*

Hora.——*Si quid*——
——*Candidus Imperti si non his vtere mecum.*

LONDON:

Printed by NICHOLAS OKES, for IOHN
WATERSON, and are to be sold at the
signe of the Crowne, in *Paules*
Church-yard, 1623.

Original title-page

priuatly, at the Black-Friers The Blackfriars Theatre, smaller than the Globe, an indoor playhouse ('private' alludes to its select fashionable ambitions) which had been home to a company of boy-actors until it was taken over by the most famous and successful adult acting company, the King's Men, whose base was the Globe Theatre. Probably from 1609 the King's Men acted at Blackfriars in winter (October to March or April when the Court was in London, and the law-courts busy) and at the Globe in summer (when the Court was in the country and the law-courts not in session).

publiquely at the Globe The Globe, a large open amphitheatre-type playhouse on Bankside, erected in 1599 with timbers transferred from the old Theatre in Shoreditch. The Globe burned down on 29 June 1613 (before the supposed date of the first performance of *The Duchess of Malfi*) and a more elaborate second Globe was built on the site; it was in use by June 1614.

perfect and exact Coppy What is really striking is this emphatic claim to present the author's fuller text, restoring the cuts made by the players for performance. It is Webster's dignity as author, not merely playwright, and of his work as literature, not as acting-script, that is given emphasis, and this is further stressed in the epigraph from Horace, in the dedicatory epistle where Webster asserts the enduring worth of his work, and in the commendatory verses from fellow authors who stress the established fame of Webster and his Duchess. The year of publication, 1623, is the same as that for the First Folio of Shakespeare, and may have appealed to Webster for that reason.

Hora . . . mecum Horace, *Epistles*, I vi 67–8: *Si quid novisti rectius istis, candidus imperti; si non, his utere mecum* ('If you know something better than these precepts, be kind and tell me; if not, practice mine with me'). As Lucas suggests, Webster presumably intends to apply this with the sense 'If you know a better play, let's hear it, if not, hear mine'.

DEDICATION

To the right honourable George Harding, Baron Berkeley
of Berkeley Castle and Knight of the Order of the Bath
to the illustrious Prince Charles.

My Noble Lord,

That I may present my excuse why, being a stranger to your 5
Lordship, I offer this poem to your patronage, I plead this warrant:
men who never saw the sea yet desire to behold that regiment of
waters, choose some eminent river to guide them thither, and
make that, as it were, their conduct or postilion; by the like
ingenious means has your fame arrived at my knowledge, 10
receiving it from some of worth who, both in contemplation and
practice, owe to your honour their clearest service. I do not
altogether look up at your title, the ancientest nobility being but a
relic of time past, and the truest honour indeed being for a man to
confer honour on himself: which your learning strives to propagate, 15
and shall make you arrive at the dignity of a great example. I am
confident this work is not unworthy your Honour's perusal: for by
such poems as this, poets have kissed the hands of great princes
and drawn their gentle eyes to look down upon their sheets of
paper, when the poets themselves were bound up in their winding- 20
sheets. The like courtesy from your Lordship shall make you live in
your grave, and laurel spring out of it, when the ignorant scorners
of the Muses, that like worms in libraries seem to live only to
destroy learning, shall wither, neglected and forgotten. This work,
and myself, I humbly present to your approved censure, it being 25
the utmost of my wishes to have your honourable self my weighty
and perspicuous comment; which grace so done me, shall ever be
acknowledged

By your Lordship's in all duty and observance,

John Webster. 30

---

1   *George Harding* (1601–58) became eighth Baron Berkeley in November 1613; the
significance of Webster's choice of this dedicatee (see Forker, p. 119) was that Harding
was a direct descendant of the first and second Lords Hunsdon, who had both been
patrons of the Chamberlain's Men, the acting company honoured in May 1603 by royal
patronage and thereafter re-named the King's Men (the King's Majesty's Servants).

9   *conduct* conductor.

25   *approved censure* seasoned judgement.

In the just worth of that well deserver Mr John Webster,
    and upon this masterpiece of tragedy.

In this thou imitat'st one rich and wise
That sees his good deeds done before he dies.
As he by works, thou by this work of fame
Hast well provided for thy living name.   5
To trust to others' honourings is worth's crime,
Thy monument is raised in thy lifetime,
And 'tis most just: for every worthy man
Is his own marble, and his merit can
Cut him to any figure, and express   10
More art than death's cathedral palaces
Where royal ashes keep their court. Thy note
Be ever plainness, 'tis the richest coat.
Thy epitaph only the title be,
Write 'Duchess': that will fetch a tear for thee,   15
For whoe'er saw this Duchess live and die
That could get off under a bleeding eye?

In Tragaediam.

Ut lux ex tenebris ictu percussa Tonantis,
Illa, ruina malis, claris fit vita poetis.   20

Thomas Middletonus,
Poëta & Chron:
Londiniensis

18–20   *In Tragaediam . . . poetis* To tragedy. As light springs from darkness at the stroke of
      the thunderer, / May it (ruin to evil) be life for famous poets.
22–3   *Chron: Londiniensis* Chronologer of London. Thomas Middleton the playwright was
      appointed to this post in 1620.

To his friend Mr John Webster
Upon his *Duchess of Malfi.*

I never saw thy Duchess till the day
That she was lively bodied in thy play:
Howe'er she answered her low-rated love,   5
Her brothers' anger did so fatal prove;
Yet my opinion is, she might speak more,
But never, in her life, so well before.

           Wil. Rowley.

To the reader of the author,   10
   and his *Duchess of Malfi.*

Crown him a poet, whom nor Rome nor Greece
Transcend in all theirs, for a masterpiece
In which, whiles words and matter change, and men
Act one another, he, from whose clear pen   15
They all took life, to memory hath lent
A lasting fame to raise his monument.

           John Ford.

---

4   *bodied* embodied.
5-6 *Howe'er . . . prove* However eloquently in her real life the Duchess may have defended that misalliance which her brothers' anger made so fatal (Lucas).
7   *speak* have spoken.
8   *But . . . before* She can never have spoken so well as in your play (Lucas).
9   *Wil. Rowley* A dramatist who collaborated at various times with Webster, Middleton and Ford.
14-15 *whiles . . . Act* while literature has its fashions and the theatre lasts (Brown).

Bosola, *J. Lowin.*
Ferdinand, 1 *R. Burbidge.* 2 *J. Taylor.*
Cardinal, 1 *H. Cundaile.* 2 *R. Robinson.*
Antonio, 1 *W. Ostler.* 2 *R. Benfield.*
Delio, *J. Underwood.*
Forobosco, *N. Towley.*
Malateste.
The Marquis of Pescara, *J. Rice.*
Silvio, *T. Pollard.*
The several mad-men, *N. Towley, J. Underwood, etc.*
The Duchess, *R. Sharpe.*
The Cardinal's Mistress, *J. Tomson.*
The Doctor, ⎤
⎥ *R Pallant.*
Cariola,   ⎦
Court Officers.
Three young Children.
Two Pilgrims.

The play's first edition strikingly dignifies the actors - it is the first in English to publish a list of the actors' names against their parts. The cast probably comprised fourteen to sixteen men and four boys, assuming some doubling. This list probably dates from a stage revival some time after the death of Burbage on 12 March 1619, perhaps near the date of publication, 1623; it is not part of the original manuscript. Two boys listed were probably too young for the first performance in 1613–14 – Sharpe (born in 1601) was apprenticed to Heminges in 1616, and Pallant, born in 1605, was apprenticed in 1620. When the play was new in 1614 Burbage (Ferdinand) and Lowin (Bosola) were certainly leading members of the company, Burbage having created the roles of Hamlet, Malevole, Othello, Lear, while Lowin, with the company since 1603, had acted Falstaff and Epicure Mammon, and as Bosola must have proved 'a formidable figure' by 1623 (so NCW). Burbage died in 1619 and Taylor took over the role of Ferdinand on joining the company. Cundall (Cardinal) a member of the company since 1598, ceased acting in 1619, after which Richard Robinson succeeded him as Cardinal. The role of the Duchess in 1613–14 may have been created by Robinson, who in 1611 had played a Lady in *The Second Maiden's Tragedy*. Ostler (Antonio) was in his twenties in 1614 and died on 16th December in that year, to be succeeded by Benfield. Underwood was in his twenties in 1613–14, Towley (or Tooley) was active before 1605, Rice was apprenticed to Heminges in 1607, Pollard (Silvio)not before 1613, probably doubled as the Doctor and a Madman. See NCW, 423–7, and Andrew Gurr, *The Shakespeare Company 1594–1642*, 2004, pp. 217–46, also David Kathman, 'How old were Shakespeare's boy actors?', *Shakespeare Survey* 58 (2005), 220–46, and 'Grocers, goldsmiths, and drapers: freemen and apprentices in the Elizabethan theater', *Shakespeare Quarterly* 55 (2004), 220-46.

1. R. Burbidge. 2. J. Taylor. That Burbidge is the first-named indicates he was in the original performance (which took place before Ostler's death on 16 Dec 1614) and the second-named, Taylor, was in a revival some time after the death of Burbage on 13 March 1619.

Forobosco He has no lines to speak and is only referred to in II.ii.29. Perhaps this is a 'ghost'

[DRAMATIS PERSONAE]

[FERDINAND, *Duke of Calabria, twin brother of the Duchess*
CARDINAL, *their brother*
BOSOLA, *formerly served the Cardinal, now returned from*
imprisonment in the galleys; then Provisor of Horse to the
Duchess, and in the pay of Ferdinand
ANTONIO, *household steward to the Duchess, then her husband*
DELIO, *his friend, a courtier*
CASTRUCHIO, *an old lord, Julia's husband*
SILVIO, *a courtier*
RODERIGO, *a courtier*
GRISOLAN, *a courtier*
PESCARA, *a marquis*
MALATESTE, *a count*
DOCTOR
DUCHESS OF MALFI, *a young widow, later Antonio's wife, and the*
twin sister of Ferdinand and sister of the Cardinal
CARIOLA, *her waiting-woman*
JULIA, *wife of Castruchio and mistress of the Cardinal*
OLD LADY
TWO PILGRIMS
The Duchess' Children – *two boys and a girl*
Eight Madmen: *an astrologer, a lawyer, a priest, a doctor, an*
English tailor, a gentleman usher, a farmer, a broker
Officers, Servants, Guards, Executioners, Attendants, Churchmen,
Ladies-in-Waiting]

character - Webster altered his original plan in the course of composition and cut the part but forgot to delete the name from this list.

Three young Children The eldest a boy, the middle child a girl, the youngest a babe in arms (see III.v.81: 'sweet armful') presumably represented by a property doll.

CASTRUCHIO The name Castruccio is in Painter who (following Belleforest) thus refers to Petrucci, Cardinal of Siena. Lucas suggests Webster saw it as a suitable name for Julia's old husband because it sounds as if it means 'castrated'. Florio defines the Italian word *castrone* as 'a gelded man . . . a cuckold'.

CARIOLA Florio lists the Italian word *carriolo* or *carriuola* as (among other things) a 'trundle-bed'. In an age when personal servants slept in trundle-beds close to their employers, this name would be apt.

The Duchess' children In III.iii.66 there is reference to a son by her first husband; the boy is called Duke of Malfi. This is possibly a 'ghost character' unless it is he who is referred to at V.v.111–12, although Ferdinand's assertion at IV.ii.270–2 seems incompatible with his existence; see also Delio's remarks, as reported by Pescara, at V.v.105–7.

ACT I, SCENE i

[*Enter* ANTONIO *and* DELIO]

DELIO

You are welcome to your country, dear Antonio;
You have been long in France, and you return
A very formal Frenchman in your habit.
How do you like the French court?

ANTONIO   I admire it:
In seeking to reduce both state and people   5
To a fixed order, their judicious king
Begins at home, quits first his royal palace
Of flatt'ring sycophants, of dissolute
And infamous persons – which he sweetly terms
His Master's masterpiece, the work of heaven –   10
Consid'ring duly that a prince's court
Is like a common fountain, whence should flow
Pure silver drops in general, but if't chance
Some cursed example poison't near the head,

---

0   s.d. ed. (*Actus Primus. Scena Prima. / Antonio, and Delio, Bosola, Cardinall. Q1*).

0   s.d. Antonio and Delio, like other courtiers, may enter 'as from a tournament' and
    be accoutred accordingly: Antonio differently from Delio – see n. 3 below. At the
    head of this and all subsequent scenes in Q1 (including the dubious Scene ii – see
    note to I.i.79 below) there is a 'massed entry' listing all the persons involved,
    irrespective of where they actually make their entrance. This is often a feature of
    manuscripts intended for literary use, and is typical of the work of the scribe Ralph
    Crane, whose practice it was to use Latin for marking Act and Scene divisions, but
    may have been following the author's particular wishes here. Webster's *Devil's Law
    Case*, a literary rather than theatrical text and also published in 1623, has Latin
    divisions, whereas the first edition of *The White Devil*, 1612, has no divisions.

2   *long in France* The historical Antonio had accompanied Federico, the last Aragonese
    king of Naples, into exile in France from 1501 until Federico's death in 1504.

3   *habit* dress: Delio says that Antonio's French clothes set him visibly apart in the
    Italian court of Malfi, but is implying that Antonio remains essentially unchanged
    by his time abroad. NCW suggest he could be wearing the sign of his office as
    steward, a gold chain: the steward's gold chain is only mentioned once, quite late in
    the play and then derisively, by an Officer, at III.ii.223, in terms recalling the ridicule
    of Malvolio in *Twelfth Night*, II.iii.119–20.

4   ed. (How . . . court / I . . . it Q1).

5   *state* ruling body, grand council (Brown).

9   *which* Referring to the policy of cleansing the court.

291

Death and diseases through the whole land spread.   15
And what is't makes this blessed government
But a most provident council, who dare freely
Inform him the corruption of the times?
Though some o'th'court hold it presumption
To instruct princes what they ought to do,   20
It is a noble duty to inform them
What they ought to foresee.

                    [*Enter* BOSOLA]

                              Here comes Bosola,
The only court-gall; yet I observe his railing
Is not for simple love of piety,
Indeed he rails at those things which he wants,   25
Would be as lecherous, covetous, or proud,
Bloody, or envious, as any man,
If he had means to be so.

                    [*Enter* CARDINAL]

                    Here's the Cardinal.

BOSOLA
I do haunt you still.

CARDINAL   So.

BOSOLA   I have done you
Better service than to be slighted thus.   30
Miserable age, where only the reward
Of doing well is the doing of it.

CARDINAL
You enforce your merit too much.

BOSOLA
I fell into the galleys in your service, where for two years

16–22   from Painter, xiii (Dent).
  23   *court-gall* 'a person who harrasses or distresses the court' (*OED*) – *gall* means bile,
        but also a sore produced by chafing. As a malcontent Bosola is presumably dressed
        in black; his appearance indicates his poor reward for service, including the hardship
        of having been a galley-slave. Antonio and Delio serve as critical commentators on
        the Duchess' Court; Webster's stagecraft is like Shakespeare's in the opening scene
        of *Antony and Cleopatra* where Demetrius and Philo, Roman officers in the General's
        retinue, observe and discuss the feminine Court of the Egyptian Queen Cleopatra
        and watch her striking entry with their obviously enamoured General, Antony.
        railing abusive language.
31–2   *the reward . . . it* Proverbial – Tilley V81.

together I wore two towels instead of a shirt, with a knot on the   35
shoulder, after the fashion of a Roman mantle. Slighted thus?
I will thrive some way: blackbirds fatten best in hard weather,
why not I, in these dog days?

CARDINAL
Would you could become honest.

BOSOLA
With all your divinity, do but direct me the way to it. I have   40
known many travel far for it, and yet return as arrant knaves as
they went forth, because they carried themselves always along
with them.

                                       [*Exit* CARDINAL]
Are you gone? Some fellows, they say, are possessed with the
devil, but this great fellow were able to possess the greatest devil   45
and make him worse.

ANTONIO
He hath denied thee some suit?

BOSOLA
He and his brother are like plum trees that grow crooked over
standing pools: they are rich, and o'erladen with fruit, but none
but crows, pies and caterpillars feed on them. Could I be one of   50
their flatt'ring panders, I would hang on their ears like a horse-
leech till I were full, and then drop off. I pray leave me. Who
would rely upon these miserable dependences, in expectation
to be advanced tomorrow? What creature ever fed worse than
hoping Tantalus? Nor ever died any man more fearfully than he   55

---

38   *dog days* A period of oppressive and unhealthy hot weather, associated with the dog-
      star Sirius (Brown).
40–3 *I have . . . them* A contradiction of the proverb that travel broadens the mind:
      Webster is recalling Montaigne, *Essayes*, p. 119.
41   *arrant* thorough.
45–6 Dent notes a borrowing from Donne, *Ignatius*, 15: Loyola was 'so indued with the
      Diuell that he was able . . . to possesse the Diuell'.
49   *standing* stagnant.
50   *pies* magpies.
51–2 *horse-leech* blood-sucker.
53   *dependences* The condition of living on promises.
55   *Tantalus* The type of the disappointed man (hence the verb 'tantalise'), punished in
      Hades by perpetual thirst, though up to his neck in water, and by hunger, though
      fruit hung just beyond his grasp.
      died (Q1b; did Q1a).

that hoped for a pardon? There are rewards for hawks and dogs
when they have done us service, but for a soldier that hazards
his limbs in a battle, nothing but a kind of geometry is his last
supportation.

DELIO

Geometry?   60

BOSOLA

Ay, to hang in a fair pair of slings, take his latter swing in
the world upon an honourable pair of crutches, from hospital to hospital. Fare ye well sir; and yet do not you scorn
us, for places in the court are but like beds in the hospital,
where this man's head lies at that man's foot, and so lower,   65
and lower.   [*Exit*]

DELIO

I knew this fellow seven years in the galleys
For a notorious murder, and 'twas thought
The Cardinal suborned it. He was released
By the French general, Gaston de Foix,   70
When he recovered Naples.

ANTONIO   'Tis great pity
He should be thus neglected, I have heard
He's very valiant. This foul melancholy
Will poison all his goodness, for, I'll tell you,
If too immoderate sleep be truly said   75
To be an inward rust unto the soul,

---

56   *pardon* (Q1b; pleadon Q1a).

       dogs ed. (dogges, and Q1).

       hawks and dogs In Q1 there is a space at the line-end after *hawkes, and dogges*,
       and   whereas the preceding and succeeding lines are printed full out right.
       Presumably Q1's second *and* is an erroneous repetition. Lucas suggests the noun
       horses had dropped out, but type could not have fallen out without movement –
       indeed disintegration – of the whole page of type (as NCW note). The parallel in
       Montaigne, *Essayes*, p. 266, is inconclusive: it is true that the first part does refer to
       men serving better, and for less entreaty, 'then wee vse vnto birdes, vnto horses, and
       vnto dogges' – but then follows the second: 'We share the fruites of our prey with our
       dogges and hawkes, as a meede of their paine and reward of their industry': here
       the word 'horses' is omitted.

64   *like* ed. (likes Q1).

70   *Foix* ed. (*Foux* Q1); Q1's *Foux* is probably a transcription error since the correct
       form of the name appears in Painter. Historically, Gaston de Foix was still a child in
       1501 when Naples was recovered (Brown).

73   *melancholy* A mental disease thought to be due to an excess of black bile (see T.
       Bright, *Treatise of Melancholy*, 1586) but also an affectation – and Ferdinand assumes
       Bosola affects melancholy as a 'garb' at I.i.269.

It then doth follow, want of action
Breeds all black malcontents, and their close rearing,
Like moths in cloth, do hurt for want of wearing.

[*Enter* CASTRUCHIO, SILVIO, RODERIGO *and* GRISOLAN]

DELIO

The presence 'gins to fill. You promised me   80
To make me the partaker of the natures
Of some of your great courtiers.

ANTONIO   The Lord Cardinal's,
And other strangers', that are now in court,
I shall.

[*Enter* FERDINAND]

Here comes the great Calabrian Duke.

FERDINAND

Who took the ring oft'nest?   85

77–9   Malcontents, having been reared in secret (like moths in cloth) are able to do damage
       precisely because of the lack of activity (NCW).

79   s.d. ed. (SCENA II. / *Antonio, Delio, Ferdinand, Cardinall, Dutchesse, Castruchio,
       Silvio, Rodocico, Grisolan, Bosola, Iulia, Cariola.* Q1).

79   s.d. No Exit s.d. is marked in Q1 here. Although lines 78–9 form a sententious couplet,
       this is not decisive evidence of a scene-end since Q1 has numerous mid-scene
       couplets which do not mark exits. In Webster's *The White Devil*, too, mid-scene
       sententious couplets are frequent: Webster evidently liked sententious couplets. The
       'massed direction' is significant: as Brown (p. lxv) remarks, no manuscript 'prepared
       for use in a theatre would have the character-names together at the head of each
       scene, rather than where they enter individually'. This s.d. is probably just such a
       massed entry prepared with readers in mind. NCW cogently suggest that the
       manuscript Ralph Crane was copying had a s.d. for several characters; Crane assumed
       this implied a scene break, which he marked, following it with one of his habitual
       massed entry directions. I omit the scene-break, so making Act I an unbroken stage
       action. It is a possible staging option to have Antonio and Delio exit here and return
       a moment later in the wake of the minor characters who enter at this point. Marcus
       opts for the scene break, suggesting it implies 'a subtle shift in time and place'.

80   *presence* the ruler's audience chamber, perhaps indicated by a chair of state upstage.

85   *took the ring* A game introduced by King James I to his court in place of jousting: the
       galloping horseman had to carry off the suspended ring on the point of his lance.
       NCW quote Nichols, *The Progresses and Public Processions of Queen Elizabeth,* (1823
       repr. New York 1966) II, 549–50: King James' son Prince Charles 'mounted as it were
       upon a Spanish jennet that takes his swiftnes from the nature of the winde, most
       couragiously and with much agilitie of hand took the ring clearly four times in five
       courses'. Webster makes rings important in the play: the Duchess puts a ring on
       Antonio's finger at the end of Act I, the Cardinal takes one off her finger in III.iv
       (see lines 35–6), Ferdinand gives the Duchess what she takes to be Antonio's severed
       hand, with a ring on it, (IV.i.42–4), and the noose (see IV.ii.235) is a ring.

SILVIO

Antonio Bologna, my lord.

FERDINAND

Our sister Duchess' great master of her household? Give him
the jewel. When shall we leave this sportive action and fall to
action indeed?

CASTRUCHIO

Methinks, my lord, you should not desire to go to war in   90
person.

FERDINAND

Now for some gravity. Why, my lord?

CASTRUCHIO

It is fitting a soldier arise to be a prince, but not necessary a
prince descend to be a captain.

FERDINAND

No?   95

CASTRUCHIO

No, my lord, he were far better do it by a deputy.

FERDINAND

Why should he not as well sleep, or eat, by a deputy? This might
take idle, offensive, and base office from him, whereas the other
deprives him of honour.

CASTRUCHIO

Believe my experience: that realm is never long in quiet where   100
the ruler is a soldier.

FERDINAND

Thou told'st me thy wife could not endure fighting.

CASTRUCHIO

True, my lord.

FERDINAND

And of a jest she broke of a captain she met full of wounds – I
have forgot it.   105

CASTRUCHIO

She told him, my lord, he was a pitiful fellow to lie like the
children of Ismael, all in tents.

---

88   *jewel* The reward for taking the ring; but again Webster may signal irony, as *jewel*
     could signify virginity and married chastity (as in *Cymbeline*, I.iv.153).
104 s.p. FERDINAND ed. (*Fred* Q1).
107 *children . . . tents* i.e. Arabs (See Genesis 21.9–21), tent-dwellers; with a pun on *tent*
     meaning a dressing for a wound.

FERDINAND

Why, there's a wit were able to undo all the surgeons of the city:
for although gallants should quarrel, and had drawn their
weapons, and were ready to go to it, yet her persuasions would   110
make them put up.

CASTRUCHIO

That she would, my lord.

[FERDINAND]

How do you like my Spanish jennet?

RODERIGO

He is all fire.

FERDINAND

I am of Pliny's opinion, I think he was begot by the wind, he   115
runs as if he were ballass'd with quicksilver.

SILVIO

True, my lord, he reels from the tilt often.

RODERIGO *and* GRISOLAN

Ha, ha, ha!

FERDINAND

Why do you laugh? Methinks you that are courtiers should be
my touchwood, take fire when I give fire, that is, laugh when I   120
laugh, were the subject never so witty.

CASTRUCHIO

True, my lord, I myself have heard a very good jest and
have scorned to seem to have so silly a wit as to understand it.

---

111 *put up* sheathe their weapons.

114 s.p. FERDINAND ed. (not in Q1); in Q1 the line is inset as for all lines with a new
speaker. Presumably the s.p. has been accidentally omitted. It is consistent to give the
line to Ferdinand in this context where he praises the animal and refers several more
times to horses and horsemanship. It is unlikely that in Ferdinand's presence
Castruchio would initiate a topic, and a *Spanish jennet* is a light sporting horse (see
85 n. above) unsuitable for an old lord like Castruchio.

115 *Pliny's opinion* Pliny writes that Portuguese mares are said to conceive by the west
wind.

116 It is as if quicksilver (mercury) endows the steed with added speed and liveliness –
a ship may, like a horse, be said to *run* (as in 'run before the wind') and has ballast
for stability; *quicksilver* suggests speed, high mobility and value, the opposite to
cheap heavy material normally used as ballast.

117 *reels from the tilt* Quibbling on *reel* (1) swing about, be unbalanced (2) stagger back;
and on *tilt* (1) the listing effect of uneven ballast on a ship (2) a blow in jousting (3)
the act of copulation.

120 *when* only when.

FERDINAND

But I can laugh at your fool, my lord.

CASTRUCHIO

He cannot speak, you know, but he makes faces, my lady cannot   125
abide him.

FERDINAND

No?

CASTRUCHIO

Nor endure to be in merry company, for she says too much
laughing and too much company fills her too full of the
wrinkle.   130

FERDINAND

I would then have a mathematical instrument made for her
face, that she might not laugh out of compass. I shall shortly
visit you at Milan, Lord Silvio.

SILVIO

Your grace shall arrive most welcome.

FERDINAND

You are a good horseman, Antonio; you have excellent riders in   135
France: what do you think of good horsemanship?

ANTONIO

Nobly, my lord; as out of the Grecian horse issued many
famous princes, so, out of brave horsemanship arise the first
sparks of growing resolution that raise the mind to noble
action.   140

FERDINAND

You have bespoke it worthily.

[*Enter* CARDINAL, DUCHESS, CARIOLA, JULIA
and Attendants]

SILVIO

Your brother the Lord Cardinal, and sister Duchess.

CARDINAL

Are the galleys come about?

GRISOLAN

They are, my lord.

FERDINAND

Here's the Lord Silvio is come to take his leave.   145

128–30   prose ed. (Nor . . . saies / Too . . . her / Too . . . wrinckle Q1).
  132   *out of compass* immoderately.
  137   *Grecian horse* the proverbial Trojan horse.

DELIO [*Aside to* ANTONIO]

    Now, sir, your promise: what's that Cardinal?
    I mean his temper? They say he's a brave fellow,
    Will play his five thousand crowns at tennis, dance,
    Court ladies, and one that hath fought single combats.

ANTONIO

    Some such flashes superficially hang on him, for form, but   150
    observe his inward character: he is a melancholy churchman.
    The spring in his face is nothing but the engend'ring of toads.
    Where he is jealous of any man he lays worse plots for them
    than ever was imposed on Hercules, for he strews in his way
    flatterers, panders, intelligencers, atheists, and a thousand such   155
    political monsters. He should have been Pope, but instead of
    coming to it by the primitive decency of the Church, he did
    bestow bribes so largely, and so impudently, as if he would have
    carried it away without heaven's knowledge. Some good he
    hath done.   160

DELIO

    You have given too much of him. What's his brother?

ANTONIO

    The Duke there? A most perverse and turbulent nature;
    What appears in him mirth is merely outside.
    If he laugh heartily, it is to laugh
    All honesty out of fashion.

DELIO   Twins?

ANTONIO   In quality.   165

---

150   *form* outward appearance. Antonio goes on to offer formal Theophrastian
        Character-sketches of Ferdinand's two siblings (162–202). Brown notes parallels
        from Hall, *Characters*, 1608, showing that Webster followed the Jacobean literary
        vogue for such Character-sketches. Later, in 1615, Webster contributed fresh sketches
        to the sixth (posthumous) edition of Sir Thomas Overbury's *Characters*.

152   *spring . . . toads* i.e. his tears, in others a sign of humanity, are a slime which breeds
        amphibians – assuming *spring* means fountain: Lucas compares Chapman, *Bussy
        d'Ambois*, III.ii.263–5 'that toadpool that stands in thy complexion'. Alternatively or
        additionally, if *spring* means Springtime, then in Ferdinand it generates nothing but
        ugliness and poison. Webster probably remembers *Troilus and Cressida*, II.iii.158–9:
        'I do hate a proud man as I do hate the engend'ring of toads'.

155   *flatterers* ed. (Flatters Q1).
        intelligencers spies.

157   *primitive decency* the pristine early period of morality (Marcus).

165   *In quality* In kind – but they are not twins, though Ferdinand and the Duchess are
        actual twins (see IV.ii.253). Nevertheless Webster probably intended close
        resemblance in appearance and age between the three of them, as visual correlation
        to their psychological and emotional involvement with one another. This physical

He speaks with others' tongues, and hears men's suits
With others' ears: will seem to sleep o'th'bench
Only to entrap offenders in their answers;
Dooms men to death, by information,
Rewards, by hearsay.

DELIO   Then the law to him   170
Is like a foul black cobweb to a spider,
He makes it his dwelling, and a prison
To entangle those shall feed him.

ANTONIO   Most true:
He ne'er pays debts, unless they be shrewd turns,
And those he will confess that he doth owe.   175
Last: for his brother there, the Cardinal,
They that do flatter him most say oracles
Hang at his lips, and verily I believe them,
For the devil speaks in them;
But for their sister, the right noble Duchess,   180
You never fixed your eye on three fair medals
Cast in one figure, of so different temper.
For her discourse, it is so full of rapture
You only will begin then to be sorry
When she doth end her speech, and wish, in wonder,   185
She held it less vainglory to talk much
Than you penance, to hear her. Whilst she speaks,
She throws upon a man so sweet a look,
That it were able raise one to a galliard
That lay in a dead palsy, and to dote   190
On that sweet countenance; but in that look
There speaketh so divine a continence

resemblance was stressed in RSC productions in 1971 and 1989. The contemporary
prejudice against widows remarrying is given extreme expression by Hamlet – see
Hamlet, III iv., for instance 68–9: 'you cannot call it love, / For at your age the heyday
in the blood is tame'.

174   *shrewd* ed. (shewed Q1).
      shrewd turns injuries.
181   *your* ed. (you Q1).
187   *you* ed. (your Q1). The parallel with Guazzo, *The civile conversation of M. Steeven
      Guazzo*, trans. G. Pettie, 1581, (cit. Dent p. 67), indicates that Q1's *your* is an error:
      the Cardinal's devilishness is contrasted to the Duchess' religious virtue. In Guazzo,
      although the Duchess' discourses are said to be 'delightful' and her smile 'sweet'
      enough to attract men, her 'continency' leads men to religious virtue.
      Than you penance Than you hold it spiritually purifying.
189   *galliard* a lively dance.

As cuts off all lascivious and vain hope.
Her days are practised in such noble virtue
That sure her nights, nay more, her very sleeps,   195
Are more in heaven than other ladies' shrifts.
Let all sweet ladies break their flatt'ring glasses
And dress themselves in her.

DELIO   Fie, Antonio,
You play the wire-drawer with her commendations.

ANTONIO
I'll case the picture up, only thus much: 200
All her particular worth grows to this sum,
She stains the time past, lights the time to come.

CARIOLA [*Aside to* ANTONIO]
You must attend my lady in the gallery
Some half an hour hence.

ANTONIO   I shall.

FERDINAND
Sister, I have a suit to you.

DUCHESS   To me, sir?   205

FERDINAND
A gentleman here, Daniel de Bosola,
One that was in the galleys.

DUCHESS   Yes, I know him.

FERDINAND
A worthy fellow h'is. Pray let me entreat for
The provisorship of your horse.

DUCHESS   Your knowledge of him
Commends him, and prefers him.

FERDINAND   Call him hither.   210

[*Exit* ATTENDANT]

We are now upon parting. Good Lord Silvio,

---

196   *shrifts* confessions.
197   *glasses* looking-glasses, mirrors.
198   *dress . . . her* (1) use her as a mirror (2) adopt her virtues as their own.
199   *play the wire-drawer* spin out to an excessive degree.
200   *case the picture up* put the picture away in its case.
202   *stains* eclipses, puts into the shade.
204–5 ed. (Some . . . hence / I shall / Sister . . . you / To me Sir Q1).
209   *provisorship of your horse* An important and valuable court appointment: Queen
       Elizabeth I gave the equivalent post in her court to her favourite, Robert Dudley,
       later Earl of Leicester.
211   *are* ed. (not in Q1).

Do us commend to all our noble friends
At the leaguer.

SILVIO   Sir, I shall.

[DUCHESS]   You are for Milan?

SILVIO   I am.

DUCHESS

Bring the caroches – we'll bring you down to the haven.

[*Exeunt* ALL *but* FERDINAND *and the* CARDINAL]

CARDINAL

Be sure you entertain that Bosola   215
For your intelligence; I would not be seen in't,
And therefore many times I have slighted him,
When he did court our furtherance – as this morning.

FERDINAND

Antonio, the great master of her household,
Had been far fitter.

CARDINAL   You are deceived in him,   220
His nature is too honest for such business.

[*Enter* BOSOLA]

He comes. I'll leave you.   [*Exit*]

BOSOLA   I was lured to you.

FERDINAND

My brother here, the Cardinal, could never
Abide you.

BOSOLA   Never since he was in my debt.

FERDINAND

May be some oblique character in your face   225
Made him suspect you?

BOSOLA   Doth he study physiognomy?
There's no more credit to be given to th'face
Than to a sick man's urine, which some call

---

213   ed. (At . . . Leagues / Sir . . . shall / You . . . *Millaine* / I am Q1).
      leaguer ed. (leagues Q1) = military camp, especially one engaged in a siege.
213   s.p. DUCHESS ed. (*Ferd* Q1). Attribution of the speech in Q1 to Ferdinand cannot be
      right since he already knows Silvio's destination (see his preceding speech and line
      132–3). If the Duchess speaks this line then her next speech at line 214 is prepared for.
214   *caroches* elegant coaches.
215–6 *entertain . . . intelligence* keep that Bosola on your payroll as your secret agent.
218   *court our furtherance* ask us for reward.
228   *a sick man's urine* Early Modern medical analysis of urine was a proverbial joke – see
      Shakespeare, *2 Henry IV*, I.ii.1–5.

The physician's whore, because she cozens him.
He did suspect me wrongfully.

FERDINAND   For that   230
You must give great men leave to take their times:
Distrust doth cause us seldom be deceived;
You see, the oft shaking of the cedar tree
Fastens it more at root.

BOSOLA   Yet take heed:
For to suspect a friend unworthily   235
Instructs him the next way to suspect you,
And prompts him to deceive you.

[FERDINAND]   There's gold.

BOSOLA   So:
What follows? Never rained such showers as these
Without thunderbolts i'th'tail of them.
Whose throat must I cut?   240

FERDINAND
Your inclination to shed blood rides post
Before my occasion to use you. I give you that
To live i'th'court here and observe the Duchess,
To note all the particulars of her haviour:
What suitors do solicit her for marriage   245
And whom she best affects. She's a young widow,
I would not have her marry again.

BOSOLA   No, sir?

FERDINAND
Do not you ask the reason, but be satisfied
I say I would not.

BOSOLA   It seems you would create me
One of your familiars.

FERDINAND   Familiar? What's that?   250

---

229 *cozens* deceives.
236 *next* nearest.
237 s.p. ed. (*Berd* Q1).
238–9 *rained . . . tail* alluding to the shower of gold, in which form Jupiter visited Danae.
230–40 ed. (one line Q1).
241 *rides post* runs ahead.
249–50 ed. (I . . . not / It . . . me / One . . . familiars / Familiar . . . that Q1).
250 *familiars* Quibbling on the senses (1) members of the household (2) familiar spirits (3) intimate friends. Presumably Ferdinand's reaction is to (3), he being at this point unmoved by the implications of (2): on which see below 302 n.

BOSOLA

   Why, a very quaint invisible devil in flesh:

   An intelligencer.

FERDINAND   Such a kind of thriving thing

   I would wish thee: and ere long thou mayst arrive

   At a higher place by't.

BOSOLA   Take your devils,

   Which hell calls angels: these cursed gifts would make   255

   You a corrupter, me an impudent traitor,

   And should I take these they'd take me to hell.

FERDINAND

   Sir, I'll take nothing from you that I have given.

   There is a place that I procured for you

   This morning, the provisorship o'th'horse.   260

   Have you heard on't?

BOSOLA   No.

FERDINAND   'Tis yours: is't not worth thanks?

BOSOLA

   I would have you curse yourself now, that your bounty,

   Which makes men truly noble, e'er should make

   Me a villain: oh, that to avoid ingratitude

   For the good deed you have done me, I must do   265

   All the ill man can invent. Thus the devil

   Candies all sins o'er: and what heaven terms vile,

   That names he complemental.

FERDINAND   Be yourself:

   Keep your old garb of melancholy, 'twill express

   You envy those that stand above your reach,   270

   Yet strive not to come near 'em. This will gain

   Access to private lodgings, where yourself

   May, like a politic dormouse –

---

251   *quaint* cunning.

255   *angels* The gold coins called nobles, familiarly known as angels, bore the image of St Michael killing a dragon. The same pun appears in *The Revenger's Tragedy*, II.i.88: 'forty angels can make four score devils'.

257   *to* ed. (not in Q1).

261   *on't* ed. (out Q1).

267   *o'er* ed. (are Q1).

268   *complemental* polite accomplishment.

273   *politic* cunning.

     dormouse According to Pliny the dormouse renews its strength and youth by sleeping all the winter.

BOSOLA   As I have seen some
Feed in a lord's dish, half asleep, not seeming
To listen to any talk, and yet these rogues   275
Have cut his throat in a dream. What's my place?
The provisorship o'th'horse? Say then my corruption
Grew out of horse dung. I am your creature.

FERDINAND
Away!

BOSOLA
Let good men, for good deeds, covet good fame,   280
Since place and riches oft are bribes of shame.
Sometimes the devil doth preach.   *Exit*

[*Enter* CARDINAL *and* DUCHESS]

CARDINAL
We are to part from you, and your own discretion
Must now be your director.

FERDINAND   You are a widow:
You know already what man is, and therefore   285
Let not youth, high promotion, eloquence –

CARDINAL
No, nor any thing without the addition, honour,
Sway your high blood.

FERDINAND   Marry? They are most luxurious
Will wed twice.

CARDINAL   O fie!

FERDINAND   Their livers are more spotted
Than Laban's sheep.

---

274   *Feed . . . dish* Dine at a lord's table. See *The Malcontent*, II.iii.42–4: 'Lay one into his
        breast shall sleep with him, / Feed in the same dish, run in self faction, / Who may
        discover any shape of danger'.
277   *provisorship* ed. (Prouisors-ship Q1).
282   Proverbial – Tilley D230 and D266.
283–4 *your . . . director* you must rely on your own judgement.
288–90 ed. (Sway . . . blood / Marry . . . luxurious / Will . . . twice / O fie / Their . . . spotted
        / Then . . . sheepe / Diamonds . . . value Q1).
288   *high blood* (1) noble lineage (2) passionate nature.
        luxurious lecherous.
289   *livers* The organ was associated with passions, from lust to love: see *As You Like It*,
        III.ii.422–4.
290   *Laban's sheep* See Genesis 30.31–43; but the phrase probably comes from Whetstone,
        Heptameron (1582): 'a company as spotted as Labans Sheepe' (Dent).

DUCHESS   Diamonds are of most value   290
  They say, that have passed through most jewellers' hands.
FERDINAND
  Whores, by that rule, are precious.
DUCHESS   Will you hear me?
  I'll never marry.
CARDINAL   So most widows say,
  But commonly that motion lasts no longer
  Than the turning of an hourglass: the funeral sermon,   295
  And it, end both together.
FERDINAND   Now hear me:
  You live in a rank pasture here, i'th'court.
  There is a kind of honey-dew that's deadly:
  'Twill poison your fame. Look to't. Be not cunning:
  For they whose faces do belie their hearts   300
  Are witches ere they arrive at twenty years,
  Ay, and give the devil suck.
DUCHESS
  This is terrible good counsel.
FERDINAND
  Hypocrisy is woven of a fine small thread
  Subtler than Vulcan's engine: yet, believe't,   305
  Your darkest actions, nay, your privat'st thoughts,
  Will come to light.
CARDINAL   You may flatter yourself
  And take your own choice: privately be married
  Under the eaves of night.
FERDINAND   Think't the best voyage

292–3   ed. (Whores ... precious / Will ... me / I'll ... marry / So ... say Q1).
  293   I assume Q1's colon after *marry* signifies a full-stop, as frequently with Crane: but
       if the colon is interpreted as indicating interruption the Duchess cannot be
       convicted of telling a bare-faced lie here.
  294   *motion* impulse.
  298   *honey-dew* sweet sticky substance found on plants, formerly supposed a kind of dew.
       In *The Malcontent*, III.ii.27–50, Malevole memorably evokes the luxury of an Italian
       court: 'The strong'st incitements to immodesty – / To have her bound, incensed with
       wanton sweets, / Her veins filled high with heating delicates ...'
  302   Witches supposedly suckled familiar spirits, usually animals, from an extra nipple.
  305   *Vulcan's engine* Vulcan used a net of very fine thread to catch Venus and Mars in
       adultery.
  309   *eaves* ed. (eves Q1) Dent compares Dekker, *The Whore of Babylon*, III.i.158,
       describing Catholic agents secretly infiltrating England, who 'Flie with the Batt under
       the eeues of night'.

That e'er you made, like the irregular crab   310
Which, though't goes backward, thinks that it goes right
Because it goes its own way; but observe:
Such weddings may more properly be said
To be executed than celebrated.
CARDINAL   The marriage night
Is the entrance into some prison.
FERDINAND   And those joys,   315
Those lustful pleasures, are like heavy sleeps
Which do forerun man's mischief.
CARDINAL   Fare you well.
Wisdom begins at the end: remember it.   [*Exit*]
DUCHESS
I think this speech between you both was studied,
It came so roundly off.
FERDINAND   You are my sister.   320
This was my father's poniard: do you see?
I'd be loath to see't look rusty, 'cause 'twas his.
I would have you to give o'er these chargeable revels;
A visor and a masque are whispering rooms
That were ne'er built for goodness. Fare ye well –   325
And women like that part which, like the lamprey,
Hath ne'er a bone in't.

314–5   ed. (To ... celibrated / The ... night / Is ... prison / And ... ioyes Q1).
314   Both these verbs could be used equally of religious rites, but Ferdinand implies the
         alternative meaning of *executed* = put to death.
318   Alluding to the proverbs 'Think on the end before you begin' (Tilley E125) and
         'Remember the end' (E128).
319   *studied* prepared in advance, rehearsed. If the brothers take positions on either side
         of the Duchess the episode's general parallels with *The Revenger's Tragedy*, IV.iv.4
         (the interrogation by Vindice and Hippolito, with daggers drawn, of their mother)
         are apparent; at the same time in Webster each brother is driven by a different
         obsession: Ferdinand's is sexual, the Cardinal's is social rank. See also II.v below.
321–2   *poniard ... rusty* If he uses the dagger to kill her, its tempered steel will be bloody
         and start to rust: see Juliet's last words, in *Romeo and Juliet*, V.iii.170. Vindice in *The
         Revenger's Tragedy*, IV.iv.45, sheathing his dagger when his mother begins to weep,
         says 'Brother it rains, 'twill spoil your dagger, house it'.
323   *chargeable revels* expensive court festivities. The elaborate masques at the court of
         James I were notoriously expensive.
324–5   In *The Revenger's Tragedy*, I.iv.27ff., Antonio describes a court masque 'last revelling
         night' where 'torchlight made an artificial noon' and a murderer wore a mask as
         disguise; and Spurio tells (I.ii.185–6) of a court feast and 'a whispering and
         withdrawing hour / When base male bawds kept sentinel at stairhead'.
326   *lamprey* an eel-like fish.

DUCHESS   Fie sir!
FERDINAND   Nay,
I mean the tongue: variety of courtship.
What cannot a neat knave with a smooth tale
Make a woman believe? Farewell, lusty widow.   [*Exit*]   330
DUCHESS
Shall this move me? If all my royal kindred
Lay in my way unto this marriage
I'd make them my low foot-steps, and even now,
Even in this hate, as men in some great battles,
By apprehending danger have achieved   335
Almost impossible actions – I have heard soldiers say so –
So I, through frights and threat'nings will assay
This dangerous venture. Let old wives report
I winked and chose a husband.

[*Enter* CARIOLA]

                    Cariola,
To thy known secrecy I have given up   340
More than my life, my fame.
CARIOLA   Both shall be safe:
For I'll conceal this secret from the world
As warily as those that trade in poison
Keep poison from their children.
DUCHESS   Thy protestation
Is ingenious and hearty: I believe it.   345
Is Antonio come?
CARIOLA   He attends you.
DUCHESS   Good dear soul.
Leave me: but place thyself behind the arras,

---

329 *tale* Punning on the sense 'penis' (as in e.g. *Romeo and Juliet*, II.iv.97).
333 *foot-steps* steps (up to the altar).
339 *winked* closed my eyes. The proverb 'You may wink and choose' (Tilley W501) meant
     'choose blind' – but *wink* also meant 'shut your eyes at wrong', in which case the
     Duchess anticipates moral condemnation and dismisses it as no better than the
     prejudice of old wives.
341 *fame* reputation.
341 s.p. CARIOLA ed. (*Carolia* Q1).
345 *ingenious and hearty* sagacious and heartfelt.
347 *arras* curtain – hung across the back of the stage (later, at IV.i.54 s.d. a curtain is
     drawn to display the figures of Antonio and the children).

Where thou mayst overhear us. Wish me good speed,
For I am going into a wilderness
Where I shall find nor path, nor friendly clew   350
To be my guide.

[CARIOLA *withdraws behind the arras*]

[*Enter* ANTONIO]

                    I sent for you. Sit down:
Take pen and ink and write. Are you ready?
ANTONIO   Yes.
DUCHESS
What did I say?
ANTONIO   That I should write somewhat.
DUCHESS
Oh, I remember:
After these triumphs and this large expense   355
It's fit – like thrifty husbands – we enquire
What's laid up for tomorrow.
ANTONIO
So please your beauteous excellence.
DUCHESS   Beauteous?
Indeed I thank you: I look young for your sake.
You have ta'en my cares upon you.
ANTONIO [*Rising*]   I'll fetch your grace   360
The particulars of your revenue and expense.
DUCHESS
Oh, you are an upright treasurer: but you mistook,
For when I said I meant to make enquiry

---

348   *Where . . . us* The staging recalls two episodes involving Polonius in *Hamlet*, III.i.54ff.
       and III.iv.6ff.
350   *clew* ball of thread used as a guide (as by Theseus to guide him through the
       labyrinth).
352–4 ed. (Take . . . ready / Yes / What . . . say / That . . . -what / Oh . . . remember Q1).
355   *these* ed. (this Q1).
       triumphs court festivities.
356   *thrifty husbands* provident managers (of the court and ducal household) – but the
       Duchess lightly hints at *husband* = marriage partner, the sense in 397.
357   *laid up* in store.
358–69 ed. (So . . . Excellence / Beauteous . . . sake / You . . . you / I'le . . . the / Particulars . . .
       expence Q1).
359   *for your sake* thanks to you – and with the hinted sense 'for love of you'.
362   *upright* Punning on the fact that Antonio has just stood up (NCW).

What's laid up for tomorrow, I did mean
What's laid up yonder for me.

ANTONIO   Where?

DUCHESS   In heaven.   365
I am making my will, as 'tis fit princes should
In perfect memory, and I pray sir, tell me
Were not one better make it smiling, thus,
Than in deep groans and terrible ghastly looks,
As if the gifts we parted with procured   370
That violent distraction?

ANTONIO   Oh, much better.

DUCHESS
If I had a husband now, this care were quit:
But I intend to make you overseer.
What good deed shall we first remember? Say.

ANTONIO
Begin with that first good deed began i'th'world   375
After man's creation, the sacrament of marriage.
I'd have you first provide for a good husband,
Give him all.

DUCHESS   All?

ANTONIO   Yes, your excellent self.

DUCHESS
In a winding sheet?

ANTONIO   In a couple.

DUCHESS
St Winifred, that were a strange will!   380

364–5   See Matthew 6 particularly 19–21: 'lay up for yourselves treasure in heaven . . . for
        where your treasure is there will your heart be also' – but the whole chapter is highly
        relevant.
370   *procured* were the cause of.
371   *distraction* Q3 (distruction Q1).
372   *quit* Under English law at the time her husband would be owner of all her assets
        (Marcus).
373   *overseer* person appointed under the terms of a will to supervise or assist its
        executors.
378–9   ed. (Give . . . all / All / Yes . . . selfe / In . . . sheete / In . . . cople Q1).
379   *winding sheet* shroud. So making her fit to accompany her dead husband. There was
        apparently a fashion for women to be buried in their wedding sheets – see Clare
        Gittings, *Death, Burial, and the Individual in Early Modern England*, 1984, pp.
        111–12, cit. Michael Neill, *Issues of Death*, 1997, p. 339.
380   *Winifred* ed. (*Winfrid* Q1); Q1 is an error since St Winfred – Wynfrith – was then
        universally known as St Boniface. *St Winifred*, a Welsh saint of the 7th century whose

ANTONIO
'Twere strange if there were no will in you
To marry again.
DUCHESS   What do you think of marriage?
ANTONIO
I take't as those that deny purgatory:
It locally contains or heaven or hell;
There's no third place in't.
DUCHESS   How do you affect it?   385
ANTONIO
My banishment, feeding my melancholy,
Would often reason thus –
DUCHESS   Pray let's hear it.
ANTONIO
Say a man never marry, nor have children,
What takes that from him? Only the bare name
Of being a father, or the weak delight   390
To see the little wanton ride a-cock-horse
Upon a painted stick, or hear him chatter
Like a taught starling.
DUCHESS   Fie, fie, what's all this?
One of your eyes is blood-shot, use my ring to't,
                                        [*Gives him the ring*]
They say 'tis very sovereign: 'twas my wedding ring,   395
And I did vow never to part with it
But to my second husband.
ANTONIO
You have parted with it now.
DUCHESS
Yes, to help your eyesight.

head, struck off by Caradoc ap Alauc for refusing his love, was restored to life by St
Bruno, and is invoked by the Duchess because she sees an apt parallel with her own
situation. Recusant Catholics made defiant pilgrimages to the well of St Winifred.
See Andrew Breeze, 'St Winifred of Wales and *The Duchess of Malfi*' N&Q (March
1998) 33–4, and Todd Borlik, 'Catholic Nostalgia in *The Duchess of Malfi*' in Luckyj,
138–9.

383–5   Protestants denied the existence of Purgatory; some proverbs averred that marriage
            was heaven or hell, others that it was purgatory or hell (Dent).
385   *affect* like, feel about.
386   *banishment* When he accompanied Federico to France (see above 2 n.).
391   *wanton* rogue.
395   *sovereign* efficacious: so gold is believed to cure a stye on an eyelid.

ANTONIO

   You have made me stark blind. 400

DUCHESS

   How?

ANTONIO

   There is a saucy and ambitious devil

   Is dancing in this circle.

DUCHESS   Remove him.

ANTONIO   How?

DUCHESS

   There needs small conjuration when your finger

   May do it: thus –

              [*She puts her ring upon his finger*]

   – is it fit?

                    He kneels

ANTONIO   What said you?

DUCHESS   Sir, 405

   This goodly roof of yours is too low built,

   I cannot stand upright in't, nor discourse,

   Without I raise it higher. Raise yourself,

   Or if you please, my hand to help you: so.

                  [*He rises*]

ANTONIO

   Ambition, madam, is a great man's madness, 410

   That is not kept in chains and close-pent rooms

   But in fair lightsome lodgings, and is girt

   With the wild noise of prattling visitants

   Which makes it lunatic beyond all cure.

   Conceive not I am so stupid but I aim 415

   Whereto your favours tend: but he's a fool

   That being a-cold would thrust his hands i'th'fire

   To warm them.

DUCHESS   So now the ground's broke

   You may discover what a wealthy mine

   I make you lord of.

ANTONIO   Oh my unworthiness. 420

DUCHESS

   You were ill to sell yourself.

   This dark'ning of your worth is not like that

---

415   *aim* guess.

420   *of* ed. (off Q1).

Which tradesmen use i'th'city: their false lights
Are to rid bad wares off; and I must tell you,
If you will know where breathes a complete man –   425
I speak it without flattery – turn your eyes
And progress through yourself.

ANTONIO   Were there nor heaven nor hell
I should be honest: I have long served virtue
And ne'er ta'en wages of her.   430

DUCHESS   Now she pays it.
The misery of us that are born great,
We are forced to woo because none dare woo us:
And as a tyrant doubles with his words,
And fearfully equivocates, so we
Are forced to express our violent passions   435
In riddles and in dreams, and leave the path
Of simple virtue which was never made
To seem the thing it is not. Go, go brag
You have left me heartless, mine is in your bosom,
I hope 'twill multiply love there. You do tremble.   440
Make not your heart so dead a piece of flesh
To fear more than to love me. Sir, be confident,
What is't distracts you? This is flesh and blood, sir,
'Tis not the figure cut in alabaster
Kneels at my husband's tomb. Awake, awake, man,   445
I do here put off all vain ceremony
And only do appear to you a young widow
That claims you for her husband; and like a widow,
I use but half a blush in't.

ANTONIO   Truth speak for me,
I will remain the constant sanctuary   450
Of your good name.

DUCHESS   I thank you, gentle love,
And 'cause you shall not come to me in debt,

424   *rid . . . off* get rid of bad wares.
443   *flesh and blood* Proverbial: 'To be flesh and blood as others are' (Tilley F367).
444–5 *figure . . . tomb* For this comparison see *Merchant of Venice*, I.i.83–4. It is a further
       unwittingly ironic anticipation of tragedy: the Duchess has referred to her will and
       winding-sheet, Antonio to imprisonment and the visits of madmen; even a cold
       hand will recur – see IV.i.50. Elizabethan sculptures were usually polychrome and
       realistic; on the stage, a stone figure could be represented by an actor, as in *The
       Winter's Tale*, V.iii, and so could a waxwork, as in IV.i.54 below.

Being now my steward, here upon your lips
I sign your *Quietus est.*

                                   [*She kisses him*]

This you should have begged now.   455
I have seen children oft eat sweet-meats thus
As fearful to devour them too soon.

ANTONIO
But for your brothers?

DUCHESS   Do not think of them.

                                  [*Embraces him*]

All discord, without this circumference,
Is only to be pitied and not feared.   460
Yet, should they know it, time will easily
Scatter the tempest.

ANTONIO   These words should be mine,
And all the parts you have spoke, if some part of it
Would not have savoured flattery.

DUCHESS   Kneel.
                  [CARIOLA *comes from behind the arras*]
ANTONIO   Ha?
DUCHESS

Be not amazed, this woman's of my counsel.   465
I have heard lawyers say a contract in a chamber,
Per verba de presenti, is absolute marriage:
Bless, heaven, this sacred Gordian, which let violence
Never untwine.

---

454 *Quietus est* Latin: 'he is discharged of payment due' – a conventional phrase
     indicating that accounts are correct; but with an ominous undertone: it could also
     refer to release from one's debt to nature, death, as in *Hamlet*, III.i.74.
459 *without this circumference* outside my arms' embrace (also perhaps referring to the
     ring).
463 *parts* particulars.
464 *Kneel* The couple might kneel here, or perhaps at 468, and rise again at 480 (Marcus).
467 *Per . . . presenti* A term in canon law, 'by words, as from the present': the Elizabethan
     church recognised as a marriage the simple declaration by a couple that they were
     man and wife, even without a witness. See *Measure for Measure*, I.ii.145ff.: Claudio
     explains how he believes his clandestine marriage to Juliet was 'upon a true contract
     . . .' but a new unjustly severe law brands them criminals. This was a topical issue in
     the year when Shakespeare's play was first performed, 1604, since that was the year
     in which English canon law about marriage was newly tightened up.
     de ed. (not in Q1).
468–9 *Bless . . . untwine* The Duchess refers to her hand clasping Antonio's.
468 *Gordian* The oracle decreed that anyone who could loose the knot tied by King
     Gordius would rule Asia. Alexander the Great had to cut it with his sword.

ANTONIO

  And may our sweet affections, like the spheres,   470

  Be still in motion –

DUCHESS   Quickening, and make

  The like soft music –

ANTONIO

  That we may imitate the loving palms,

  Best emblem of a peaceful marriage,

  That ne'er bore fruit divided.   475

DUCHESS

  What can the Church force more?

ANTONIO

  That Fortune may not know an accident

  Either of joy, or sorrow, to divide

  Our fixed wishes.

DUCHESS   How can the Church build faster?

  We now are man and wife, and 'tis the Church   480

  That must but echo this. Maid, stand apart,

  I now am blind.

ANTONIO   What's your conceit in this?

DUCHESS

  I would have you lead your Fortune by the hand

  Unto your marriage bed.

  You speak in me this, for we now are one.   485

  We'll only lie, and talk, together, and plot

  T'appease my humorous kindred; and if you please,

  Like the old tale in Alexander and Lodowick,

  Lay a naked sword between us, keep us chaste.

470–2 The planetary spheres supposedly created music by their perpetual (*still*), stimulating (*Quickening*) and unheard (*soft*) harmonious motion.

476 *force* enforce.

479 *build* Q1 (bind Brown) Some editors conjecture that 'bind' stood in Crane's copy but that in transcribing he erroneously used too many minim strokes; these the compositor interpreted as 'uil': but this is unconvincing – why add a letter 'l' which is not a minim? Q1 makes sense (a marriage needs to be firmly built) and should stand, even though as some editors argue, 'bind' better relates to the passage's concern with tying together.

      faster more strongly and firmly.

487 *humorous* ill-humoured, difficult.

488 i.e. The two friends were so alike they were mistaken for each other. When Lodowick married a princess in Alexander's name, he laid a naked (unsheathed) sword each night between himself and the princess, because he would not wrong his friend. This story of 'The Two Faithful Friends' was made into a ballad, and was the subject of a play staged by The Admiral's Men in 1597 (NCW).

Oh, let me shroud my blushes in your bosom,   490
Since 'tis the treasury of all my secrets.

[Exeunt DUCHESS *and* ANTONIO]

CARIOLA

Whether the spirit of greatness or of woman
Reign most in her, I know not, but it shows
A fearful madness. I owe her much of pity.   [*Exit*]

---

490   *shroud* hide from view; but the verb also had the ominous sense 'prepare for burial'
      (OED v.7).
491   s.d. If Cariola remains on stage alone (like the solitary Duchess at 331–9), then added
      emphasis is given to her anxiety that her mistress is showing a *fearful madness.*
      Marcus prefers Q1, where all three remain until 494, as truer to the 'whispering
      room' atmosphere of the play.
494   [*Exit*] ed. (*Exeunt* Q1).

ACT II, SCENE i

[*Enter* BOSOLA *and* CASTRUCHIO]

BOSOLA

You say you would fain be taken for an eminent courtier?

CASTRUCHIO

'Tis the very main of my ambition.

BOSOLA

Let me see: you have a reasonable good face for't already, and
your night-cap expresses your ears sufficient largely. I would
have you learn to twirl the strings of your band with a good   5
grace; and in a set speech, at th'end of every sentence, to hum
three or four times, or blow your nose till it smart again, to
recover your memory. When you come to be a president in
criminal causes, if you smile upon a prisoner, hang him, but if
you frown upon him, and threaten him, let him be sure to   10
'scape the gallows.

CASTRUCHIO

I would be a very merry president.

BOSOLA

Do not sup a-nights, 'twill beget you an admirable wit.

CASTRUCHIO

Rather it would make me have a good stomach to quarrel, for
they say your roaring boys eat meat seldom, and that makes   15
them so valiant. But how shall I know whether the people take
me for an eminent fellow?

---

 0   s.d. ed. (ACTUS II. SCENA I. / Bosola, Castruchio, an Old Lady, Antonio, Delio,
       Duchesse, Rodorico, Grisolan. Q1).
 1   *courtier* lawyer, judge, identified by the white coif or skull-cap (see line 4 below, *your
       night-cap*) worn by a sergeant-at-law. The usual sense of *courtier* may also apply, as
       senior lawyers might well attend the ruler's court.
 2   *main* purpose.
3–11 prose ed. (*Q1 lines ending* already / largely / a / sentence / againe / in / if / scape).
 4   *expresses . . . largely* shows off your long ears (and makes you look a complete ass).
 5   *twirl . . . band* collar-bands with a string attached were fashionable among courtiers
       and lawyers – Brown cites Jonson, *Cynthia's Revels*, V.iv.158.
14–20 prose ed. (*Q1 lines ending* quarrel / seldome / valiant / me / fellow / it / you / you /
       -caps).
 15   *roaring boys* rowdies, yobs, louts.

317

BOSOLA

I will teach a trick to know it: give out you lie a-dying, and if
you hear the common people curse you, be sure you are taken
for one of the prime night-caps.   20

[*Enter* OLD LADY]

You come from painting now?

OLD LADY

From what?

BOSOLA

Why, from your scurvy face physic. To behold thee not painted
inclines somewhat near a miracle. These in thy face, here, were
deep ruts and foul sloughs the last progress. There was a lady in   25
France that, having had the smallpox, flayed the skin off her
face to make it more level; and whereas before she looked like a
nutmeg grater, after she resembled an abortive hedgehog.

OLD LADY

Do you call this painting?

BOSOLA

No, no, but careening of an old morphewed lady, to make her   30
disembogue again. There's rough cast phrase to your plastic.

OLD LADY

It seems you are well acquainted with my closet?

BOSOLA

One would suspect it for a shop of witchcraft, to find in it the
fat of serpents, spawn of snakes, Jews' spittle, and their young
children's ordures, and all these for the face: I would sooner eat   35
a dead pigeon, taken from the soles of the feet of one sick of the

---

23–8 prose ed. (*Q1 lines ending* -physicke / neere / rutts / progresse / pockes / leuell /
      Nutmeg-grater / hedge-hog).
25   *sloughs* muddy holes in the road.
      progress ceremonious royal journey.
30–1 prose ed. (*Q1 lines ending* old / againe / plastique).
30   *but* ed. (but you call Q1; but you call it Q3; but I call it Lucas).
      careening . . . lady giving an old lady's leprous hull a good scraping.
31   *disembogue* put out to sea, on the war-path.
      There's . . . plastic That's coarsely put – rough-cast (lime and gravel) crudely
      plastered, not your smooth finish.
33–41 prose ed. (*Q1 lines ending* witch-craft / spittle / face / feete / fasting / very / his / his
      / leafe / -selues).
35   *children's* ed. (children Q1).
36–7 *dead . . . plague* In 1612 when the heir to the English throne Prince Henry lay
      mortally ill, freshly killed pigeons were applied to the soles of his feet. The same
      treatment is recommended (for the plague) in *The English Huswife*, 1615.

plague, than kiss one of you fasting. Here are two of you whose
sin of your youth is the very patrimony of the physician, makes
him renew his foot-cloth with the spring, and change his high-
priced courtesan with the fall of the leaf. I do wonder you do   40
not loathe yourselves.
Observe my meditation now.
What thing is in this outward form of man
To be beloved? We account it ominous
If nature do produce a colt, or lamb,   45
A fawn, or goat, in any limb resembling
A man; and fly from't as a prodigy.
Man stands amazed to see his deformity
In any other creature but himself;
But in our own flesh, though we bear diseases   50
Which have their true names only ta'en from beasts –
As the most ulcerous wolf, and swinish measle –
Though we are eaten up of lice, and worms,
And though continually we bear about us
A rotten and dead body, we delight   55
To hide it in rich tissue; all our fear –
Nay all our terror – is, lest our physician
Should put us in the ground, to be made sweet.
[*To* CASTRUCHIO] Your wife's gone to Rome: you two couple
and get you to the wells at Lucca, to recover your aches.   60
                    [*Exeunt* CASTRUCHIO *and* OLD LADY]

37   kiss . . . fasting Fasting supposedly makes bad breath even worse.
39   foot-cloth a rich cloth laid over the horse's back and hanging down to the ground,
      protecting the rider from dirt: a mark of high status.
39–40 high-priced She is, like the foot-cloth, an expensive status-symbol.
42–58 See *Measure for Measure*, III.i.5ff., where the Duke-as-Friar delivers to young Claudio
      similar advocacy: 'Be absolute for death'. The difference here is that instead of a
      young man there is an old lord and old lady. In performance, if Bosola addresses
      them directly his words will seem calculatedly cruel, but if he stands apart and
      addresses the audience, the two old people will serve as visible instances of man's
      deformity.
52   *ulcerous wolf* The Elizabethan name for a type of ulcer was 'wolf': Webster perhaps
      also makes a covert anticipatory allusion to Ferdinand's lycanthropia.
      measle The disease of measles in humans, also a disease in swine: both diseases
      etymologically confused with *mesel* = leprous (*OED*).
56   *tissue* delicate cloth.
58   *sweet* benign in effect.
59–60 ed. (Your . . . you / To . . . aches Q1).
60   *wells at Lucca* The Italian city was famous as a spa.
      recover your aches The waters are to alleviate the symptoms of venereal disease
      (commonly called 'the bone-ache').

I have other work on foot. I observe our Duchess
Is sick a-days, she pukes, her stomach seethes,
The fins of her eyelids look most teeming blue,
She wanes i'th'cheek, and waxes fat i'th'flank;
And contrary to our Italian fashion   65
Wears a loose-bodied gown. There's somewhat in't.
I have a trick may chance discover it,
A pretty one: I have bought some apricots,
The first our spring yields.

    [*Enter* ANTONIO *and* DELIO *talking apart*]

DELIO   And so long since married?
You amaze me.
ANTONIO   Let me seal your lips for ever,   70
For did I think that anything but th'air
Could carry these words from you, I should wish
You had no breath at all.
 [*To* BOSOLA] Now sir, in your contemplation? You are studying
to become a great wise fellow?   75
BOSOLA
Oh sir, the opinion of wisdom is a foul tetter that runs all over
a man's body: if simplicity direct us to have no evil, it directs us
to a happy being. For the subtlest folly proceeds from the
subtlest wisdom. Let me be simply honest.
ANTONIO
I do understand your inside.   80
BOSOLA
Do you so?
ANTONIO
Because you would not seem to appear to th'world puffed
up with your preferment, you continue this out-of-fashion
melancholy; leave it, leave it.

---

 63 The edges of her eyelids are blue, like those of a pregnant woman (Lucas).
65–6 *contrary . . . gown* Bosola, having listed physical signs associated with pregnancy,
   then observes the Duchess' unusual choice of gown, which could conceal the most
   obvious sign; there is an innuendo in *loose-bodied* = morally loose.
 68 *apricots* ed (apricocks Q1). In Q1's period spelling 'Apricocks' Marcus sees a bawdy
   pun ('cock' = penis) and compares lines 22–6 of Webster's Induction to *The
   Malcontent*.
74–90 prose ed. (*Q1 lines ending* contemplation / fellow / tettor / simplicity / happy / from
   the / honest / in-side / so / world / continue / leave it / any / you / reach / horses /
   suit / me / gallop / tyre).
 76 *tetter* skin eruption.

BOSOLA

Give me leave to be honest in any phrase, in any compliment 85
whatsoever. Shall I confess myself to you? I look no higher than
I can reach: they are the gods that must ride on winged horses,
a lawyer's mule of a slow pace will both suit my disposition and
business, for, mark me, when a man's mind rides faster than his
horse can gallop, they quickly both tire. 90

ANTONIO

You would look up to heaven, but I think
The devil that rules i'th'air stands in your light.

BOSOLA

Oh, sir, you are lord of the ascendant, chief man with the
Duchess, a duke was your cousin-german, removed. Say you
were lineally descended from King Pippin, or he himself, what 95
of this? Search the heads of the greatest rivers in the world, you
shall find them but bubbles of water. Some would think the
souls of princes were brought forth by some more weighty
cause than those of meaner persons; they are deceived, there's
the same hand to them, the like passions sway them; the same 100
reason that makes a vicar go to law for a tithe-pig, and undo his
neighbours, makes them spoil a whole province, and batter
down goodly cities with the cannon.

[*Enter* DUCHESS *with* ATTENDANTS]

DUCHESS

Your arm, Antonio. Do I not grow fat?
I am exceeding short-winded. Bosola, 105
I would have you, sir, provide for me a litter,
Such a one as the Duchess of Florence rode in.

BOSOLA

The Duchess used one when she was great with child.

92   *devil . . . air* So referred to in the Bishop's Bible, Ephesians 2.2: he 'that ruleth in the
       ayre'.
93–103 prose ed. (*Q1 lines ending* ascendant / your / lineally / himselfe / in / water / brought
       / persons / them / makes / tithe-pig / spoile / goodly / Cannon).
93   *lord of the ascendant* the dominant influence, the rising star. In astrology the *lord* is
       the planet of which the associated zodiac sign is at the moment *the ascendant* – is
       entering the 'first house', that part of the sky which is rising above the horizon.
94   *cousin-german, removed* first cousin, once removed.
95   *King Pippin* Died 768: King of the Franks and father of Charlemagne.
97–103 Derived from Montaigne, *Essayes*, p. 274.
103   s.d. The entrance would have added effect if placed at line 97 'Some . . .' (Brown).
104   *fat* An attempt to explain away her advanced state of pregnancy.

DUCHESS
    I think she did – come hither, mend my ruff,
    Here, when? Thou art such a tedious lady –   110
    And thy breath smells of lemon peels – would thou hadst
       done –
    Shall I swoon under thy fingers? I am
    So troubled with the mother.
BOSOLA [*Aside*]   I fear too much.
DUCHESS [*To* ANTONIO]
    I have heard you say that the French courtiers
    Wear their hats on 'fore the King.
ANTONIO   I have seen it.   115
DUCHESS
    In the presence?
ANTONIO
    Yes.
[DUCHESS]
    Why should not we bring up that fashion?
    'Tis ceremony more than duty that consists
    In the removing of a piece of felt.   120
    Be you the example to the rest o'th'court,
    Put on your hat first.
ANTONIO   You must pardon me:
    I have seen, in colder countries than in France,
    Nobles stand bare to th'prince; and the distinction
    Methought showed reverently.   125
BOSOLA
    I have a present for your grace.
DUCHESS   For me sir?
BOSOLA
    Apricots, madam.
DUCHESS   Oh sir, where are they?
    I have heard of none to-year.
BOSOLA [*Aside*]   Good, her colour rises.

111   *peels* ed. (pils Q1; peel Q4).
113   *the mother* hysteria.
      too ed. (to Q1).
114   *courtiers* ed. (courties Q1).
118   s.p. ed. (not in Q1, but added by hand in many copies).
125   *Methought* ed. (My thought Q1).
126–8 ed. (I . . . Grace / For me sir / Apricocks Madam / O . . . they / I . . . yeare / Good . . .
      rises Q1).

DUCHESS

    Indeed I thank you, they are wondrous fair ones.

    What an unskilful fellow is our gardener,   130

    We shall have none this month.

BOSOLA

    Will not your grace pare them?

DUCHESS

    No – they taste of musk, methinks, indeed they do.

BOSOLA

    I know not: yet I wish your grace had pared 'em.

DUCHESS

    Why?   135

BOSOLA

    I forgot to tell you, the knave gardener,

    Only to raise his profit by them the sooner,

    Did ripen them in horse dung.

DUCHESS   Oh you jest.

    You shall judge: pray taste one.

ANTONIO   Indeed madam,

    I do not love the fruit.

DUCHESS   Sir, you are loath   140

    To rob us of our dainties: 'tis a delicate fruit,

    They say they are restorative?

BOSOLA

    'Tis a pretty art, this grafting.

DUCHESS

    'Tis so: a bett'ring of nature.

BOSOLA

    To make a pippin grow upon a crab,   145

    A damson on a blackthorn.

    [*Aside*]   – How greedily she eats them!

    A whirlwind strike off these bawd farthingales!

138–40   ed. (Did . . . –doung / Oh . . . iest / You . . . one / Indeed Madam / I . . . fruit / Sir . . .
        loath).

    141   *dainties* (1) choice foods (2) luxuries – with a sexual innuendo.

    143   *grafting* Ironically alluding to the union of the Duchess with someone of inferior
        stock (see *The Winter's Tale*, IV.iv.86ff.); this verb also had an indecent sense, played
        upon here.

145–6   An instance of Webster's detailed use of sources, here Breton, *Wil of Wit*, 1606, Iir:
        'Is not the Damson tree . . . aboue the Blackthorne tree? is not the Pippin . . . aboue
        the crabtree? the Abricock above the common plum?' (cited by Dent).

    147   *farthingales* hooped petticoats.

For, but for that, and the loose-bodied gown,
I should have discovered apparently
The young springal cutting a caper in her belly.   150

DUCHESS
I thank you, Bosola, they were right good ones,
If they do not make me sick.

ANTONIO   How now madam?

DUCHESS
This green fruit and my stomach are not friends.
How they swell me!

BOSOLA [*Aside*]   Nay, you are too much swelled already.

DUCHESS
Oh, I am in an extreme cold sweat.

BOSOLA   I am very sorry.   155

DUCHESS
Lights to my chamber. Oh, good Antonio,
I fear I am undone.   *Exit*

DELIO   Lights there, lights.
                    [*Exeunt all but* ANTONIO *and* DELIO]

ANTONIO
O my most trusty Delio, we are lost.
I fear she's fall'n in labour, and there's left
No time for her remove.

DELIO   Have you prepared   160
Those ladies to attend her, and procured
That politic safe conveyance for the midwife
Your Duchess plotted?

ANTONIO   I have.

DELIO
Make use then of this forced occasion.
Give out that Bosola hath poisoned her   165
With these apricots: that will give some colour
For her keeping close.

ANTONIO   Fie, fie, the physicians
Will then flock to her.

DELIO   For that you may pretend
She'll use some prepared antidote of her own,
Lest the physicians should re-poison her.   170

---

149   *apparently* clearly.
150   *springal* stripling.

ANTONIO

I am lost in amazement. I know not what to think on't.

Exeunt

[ACT II,] SCENE ii

[*Enter* BOSOLA]

BOSOLA

So, so: there's no question but her tetchiness, and most vulturous eating of the apricots, are apparent signs of breeding.

[*Enter* OLD LADY]

Now?

OLD LADY

I am in haste, sir.

BOSOLA

There was a young waiting-woman had a monstrous desire to   5
see the glass-house –

OLD LADY

Nay, pray let me go –

BOSOLA

And it was only to know what strange instrument it was should swell up a glass to the fashion of a woman's belly.

OLD LADY

I will hear no more of the glass-house, you are still abusing   10
women.

BOSOLA

Who I? No, only by the way, now and then, mention your frailties. The orange tree bears ripe and green fruit and blossoms altogether, and some of you give entertainment for

---

  0   s.d. ed. (*SCENA. II. / Bosola, old Lady, Antonio, Rodorigo, Grisolan: seruants, Delio, Cariola. Q1*).

1–3 prose ed. (*Q1 lines ending* teatchiues / apparant / now).

  4   This Old Lady is in haste to act as midwife to the Duchess: entering by one door, she is crossing the stage to exit at another when Bosola blocks her way.

  6   *glass-house* glass factory: Webster alludes to the Blackfriars glass factory in *The White Devil*, I.ii.132.

 13 *bears* ed. (beare Q1).

 14 *altogether* both together, simultanously.
      entertainment sexual pleasure.

pure love; but more, for more precious reward. The lusty spring   15
smells well, but drooping autumn tastes well. If we have the
same golden showers that rained in the time of Jupiter the
Thunderer, you have the same Danaes still, to hold up their laps
to receive them. Didst thou never study the mathematics?

OLD LADY

What's that, sir?   20

BOSOLA

Why, to know the trick how to make a many lines meet in one
centre. Go, go; give your foster-daughters good council: tell
them that the devil takes delight to hang at a woman's girdle
like a false rusty watch, that she cannot discern how the time
passes.   25

[*Exit* OLD LADY]

[*Enter* ANTONIO, DELIO, RODERIGO, GRISOLAN]

ANTONIO

Shut up the court gates.

RODERIGO   Why sir, what's the danger?

ANTONIO

Shut up the posterns presently, and call
All the officers o'th'court.

GRISOLAN   I shall, instantly.   [*Exit*]

ANTONIO

Who keeps the key o'th'park gate?

RODERIGO   Forobosco.

ANTONIO

Let him bring't presently.   30

[*Exeunt* ANTONIO *and* RODERIGO]

[*Enter* SERVANTS]

SERVANT

Oh gentlemen o'th'court, the foulest treason!

---

15   *precious reward* gold.
17–19   Receiving Jupiter in the form of a shower of gold, Danae became a synonym for a
mercenary woman. See I.i.238.
18   *Danaes* ed. (Danes Q1).
21–2   *many . . . centre* Proverbial; as in Montaigne, *Essayes*, p. 514: 'a Centre whereto all
lines come'.
27   *presently* at once.

BOSOLA

If that these apricots should be poisoned, now, without my
knowledge!

SERVANT

There was taken even now a Switzer in the Duchess'
bedchamber.   35

2 SERVANT

A Switzer?

SERVANT

With a pistol in his great codpiece!

BOSOLA

Ha, ha, ha.

SERVANT

The codpiece was the case for't.

2 SERVANT

There was a cunning traitor: who would have searched his   40
codpiece?

SERVANT

True, if he had kept out of the ladies' chambers; and all the
moulds of his buttons were leaden bullets.

2 SERVANT

Oh wicked cannibal: a fire-lock in's codpiece?

SERVANT

'Twas a French plot, upon my life!   45

2 SERVANT

To see what the devil can do!

[*Enter* ANTONIO, RODERIGO, GRISOLAN]

ANTONIO

All the officers here?

SERVANTS   We are.

ANTONIO   Gentlemen,

We have lost much plate, you know; and but this evening

37   *pistol . . . codpiece* The Elizabethan pronunciation of *pistol* omitted the medial 't' –
      so Kökeritz, *Shakespeare's Pronunciation*, 1953, p. 135 – making the pun on *pizzle* =
      penis clearer. The *codpiece*, no longer fashionable by 1612, was sometimes
      exaggerated in size and ornamentation – Rabelais has a memorable passage on
      Gargantua's opulent codpiece. Perhaps the joke involves not only the exaggerated
      size of the codpiece but also the unduly modest endowment of the Switzer in this
      department.

44   *cannibal* Marcus suggests a pun on 'cannonball'.

45   *French* Presumably alluding to the 'French disease', syphilis.

47   *All* Q1 (Are all Q4); *officers* Q2 (offices Q1).

327

Jewels to the value of four thousand ducats
Are missing in the Duchess' cabinet. 50
Are the gates shut?
SERVANT   Yes.
ANTONIO   'Tis the Duchess' pleasure
Each officer be locked into his chamber
Till the sun-rising, and to send the keys
Of all their chests, and of their outward doors,
Into her bedchamber: she is very sick. 55
RODERIGO
At her pleasure.
ANTONIO
She entreats you take't not ill. The innocent
Shall be the more approved by it.
BOSOLA
Gentleman o'th'wood-yard, where's your Switzer now?
SERVANT
By this hand, 'twas credibly reported by one o'th'Black-guard. 60
                    [*Exeunt all but* DELIO *and* ANTONIO]
DELIO
How fares it with the Duchess?
ANTONIO   She's exposed
Unto the worst of torture, pain, and fear.
DELIO
Speak to her all happy comfort.
ANTONIO
How I do play the fool with mine own danger!
You are this night, dear friend, to post to Rome, 65
My life lies in your service.
DELIO   Do not doubt me.
ANTONIO
Oh, 'tis far from me: and yet fear presents me
Somewhat that looks like danger.
DELIO   Believe it,
'Tis but the shadow of your fear, no more:
How superstitiously we mind our evils: 70

---

50   *cabinet* private chamber.
59   *Gentleman o'th' wood-yard* Bosola is clearly mocking the Servant's first words (lines
       31 and 34–5 above), so presumably the *wood-yard* has base and menial associations,
       like the next line's joke on *Black-guard* = scullions and greasy turnspits.
68   *looks* Q2 (looke Q1).

The throwing down salt, or crossing of a hare,
Bleeding at nose, the stumbling of a horse
Or singing of a cricket, are of power
To daunt whole man in us. Sir, fare you well:
I wish you all the joys of a blessed father   75
And, for my faith, lay this unto your breast:
Old friends, like old swords, still are trusted best.   [*Exit*]

[*Enter* CARIOLA]

CARIOLA
Sir, you are the happy father of a son.
Your wife commends him to you.
ANTONIO   Blessed comfort:
For heaven' sake tend her well. I'll presently   80
Go set a figure for's nativity.

                                                Exeunt

[ACT II,] SCENE iii

[*Enter* BOSOLA *with a dark lantern*]

BOSOLA
Sure I did hear a woman shriek: list, ha?
And the sound came, if I received it right,
From the Duchess' lodgings. There's some stratagem
In the confining all our courtiers
To their several wards. I must have part of it,   5
My intelligence will freeze else. List again:
It may be 'twas the melancholy bird,

74   *whole man* resolution.
77   s.d. Q4 adds *with a Child*, but this is superfluous: Cariola's appearance is momentary
        and the dramatic function is not to display the child but to prompt Antonio to make
        the horoscope, since this is the focus of the next piece of plot.
81   *set . . . nativity* cast his horoscope.

 0   s.d. ed. (SCENA. III. / Bosola, Antonio. Q1; Bosola, Antonio, with a dark lanthorn
        Q4).
 0   s.d. *dark lantern* A lantern with an arrangement for concealing its light. On the
        Elizabethan stage the conventional signal that a scene takes place by night was for
        actors to carry a light. A dark lantern features again in V.iv.50ff., offering an ironic
        comment on Bosola's nocturnal and murky career in the play.

Best friend of silence, and of solitariness,
The owl, that screamed so –

[*Enter* ANTONIO, *with a horoscope*]

Ha? Antonio?

ANTONIO
I heard some noise: who's there? What art thou? Speak.　　　10
BOSOLA
Antonio? Put not your face nor body
To such a forced expression of fear;
I am Bosola, your friend.
ANTONIO　　　　　　　　　Bosola?
[*Aside*] This mole does undermine me – heard you not
A noise even now?
BOSOLA　　　　　　From whence?
ANTONIO　　　　　　　　　　　From the Duchess' lodging.　　　15
BOSOLA
Not I. Did you?
ANTONIO　　　　　I did, or else I dreamed.
BOSOLA
Let's walk towards it.
ANTONIO　　　　　　No. It may be 'twas
But the rising of the wind.
BOSOLA　　　　　　　　Very likely.
Methinks 'tis very cold, and yet you sweat.
You look wildly.
ANTONIO　　　　　I have been setting a figure　　　20
For the Duchess' jewels.
BOSOLA　　　　　　　Ah: and how falls your question?
Do you find it radical?
ANTONIO　　　　　　What's that to you?
'Tis rather to be questioned what design,

9　s.d. ed. (Enter *Antonio*, with a Candle his sword drawn Q4).
15–18　ed. (A . . . now / From whence / From . . . lodging / Not . . . you / I . . . dream'd / Let's
　　　. . . it / No . . . 'twas / But . . . winde / Very likely Q1).
17　*it* The door by which Antonio entered, and which leads to the Duchess' apartments.
20–2　ed. (You . . . wildly / I . . . figure / For . . . Iewells / Ah . . question / Doe . . radicall /
　　　What's . . you Q1).
20–1　*setting . . . jewels* Recourse to astrology supposedly enabled the discovery of lost
　　　goods. Antonio backs up this lie by referring to his earlier – false – claim (see
　　　II.ii.48ff.) that jewels had been stolen.
22　*radical* fit to be judged.

When all men were commanded to their lodgings,
Makes you a night-walker.

BOSOLA   In sooth I'll tell you: 25
Now all the court's asleep, I thought the devil
Had least to do here. I came to say my prayers,
And if it do offend you I do so,
You are a fine courtier.

ANTONIO [*Aside*]   This fellow will undo me. –
You gave the Duchess apricots today,   30
Pray heaven they were not poisoned.

BOSOLA   Poisoned?
A Spanish fig for the imputation.

ANTONIO
Traitors are ever confident till they
Are discovered. There were jewels stolen too.
In my conceit none are to be suspected   35
More than yourself.

BOSOLA   You are a false steward.

ANTONIO
Saucy slave, I'll pull thee up by the roots!

BOSOLA
May be the ruin will crush you to pieces.

ANTONIO
You are an impudent snake indeed, sir!
Are you scarce warm and do you show your sting?   40

[BOSOLA
    …]

ANTONIO
You libel well, sir.

---

25   *night-walker* nocturnal rogue or criminal.
31–4   ed. (Pray . . poysond / Poysond . . . figge / For . . . imputation / Traitors . . . confident
       / Till . . . too Q1).
32   *Spanish fig* An indecent gesture, thrusting the thumb between the first two fingers –
       and with a pun on the other meaning, poison (as in *The White Devil*, IV.ii.60).
41   s.p. *BOSOLA* ed. (not in Q1) In Q1 two consecutive speeches are given to Antonio,
       probably implying that a speech by Bosola is missing, one provoking Antonio's angry
       response 'You libel well, sir' (Lucas). Brown speculates that 39–40 might have
       belonged to Bosola, referring to Antonio the upstart, but Compositor A, who has
       trouble with s.p.s elsewhere, might have misplaced a s.p. Marcus (presumably
       developing this idea of Brown's) does assign line 40 'Are . . . sting' to Bosola, assuming
       a missing s.p. rather than a missing speech.
42–4   ed. (You . . . sir / No sir / Copy . . . to't / My . . . count Q1).

BOSOLA   No, sir. Copy it out
   And I will set my hand to't.
ANTONIO [*Aside*]   My nose bleeds.
                        [*Takes out handkerchief and drops paper*]
   One that were superstitious would count
   This ominous, when it merely comes by chance: 45
   Two letters that are wrought here for my name
   Are drowned in blood:
   Mere accident. [*Aloud*] For you, sir, I'll take order:
   I'th'morn you shall be safe. [*Aside*] 'Tis that must colour
   Her lying in: [*Aloud*] sir, this door you pass not.   50
   I do not hold it fit that you come near
   The Duchess' lodgings till you have quit yourself.
   'The great are like the base, nay, they are the same,
   When they seek shameful ways to avoid shame'.   *Exit*
BOSOLA
   Antonio here about did drop a paper: 55
   Some of your help, false friend:
                   [*Searches with the lantern and finds paper*]
                        – oh, here it is.
   What's here? A child's nativity calculated?
   [*Reads*] *The Duchess was delivered of a son, 'tween the hours twelve*
        and one, in the night, Anno Dom: 1504, (that's this year)
        decimo nono Decembris, (that's this night) *taken according to*   60
        the meridian of Malfi (that's our Duchess: happy discovery).

42–3   *Copy . . . to't* If Antonio will write down the supposed libel Bosola will sign it.
  43   s.d. Developed from the implications in the text: the two letters are *wrought* (46), that
        is, embroidered, *here,* in the handkerchief with which Antonio stanches his nose
        bleed. Antonio drops *a paper* – identified by Bosola as the horoscope in line 57 – and
        it is simple and plausible that he does so when getting out his handkerchief).
        Webster's use of the handkerchief is no doubt intended to recall *Othello* – both the
        likeness and difference are significant.
47–8   ed. (Are . . . order Q1).
  50   *this door* The one to the Duchess' lodging, referred to in line 17 above.
  56   *false friend* The dark lantern.
58–65   As it turns out, this first-born child survives at the end of the play – but for how
        much longer? The prediction for a short life and a violent death remains; *Caetera non*
        scrutantur ('the rest is not examined') means only that the horoscope has not been
        completed, not that its validity is uncertain. Webster's main interest is in what the
        astrological terminology can contribute to the general atmosphere of menace; the
        horoscope is implausible, astrologically speaking: NCW refer to J. C. Eade, *The*
        Forgotten Sky, 1984, pp. 188–9.

> *The Lord of the first house, being combust in the ascendant,*
> *signifies short life; and Mars being in a human sign, joined to*
> *the tail of the Dragon, in the eighth house, doth threaten a*
> *violent death. Caetera non scrutantur.* 65

Why now 'tis most apparent. This precise fellow
Is the Duchess' bawd. I have it to my wish.
This is a parcel of intelligency
Our courtiers were cased up for. It needs must follow
That I must be committed on pretence 70
Of poisoning her, which I'll endure, and laugh at.
If one could find the father now: but that
Time will discover. Old Castruchio
I'th'morning posts to Rome; by him I'll send
A letter that shall make her brothers' galls 75
O'erflow their livers. This was a thrifty way.
'Though lust do masque in ne'er so strange disguise
She's oft found witty, but is never wise'. [*Exit*]

[ACT II,] SCENE iv

[*Enter* CARDINAL *and* JULIA]

CARDINAL
Sit: thou art my best of wishes. Prithee tell me
What trick didst thou invent to come to Rome

---

62   *Lord . . . house* See II.i.93 n. This planet was supposed to be particularly influential in the life of the child then born.
    combust burnt up. This signifies a planet positioned within 8 degrees of the sun, whereby its influence is destroyed.
63   *human sign* Aquarius, Gemini, Virgo or Sagittarius.
64   *tail of the Dragon* This lay where the moon traverses the ecliptic in its descent. It had a sinister influence.
    eighth ed. (eight Q1).
    eighth house This regularly signified death.
66   *precise* strict, puritanical.
69   *cased* ed. (caside Q1).

0   s.d. ed. (SCENA. IIII. / Cardinall, and Iulia, Seruant, and Delio. Q1).
1   *Sit* Orazio Busino (7 Feb 1618) reports seeing a performance where the Cardinal, presumably at this point, was shown 'with a harlot on his knee'. Recent productions have developed such possibilities further: in the Manchester Royal Exchange

Without thy husband.

JULIA   Why, my lord, I told him
I came to visit an old anchorite
Here, for devotion.

CARDINAL   Thou art a witty false one –   5
I mean, to him.

JULIA   You have prevailed with me
Beyond my strongest thoughts; I would not now
Find you inconstant.

CARDINAL   Do not put thyself
To such a voluntary torture, which proceeds
Out of your own guilt.

JULIA   How, my lord?   10

CARDINAL
You fear my constancy because you have approved
Those giddy and wild turnings in yourself.

JULIA
Did you e'er find them?

CARDINAL   Sooth, generally, for women,
A man might strive to make glass malleable
Ere he should make them fixed.

JULIA   So, my lord.   15

CARDINAL
We had need go borrow that fantastic glass
Invented by Galileo the Florentine
To view another spacious world i'th'moon,
And look to find a constant woman there.

JULIA
This is very well, my lord.

CARDINAL   Why do you weep?   20
Are tears your justification? The self-same tears
Will fall into your husband's bosom, lady,
With a loud protestation that you love him
Above the world. Come, I'll love you wisely,
That's jealously, since I am very certain   25

production 1980 the couple mimed sexual coition before speaking, in the RSC
production of 1989/90 Julia advanced on the Cardinal, raising her skirts by degrees
before sitting astride a chair to display her legs to him.

12   *turnings* ed. (turning Q1).

16   *fantastic glass* The telescope built by Galileo in 1609.

18   Dent compares Donne, *Ignatius*, 116–7: 'hills woods, and Cities in the new world, the
Moone'.

You cannot me make cuckold.

JULIA   I'll go home
To my husband.

CARDINAL   You may thank me, lady:
I have taken you off your melancholy perch,
Bore you upon my fist, and showed you game,
And let you fly at it. I pray thee kiss me.   30
When thou wast with thy husband thou wast watched
Like a tame elephant – still you are to thank me –
Thou hadst only kisses from him, and high feeding,
But what delight was that? 'Twas just like one
That hath a little fingering on the lute,   35
Yet cannot tune it – still you are to thank me.

JULIA
You told me of a piteous wound i'th'heart
And a sick liver, when you wooed me first,
And spake like one in physic.

                                 [*Knocking*]

CARDINAL   Who's that?
Rest firm: for my affection to thee,   40
Lightning moves slow to't.

                 [*Enter* SERVANT]

SERVANT   Madam, a gentleman
That's come post from Malfi, desires to see you.

CARDINAL
Let him enter, I'll withdraw.   *Exit*

SERVANT   He says
Your husband Old Castruchio is come to Rome,
Most pitifully tired with riding post.   [*Exit*] 45

                  [*Enter* DELIO]

JULIA

28–30   *perch . . . at it* As if she were a falcon.

30   *thee* ed. (the Q1).

31–2   *watched . . . elephant* The comparison of Julia to an elephant is grotesque, with *tame* implying 'sexually frustrated'; *watched* could mean 'tamed by being kept awake' and also 'looked at' (like the real elephant put on public exhibition in London in 1594, which attracted great attention).

38   *liver* The seat of love and the passions.

Signior Delio? [*Aside*] 'Tis one of my old suitors.

DELIO

I was bold to come and see you.

JULIA   Sir, you are welcome.

DELIO

Do you lie here?

JULIA   Sure, your own experience
Will satisfy you no, our Roman prelates
Do not keep lodging for ladies.

DELIO   Very well: 50
I have brought you no commendations from your husband,
For I know none by him.

JULIA   I hear he's come to Rome?

DELIO

I never knew man and beast, of a horse and a knight,
So weary of each other; if he had had a good back
He would have undertook to have borne his horse,   55
His breech was so pitifully sore.

JULIA   Your laughter
Is my pity.

DELIO   Lady, I know not whether
You want money, but I have brought you some.

JULIA

From my husband?

DELIO   No, from mine own allowance.

JULIA

I must hear the condition ere I be bound to take it.   60

DELIO

Look on't, 'tis gold, hath it not a fine colour?

JULIA

I have a bird more beautiful.

DELIO

Try the sound on't.

JULIA   A lute-string far exceeds it,
It hath no smell, like cassia or civet,
Nor is it physical, though some fond doctors   65

47–8   ed. (I . . . you / Sir . . . wel-come / Do . . . here / Sure . . . experience Q1).
47   *you* ed. (your Q1).
65   *physical* used as medicine.

336

Persuade us seeth't in cullisses; I'll tell you,
This is a creature bred by –

[*Enter* SERVANT]

SERVANT   Your husband's come,
Hath delivered a letter to the Duke of Calabria that,
To my thinking, hath put him out of his wits.   [*Exit*]

JULIA
Sir, you hear: 70
Pray let me know your business, and your suit,
As briefly as can be.
DELIO   With good speed. I would wish you,
At such time as you are non-resident
With your husband, my mistress.

JULIA
Sir, I'll go ask my husband if I shall,   75
And straight return your answer.   *Exit*
DELIO   Very fine.
Is this her wit, or honesty, that speaks thus?
I heard one say the Duke was highly moved
With a letter sent from Malfi. I do fear
Antonio is betrayed. How fearfully   80
Shows his ambition now: unfortunate Fortune!
'They pass through whirlpools, and deep woes do shun,
Who the event weigh, ere the action's done'.   *Exit*

66   *seeth't* ed. (seeth's Q1).
      cullisses broths.
77–80   This soliloquy seems to suggest that Delio is on a mission of espionage, and possibly
        plans to manipulate Julia (indeed in V.ii Bosola succeeds in doing this); but no more
        emerges of the present intrigue. This may be deliberate on Webster's part, and
        designed to create an atmosphere of secret plotting.
82   *pass through* successfully cross.

[ACT II,] SCENE v

[Enter] CARDINAL, *and* FERDINAND *with a letter*

FERDINAND
 I have this night digged up a mandrake.
CARDINAL   Say you?
FERDINAND
 And I am grown mad with't.
CARDINAL   What's the prodigy?
FERDINAND
 Read there: a sister damned, she's loose i'th'hilts,
 Grown a notorious strumpet!
CARDINAL   Speak lower.
FERDINAND   Lower?
 Rogues do not whisper't now, but seek to publish't,   5
 As servants do the bounty of their lords,
 Aloud; and with a covetous searching eye
 To mark who note them. Oh confusion seize her!
 She hath had most cunning bawds to serve her turn,
 And more secure conveyances for lust   10
 Than towns of garrison, for service.
CARDINAL   Is't possible?
 Can this be certain?
FERDINAND   Rhubarb, oh, for rhubarb
 To purge this choler! Here's the cursed day
 To prompt my memory, and here it shall stick
 Till of her bleeding heart I make a sponge   15
 To wipe it out.

---

 0   s.d. ed. (SCENA V. / Cardinall, and Ferdinand, with a letter. Q1).
 1   *digged* Q1b (dig Q1a).
      mandrake The forked root of the plant mandragora, supposedly resembling a man,
      gave rise to the superstition that when dug up it emitted a shriek which induced
      madness.
 2   *prodigy* ed. (progedy Q1).
 3   *loose i'the hilts* unchaste.
 4   ed. (Growne . . . Strumpet / Speak lower / Lower Q1).
 11 *service* supplies (including sexual services).
 12 *rhubarb* A recognised antidote to choler.

CARDINAL   Why do you make yourself
So wild a tempest?
FERDINAND   Would I could be one,
  That I might toss her palace 'bout her ears,
  Root up her goodly forests, blast her meads,
  And lay her general territory as waste   20
  As she hath done her honours.
CARDINAL   Shall our blood,
  The royal blood of Aragon and Castile,
  Be thus attainted?
FERDINAND   Apply desperate physic!
  We must not now use balsamum, but fire,
  The smarting cupping glass, for that's the mean   25
  To purge infected blood, such blood as hers.
  There is a kind of pity in mine eye,
  I'll give it to my handkercher –
       [*He wipes away the tears with a handkerchief*]
              and now 'tis here,
  I'll bequeath this to her bastard.
CARDINAL   What to do?
FERDINAND
  Why, to make soft lint for his mother's wounds,   30
  When I have hewed her to pieces.
CARDINAL   Cursed creature!
  Unequal nature, to place women's hearts
  So far upon the left side.
FERDINAND   Foolish men,
  That e'er will trust their honour in a bark
  Made of so slight weak bullrush as is woman,   35
  Apt every minute to sink it!
CARDINAL   Thus
  Ignorance, when it hath purchased honour,
  It cannot wield it.

---

23   *attainted* The Cardinal intends the legal term referring to lineage stained or corrupted; Ferdinand takes it literally, referring to blood infected with disease (with the added sense of *blood* = passion).

28   s.d. Webster stresses the action, ironically recalling Antonio's fatal use of his handkerchief for the nosebleed in II.iii.

30   *mother's* ed. (mother Q1).

33   *left* Probably to be understood figuratively, as sinister, not right (see III.i.28–9).

36–7   ed. (Apt . . . it / Thus / Ignorance . . . honour Q1).

FERDINAND   Methinks I see her laughing –
Excellent hyena! Talk to me somewhat quickly,
Or my imagination will carry me   40
To see her in the shameful act of sin.
CARDINAL   With whom?
FERDINAND
Happily with some strong-thighed bargeman;
Or one o'th'woodyard that can quoit the sledge
Or toss the bar; or else some lovely squire
That carries coals up to her privy lodgings.   45
CARDINAL
You fly beyond your reason.
FERDINAND   Go to, mistress,
Tis not your whore's milk that shall quench my wild-fire,
But your whore's blood!
CARDINAL
How idly shows this rage, which carries you
As men conveyed by witches through the air   50
On violent whirlwinds! This intemperate noise
Fitly resembles deaf men's shrill discourse,
Who talk aloud, thinking all other men
To have their imperfection.
FERDINAND   Have not you
My palsy?
CARDINAL   Yes. I can be angry   55
Without this rupture; there is not in nature
A thing that makes man so deformed, so beastly,
As doth intemperate anger. Chide yourself.
You have diverse men who never yet expressed
Their strong desire of rest, but by unrest –   60
By vexing of themselves. Come, put yourself
In tune.
FERDINAND   So, I will only study to seem

---

43   *o'th'* ed. (the Q1).
      quoit the sledge throw the hammer.
45   *carries coals* With a subsidiary (proverbial) sense 'do any dirty or menial work' – see
      next note.
      privy lodgings private apartment (with puns on *privy* parts = genitals, and *lodgings*
      = sexual penetrations).
48–50 ed. (But ... blood / How ... rage / Which ... ayre Q1).
55   *palsy* the shaking palsy, involuntary tremors (*OED* sb 1a).
56   *rupture* Q1 (rapture conj. Dyce).

The thing I am not. I could kill her now
In you, or in myself, for I do think
It is some sin in us heaven doth revenge   65
By her.
CARDINAL Are you stark mad?
FERDINAND   I would have their bodies
   Burnt in a coal pit with the ventage stopped,
   That their cursed smoke might not ascend to heaven;
   Or dip the sheets they lie in, in pitch or sulphur,
   Wrap them in't and then light them like a match;   70
   Or else to boil their bastard to a cullis
   And give't his lecherous father to renew
   The sin of his back.
CARDINAL   I'll leave you.
FERDINAND   Nay, I have done.
   I am confident, had I been damned in hell
   And should have heard of this, it would have put me   75
   Into a cold sweat. In, in, I'll go sleep.
   Till I know who leaps my sister, I'll not stir:
   That known, I'll find scorpions to string my whips,
   And fix her in a general eclipse.
                                              Exeunt

ACT III, SCENE i

[*Enter* ANTONIO *and* DELIO]

ANTONIO
Our noble friend, my most beloved Delio,
Oh you have been a stranger long at court;
Came you along with the Lord Ferdinand?

DELIO
I did sir; and how fares your noble Duchess?

ANTONIO
Right fortunately well. She's an excellent   5
Feeder of pedigrees: since you last saw her,
She hath had two children more, a son, and daughter.

DELIO
Methinks 'twas yesterday – let me but wink
And not behold your face, which to mine eye
Is somewhat leaner, verily I should dream   10
It were within this half hour.

ANTONIO
You have not been in law, friend Delio,
Nor in prison, nor a suitor at the court,
Nor begged the reversion of some great man's place,
Nor troubled with an old wife, which doth make   15
Your time so insensibly hasten.

DELIO   Pray sir tell me,
Hath not this news arrived yet to the ear
Of the Lord Cardinal?

ANTONIO   I fear it hath.
The Lord Ferdinand that's newly come to court
Doth bear himself right dangerously.

---

0   s.d. ed. (ACTVS III. SCENA I. / Antonio, and Delio, Duchesse, Ferdinand, Bosola. Q1).

2   Delio has been away in Rome since the end of II.ii.

6–11   Comic-ironic in-jokes on the conventions of theatrical illusion, by which some two years must be imagined to have passed since II.ii – in performance time, it certainly is 'within the half-hour' that Antonio and Delio last met! (See Lopez, pp. 75–6).

17ff.   This discussion is clearly parallel to that between Delio and Antonio about good government in Act I, but here Antonio seems to be admitting that keeping the marriage secret has seriously weakened the Duchess as ruler, even without the new danger of Ferdinand's presence.

DELIO   Pray why?   20

ANTONIO

He is so quiet that he seems to sleep
The tempest out as dormice do in winter.
Those houses that are haunted are most still
Till the devil be up.

DELIO   What say the common people?

ANTONIO

The common rabble do directly say   25
She is a strumpet.

DELIO   And your graver heads,
Which would be politic, what censure they?

ANTONIO

They do observe I grow to infinite purchase
The left-hand way, and all suppose the Duchess
Would amend it if she could. For, say they,   30
Great princes, though they grudge their officers
Should have such large and unconfined means
To get wealth under them, will not complain
Lest thereby they should make them odious
Unto the people; for other obligation –   35
Of love, or marriage, between her and me –
They never dream of.

> [*Enter* DUCHESS, FERDINAND *and* BOSOLA]

DELIO   The Lord Ferdinand
Is going to bed.

FERDINAND   I'll instantly to bed,
For I am weary. I am to bespeak
A husband for you.

DUCHESS   For me, sir? Pray who is't?   40

FERDINAND

The great Count Malateste.

DUCHESS   Fie upon him!
A Count? He's a mere stick of sugar candy,

---

27   *be* ed. (he Q1).
28   *purchase* wealth.
29   *left-hand* corrupt.
31–5 Dent compares the close parallel in Donne, *Ignatius*, 92.
37   *of* ed. (off Q1).
39   *bespeak* ed. (be be-speake Q1).

You may look quite thorough him. When I choose
A husband, I will marry for your honour.
FERDINAND
You shall do well in't. – How is't, worthy Antonio?   45
DUCHESS
But, sir, I am to have private conference with you
About a scandalous report is spread
Touching mine honour.
FERDINAND   Let me be ever deaf to't:
One of Pasquil's paper bullets, court calumny,
A pestilent air which princes' palaces   50
Are seldom purged of. Yet, say that it were true:
I pour it in your bosom, my fixed love
Would strongly excuse, extenuate, nay deny
Faults, were they apparent in you. Go be safe
In your own innocency.
DUCHESS   Oh bless'd comfort,   55
This deadly air is purged.

> *Exeunt* [*all but* FERDINAND *and* BOSOLA]

FERDINAND   Her guilt treads on
Hot burning coulters. Now Bosola,
How thrives our intelligence?
BOSOLA   Sir, uncertainly:
'Tis rumoured she hath had three bastards, but
By whom, we may go read i'th'stars.
FERDINAND   Why some   60
Hold opinion all things are written there.
BOSOLA
Yes, if we could find spectacles to read them.
I do suspect there hath been some sorcery
Used on the Duchess.
FERDINAND   Sorcery? To what purpose?

---

49   *Pasquil's paper bullets* satires or lampoons (*Pasquin* or *Pasquil* became a popular
     name for a satirist, following the custom in 16th century Rome of attaching
     lampoons to a statue named after one Pasquino or Pasquillo, a sharp-tongued
     schoolmaster or cobbler).
54   *were* ed. (where Q1).
56–7 *reads . . . coulters* An ordeal decreed as a trial of chastity in Old English law; the
     mother of Edward the Confessor is reputed to have walked barefoot upon nine
     coulters red hot. The coulter is the cutting blade in front of a ploughshare.
57   *coulters* ed. (cultures Q1).

BOSOLA

To make her dote on some desertless fellow   65
She shames to acknowledge.

FERDINAND   Can your faith give way
To think there's power in potions or in charms
To make us love, whether we will or no?

BOSOLA

Most certainly.

FERDINAND

Away! These are mere gulleries, horrid things   70
Invented by some cheating mountebanks
To abuse us. Do you think that herbs or charms
Can force the will? Some trials have been made
In this foolish practice, but the ingredients
Were lenitive poisons, such as are of force   75
To make the patient mad; and straight the witch
Swears, by equivocation, they are in love.
The witchcraft lies in her rank blood. This night
I will force confession from her. You told me
You had got, within these two days, a false key   80
Into her bedchamber?

BOSOLA   I have.

FERDINAND   As I would wish.

BOSOLA

What do you intend to do?

FERDINAND   Can you guess?

BOSOLA   No.

FERDINAND

Do not ask then.
He that can compass me, and know my drifts,
May say he hath put a girdle 'bout the world   85

---

75 *lenitive poisons* drugs seemingly aphrodisiac but inducing madness. N. W. Bawcutt
    in MLR 66, (1971) 488–91, claims that Webster is recalling Shelton's translation of
    Don Quixote, I.iii.8: 'poysons . . . cause men runne mad, and in the meane while
    perswade us they have force to make one love well'. Lucas notes that Webster in
    Anything for a Quiet Life, I.i.91, uses *lenitive* to mean 'soothing', but finds this goes
    oddly with *poisons*: is Webster guilty of false etymology, via Latin *lenare* = to
    prostitute? The phrase could then mean 'violent aphrodisiac'.

And sounded all her quicksands.

BOSOLA   I do not
Think so.

FERDINAND
What do you think then, pray?

BOSOLA   That you are
Your own chronicle too much, and grossly
Flatter yourself.

FERDINAND   Give me thy hand, I thank thee.   90
I never gave pension but to flatterers
Till I entertained thee: farewell.
'That friend a great man's ruin strongly checks,
Who rails into his belief, all his defects'.

                                                        Exeunt

[ACT III,] SCENE ii

[*Enter* DUCHESS, ANTONIO *and* CARIOLA]

DUCHESS
Bring me the casket hither, and the glass.
You get no lodging here tonight my lord.

ANTONIO
Indeed I must persuade one.

DUCHESS   Very good.
I hope in time 'twill grow into a custom
That noblemen shall come with cap and knee   5
To purchase a night's lodging of their wives.

ANTONIO
I must lie here.

86–90   ed. (And . . . -sands / I . . . not / Thinke so / What . . . pray / That . . . are / Your . . .
         grosly / Flatter . . . selfe / Give . . . thee Q1).

Act III scene ii
    0   s.d. ed. (*SCENA. II. / Dutchesse, Antonio, Cariola, Ferdinand, Bosola, Officers. Q1*).
    0   s.d. The Duchess will remove her jewellery and brush her hair in preparation for
         bed; candles or torches would indicate that it is night.

DUCHESS Must? You are a Lord of Misrule.

ANTONIO
Indeed, my rule is only in the night.

DUCHESS
To what use will you put me?

ANTONIO We'll sleep together.

DUCHESS
Alas, what pleasure can two lovers find in sleep? 10

CARIOLA
My lord, I lie with her often and I know
She'll much disquiet you –

ANTONIO See, you are complained of –

CARIOLA
For she's the sprawling'st bedfellow.

ANTONIO
I shall like her the better for that.

CARIOLA
Sir, shall I ask you a question?

ANTONIO I pray thee Cariola. 15

CARIOLA
Wherefore still when you lie with my lady
Do you rise so early?

ANTONIO Labouring men
Count the clock oft'nest, Cariola,
Are glad when their task's ended.

DUCHESS I'll stop your mouth.
[*Kisses him*]

ANTONIO
Nay, that's but one, Venus had two soft doves 20
To draw her chariot: I must have another.
[*She kisses him*]
When wilt thou marry, Cariola?

CARIOLA Never, my lord.

ANTONIO
Oh fie upon this single life! Forgo it:

---

7   *Misrule* ed. (Misse-rule Q); *Lord of Misrule* (1) Someone very young or of low degree,
    traditionally chosen to preside over feasts and revels at court, reversing the usual
    hierarchies (2) Punning on *Mis* / *misse* = kept mistress. On the retrospectively bittter
    irony of this joke about the Lord of Misrule, see below, note to IV.ii.1.
22 *Never* An ironically prophetic answer: this dialogue recalls *Antony and Cleopatra*,
    I.ii, where the Soothsayer converses with Charmian, Iras and Alexas.

We read how Daphne, for her peevish flight,
Became a fruitless bay-tree, Syrinx turn'd   25
To the pale empty reed, Anaxarete
Was frozen into marble, whereas those
Which married, or proved kind unto their friends,
Were by a gracious influence transshaped
Into the olive, pomegranate, mulberry,   30
Became flowers, precious stones or eminent stars.

CARIOLA
This is a vain poetry; but I pray you tell me,
If there were proposed me wisdom, riches, and beauty,
In three several young men, which should I choose?

ANTONIO
'Tis a hard question. This was Paris' case   35
And he was blind in't, and there was great cause:
For how was't possible he could judge right,
Having three amorous goddesses in view,
And they stark naked? 'Twas a motion
Were able to be-night the apprehension   40
Of the severest counsellor of Europe.
Now I look on both your faces so well formed
It puts me in mind of a question I would ask.

CARIOLA
What is't?

ANTONIO   I do wonder why hard-favoured ladies
For the most part keep worse-favoured waiting-women   45
To attend them, and cannot endure fair ones.

DUCHESS
Oh, that's soon answered.
Did you ever in your life know an ill painter
Desire to have his dwelling next door to the shop
Of an excellent picture-maker? 'Twould disgrace   50
His face-making, and undo him. – I prithee
When were we so merry? My hair tangles.

ANTONIO [*Aside to* CARIOLA]
Pray thee, Cariola, let's steal forth the room

24   *flight* ed. (slight Q1).
25   *Syrinx* ed. (Siriux Q1b, Sirina Q1a).
28   *friends* lovers.
39   *motion* show.
40   *apprehension* Q1b (approbation Q1a).
49   *his* Q1b (the Q1a).

And let her talk to herself. I have divers times
Served her the like, when she hath chafed extremely.   55
I love to see her angry. Softly Cariola.

Exeunt [ANTONIO *and* CARIOLA]

DUCHESS

Doth not the colour of my hair 'gin to change?
When I wax grey I shall have all the court
Powder their hair with arras, to be like me:

[*Enter* FERDINAND, *behind*]

You have cause to love me, I enter'd you into my heart   60
Before you would vouchsafe to call for the keys.
We shall one day have my brothers take you napping:
Methinks his presence, being now in court,
Should make you keep your own bed; but you'll say
Love mixed with fear is sweetest. I'll assure you   65
You shall get no more children till my brothers
Consent to be your gossips. – Have you lost your tongue?

[*She sees* FERDINAND]

'Tis welcome:
For know, whether I am doomed to live, or die,
I can do both like a prince.

FERDINAND *gives her a poniard*

FERDINAND   Die then, quickly!   70
Virtue, where art thou hid? What hideous thing
Is it that doth eclipse thee?

DUCHESS   Pray sir hear me.

FERDINAND

Or is it true thou art but a bare name,
And no essential thing?

56   s.d., 59 s.d. An ironic parallel with I.i.352–464 where, after hiding behind the arras,
      Cariola appears, surprising Antonio. Lucas unpersuasively suggests (in view of line
      145 below) that here Webster intends Ferdinand to be seen crossing the upper stage
      before descending out of sight and then making this entrance on the main stage.
59   *arras* powdered orris-root, white and smelling of violets, used on the hair.
67   *gossips* godparents for the children.
67–8 Q4 (Consent . . . welcome Q1).
67   s.d. The staging is especially powerful if the Duchess catches sight of Ferdinand in
      the mirror. There is a visual allusion to the Dance of Death, where the figure of
      Death arrests men and women of various ages and ranks, including youthful queens
      and duchesses. The mirror in such cases is an emblem of female vanity.
70   ed. (I . . . Prince / Die . . quickle Q1).
70   s.d. Q1b (not in Q1a); *poniard* Presumably the dagger is his father's, the one with
      which he threatened the Duchess in I.i.321.

349

DUCHESS	Sir –
FERDINAND	Do not speak.

DUCHESS

No sir: 75
I will plant my soul in mine ears to hear you.

FERDINAND

Oh most imperfect light of human reason,
That mak'st so unhappy to foresee
What we can least prevent, pursue thy wishes
And glory in them: there's in shame no comfort   80
But to be past all bounds and sense of shame.

DUCHESS

I pray sir, hear me: I am married.

FERDINAND   So.

DUCHESS

Happily, not to your liking; but for that,
Alas, your shears do come untimely now
To clip the bird's wings that's already flown.   85
Will you see my husband?

FERDINAND   Yes, if I could change
Eyes with a basilisk.

DUCHESS   Sure, you came hither
By his confederacy.

FERDINAND   The howling of a wolf
Is music to thee, screech owl, prithee peace.
What e'er thou art that hast enjoyed my sister –   90
For I am sure thou hear'st me – for thine own sake
Let me not know thee. I came hither prepared
To work thy discovery, yet am now persuaded
It would beget such violent effects
As would damn us both. I would not for ten millions   95
I had beheld thee, therefore use all means
I never may have knowledge of thy name.
Enjoy thy lust still, and a wretched life,
On that condition; and for thee, vile woman,

---

83   *Happily* Perhaps.
86–8   ed. (Will . . . Husband / Yes . . . I / Could . . . Basilisque / Sure . . . hither / By . . .
        consideracy / The . . . Wolfe Q1).
87   *basilisk* a mythical kind of serpent: its breath, or the sight of it, was supposedly fatal.
88   *confederacy* ed. (consideracy Q1).
89   *to thee* compared to thee.

If thou do wish thy lecher may grow old   100
In thy embracements, I would have thee build
Such a room for him as our anchorites
To holier use inhabit. Let not the sun
Shine on him till he's dead, let dogs and monkeys
Only converse with him, and such dumb things   105
To whom nature denies use to sound his name.
Do not keep a paraquito lest she learn it.
If thou do love him cut out thine own tongue
Lest it bewray him.
DUCHESS   Why might not I marry?
I have not gone about in this to create   110
Any new world or custom.
FERDINAND   Thou art undone;
And thou hast ta'en that massy sheet of lead
That hid thy husband's bones, and folded it
About my heart.
DUCHESS   Mine bleeds for't.
FERDINAND   Thine? Thy heart?
What should I name't, unless a hollow bullet   115
Filled with unquenchable wild-fire?
DUCHESS   You are in this
Too strict, and were you not my princely brother
I would say too wilful. My reputation
Is safe.
FERDINAND Dost thou know what reputation is?
I'll tell thee – to small purpose, since th'instruction   120
Comes now too late.
Upon a time Reputation, Love, and Death
Would travel o'er the world; and it was concluded
That they should part, and take three several ways:
Death told them they should find him in great battles   125
Or cities plagued with plagues; Love gives them counsel
To enquire for him 'mongst unambitious shepherds,
Where dowries were not talked of, and sometimes
'Mongst quiet kindred that had nothing left
By their dead parents. 'Stay', quoth Reputation,   130

---

115   *What . . . unless* What else should I call it but.
        hollow bullet cannon-ball filled with explosive, not the older type which was a solid
        iron ball.
118   *too* ed. (to Q1).

'Do not forsake me: for it is my nature
If once I part from any man I meet
I am never found again'; and so for you:
You have shook hands with Reputation
And made him invisible. So fare you well.   135
I will never see you more.

DUCHESS   Why should only I
Of all the other princes of the world
Be cased up like a holy relic? I have youth,
And a little beauty.

FERDINAND   So you have some virgins
That are witches. I will never see thee more.   *Exit*   140

              Enter ANTONIO *with a pistol* [*and* CARIOLA]

DUCHESS
You saw this apparition?

ANTONIO   Yes, we are
Betrayed. How came he hither? I should turn
This to thee, for that.

                              [*Points the pistol at* CARIOLA]
CARIOLA   Pray sir do: and when
That you have cleft my heart you shall read there
Mine innocence.

DUCHESS   That gallery gave him entrance.   145

ANTONIO
I would this terrible thing would come again
That, standing on my guard, I might relate
My warrantable love. Ha, what means this?

DUCHESS
He left this with me –

                              She shows the poniard
ANTONIO   And it seems did wish
You would use it on yourself?

---

134   *shook* Q1c (shooked Q1a, Q1b).
145   *gallery* It is not likely that *gallery* refers to the stage's upper playing space, since
      'above' is how the Elizabethans referred to this part of the tiring-house: more
      probably it is one of the play's numerous references to specific rooms and parts of
      palaces and houses in the named cities – Malfi, Rome, Loreto, Ancona, Milan. As
      with IV.ii.31 where the Duchess' portrait is said to hang in the gallery, the effect is
      impressionistic rather than exactly realistic in the nineteenth-century manner of
      Ibsen.

DUCHESS His action 150
  Seemed to intend so much.
ANTONIO This hath a handle to't
  As well as a point, turn it towards him
  And so fasten the keen edge in his rank gall.

  [*Knocking*]

  How now? Who knocks? More earthquakes?
DUCHESS I stand
  As if a mine beneath my feet were ready 155
  To be blown up.
CARIOLA 'Tis Bosola.
DUCHESS Away!
  Oh misery, methinks unjust actions
  Should wear these masks and curtains, and not we:
  You must instantly part hence: I have fashioned it already.

  Exit ANTONIO

  [*Enter* BOSOLA]

BOSOLA
  The Duke your brother is ta'en up in a whirlwind: 160
  Hath took horse and's rid post to Rome.
DUCHESS So late?
BOSOLA
  He told me as he mounted into th'saddle
  You were undone.
DUCHESS Indeed I am very near it.
BOSOLA
  What's the matter?
DUCHESS
  Antonio, the master of our household 165
  Hath dealt so falsely with me in's accounts.
  My brother stood engaged with me for money
  Ta'en up of certain Neapolitan Jews,
  And Antonio lets the bonds be forfeit.
BOSOLA
  Strange! [*Aside*] This is cunning.
DUCHESS And hereupon 170

165–72 A similar feeble excuse, of theft, to that in II.ii.48ff., where Bosola was also present.
167–8   *stood . . . up* was security for money I borrowed.
169   *lets . . . forfeit* Presumably by failing to make the payments.

My brother's bills at Naples are protested
Against. Call up our officers.

BOSOLA   I shall.   *Exit*

[*Enter* ANTONIO]

DUCHESS
The place that you must fly to is Ancona:
Hire a house there. I'll send after you
My treasure and my jewels. Our weak safety   175
Runs upon enginous wheels, short syllables
Must stand for periods. I must now accuse you
Of such a feigned crime as Tasso calls
Magnanima mensogna, a noble lie,
'Cause it must shield our honours. Hark, they are coming!   180

[*Enter* BOSOLA *and* OFFICERS]

ANTONIO
Will your grace hear me?

DUCHESS
I have got well by you: you have yielded me
A million of loss; I am like to inherit
The people's curses for your stewardship.
You had the trick in audit time to be sick   185
Till I had signed your *Quietus*; and that cured you
Without help of a doctor. Gentlemen,
I would have this man be an example to you all,
So shall you hold my favour. I pray let him,
For h'as done that, alas, you would not think of,   190
And, because I intend to be rid of him,
I mean not to publish. – Use your fortune elsewhere.

171–2   *bills . . . Against* promissory notes are not accepted.
173   But see below 300–306 and n.
176   *enginous* ed. (engenous Q1).
        enginous wheels Like those of a clock where a small, almost imperceptible movement
        produces obvious motion in the hands (Brennan).
178   *Tasso* Alluding to *Gerusalemme Liberata*, 2.22, where Soprina falsely confesses taking
        a statue of the Virgin Mary from a mosque, in order to prevent wholesale
        persecution of her fellow Christians.
182   *got well* This double entendre is the first of a series down to 207 in which the Duchess
        and Antonio covertly affirm their love. For a memorable instance in Shakespeare
        see *Romeo and Juliet*, III.v.68–102.
189   *let him* let him go free (but *let* could also mean 'stop').

ANTONIO

    I am strongly armed to brook my overthrow,
    As commonly men bear with a hard year.
    I will not blame the cause on't but do think   195
    The necessity of my malevolent star
    Procures this, not her humour. Oh the inconstant
    And rotten ground of service you may see:
    Tis ev'n like him that in a winter night
    Takes a long slumber o'er a dying fire   200
    As loth to part from't, yet parts thence as cold
    As when he first sat down.

DUCHESS   We do confiscate,

    Towards the satisfying of your accounts,
    All that you have.

ANTONIO   I am all yours: and 'tis very fit

    All mine should be so.

DUCHESS   So, sir; you have your pass.   205

ANTONIO

    You may see, gentlemen, what 'tis to serve
    A prince with body and soul.   *Exit*

BOSOLA

    Here's an example for extortion! What moisture is drawn out of
    the sea, when foul weather comes, pours down and runs into
    the sea again.   210

DUCHESS

    I would know what are your opinions of this Antonio.

2 OFFICER

    He could not abide to see a pig's head gaping; I thought your
    grace would find him a Jew.

3 OFFICER

    I would you had been his officer, for your own sake.

4 OFFICER

    You would have had more money.   215

---

201   *As loth* Q1c (A-loth Q1a, Q1b).

212–23   prose ed. (*Q1 lines ending* gaping / Iew / sake / money / came / hearing / woman /
        full / goe / him / Chaine).

212–13   *pig's head … Jew* A crudely racist way of saying Antonio is financially untrustworthy
        – the sycophantic Officer takes the hint of line 168's reference to Neapolitan Jews.
        Webster is again drawing on *Merchant of Venice*: in IV.i Shylock refers twice to one
        who 'cannot abide a gaping pig'. A Christian proverb is 'Invite not a Jew either to
        pig or pork' (Tilley P310).

1 OFFICER

He stopped his ears with black wool, and to those came to him
for money, said he was thick of hearing.

2 OFFICER

Some said he was an hermaphrodite, for he could not abide a
woman.

4 OFFICER

How scurvy proud he would look when the treasury was full!   220
Well, let him go.

1 OFFICER

Yes, and the chippings of the butt'ry fly after him, to scour his
gold chain!

DUCHESS

Leave us.

Exeunt [OFFICERS]

[*To* BOSOLA] What do you think of these?

BOSOLA

That these are rogues that, in's prosperity,   225
But to have waited on his fortune, could have wished
His dirty stirrup riveted through their noses
And followed after's mule like a bear in a ring;
Would have prostituted their daughters to his lust,
Made their first born intelligencers, thought none happy   230
But such as were born under his blessed planet
And wore his livery; and do these lice drop off now?
Well, never look to have the like again.
He hath left a sort of flatt'ring rogues behind him:
Their doom must follow. Princes pay flatterers   235
In their own money: flatterers dissemble their vices,
And they dissemble their lies: that's justice.
Alas, poor gentleman.

DUCHESS

Poor? He hath amply filled his coffers.

---

222   *chippings* parings of the crust of a loaf.
223   *gold chain* The steward's official chain of office. In *Twelfth Night*, II.iii.119–20,
         Malvolio is mockingly told to rub his chain 'with crumbs'.
225ff.   Bosola's praise of Antonio is an elaborate and over-extended ploy, yet it persuades
         the Duchess to confide in him. Perhaps she is so surprised to hear praise from this
         wonted malcontent that she is disarmed; but even if Bosola's estimation of Antonio
         is sincere, he continues to serve Ferdinand.
230   *intelligencers* Q1c (and intelligencers Q1a, Q1b).

BOSOLA

Sure he was too honest. Pluto the god of riches,   240

When he's sent by Jupiter to any man,

He goes limping, to signify that wealth

That comes on god's name, comes slowly; but when he's sent

On the devil's errand he rides post and comes in by scuttles.

Let me show you what a most unvalued jewel   245

You have in a wanton humour thrown away

To bless the man shall find him. He was an excellent

Courtier, and most faithful, a soldier that thought it

As beastly to know his own value too little

As devilish to acknowledge it too much;   250

Both his virtue and form deserved a far better fortune;

His discourse rather delighted to judge itself than show itself,

His breast was filled with all perfection

And yet it seemed a private whisp'ring room,

It made so little noise of't.

DUCHESS   But he was basely descended.   255

BOSOLA

Will you make yourself a mercenary herald,

Rather to examine men's pedigrees than virtues?

You shall want him,

For know: an honest statesman to a prince

Is like a cedar planted by a spring;   260

The spring bathes the tree's root, the grateful tree

Rewards it with his shadow. You have not done so:

I would sooner swim to the Bermoothes on

Two politicians' rotten bladders, tied

Together with an intelligencer's heart-string,   265

Than depend on so changeable a prince's favour!

Fare thee well, Antonio: since the malice of the world

Would needs down with thee, it cannot be said yet

That any ill happened unto thee,

Considering thy fall was accompanied with virtue.   270

240   *Pluto* The god of riches was Plutus, whereas Pluto was god of the underworld. Lucas
      suggests that the link of association was that wealth came from underground.

244   *On* ed. (One Q1).
      scuttles The meaning is uncertain: 'short hurried runs' (*OED*) or 'large baskets'
      (Brown).

245   *unvalued* priceless, very valuable.

263   *Bermoothes* The reports of the wreck of Sir George Somers on the Bermudas in 1609
      were topical and famous, and were used by Shakespeare in writing *The Tempest*.

DUCHESS

    Oh, you render me excellent music.

BOSOLA   Say you?

DUCHESS

    This good one that you speak of is my husband.

BOSOLA

    Do I not dream? Can this ambitious age
    Have so much goodness in't as to prefer
    A man merely for worth, without these shadows   275
    Of wealth and painted honours? Possible?

DUCHESS

    I have had three children by him.

BOSOLA   Fortunate lady,

    For you have made your private nuptial bed
    The humble and fair seminary of peace,
    No question but many an unbeneficed scholar   280
    Shall pray for you, for this deed, and rejoice
    That some preferment in the world can yet
    Arise from merit. The virgins of your land
    That have no dowries, shall hope your example
    Will raise them to rich husbands; should you want   285
    Soldiers 'twould make the very Turks and Moors
    Turn Christians and serve you, for this act;
    Last, the neglected poets of your time,
    In honour of this trophy of a man
    Raised by that curious engine, your white hand,   290
    Shall thank you, in your grave, for't, and make that
    More reverend than all the cabinets
    Of living princes. For Antonio,
    His fame shall likewise flow from many a pen
    When heralds shall want coats to sell to men.   295

DUCHESS

    As I taste comfort in this friendly speech,
    So would I find concealment.

BOSOLA

    Oh the secret of my prince,
    Which I will wear on th'inside of my heart!

---

290   *curious* delicate, dainty.
295   The sale of honours (involving the devising of coats of arms) was a subject of much
      attack by satirists in the early Jacobean age.

DUCHESS
You shall take charge of all my coin, and jewels,   300
And follow him, for he retires himself
To Ancona.
BOSOLA   So.
DUCHESS   Whither, within few days,
I mean to follow thee.
BOSOLA   Let me think:
I would wish your grace to feign a pilgrimage
To Our Lady of Loreto, scarce seven leagues   305
From fair Ancona: so may you depart
Your country with more honour, and your flight
Will seem a princely progress, retaining
Your usual train about you.
DUCHESS   Sir, your direction
Shall lead me by the hand.
CARIOLA   In my opinion   310
She were better progress to the baths
At Lucca, or go visit the Spa
In Germany, for, if you will believe me,
I do not like this jesting with religion,
This feigned pilgrimage.   315
DUCHESS
Thou art a superstitious fool.
Prepare us instantly for our departure.
Past sorrows, let us moderately lament them,
For those to come, seek wisely to prevent them.
                    Exeunt [DUCHESS *and* CARIOLA]

BOSOLA
A politician is the devil's quilted anvil,   320
He fashions all sins on him and the blows
Are never heard – he may work in a lady's chamber,
As here for proof. What rests, but I reveal

300–6   According to 173 above, Antonio was to go directly to Ancona and by now might be
        supposed to be on the way, but when she changes the plan the Duchess does not
        refer to Antonio; nevertheless in III.iv.6 s.d. Antonio is with her at Loreto. Either
        this is an error by Webster or we are tacitly to assume that Antonio came from
        Ancona to meet her.

309   *usual train* The number of attendants was (and still is) a sign of power and prestige:
        Shakespeare's King Lear requires a hundred knights.

312   *the Spa* In Belgium, a famous watering-place; Webster could have found in
        Montaigne, *Essayes*, II.xv, p. 357, adjacent references to Ancona, Lucca, Loreto and
        Spa.

All to my lord? Oh, this base quality
Of intelligencer! Why, every quality i'th'world   325
Prefers but gain or commendation:
Now for this act I am certain to be raised,
And men that paint weeds – to the life – are praised.   *Exit*

[ACT III,] SCENE iii

[*Enter* CARDINAL, FERDINAND, MALATESTE,
PESCARA, SILVIO, *and* DELIO]

CARDINAL
Must we turn soldier then?
MALATESTE   The Emperor
Hearing your worth that way, ere you attained
This reverend garment, joins you in commission
With the right fortunate soldier, the Marquis of Pescara,
And the famous Lannoy.
CARDINAL   He that had the honour   5
Of taking the French King prisoner?
MALATESTE   The same.
[*Shows plan*] Here's a plot drawn for a new fortification,
At Naples.
FERDINAND This great Count Malateste I perceive
Hath got employment?
DELIO   No employment, my lord,
A marginal note in the muster-book that he is   10
A voluntary lord.
FERDINAND   He's no soldier?
DELIO
He has worn gunpowder in's hollow tooth,

---

326   *Prefers* Assists in bringing about (*OED*).

0   s.d. ed. (*SCENA III. / Cardinall, Ferdinand, Mallateste, Pescara, Silvio, Delio, Bosola. Q1*)
1   *Emperor* Charles V.
3   *reverend garment* the robes of a Cardinal.
5   *famous Lannoy* The historical figure Charles de Lannoy (c.1487–1527) received the
      surrendered sword of Francis I of France at the battle of Pavia in 1525.
7   *plot* ground-plan.

For the tooth-ache.
SILVIO
　He comes to the leaguer with a full intent
　To eat fresh beef and garlic, means to stay　　　　　　　　15
　Till the scent be gone, and straight return to court.
DELIO
　He hath read all the late service,
　As the city chronicle relates it,
　And keeps two painters going, only to express
　Battles in model.
SILVIO　　　　　　　Then he'll fight by the book.　　　　20
DELIO
　By the almanac, I think,
　To choose good days and shun the critical. –
　That's his mistress' scarf.
SILVIO　　　　　　　　　　Yes, he protests
　He would do much for that taffeta.
DELIO
　I think he would run away from a battle　　　　　　　　25
　To save it from taking prisoner.
SILVIO　　　　　　　　　　He is horribly afraid
　Gunpowder will spoil the perfume on't.
DELIO
　I saw a Dutchman break his pate once
　For calling him pot-gun: he made his head
　Have a bore in't like a musket.　　　　　　　　　　30
SILVIO
　I would he had made a touch-hole to't.

14　*leaguer* army camp.
17　*service* military campaign.
19　*keeps* ed. (keepe Q1).
　　painters Q1c (pewterers Q1a-b) 'Press-corrections in this forme are probably
　　authorial' (Brown).
20　*model* drawings made to scale.
　　by the book only theoretically. The phrase means 'strictly according to the rules',
　　whether in a good sense or bad – see *Romeo and Juliet*, I.v.110, III.i.102.
29　*pot-gun* a term for a short-barrelled pot-shaped artillery-piece, contemptuously
　　applied to a pistol (OED sb, 2b) or figuratively, as here, to a braggart (OED sb. 3).
　　English dramatists of the period caricature Dutch indulgence in butter and beer.
31　*touch-hole* hole in the breech for igniting the charge.

[DELIO]

He is indeed a guarded sumpter-cloth
Only for the remove of the court.

[*Enter* BOSOLA, *who speaks apart to* FERDINAND
and the CARDINAL]

PESCARA

Bosola arriv'd? What should be the business?
Some falling-out amongst the cardinals.   35
These factions amongst great men, they are like
Foxes: when their heads are divided
They carry fire in their tails, and all the country
About them goes to wrack for't.

SILVIO   What's that Bosola?

DELIO

I knew him in Padua, a fantastical scholar, like such who study   40
to know how many knots was in Hercules' club, of what colour
Achilles' beard was, or whether Hector were not troubled with
the tooth-ache. He hath studied himself half blear-eyed to
know the true symmetry of Caesar's nose by a shoeing-horn,
and this he did to gain the name of a speculative man.   45

PESCARA

Mark Prince Ferdinand,
A very salamander lives in's eye
To mock the eager violence of fire.

SILVIO

That Cardinal hath made more bad faces with his oppression
than ever Michael Angelo made good ones; he lifts up's nose   50
like a foul porpoise before a storm.

PESCARA

The Lord Ferdinand laughs.

32   DELIO *He* ed. (He Q1) The catchword at the bottom of the preceding page, G4v, is
      Del. NCW suggest the omission of the s.p. occurred because the compositor went
      from G4v to the inner forme of H (H1v and H2r) before returning to H1r, when he
      overlooked it.
      guarded sumpter-cloth ornamented cloth covering a pack-horse or mule.
37–8 Alluding to Judges 15.4, the trick of Samson who tied pairs of foxes together by their
      tails, attached firebrands to them, and sent them into the Philistines' crops to destroy
      them.
40–5 prose ed. (*Q1 lines ending* scholler / in / was / – ach / the / this / man).
47   *salamander* supposed to live in fire, the element of passion, destruction or torment.
49–51 prose ed (*Q1 lines ending* oppression / ones / storme).
51   *porpoise* (por-pisse Q1).

DELIO   Like a deadly cannon
That lightens ere it smokes.

PESCARA
These are your true pangs of death,
The pangs of life that struggle with great statesmen.   55

DELIO
In such a deformed silence witches whisper their charms.

CARDINAL
Doth she make religion her riding-hood
To keep her from the sun, and tempest?

FERDINAND   That –
That damns her: Methinks her fault and beauty,
Blended together, show like leprosy,   60
The whiter, the fouler: I make it a question
Whether her beggarly brats were ever christened.

CARDINAL
I will instantly solicit the state of Ancona
To have them banished.

FERDINAND   You are for Loreto?
I shall not be at your ceremony: fare you well.   65
[*To* BOSOLA] Write to the Duke of Malfi, my young nephew
She had by her first husband, and acquaint him
With's mother's honesty.

BOSOLA   I will.

FERDINAND   Antonio?
A slave that only smelled of ink and counters,
And ne'er in's life looked like a gentleman   70
But in the audit time! Go, go presently,
Draw me out an hundred and fifty of our horse,
And meet me at the fort bridge.

                                                          Exeunt

---

56–60   ed. (In . . . charmes / Doth . . . hood / To . . . tempest / That . . . and / Beauty . . .
        leaprosie Q1).

66–7   This is the only reference to this son. Perhaps he is a 'ghost character' from an early
        draft whom Webster forgot to delete. His existence seems incompatible with
        Ferdinand's hope at IV.ii.269–71 of inheriting a mass of treasure at the Duchess'
        death.

69   *counters* small discs used in accounting.

70   *life* ed. (like Q1).

72   *hundred* ed. (hundreth Q1).

[ACT III,] SCENE iv

[Enter] TWO PILGRIMS *to the shrine*
of Our Lady of Loretto

1 PILGRIM
I have not seen a goodlier shrine than this,
Yet I have visited many.

2 PILGRIM   The Cardinal of Aragon
Is this day to resign his cardinal's hat,
His sister Duchess likewise is arrived
To pay her vow of pilgrimage. I expect   5
A noble ceremony.

1 PILGRIM   No question. – They come.

Here the ceremony of the Cardinal's instalment
in the habit of a soldier: performed in delivering up
his cross, hat, robes and ring, at the shrine; and investing
him with sword, helmet, shield, and spurs: then ANTONIO,
the DUCHESS *and their children, having presented themselves*
at the shrine, are by a form of banishment in dumb-show,
expressed towards them by the CARDINAL *and the*
State of Ancona, banished; during all which ceremony,
this ditty is sung to very solemn music, by divers churchmen;
and then

Exeunt.

0   s.d. ed. (SCENA IIII. / Two Pilgrimes to the Shrine of our Lady of Loreto. Q1).
0   s.d. 1 PILGRIMS The traditional dress of a pilgrim consisted of a gown, staff, scallop-shell, scrip and bottle, as described in Sir Walter Raleigh's poem 'The passionate man's Pilgrimage'.
0   s.d. 1 *shrine* The actual Loreto shrine featured a black madonna with child, and Webster may have intended an elaborate imitation, a spectacle composing a pattern with the later spectacular staging of the bodies (IV.i) and the tomb (V.iii).
6   s.d. 2 *habit* Q1b (*order* Q1a); *of a* ed. (*a* Q1).
     s.d. 5 *children* A boy, a girl old enough to say her prayers (see IV.ii.191–2) and a babe in arms.
6   s.d. 6 *in dumb-show* Q1b (not in Q1a). This dumb-show must include the violent removal of the wedding-ring from the finger of the Duchess, as lines 35–6 indicate. The dumb-show signals a decisive turning point with the Cardinal's transformation into soldier and the simultaneous subjection suffered by the Duchess. The presence of Antonio seems to contradict III.ii.173 where the Duchess tells him to go to Ancona. See above, III.ii.300–306 n.
6   s.d. 9 *ditty* Q1b (*Hymne* Q1a).

Arms, and honours, deck thy story
To thy fame's eternal glory,
Adverse fortune ever fly thee,
No disastrous fate come nigh thee.   The author   10
                                                        disclaims
I alone will sing thy praises,   this ditty
Whom to honour, virtue raises;   to be his
And thy study, that divine is,
Bent to martial discipline is.
Lay aside all those robes lie by thee,   15
Crown thy arts with arms: they'll beautify thee.

Oh worthy of worthiest name, adorned in this manner,
Lead bravely thy forces on, under war's warlike banner:
Oh mayest thou prove fortunate in all martial courses,
Guide thou still, by skill, in arts and forces: 20
Victory attend thee nigh whilst fame sings loud thy powers,
Triumphant conquest crown thy head, and blessings pour down
    showers.

1 PILGRIM
    Here's a strange turn of state: who would have thought
    So great a lady would have matched herself
    Unto so mean a person? Yet the Cardinal   25
    Bears himself much too cruel.
2 PILGRIM   They are banished.
1 PILGRIM
    But I would ask what power hath this state
    Of Ancona to determine of a free prince?
2 PILGRIM
    They are a free state sir, and her brother showed
    How that the Pope, forehearing of her looseness,   30

---

    7   *Arms* Q1b (The Hymne. / *Armes* Q1a) (but the catch-word in Q1b is not corrected
         and reads 'The').
 10–13   *The . . . his* Q1b (opposite line 3 on sig H2r – not in Q1a). Added, presumably by
         Webster, when the text was read in proof. The author of the ditty has not been
         identified.
    19   *courses* encounters.
    29   *free state* Ancona had been an independent republic but by Webster's time was one
         of the Papal States, and as 2 Pilgrim explains, this gives the Cardinal an excuse to act
         ostensibly in the name of the Papacy to gain his revenge.
         state sir Q1b (state Q1).

Hath seized into the protection of the Church
The dukedom which she held as dowager.

1 PILGRIM
But by what justice?

2 PILGRIM   Sure I think by none,
Only her brother's instigation.

1 PILGRIM
What was it with such violence he took   35
Off from her finger?

2 PILGRIM   'Twas her wedding ring,
Which he vowed shortly he would sacrifice
To his revenge.

1 PILGRIM   Alas, Antonio,
If that a man be thrust into a well,
No matter who sets hand to't, his own weight   40
Will bring him sooner to th'bottom. Come, let's hence.
Fortune makes this conclusion general,
'All things do help th'unhappy man to fall'.

Exeunt

[ACT III,] SCENE v

[*Enter* ANTONIO, DUCHESS, CHILDREN,
CARIOLA, *and* SERVANTS]

DUCHESS
Banished Ancona?

ANTONIO   Yes, you see what power
Lightens in great men's breath.

---

31   *Hath* Q1b (Had Q1a).
36   *Off* ed. (Of Q1).

0   s.d. ed. (*SCENA V. / Antonio, Duchesse, Children, Cariola, Seruants, Bosola, Souldiers, with Vizards.* Q1).
0   s.d. 1 *CARIOLA* As line 81 indicates, Cariola has the baby in her arms.
1–3   ed. (Banish'd *Ancona* / Yes . . . powre / Lightens . . . breath / Is . . . traine / Shrunke . . . remainder / These . . . men Q1).
2   *Lightens* An intransitive verb, 'flashes like lightning' – as at III.iii.53.

DUCHESS   Is all our train
    Shrunk to this poor remainder?
ANTONIO   These poor men,
    Which have got little in your service, vow
    To take your fortune; but your wiser buntings,   5
    Now they are fledged, are gone.
DUCHESS   They have done wisely.
    This puts me in mind of death: physicians thus,
    With their hands full of money, use to give o'er
    Their patients.
ANTONIO   Right the fashion of the world:
    From decayed fortunes every flatterer shrinks,   10
    Men cease to build where the foundation sinks.
DUCHESS
    I had a very strange dream tonight.
ANTONIO   What was't?
DUCHESS
    Methought I wore my coronet of state,
    And on a sudden all the diamonds
    Were changed to pearls.
ANTONIO   My interpretation   15
    Is, you'll weep shortly, for to me the pearls
    Do signify your tears.
DUCHESS   The birds that live i'th'field
    On the wild benefit of nature, live
    Happier than we; for they may choose their mates
    And carol their sweet pleasures to the spring.   20

            [*Enter* BOSOLA *with a letter*
            which he presents to the DUCHESS]

BOSOLA
    You are happily o'er-ta'en.
DUCHESS   From my brother?
BOSOLA
    Yes, from the Lord Ferdinand your brother,
    All love, and safety.

---

    5   *buntings* small birds related to the lark but without their song: here applied to the
        servants who have had the wit to see that it is time to leave and have the means to
        do so.
    9   *Right* Just.
   18   *benefit* gift.

DUCHESS   Thou dost blanch mischief,
    Wouldst make it white. See, see, like to calm weather
    At sea before a tempest, false hearts speak fair   25
    To those they intend most mischief.
    [*Reads*] *Send Antonio to me, I want his head in a business* –
    A politic equivocation:
    He doth not want your counsel but your head:
    That is, he cannot sleep till you be dead;   30
    And here's another pitfall that's strewed o'er
    With roses: mark it, 'tis a cunning one:
    [*Reads*] *I stand engaged for your husband, for several debts, at*
       Naples; let not that trouble him, I had rather have his heart
       than his money.   35
    And I believe so too.
BOSOLA   What do you believe?
DUCHESS
    That he so much distrusts my husband's love
    He will by no means believe his heart is with him
    Until he see it. The devil is not cunning enough
    To circumvent us in riddles.   40
BOSOLA
    Will you reject that noble and free league
    Of amity and love which I present you?
DUCHESS
    Their league is like that of some politic kings
    Only to make themselves of strength and power
    To be our after-ruin: tell them so.   45
BOSOLA
    And what from you?
ANTONIO   Thus tell him: I will not come.
BOSOLA
    And what of this?
ANTONIO   My brothers have dispersed
    Bloodhounds abroad; which till I hear are muzzled,
    No truce, though hatched with ne'er such politic skill,
    Is safe, that hangs upon our enemies' will.   50

33–5   This was the (invented) reason the Duchess gave for dismissing Antonio at III.ii.165–9.
       Presumably Bosola, who was present then, reported it like a dutiful spy.
33   s.d. Q4 (A Letter Q1).
37–8 Dent compares Donne, *Ignatius*, 89.
47   *brothers* i.e. brothers-in-law.

I'll not come at them.

BOSOLA   This proclaims your breeding.
Every small thing draws a base mind to fear
As the adamant draws iron. Fare you well sir,
You shall shortly hear from's.   *Exit*

DUCHESS   I suspect some ambush:
Therefore by all my love I do conjure you   55
To take your eldest son and fly towards Milan;
Let us not venture all this poor remainder
In one unlucky bottom.

ANTONIO   You counsel safely:
Best of my life, farewell; since we must part
Heaven hath a hand in't; but no other wise   60
Than as some curious artist takes in sunder
A clock, or watch, when it is out of frame,
To bring't in better order.

DUCHESS   I know not which is best,
To see you dead, or part with you: farewell boy,
Thou art happy that thou hast not understanding   65
To know thy misery; for all our wit
And reading brings us to a truer sense
Of sorrow. In the eternal Church, sir,
I do hope we shall not part thus.

ANTONIO   Oh, be of comfort.
Make patience a noble fortitude,   70
And think not how unkindly we are used:
'Man, like to cassia, is proved best, being bruised'.

DUCHESS
Must I like to a slave-born Russian
Account it praise to suffer tyranny?

---

53   *adamant* magnet.

57–8   *venture . . . bottom* Alluding to the proverb, 'Venture not all in one bottom' i.e. do not
risk all your wealth in one ship.

64   *boy* Addressing her son.

68   *the eternal Church* The congregation of the saved in Heaven. The phrase occurs in
Sidney, *Arcadia* (*Works* I. 233), one of a small cluster of borrowings at this point by
Webster from Sidney.

72   '*Man* Q1b (Man Q1a).

72   *bruised'* ed. (bruiz'd Q1a, Q1b).

73–4   From Sidney, *Astrophil and Stella*, Sonnet 2: 'and now like slave-borne *Muscovite* / I
call it praise to suffer Tyrannie'. *Astrophil and Stella* would have become even better
known after it was included with the *Arcadia* in editions from 1598 on – see William
A. Ringler Jr., ed. *The Poems of Sir Philip Sidney*, 1962, p. lxii.

And yet, oh heaven, thy heavy hand is in't.   75
I have seen my little boy oft scourge his top
And compared myself to't: nought made me e'er
Go right but heaven's scourge-stick.

ANTONIO   Do not weep:
Heaven fashioned us of nothing; and we strive
To bring ourselves to nothing. Farewell Cariola   80
And thy sweet armful. –
[*To* DUCHESS]   If I do never see thee more,
Be a good mother to your little ones,
And save them from the tiger. Fare you well.

DUCHESS
Let me look upon you once more: for that speech
Came from a dying father. Your kiss is colder   85
Than that I have seen an holy anchorite
Give to a dead man's skull.

ANTONIO
My heart is turned to a heavy lump of lead,
With which I sound my danger: fare you well.

                              Exit [*with his eldest son*]

DUCHESS
My laurel is all withered.   90

CARIOLA
Look, madam, what a troop of armed men
Make toward us.

76–8   Compare Sidney, *Arcadia* (*Works* I. 227): 'Griefe onely makes his wretched state to
       see / (Even like a toppe which nought but whipping moves)'.
77–8   ed. (And . . . right / But . . . -sticke / Doe . . . weepe Q1).
78   *scourge-stick* whip used to make a child's top spin.
79–80 Lucas compares Donne, *An Anatomy of the World*, lines 155–7, but Donne's 'God' has
       been altered to 'Heaven'. A Jacobean statute (3 Jac. I) forbade profanities; and this has
       been thought to explain the substitution. Brown observes (pp.lxviii–lxix) that in the
       play's other instances 'heaven' refers to the skies or the heavenly world and is not
       plausible as a substitution for an original 'God'; moreover it is the fact of a complete
       absence of oaths involving 'God' which is strange in Q1 and strongly suggests
       censorship.
81   *sweet armful* The Duchess' youngest child.
       never see thee more The phrase is an echo of III.ii.140 and recurs at IV.i.24 and
       V.iii.41.
86   *anchorite* hermit.
88–9   As the depth of water is gauged (*sounded*) with a lead-weighted line, so the weight
       of Antonio's heavy heart can sound the danger.
90   An ominous sign, referred to in Shakespeare, *Richard II*, II.iv.7–8.

[Enter BOSOLA *with a guard with vizards]*

DUCHESS   Oh they are very welcome:
When Fortune's wheel is overcharged with princes
The weight makes it move swift. I would have my ruin
Be sudden. [*To* BOSOLA] I am your adventure, am I not?   95

BOSOLA
You are. You must see your husband no more.

DUCHESS
What devil art thou that counterfeits heaven's thunder?

BOSOLA
Is that terrible? I would have you tell me
Whether is that note worse that frights the silly birds
Out of the corn, or that which doth allure them   100
To the nets? You have harkened to the last too much.

DUCHESS
Oh misery: like to a rusty o'er-charged cannon,
Shall I never fly in pieces? Come: to what prison?

BOSOLA
To none.

DUCHESS   Whither then?

BOSOLA   To your palace.

DUCHESS
I have heard that Charon's boat serves to convey   105
All o'er the dismal lake, but brings none back again.

BOSOLA
Your brothers mean you safety and pity.

DUCHESS   Pity?

92   s.d. The use of masks by the soldiers, and Bosola, is menacing. The play contains
      many textual references to disguise and masks, reinforced in visual terms by this
      episode, by the stage presentation of a masque of madmen, and Bosola's various
      disguises.
94   *move* Q1b (*more* Q1a).
95   *I am your adventure* I am your target (but possibly in an ironic sense, 'You aim to find
      me as if by chance').
98   s.p. Q1b (not in Q1a).
99   *silly* weak, defenceless.
101   s.p. Q1b (*Ant.* Q1a).
102   *o'er-charged* ed. (ore-char'd Q1).
102–3 The image is used for the soul leaving the body at death by Donne, *Of the Progress
      of the Soul: The Second Anniversary*, lines 181–2.
105   *Charon's boat* In Classical mythology Charon was the ferryman who conveyed the
      dead across the river Styx to Hades.
107–8 ed. (Your . . . pitie / Pitie. . . aliue Q1).

371

With such a pity men preserve alive
Pheasants and quails, when they are not fat enough
To be eaten.

BOSOLA   These are your children?

DUCHESS   Yes.

BOSOLA   Can they prattle?

DUCHESS   No: 110
But I intend, since they were born accursed,
Curses shall be their first language.

BOSOLA   Fie, madam,
Forget this base, low fellow.

DUCHESS   Were I a man
I'd beat that counterfeit face into thy other.

BOSOLA
One of no birth.

DUCHESS   Say that he was born mean: 115
Man is most happy when's own actions
Be arguments and examples of his virtue.

BOSOLA
A barren, beggarly virtue.

DUCHESS
I prithee who is greatest, can you tell?
Sad tales befit my woe: I'll tell you one.   120
A salmon as she swam unto the sea
Met with a dog-fish who encounters her
With this rough language: 'Why art thou so bold
To mix thyself with our high state of floods,
Being no eminent courtier, but one   125
That for the calmest and fresh time o'th'year
Dost live in shallow rivers, rank'st thyself
With silly smelts and shrimps? And darest thou
Pass by our dog-ship without reverence?'
'Oh', quoth the salmon, 'sister be at peace: 130
Thank Jupiter we both have passed the net,
Our value never can be truly known
Till in the fisher's basket we be shown.
I'th'market then my price may be the higher

108   *a* Q1b (*not in* Q1a).
110   ed. (To ... eaten / These ... children / Yes / Can ... prattle / No Q1).
112–3 ed. (Curses ... language / Fye Madam / Forget ... -fellow / Were ... man Q1).
114   *counterfeit face* vizard.

Even when I am nearest to the cook, and fire'.   135
So to great men the moral may be stretched:
'Men oft are valued high, when th'are most wretched'.
But come, whither you please: I am armed 'gainst misery,
Bent to all sways of the oppressor's will.
'There's no deep valley, but near some great hill'.   140

Exeunt

ACT IV, SCENE i

[*Enter* FERDINAND, BOSOLA, *and* SERVANTS *with torches*]

FERDINAND
How doth our sister Duchess bear herself
In her imprisonment?

BOSOLA   Nobly; I'll describe her:
She's sad, as one long used to't, and she seems
Rather to welcome the end of misery
Than shun it: a behaviour so noble   5
As gives a majesty to adversity:
You may discern the shape of loveliness
More perfect in her tears than in her smiles;
She will muse four hours together, and her silence,
Methinks, expresseth more than if she spake.   10

FERDINAND
Her melancholy seems to be fortified
With a strange disdain.

BOSOLA   'Tis so: and this restraint,
Like English mastiffs that grow fierce with tying,
Makes her too passionately apprehend

---

0   s.d. ed. (ACTVS IIII. SCENA. I. / Ferdinand, Bosola, Dutchesse, Cariola, Seruants. Q1).

0   s.d. Torches and candles, brought on stage, would indicate that this is a night-scene (see line 24).

2   *imprisonment* This presumably means (for the moment at least) house-arrest, since in III.v.104 Bosola tells the Duchess she is to be taken to her palace not some prison; but she may be imagined as moved to a dungeon for her killing (see IV.ii.11 and n.). There is a general parallel between the fate of the Duchess and the royal figure of Richard II in Shakespeare, except that Webster's Duchess is brought not at once but by progressive degrees to mortification: here she is still dressed with the dignity proper to her rank, but Bosola commands (IV.i.115ff.) that she is to wear a penitential garment next her skin and have beads and a prayer-book, and this may indicate how she is to appear in the next scene – her last – IV.ii.

3–5   From Sidney, *Arcadia* (*Works* I. 332).

5–6   Taken from Sidney, *Arcadia* (*Works* I. 16): 'a behaviour so noble, as gave a majestie to adversitie'.

7–8   The cadence is close to Sidney, *Arcadia* (*Works* I. 333): 'perceyve the shape of lovelinesse more perfectly in wo, then in joyfulnesse' – and Webster's words also recall *King Lear*, IV.iii.16–22.

9   *four hours* A common expression for 'several hours' as in *Hamlet*, 2.2.160.

12–15   From Sidney, *Arcadia* (*Works* I. 25).

Those pleasures she's kept from.

FERDINAND   Curse upon her: 15
  I will no longer study in the book
  Of another's heart: inform her what I told you.   *Exit*

   [*Enter* DUCHESS *and* CARIOLA]

BOSOLA
  All comfort to your grace.

DUCHESS   I will have none:
  Pray thee, why dost thou wrap thy poisoned pills
  In gold and sugar?   20

BOSOLA
  Your elder brother the Lord Ferdinand
  Is come to visit you, and sends you word,
  'Cause once he rashly made a solemn vow
  Never to see you more, he comes i'th'night:
  And prays you, gently, neither torch nor taper   25
  Shine in your chamber. He will kiss your hand
  And reconcile himself, but, for his vow,
  He dares not see you.

DUCHESS   At his pleasure:
  Take hence the lights.

      [*Exeunt* SERVANTS *with torches*]

   [*Enter* FERDINAND]

   He's come.

FERDINAND
  Where are you?

DUCHESS   Here, sir.

FERDINAND   This darkness suits you well. 30

DUCHESS
  I would ask you pardon.

FERDINAND   You have it;
  For I account it the honorabl'st revenge,

---

21 *elder brother* Since in IV.ii.253 Ferdinand declares he is her twin, here presumably
  Bosola must be supposed mistaken, or to mean that Ferdinand was the first twin to
  be born, or Webster is being careless.

24 *i'th'night* Conventionally indicated on the Elizabethan stage by the bringing on of
  torches or candles.

28–9 ed. (He . . . you / At . . . pleasure / Take . . . come Q1).

30–31 ed. (Where . . . you / Here sir / This . . . well / I . . . pardon / You . . . it Q1).

Where I may kill, to pardon. Where are your cubs?
DUCHESS
Whom?
FERDINAND Call them your children;
For though our national law distinguish bastards   35
From true legitimate issue, compassionate nature
Makes them all equal.
DUCHESS   Do you visit me for this?
You violate a sacrament o'th'Church
Shall make you howl in hell for't.
FERDINAND   It had been well
Could you have lived thus always, for indeed   40
You were too much i'th'light. But no more.
I come to seal my peace with you. Here's a hand
To which you have vowed much love: the ring upon't
You gave.

Gives her a dead man's hand
DUCHESS   I affectionately kiss it.
FERDINAND
Pray do, and bury the print of it in your heart.   45
I will leave this ring with you for a love token,
And the hand, as sure as the ring; and do not doubt
But you shall have the heart too. When you need a friend
Send it to him that owned it: you shall see
Whether he can aid you.
DUCHESS   You are very cold.   50
I fear you are not well after your travel –
Ha? Lights! – Oh horrible!
FERDINAND   Let her have lights enough.   *Exit*

[*Enter* SERVANTS *with torches*]

---

33   *cubs* The first touch of the Duke's future lycanthropia? (Lucas).
41   *i'th'light* in the public eye (and with a play upon *light* = wanton).
43   *the ring upon't* Recalling I.i.405 when the Duchess put a ring on Antonio's finger. In
      most productions until the twentieth century the dead man's hand was not used –
      in 1850 it was Ferdinand's own 'cold hand' which was kissed. In the 1980 production
      the shocked Duchess threw the horribly realistic hand into the audience. (PinP,
      p. 151).
44   The Duchess assumes it is Ferdinand's own hand. Her concerned reaction that he
      feels cold shows by the starkest contrast how cruel and perverse he has become. M.
      C. Bradbrook, MLR (1947), 283–94, points out that, ironically, a dead man's hand
      was a charm supposed to cure madness.

DUCHESS

What witchcraft doth he practise, that he hath left
A dead man's hand here?

Here is discovered behind a traverse the artificial figures
of ANTONIO *and his children, appearing*
as if they were dead.

BOSOLA

Look you, here's the piece from which 'twas ta'en.   55
He doth present you this sad spectacle,
That now you know directly they are dead.
Hereafter you may, wisely, cease to grieve
For that which cannot be recovered.

DUCHESS

There is not between heaven and earth one wish   60
I stay for after this: it wastes me more
Than were't my picture, fashioned out of wax,
Stuck with a magical needle, and then buried
In some foul dung-hill; and yond's an excellent property
For a tyrant, which I would account mercy.

BOSOLA   What's that?   65

DUCHESS

If they would bind me to that lifeless trunk
And let me freeze to death.

BOSOLA   Come, you must live.

DUCHESS

That's the greatest torture souls feel in hell,
In hell: that they must live, and cannot die.

54   s.d. *traverse* A curtain drawn back to discover the tableau. This spectacle of the dead
      bodies of Antonio and the children is the severest test of the Duchess' sanity and
      faith. Fifty-five lines later, Webster allows the audience (but not the Duchess) to
      learn that these figures were waxwork not real. In Jacobean performances they could,
      as with the stone statue *The Winter's Tale*, have been represented by real actors and
      this would have been the simplest method, the audience taking their cue from the
      Duchess and accepting the figures as dead. Webster makes a point about the
      deceptive illusionism of theatre: the identical theatrical sign can be treacherously
      unstable, can be interpreted in opposite ways. Lopez, p. 109, compares George F.
      Reynolds' view in *The Staging of Elizabethan Plays at the Red Bull Theatre*, p. 40, that
      Elizabethan playwrights 'did, at least in some particulars, delight in realism to an
      extraordinary degree'.
66   In emblem books the image of a live person bound to a corpse symbolised ill-
      matched marriages, but the Duchess characteristically defies commonplace
      attitudes, outfacing horror with her love for her husband: perhaps she moves
      towards the corpse and is restrained by Bosola.

Portia, I'll new kindle thy coals again 70
And revive the rare and almost dead example
Of a loving wife.

BOSOLA Oh fie: despair? Remember
You are a Christian.

DUCHESS The Church enjoins fasting:
I'll starve myself to death.

BOSOLA Leave this vain sorrow.
Things being at the worst, begin to mend: 75
The bee, when he hath shot his sting into your hand,
May then play with your eye-lid.

DUCHESS Good comfortable fellow,
Persuade a wretch that's broke upon the wheel
To have all his bones new set: entreat him live,
To be executed again. Who must dispatch me? 80
I account this world a tedious theatre,
For I do play a part in't 'gainst my will.

BOSOLA
Come, be of comfort, I will save your life.

DUCHESS
Indeed I have not leisure to tend so small a business.

BOSOLA
Now, by my life, I pity you.

DUCHESS Thou art a fool then, 85
To waste thy pity on a thing so wretch'd
As cannot pity itself. I am full of daggers –
Puff – let me blow these vipers from me.
[To a SERVANT] What are you?

SERVANT One that wishes you long life.

---

70   *Portia* Brutus' wife, who choked herself by putting live coals in her mouth after
hearing of her husband's defeat and death at Philippi.

81–2   From Sidney, *Arcadia* (*Works* I. 333) and see *Richard II*, V.ii.23–5 where York
describes the deposed king: 'As in a theatre the eyes of men, / After a well-graced
actor leaves the stage, /Are idly bent on him that enters next, / Thinking his prattle
to be tedious'.

87   *itself* ed. (it Q1).

88   *vipers* Q1 (vapours Brown). Brown supposes the scribe misread ms 'vapors'.
let . . . me let me blow away these poisonous thoughts. The pressure of emotion
transforms the Duchess' metaphor as she speaks: the daggers become the stings of
snakes (a supplementary image of stinging pain) which she would blow off (as if
they were burrs).

89–91   *What . . . me* From Sidney, *Arcadia* (*Works* I. 485).

DUCHESS

    I would thou wert hanged for the horrible curse   90

    Thou hast given me! I shall shortly grow one

    Of the miracles of pity. I'll go pray – no,

    I'll go curse.

BOSOLA   Oh fie.

DUCHESS   I could curse the stars.

BOSOLA   Oh fearful!

DUCHESS

    And those three smiling seasons of the year

    Into a Russian winter, nay the world   95

    To its first chaos.

BOSOLA

    Look you, the stars shine still.

DUCHESS   Oh, but you must

    Remember, my curse hath a great way to go.

    Plagues, that make lanes through largest families,

    Consume them.

BOSOLA   Fie, lady:

DUCHESS   Let them like tyrants   100

    Never be remembered but for the ill they have done:

    Let all the zealous prayers of mortified

    Churchmen forget them.

BOSOLA   Oh uncharitable.

DUCHESS

    Let heaven a little while cease crowning martyrs

    To punish them.   105

    Go howl them this and say I long to bleed:

    'It is some mercy, when men kill with speed'.

                   Exeunt [DUCHESS *and* CARIOLA]

          [*Enter* FERDINAND]

FERDINAND

    Excellent, as I would wish, she's plagued in art.

    These presentations are but framed in wax

    By the curious master in that quality,   110

    Vincentio Lauriola, and she takes them

---

99   *make lanes* As does a cannon-ball through a formation of troops in battle.
      them the brothers.

108 Ferdinand has evidently watched and heard everything from concealment, a solitary
      voyeur.

110 *curious* ingenious.

For true substantial bodies.

BOSOLA   Why do you do this?

FERDINAND

To bring her to despair.

BOSOLA   Faith, end here
And go no farther in your cruelty.
Send her a penitential garment to put on   115
Next to her delicate skin, and furnish her
With beads and prayer books.

FERDINAND   Damn her, that body of hers,
While that my blood ran pure in't, was more worth
Than that which thou wouldst comfort, called a soul.
I will send her masques of common courtesans,   120
Have her meat served up by bawds and ruffians,
And, 'cause she'll needs be mad, I am resolved
To remove forth the common hospital
All the mad-folk and place them near her lodging;
There let them practise together, sing and dance   125
And act their gambols to the full o'th'moon.
If she can sleep the better for it, let her.
Your work is almost ended.

BOSOLA

Must I see her again?

FERDINAND   Yes.

BOSOLA   Never.

FERDINAND   You must.

BOSOLA

Never in mine own shape,   130
That's forfeited by my intelligence
And this last cruel lie. When you send me next
The business shall be comfort.

FERDINAND   Very likely.
Thy pity is nothing of kin to thee. Antonio
Lurks about Milan, thou shalt shortly thither   135
To feed a fire as great as my revenge,

115–17   See below, note to IV.ii.0 s.d.
  131   *intelligence* spying.
  133   *Very likely* This is said and meant ironically – a small touch by which Webster stresses
         that Ferdinand does not detect the growing crisis in Bosola's personality, the split
         between cynicism and compassion.

Which ne'er will slack till it have spent his fuel:
'Intemperate agues make physicians cruel'.

Exeunt

[ACT IV,] SCENE ii

[*Enter* DUCHESS *and* CARIOLA]

DUCHESS
What hideous noise was that?

CARIOLA   'Tis the wild consort
Of madmen, lady, which your tyrant brother
Hath placed about your lodging; this tyranny
I think was never practised till this hour.

0   s.d. ed. (*SCENA II. / Duchesse, Cariola, Seruant, Mad-men, Bosola, Executioners,*
     Ferdinand. Q1).

0   s.d. The Duchess may be dressed as a penitent (see IV.i.115–7). Brennan notes that
     ecclesiastical courts sentenced adulteresses to walk through the streets in a
     penitential garment of white, with hair unbound and carrying a lighted taper. Jane
     Shore appears thus in Heywood's play of 1599, *The Second Part of King Edward the*
     Fourth. It is not clear whether in line 11 ('this is a prison') the Duchess is saying that
     she finds her loss of liberty generally depressing, or that she has been moved to an
     actual prison – which would be something very ominous, a suitable place for a
     killing, as in Shakespeare's *Richard II*. In Webster's time such a location would be left
     to the imagination of the spectators, perhaps aided by simple props.

1   *consort* company – with a play on the sense 'group of musicians' – and there may be
     play on *noise* which also could mean 'group of musicians'. Webster may have thus
     intended to alert his audience to the parodies of a Jacobean court wedding masque
     and of a charivari (a mock-masque baiting the bride who married too soon after the
     death of her husband, or who made an unequal match: or a ruffianly band showed
     their disapproval by making clamour and antic dances). The anti-masque precisely
     inverted, in grotesque manner, the harmonies and costly elegance of the main
     masque, in music, words, dance and costume. The Lord of Misrule (see III.ii.7 and
     note) presided at feasts and was chosen for his youth or low degree, inverting the
     normal hierarchy in the spirit of foolery, festive licence and anarchy. See Inga-Stina
     Ekeblad, 'The "impure art" of John Webster', *RES* 9, (1958), 253–67, who argues that
     the masque of Madmen in IV.ii is related to the charivari. Brown (p.xxxvi) makes a
     connection with actual masques of 1613, Campion's *Lords' Masque* and Beaumont's
     Masque of the Inner Temple and Gray's Inn.
         More broadly, the use of masks in festivals is an ancient tradition formalised in
     comedy, where the temporary release from fixed, normal identity by wearing
     disguise, often in the form of fantastic masks, liberates repressed energies and effects
     positive transformation. Shakespeare gives concentrated attention to these elements
     in *Twelfth Night*, which is occasionally in Webster's mind in this play.

DUCHESS

    Indeed I thank him: nothing but noise and folly   5
    Can keep me in my right wits, whereas reason
    And silence make me stark mad. Sit down,
    Discourse to me some dismal tragedy.

CARIOLA

    Oh 'twill increase your melancholy.

DUCHESS   Thou art deceived,
    To hear of greater grief would lessen mine.   10
    This is a prison?

CARIOLA   Yes, but you shall live
    To shake this durance off.

DUCHESS   Thou art a fool,
    The robin redbreast and the nightingale
    Never live long in cages.

CARIOLA   Pray dry your eyes.
    What think you of, madam?

DUCHESS   Of nothing: 15
    When I muse thus, I sleep.

CARIOLA

    Like a madman, with your eyes open?

DUCHESS

    Dost thou think we shall know one another
    In th'other world?

CARIOLA   Yes, out of question.

DUCHESS

    Oh that it were possible we might   20
    But hold some two days conference with the dead,
    From them I should learn somewhat I am sure
    I never shall know here. I'll tell thee a miracle,
    I am not mad yet, to my cause of sorrow.
    Th'heaven o'er my head seems made of molten brass,   25
    The earth of flaming sulphur, yet I am not mad;
    I am acquainted with sad misery
    As the tanned galley-slave is with his oar.
    Necessity makes me suffer constantly,
    And custom makes it easy. Who do I look like now?   30

---

11   At Blackfriars and the Globe simple props such as chains and fetters could have been
      enough to suggest a prison cell.

15–17 ed. (What . . . Madam / Of nothing / When . . . sleepe / Like . . . open Q1).

25–6   From Deuteronomy 28.15, 23.

CARIOLA
　　Like to your picture in the gallery,
　　A deal of life in show but none in practice;
　　Or rather like some reverend monument
　　Whose ruins are even pitied.
DUCHESS　　　　　　　　　Very proper:
　　And Fortune seems only to have her eye-sight　　　　　35
　　To behold my tragedy. How now,
　　What noise is that?

　　　　　　　[*Enter* SERVANT]

SERVANT　　　　　　I am come to tell you
　　Your brother hath intended you some sport:
　　A great physician, when the Pope was sick
　　Of a deep melancholy, presented him　　　　　　40
　　With several sorts of madmen, which wild object,
　　Being full of change and sport, forced him to laugh,
　　And so th'imposthume broke; the self-same cure
　　The Duke intends on you.
DUCHESS　　　　　　　　Let them come in.
SERVANT
　　There's a mad lawyer, and a secular priest,　　　　45
　　A doctor that hath forfeited his wits
　　By jealousy, an astrologian
　　That in his works said such a day o'th'month
　　Should be the day of doom, and failing oft,
　　Ran mad; an English tailor crazed i'th'brain　　　　50
　　With the study of new fashion, a gentleman usher
　　Quite beside himself with care to keep in mind
　　The number of his lady's salutations,
　　Or how do you, she employed him in each morning;
　　A farmer too, an excellent knave in grain,　　　　55
　　Mad 'cause he was hind'red transportation;

31–2　From Sidney, *Arcadia* (*Works* I. 90).
33–4　Anticipating the setting of V.iii: to describe the ruins as 'reverend' implies that they
　　remain sacred (though at the Dissolution, English monasteries were deconsecrated).
43　*imposthume* abscess.
45　*secular priest* One living in the world as contrasted with those who lived in monastic
　　seclusion.
55　*knave in grain* incorrigible rogue (and crooked dealer in corn or wheat).
56　*transportation* export. Lucas notes a specific ruling of 1613 forbidding export of
　　grain because of its high domestic price and fear of scarcity.

And let one broker that's mad loose to these,
You'd think the devil were among them!

DUCHESS

Sit, Cariola. [*To* SERVANT] – Let them loose when you please,
For I am chained to endure all your tyranny.   60

[*Enter* MADMEN]

*Here, by a madman, this song is sung
to a dismal kind of music.*

*Oh let us howl some heavy note,
    some deadly dogged howl,
Sounding, as from the threat'ning throat
    of beasts and fatal fowl.
As ravens, screech-owls, bulls, and bears,*   65
    *we'll bill and bawl our parts,
Till irksome noise have cloyed your ears
    and corrosived your hearts.
At last whenas our choir wants breath,
    our bodies being blest,*   70
*We'll sing like swans to welcome death,
    and die in love and rest.*

1 MADMAN

Doomsday not come yet? I'll draw it nearer by a perspective, or
make a glass that shall set all the world on fire upon an instant.
I cannot sleep, my pillow is stuffed with a litter of porcupines.   75

2 MADMAN

Hell is a mere glass-house, where the devils are continually
blowing up women's souls on hollow irons, and the fire never
goes out.

57 *broker* dealer, retailer.
60 s.d. The servant describes eight Madmen and Q1 assigns eight to dance, but allots
    the song only to one and speeches to four. Only the doctor is characterised
    consistently, and the text leaves open the choice, in performance, of the number of
    madmen and the way they are dressed.
60 s.d. 2 *song* The music, probably by Robert Johnson, has survived in several mss, and
    is in Brown and NCW.
66 *bill* Probably a nonce-word referring to the birds, meaning 'to utter through the bill
    or beak'; alternative readings such as *bell* (bellow) or *bawl* are appropriate to animals
    not birds.
73 *perspective* telescope, magnifying glass.
76 *glass-house* There was a glass factory in Blackfriars, and Webster refers to blown
    glass, shaped like a pregnant woman's belly, at II.ii.6–10.

3 MADMAN

I will lie with every woman in my parish the tenth night: I will
tithe them over like hay-cocks. 80

4 MADMAN

Shall my pothecary out-go me, because I am a cuckold? I have
found out his roguery: he makes allum of his wife's urine, and
sells it to Puritans that have sore throats with over-straining.

1 MADMAN

I have skill in heraldry.

2 MADMAN

Hast? 85

1 MADMAN

You do give for your crest a woodcock's head, with the brains
picked out on't: you are a very ancient gentleman.

3 MADMAN

Greek is turned Turk, we are only to be saved by the Helvetian
translation.

1 MADMAN

Come on sir, I will lay the law to you. 90

2 MADMAN

O, rather lay a corrosive, the law will eat to the bone.

3 MADMAN

He that drinks but to satisfy nature is damned.

4 MADMAN

If I had my glass here, I would show a sight should make all the
women here call me mad doctor.

1 MADMAN

What's he, a rope-maker? 95

2 MADMAN

No, no, no, a snuffling knave, that while he shows the tombs
will have his hand in a wench's placket.

---

86   *woodcock's* This bird was proverbially stupid and easy to catch.

87   *picked out* removed (and playing on the sense 'embroidered', associated with the idea
of the heraldic crest).

88   *turned Turk* become an infidel (i.e. the Greek text of the Bible has been used to
promote false religion).

88–9   The third Madman is apparently a Puritan, and Puritans were a frequent object of
satire in the theatre of Webster's day: the Helvetian translation of the Bible – the
Geneva Bible – of 1560, by Coverdale, Knox, and others, was strongly Calvinist in
tone. It was condemned by King James I in 1603 as 'partial' and 'seditious'.

90   *lay the law* (1) expound the law (2) apply the law as a medicine, make a legal charge.

96   *snuffling* Probably alluding to the nasal whine affected by Puritans.

97   *placket* slit at the top of a skirt.

3 MADMAN

Woe to the caroche that brought home my wife from the
masque at three o'clock in the morning, it had a large feather-
bed in it.   100

4 MADMAN

I have pared the devil's nails forty times, roasted them in raven's
eggs, and cured agues with them.

3 MADMAN

Get me three hundred milch bats, to make possets to procure
sleep.

4 MADMAN

All the college may throw their caps at me, I have made a soap   105
boiler costive. It was my masterpiece.

Here the dance consisting of eight madmen,
with music answerable thereunto, after which

BOSOLA, *like an old man, enters*

DUCHESS

Is he mad too?

SERVANT   Pray question him: I'll leave you.

                                   [*Exeunt* SERVANT *and* MADMEN]

BOSOLA

I am come to make thy tomb.

DUCHESS   Ha, my tomb?

Thou speak'st as if I lay upon my death bed
Gasping for breath: do'st thou perceive me sick?   110

BOSOLA

Yes, and the more dangerously since thy sickness is insensible.

DUCHESS

Thou art not mad sure; dost know me?

BOSOLA

Yes.

---

103   *possets* drinks of hot milk curdled by spiced wine or ale.
105   *throw their caps at me* concede my superiority.
105–6 *soap boiler costive* Diarrhoea was an occupational hazard in making soap; *costive* =
       constipated.
106   s.d. A parodic inversion of the form and values of the climactic dance in a marriage
       masque (where harmony, unity and order were symbolically expressed).
106   s.d. 3 *old man* Conventionally symbolic of Time and Death.
111   *insensible* Montaigne, *Essayes,* p. 397: 'And onely because we perceive not to be sicke,
       makes our recoverie to be more difficult'.

DUCHESS

Who am I?

BOSOLA

Thou art a box of worm-seed, at best, but a salvatory of green   115
mummy. What's this flesh? A little cruded milk, fantastical puff
paste: our bodies are weaker than those paper prisons boys use
to keep flies in – more contemptible, since ours is to preserve
earth worms. Didst thou ever see a lark in a cage? Such is the
soul in the body: this world is like her little turf of grass, and   120
the heaven o'er our heads like her looking-glass, only gives us a
miserable knowledge of the small compass of our prison.

DUCHESS

Am not I thy Duchess?

BOSOLA

Thou art some great woman sure, for riot begins to sit on thy
forehead, clad in grey hairs, twenty years sooner than on a   125
merry milkmaid's. Thou sleep'st worse than if a mouse should
be forced to take up her lodging in a cat's ear; a little infant that
breeds its teeth, should it lie with thee, would cry out as if thou
wert the more unquiet bed-fellow.

DUCHESS

I am Duchess of Malfi still.   130

BOSOLA

That makes thy sleeps so broken:
'Glories, like glow worms, afar off shine bright,
But looked to near, have neither heat nor light'.

DUCHESS

Thou art very plain.

---

115   *worm-seed* dried flower-heads of the plant were used as a remedy for intestinal
       worms: and, alluding to the proverbial association of worms with corpses, there is
       word-play on *seed* = germ, origin.
       salvatory ointment box.
115–16 *green mummy* medicine from mummified corpses; it was also believed that fresh
       corpses could yield a medicinal balsam: this may explain *green*, although the colour
       and its association with mouldy bones has a Websterian gruesomeness all its own.
116   *cruded* curded. Compare Donne, *Second Anniversary*, 165 (alluding to Job 10.10).
117   It was proverbial that 'the body is the prison of the soul' (Tilley B497). Webster may
       also be recalling Shakespeare, *King Lear*, V.iii.8–9, where Lear, reunited with his
       beloved daughter but captured, cries 'Come let's away to prison: / We two alone will
       sing like birds i' th' cage'.
124   *riot* wantonness.
132–3 From *The White Devil*, V.i.40–41.

BOSOLA

My trade is to flatter the dead, not the living.   135
I am a tomb-maker.

DUCHESS

And thou com'st to make my tomb?

BOSOLA

Yes.

DUCHESS

Let me be a little merry. Of what stuff wilt thou make it?

BOSOLA

Nay, resolve me first, of what fashion?   140

DUCHESS

Why, do we grow fantastical in our death-bed, do we affect
fashion in the grave?

BOSOLA

Most ambitiously: princes' images on their tombs do not lie as
they were wont, seeming to pray up to heaven, but with their
hands under their cheeks as if they died of the toothache. They   145
are not carved with their eyes fixed upon the stars, but as their
minds were wholly bent upon the world the self-same way they
seem to turn their faces.

DUCHESS

Let me know fully therefore the effect
Of this thy dismal preparation,   150
This talk fit for a charnel.

BOSOLA   Now I shall.

[*Enter* EXECUTIONERS *with*] *a* [*shrouded*] *coffin,
cords and a bell*

Here is a present from your princely brothers,
And may it arrive welcome, for it brings
Last benefit, last sorrow.

DUCHESS   Let me see it,
I have so much obedience in my blood   155
I wish it in their veins, to do them good.

BOSOLA

This is your last presence chamber.   [*Reveals the coffin*]

141–8   prose ed. (*Q1 lines ending* -bed / graue / tombes / pray / cheekes / carued / their /
        world / faces).
  152   s.d. The coffin is concealed under a pall or cloth.

CARIOLA
  Oh my sweet lady.
DUCHESS   Peace, it affrights not me.
BOSOLA
  I am the common bell-man,
  That usually is sent to condemned persons   160
  The night before they suffer.
DUCHESS   Even now thou said'st
  Thou wast a tomb-maker.
BOSOLA   'Twas to bring you
  By degrees to mortification. Listen:
    Hark now everything is still,
    The screech owl and the whistler shrill   165
    Call upon our dame, aloud,
    And bid her quickly don her shroud.
    Much you had of land and rent,
    Your length in clay's now competent;
    A long war disturbed your mind,   170
    Here your perfect peace is signed.
    Of what is't fools make such vain keeping?
    Sin their conception, their birth, weeping;
    Their life a general mist of error,
    Their death a hideous storm of terror.   175
    Strew your hair with powders sweet,
    Don clean linen, bathe your feet,
    And (the foul fiend more to check)

159   *bell-man* Here specified apparently to refer to a charity established by the Common
       Council of the Merchant Tailors guild (of which Webster's father was a member)
       which endowed a bell-man at Newgate Prison to make a speech outside the cell of
       condemned men the night before execution and another as they were taken to be
       hanged at Tyburn. Both speeches (accompanied by the tolling of a hand-bell) were
       to put them in mind of their mortality and urge them to save their souls. The bell
       is still extant, and on view in St Sepulchre's church – See Forker, pp. 21–4.
163   *mortification* The spiritual process ending in transcendence of one's earthly concerns
       and appetites (with a play on the sense 'the state of torpor and insensibility preceding
       death').
165   *whistler* Referred to as a fatal bird in Spenser, *Faerie Queene*, 2.12.36.
166   This invocation is the very opposite of that in an epithalamion or marriage-song,
       which conventionally bade such birds be silent on the wedding night.
169   *competent* appropriate, sufficient.
176   The Duchess is to prepare herself for burial in the same manner as a bride – in
       epithalamia brides are bid to strew their hair with sweet powders. A further irony is
       the echo of the Duchess' words at III.ii.58–9.

A crucifix let bless your neck.
'Tis now full tide 'tween night and day,   180
End your groan and come away.

CARIOLA
Hence villains, tyrants, murderers! Alas,
What will you do with my lady? Call for help!

DUCHESS
To whom? To our next neighbours? They are mad folks.

BOSOLA
Remove that noise.

                              [EXECUTIONERS *seize* CARIOLA]

DUCHESS   Farewell Cariola,   185
In my last will I have not much to give:
A many hungry guests have fed upon me.
Thine will be a poor reversion.

CARIOLA
I will die with her.

DUCHESS
I pray thee look thou giv'st my little boy   190
Some syrup for his cold, and let the girl
Say her prayers ere she sleep.

                      [EXECUTIONERS *force* CARIOLA *off*]
                              Now what you please:
What death?

BOSOLA   Strangling. Here are your executioners.

DUCHESS
I forgive them.
The apoplexy, catarrh, or cough o'th'lungs   195
Would do as much as they do.

BOSOLA
Doth not death fright you?

DUCHESS   Who would be afraid on't,
Knowing to meet such excellent company
In th'other world?

BOSOLA   Yet, methinks,
The manner of your death should much afflict you: 200
This cord should terrify you?

DUCHESS   Not a whit.
What would it pleasure me to have my throat cut

188   *reversion* bequest.
197–9 From Montaigne, *Essayes*, p. 75.

With diamonds, or to be smothered
With cassia, or to be shot to death with pearls?
I know death hath ten thousand several doors   205
For men to take their exits; and 'tis found
They go on such strange geometrical hinges,
You may open them both ways – any way, for heaven' sake,
So I were out of your whispering. Tell my brothers
That I perceive death, now I am well awake,   210
Best gift is they can give, or I can take.
I would fain put off my last woman's fault,
I'd not be tedious to you.

EXECUTIONER   We are ready.

DUCHESS
Dispose my breath how please you, but my body
Bestow upon my women: will you?

EXECUTIONER   Yes.   215

DUCHESS
Pull, and pull strongly, for your able strength
Must pull down heaven upon me –
Yet stay, heaven gates are not so highly arched
As princes' palaces: they that enter there
Must go upon their knees. [*Kneels*] Come violent death,   220
Serve for mandragora, to make me sleep.
Go tell my brothers when I am laid out,
They then may feed in quiet.

                                    They strangle her

BOSOLA
Where's the waiting woman?
Fetch her. Some other strangle the children.   225

                    [EXECUTIONERS *fetch* CARIOLA,
                     one goes to strangle the CHILDREN]

Look you, there sleeps your mistress.

CARIOLA   Oh you are damned
Perpetually for this! My turn is next,
Is't not so ordered?

BOSOLA   Yes, and I am glad
You are so well prepared for't.

CARIOLA   You are deceived, sir,
I am not prepared for't! I will not die!   230

205–6   *death . . . exits* From Seneca, and proverbial.
221   *mandragora* mandrake root, used as a narcotic (see II.v.1).

391

I will first come to my answer and know
How I have offended.

BOSOLA   Come, dispatch her.
You kept her counsel, now you shall keep ours.

CARIOLA
I will not die, I must not, I am contracted
To a young gentleman!

EXECUTIONER [*Shows noose*] Here's your wedding ring.   235

CARIOLA
Let me but speak with the Duke: I'll discover
Treason to his person.

BOSOLA   Delays: throttle her.

EXECUTIONER
She bites and scratches!

CARIOLA   If you kill me now
I am damned! I have not been at confession
This two years.

BOSOLA   When.

CARIOLA   I am quick with child.

BOSOLA   Why then,   240
Your credit's saved.

                                        [*They strangle her*]
                        Bear her into th'next room.
Let this lie still.

                        [*Exeunt* EXECUTIONERS *with* CARIOLA'*s body*]

                        [*Enter* FERDINAND]

FERDINAND   Is she dead?

BOSOLA   She is what
You'd have her. But here begin your pity.
                        [*Draws the traverse and*] *shows the children strangled*
Alas, how have these offended?

FERDINAND   The death
Of young wolves is never to be pitied.   245

BOSOLA
Fix your eye here.

FERDINAND   Constantly.

BOSOLA   Do you not weep?

---

241   *credit* reputation.
242–6 ed. (Let . . . still / Is . . . dead / She is what / You'll'd . . . pitty / Alas . . . offended / The
       death / Of . . . pittied / Fix . . . here / Constantly / Do . . . weepe Q1).
243   s.d. A grim repetition of the s.d. at IV.i.54.

Other sins only speak; murder shrieks out.
The element of water moistens the earth,
But blood flies upwards and bedews the heavens.

FERDINAND
Cover her face. Mine eyes dazzle. She died young.   250

BOSOLA
I think not so; her infelicity
Seemed to have years too many.

FERDINAND   She and I were twins,
And should I die this instant I had lived
Her time to a minute.

BOSOLA   It seems she was born first: 255
You have bloodily approved the ancient truth
That kindred commonly do worse agree
Than remote strangers.

FERDINAND   Let me see her face again.
Why didst not thou pity her? What an excellent
Honest man might'st thou have been   260
If thou hadst borne her to some sanctuary
Or, bold in a good cause, opposed thyself
With thy advanced sword above thy head
Between her innocence and my revenge!
I bade thee, when I was distracted of my wits,   265
Go kill my dearest friend, and thou hast done't!
For let me but examine well the cause:
What was the meanness of her match to me?
Only, I must confess, I had a hope –
Had she continued widow – to have gained   270
An infinite mass of treasure by her death:

---

250   *Mine eyes dazzle* In IV.i The Duchess is associated with light, Ferdinand with
       darkness both spiritual and actual: he insists on visiting her in darkness, and later,
       in V.ii.62 speaks of his cruel sore eyes. See also lines 320–1 below; *dazzle* could also
       refer to the welling up of tears in Ferdinand's eyes – see Martin Wiggins, N&Q (Sep.
       1995) 372.

269–71 This constitutes an anomaly. At III.iii.66–7 it is asserted that the Duchess has a son
       by her first marriage. This corresponds to the sources but could be a relic of an early
       draft, a detail Webster accidentally failed to cancel, since if it is accepted it means that
       here Ferdinand – of all people – has somehow forgotten about his existence,
       although Webster makes Ferdinand the only person elsewhere in the play (III.iii.67)
       who refers to him: 'the Duke of Malfi, my young nephew'. Brown assumes Webster
       did intend to retain this son by the first marriage of the Duchess, and that here
       Ferdinand is deliberately trying to deceive Bosola or is making 'an instinctive'

And that was the main cause. Her marriage,
That drew a stream of gall quite through my heart.
For thee – as we observe in tragedies
That a good actor many times is cursed   275
For playing a villain's part – I hate thee for't;
And for my sake say, thou hast done much ill, well.

BOSOLA

Let me quicken your memory, for I perceive
You are falling into ingratitude: I challenge
The reward due to my service.

FERDINAND   I'll tell thee   280
What I'll give thee.

BOSOLA   Do.

FERDINAND   I'll give thee a pardon
For this murder.

BOSOLA   Ha?

FERDINAND   Yes: and 'tis
The largest bounty I can study to do thee.
By what authority did'st thou execute
This bloody sentence?

BOSOLA   By yours.

FERDINAND   Mine? Was I her judge?   285
Did any ceremonial form of law
Doom her to not-being? Did a complete jury
Deliver her conviction up i'th'court?
Where shalt thou find this judgement registered
Unless in hell? See, like a bloody fool   290
Th'hast forfeited thy life, and thou shalt die for't.

BOSOLA

The office of justice is perverted quite
When one thief hangs another. Who shall dare
To reveal this?

---

attempt to 'cover up' feelings of 'guilt'. Yet if it is assumed that Webster intends there
to be this son by the first marriage, then the first child the audience know about,
the first-born to the Duchess and Antonio, could inherit nothing except such
personal property as the Duchess is entitled to by her first marriage settlement and
/ or the dower after her first husband's death – scarcely an 'infinite mass of treasure'.
But the son born in Act II is presented in the closing moments of the play as a
symbol of hope for the future, so in performance it looks as if Webster did intend
to cancel the son by the first marriage.

274–91 A close parallel to Shakespeare, *Richard II*, V.vi.30–44, where Bolingbroke refuses to
reward the murderer of the King.

FERDINAND   Oh, I'll tell thee:
  The wolf shall find her grave and scrape it up,   295
  Not to devour the corpse but to discover
  The horrid murder.
BOSOLA   You, not I, shall quake for't.
FERDINAND
  Leave me.
BOSOLA   I will first receive my pension.
FERDINAND
  You are a villain.
BOSOLA   When your ingratitude
  Is judge, I am so.
FERDINAND   O horror,   300
  That not the fear of him which binds the devils
  Can prescribe man obedience.
  Never look upon me more.
BOSOLA   Why fare thee well.
  Your brother and yourself are worthy men,
  You have a pair of hearts are hollow graves,   305
  Rotten, and rotting others; and your vengeance,
  Like two chained bullets, still goes arm in arm.
  You may be brothers: for treason, like the plague,
  Doth take much in a blood. I stand like one
  That long hath ta'en a sweet and golden dream: 310
  I am angry with myself now that I wake.
FERDINAND
  Get thee into some unknown part o'th'world
  That I may never see thee.
BOSOLA   Let me know
  Wherefore I should be thus neglected. Sir,
  I served your tyranny, and rather strove   315
  To satisfy yourself than all the world;
  And though I loathed the evil yet I loved
  You, that did counsel it, and rather sought
  To appear a true servant than an honest man.

295–7   This superstition is referred to in *The White Devil*, V.iv.100–101.
   307   *chained bullets* Cannon-balls linked by chain were used mainly in naval warfare to
          destroy masts and rigging but would also cut swathes through infantry in close
          order.
   309   *take . . . blood* take hold in certain families.

FERDINAND

> I'll go hunt the badger, by owl-light: 320
> 'Tis a deed of darkness. *Exit*

BOSOLA

> He's much distracted. Off, my painted honour;
> While with vain hopes our faculties we tire,
> We seem to sweat in ice, and freeze in fire;
> What would I do, were this to do again? 325
> I would not change my peace of conscience
> For all the wealth of Europe –
>
> [DUCHESS *moves*]
> She stirs! Here's life!
> Return fair soul from darkness, and lead mine
> Out of this sensible hell! She's warm, she breathes:
> Upon thy pale lips I will melt my heart 330
> To store them with fresh colour. [*Kisses her*] Who's there –
> Some cordial drink! – Alas, I dare not call;
> So pity would destroy pity. Her eye opes,
> And heaven in it seems to ope, that late was shut,
> To take me up to mercy.

DUCHESS Antonio. 335

BOSOLA

> Yes Madam he is living,
> The dead bodies you saw were but feigned statues,
> He's reconciled to your brothers, the Pope hath wrought
> The atonement.

DUCHESS Mercy. *She dies*

BOSOLA

> Oh, she's gone again: there the cords of life broke. 340
> Oh sacred innocence that sweetly sleeps
> On turtles' feathers, whilst a guilty conscience
> Is a black register wherein is writ
> All our good deeds and bad, a perspective

320 *owl-light* dusk.
327 s.d. Recalling the momentary revival of Desdemona in *Othello*, V.ii.117–25.
329 *sensible* perceptible, palpable.
332 *cordial* invigorating to the heart, reviving.
335 *mercy* ed. (merry Q1).
340 *cords of life* heart-strings.
344 *perspective* An optical device using mirrors, lenses etc. to produce special or fantastic effects. The effect of a guilty conscience is to rearrange past deeds, both good and bad, into a distorted prospect showing hell.

That shows us hell – that we cannot be suffered   345
To do good when we have a mind to it!
This is manly sorrow:
These tears, I am very certain, never grew
In my mother's milk. My estate is sunk
Below the degree of fear: where were   350
These penitent fountains while she was living?
Oh, they were frozen up. Here is a sight
As direful to my soul as is the sword
Unto a wretch hath slain his father.
Come, I'll bear thee hence   355
And execute thy last will; that's deliver
Thy body to the reverend dispose
Of some good women: that the cruel tyrant
Shall not deny me: then I'll post to Milan,
Where somewhat I will speedily enact   360
Worth my dejection.

Exit [*with the* DUCHESS' *body*]

354–5   ed. (*one line* Q1).
   361   *dejection* dismissal, humiliation.

ACT V, SCENE i

[*Enter* ANTONIO, DELIO]

ANTONIO

What think you of my hope of reconcilement
To the Aragonian brethren?

DELIO   I misdoubt it;
For though they have sent their letters of safe conduct
For your repair to Milan, they appear
But nets to entrap you. The Marquis of Pescara,   5
Under whom you hold certain land in cheat,
Much 'gainst his noble nature hath been moved
To seize those lands, and some of his dependants
Are at this instant making it their suit
To be invested in your revenues.   10
I cannot think they mean well to your life
That do deprive you of your means of life –
Your living.

ANTONIO   You are still an heretic
To any safety I can shape myself.

[*Enter* PESCARA]

DELIO

Here comes the Marquis: I will make myself   15
Petitioner for some part of your land,
To know whether it is flying.

ANTONIO   I pray do.   [*Withdraws*]

DELIO

Sir, I have a suit to you.

PESCARA   To me?

DELIO   An easy one:
There is the citadel of Saint Bennet,
With some demesnes, of late in the possession   20
Of Antonio Bologna; please you bestow them on me?

---

  0   s.d. ed. (ACTVS V. SCENA. I. / *Antonio, Delio, Pescara, Iulia.* Q1).
  6   *in cheat* The property would revert to Pescara should Antonio be convicted of
      treason or felony (as seems to be the case).
11–12 Recalling *Merchant of Venice*, IV.i.376–7.
 13   ed. (Your living / You . . . heretique Q1).

PESCARA
  You are my friend: But this is such a suit
  Nor fit for me to give nor you to take.
DELIO
  No sir?

[*Enter* JULIA]

PESCARA
  I will give you ample reason for't   25
  Soon in private. Here's the Cardinal's mistress.
JULIA
  My lord, I am grown your poor petitioner,
  And should be an ill beggar, had I not
  A great man's letter, here, the Cardinal's,   [*Presents letter*]
  To court you in my favour.
PESCARA   He entreats for you   30
  The citadel of Saint Bennet, that belonged
  To the banished Bologna.
JULIA   Yes.
PESCARA
  I could not have thought of a friend I could
  Rather pleasure with it: 'tis yours.
JULIA   Sir, I thank you,
  And he shall know how doubly I am engaged   35
  Both in your gift and speediness of giving,
  Which makes your grant the greater.   *Exit*
ANTONIO [*Aside*]   How they fortify
  Themselves with my ruin!
DELIO   Sir, I am
  Little bound to you.
PESCARA   Why?
DELIO
  Because you denied this suit to me, and gave't   40
  To such a creature.
PESCARA   Do you know what it was?
  It was Antonio's land: not forfeited
  By course of law but ravished from his throat
  By the Cardinal's entreaty: it were not fit
  I should bestow so main a piece of wrong   45
  Upon my friend, 'tis a gratification
  Only due to a strumpet, for it is injustice.

Shall I sprinkle the pure blood of innocents
To make those followers I call my friends
Look ruddier upon me? I am glad   50
This land, ta'en from the owner by such wrong,
Returns again unto so foul an use
As salary for his lust. Learn, good Delio,
To ask noble things of me, and you shall find
I'll be a noble giver.

DELIO   You instruct me well.   55

ANTONIO [Aside]
Why, here's a man, now, would fright impudence
From sauciest beggars.

PESCARA   Prince Ferdinand's come to Milan
Sick, as they give out, of an apoplexy;
But some say, 'tis a frenzy. I am going
To visit him.   Exit

ANTONIO [Coming forward] 'Tis a noble old fellow.   60

DELIO
What course do you mean to take, Antonio?

ANTONIO
This night I mean to venture all my fortune
Which is no more than a poor lingering life
To the Cardinal's worst of malice. I have got
Private access to his chamber and intend   65
To visit him about the mid of night
As once his brother did our noble Duchess.
It may be that the sudden apprehension
Of danger – for I'll go in mine own shape –
When he shall see it fraught with love and duty,   70
May draw the poison out of him, and work
A friendly reconcilement. If it fail,
Yet it shall rid me of this infamous calling:
For better fall once than be ever falling.

DELIO
I'll second you in all danger, and howe'er,   75
My life keeps rank with yours.

ANTONIO
You are still my loved and best friend.

                                                    Exeunt

59   *frenzy* inflammation of the brain.
70   *fraught* ed. (fraight Q1).

[ACT V,] SCENE ii

[*Enter* PESCARA *and a* DOCTOR]

PESCARA

Now Doctor, may I visit your patient?

DOCTOR

If 't please your lordship: but he's instantly
To take the air here in the gallery,
By my direction.

PESCARA   Pray thee, what's his disease?

DOCTOR

A very pestilent disease, my lord,   5
They call lycanthropia.

PESCARA   What's that?

I need a dictionary to't.

DOCTOR   I'll tell you:

In those that are possessed with't there o'er-flows
Such melancholy humour they imagine
Themselves to be transformed into wolves: 10
Steal forth to church-yards in the dead of night
And dig dead bodies up: as two nights since
One met the Duke 'bout midnight in a lane
Behind St Mark's church, with the leg of a man
Upon his shoulder; and he howled fearfully;   15
Said he was a wolf, only the difference
Was, a wolf's skin was hairy on the outside,
His on the inside; bad them take their swords,

---

0   s.d. ed. (*SCENA. II. / Pescara, a Doctor, Ferdinand, Cardinall, Malateste, Bosola, Iulia.*
     Q1).

6   *lycanthropia* The name and the details in lines 8–19 come from Simon Goulart,
     Admirable and Memorable Histories (1607). Apparently lycanthropia was a
     fashionable subject for intellectuals: Donne owned a copy of Claude Prieur's
     *Dialogue de la lycanthropie, ou transformation d'hommes en loups, vulgairement dits
     loups-garous, et si telle se peut faire: auquel en discourant est traicté de la maniere de
     se contregarder des enchantements et sorcelleries, ensemble de plusiers abus et
     superstitions, lesquelles se commettent en ce temps*, Louvain, 1596 – see Jonathan Bate
     and Dora Thornton, *Shakespeare Staging the World*, 2012, p. 246.

14   *St Mark's church* Since no such church was located within the City of London,
     Marcus speculates that for audiences unfamiliar with Italy the name would probably
     have suggested the famous St Mark's in Venice rather than the less prominent one
     in Milan.

Rip up his flesh, and try. Straight I was sent for,
And having ministered to him, found his grace   20
Very well recovered.

PESCARA   I am glad on't.

DOCTOR

Yet not without some fear of a relapse:
If he grow to his fit again I'll go
A nearer way to work with him than ever
Paracelsus dreamed of: if they'll give me   25
Leave I'll buffet his madness out of him.
Stand aside, he comes.

[*Enter* CARDINAL, FERDINAND, MALATESTE,
and BOSOLA, *who stays apart*]

FERDINAND

Leave me.

MALATESTE

Why doth your lordship love this solitariness?

FERDINAND

Eagles commonly fly alone: they are crows, daws and starlings   30
that flock together. – Look, what's that follows me?

MALATESTE

Nothing, my lord.

FERDINAND

Yes.

MALATESTE

'Tis your shadow.

FERDINAND

Stay it, let it not haunt me.   35

MALATESTE

Impossible, if you move, and the sun shine.

FERDINAND

I will throttle it.

[*Throws himself on the ground*]

MALATESTE

---

25   *Paracelsus* Swiss physician and alchemist (1493–1541), famous as a serious scientist
     and physician while also the subject of many tall stories.
30–35   prose ed. (*Q1 lines ending* and / that / me / Lord / Yes / shadow / me).
31   *what's . . . me* There are proverbs, 'to be afraid of one's own shadow' and 'to fight with
     one's own shadow', but closer to the case of Ferdinand is an emblem for guilt in
     Whitney's *Choice of Emblemes* showing a man holding a sword fearing his own
     shadow. See R. E. R. Madeleine, *N&Q* (1982) 146.

Oh, my lord, you are angry with nothing.

FERDINAND

You are a fool. How is't possible I should catch my shadow
unless I fall upon't? When I go to hell, I mean to carry a bribe,   40
for look you, good gifts evermore make way for the worst
persons.

PESCARA

Rise, good my lord.

FERDINAND

I am studying the art of patience.

PESCARA

'Tis a noble virtue.   45

FERDINAND

To drive six snails before me, from this town to Moscow –
neither use goad nor whip to them, but let them take their own
time – the patient'st man i'th'world match me for an experi-
ment – and I'll crawl after like a sheep-biter.

CARDINAL

Force him up.   50

                              [*They get* FERDINAND *to his feet*]

FERDINAND

Use me well, you were best: what I have done, I have done, I'll
confess nothing.

DOCTOR

Now let me come to him. Are you mad, my lord? Are you out
of your princely wits?

FERDINAND

What's he?   55

PESCARA

Your doctor.

FERDINAND

Let me have his beard sawed off, and his eye-brows filed more
civil.

39–42   prose ed. (*Q1 lines ending* foole / shadow / Hell / you / persons).
46–9   prose ed. (*Q1 lines ending* towne / them / world / after / -biter).
   49   *sheep-biter* dog that bites or worries sheep.
51–2   *what . . . nothing* Recalling *Othello*, V.ii.303–4.
51–4   prose ed. (*Q1 lines ending* best / nothing / mad / wits).
57–61   prose ed. (*Q1 lines ending* eye /civill / him / brought / you / -burning).
56–7   NCW suggest that if the part of Doctor is doubled by the boy-actor who earlier
        played Cariola, the exaggerated false beard and eyebrows (conventional comedy
        make-up) make appropriate heavy disguise for the actor.

DOCTOR

I must do mad tricks with him, for that's the only way on't. I
have brought your grace a salamander's skin, to keep you from   60
sun-burning.

FERDINAND

I have cruel sore eyes.

DOCTOR

The white of a cocatrice's egg is present remedy.

FERDINAND

Let it be a new laid one, you were best. – Hide me from him.
Physicians are like kings, they brook no contradiction.   65

DOCTOR

Now he begins to fear me, now let me alone with him.

CARDINAL

How now, put off your gown?

DOCTOR

Let me have some forty urinals filled with rose water: he and
I'll go pelt one another with them. Now he begins to fear me. –
Can you fetch a frisk, sir? – Let him go, let him go, upon my   70
peril.

                              [*They release* FERDINAND]
I find by his eye he stands in awe of me, I'll make him as tame
as a dormouse.

                              [FERDINAND *attacks the* DOCTOR]
FERDINAND

Can you fetch your frisks, sir? I will stamp him into a cullis, flay
off his skin to cover one of the anatomies this rogue hath set   75
i'th'cold yonder – in Barber Surgeons' hall! Hence! Hence! You
are all of you like beasts for sacrifice! There's nothing left of you
but tongue and belly, flattery and lechery!   [*Exit*]

---

60 *salamander's* The salamander was believed to live in fire.
63 *cockatrice's* the basilisk – see III.ii.87 n.
64–6 prose ed. (*Q1 lines ending* best / Kings / contradiction / me / him).
68–78 prose ed. (*Q1 lines ending* water / them / sir / perill / me / Dormouse / Cullice /
      Anotomies / hall / sacrifice / belly / leachery).
70 *fetch a frisk* cut a caper.
74 *cullis* meat broth.
75 *anatomies* skeletons.
76 *Barber Surgeons' hall* This chartered company was entitled to claim four corpses of
      executed felons per year for surgical dissection and experiment: it displayed
      specimen skeletons in the company's hall in Monkswell Street, Cripplegate.

PESCARA
    Doctor, he did not fear you throughly.
DOCTOR
    True, I was somewhat too forward.   [*Exit*]   80
BOSOLA [*Aside*]
    Mercy upon me, what a fatal judgement
    Hath fallen upon this Ferdinand.
PESCARA   Knows your grace
    What accident hath brought unto the Prince
    This strange distraction?
CARDINAL [*Aside*]
    I must feign somewhat. [*Aloud*] Thus they say it grew: 85
    You have heard it rumoured for these many years,
    None of our family dies but there is seen
    The shape of an old woman, which is given
    By tradition to us, to have been murdered
    By her nephews for her riches. Such a figure   90
    One night, as the Prince sat up late at's book,
    Appeared to him: when crying out for help,
    The gentlemen of 's chamber found his grace
    All on a cold sweat, altered much in face
    And language; since which apparition   95
    He hath grown worse and worse, and I much fear
    He cannot live.
BOSOLA [*To* CARDINAL]
    Sir, I would speak with you.
PESCARA   We'll leave your grace,
    Wishing to the sick Prince, our noble lord,
    All health of mind and body.
CARDINAL   You are most welcome.   100
                    [*Exeunt all except* CARDINAL *and* BOSOLA]
    Are you come? [*Aside*] So: this fellow must not know
    By any means I had intelligence
    In our Duchess' death, for though I counselled it,
    The full of all th'engagement seemed to grow
    From Ferdinand. [*To* BOSOLA] Now sir, how fares our sister?   105
    I do not think but sorrow makes her look
    Like to an oft-dyed garment: she shall now
    Taste comfort from me. Why do you look so wildly?
    Oh, the fortune of your master here, the Prince,

104   *engagement* employment (of Bosola).

405

Dejects you? But be you of happy comfort. 110
If you'll do one thing for me, I'll entreat
Though he had a cold tombstone o'er his bones
I'd make you what you would be.

BOSOLA   Any thing:
Give it me in a breath, and let me fly to't.
They that think long, small expedition win, 115
For musing much o'th'end, cannot begin.

                    [*Enter* JULIA]

JULIA
Sir, will you come in to supper?
CARDINAL   I am busy, leave me.
JULIA [*Aside*]
What an excellent shape hath that fellow!   *Exit*
CARDINAL
'Tis thus: Antonio lurks here in Milan,
Enquire him out, and kill him. While he lives 120
Our sister cannot marry, and I have thought
Of an excellent match for her. Do this, and style me
Thy advancement.
BOSOLA   But by what means shall I find him out?
CARDINAL
There is a gentleman called Delio
Here in the camp, that hath been long approved 125
His loyal friend: set eye upon that fellow,
Follow him to Mass; may be Antonio,
Although he do account religion
But a school-name, for fashion of the world,
May accompany him; or else go enquire out 130
Delio's confessor, and see if you can bribe
Him to reveal it. There are a thousand ways
A man might find to trace him, as to know
What fellows haunt the Jews for taking up
Great sums of money – for sure he's in want – 135

---

111   *one* ed. (on Q1).
125   *camp* Reminding the audience that the Cardinal has turned soldier (Brennan).
129   *school-name* From Sidney, *Arcadia* (*Works* II. 133): 'As for vertue, hee counted it but
        a schoole name' – a disparaging reference to the 'Schoolmen' of scholastic
        philosophy. Brown cites Bacon's view (*Advancement of Learning* I) that they
        produced 'cobwebs of learning, admirable for the fineness of thread and work, but
        of no substance or profit'.

Or else to go to th'picture makers and learn
Who brought her picture lately – some of these
Happily may take.

BOSOLA   Well, I'll not freeze i'th' business,
I would see that wretched thing Antonio
Above all sights i'th'world.

CARDINAL   Do, and be happy.   *Exit*   140

BOSOLA
This fellow doth breed basilisks in's eyes,
He's nothing else but murder; yet he seems
Not to have notice of the Duchess' death.
'Tis his cunning: I must follow his example,
There cannot be a surer way to trace   145
Than that of an old fox.

                    [*Enter* JULIA *pointing a pistol at him*]

JULIA   So, sir, you are well met.

BOSOLA
How now?

JULIA   Nay, the doors are fast enough.
Now sir, I will make you confess your treachery.

BOSOLA
Treachery?

JULIA   Yes, confess to me
Which of my women 'twas you hired, to put   150
Love-powder into my drink?

BOSOLA   Love powder?

JULIA
Yes, when I was at Malfi,
Why should I fall in love with such a face else?
I have already suffered for thee so much pain,
The only remedy to do me good   155
Is to kill my longing.

BOSOLA   Sure your pistol holds
Nothing but perfumes or kissing comfits; excellent lady,
You have a pretty way on't to discover

---

141   *basilisks* See III.ii.87 n.
146   s.d. Webster's stagecraft makes Julia's return parallel with Antonio's return, also
       carrying a pistol, at III.ii.140. Then Julia's wooing of Bosola is parallel (though clearly
       contrasting) to that of the Duchess' wooing of Antonio in Act I.
157   *kissing comfits* sweets perfumed to sweeten the breath.

Your longing: come, come, I'll disarm you,
And arm you thus.   [*Embracing her*]
                    Yet this is wondrous strange.   160

JULIA

Compare thy form and my eyes together,
You'll find my love no such great miracle. Now you'll say
I am wanton; this nice modesty in ladies
Is but a troublesome familiar
That haunts them.   165

BOSOLA

Know you me. I am a blunt soldier.

JULIA   The better,
Sure. There wants fire, where there are no lively sparks
Of roughness.

BOSOLA   And I want compliment.

JULIA   Why, ignorance
In courtship cannot make you do amiss
If you have a heart to do well.

BOSOLA   You are very fair.   170

JULIA

Nay, if you lay beauty to my charge
I must plead unguilty.

BOSOLA   Your bright eyes
Carry a quiver of darts in them sharper
Than sun-beams.

JULIA   You will mar me with commendation,
Put yourself to the charge of courting me,   175
Whereas now I woo you.

BOSOLA [*Aside*]

I have it, I will work upon this creature. –
[*To* JULIA] Let us grow most amorously familiar.
If the great Cardinal now should see me thus,
Would he not count me a villain?   180

JULIA

No, he might count me a wanton,
Not lay a scruple of offence on you:
For if I see and steal a diamond,
The fault is not i'th'stone but in me the thief

167–8   *fire ... roughness* From Sidney, *Arcadia* (*Works* I. 452–3).
168–9   ed. (Of ... roughnes / And ... compliment / Why ... amisse Q1).
168–70 *ignorance ... well* From Sidney, *Arcadia* (*Works* I. 106).

That purloins it. I am sudden with you: 185
We that are great women of pleasure, use to cut off
These uncertain wishes and unquiet longings
And in an instant join the sweet delight
And the pretty excuse together. Had you been in th'street,
Under my chamber window, even there 190
I should have courted you.
BOSOLA   Oh, you are an excellent lady.
JULIA
Bid me do somewhat for you presently
To express I love you.
BOSOLA   I will; and if you love me,
Fail not to effect it.
The Cardinal is grown wondrous melancholy: 195
Demand the cause, let him not put you off
With feigned excuse; discover the main ground on't.
JULIA
Why would you know this?
BOSOLA   I have depended on him,
And I hear that he is fallen in some disgrace
With the Emperor. If he be, like the mice 200
That forsake falling houses, I would shift
To other dependence.
JULIA   You shall not need follow the wars,
I'll be your maintenance.
BOSOLA   And I your loyal servant;
But I cannot leave my calling.
JULIA   Not leave an
Ungrateful general, for the love of a sweet lady? 205
You are like some cannot sleep in feather-beds,
But must have blocks for their pillows.
BOSOLA   Will you do this?
JULIA
Cunningly.
BOSOLA   Tomorrow I'll expect th'intelligence.
JULIA
Tomorrow? Get you into my cabinet,

187–9   *wishes . . . excuse* From Sidney, *Arcadia* (*Works* I. 452).
191   ed. (I . . . you / Oh . . . Lady Q1).
193   ed. (To . . . you / I . . . me Q1).
194–5   ed. (Fail . . . mellancholly Q1).

You shall have it with you. Do not delay me, 210
No more than I do you. I am like one
That is condemned: I have my pardon promised,
But I would see it sealed. Go, get you in,
You shall see me wind my tongue about his heart
Like a skein of silk. 215

[*Exit* BOSOLA]

[*Enter* CARDINAL *followed by* SERVANTS]

CARDINAL
    Where are you?
SERVANTS   Here.
CARDINAL   Let none upon your lives
    Have conference with the Prince Ferdinand
    Unless I know it.

                        [*Exeunt* SERVANTS]

    [*Aside*]   In this distraction
    He may reveal the murder.
    Yond's my lingering consumption: 220
    I am weary of her and by any means
    Would be quit off.
JULIA   How now, my lord,
    What ails you?
CARDINAL   Nothing.
JULIA   Oh, you are much altered.
    Come, I must be your secretary and remove
    This lead from off your bosom. What's the matter? 225
CARDINAL
    I may not tell you.
JULIA   Are you so far in love with sorrow
    You cannot part with part of it? Or think you
    I cannot love your grace when you are sad,
    As well as merry? Or do you suspect
    I, that have been a secret to your heart 230
    These many winters, cannot be the same
    Unto your tongue?
CARDINAL   Satisfy thy longing,
    The only way to make thee keep my counsel
    Is not to tell thee.

_____

210–13 *delay . . . sealed* From Sidney, *Arcadia* (*Works* II. 31).

JULIA   Tell your echo this –
  Or flatterers, that like echoes still report   235
  What they hear, though most imperfect – and not me:
  For if that you be true unto yourself,
  I'll know.
CARDINAL   Will you rack me?
JULIA   No, judgement shall
  Draw it from you. It is an equal fault,
  To tell one's secrets unto all, or none.   240
CARDINAL
  The first argues folly.
JULIA   But the last tyranny.
CARDINAL
  Very well – why, imagine I have committed
  Some secret deed which I desire the world
  May never hear of.
JULIA   Therefore may not I know it?
  You have concealed for me as great a sin   245
  As adultery: sir, never was occasion
  For perfect trial of my constancy
  Till now: sir, I beseech you.
CARDINAL   You'll repent it.
JULIA   Never.
CARDINAL
  It hurries thee to ruin. I'll not tell thee,
  Be well advised, and think what danger 'tis   250
  To receive a prince's secrets: they that do
  Had need have their breasts hooped with adamant
  To contain them. I pray thee yet be satisfied,
  Examine thine own frailty; 'tis more easy
  To tie knots than unloose them: 'tis a secret   255
  That like a ling'ring poison may chance lie
  Spread in thy veins, and kill thee seven year hence.
JULIA
  Now you dally with me.
CARDINAL   No more: thou shalt know it.
  By my appointment the great Duchess of Malfi
  And two of her young children, four nights since   260
  Were strangled.
JULIA   Oh heaven! Sir, what have you done!

CARDINAL
   How now, how settles this? Think you, your
   Bosom will be a grave dark and obscure enough
   For such a secret?
JULIA   You have undone yourself, sir.
CARDINAL
   Why?
JULIA   It lies not in me to conceal it.   265
CARDINAL
   No? Come, I will swear you to't upon this book.
JULIA
   Most religiously.
CARDINAL   Kiss it.

                                 [She kisses the book]
   Now you shall never utter it. Thy curiosity
   Hath undone thee. Thou'rt poisoned with that book;
   Because I knew thou couldst not keep my counsel,   270
   I have bound thee to't by death.

               [Enter BOSOLA*]*

BOSOLA
   For pity sake, hold!
CARDINAL   Ha, Bosola!
JULIA   I forgive you
   This equal piece of justice you have done,
   For I betrayed your counsel to that fellow,
   He overheard it: that was the cause I said   275
   It lay not in me to conceal it.
BOSOLA   Oh foolish woman,
   Couldst not thou have poisoned him?
JULIA   'Tis weakness
   Too much to think what should have been done.
   I go I know not whither.   *[She dies]*
CARDINAL
   Wherefore com'st thou hither?   280
BOSOLA
   That I might find a great man like yourself,

---

267   *religiously* If Julia kneels the spectators will recognise a visual parallel with the death
      of the Duchess; at the same time Julia dies with the conventional words of a dying
      sinner, contrasting to the firm faith of the Duchess.
271   *thee* ed. (the Q1).

Not out of his wits as the Lord Ferdinand,
To remember my service.

CARDINAL   I'll have thee hewed in pieces!

BOSOLA
Make not yourself such a promise of that life
Which is not yours to dispose of.   285

CARDINAL
Who placed thee here?

BOSOLA   Her lust, as she intended.

CARDINAL
Very well, now you know me for your fellow murderer.

BOSOLA
And wherefore should you lay fair marble colours
Upon your rotten purposes to me,
Unless you imitate some that do plot great treasons   290
And, when they have done, go hide themselves i'th'graves
Of those were actors in't?

CARDINAL   No more,
There is a fortune attends thee.

BOSOLA
Shall I go sue to Fortune any longer?
'Tis the fool's pilgrimage.   295

CARDINAL
I have honours in store for thee.

BOSOLA
There are a many ways that conduct to seeming
Honour, and some of them very dirty ones.

CARDINAL
Throw to the devil
Thy melancholy. The fire burns well,   300
What need we keep a stirring of it, and make
A greater smother? Thou wilt kill Antonio?

BOSOLA
Yes.

CARDINAL Take up that body.

BOSOLA   I think I shall
Shortly grow the common bier for church-yards.

288–9   A further metaphor from painting, the wording close to Sidney, *Arcadia*, (*Works* I. 260).

297–8   For the proverbial quality of this remark compare Francis Bacon's observation that the roads to riches are many and most of them foul.

CARDINAL

    I will allow thee some dozen of attendants   305
    To aid thee in the murder.

BOSOLA   Oh, by no means.

    Physicians that apply horse-leeches to any rank swelling, use
    to cut off their tails, that the blood may run through them the
    faster: let me have no train when I go to shed blood, lest it make
    me have a greater when I ride to the gallows.   310

CARDINAL

    Come to me after midnight to help to remove that body to her
    own lodging: I'll give out she died o'th'plague, 'twill breed the
    less enquiry after her death.

BOSOLA

    Where's Castruchio, her husband?

CARDINAL

    He's rode to Naples to take possession of Antonio's citadel.   315

BOSOLA

    Believe me, you have done a very happy turn.

CARDINAL

    Fail not to come. There is the master-key
    Of our lodgings, and by that you may conceive
    What trust I plant in you.   *Exit*

BOSOLA   You shall find me ready.

    Oh poor Antonio, though nothing be so needful   320
    To thy estate as pity, yet I find
    Nothing so dangerous. I must look to my footing;
    In such slippery ice-pavements men had need
    To be frost-nailed well, they may break their necks else.
    The precedent's here afore me: how this man   325
    Bears up in blood, seems fearless! Why, 'tis well:
    Security some men call the suburbs of hell,
    Only a dead wall between. Well, good Antonio,
    I'll seek thee out, and all my care shall be

307–13 prose ed. (*Q1 lines ending* swelling / them / blood / Gallowes / body / Plague / death).
317 *master-key* A parallel to Bosola's procuring for Ferdinand the key to the Duchess'
      bedchamber in III.i.80.
325 *precedent's* ed. (President's Q1).
326 *Bears up in blood* Probably deriving from hunting terms – 'keeps his courage' (so
      Lucas); Brown suggests 'persists in shedding blood'.
327 *Security* If of the spiritual kind, security was believed dangerous because implying
      undue confidence in salvation; if carnal, dangerous because implying undue concern
      for this life and indifference to the next world.
328 *dead* continuous.

To put thee into safety from the reach 330
Of these most cruel biters that have got
Some of thy blood already. It may be
I'll join with thee in a most just revenge:
The weakest arm is strong enough that strikes
With the sword of justice. – Still methinks the Duchess 335
Haunts me! There there, 'tis nothing but my melancholy.
O penitence, let me truly taste thy cup,
That throws men down, only to raise them up.

Exit [*with* JULIA's *body*]

[ACT V,] SCENE iii

[*Enter* ANTONIO *and* DELIO]

DELIO
Yond's the Cardinal's window. This fortification
Grew from the ruins of an ancient abbey,
And to yond side o'th'river lies a wall,
Piece of a cloister, which in my opinion
Gives the best echo that you ever heard, 5

---

338   s.d. A visual parallel to Bosola's previous exit with the Duchess' body in IV.ii.

0   s.d. ed. (SCENA III. / *Antonio, Delio, Eccho, (from the Dutchesse Graue.*) Q1).

0   s.d. The s.d. for Echo seems to be directed to readers; it makes no reference to any
visual special effect, and Delio does say (45) that Antonio only imagines seeing the
Duchess' face; but Antonio's description (44–5), as Brown notes, corresponds to a
s.d. in *The Second Maiden's Tragedy* (acted by the King's Men in 1611):
>   *On a sodayne in a kinde of Noyse like a Wynde, the dores clattering, the Toombstone
>   flies open, and a great light appears in the midst of the Toombe; His Lady as went
>   owt, standing iust before hym all in white, Stuck with Iewells and a great crucifex
>   on her brest.*

Webster perhaps saw this piece of machinery among the properties of the King's
Men.

1   *Yond* In the original performance Delio presumably would point to the tiring-house
backing the stage (with its openings at the upper level) to indicate the exterior of the
Cardinal's house. Antonio's reference to *here in this open court* presumably indicates
the main stage where they stand; other features – the wall and *piece of a cloister* –
could be left wholly to the spectator's imagination. The echoes would be spoken offstage by the actor who played the Duchess. If an actual tomb-property was used, it
was probably placed in the central opening in the tiring-house.

So hollow and so dismal and withal
So plain in the distinction of our words
That many have supposed it is a spirit
That answers.
ANTONIO   I do love these ancient ruins.
We never tread upon them but we set   10
Our foot upon some reverend history,
And questionless, here in this open court
Which now lies naked to the injuries
Of stormy weather, some men lie interred
Loved the church so well, and gave so largely to't,   15
They thought it should have canopied their bones
Till doomsday; but all things have their end:
Churches and cities, which have diseases like to men,
Must have like death that we have.
ECHO   *Like death that we have.*
DELIO
Now the echo hath caught you.
ANTONIO   It groaned, methought, and gave   20
A very deadly accent.
ECHO   *Deadly accent.*
DELIO
I told you 'twas a pretty one: you may make it
A huntsman, or a falconer, a musician,
Or a thing of sorrow.
ECHO   *A thing of sorrow.*
ANTONIO
Ay sure, that suits it best.
ECHO   *That suits it best.*   25
ANTONIO
'Tis very like my wife's voice.
ECHO   *Ay, wife's voice.*
DELIO
Come: let's walk farther from't.
I would not have you go to th'Cardinal's tonight:
Do not.
ECHO   *Do not.*

9–11   From Montaigne, *Essayes*, pp. 596–7.
19   Echo's lines are italicised in Q1.
27   *let's* ed. (let's us Q1).
28   *go* Q1b (too Q1a).

DELIO

  Wisdom doth not more moderate wasting sorrow   30

  Than time: take time for't, be mindful of thy safety.

ECHO

  Be mindful of thy safety.

ANTONIO   Necessity compels me.

  Make scrutiny throughout the passes

  Of your own life; you'll find it impossible

  To fly your fate.

[ECHO]   *O fly your fate.*   35

DELIO

  Hark: the dead stones seem to have pity on you

  And give you good counsel.

ANTONIO

  Echo, I will not talk with thee,

  For thou art a dead thing.

ECHO   *Thou art a dead thing.*

ANTONIO

  My Duchess is asleep now,   40

  And her little ones, I hope sweetly: oh heaven

  Shall I never see her more?

ECHO   *Never see her more.*

ANTONIO

  I marked not one repetition of the echo

  But that: and on the sudden a clear light

  Presented me a face folded in sorrow.   45

DELIO

  Your fancy, merely.

ANTONIO   Come, I'll be out of this ague;

  For to live thus is not indeed to live:

  It is a mockery and abuse of life.

  I will not henceforth save myself by halves,

  Lose all, or nothing.

DELIO   Your own virtue save you!   50

  I'll fetch your eldest son and second you:

  It may be that the sight of his own blood

  Spread in so sweet a figure, may beget

---

33   *passes* events.

35   s.p. ed. (not in Q1).

42   *never see her more* Antonio echoes his own words at III.v.81.

44–5 See n. to line 1 above.

417

The more compassion.

[ANTONIO]   How ever, fare you well.
Though in our miseries Fortune have a part,   55
Yet in our noble suff'rings she hath none.
Contempt of pain – that we may call our own.

Exeunt

[ACT V,] SCENE iv

[*Enter* CARDINAL, PESCARA, MALATESTE,
RODERIGO, *and* GRISOLAN]

CARDINAL
You shall not watch tonight by the sick Prince,
His grace is very well recovered.

MALATESTE
Good my lord, suffer us.

CARDINAL   Oh, by no means.
The noise, and change of object in his eye,
Doth more distract him. I pray, all to bed,   5
And though you hear him in his violent fit,
Do not rise, I entreat you.

PESCARA   So sir, we shall not.

CARDINAL
Nay, I must have your promise
Upon your honours, for I was enjoined to't
By himself; and he seemed to urge it sensibly.   10

---

54   s.p. ed. (not in Q1) follows Q1 where the page ends at 'compassion' and the
     catchword is 'How' with no sign that a s.p. has been omitted. Nevertheless I consider
     a compositor's error is likely: the change of speaker would allow this scene to end
     focused on Antonio, which seems dramatically right.

0   s.d. ed. (SCENA. IIII. / *Cardinall, Pescara, Malateste, Rodorigo, Grisolan, Bosola,
     Ferdinand, Antonio, Seruant.* Q1).

1   *tonight* The time is close to midnight (see line 23). Since performances at the open
     amphitheatre playhouses took place in daylight, and the Blackfriars theatre
     auditorium was candle-lit not darkened, actors carried torches, candles or (as here)
     lanterns, as conventional indication of night.

PESCARA
  Let our honours bind this trifle.
CARDINAL
  Nor any of your followers.
MALATESTE   Neither.
CARDINAL
  It may be, to make trial of your promise
  When he's asleep, myself will rise and feign
  Some of his mad tricks, and cry out for help,   15
  And feign myself in danger.
MALATESTE   If your throat were cutting
  I'd not come at you, now I have protested against it.
CARDINAL
  Why, I thank you.   [*Walks apart*]
GRISOLAN   'Twas a foul storm tonight.
RODERIGO
  The Lord Ferdinand's chamber shook like an osier.
MALATESTE
  'Twas nothing but pure kindness in the devil,   20
  To rock his own child.
                          Exeunt [*all but* CARDINAL]

CARDINAL
  The reason why I would not suffer these
  About my brother, is, because at midnight
  I may with better privacy convey
  Julia's body to her own lodging.   25
  Oh, my conscience!
  I would pray now, but the devil takes away my heart
  For having any confidence in prayer.

                    [*Enter* BOSOLA *behind*]

  About this hour I appointed Bosola
  To fetch the body: when he hath served my turn,   30
  He dies.   *Exit*
BOSOLA
  Ha? 'Twas the Cardinal's voice: I heard him name
  Bosola, and my death. – Listen, I hear one's footing.

  10   *sensibly* with strong feeling.
  11   *our* ed. (out Q1).
  16   *cutting* being cut.
  25–6 ed. (*one line* Q1).

[Enter FERDINAND]

FERDINAND
Strangling is a very quiet death.
BOSOLA *[Aside]*
Nay then, I see I must stand upon my guard.   35
FERDINAND
What say to that? Whisper, softly: do you agree to't?
So. It must be done i'th'dark – the Cardinal
Would not for a thousand pounds the Doctor should see it.
                                                        Exit
BOSOLA
My death is plotted. Here's the consequence of murder.
'We value not desert, nor Christian breath,   40
When we know black deeds must be cured with death'.

[Enter ANTONIO *and* SERVANT]

SERVANT
Here stay sir, and be confident, I pray.
I'll fetch you a dark lantern.   *Exit*
ANTONIO
Could I take him at his prayers,
There were hope of pardon.
BOSOLA   Fall right my sword: 45
I'll not give thee so much leisure as to pray.
                                   [BOSOLA *wounds* ANTONIO]
ANTONIO
Oh, I am gone! Thou hast ended a long suit
In a minute.
BOSOLA   What art thou?
ANTONIO   A most wretched thing,
That only have thy benefit in death,
To appear myself.

[Enter SERVANT *with a lantern]*

SERVANT   Where are you sir?   50

---

34   *quiet* ed. (quiein Q1).
44–5   Bosola, unable to identify the speaker in the darkness, mistakes Antonio for a cut-
       throat and misinterprets his words as meaning 'If I could kill Bosola at his prayers
       the Cardinal would give me a pardon'.
50   NCW suggest that the servant brings a light (a theatrical signal that the action must
      be imagined as in darkness) so enabling Antonio and Bosola to recognise each other.

ANTONIO

Very near my home. – Bosola?

SERVANT   Oh misfortune!

BOSOLA

Smother thy pity, thou art dead else. – Antonio?
The man I would have saved 'bove mine own life?
We are merely the stars' tennis balls, struck and banded
Which way please them. Oh good Antonio,   55
I'll whisper one thing in thy dying ear
Shall make thy heart break quickly: thy fair Duchess
And two sweet children –

ANTONIO   Their very names

Kindle a little life in me –

BOSOLA   Are murdered!

ANTONIO

Some men have wished to die   60
At the hearing of sad tidings. I am glad
That I shall do't in sadness. I would not now
Wish my wounds balmed, nor healed, for I have no use
To put my life to: in all our quest of greatness,
Like wanton boys whose pastime is their care,   65
We follow after bubbles blown in the air.
Pleasure of life, what is't? Only the good hours
Of an ague; merely a preparative to rest,
To endure vexation. I do not ask
The process of my death: only commend me   70
To Delio.

BOSOLA   Break heart.

ANTONIO

And let my son fly the courts of princes.   [*Dies*]

BOSOLA

Thou seem'st to have loved Antonio?

SERVANT   I brought him hither

To have reconciled him to the Cardinal.

54–5   A Renaissance tag, but the phrasing is very close to Sidney, *Arcadia* (*Works* II. 177),
        where men 'are but like tenisballs, tossed by the racket of the hyer powers'; see also
        Sir William Alexander, *The Alexandraean Tragedy*, 5.1 in *The Monarchicke Tragedies*,
        1607. 'I thinke the world is but a tennis-court, / Where men are tossde by fortune as
        her balls'.
59   A contrast to the comforting words Bosola speaks to the dying Duchess at IV.ii.336–9.
        Delivered abruptly, the line can provoke laughter in an audience.
62   *sadness* earnest.

BOSOLA

I do not ask thee that: 75
Take him up, if thou tender thine own life,
And bear him where the Lady Julia
Was wont to lodge. Oh, my fate moves swift.
I have this Cardinal in the forge already,
Now I'll bring him to th'hammer. Oh direful misprision, 80
I will not imitate things glorious
No more than base; I'll be mine own example.
[*To* SERVANT] On, on, and look thou represent, for silence,
The thing thou bear'st.

Exeunt [BOSOLA *and* SERVANT *with* ANTONIO's *body*]

[ACT V,] SCENE v

[*Enter* CARDINAL, *with a book*]

CARDINAL

I am puzzled in a question about hell:
He says, in hell there's one material fire,
And yet it shall not burn all men alike.
Lay him by. How tedious is a guilty conscience!
When I look into the fish-ponds in my garden 5
Methinks I see a thing armed with a rake
That seems to strike at me.

[*Enter* BOSOLA *and* SERVANT *with* ANTONIO's *body*]

Now! Art thou come? Thou look'st ghastly:
There sits in thy face some great determination,

---

80   *misprision* mistake.
84   s.d. Webster's stagecraft makes a point by repetition: Bosola has already carried out
     the dead bodies of the Duchess (IV.ii) and Julia (V.ii).

0   s.d. ed. (SCENA. V. / *Cardinall* (*with a Booke*) *Bosola, Pescara, Malateste, Rodorigo,*
     Ferdinand, Delio, Seruant with Antonio's body. Q1).
0   s.d. *with a book* A conventional stage sign of melancholy (as in *Hamlet*, 2.2.167).
4   *tedious* If the Cardinal uses the word in the sense 'tiresome' he is being cynical, if in
     the sense 'painful', he is seriously troubled. Either is possible.

Mixed with some fear.

BOSOLA   Thus it lightens into action: 10
I am come to kill thee.

CARDINAL   Ha? Help! Our guard!

BOSOLA
Thou art deceived, they are out of thy howling.

CARDINAL
Hold: and I will faithfully divide
Revenues with thee.

BOSOLA   Thy prayers and proffers
Are both unseasonable.

CARDINAL   Raise the watch!   15
We are betrayed!

BOSOLA   I have confined your flight:
I'll suffer your retreat to Julia's chamber,
But no further.

CARDINAL   Help! We are betrayed!

[*Enter, above,* PESCARA, MALATESTE, RODERIGO,
GRISOLAN]

MALATESTE   Listen.

CARDINAL
My dukedom, for rescue!

RODERIGO   Fie upon his counterfeiting.

MALATESTE
Why, 'tis not the Cardinal.

RODERIGO   Yes, yes, 'tis he: 20
But I'll see him hanged ere I'll go down to him.

CARDINAL
Here's a plot upon me! I am assaulted! I am lost
Unless some rescue!

GRISOLAN   He doth this pretty well,
But it will not serve to laugh me out of mine honour.

CARDINAL
The sword's at my throat!

RODERIGO   You would not bawl so loud then.   25

MALATESTE

10–12   ed. (Mixed . . . feare / Thus . . . Action / I . . . thee / Hah . . . Guard / Thou . . . deceiu'd
/ They . . . howling Q1).

14–16   ed. (Revenewes . . . thee / Thy . . . proffers / Are . . . vnseasonable / Raise . . . betraid
/ I . . . flight Q1).

19   *My . . . rescue* Recalling *Richard III*, V.iv.1–7.

Come, come, let's go to bed, he told us thus much aforehand.
PESCARA
    He wished you should not come at him, but believe't,
    The accent of the voice sounds not in jest.
    I'll down to him, howsoever, and with engines
    Force ope the doors.   *[Exit above]*
RODERIGO   Let's follow him aloof,   30
    And note how the Cardinal will laugh at him.
                        [Exeunt above]
BOSOLA
    There's for you first –

                 He kills the SERVANT
    'Cause you shall not unbarricade the door
    To let in rescue.
CARDINAL
    What cause hast thou to pursue my life?
BOSOLA   Look there.   35
CARDINAL
    Antonio?
BOSOLA   Slain by my hand unwittingly.
    Pray, and be sudden. When thou kill'dst thy sister
    Thou took'st from Justice her most equal balance
    And left her nought but her sword.
CARDINAL   Oh mercy!
BOSOLA
    Now it seems thy greatness was only outward,   40
    For thou fall'st faster of thyself than calamity
    Can drive thee. I'll not waste longer time – there!
                [BOSOLA *wounds the* CARDINAL]
CARDINAL
    Thou hast hurt me.
BOSOLA   Again!
                  [Wounds him again]
CARDINAL   Shall I die like a leveret
    Without any resistance? Help! Help! Help!
    I am slain!   45

        [Enter FERDINAND]

32–5   ed. (There's ... doore / To ... rescew / What ... life / Looke there Q1).

FERDINAND

    Th'alarum? Give me a fresh horse!
    Rally the vaunt-guard, or the day is lost!
    Yield! Yield! I give you the honour of arms,
    Shake my sword over you. Will you yield?

CARDINAL

    Help me! I am your brother.

FERDINAND   The devil?   50

    My brother fight upon the adverse party?
    There flies your ransom!

               He wounds the CARDINAL, *and (in the scuffle)*
               gives BOSOLA *his death wound*

CARDINAL

    Oh justice!
    I suffer now for what hath former been:
    'Sorrow is held the eldest child of sin'.   55

FERDINAND

    Now you're brave fellows: Caesar's fortune was harder than
    Pompey's, Caesar died in the arms of prosperity, Pompey at the
    feet of disgrace: you both died in the field. The pain's nothing:
    pain, many times, is taken away with the apprehension of
    greater – as the tooth-ache with the sight of a barber that comes   60
    to pull it out. There's philosophy for you.

BOSOLA

    Now my revenge is perfect: sink, thou main cause
    Of my undoing!

                     He kills FERDINAND

           The last part of my life
    Hath done me best service.

FERDINAND

    Give me some wet hay, I am broken winded.   65

---

46   Ferdinand (to grotesque and absurd effect) imagines he is on the battlefield (see
       Richard III, V.iii.177, where Richard starts up out of a nightmare crying 'Give me
       another horse!'). For those spectators who recognise the quotation the absurdity
       will be doubled – Ferdinand believing himself to be a king in a famous Shakespeare
       play and speaking lines from it. In the original production the effect would have
       been further enhanced for those spectators who recognised that the actor playing
       Ferdinand (Burbage), had himself played the Shakespearean role of Richard III.

51   This scuffle is evidently to be as clumsy and confused as possible, the very opposite
       of high tragic style.

56–61   prose ed. (*Q1 lines ending* fellowes / *Pompey's* / prosperity / field / with / sight / you).

65   *wet hay* Treatment for broken-winded horses recommended in Gervase Markham,
       Markham's Maister-peece, 1610, p. 101 (so Lucas).

I do account this world but a dog-kennel:
I will vault credit and affect high pleasures
Beyond death.

BOSOLA   He seems to come to himself
Now he's so near the bottom.

FERDINAND
My sister! Oh my sister, there's the cause on't!   70
'Whether we fall by ambition, blood, or lust,
Like diamonds we are cut with our own dust'.   [*Dies*]

CARDINAL
Thou hast thy payment too.

BOSOLA
Yes, I hold my weary soul in my teeth,
'Tis ready to part from me. I do glory   75
That thou, which stood'st like a huge pyramid
Begun upon a large and ample base,
Shalt end in a little point, a kind of nothing.

[*Enter* PESCARA, MALATESTE, RODERIGO, GRISOLAN]

PESCARA
How now, my lord?

MALATESTE   Oh sad disaster.

RODERIGO   How comes this?

BOSOLA
Revenge for the Duchess of Malfi, murdered   80
By th'Aragonian brethren; for Antonio,
Slain by this hand; for lustful Julia,
Poisoned by this man; and lastly, for myself,
That was an actor in the main of all,
Much 'gainst mine own good nature, yet i'th'end   85
Neglected.

PESCARA   How now, my lord?

CARDINAL   Look to my brother.
He gave us these large wounds as we were struggling
Here i'th'rushes. And now, I pray, let me
Be laid by, and never thought of.

68–9   ed. (Beyond death. / He ... bottom. Q1).
74   *soul in my teeth* From Montaigne, *Essayes*, II. p. 430.
82   this ed. (his Q1).
88   *rushes* Customarily strewn on the Elizabethan stage.

PESCARA
    How fatally, it seems, he did withstand   90
    His own rescue!
MALATESTE   Thou wretched thing of blood,
    How came Antonio by his death?

BOSOLA
    In a mist: I know not how;
    Such a mistake as I have often seen
    In a play. Oh I am gone.   95
    We are only like dead walls, or vaulted graves,
    That ruined, yields no echo. Fare you well.
    It may be pain but no harm to me, to die
    In so good a quarrel. Oh this gloomy world!
    In what a shadow, or deep pit of darkness,   100
    Doth womanish and fearful mankind live!
    Let worthy minds ne'er stagger in distrust
    To suffer death or shame for what is just.
    Mine is another voyage.   [*Dies*]

PESCARA
    The noble Delio, as I came to th'palace,   105
    Told me of Antonio's being here, and showed me
    A pretty gentleman, his son and heir.

        [*Enter* DELIO *with* ANTONIO's SON]

MALATESTE
    Oh sir, you come too late.
DELIO   I heard so, and
    Was armed for't ere I came. Let us make noble use
    Of this great ruin; and join all our force   110
    To establish this young hopeful gentleman
    In's mother's right. These wretched eminent things

---

   96   *dead* continuous, unbroken.
100–1   *shadow . . . live* From Sidney, *Arcadia* (*Works* II 177): 'such a shadowe, or rather pit
        of darkenes, the wormish mankinde lives'.
  112   *mother's right* See IV.ii.269–71 n. There is a reference at III.iii.66–7 to the Duchess
        having had a son by her first marriage: a child who, though a minor, is Duke of
        Malfi. Yet the Duchess never refers to any such son by her first marriage nor, of
        course, do the audience see one, whereas Webster stresses the Duchess' exceptional
        concern for her children born of the marriage to Antonio, and their presence in
        several scenes of the play is very significant. Delio here presents Antonio's son, as sole
        survivor, in public as a symbol of political hope, as successor to his mother. His
        horoscope – see II.iii.57–65 – may give cause for anxiety, but Webster's treatment of
        it in Act II is ambivalent. Given the importance of this final theatrical and narrative

Leave no more fame behind 'em than should one
Fall in a frost and leave his print in snow:
As soon as the sun shines, it ever melts,   115
Both form, and matter. I have ever thought
Nature doth nothing so great, for great men,
As when she's pleased to make them lords of truth:
'Integrity of life is fame's best friend,
Which nobly, beyond death, shall crown the end'.   120

Exeunt

FINIS

emphasis on the surviving son it seems likely that Webster changed his mind during
composition of the play and decided to diverge from his sources, making the
Duchess childless until she married Antonio, but he failed to correct the text
accordingly. Otherwise the *mother's right* would refer, lamely, not to the dukedom,
since this has already passed to her son by her first marriage (she has only been
administering it during his minority); it would refer only to such property as the
Duchess retained personally after her marriages. This boy would then represent the
(fragile) survival of his parents' spiritual values and their love.

117–18   From Sidney, *Arcadia* (*Works* I. 190).
119–20   Alluding to Horace, *Odes* I xxii. Horace's phrase 'integer vitae' was itself a
commonplace, so probably the implied irony would be appreciated only by the more
understanding members of Webster's audience. Yet this quotation is bedevilled by
the ironic sting in the quotation's tail, for Horace later in the Ode also says that not
even a wolf would attack a man possessed of integrity of life. The Duchess certainly
was attacked by the wolf-man Ferdinand, and she does resort to public deceptions:
but against that an audience can balance her unwavering constancy to a private faith.

The Witch of Edmonton

A known true STORY.

Composed into

A TRAGI-COMEDY

By divers well-esteemed Poets;

William Rowley, Thomas Dekker, John Ford, &c

Acted by the Princes Servants, often at the Cock-Pit in *Drury-Lane,*
once at Court, with singular Applause.

Never printed till now.

London, *Printed by* J. Cottrel, *for* Edward Blackmore, *at the Angel in*
Paul's *Church-yard.* 1658.

ARGUMENT

The whole Argument is this Distich:

Forced Marriage, Murder; Murder, Blood requires.
Reproach, Revenge; Revenge, Hell's help desires.

Distich couplet; line 1 gives precedent to the overplot; line 2, to the underplot

Sir Arthur Clarington
Old Thorney, a Gentleman
Old Carter, a rich Yeoman
Old Banks, a Countryman
W. Mago, } two Countrymen
W. Hamluc, }   5
Three other Countrymen
Warbeck, } suitors to [Old] Carter's daughters
Somerton, }
Frank, [Old] Thorney's son   10
Young Cuddy Banks, the Clown
Four Morris Dancers
Old Ratcliffe
Sawgut, an old Fiddler
Poldavis, a Barber's boy   15
Justice
Constable
Officers
Servingmen
Dog, a Familiar   20
A Spirit
Mother Sawyer, the Witch
Anne, [Old] Ratcliffe's Wife
Susan,   } [Old] Carter's daughters
Katherine, }   25
Winifred, Sir Arthur's Maid
[Jane, a Maid]

4 *Old Banks* Sugden notes a Banks also appears as the Miller of Waltham in *The Merry Devil of Edmonton*; it 'seems to indicate that he was a study from life'

5 *W. Mago* Bentley identifies him as an actor in the King's Company in 1624 and 1631. He is named only twice, and both times elsewhere – as a 'Carthaginian Officer' and an attendant on the Prussian king in the King's Men's production of Massinger's *Believe as You List* (1631). Bowers argues that Mago and Hamluc (below) were members of Henrietta Maria's Men in the revival in the 1630s

6 *W. Hamluc* Bentley argues this is an error, listing an actor who is given two short speeches in IV.i

11 *Cuddy* derived from Cudden or fool, ass

15 *Poldavis* Probably an actor's name; he is referred to at III.i.59, but has no clear role and is not mentioned in the stage direction

PROLOGUE

The Town of Edmonton hath lent the Stage
A Devil and a Witch, both in an age.
To make comparisons it were uncivil,
Between so even a pair, a Witch and Devil.
But as the year doth with his plenty bring   5
As well a latter as a former Spring;
So has this Witch enjoyed the first, and reason
Presumes she may partake the other season.
In Acts deserving name, the Proverb says,
Once good, and ever; Why not so in Plays?   10
Why not in this? since (Gentlemen) we flatter
No Expectations. Here is Mirth and Matter.

                                      Master Bird

Prologue Clearly written for a revival of the play c. 1635 when Theophilus Bird and
   Ezekiel Fenn (Winifred) were both in Queen Henrietta's Company. Bentley and
   Hoy speculate the revival was around 1635 at the Cockpit in London
 1 *Edmonton* Then a village in Middlesex about 7 miles north of London
 2 *Devil* Thought to refer to an earlier play, *The Merry Devil of Edmonton*, but see
   also I.i.19. *The Merry Devil* was frequently staged and printed from 1608 to 1631
   and is also referred to in two works of Middleton and two of Jonson; it was staged
   by 1604 and given a performance at court in 1613. In 1653 the printer Humphrey
   Moseley mistakenly attributed this anonymous work to Shakespeare. Performances and publication continued until 1691. The plot may well have influenced the
   Thorney overplot
12 *Matter* serious material
13 *Master Bird* Presumably the actor who spoke these lines, probably the son of
   William Bird. He first played female roles, graduating to male roles by the 1630s;
   with Andrew Penncuicke he signed the dedication to Dekker and Ford's *The Sun's
   Darling*

ACT I, SCENE i

Enter [YOUNG] FRANK THORNEY, WINIFRED *with child*

FRANK
    Come, wench; why here's a business soon dispatched.
    Thy heart I know is now at ease. Thou needst not
    Fear what the tattling gossips in their cups
    Can speak against thy fame. Thy child shall know
    Who to call Dad now.

WINIFRED   You have discharged   5
    The true part of an honest man; I cannot
    Request a fuller satisfaction
    Than you have freely granted. Yet methinks
    'Tis a hard case, being lawful man and wife,
    We should not live together.

FRANK   Had I failed   10
    In promise of my truth to thee, we must
    Have then been ever sundered; now the longest
    Of our forbearing either's company,
    Is only but to gain a little time
    For our continuing thrift, that so hereafter   15
    The heir that shall be born may not have cause
    To curse his hour of birth, which made him feel
    The misery of beggary and want;
    Two devils that are occasions to enforce

Scene i This scene – because of its style and situation – is generally attributed to Ford,
    but from the start of his career, Dekker was known for his structural craftsman-
    ship in beginning plays forcefully and thematically. Here the exposition of events
    previous to the play is skilfully released for dramatic effectiveness and irony

  0 s.d. 1 *with child* pregnant
  1 *wench* woman; here a neutral or even affectionate term
    dispatched taken care of
  3 *gossips* slang for newsmongers
    in their cups in drunkenness
 13 *forbearing* giving up
 15 *thrift* well-being
 19 *Two devils* Beggary and want link overplot and subplot here
    occasions causes

A shameful end. My plots aim but to keep   20
My father's love.

WINIFRED   And that will be as difficult
To be preserved, when he shall understand
How you are married, as it will be now,
Should you confess it to him.

FRANK   Fathers are
Won by degrees, not bluntly, as our masters   25
Or wronged friends are; and besides, I'll use
Such dutiful and ready means, that ere
He can have notice of what's past, th'inheritance
To which I am born heir shall be assured.
That done, why let him know it; if he likes it not,   30
Yet he shall have no power in him left
To cross the thriving of it.

WINIFRED   You who had
The conquest of my maiden-love, may easily
Conquer the fears of my distrust. And whither
Must I he hurried?

FRANK   Prithee do not use   35
A word so much unsuitable to the constant
Affections of thy husband. Thou shalt live
Near Waltham Abbey, with thy Uncle Selman.
I have acquainted him with all at large.
He'll use thee kindly. Thou shalt want no pleasures,   40
Nor any other fit supplies whatever
Thou canst in heart desire.

WINIFRED   All these are nothing
Without your company.

FRANK   Which thou shalt have
Once every month at least.

WINIFRED   Once every month!
Is this to have an husband?

FRANK   Perhaps oftener.   45
That's as occasion serves.

WINIFRED   Ay, ay; in case

32 *cross* prevent

33 *conquest of my maiden-love* ended my virginity (by conquering my maidenhead)

38 *Waltham Abbey* Then 12 miles north of London across the border from the village of Waltham, or Waltham Cross, Hertfordshire

39 *large* length

46 *Ay, ay* (I, I Q (quarto publication of the text))

No other beauty tempt your eye, whom you
Like better, I may chance to be remembered,
And see you now and then. Faith, I did hope
You'd not have used me so. 'Tis but my fortune.   50
And yet, if not for my sake, have some pity
Upon the child I go with, that's your own.
And, 'less you'll be a cruel-hearted father,
You cannot but remember that.
Heaven knows how –
FRANK   To quit which fear at once,   55
As by the ceremony late performed,
I plighted thee a faith, as free from challenge,
As any double thought; once more in hearing
Of heaven and thee, I vow, that never henceforth
Disgrace, reproof, lawless affections, threats,   60
Or what can be suggested 'gainst our marriage,
Shall cause me falsify that bridal oath
That binds me thine. And, Winifred, whenever
The wanton heat of youth by subtle baits
Of beauty, or what woman's art can practise,   65
Draw me from only loving thee; let heaven
Inflict upon my life some fearful ruin.
I hope thou dost believe me.
WINIFRED   Swear no more;
I am confirmed, and will resolve to do
What you think most behooveful for us.
FRANK   Thus then;   70
Make thyself ready. At the furthest house
Upon the green, without the town, your uncle
Expects you. For a little time farewell.
WINIFRED   Sweet,

---

50 *You'd* (Youl'd Q)
55 *how –* (how. Q)
57 *plighted* vowed
      plighted thee a faith In Rowley's *All's Lost for Lust* (c. 1607, published 1633),
      the nobleman Antonio pledges the country girl Marguerite to a secret marriage;
      as Frank will, he later denies the marriage by marrying a girl of a higher social
      class
58 *double* strong; also possibly duplicitous
67 *ruin* Ironic anticipation following Frank's betrayal of Winifred
69 *I am confirmed* Winifred's staunch loyalty to Frank will be complicated by later
      revelations
70 *most behooveful* advantageous

We shall meet again as soon as thou canst possibly?
FRANK
We shall. One kiss. [*Kisses her*] Away.

[*Exit* WINIFRED]

Enter SIR ARTHUR CLARINGTON

SIR ARTHUR	Frank Thorney.
FRANK	Here Sir.	75

SIR ARTHUR
Alone? Then must I tell thee in plain terms,
Thou hast wronged thy master's house basely and lewdly.
FRANK
Your house, sir?
SIR ARTHUR   Yes, sir. If the nimble devil
That wantoned in your blood rebelled against
All rules of honest duty, you might, sir,   80
Have found out some more fitting place than here
To have built a stews in. All the country whispers
How shamefully thou hast undone a maid,
Approved for modest life, for civil carriage,
Till thy prevailing perjuries enticed her   85
To forfeit shame. Will you be honest yet?
Make her amends and marry her?

---

74 s.d. *SIR* The basis of Clarington's title – and thus his precise social status – is never explained; it might derive from an hereditary baronetcy or an individual knighthood awarded for life. By 1621, however, the title no longer signified military or political service to the king and had become diluted by James I who sold the honour to produce royal income; he created more knights in his first four months in office than Elizabeth I had in her entire reign of 44 years. Here it has been used as a social marker to give Sir Arthur the highest social status in the play (cf. V.iii.157 ff.) and thus potentially the most exploitative

77 *Thou* A formal and more distant term used to address lower classes
thy master's That a gentleman like Frank is in service to Sir Arthur as an eldest (or only) rather than a younger son indicates his father's low financial state. Boys and girls normally entered service between the ages of 12 and 15; length and terms of service varied with the master, as well as treatment, from strict authoritarianism to developing dependency. If girls did not marry when their term of service ended, they often stayed on with their employer. Frank's ability here to keep his distance from Sir Arthur (unlike Winifred) argues for his difference in gender, class and possibly maturity

82 *stews* brothel

84 *civil* courteous, proper

85 *prevailing perjuries* successful false arguments

FRANK   So, sir,
I might bring both myself and her to beggary;
And that would be a shame worse than the other.

SIR ARTHUR
You should have thought on this before, and then   90
Your reason would have overswayed the passion
Of your unruly lust. But that you may
Be left without excuse, to salve the infamy
Of my disgraced house, and 'cause you are
A gentleman, and both of you my servants,   95
I'll make the maid a portion.

FRANK   So you promised me
Before, in case I married her. I know
Sir Arthur Clarington deserves the credit
Report hath lent him; and presume you are
A debtor to your promise. But upon   100
What certainty shall I resolve? Excuse me
For being somewhat rude.

SIR ARTHUR   'Tis but reason.
Well, Frank, what thinkest thou of two hundred pound
And a continual friend?

FRANK   Though my poor fortunes
Might happily prefer me to a choice   105
Of a far greater portion; yet to right
A wronged maid, and to preserve your favour,
I am content to accept your proffer.

SIR ARTHUR   Art thou?

FRANK
Sir, we shall every day have need to employ
The use of what you please to give.

SIR ARTHUR   Thou shalt hav't.   110

FRANK
Then I claim your promise. We are man and wife.

SIR ARTHUR
Already?

FRANK   And more than so, I have promised her
Free entertainment in her uncle's house,
Near Waltham Abbey, where she may securely
Sojourn, till time and my endeavours work   115

---

92 *But that* because
95 *gentleman* Children of gentry were often educated by serving in households of
   social superiors; Sir Arthur's generosity will soon reveal darker motives
96 *portion* dowry
100–1 *But ... resolve?* How should I be certain?
113 *entertainment* hospitality

My father's love and liking.

SIR ARTHUR   Honest Frank.

FRANK

I hope, sir, you will think I cannot keep her
Without a daily charge.

SIR ARTHUR   As for the money,
'Tis all thine own; and though I cannot make thee
A present payment, yet thou shalt be sure   120
I will not fail thee.

FRANK   But our occasions –

SIR ARTHUR   Nay, nay,
Talk not of your occasions, trust my bounty.
It shall not sleep. Hast married her, i'faith, Frank?
'Tis well, 'tis passing well. [*Aside*] Then Winifred,
Once more thou art an honest woman. [*To* FRANK] Frank,   125
Thou hast a jewel. Love her, she'll deserve it.
And when to Waltham?

FRANK   She is making ready.
Her uncle stays for her.

SIR ARTHUR   Most provident speed.
Frank, I will be thy friend, and such a friend.
Thou'lt bring her thither?

FRANK   Sir, I cannot. Newly   130
My father sent me word I should come to him.

SIR ARTHUR

Marry, and do. I know thou hast a wit
To handle him.

FRANK   I have a suit t'ye.

SIR ARTHUR   What is't?
Anything, Frank, command it.

FRANK   That you'll please
By letters to assure my father that   135
I am not married.

SIR ARTHUR   How?

FRANK   Some one or other
Hath certainly informed him that I purposed
To marry Winifred, on which he threatened
To disinherit me; to prevent it,

120 *present payment* Cf. V.iii.158; presumably Sir Arthur is not telling Frank the
   truth, whereas he will the Justice
121 *occasions* – (occasions. Q) needs
128 *stays* waits
130 *Newly* just now
132 *Marry* A term of strong agreement
133 *suit* request (of a social superior)

Lowly I crave your letters, which he seeing   140
Will credit; and I hope, ere I return,
On such conditions as I'll frame, his lands
Shall be assured.
SIR ARTHUR   But what is there to quit
My knowledge of the marriage?
FRANK   Why you were not
A witness to it.
SIR ARTHUR   I conceive. And then,   145
His land confirmed, thou wilt acquaint him thoroughly
With all that's passed.
FRANK   I mean no less.
SIR ARTHUR   Provided,
I never was made privy to it.
FRANK   Alas, sir,
Am I a talker?
SIR ARTHUR   Draw thyself the letter,
I'll put my hand to it. I commend thy policy.   150
Thou'rt witty, witty Frank; nay, nay, 'tis fit,
Dispatch it.
FRANK
I shall write effectually.   *Exit*
SIR ARTHUR
Go thy way, cuckoo; have I caught the young man?
One trouble then is freed. He that will feast   155
At others' cost, must be a bold-faced guest.

Enter WINIFRED *in a riding suit*

I have heard the news, all now is safe,
The worst is past. Thy lip, wench. [*Kisses her*] I must bid

140 *Lowly* humbly
143 *assured* secured (for myself)
143–4 *But ... marriage?* What grounds do I have not to know about the marriage?
145 *conceive* understand
148 *made privy to* given knowledge of
149–50 *Draw ... it.* Write the letter; I'll sign it
150 *policy* strategy
151 *witty* crafty
154 *cuckoo* (Cuckow Q, as homonym to cuckold) cuckold; also slang for fool; Sir
       Arthur's character is first revealed here (cf. 194–6 below)
       caught trapped
157–8 *I ... past.* (*Winifred* Q) This speech prefix must be in error; the conspiratorial
       tone is in keeping with Sir Arthur's attitude but is never shown by Winifred. Her
       situation resembles that of Jacinta in Rowley's *All's Lost by Lust*; Dekker treats
       adultery in *The Honest Whore Part II*

Farewell, for fashion's sake; but I will visit thee
Suddenly, girl. This was cleanly carried.   160
Ha, was't not Win?
WINIFRED   Then were my happiness,
That I in heart repent I did not bring him
The dower of virginity. Sir, forgive me;
I have been much to blame. Had not my lewdness
Given way to your immoderate waste of virtue,   165
You had not with such eagerness pursued
The error of your goodness.
SIR ARTHUR   Dear, dear Win.
I hug this art of thine, it shows how cleanly
Thou canst beguile, in case occasion serve
To practise. It becomes thee, now we share   170
Free scope enough, without control or fear,
To interchange our pleasures; we will surfeit
In our embraces, wench. Come, tell me, when
Wilt thou appoint a meeting?
WINIFRED   What to do?
SIR ARTHUR
Good, good, to con the lesson of our loves,   175
Our secret game.

---

160 *Suddenly* very soon
   cleanly carried well done
161–4 *Then ... blame* Winifred's change of heart suggests moral transformation and
   underscores Sir Arthur's continuing complicity
164 *lewdness* (laundress Q)
164–7 *Had not ... goodness* Had not my lust surrendered to your advances, you had
   not so eagerly pursued this bad behaviour. While consummation before or outside marriage was not sanctioned, it was also not uncommon
169 *Thou canst beguile* Sir Arthur thinks Winifred has decided to marry Frank to
   conceal the truth of her pregnancy and continue their affair; the rest of this scene
   encodes lines about their liaison
   beguile, (beguile Q)
170 *practise* scheme, plot
   becomes suits
175 *con* learn, memorise
175–8 *con ... monstrous* Sir Arthur sees this marriage as a way to pursue his sexual
   alliance with Winifred – something Frank does not know – but following her
   marriage she declines any further relationship with Sir Arthur. The tragedy of the
   couple stems from this interchange
176 *Our secret* Sir Arthur sees his alliance as sport. In 1633 – after the play was written but before it was printed – Archbishop Laud introduced the punishment of
   such adulterous nobility by requiring them to stand in a white sheet before the
   congregation of their parish church as a sign of their sexual misconduct

WINIFRED   O blush to speak it further!
  As y'are a noble gentleman, forget
  A sin so monstrous. 'Tis not gently done,
  To open a cured wound. I know you speak
  For trial; troth, you need not.
SIR ARTHUR   I for trial?   180
  Not I, by this good sunshine!
WINIFRED   Can you name
  That syllable of good, and yet not tremble,
  To think to what a foul and black intent,
  You use it for an oath? Let me resolve you,
  If you appear in any visitation   185
  That brings not with it pity for the wrongs
  Done to abused Thorney, my kind husband;
  If you infect mine ear with any breath
  That is not thoroughly perfumed with sighs
  For former deeds of lust, may I be cursed   190
  Even in my prayers, when I vouchsafe
  To see or hear you. I will change my life,
  From a loose whore to a repentant wife.

SIR ARTHUR
  Wilt thou turn monster now? Are not ashamed
  After so many months to be honest at last?   195
  Away, away, fie on't!
WINIFRED   My resolution
  Is built upon a rock. This very day
  Young Thorney vowed with oaths not to be doubted,
  That never any change of love should cancel
  The bonds, in which we are to either bound,   200
  Of lasting truth. And shall I then for my part
  Unfile the sacred oath set on record
  In heaven's book? Sir Arthur, do not study
  To add to your lascivious lust the sin
  Of sacrilege. For if you but endeavour   205
  By any unchaste word to tempt my constancy,
  You strive as much as in you lies to ruin
  A temple hallowed to the purity
  Of holy marriage. I have said enough.
  You may believe me.

184 *resolve you* end your doubts
190 *lust,* (lust: Q)
191 *vouchsafe* allow myself
202 *Unfile* retract
203 *study* attempt

SIR ARTHUR Get you to your nunnery, 210
There freeze in your cold cloister. This is fine.

WINIFRED
Good angels guide me. Sir you'll give me leave
To weep and pray for your conversion?

SIR ARTHUR Yes,
Away to Waltham! Pox on your honesty.
Had you no other trick to fool me? Well, 215
You may want money yet.

WINIFRED None that I'll send for
To you, for hire of a damnation.
When I am gone, think on my just complaint.
I was your devil, O be you my saint! *Exit* WIN[IFRED]

SIR ARTHUR
Go, go thy ways, as changeable a baggage 220
As ever cozened knight. I'm glad I'm rid of her.
Honest? Marry, hang her! Thorney is my debtor,
I thought to have paid him too. But fools have fortune.

Exit S[IR] A[RTHUR]

ACT I, SCENE ii

Enter OLD THORNEY, *and* OLD CARTER

OLD THORNEY
You offer, Master Carter, like a gentleman;
I cannot find fault with it, 'tis so fair.

210 *Get ... nunnery* Probably an allusion to *Hamlet* III.i.120
211 *cold* (old Q)
    fine cunning
214 *Pox* syphilis; plague (an idiomatic term of annoyance)
217 *for hire of a* to be rewarded with
220 *baggage* immoral woman
221 *cozened* cheated
222 *Marry,* (Marry Q) A term of surprise; originally an oath, 'By the Virgin Mary'
223 *fools have fortune* Proverbial; F536 (Tilley)

  1 *offer* Old Thorney's arrangement of his son's marriage, like Old Carter's of his
    daughter's, is not unusual among aristocrats and gentry nor is it unkind; Old
    Thorney will not only regain solvency but assure Frank of an inheritance
    like a gentleman The play continues to make social class an issue, but here the
    scene reverses I.i: whereas Sir Arthur used his superior status to subjugate Frank
    and Winifred, Old Thorney pleads with his yeoman inferior Old Carter by flat-
    tering him with this form of address
    gentleman; (gentleman, Q)

OLD CARTER

No gentleman I, Master Thorney; spare the Mastership,
call me by my name, John Carter; Master is a title my
father, nor his before him, were acquainted with. Honest 5
Hertfordshire yeomen, such an one am I; my word and my
deed shall be proved one at all times. I mean to give you no
security for the marriage-money.

OLD THORNEY

How? No security?
Although it need not, so long as you live; 10
Yet who is he has surety of his life one hour?
Men, the proverb says, are mortal. Else, for my part,
I distrust you not, were the sum double.

OLD CARTER

Double, treble, more or less; I tell you, Master Thorney, I'll
give no security. Bonds and bills are but tarriers to catch 15
fools, and keep lazy knaves busy; my security shall be present payment. And we here, about Edmonton, hold present
payment as sure as an alderman's bond in London, Master
Thorney.

OLD THORNEY

I cry you mercy, sir, I understand you not. 20

OLD CARTER

I like young Frank well, so does my Susan too. The girl has
a fancy to him, which makes me ready in my purse. There
be other suitors within, that make much noise to little purpose. If Frank love Sue, Sue shall have none but Frank. 'Tis
a mannerly girl, Master Thorney, though but an homely 25

---

6 *Hertfordshire* Old Carter reliably lays claim to being a local landlord of some
means
yeomen farming class; Thomas Wilson in 1601 distinguishes yeoman class and
below from aristocrats and gentry because they labour with their hands

7 *give you* require

12 *Men ... mortal* Proverbial; M502

15–16 *Bonds ... busy* Dekker in particular was concerned with mercantile arrangements; but interest in the power of capital was by this time becoming commonplace

15 *tarriers* obstructions; hindrances

16–17 *present* immediate

18 *alderman* governing authority

20 *I ... mercy* I beg forgiveness; Old Thorney's sense of status has harboured a mistrust of yeomen generally, but here it would defeat his purpose

22 *ready in my purse* willing to pay the dowry; Old Carter maintains his dignity at
the proposal of improved social status by marriage; his continual use of proverbs
betrays his lower social status throughout

man's daughter. There have worse faces looked out of
black bags, man.

OLD THORNEY

You speak your mind freely and honestly.
I marvel my son comes not. I am sure he will be
Here sometime today.   30

OLD CARTER

Today or tomorrow, when he comes he shall be welcome to
bread, beer, and beef, yeoman's fare; we have no kickshaws. Full dishes, whole bellyfulls. Should I diet three days
at one of the slender city-suppers, you might send me to
Barber-Surgeons' Hall the fourth day, to hang up for an   35
anatomy. Here come they that –

Enter WARBECK *with* SUSAN, SOMERTON *with*
KATHERINE

How now girls? Every day play-day with you? Valentine's
day too, all by couples? Thus will young folks do when we
are laid in our graves, Master Thorney. Here's all the care
they take. And how do you find the wenches, gentlemen?   40
Have they any mind to a loose gown and a strait shoe? Win
'em, and wear 'em. They shall choose for themselves by my
consent.

27 *bags* Perhaps masks worn by women out of doors to protect complexions and
   indoors at balls and banquets; see *Measure for Measure* II.iv.94
28–30 (set as prose Q)
32 *yeoman's fare* Old Carter is self-conscious about his class while insisting he is a
   good provider
32–3 *kickshaws* fancy food (from French *quelque chose*). This speech complicates
   Old Carter's character; having located a suitor for Katherine as far away as West
   Ham and being willing to dismiss the engagement of Susan to Warbeck for a
   better match with Frank, Old Carter is essentially selfish, a good provider in a
   double sense
35 *Barber-Surgeons* Trade guild of men who performed simple operations; their
   Hall was built in Monkswell Street near Cripplegate in the reign of Edward IV
   as a special place for the dissection of corpses, and, in some instances, for the
   preservation of skeletons
36 *anatomy* skeleton, or a skeleton with its skin still remaining
36 s.d. (set one line later Q) A visual clue subsequent events will challenge
37–8 *Valentine's day* 14 February, a traditional time for the mating of birds
41 *loose gown* Probably a sexual joke
41–2 *Win 'em, and wear 'em* Proverbial; cf. 'woo her, win her, wear her' (W408)
   with *wear* meaning consummation
42–3 *by my consent* Old Carter's confession of his social and economic ambitions;
   he has, however, already opposed Warbeck in his agreement with Old Thorney

WARBECK
  You speak like a kind father. Sue, thou hearest
  The liberty that's granted thee. What sayest thou?   45
  Wilt thou be mine?
SUSAN   Your what, sir? I dare swear,
  Never your wife.
WARBECK   Canst thou be so unkind?
  Considering how dearly I affect thee;
  Nay, dote on thy perfections.
SUSAN   You are studied
  Too scholar-like in words I understand not.   50
  I am too coarse for such a gallant's love
  As you are.
WARBECK   By the honour of gentility –
SUSAN
  God sir, no swearing. Yea and nay with us
  Prevails above all oaths you can invent.
WARBECK
  By this white hand of thine –
SUSAN   Take a false oath?   55
  Fie, fie, flatter the wise. Fools not regard it;
  And one of these am I.
WARBECK   Dost thou despise me?
OLD CARTER
  Let 'em talk on, Master Thorney. I know Sue's mind. The
  fly may buzz about the candle, he shall but singe his wings
  when all's done. Frank, Frank is he has her heart.   60
SOMERTON
  But shall I live in hope, Kate?
KATHERINE
  Better so, than be a desperate man.

47 *Never your wife* Old Carter's previous line suggests Susan is in on his plan with
    Old Thorney
48 *affect* love
49 *Nay, dote* A construction familiar in Ford's work and grounds on which this
    scene has been at least partially attributed to him
51 *gallant* as a social ne'er-do-well
52 *gentility* Warbeck claims the same social status as Frank Thorney
53 *no swearing* Susan's sharp wit with Warbeck counters her earlier self-description
    (lines 49–52) and its later absence with Frank signals her serious interest in him
    Yea and nay A particularly serious oath (derived from Matthew 5:37)
59 *fly ... wings* Proverbial; F394

SOMERTON
    Perhaps thou thinkest it is thy portion
    I level at. Wert thou as poor in fortunes
    As thou art rich in goodness, I would rather   65
    Be suitor for the dower of thy virtues
    Than twice thy father's whole estate; and prithee
    Be thou resolved so.
KATHERINE   Master Somerton,
    It is an easy labour to deceive
    A maid that will believe men's subtle promises.   70
    Yet I conceive of you as worthily
    As I presume you do deserve.
SOMERTON   Which is
    As worthily in loving thee sincerely,
    As thou art worthy to be so beloved.
KATHERINE
    I shall find time to try you.
SOMERTON   Do, Kate, do.   75
    And when I fail, may all my joys forsake me.
OLD CARTER
    Warbeck and Sue are at it still. I laugh to myself, Master
    Thorney, to see how earnestly he beats the bush, while the
    bird is flown into another's bosom. A very unthrift, Master
    Thorney, one of the country roaring-lads. We have such as   80
    well as the city, and as arrant rake-hells as they are, though
    not so nimble at their prizes of wit. Sue knows the rascal to
    an hair's breadth, and will fit him accordingly.
OLD THORNEY
    What is the other gentleman?

63–8 *Perhaps ... so* Somerton senses the importance of status in courting Old
    Carter's other daughter; he may be responding directly to the previous conver-
    sation between Warbeck and Susan
64 *level* aim
67 *prithee* Shortened version of 'I pray thee'
75 *try* test
78–9 *he ... bosom* Proverbial; B740
79 *unthrift* (and therefore undeserving); Old Carter will not lose the prospect of a
    better marriage for Susan
80 *country roaring-lads* Such riotous young men were usually associated with
    London; perhaps his accusation is meant to appear false
81 *arrant rake-hells* dissolute rascals
82 *prizes* contests
    Sue Old Carter gives to his daughter interest in arranging a good match
83 *fit* reward

OLD CARTER

One Somerton, the honester man of the two, by five pound   85
in every stone-weight. A civil fellow. He has a fine con-
venient estate of land in West Ham by Essex. Master
Ranges, that dwells by Enfield, sent him hither. He likes
Kate well. I may tell you, I think she likes him as well. If
they agree, I'll not hinder the match for my part. But that   90
Warbeck is such another –. I use him kindly for Master
Somerton's sake, for he came hither first as a companion of
his. Honest men, Master Thorney, may fall into knaves'
company, now and then.

WARBECK

Three hundred a year jointure, Sue.   95

SUSAN

Where lies it, by sea or by land? I think by sea.

WARBECK

Do I look a captain?

SUSAN   Not a whit, sir.

Should all that use the seas be reckoned captains,
There's not a ship should have a scullion in her
To keep her clean.

WARBECK   Do you scorn me, Mistress Susan?   100

Am I subject to be jeered at?

SUSAN   Neither

Am I property for you to use
As stale to your fond wanton loose discourse.
Pray sir be civil.

WARBECK   Wilt be angry, wasp?

---

86 *stone-weight* 14 pounds; Old Carter is thus sceptical of Warbeck

87 *West Ham* Then a village 4½ miles north of London; this distinction is what
seems to make him attractive to Old Carter, 'the honester man of the two' (85)
by near, bordering on

88 *Enfield* Then about 11 miles from London in Middlesex

92 *sake,* (sake: Q)

93–4 *Honest ... company* Proverbial; BM528

95 *Three ... jointure* Joint ownership of his income of £300 a year with a provision
for her if she is widowed

96 *by sea* That is, the fortune is less certain

103 *stale* decoy; pretext
fond foolish

104 *Wilt ... wasp?* 'As angry as a wasp' (Proverbial; W76)

OLD CARTER

God-a-mercy, Sue. She'll firk him on my life, if he fumble   105
with her.

Enter FRANK

Master Francis Thorney, you are welcome indeed. Your
father expected your coming. How does the right worshipful knight, Sir Arthur Clarington, your master?

FRANK

In health this morning. Sir, my duty.

OLD THORNEY   Now   110
You come as I could wish.

WARBECK   Frank Thorney, ha!

SUSAN

You must excuse me.

FRANK   Virtuous Mistress Susan.
Kind Mistress Katherine. Gentlemen, to both *Salutes them*
Good time o'th' day.

SOMERTON   The like to you.

WARBECK   'Tis he.
A word, friend [*To* SOMERTON] On my life, this is the man   115
Stands fair in crossing Susan's love to me.

SOMERTON

[*To* WARBECK] I think no less. Be wise, and take no notice
on't.
He that can win her, best deserves her.

WARBECK   [*To* SOMERTON] Marry
A serving-man? Mew.

SOMERTON   [*To* WARBECK] Prithee friend no more.

OLD CARTER

Gentlemen all, there's within a slight dinner ready, if you   120
please to taste of it. Master Thorney, Master Francis,
Master Somerton. Why, girls? What, huswives, will you
spend all your forenoon in tittle-tattles? Away. It's well,
i'faith. Will you go in, gentlemen?

---

105 *God-a-mercy* God have mercy (a phrase of approval)
   firk beat
   fumble grope
110 *my duty* Signal that he bows in courtesy
113 s.d. *Salutes* greets with a kiss
116 *crossing* getting in the way of
119 *Mew* a word of social contempt
122 *huswives* loose women (a term of contempt)
123 *tittle-tattles* gossip

OLD THORNEY
  We'll follow presently. My son and I   125
  Have a few words of business.
OLD CARTER   At your pleasure.

                              Ex[eunt] the rest

OLD THORNEY
  I think you guess the reason, Frank, for which
  I sent for you.
FRANK   Yes, sir.
OLD THORNEY   I need not tell you
  With what a labyrinth of dangers daily
  The best part of my whole estate's encumbered.   130
  Nor have I any clew to wind it out,
  But what occasion proffers me. Wherein
  If you should falter, I shall have the shame,
  And you the loss. On these two points rely
  Our happiness or ruin. If you marry   135
  With wealthy Carter's daughter, there's a portion
  Will free my land. All which I will instate
  Upon the marriage to you. Otherwise,
  I must be of necessity enforced
  To make a present sale of all. And yet,   140
  For ought I know, live in as poor distress,
  Or worse, than now I do. You hear the sum.
  I told you thus before. Have you consider'd on't?
FRANK
  I have, sir. And however I could wish
  To enjoy the benefit of single freedom,   145
  For that I find no disposition in me
  To undergo the burden of that care
  That marriage brings with it; yet to secure
  And settle the continuance of your credit,
  I humbly yield to be directed by you   150

131 *clew* a ball of thread
    wind it out discover (referring to the thread Theseus unwound when entering the Minotaur's labyrinth so that he could later find his way back out by following it)
134 *you the loss* Old Thorney's reasoning includes securing his son's future, but the appeal is also aimed at Frank's self-interest
137 *instate* bestow
148–50 *secure ... you* Frank assigns responsibility for his bigamous act to his father's wishes, as Old Carter has assigned any blame to Susan

In all commands.

OLD THORNEY   You have already used
Such thriving protestations to the maid,
That she is wholly yours. And speak the truth,
You love her, do you not?

FRANK   'Twere pity, sir,
I should deceive her.

OLD THORNEY   Better y'had been unborn.   155
But is your love so steady that you mean,
Nay, more, desire to make her your wife?

FRANK   Else, sir,
It were a wrong not to be righted.

OLD THORNEY   True,
It were. And you will marry her?

FRANK   Heaven prosper it.
I do intend it.

OLD THORNEY O thou art a villain!   160
A devil like a man! Wherein have I
Offended all the powers so much, to be
Father to such a graceless godless son?

FRANK
To me, sir, this? O my cleft heart!

OLD THORNEY   To thee,
Son of my curse. Speak with truth, and blush, thou mon-
ster,   165
Hast thou not married Winifred, a maid
Was fellow-servant with thee?

FRANK   [Aside] Some swift spirit
Has blown this news abroad. I must outface it.

OLD THORNEY
D'you study for excuse? Why all the country
Is full on't.

FRANK   With your licence, 'tis not charitable,   170
I am sure it is not fatherly, so much
To be o'erswayed with credulous conceit
Of mere impossibilities. But fathers
Are privileged to think and talk at pleasure.

168 *outface* boldly deny
169 *study* search
170 *full on't* aware of it
    licence permission
172 *conceit* imagination

OLD THORNEY 175
  Why canst thou yet deny thou hast no wife?

FRANK
  What do you take me for? An atheist?
  One that nor hopes the blessedness of life
  Hereafter, neither fears the vengeance due
  To such as make the marriage-bed an inn, 180
  Which travellers day and night,
  After a toilsome lodging leave at pleasure?
  Am I become so insensible of losing
  The glory of creation's work? My soul!
  O, I have lived too long!

OLD THORNEY   Thou hast, dissembler;
  Darest thou persevere yet? and pull down wrath 185
  As hot as flames of hell, to strike thee quick
  Into the grave of horror? I believe thee not.
  Get from my sight.

FRANK   Sir, though mine innocence
  Needs not a stronger witness than the clearness
  Of an unperished conscience; yet for that 190
  I was informed, how mainly you had been
  Possessed of this untruth. To quit all scruple
  Please you peruse this letter. 'Tis to you.

OLD THORNEY
  From whom?

FRANK   Sir Arthur Clarington my master.

OLD THORNEY
  Well, sir. [*Reads letter*]

FRANK   [*Aside*] On every side I am distracted, 195
  Am waded deeper into mischief,
  Than virtue can avoid. But on I must.
  Fate leads me. I will follow. [*To his father*] There you read

---

176 *atheist* one without any scruples

179 *marriage-bed an inn* That is, marriage as a night of sexual bliss only

180 *Which ... night* The short line may indicate some corruption in the text, but it makes sense and emendation seems unwise

186 *quick* living

190 *unperished* clear

191 *mainly* strongly

192 *quit* get rid of

197 *Than ... avoid* Frank continues to avoid full self-knowledge by seeing himself as virtuous and only wrong in his choice, 'mischief' (196); this line introduces a parallel to Mother Sawyer who will see herself as forced to make a pact with Dog because of other people's attitudes (cf. II.i.1–2)

What may confirm you.

OLD THORNEY   Yes, and wonder at it.
Forgive me, Frank. Credulity abused me.   200
My tears express my joy. And I am sorry
I injured innocence.

FRANK   Alas! I knew
Your rate and grief proceeded from your love
To me. So I conceived it.

OLD THORNEY   My good son.
I'll bear with many faults in thee hereafter.   205
Bear thou with mine.

FRANK   The peace is soon concluded.

Enter OLD CARTER [*and* SUSAN]

OLD CARTER
Why, Master Thorney, d'ye mean to talk out your dinner?
The company attends your coming. What must it be,
Master Frank, or son Frank? I am plain Dunstable.

OLD THORNEY
Son, brother, if your daughter like to have it so.   210

FRANK
I dare be confident she's not altered
From what I left her at our parting last.
Are you, fair maid?

SUSAN   You took too sure possession
Of an engaged heart.

FRANK   Which now I challenge.

OLD CARTER
Marry and much good may it do thee, son. Take her to   215
thee. Get me a brace of boys at a burden, Frank. The nursing shall not stand thee in a pennyworth of milk. Reach her
home and spare not. When's the day?

199 *confirm* convince
199–202 *Yes ... innocence* (prose Q)
204 *conceived* understood
209 *plain Dunstable* Proverbial for direct, plainspoken, after the Dunstable–London
  road known for its straight and even route (D646)
210 *Son, brother* son-in-law, brother-in-law
214 *engaged heart* heart already won
  challenge claim
216 *brace* pair   *boys* That is, grandsons
  at a burden at the same time
216–17 *nursing ... milk* the cost of nursing will not be yours
217 *Reach* take
218 *spare not* waste no time

OLD THORNEY
Tomorrow, if you please. To use ceremony
Of charge and custom, were to little purpose.   220
Their loves are married fast enough already.

OLD CARTER
A good motion. We'll e'en have an household dinner; and
let the fiddlers go scrape. Let the bride and bridegroom
dance at night together. No matter for the guests.
Tomorrow, Sue, tomorrow. Shall's to dinner now?   225

OLD THORNEY
We are on all sides pleased, I hope.

SUSAN
Pray heaven I may deserve the blessing sent me.
Now my heart is settled.   FRANK So is mine.

OLD CARTER
Your marriage-money shall be received before your
wedding-shoes can be pulled on. Blessing on you both.   230

FRANK
[*Aside*] No man can hide his shame from heaven that
  views him.
In vain he flees, whose destiny pursues him.

Exeunt All

220 *Of ... purpose* By village custom, there should be a waiting period and public
  announcements of their intentions (banns). This unseemly haste of both parents
  and children will contribute to the tragedy (a variant on *Romeo and Juliet*); cf.
  Mother Sawyer's swift reaction to Old Banks (II.i)
222 *motion* proposal
223 *let ... scrape* dismiss the musicians. The Fiddler, later assigned to a morris dance,
  will (by parallel) be dismissed when he is replaced by Dog
224 *dance at night* May allude to the common tune 'The Shaking of the Sheets' with
  its sexual overtones
225 *Shall's* shall we (contraction of 'shall us')
232 *destiny* Frank defines destiny as guilt, not fate, concerning his agreement to
  marry Susan

ACT II, SCENE i

Enter ELIZABETH SAWYER, *gathering sticks*

SAWYER

And why on me? Why should the envious world
Throw all their scandalous malice upon me?
'Cause I am poor, deformed and ignorant,
And like a bow buckled and bent together,
By some more strong in mischiefs than myself?   5
Must I for that be made a common sink,
For all the filth and rubbish of men's tongues
To fall and run into? Some call me witch;
And being ignorant of myself, they go
About to teach me how to be one: urging   10
That my bad tongue (by their bad usage made so)
Forespeaks their cattle, doth bewitch their corn,

1–2 *why ... me?* Mother Sawyer sees her virtue displaced by the accusations of others and herself as a hopeless victim despite her good intentions. Her social oppression is the kind of role that Dekker specialized in throughout his career, beginning with his first surviving play, *Old Fortunatus*, in 1599. Mother Sawyer has most of the soliloquies in this play, emphasizing her social isolation. More strangely, given her class, her lines are largely in poetry rather than prose, and all are given as poetry here

3–4 *'Cause ... together* Goodcole writes that 'Her body was crooked and deformed, even bending together' (sig. A4v); 'she was a very ignorant woman' (sig. C1). Mother Sawyer's sympathetic characterization may therefore owe even more to Reginald Scot's description of witches generally in *The Discouerie of Witchcraft* as 'women who are commonly old, lame, blear-eied, pale, fowle, and full of wrinkles; poore, sullen, superstitious ... They are leane and deformed, shewing melancholie in their faces ... They are doting, scolds, mad, divelish' (1.3). She is thus unlike the title character of Middleton's *The Witch* (1615–16) whom the Mermaid editor finds a 'fantastic', 'tongue-in-cheek caricature' (p. xx)

6 *sink* pit for sewage

11 *That ... so* The witch was known for the power of her tongue and her speeches were often considered curses; cf. Shakespeare's Caliban on Prospero (I.ii.365–6) *bad usage* Thomas notes (p. 674) that powerless women might assume the position of witch to gain some authority and even respect in the community; cf. George Gifford, *A Dialogue Concerning Witches and Witchcraftes* (1593), sig. B1

12 *Forespeaks* bewitches

12–13 *Forespeaks ... nurse* According to Goodcole, Mother Sawyer confessed that 'I have bene by the helpe of the Divell, the meanes of many Christians and beasts death; the cause that moved mee to do it, was malice and envy, for if any body had angred me in any manner, I would be so revenged of them and of their

Themselves, their servants and their babes at nurse.
This they enforce upon me. And in part
Make me to credit it. And here comes one   15
Of my chief adversaries.

Enter OLD BANKS

OLD BANKS
  Out, out upon thee, witch.
SAWYER   Dost call me witch?
OLD BANKS
  I do, witch, I do. And worse I would, I knew I a name more
  hateful. What makest thou upon my ground?
SAWYER
  Gather a few rotten sticks to warm me.   20
OLD BANKS
  Down with them when I bid thee, quickly; I'll make thy
  bones rattle in thy skin else.
SAWYER
  You won't, churl, cut-throat, miser. [*Throws down sticks*]
  There they be. Would they stuck 'cross thy throat,
  Thy bowels, thy maw, thy midriff.   25
OLD BANKS
  Sayest thou me so? Hag, out of my ground. [*Hits her*]

---

cattell. And do now further confess, that I was the cause of those two nurse-
childrens death' (sig. C2)

17 *witch* Old Banks is speaking colloquially, not literally. In England (unlike the
Continent), Thomas writes, 'Most accusations of witchcraft related to supposed
maleficium and did not suggest that the accused person had contemplated even
a mental transfer of allegiance to the Devil' (p. 627)

18 *worse ... name* 'The conflict between resentment and a sense of obligation produced the ambivalence which made it possible for men to turn begging women
brusquely from the door, and yet suffer torments of conscience after having done
so. This ensuing guilt was fertile ground for witchcraft accusations ... and it
should be emphasised that these conflicts were not between the very rich and the
very poor, but between fairly poor and very poor' (Thomas, p. 673)

19 *makest thou upon* brings you to

20-2 (prose Q)
  Gather ... else The discrepancy between Mother Sawyer's minimal needs and
  Old Banks' severe punishment creates immediate sympathy for her and confirms
  her view of events in her opening soliloquy

23 *You ... miser* Resorting to curses as Mother Sawyer does here was commonly
  taken as proof of witchcraft
  churl villain

25 *maw* belly

26 *Hag* (1) an evil spirit or daemon; (2) a witch; (3) an ugly old woman

SAWYER

Dost strike me, slave? Curmudgeon,
Now thy bones aches, thy joints cramps, and
Convulsions stretch and crack thy sinews!

OLD BANKS

Cursing, thou hag! Take that, and that.   30

[Strikes her and] exit

SAWYER

Strike, do, and withered may that hand and arm
Whose blows have lamed me, drop from the rotten trunk.
Abuse me! Beat me! Call me hag and witch!
What is the name? Where and by what art learned?
What spells, what charms, or invocations?   35
May the thing called Familiar be purchased?

Enter YOUNG [CUDDY] BANKS, *and three or four more*

YOUNG BANKS

A new head for the tabor, and silver tipping for the pipe.
Remember that, and forget not five leash of new bells.

FIRST DANCER

Double bells. Crooked Lane, ye shall have 'em straight in
Crooked Lane. Double bells all, if it be possible.   40

28–9 *Now ... sinews* Mother Sawyer's initial retort has now been transformed into
a full curse, displaying the social construction of witches; Dog is thus a natural
consequence when he appears and can be interpreted as a self-projection of guilt
(cf. Susan to Frank, IV.ii.s.d.69)

36 *Familiar* Technical term for the demonic companion of a witch, often in the form
of an animal; this belief was largely exclusive to English and Scottish accounts of
witchcraft

s.d. *YOUNG BANKS* The author William Rowley probably played (and wrote)
the part of Cuddy since he normally took clown roles, beginning in 1609; some
of his dialogue may first have begun in extemporaneous remarks or actions that
were successful in performance

37 *tabor* small drum

38 *leash* set of three

bells Morris dancers made (and still make) music by dancing vigorously while
wearing bells strapped around their legs; this was common entertainment

39 *Double* bass

40 *Crooked Lane* (speech prefix Q) A street near London Bridge that ran from New
Fish Street to St Michael's Lane, with the Black Bell, an inn, at one end. The
playwrights clearly know London in more intimate detail than they know
Edmonton

YOUNG BANKS
    Double bells? Double coxcombs; trebles: buy me trebles, all
    trebles: for our purpose is to be in the altitudes.
SECOND DANCER
    All trebles? Not a mean?
YOUNG BANKS
    Not one. The morris is so cast we'll have neither mean nor
    base in our company, fellow Rowland.   45
THIRD DANCER
    What? Not a counter?
YOUNG BANKS
    By no means, no hunting counter; leave that to Enville
    Chase men. All trebles, all in the altitudes. Now for the dis-
    posing of parts in the morris, little or no labour will serve.
SECOND DANCER
    If you that be minded to follow your leader, know me, an   50
    ancient honour belonging to our house, for a fore-horse
    team, and fore-gallant in a morris. My father's stable is not
    unfurnished.
THIRD DANCER
    So much for the fore-horse. But how for a good hobby-
    horse?   55
YOUNG BANKS
    For a hobby-horse? Let me see an almanac. [Reads

41 *coxcombs* fools (from the hat shaped like a cock's comb worn by jesters and pro-
    fessional fools)
    trebles voices or instruments highest in pitch
42 *altitudes* high notes
43 *mean* Intermediate range of sound; cf. Cuddy's pun in the following line
44 *morris* A round dance that takes its name from the homonym 'Moorish', since
    originally the dancers blackened their faces
45 *fellow Rowland* Presumably the second dancer. The name may be a slip of the
    pen, referring to Rowland Doyle, an actor in the King's Men's company
46 *counter* counter-tenor
47 *hunting counter* a hunting term for chasing the trail in the opposite direction
    from the quarry
47–8 *Enville Chase* a royal hunting preserve (also known as Enfield Chase) then 12
    miles north of London stocked by Elizabeth I and James I
51 *fore-horse* lead horse in a team
52 *fore-gallant* chief performer
53 *unfurnished* ill-equipped
54–5 *hobby-horse* one dancer was costumed as an especially high-spirited horse
    with a light frame about his waist; he walked and pranced carrying the framed
    costume. Cuddy thinks this is a most desirable part
56 *almanac* an annual book of astrological predictions

almanac] Midsummer-moon, let me see ye. When the moon's in the full, then's wit in the wane. No more. Use your best skill. Your morris will suffer an eclipse.

FIRST DANCER
An eclipse?   60

YOUNG BANKS
A strange one.

SECOND DANCER
Strange?

YOUNG BANKS
Yes, and most sudden. Remember the fore-gallant, and forget the hobby-horse. The whole body of your morris will be darkened. There be of us – but 'tis no matter. Forget the   65
hobby-horse.

FIRST DANCER
Cuddy Banks, have you forgot since he paced it from Enville Chase to Edmonton? Cuddy, honest Cuddy, cast thy stuff.

YOUNG BANKS
Suffer may ye all. It shall be known, I can take mine ease as   70
well as another man. Seek your hobby-horse where you can get him.

FIRST DANCER
Cuddy, honest Cuddy, we confess, and are sorry for our neglect.

SECOND DANCER
The old horse shall have a new bridle.   75

THIRD DANCER
The caparisons new painted.

FOURTH DANCER
The tail repaired.

57   *Midsummer* The summer solstice (now 21 June), a time of madness or strangeness; cf. proverb 'it is midsummer moon with you' (M1117) and Shakespeare's use of the idea in *A Midsummer Night's Dream* and *Twelfth Night*

57–8   *When . . . wane* The passage in the almanac which Young Banks quotes is proverbial (W555)

65-6   *Forget the hobby-horse* The allusion is to the phrase 'The hobby-horse is forgot', from a popular ballad on the Puritans' condemnation of morris dancing. Cf. *Love's Labour's Lost* III.i.129; *Hamlet* III.ii.135. There was a period when the hobby-horse was omitted from games played on May Day

68-9   *cast thy stuff* don't be that way; stop being moody

76   *caparisons* coverings for the horse

FIRST DANCER
The snaffle and the bosses new saffroned o'er. Kind:

SECOND DANCER
Honest:

THIRD DANCER   80
Loving, ingenious:

FOURTH DANCER
Affable Cuddy.

YOUNG BANKS
To show I am not flint, but affable, as you say, very well
stuffed, a kind of warm dough or puff-paste, I relent, I con-
nive, most affable Jack. Let the hobby-horse provide a
strong back, he shall not want a belly when I am in 'em. But   85
'uds me, Mother Sawyer.

FIRST DANCER
The old Witch of Edmonton. If our mirth be not crossed –

SECOND DANCER
Bless us, Cuddy, and let her curse her t'other eye out. What
dost now?

YOUNG BANKS
Ungirt, unblessed, says the proverb. But my girdle shall   90
serve a riding knot. And a fig for all the witches in
Christendom. What wouldst thou?

FIRST DANCER
The devil cannot abide to be crossed.

78 *snaffle and the bosses* A bit with studs on each side
   saffroned Dyed orange
82 *flint* hard, unforgiving
83 *puff-paste* Light and flaky flour paste that has been heavily pounded
85 *want* lack
86 *'uds me* Slang abbreviation for 'God save me'
88 *t'other eye* Mother Sawyer had only one eye. Goodcole records this examination:
   '*Quest[ion]. How came your eye to be put out? Answ[er]*. With a stick which one
   of my children had in the hand, that night my mother did dye it was done; for I
   was stooping by the bed side, and I by chance did hit my eye on the sharpe end
   of the sticke' (sig. D1). Similar deformities were often seen as a mark of witches;
   see Harris, p. 55
90 *Ungirt* unbelted; proverbial, U10   *girdle* belt
91 *riding knot* A running knot used for making nooses and snares
   knot (knit Q)
   a fig for A phrase of contempt; Cuddy pretends not to be frightened when pulling
   off his belt to defend himself from the witch
93 *crossed* opposed; this alludes to the popular belief that to cross the Devil's path
   will lead to harm from him; it may also allude to the protection from the Devil
   by carrying or brandishing a cross; cf. *Hamlet* I.i.127

SECOND DANCER
  And scorns to come at any man's whistle.
THIRD DANCER
  Away –   95
FOURTH DANCER
  With the witch.
ALL
  Away with the Witch of Edmonton.

                         Ex[eunt] in strange postur[es]

SAWYER
  Still vexed? Still tortured? That curmudgeon Banks
  Is ground of all my scandal. I am shunned
  And hated like a sickness. Made a scorn   100
  To all degrees and sexes. I have heard old beldams
  Talk of familiars in the shape of mice,
  Rats, ferrets, weasels and I wot not what,
  That have appeared, and sucked, some say, their blood.
  But by what means they came acquainted with them,   105
  I'm now ignorant. Would some power good or bad
  Instruct me which way I might be revenged
  Upon this churl, I'd go out of myself,

97 s.d. *strange postures* Cuddy and the dancers have either been affected by Mother Sawyer or the Devil or else assume such postures in an attempt to protect themselves

99 *scandal* embarrassment; false charges

101 *degrees* social classes
    beldams hags

103 *wot* know

104 *sucked* According to popular belief, witches fed their familiars with their blood either by scratching themselves or allowing the familiar to suck blood from them, raising the skin and marking it with the 'witch's mark' so that what remained resembled a teat. Goodcole notes of witnesses, 'And they all three said, that they a little above the Fundiment [anus] of *Elizabeth Sawyer* the prisoner, there indited before the Bench for a Witch, found a thing like a Teate the bignesse of the little finger, and the length of halfe a finger, which was branched at the top like a teate, and seemed as though one had suckt it, and that the bottome thereof was blew, and the top of it was redd' (sig. B3v). The Witchcraft Act of 1604 refers to the feeding of familiars, for which see Thomas, p. 530. Mother Sawyer testified, 'The place where the Diuell suckt my bloud was a little above my fundiment, and that place chosen by himselfe; and in that place chosen by himself by continuall drawing, there is a thing in the forme of a Teate, at which the diuell would sucke mee. And I asked the Diuell why hee would sucke my bloud, and hee sayd it was to nourish him' (sigs. C3–C3v); cf. Harris, pp. 21–2

And give this fury leave to dwell within
This ruined cottage, ready to fall with age.   110
Abjure all goodness. Be at hate with prayer,
And study curses, imprecations,
Blasphemous speeches, oaths, detested oaths,
Or anything that's ill; so I might work
Revenge upon this miser, this black cur,   115
That barks and bites, and sucks the very blood
Of me, and of my credit. 'Tis all one,
To be a witch as to be counted one.
Vengeance, shame, ruin, light upon that canker.

Enter DOG

DOG
   Ho! Have I found thee cursing? Now thou art mine own.   120
SAWYER
   Thine? What art thou?
DOG   He thou hast so often importuned
   To appear to thee, the Devil.
SAWYER   Bless me! The Devil?

---

110 *This ruined cottage* Mother Sawyer is referring to her body
117 *credit* reputation
119 s.d. *Enter* DOG A dog was a conventional familiar and of the choices available
(dog, cat, spider, toad) may have been the easiest (and most visible) to stage; cf.
Goodcole: '*Question.* In what shape would the Diuell come vnto you? *Answere.*
Alwayes in the shape of a dogge, and of two collars, sometimes of blacke and
sometimes of white' (sig. C2v). Hoy argues that the audience must decide if Dog
is the Devil or can be Mother Sawyer's overwrought imagination (III, 238) but
the actual appearance and dialogue of Dog on stage might more strongly support
the former
120 *cursing* So Goodcole's *Wonderful Discouerie*: '*Question. By what meanes came
you to haue acquaintance with the Diuell, and when was the first time that you
saw him, and how did you know that it was the Diuell? Answere.* The first time
that the Diuell came vnto me was, when I was cursing, swearing and blasphem-
ing; he then rushed in vpon me, and neuer before that time did I see him, or he
me; and when he, namely the Diuel, came to me, the first words that hee spake
vnto me were these: *Oh! haue I now found you cursing, swearing, and blas-
pheming? now you are mine*' (sigs. C1–C1v). James I noted in his *Daemonologie*
(1597; 1603) that desperate persons calling on the Devil often met him in familiar shapes
121 *importuned* pleaded with
122 *appear* Thomas remarks that contemporary religion emphasized the continual
presence of the Devil and his agents (pp. 638ff.)

DOG

> Come, do not fear, I love thee much too well
> To hurt or fright thee. If I seem terrible,
> It is to such as hate me. I have found   125
> Thy love unfeigned; have seen and pitied
> Thy open wrongs, and come out of my love
> To give thee just revenge against thy foes.

SAWYER

> May I believe thee?

DOG

>   To confirm't, command me
> Do any mischief unto man or beast,   130
> And I'll effect it, on condition,
> That uncompelled thou make a deed of gift
> Of soul and body to me.

SAWYER

>   Out, alas!

123 *do not fear* Thus Goodcole: '*Question. What sayd you to the Diuell, when hee came vnto you and spake vnto you, were you not afraide of him? If you did feare him, what sayd the Diuell then vnto you? Answere.* I was in a very greate feare, when I saw the Diuell, but hee did bid me not to feare him at all, for hee would do me no hurt at all, but would do for mee whatsoeuer I should require of him, and as he promised vnto me, he alwayes did such mischiefes as I did bid him to do, both on the bodies of Christians and beastes: if I did bid him vexe them to death, as oftentimes I did so bid him, it was then presently by him so done' (sigs. C1v–C2)

127 *out of my love* Dog gains power over Mother Sawyer by offering her the only love (and pity) she knows. 'These creatures may have been the only friends these lonely old women possessed' (Thomas, p. 626)

132–5 *make a deed ... seal it with thy blood* Cf. Goodcole: '*Question.* What talke had the Diuel and you together, when that he appeared to you, and what did he aske of you, and what did you desire of him? *Answere.* He asked of me, when hee came vnto me, how I did, and what he should doe for mee, and demanded of mee my soule and body; threatning then to teare me in peeces, if that I did not grant vnto him my soule and my body which he asked of me. *Question. What did you after such the Diuells asking of you, to haue your Soule and Body, and after this his threatning of you, did you for feare grant vnto the Diuell his desire? Answer.* Yes, I granted for feare vnto the Diuell his request of my Soule and body; and to seale this my promise made vnto him, I then gaue him leaue to sucke of my bloud, the which hee asked of me' (sigs. C2v–C3)

132 *deed of gift* Mother Sawyer seems to sign over her soul here to Dog as the Devil despite a common belief that no person could so easily undo baptismal rites. In *A Discourse of the Damned Art of Witchcraft* (1608) William Perkins writes that 'consenting to use the help of the devil, either by open or secret league, wittingly and willingly: wherein standeth the very thing that maketh a witch to be a witch, the yielding of consent upon covenant'

My soul and body?
DOG   And that instantly,   135
  And seal it with thy blood. If thou deniest,
  I'll tear thy body in a thousand pieces.
SAWYER
  I know not where to seek relief. But shall I
  After such covenants sealed, see full revenge
  On all that wrong me?
DOG   Ha, ha, silly woman!   140
  The Devil is no liar to such as he loves.
  Didst ever know or hear the Devil a liar
  To such as he affects?
SAWYER   Then I am thine, at least
  So much of me as I can call mine own.
DOG   Equivocations?
  Art mine or no? Speak, or I'll tear –
SAWYER   All thine.
DOG
  Seal't with thy blood.

Sucks her arm, thunder and lightning

           See, now I dare call thee mine;   145
  For proof, command me. Instantly I'll run
  To any mischief, goodness can I none.
SAWYER
  And I desire as little. There's an old churl,
  One Banks –
DOG   That wronged thee.
  He lamed thee, called thee witch.   150
SAWYER
  The same. First upon him I'd be revenged.
DOG
  Thou shalt. Do but name how.
SAWYER   Go, touch his life.
DOG
  I cannot.

136 *tear thy body* Mother Sawyer does not agree to make a pact with Dog until he threatens her with bodily harm

145 s.d. *Sucks her arm* Mother Sawyer must draw blood to seal their pact; in the 1981 RSC production she produced blood by scratching her chest

150 *lamed thee* Dog confirms Mother Sawyer's sense of herself as the victim of Old Banks especially

152 *touch his life* kill him

153 *cannot* Thomas notes that common belief held the Devil was powerless before virtue (p. 592)

SAWYER
Hast thou not vowed? Go, kill the slave.

DOG
I wonnot.   155

SAWYER
I'll cancel then my gift.

DOG   Ha, ha!

SAWYER   Dost laugh?
Why wilt not kill him?

DOG   Fool, because I cannot.
Though we have power, know, it is circumscribed,
And tied in limits. Though he be cursed to thee,
Yet of himself he is loving to the world,   160
And charitable to the poor. Now men
That, as he, love goodness, though in smallest measure,
Live without compass of our reach. His cattle
And corn I'll kill and mildew. But his life,
(Until I take him as I late found thee,   165
Cursing and swearing) I have no power to touch.

SAWYER
Work on his corn and cattle then.

DOG   I shall.
The Witch of Edmonton shall see his fall.
If she at least put credit in my power,
And in mine only; make orisons to me,   170
And none but me.

SAWYER   Say how, and in what manner?

DOG
I'll tell thee, when thou wishest ill;
Corn, man or beast, would spoil or kill,
Turn thy back against the sun,
And mumble this short orison: 175

---

155 *wonnot* (1) don't know how; (2) I will not

156 *cancel ... gift* Despite Dog's accusation of Old Banks' persecution of Mother
    Sawyer, he will not grant her the one wish for which she agreed to the pact with
    him; she is thus (despite her 'virtue') in a dilemma similar to Frank's when he
    consents to marry Susan. Both have made mistaken moral choices and commit-
    ments for understandable reasons

159 *cursed* evil

163 *without compass of* beyond

166 *touch* harm

170 *orisons* prayers

175–83 *orison ... Speak Latin* Thus Goodcole's account of Mother Sawyer's exam-
    ination: 'Quest. Did the Diuell at any time find you praying when he came vnto
    you, and did not the Diuell forbid you to pray to Iesus Christ, but to him alone?

If thou to death or shame pursue 'em,
Sanctibicetur nomen tuum.

SAWYER
If thou to death or shame pursue 'em,
Sanctibecetur nomen tuum.

DOG
Perfect. Farewell. Our first-made promises   180
We'll put in execution against Banks.   *Exit*

SAWYER
Contaminetur nomen tuum. I'm an expert scholar;
Speak Latin, or I know not well what language,
As well as the best of 'em.

Enter YOUNG BANKS

But who comes here?   185
The son of my worst foe. *To death pursue 'em,*
Et sanctabecetur nomen tuum.

YOUNG BANKS
What's that she mumbles? The Devil's *pater noster*? Would
it were else. Mother Sawyer, good morrow.

SAWYER
Ill morrow to thee, and all the world,   190
That flout a poor old woman.

---

and did not he bid you pray to him the Divell, as he taught you? Answ. Yes, he
found me once praying, and he asked of me to whom I prayed, and I answered
him, to Iesus Christ; and he charged me then to pray no more to Iesus Christ, but
to him the Diuell, and he the Diuell taught me this prayer, *Sanctibicetur nomen*
tuum. Amen. Quest. Were you euer taught these Latine words before by any
person else, or did you euer heare it before of anybody, or can you say more of
it? Answ. No, I was not taught it by any body else, but by the Diuell alone;
neither doe I vnderstand the meaning of these words, nor can speake any more
Latine words' (sig. C4v)

177 *Sanctibicetur nomen tuum* In a parody of the phrase 'Hallowed be thy name'
from the Lord's Prayer, *sanctibicetur* is substituted for *sanctificetur*; as the Devil,
Dog is unable to teach the Lord's Prayer correctly

179 *Sanctibecetur* That Mother Sawyer instantly makes a mistake shows her ignorance (and perhaps a residual innocence) as well as the weak hold she has on the
charm Dog has tried to teach her. Alternatively, it may be a sign of her damnation

180 *Perfect* Either Dog lies or he fails to notice his disciple's error

182 *Contaminetur ... scholar* In a further joke, Mother Sawyer uses a correct term
(*contaminetur* means polluted or defiled) she has not been taught; this may continue to suggest residual grace or self-damnation

183 *Speak Latin* Knowledge of Latin was restricted to the educated classes and clergy

188 *pater noster* prayer (literally, 'Our Father', signifying the Lord's Prayer)

To death pursue 'em,
And sanctabacetur nomen tuum.

YOUNG BANKS
Nay, Good Gammer Sawyer, whate'er it please my father
to call you, I know you are –   195

SAWYER
A witch.

YOUNG BANKS
A witch? Would you were else i'faith.

SAWYER
Your father knows I am by this.

YOUNG BANKS
I would he did.

SAWYER
And so in time may you.   200

YOUNG BANKS
I would I might else. But witch or no witch, you are a moth-
erly woman. And though my father be a kind of God-bless-
us, as they say, I have an earnest suit to you; and if you'll
be so kind to ka me one good turn, I'll be so courteous as
to kob you another.   205

SAWYER
What's that? To spurn, beat me,
And call me witch, as your
Kind father doth?

YOUNG BANKS
My father? I am ashamed to own him. If he has hurt the
head of thy credit, there's money to buy thee a plaster.   210
[*Gives her money*] And a small courtesy I would require at
thy hands.

SAWYER
You seem a good young man. [*Aside*] And
I must dissemble, the better to accomplish

---

194 *Gammer* Grandmother (a term of familiarity)
198 *by this* by this time; Mother Sawyer assumes that by now Dog will have seen to
Old Banks
201–2 *you ... woman* Ironically, Young Banks gives Mother Sawyer more unso-
licited respect than she received from soliciting the help of Dog; cf. Winifred's
sympathy for Frank in Act IV
202–3 *God-bless-us* religious man
203 *suit* request (indicating respect)
203–5 *if ... another* Proverbial for mutual help; cf. 'scratch my back and I'll scratch
yours' (K1)
204 *ka* give
205 *kob* give

My revenge. [*To him*] But for this silver,   215
What wouldst have me do? Bewitch thee?

YOUNG BANKS
No, by no means; I am bewitched already. I would have
thee so good as to unwitch me, or witch another with me
for company.

SAWYER
I understand thee not. Be plain, my son.   220

YOUNG BANKS
As a pike-staff, Mother. You know Kate Carter.

SAWYER
The wealthy yeoman's daughter. What of her?

YOUNG BANKS
That same party has bewitched me.

SAWYER
Bewitched thee?

YOUNG BANKS
Bewitched me, *hisce auribus*. I saw a little Devil fly out of   225
her eye like a burbolt, which sticks at this hour up to the
feathers in my heart. Now my request is to send one of thy
what-d'ye-call-'ems, either to pluck that out, or stick
another as fast in hers. Do, and here's my hand, I am thine
for three lives.   230

SAWYER
[*Aside*] We shall have sport. [*To him*] Thou art
In love with her?

YOUNG BANKS
Up to the very hilts, Mother.

SAWYER
And thou'dst have me make her love thee too.

YOUNG BANKS
[*Aside*] I think she'll prove a witch in earnest. [*To her*] Yes,   235
I could find in my heart to strike her three quarters deep in
love with me too.

---

221 *pike-staff* straight walking-stick; proverbial (P322)
223 *bewitched me* This line, which anticipates Young Banks' sight of Katherine's
    Spirit created by Dog (III.i.s.d.73), has particular force for Mother Sawyer
225 *hisce auribus* 'in these very ears' (Latin)
226 *burbolt* blunt-headed arrow for hunting birds
230 *for three lives* Allusion to the law concerning property held for three generations
233 *hilts* handles (of swords and daggers)
234 *And ... too* Mother Sawyer's unconscious echo of Dog here signals her servitude
    to him

SAWYER
But dost thou think that I can do't,
And I alone?

YOUNG BANKS
Truly, Mother Witch, I do verily believe so. And when I see   240
it done, I shall be half persuaded so too.

SAWYER
It's enough. What art can do, be sure of.
Turn to the west, and whatso'er thou hearest or seest,
Stand silent, and be not afraid.

She stamps. Enter the DOG; *he fawns and leaps*
upon her

YOUNG BANKS
Afraid, Mother Witch? Turn my face to the west? [*Aside*] I   245
said I should always have a back-friend of her; and now it's
out. And her little Devil should be hungry, come sneaking
behind me, like a cowardly catchpole, and clap his talons
on my haunches. 'Tis woundy cold sure. I dudder and
shake like an aspen-leaf every joint of me.   250

SAWYER
To scandal and disgrace pursue 'em,
Et sanctabicetur nomen tuum.
How now, my son, how is't?

Exit DOG

YOUNG BANKS
Scarce in a clean life, Mother Witch. But did your goblin
and you spout Latin together?   255

SAWYER
A kind of charm I work by. Didst thou hear me?

---

244 s.d. *She stamps* According to the Witchcraft Statute of 1604, the invocation of
evil spirits was a felony; at this point, Mother Sawyer is being identified as a
criminal (the law was in effect until 1736)

246 *back-friend* supporter, ally

247 *out* occurred
And suppose

248 *catchpole* constable or sergeant (with pun on 'back-friend')

249 *woundy* excessively
dudder shiver

250 *aspen-leaf* Proverbial; L140

256 *charm* That Mother Sawyer uses Dog's power against kindly Young Banks
shows both her desperation and her self-condemnation; she has acted the part of
a witch for ridiculously low stakes

YOUNG BANKS

I heard I know not the Devil what mumble in a scurvy base
tone, like a drum that had taken cold in the head the last
muster. Very comfortable words. What were they? And
who taught them you?   260

SAWYER

A great learned man.

YOUNG BANKS

Learned man? Learned Devil it was as soon? But what?
What comfortable news about the party?

SAWYER

Who? Kate Carter? I'll tell thee,
Thou knowst the stile at the west end   265
Of thy father's peas-field. Be there
Tomorrow night after sunset;
And the first live thing thou seest,
Be sure to follow, and that
Shall bring thee to thy love.   270

YOUNG BANKS

In the peas-field? Has she a mind to codlings already? The
first living thing I meet, you say, shall bring me to her?

SAWYER

To a sight of her, I mean. She will seem
Wantonly coy, and flee thee. But
Follow her close, and boldly.   275
Do but embrace her in thy arms
Once, and she is thine own.

YOUNG BANKS

At the stile, at the west end of my father's peas-land, the
first live thing I see, follow and embrace her, and she shall
be thine. Nay, and I come to embracing once, she shall be   280
mine; I'll go near to make at eaglet else.   *Exit*

SAWYER

A ball well bandied. Now the set's half won.
The father's wrong I'll wreak upon the son.   *Exit*

---

258 *cold … head* Young Banks cannot avoid a pun; it is the parallel characteristic to
Old Carter's proverbs

259 *muster* calling of troops

262 *soon* likely

271 *codlings* peas (with a pun on codpiece that covers the scrotum in man's dress)

281 *at eaglet* act as amateur (the eaglet was trained by its parent before acting on its
own)

282 *bandied* thrown to and fro
set a fixed number of games (as in tennis)

ACT II, SCENE ii

Enter [OLD] CARTER, WARBECK, SOMERTON

OLD CARTER
How now, gentlemen, cloudy? I know, Master Warbeck,
you are in a fog about my daughter's marriage.
WARBECK
And can you blame me, sir?
OLD CARTER
Nor you me justly. Wedding and hanging are tied up both
in a proverb, and destiny is the juggler that unties the knot.   5
My hope is, you are reserved to a richer fortune than my
poor daughter.
WARBECK
However, your promise –
OLD CARTER
Is a kind of debt, I confess it.
WARBECK
Which honest men should pay.   10
OLD CARTER
Yet some gentlemen break in that point, now and then, by
your leave, sir.
SOMERTON
I confess thou hast had a little wrong
In the wench. But patience is the only salve
To cure it. Since Thorney has won the wench,   15
He has most reason to wear her.
WARBECK
Love in this kind admits no reason to wear her.
OLD CARTER
Then love's a fool, and what wise man will take exception?
SOMERTON
Come, frolic. Ned, were every man master
Of his own fortune, Fate might pick straws,   20
And Destiny go a-wool-gathering.

---

1 *cloudy* troubled
5 *proverb* 'Wedding and hanging go by destiny' (W232); another forewarning
8 *promise* – (promise. Q)
8–9 *promise ... debt* Proverbial; P603
19 *frolic* carefree
20 *pick straws* become tired
21 *a-wool-gathering* absent-minded

WARBECK
  You hold yours in a string, though.
  'Tis well. But if there be any equity,
  Look thou to meet the like usage ere long.
SOMERTON   25
  In my love to her sister Katherine? Indeed,
  They are a pair of arrows drawn out of one quiver,
  And should fly at an even length, if she do run
  After her sister.
WARBECK   Look for the same mercy
  At my hands, as I have received at thine.
SOMERTON   30
  She'll keep a surer compass. I have
  Too strong a confidence to mistrust her.
WARBECK
  And that confidence is a wind,
  That has blown many a married man ashore at Cuckold's
      Haven,
  I can tell you. I wish yours more prosperous though.
OLD CARTER   35
  Whate'er you wish, I'll master my promise to him.
WARBECK
  Yes, as you did to me.
OLD CARTER
  No more of that, if you love me. But for the more assur-
  ance, the next offered occasion shall consummate the
  marriage. And that once sealed—

            Enter YOUNG [FRANK] THORNEY *and* SUSAN

22 *hold ... string* be in absolute control (from the proverb 'hold the world on a
   string', W886)
27 *run* take
30 *compass* (1) measure (from space denoted by the markings of a compass); (2)
   direction (compass-wise meant going steadily to the mark)
33 *Cuckold's Haven* Land along the Kent/south side of the Thames about a mile
   below Rotherhithe Church said to have been granted by King John to a man in
   recompense for having seduced his wife, a tale commemorated by an Eastcheap
   butcher on St Luke's Day, 18 October, by erecting a pair of horns on a pole there
   (see *Eastward Ho!* IV.i); also, more generally, a place of safety or refuge
35 *master* keep

SOMERTON
Leave the manage of the rest to my care. 40
But see, the bridegroom and bride comes;
The new pair of Sheffield knives fitted both
To one sheath.
WARBECK   The sheath might have been better fitted,
If somebody had their due. But –
SOMERTON
No harsh language, if thou lovest me. 45
Frank Thorney has done –
WARBECK
No more than I, or thou, or any man,
Things so standing, would have attempted.
SOMERTON
Good morrow, Master Bridegroom.
WARBECK
Come, give thee joy. Mayst thou live 50
Long and happy in thy fair choice.
FRANK
I thank ye gentlemen. Kind Master Warbeck,
I find you loving.
WARBECK   Thorney, that creature,
[*Aside*] (much good do thee with her)
[*To him*] Virtue and beauty hold fair mixture in her. 55
She's rich no doubt, in both. Yet were she fairer,
Thou art right worthy of her. Love her, Thorney,
'Tis nobleness in thee, in her but duty.
The match is fair and equal. The success
I leave to censure. Farewell, Mistress Bride: 60
Till now elected, thy old scorn deride.   *Exit*
SOMERTON
Good, Master Thorney.   [*Exit*]

42–3 *Sheffield knives ... one sheath* (1) A traditional emblem for marriage (as two
    made one); (2) a customary wedding present, Sheffield having a reputation for
    producing especially fine knives
45–6 *No ... done* Q assigns these lines to Old Carter, but *thou* would be an inap-
    propriate word for one of his class
 60 *censure* That is, censure opinions (of others)

OLD CARTER
  Nay, you shall not part till you see the barrels run a-tilt,
  gentlemen.   *Exit*

SUSAN
  Why change you your face, sweetheart?

FRANK   Who? I?   65
  For nothing.

SUSAN   Dear, say not so. A spirit of your
  Constancy cannot endure this change for nothing.
  I have observed strange variations in you.

FRANK   In me?

SUSAN
  In you, sir. Awake, you seem to dream,
  And in your sleep you utter sudden and   70
  Distracted accents, like one at enmity
  With peace. Dear loving husband, if I may dare
  To challenge any interest in you,
  Give me the reason fully. You may trust
  My breast as safely as your own.

FRANK   With what?   75
  You half amaze me, prithee.

SUSAN   Come, you shall not;
  Indeed, you shall not shut me from partaking
  The least dislike that grieves you. I am all yours.

FRANK
  And I all thine.

SUSAN   You are not, if you keep
  The least grief from me. But I find the cause;   80
  It grew from me.

FRANK   From you?

SUSAN   From some distaste
  In me or my behaviour. You are not kind
  In the concealment. 'Las, sir, I am young,
  Silly and plain; more, strange to those contents
  A wife should offer. Say but in what I fail,   85
  I'll study satisfaction.

FRANK   Come, in nothing.

SUSAN
  I know I do. Knew I as well in what,

---

63 *barrels run a-tilt* A tilting contest using spears aimed at barrels, here made a wed-
    ding festivity; by tradition, this was a skilled match used by burgesses and
    yeomen who were barred as combatants in jousts and tournaments since they
    were not of sufficiently high rank (esquire)

71 *accents* words

86 *study* learn

You should not long be sullen. Prithee love,
If I have been immodest or too bold,
Speak't in a frown. If peevishly too nice,   90
Show't in a smile. Thy liking is the glass
By which I'll habit my behaviour.

FRANK
Wherefore dost weep now?

SUSAN   You, sweet, have the power
To make me passionate as an April day.
Now smile, then weep, now pale, then crimson red.   95
You are the powerful moon of my blood's sea,
To make it ebb or flow into my face,
As your looks change.

FRANK   Change thy conceit, I prithee.
Thou art all perfection. Diana herself
Swells in thy thoughts, and moderates thy beauty.   100
Within thy left eye amorous Cupid sits
Feathering love-shafts, whose golden heads he dipped
– In thy chaste breast. In the other lies
Blushing Adonis scarfed in modesties.
And still as wanton Cupid blows love-fires,   105
Adonis quenches out unchaste desires.
And from these two I briefly do imply
A perfect emblem of thy modesty.
Then, prithee, dear, maintain no more dispute,
For when thou speakest, it's fit all tongues be mute.   110

SUSAN
Come, come, those golden strings of flattery
Shall not tie up my speech, sir; I must know
The ground of your disturbance.

FRANK   Then look here;
For here, here is the fen in which this Hydra
Of discontent grows rank.

SUSAN   Heaven shield it. Where?   115

---

90 *nice* coy
98 *conceit* example; forceful idea
99 *Diana* As goddess of chastity
101 *Cupid* The child-god of love whose golden arrows caused love and whose lead
    arrows repelled it
104 *Adonis* Exemplary of beauty; he attracted Venus
    scarfed clothed
114 *fen* marshy ground
    Hydra The many-headed beast that according to myth grew back two snake
    heads for every one cut off

FRANK
In mine own bosom. Here the cause has root;
The poisoned leeches twist about my heart,
And will, I hope, confound me.
SUSAN   You speak riddles.
FRANK
Take't plainly then. 'Twas told me by a woman   120
Known and approved in palmistry,
I should have two wives.
SUSAN   Two wives? Sir, I take it
Exceeding likely. But let not conceit hurt you.
You are afraid to bury me?
FRANK   No, no, my Winifred.
SUSAN
How say you? Winifred? You forget me.
FRANK
No, I forget myself, Susan.
SUSAN   In what?   125
FRANK
Talking of wives, I pretend Winifred,
A maid that at my mother's waited on me
Before thyself.
SUSAN   I hope, sir, she may live
To take my place. But why should all this move you?
FRANK
[Aside] The poor girl, she has't before thee,   130
And that's the fiend torments me.
SUSAN   Yet why should this
Raise mutiny within you? Such presages
Prove often false. Or say it should be true?

117 *leeches* Worms used in medicine to suck bad blood from the sick

118 *confound* undo, ruin

119–21 *woman ... wives* Frank associates himself with palmistry, a pseudo-science not unrelated to witchcraft

122 *likely* That is, unlikely; Susan is mocking Frank

126 *pretend* (1) lay claim to; (2) use as a pretext
Winifred Ambiguous; (1) a slip of the tongue, suggesting an unexpected act of conscience; (2) an attempt to confess – the virtue Frank earlier claimed for himself (I.ii.197)

130 *poor girl* The Revels editor thinks Susan deciphers this as a reference to the former wife's death, but the context implies she is thinking of other future wives; either way, Susan is shown as ignorant of the real situation despite the slip of Frank's tongue. Q does not make this speech an aside
has't That is, has my marriage vow

FRANK
  That I should have another wife?
SUSAN   Yes, many;
  If they be good, the better.
FRANK   Never any equal   135
  To thee in goodness.
SUSAN   Sir, I could wish I were
  Much better for you; yet if I knew your fate
  Ordained you for another, I could wish
  (So well I love you and your hopeful pleasure)
  Me in my grave, and my poor virtues added   140
  To my successor.
FRANK   Prithee, prithee, talk not
  Of death or graves; thou art so rare a goodness,
  As death would rather put itself to death
  Than murder thee. But we, as all things else,
  Are mutable and changing.
SUSAN   Yet you still move   145
  In your first sphere of discontent. Sweet, chase
  Those clouds of sorrow, and shine clearly on me.
FRANK
  At my return I will.
SUSAN   Return? Ah me!
  Will you then leave me?
FRANK   For a time I must.
  But how? As birds their young, or loving bees   150
  Their hives, to fetch home richer dainties.
SUSAN   Leave me?
  Now has my fear met its effect. You shall not,
  Cost it my life, you shall not.
FRANK   Why? Your reason?
SUSAN
  Like to the lapwing have you all this while
  With your false love deluded me? Pretending   155
  Counterfeit senses for your discontent,
  And now at last it is by chance stole from you.

---

134 *That ... wife?* Frank is recalling the falsely claimed prophecy that he will have
  two wives

  Yes, many Susan has innocently hit upon the truth, her intuition meeting his suddenly guilty conscience
140 *Me in my grave* Another ironic anticipation; cf. 153 below
152 *met its effect* come to pass
154 *lapwing* A bird known for decoying intruders away from its nest; proverbial
  (L68)

FRANK
  What? What by chance?
SUSAN   Your pre-appointed meeting
  Of single combat with young Warbeck.
FRANK   Ha!
SUSAN
  Even so. Dissemble not, 'tis too apparent.   160
  Then in his look I read it. Deny it not;
  I see't apparent. Cost it my undoing,
  And unto that my life, I will not leave you.
FRANK
  Not until when?
SUSAN   Till he and you be friends.
  Was this your cunning? and then flam me off   165
  With an old witch, two wives, and Winifred?
  You're not so kind indeed as I imagined.
FRANK
  And you more fond by far than I expected.
  It is a virtue that attends thy kind.
  But of our business within. And by this kiss   170
  I'll anger thee no more; troth chuck I will not.

                    [*Kisses her*]

SUSAN
  You shall have no just cause.
FRANK   Dear Sue, I shall not.

                                        Exeunt

ACT III, SCENE i

Enter CUDDY BANKS *and Morris dancers*

FIRST DANCER
  Nay, Cuddy, prithee do not leave us now. If we part all this
  night, we shall not meet before day.
SECOND DANCER
  I prithee, Banks, let's keep together now.

---

163 *unto that* even
165 *flam* Trick by distracting
168 *fond* Perhaps deliberately ambiguous, answering Frank's divided conscience, as
    'loving' and 'foolish' (both in reference to Susan)
171 *troth* Elision of 'by my truth', a common pledge
    chuck A common term of affection

YOUNG BANKS

If you were wise, a word would serve. But as you are, I must be forced to tell you again, I have a little private business, an hour's work; it may prove but an half hour's, as luck may serve; and then I take horse and along with you. Have we e'er a witch in the morris? 5

FIRST DANCER

No, no; no woman's part but Maid Marian, and the hobby-horse. 10

YOUNG BANKS

I'll have a witch; I love a witch.

FIRST DANCER

Faith, witches themselves are so common now-a-days, that the counterfeit will not be regarded. They say we have three or four in Edmonton, besides Mother Sawyer.

SECOND DANCER

I would she would dance her part with us. 15

THIRD DANCER

So would not I, for, if she comes, the Devil and all comes along with her.

YOUNG BANKS

Well, I'll have a witch. I have loved a witch ever since I played at cherry-pit. Leave me, and get my horse dressed. Give him oats; but water him not till I come. Whither do 20 we foot it first?

SECOND DANCER

To Sir Arthur Clarington's first, then whither thou wilt.

YOUNG BANKS

Well, I am content. But we must up to Carter's, the rich yeoman. I must be seen on hobby-horse there.

4 *YOUNG BANKS* Q begins here to use the speech prefix 'Clow[n]' for Young Banks

If ... serve Proverbial ('A word to the wise man is enough', W781)

7 *horse* hobby-horse (see note to II.i.54–5); it was sometimes associated with the witch's broomstick and is therefore especially appropriate for Young Banks to bring

8 *witch* Perhaps also a reference to Maid Marian, originally queen of the witch's coven before becoming the companion of Robin Hood and frequently played by a man in morris dances

19 *cherry-pit* A traditional children's game in which cherry stones were tossed into a small hole

21 *foot it* (1) walk; (2) dance

FIRST DANCER
　O, I smell him now. I'll lay my ears Banks is in love, and　25
that's the reason he would walk melancholy by himself.

YOUNG BANKS
　Ha! Who was that said I was in love?

FIRST DANCER
　Not I.

SECOND DANCER
　Not I.

YOUNG BANKS
　Go to. No more of that. When I understand what you　30
speak, I know what you say. Believe that.

FIRST DANCER
　Well, 'twas I, I'll not deny it. I meant no hurt in't. I have
seen you walk up to Carter's of Chessum. Banks, were not
you there last Shrovetide?

YOUNG BANKS
　Yes, I was ten days together there the last Shrovetide.　35

SECOND DANCER
　How could that be, when there are but seven days in the
week?

YOUNG BANKS
　Prithee peace, I reckon *stila nova* as a traveller. Thou
understandest as a fresh-water farmer, that never sawest a
week beyond sea. Ask any soldier that ever received his pay　40
but in the Low Countries, and he'll tell thee there are eight
days in the week there, hard by. How dost thou think they
rise in High Germany, Italy, and those remoter places?

THIRD DANCER
　Ay, but simply there are but seven days in the week yet.

25　*smell him* know what he's up to
　　lay bet
30　*Go to* go on with you (common expression)
33　*Chessum* Probably Cheshunt, Hertfordshire, then four miles north of Edmonton
34　*Shrovetide* The week before Lent, often marked by festivity
38　*stila nova* new style; a learned joke since the new Gregorian calendar introduced
　　on the Continent in 1582, seven days ahead of the English calendar, was not
　　adopted in England until 1752
39　*fresh-water* inexperienced (in analogy to a 'fresh-water sailor' who has never
　　been to sea)
40–2　*soldier ... hard by* Time went slowly for ill-paid ('hard by') soldiers, hence
　　weeks appear to have eight days
41　*Low Countries* the Netherlands (then 18 separate provinces)

YOUNG BANKS

No, simply as thou understandest. Prithee, look but in the   45
lover's almanac; when he has been but three days absent,
'Oh', says he, 'I have not seen my love these seven years.
There's a long cut.' When he comes to her again, and
embraces her, 'O', says he, 'now methinks I am in heaven';
and that's a pretty step. He that can get up to heaven in ten   50
days, need not repent his journey. You may ride a hundred
days in a caroche, and be further off than when you set
forth. But I pray you, good morris-mates, now leave me. I
will be with you by midnight.

FIRST DANCER

Well, since he will be alone, we'll back again, and trouble   55
him no more.

ALL

But remember, Banks.

YOUNG BANKS

The hobby-horse shall be remembered. But hark you. Get
Poldavis, the barber's boy, for the witch; because he can
show his art better than another.   60

Exeunt [all but YOUNG BANKS]

Well, now to my walk. I am near the place where I should
meet I know not what. Say I meet a thief, I must follow
him, if to the gallows. Say I meet a horse, or hare, or hound,
still I must follow; some slow-paced beast, I hope. Yet love
is full of lightness in the heaviest lovers.   65

[Enter DOG]

Ha! My guide is come. A water-dog. I am thy first man,
Sculler. I go with thee. Ply no other but myself. Away with

---

48 *cut* misfortune
52 *caroche* gentleman's coach
59 *Poldavis* Cf. Actors' Names, line 15. Hoy sees an allusion to poldavy, a coarse
canvas used for sailcloth – hence clown, rustic or lower order of tradesman, a
social slur (Hoy, III, 254)
62 *Say* suppose
65 *heaviest* (1) most serious; (2) overweight (as Young Banks' self-reference)
66 *water-dog* A dog, often a spaniel, taught by hunters to retrieve ducks and other
waterbirds
67 *Sculler* oarsman (cf. line 72)
   Ply take as passenger

the boat. Land me but at Katherine's Dock, my sweet
Katherine's Dock, and I'll be a fare to thee. [DOG *leads*]
That way? Nay, which way thou wilt, thou knowst the way   70
better than I. [*Aside*] Fine gentle cur it is, and well brought
up, I warrant him. [*To* DOG] We go a-ducking, spaniel;
thou shalt fetch me the ducks, pretty kind rascal.

Enter SPIRIT *in shape of* KATHERINE, *vizarded, and
takes it off*

SPIRIT
[*Aside*] Thus throw I off mine own essential horror,
And take the shape of a sweet lovely maid   75
Whom this fool dotes on. We can meet his folly,
But from his virtues must be runaways.
We'll sport with him. But when we reckoning call,
We know where to receive. Th' witch pays for all.

DOG *barks*

YOUNG BANKS
Ay? Is that the watchword? She's come. Well, if ever we be   80
married, it shall be at Barking Church, in memory of thee.
Now come behind, kind cur.
    And have I met thee, sweet Kate?
    I will teach thee to walk so late.
O see, we meet in metre. What? Dost thou trip from me?   85
Oh that I were upon my hobby-horse, I would mount after
thee so nimble.

68 *Katherine's Dock* A landing place along the Thames near St Katherine's
Hospital, east of the Tower of London; but Young Banks is also fixated here on
his love for Katherine
73 s.d. *vizarded* masked
75 *shape* Spirits were believed to appear as living or dead persons having no shape
of their own; here as later with the Spirit of Susan (IV.ii.s.d.69) the boy playing
Katherine doubled as the Spirit
80 *She's come* Young Banks' simplicity, by which he loves everyone including
Mother Sawyer, now proves his weakness. He thinks he sees Katherine; later, he
will spontaneously love Dog (117–18). A central theme of the play is the danger
of indiscriminate love as well as (with Sir Arthur and Mother Sawyer) indiscriminate dislike
81 *Barking Church* (1) Allhallows, Barking, a church in east London at the east end
of Great Tower Street; (2) a pun on 'bark'. Punning is also characteristic in
Rowley's madhouse scenes in *The Changeling*
85 *metre* (1) a reference to lovers, whose language is poetry; (2) a self-referring pun
on the previous (and subsequent) lines

'Stay nymph, stay, nymph', singed Apollo.
Tarry and kiss me; sweet nymph, stay.
Tarry and kiss me, sweet.   90
We will to Chessum Street,
And then to the house stands in the highway.
Nay, by your leave, I must embrace you.

Ex[eunt] SPIR[IT] *and* [YOUNG] BANKS

[*Off stage*] O, help, help, I am drowned, I am drowned.

Enter [YOUNG BANKS] *wet*

DOG
Ha, ha, ha, ha!   95
YOUNG BANKS
This was an ill night to go a-wooing in; I find it now in
Pond's almanac. Thinking to land at Katherine's Dock, I
was almost at Gravesend. I'll never go to a wench in the
dog-days again. Yet 'tis cool enough. Had you never a paw
in this dog-trick? A mangie take that black hide of yours.   100
I'll throw you in at Limehouse in some tanner's pit or other.

88–90 *Stay ... sweet* The chorus of a ballad then popular entitled 'When Daphne
    Did from Phoebus Fly':
    When Daphne from fair Phoebus did fly,
    The west wind most sweetly did blow in her face:
    Her silken scarf scarce shadowed her eyes;
    The god cried 'O pitie', and held her in chase.
    'Stay, nymph, stay nymph,' cries Apollo,
    'Tarry and turn thee; sweet nymph stay!'
88–92 (prose Q)
94 *drowned* Wiggin claims it is characteristic of Rowley to introduce 'whimsical
    burlesque which only too often degenerates into buffoonery and horseplay' (p.
    19); this may be the climax of an extended farcical line which is the core of the
    Young Banks plot
97 *Pond's almanac* (1) An almanac entitled *Enchiridion, or Edward Pond his
    Eutheca*, popular at the time and published each year beginning in 1604 (Pond
    died in 1629); (2) a pun on 'pond'
98 *Gravesend* (1) A port on the south bank of the Thames then 30 miles below
    London; (2) a pun on 'grave'
99 *dog-days* The hottest summer days, from early July to mid-August; dogs were
    thought to go mad at this time (another textual anticipation of later action; cf.
    Anne Ratcliffe, s.d. IV.i.182)
100 *dog-trick* spiteful practical joke
    mangie mange, a disease of a dog's skin
101 *Limehouse* An area then east of London opposite Cuckold's Haven known for
    its tanneries

DOG
Ha, ha, ha, ha.

YOUNG BANKS
How now? Who's that laughs at me? Hist to him. [DOG
barks.] Peace, peace; thou didst but thy kind neither. 'Twas
my own fault.   105

DOG
Take heed how thou trustest the Devil another time.

YOUNG BANKS
How now? Who's that speaks? I hope you have not your
reading tongue about you.

DOG
Yes, I can speak.

YOUNG BANKS
The Devil you can. You have read Aesop's fables then. I   110
have played one of your parts then: the dog that catched at
the shadow in the water. Pray you, let me catechise you a
little. What might one call your name, Dog?

DOG
My dame calls me Tom.

YOUNG BANKS
'Tis well; and she may call me Ass. So there's an whole one   115
betwixt us, Tom-Ass. She said I should follow you, indeed.
Well, Tom, give me thy fist; we are friends. You shall be
mine ingle. I love you, but I pray you let's have no more of
these ducking devices.

DOG   120
Not, if you love me. Dogs love
Where they are beloved. Cherish me,
And I'll do anything for thee.

103 *Hist* listen
104 *but ... neither* what comes naturally to you
108 *reading tongue* preaching tongue
110 *Aesop's fables* Moral tales where animals behave like people
111 *then* (there Q)
111–12 *dog ... water* One of Aesop's tales, in which a dog drops the bone it is carry-
      ing in order to fight its reflection which also carries a bone
112 *catechise* systematically enquire
114 *My ... Tom* From Goodcole: '*Quest. By what name did you call the Diuell, and
      what promises did he make to you? Answ.* I did call the Diuell by the name of
      Tom, and he promised to doe for me whatsoeuer I should require of him' (sig.
      C4)
115 *Ass* foolish (like the animal)
116 *Tom-Ass* Playing on Thomas, the name of Dog never used in the play
118 *ingle* close companion (with homosexual overtones)

YOUNG BANKS

Well you shall have jowls and livers. I have butchers to my
friends that shall bestow 'em. And I will keep crusts and
bones for you, if you'll be a kind dog, Tom.   125

DOG

Anything. I'll help thee to thy love.

YOUNG BANKS

Wilt thou? That promise shall cost me a brown loaf, though
I steal if out of my father's cupboard. You'll eat stolen
goods, Tom, will you not?

DOG

Oh best of all. The sweetest bits, those.   130

YOUNG BANKS

You shall not starve, Ningle Tom; believe that, if you love
fish, I'll help you to maids and soles. I'm acquainted with a
fishmonger.

DOG

Maids and soles? Oh, sweet bits!
Banqueting stuff, those.   135

YOUNG BANKS

One thing I would request you. Ningle, as you have played
the knavish cur with me a little, that you would mingle
amongst our morris-dancers in the morning. You can
dance?

DOG

Yes, yes, anything, I'll be there,   140
But unseen to any but thyself.
Get thee gone before. Fear not my presence.
I have work tonight. I serve more masters,

---

123 *jowls* fish heads (cf. soles, line 132)
  to among
131 *Ningle* ingle (line 118)
131–2 *if ... soles* Young Banks innocently offers food to his new companion, but
  Dog may be attracted by the prurient double meanings by which 'fish' could
  mean 'prostitute', 'maid' a flat fish or harlot and 'soles' souls for the taking. Cf.
  Rowley in *A New Wonder, A Woman Never Vext* (1632):
  Wid[ow]. What fish is there Sirra?
  Clo[wn]. Marry there is Sammon, Pike, and fresh Cod,
        Soles, Maides, and Playce.
  Wid. Bid, 'm haste to dress 'm them.
  Clo. Nay mistris, I'le helpe 'm too; the maides shall first
        Dresse the Pike, and the Cod, and then I'le dresse
        The maides in the place you wot on (sig. B2v)
142 *Get ... before* go on ahead
143–4 *I ... one* Cf. 'No servant can serve two masters' (Luke 16:13)

More dames than one.

YOUNG BANKS
[*Aside*] He can serve Mammon and the Devil too.   145

DOG
It shall concern thee, and thy love's purchase.
There's a gallant rival loves the maid;
And likely is to have her. Mark what a mischief
Before the morris ends, shall light on him.

YOUNG BANKS
Oh sweet Ningle, thy neuf once again. Friends must part for   150
a time. Farewell, with this remembrance; shalt have bread
too when we meet again. If ever there were an honest Devil,
'twill be the Devil of Edmonton, I see. Farewell Tom. I
prithee dog me as soon as thou canst.

Ex[*it*] [YOUNG] BANKS

DOG
I'll not miss thee, and be merry with thee.   155
Those that are joys denied must take delight
In sins and mischiefs, 'tis the Devil's right.   *Ex*[*it*] DOG

ACT III, SCENE ii

Enter YOUNG [FRANK] THORNEY, WINIFRED *as a boy,*
[*crying*]

FRANK
Prithee no more. Those tears give nourishment
To weeds and briars in me, which shortly will
O'ergrow and top my head. My shame will sit

---

145 *Mammon* The god of riches; cf. 'Ye cannot serve God and Mammon' (Matthew 6:24);
also proverbial (M322)

150 *neuf* fist; cf. *A Midsummer Night's Dream*, IV.i.19

153 *Devil of Edmonton* A reference to Peter Fabell, the devil in the other Edmonton play, *The
Merry Devil of Edmonton* (1607), a source for this play. Fabell performs harmless tricks
to bring about a marriage that faces parental opposition

154 *dog* follow

0 s.d. 1 (no scene break Q). Winifred's disguise as a boy page is a common theatrical convention; cf. Viola in *Twelfth Night* or Ganymede in *As You Like It*.
Dekker commonly uses disguises in his plays

1 *FRANK* Speech prefix in Q reads 'Frank', but in all other cases here 'Y[oung]
Thor[ney]'

And cover all that can be seen of me.

WINIFRED

I have not shown this cheek in company, 5
Pardon me now. Thus singled with yourself,
It calls a thousand sorrows round about.
Some going before and some on either side;
But infinite behind, all chained together.
Your second adulterous marriage leads; 10
That's the sad eclipse, the effects must follow,
As plagues of shame, spite, scorn and obloquy.

FRANK

Why? Hast thou not left one hour's patience
To add to all the rest? One hour bears us
Beyond the reach of all these enemies. 15
Are we not now set forward in the flight,
Provided with the dowry of my sin,
To keep us in some other nation?
While we together are, we are at home
In any place.

WINIFRED   'Tis foul ill-gotten coin, 20
Far worse than usury or extortion.

FRANK

Let my father then make the restitution,
Who forced me take the bribe. It is his gift
And patrimony to me; so I receive it.
He would not bless, nor look a father on me, 25
Until I satisfied his angry will.
When I was sold, I sold myself again
(Some knaves have done't in lands, and I in body)

5 *cheek* That is, her cheek is covered with tears
6 *singled* alone
7 *It* the cheek
10 *adulterous marriage* While Winifred weeps for Frank's situation she may also be thinking of her own illicit relationship with Sir Arthur
11 *sad eclipse* Often seen as an omen of misfortune; cf. *King Lear*, I.ii.100ff.
14–15 *One ... reach* A Match at Midnight (1607? published 1633), ascribed to Rowley alone, reverses this situation almost exactly: Bloodhound wishes to marry his daughter Moll to a rich informer, but she falls in love with a penniless man whom her father cheated out of his land and runs away with him at midnight, taking with her the deeds to the stolen property. Wiggin claims that some lines are taken from Middleton's plays; Rowley also collaborated with Middleton (Wiggin, pp. 10–11)
27–9 *When ... hire* Frank sees himself as a male prostitute, with his own father as the pander (cf. 95 below)

For money, and I have the hire. But, sweet, no more,   30
'Tis hazard of discovery, our discourse;
And then prevention takes off all our hopes.
For only but to take her leave of me,
My wife is coming.
WINIFRED   Who coming? Your wife?
FRANK
No, no, thou art here. The woman, I knew   35
Not how to call her now: but after this day
She shall be quite forgot, and have no name
In my remembrance. See, see, she's come.

Enter SUSAN

                              Go lead
The horses to the hill's top, there I'll meet thee.
SUSAN
Nay, with your favour, let him stay a little.
I would part with him too, because he is   40
Your sole companion; and I'll begin with him,
Reserving you the last.
FRANK   Ay, with all my heart.
SUSAN
You may hear, if it please you, sir.
FRANK   No, 'tis not fit.
Some rudiments, I conceive, they must be,
To overlook my slippery footings. And so –   45
SUSAN
No, indeed, sir.
FRANK   Tush, I know it must be so,
And 'tis necessary. On, but be brief.   [*Walks off a little*]
WINIFRED
What charge so'er you lay upon me, mistress,
I shall support it faithfully (being honest)
To my best strength.   50
SUSAN
Believe't shall be no other. I know you were
Commended to my husband by a noble knight.
WINIFRED
Oh gods! Oh, mine eyes!
SUSAN   How now? What ail'st thou, lad?

29 *hire* wages, payment
33 *wife* (1) a slip of the tongue; (2) an act of conscience (cf. II.ii.125)
40 *part with* say farewell to
44 *rudiments* basic instructions
45 *so* – (so. Q)
46 *Tush* A common expression of impatience

WINIFRED

  Something hit mine eye, it makes it water still,
  Even as you said 'commended to my husband'.   55
  Some dor I think it was. I was, forsooth,
  Commended to him by Sir Arthur Clarington.

SUSAN

  Whose servant once my Thorney was himself.
  The title methinks should make you almost fellows,
  Or at the least much more than a servant;   60
  And I am sure he will respect you so.
  Your love to him then needs no spur from me,
  And what for my sake you will ever do,
  'Tis fit it should be bought with something more
  Than fair entreats. Look! Here's a jewel for thee,   65
  A pretty wanton label for thine ear;
  And I would have it hang there, still to whisper
  These words to thee, 'Thou hast my jewel with thee'.
  It is but earnest of a larger bounty,
  When thou returnest, with praises of thy service,   70
  Which I am confident thou wilt deserve.
  Why, thou art many now, besides thyself.
  Thou mayst be servant, friend, and wife to him.
  A good wife is them all. A friend can play
  The wife and servant's part, and shift enough.   75
  No less the servant can the friend and wife.
  'Tis all but sweet society, good counsel,
  Interchanged loves, yes; and counsel-keeping.

FRANK [*Returns*] Not done yet?

SUSAN   Even now, sir.

WINIFRED

  Mistress, believe my vow. Your severe eye   80
  Were it present to command; your bounteous hand,
  Were it then by to buy or bribe my service,

---

56 *dor* flying beetle

66 *label* A token to remind Winifred of her pledge to look after Frank; the gift is given with mixed feelings and intentions. Cf. Rowley's *All's Lost by Lust* I.ii.69–72

68 *my jewel* my chastity; she gave her invaluable virginity to Frank, as compared to the money her father has given his father

69 *earnest* (1) instalment; (2) indication

75 *shift* (1) manage; (2) evade; (3) practise fraudulence

79 *Even* just

80 *Your severe eye* In contrast to Mother Sawyer's tongue (as a means of cursing and condemning)

Shall not make me more dear or near unto him,
Than I shall voluntary. I'll be all your charge.
Servant, friend, wife to him.

SUSAN   Wilt thou?   85
Now blessings go with thee for't. Courtesies
Shall meet thee coming home.

WINIFRED   Pray you say plainly,
Mistress. Are you jealous of him? If you be,
I'll look to him that way too.

SUSAN   Sayest thou so?
I would thou hadst a woman's bosom now.   90
We have weak thoughts within us. Alas,
There's nothing so strong in us as suspicion.
But I dare not, nay, I will not think
So hardly of my Thorney.

WINIFRED   Believe it, mistress,
I'll be no pander to him; and if I find   95
Any loose lubric scapes in him, I'll watch him,
And at my return, protest I'll show you all.
He shall hardly offend without my knowledge.

SUSAN
Thine own diligence is that I press,
And not the curious eye over his faults.   100
Farewell. If I should never see thee more,
Take it forever.

          [FRANK] *gives his sword*

FRANK
Prithee take that along with thee,
And haste thee to the hill's top;
I'll be there instantly.   *Ex[it]* WIN[IFRED] 105

SUSAN
No haste I prithee, slowly as thou canst.
Pray let him obey me now. 'Tis happily
His last service to me. My power is e'en
A-going out of sight.   Why would you delay?

FRANK
We have no other business now but to part. 110

---

84 *be all your charge* obey your every command
89 *look to* keep watch of
95 *pander* Cf. 27–9 above
96 *lubric scapes* lusty acts of unfaithfulness
102 *it* That is, the label or token
107 *happily* perhaps (by happenstance)

SUSAN
And will not that, sweetheart, ask a long time?
Methinks it is the hardest piece of work
That e'er I took in hand.
FRANK   Fie, fie, why look,
I'll make it plain and easy to you. Farewell.

Kisses [her]

SUSAN
Ah, 'las! I am not half perfect in it yet.   115
I must have it read over an hundred times.
Pray you take some pains, I confess my dullness.
FRANK
[*Aside*] What a thorn this rose grows on! Parting were
  sweet,
But what a trouble 'twill be to obtain it!
[*To her*] Come, again and again, farewell.

Kisses [her]

                                      Yet wilt return?   120
All questions of my journey, my stay, employment,
And revisitation, fully I have answered all.
There's nothing now behind, but nothing.
SUSAN
And that nothing is more hard than anything,
Than all the everythings. This request –
FRANK   What is it?   125
SUSAN
That I may bring you through one pasture more
Up to yon knot of trees. Amongst those shadows
I'll vanish from you, they shall teach me how.
FRANK
Why, 'tis granted. Come, walk then.
SUSAN   Nay, not too fast.
They say slow things have best perfection.   130
The gentle shower wets to fertility.

111 *ask* take
117 *take some pains* be patient (with me)
118–19 (Q makes both statements questions)
123 *behind* hidden
127 *yon* yonder
130–4 *They … long* Susan's nervous retreat to proverbial lore resembles her father's
  speech

The churlish storm may mischief with his bounty.
The baser beasts take strength, even from the womb.
But the lord lion's whelp is feeble long.   *Exeunt*

ACT III, SCENE iii

Enter DOG

DOG
Now for an early mischief and a sudden.
The mind's about it now. One touch from me
Soon sets the body forward.

Enter YOUNG [FRANK] THORNEY, SUSAN

FRANK
Your request is out. Yet will you leave me?

SUSAN
What? So churlishly? You'll make me stay for ever,   5
Rather than part with such a sound from you.

FRANK
Why you almost anger me. Pray you be gone.
You have no company, and 'tis very early;
Some hurt may betide you homewards.   Tush, I fear none.

SUSAN
To leave you is the greatest hurt I can suffer.   10
Besides, I expect your father and mine own,
To meet me back, or overtake me with you.
They began to stir when I came after you.

132 *mischief* do damage
134 *lord lion's whelp* Both Pliny in his *Natural History*, VIII.16 (translated by
    Philemon Holland [1601], p. 201), and Topsell, *The Historie of Foure-Footed
    Beastes* (1607), p. 466, comment on the weakness of young lions

  0 s.d. (no new scene in Q)
    Enter DOG Dog, always visible to the audience, is invisible to all the characters
    except Mother Sawyer and Young Banks (and so limited to the underplot); he is
    invisible to characters in the overplot
1-3 *Now ... forward* Dog's speech suggests he bears final responsibility for the
    death of Susan by bewitching Frank (cf. s.d.14)
  4 *Your ... out* This is as far as you wished to come
    Yet now
  9 *betide* befall
 12 *back* on the way back

I know they'll not be long.

FRANK   [*Aside*] So, I shall have more trouble.

DOG *rubs him*

Thank you for that. Then I'll ease all at once.   15
'Tis done now. What I ne'er thought on.
[*To her*] You shall not go back.

SUSAN   Why?
Shall I go along with thee? Sweet music!

FRANK
No, to a better place.

SUSAN   Any place, I.
I'm there at home, where thou pleasest to have me.   20

FRANK
At home? I'll leave you in your last lodging.
I must kill you.

SUSAN   Oh fine! You'd fright me from you.

FRANK
You see I had no purpose. I'm unarmed.
'Tis this minute's decree, and it must be.
Look, this will serve your turn.

[*Draws his knife*]

SUSAN   I'll not turn from it,   25
If you be earnest, sir. Yet you may tell me
Wherefore you'll kill me.

FRANK   Because you are a whore.

SUSAN
There's one deep wound already. A whore?
'Twas ever further from me than the thought
Of this black hour. A whore?

FRANK   Yes, I'll prove it.   30
And you shall confess it. You are my whore,
No wife of mine. The word admits no second.
I was before wedded to another, have her still.
I do not lay the sin unto your charge,

---

14 s.d. *DOG* The appearance of Dog in Frank's time of need parallels his appearance to Mother Sawyer (II.i.119); it also betrays his inner desires as it does her
more articulated ones; cf. the next line. 'Of those who ... mentally allied themselves with Satan ... some may have been sinners obsessed by their guilt'
(Thomas, p. 626)

19 *a better place* heaven

21 *last lodging* coffin

23 *purpose* intention, plan

25 *this* Frank's knife

'Tis all mine own. Your marriage was my theft.   35
For I espoused your dowry, and I have it.
I did not purpose to have added murder;
The Devil did not prompt me. Till this minute
You might have safe returned; now you cannot.
You have dogged your own death.

Stabs her

SUSAN   And I deserve it.   40
I'm glad my fate was so intelligent.
'Twas some good spirit's motion. Die? Oh, 'twas time!
How many years might I have slept in sin?
Sin of my most hatred too, adultery?

FRANK
Nay, sure, 'twas likely that the most was past;   45
For I meant never to return to you
After this parting.
SUSAN   Why then I thank you more,
You have done lovingly, leaving yourself,
That you would thus bestow me on another.
Thou art my husband, Death, and I embrace thee   50
With all the love I have. Forget the stain
Of my unwitting sin. And then I come
A crystal virgin to thee. My soul's purity
Shall with bold wings ascend the doors of Mercy;
For Innocence is ever her companion.   55

FRANK
Not yet mortal? I would not linger you,
Or leave you a tongue to blab.

[Stabs her again]

SUSAN
Now Heaven reward you ne'er the worse for me.
I did not think that death had been so sweet;
Nor I so apt to love him. I could ne'er die better,   60
Had I stayed forty years for preparation.
For I'm in charity with all the world.

40 *dogged* persisted in; relentlessly followed to (as in 'dogging my footsteps')
41 *intelligent* clear, understandable
42 *'Twas ... motion* Ironic, since Frank has clearly been at one with Dog; such
   'guardian spirits' were common to witchcraft and Catholic belief but disputed by
   Protestants
45 *the most* the worst
56 *mortal* ready for death   *linger* delay
62 *in charity* at peace

Let me for once be thine example, Heaven;
Do to this man as I him free forgive.
And may he better die, and better live. 65

Moritur [*She dies*]

FRANK
'Tis done; and I am in. Once past our height,
We scorn the deep'st abyss. This follows now,
To heal her wounds by dressing of the weapon.
Arms, thighs, hands, any place; we must not fail,

Wounds himself

Light scratches giving such deep ones. The best I can 70
To bind myself to this tree. Now's the storm,
Which if blown o'er, many fair days may follow.

DOG *ties him*

So, so, I'm fast; I did not think I could
Have done so well behind me. How prosperous
And effectual mischief sometimes is. Help, help; 75
Murder, murder, murder.

[*Exit* DOG]

Enter [OLD] CARTER *and* OLD THORNEY

OLD CARTER
Ha! Whom tolls the bell for?
FRANK   Oh, oh!
OLD THORNEY   Ah me!

---

65 s.d. *Moritur*. The majority of published accounts in England between 1590 and 1630 dealing with spousal murder recount the deaths of husbands at the hands of their wives. It is likely that the more romantic story of Frank and Susan has its roots in the ballad tradition rather than in contemporary history. Lena Cowen Orlin notes (p. 252) that 'early domestic tragedy is man-centered, that is, concerned with men's issues. Principal among these issues is the management of troublesome women.' This is in inverse parallel to the position of Mother Sawyer: nearly all suspected and condemned witches were women, not men
66 *I am in* there is no turning back now
68 *To … weapon* to cover up the wounds by putting my blood on the knife
76 s.d. *Exit DOG* (Not in Q; follows RSC production)
77 *tolls the bell* Reference is to the tolling of parish church bells to proclaim a death; (1) Old Carter has a premonition in agreement with other anticipations in the play; (2) (less likely) Frank's shouts toll like the church bell; (3) (ironically) the familiar saying, 'Who does the bell toll for? It tolls for thee' indicating the death of his daughter

The cause appears too soon. My child, my son.

OLD CARTER
Susan, girl, child. Not speak to thy father? Ha!

FRANK   80
O lend me some assistance to o'ertake
This hapless woman.

OLD THORNEY   Let's o'ertake the murderers.
Speak whilst thou canst; anon may be too late.
I fear thou hast death's mark upon thee too.

FRANK
I know them both; yet such an oath is passed,
As pulls damnation up if it be broke;   85
I dare not name 'em. Think what forced men do.

OLD THORNEY
Keep oath with murderers? That were a conscience
To hold the Devil in.

FRANK   Nay, sir, I can describe 'em;
Shall show them as familiar as their names.
The taller of the two at this time wears   90
His satin doublet white, but crimson lined;
Hose of black satin, cloak of scarlet.

OLD THORNEY
Warbeck, Warbeck, Warbeck. Do you list to this, sir?

OLD CARTER
Yes, yes, I listen you. Here's nothing to be heard.

FRANK   95
Th'other's cloak branched velvet, black, velvet-lined
His suit.

OLD THORNEY I have 'em already. Somerton, Somerton.
Binal revenge, all this. Come, sir, the first work
Is to pursue the murderers, when we have removed
These mangled bodies hence.   100

OLD CARTER
Sir, take that carcass there, and give me this. I'll not own
her now; she's none of mine. Bob me off with a dumb-

---

86 *forced* (1) desperate; (2) play on Frank's own condition of forced marriage and
   thus self-referential (cf. II.ii.123ff.)

91 *doublet* tight jacket

94 *Here's ... heard* Old Carter is tragically listening to his dead daughter for signs
   of life (cf. *King Lear*, V.iii.264ff.)

95 *branched* embroidered; Frank is proposing a means of identification

98 *Binal* twofold

102 *Bob me off* dismiss me

102–3 *dumb-show* (1) speechless action – here, Susan's body; (2) dumb as silent,
   referring to Frank's refusal to name his alleged attackers

show? No, I'll have life. This is my son too, and while
there's life in him, 'tis half mine; take you half that silence
for't. When I speak, I look to be spoken to: forgetful slut! 105

OLD THORNEY
Alas! what grief may do now?
Look, sir, I'll take this load of sorrow with me.

[*Picks up* SUSAN]

OLD CARTER
Ay, do, and I'll have this.

[*Picks up* FRANK]

How do you, sir?

FRANK   O, very ill, sir.
OLD CARTER
Yes, I think so; but 'tis well you can speak yet. There's no
music but in sound, sound it must be. I have not wept these 110
twenty years before, and that I guess was ere that girl was
born. Yet now methinks, if I but knew the way, my heart's
so full, I could weep night and day.

Exeunt

ACT III, SCENE iv

Enter SIR ARTHUR CLARINGTON, WARBECK, SOMERTON

SIR ARTHUR
Come, gentlemen, we must all help to grace
The nimble-footed youth of Edmonton,
That are so kind to call us up today
With an high morris.

103 *son* son-in-law
107 *load of sorrow* Old Thorney carries Susan

 0 s.d. (no new scene in Q). Although this is a relatively short scene, it is crucial and
   climactic. The morris dance is a spectacle alongside the on-stage murder of Susan
   and must be jolting in its abrupt change of mood. Dog in displacing the Fiddler
   Sawgut restores his first victim (Young Banks) as two other innocent men
   (Warbeck and Somerton) are falsely arrested, ironically bringing both plots
   together
 4 *high* especially merry

WARBECK   5
    I could wish it for the best, it were
    The worst now. Absurdity's in my opinion
    Ever the best dancer in a morris.
SOMERTON
    I could rather sleep than see 'em.
SIR ARTHUR   Not well, sir?
SOMERTON
    Faith not ever thus leaden; yet I know
    No cause for't.
WARBECK   Now am I beyond   10
    Mine own condition highly disposed to mirth.
SIR ARTHUR
    Well, you may have yet a morris to help both;
    To strike you in a dump, and make him merry.

       Enter [SAWGUT *the*] *Fiddler and* [*the*] *Morris; all but*
                [YOUNG] BANKS

SAWGUT
    Come, will you set yourselves in morris-ray? The fore-bell,
    second-bell, tenor and great-bell; Maid Marian for the   15
    same bell. But where's the weather-cock now? The hobby-
    horse?
FIRST DANCER
    Is not Banks come yet? What a spite 'tis?
SIR ARTHUR
    When set you forward, gentlemen?
FIRST DANCER
    We stay but for the hobby-horse, sir. All our foot-men are   20
    ready.
SOMERTON
    'Tis marvel your horse should be behind your foot.

---

  9 *not ... leaden* I have never been more depressed
 10–11 *beyond ... condition* despite my circumstances
 13 *dump* fit of melancholy
 14 *SAWGUT* (Fid[d]l[er] Q; also 37–9, 44–7)
    ray array; costumes
 16 *weather-cock* The hobby-horse, which shifted like a weather-cock because the
    frame is made of light wood
 18 *FIRST* (Second Q)
 20 *stay* wait
 22 *marvel ... foot* In the military, the cavalry preceded the foot-soldiers into battle

SECOND DANCER

Yes, sir. He goes further about. We can come in at the wicket, but the broad gate must be opened for him.

Enter [YOUNG] BANKS, [*as*] *Hobby-horse and* DOG

SIR ARTHUR

O, we stayed for you, sir.   25

YOUNG BANKS

Only my horse wanted a shoe, sir. But we shall make you amends ere we part.

SIR ARTHUR

Ay? Well said, make 'em drink ere they begin.

Enter SERV[ANTS] *with beer*

YOUNG BANKS

A bowl, I prithee, and a little for my horse, he'll mount the better. Nay, give me, I must drink to him, he'll not pledge   30
else. [*Drinks*] Here, hobby.

Holds him the bowl

I pray you. No? Not drink? You see, gentlemen, we can but bring our horse to the water; he may choose whether he'll drink or no.

SOMERTON

A good moral made plain by history.   35

FIRST DANCER

Strike up, Father Sawgut, strike up.

SAWGUT

E'en when you will, children. Now in the name of the best foot forward. How now? Not a word in thy guts? I think, children, my instrument has caught cold on the sudden.

YOUNG BANKS

[*Aside*] My ningle's knavery. Black Tom's doing.   40

ALL

Why, what mean you, Father Sawgut?

YOUNG BANKS

Why what would you have him do? You hear his fiddle is speechless.

---

23 *goes further about* takes the long way around
24 *wicket* small gate
30 *pledge* drink to my health; he offers himself a drink inside the hobby-horse costume
32–4 *we ... no* Proverbial; M262
38 *guts* (1) inner selves; (2) violin strings (made of gut, or animal intestines)

SAWGUT

I'll lay mine ear to my instrument, that my poor fiddle is
bewitched. I played 'The Flowers in May', e'en now, as   45
sweet as a violet; now 'twill not go against the hair. You see
I can make no more music than a beetle of a cow-turd.

YOUNG BANKS

Let me see, Father Sawgut; say, once you had a brave
hobby-horse that you were beholding to. I'll play and dance
too. [Aside] Ningle, away with it.   50

ALL

Ay marry, sir!

DOG *plays the morris; which ended, enter a*
CONSTABLE *and* OFFICERS

CONSTABLE

Away with jollity, 'tis too sad an hour.
Sir Arthur Clarington, your own assistance,
In the King's name, I charge, for apprehension
Of these two murderers, Warbeck and Somerton.   55

SIR ARTHUR

Ha! Flat murderers?

SOMERTON

Ha, ha, ha, this has awakened my melancholy.

WARBECK

And struck my mirth down flat. Murderers?

CONSTABLE

The accusation is flat against you, gentlemen.
Sir, you may be satisfied with this.   60

[*Shows warrant for their arrest*]

I hope you'll quietly obey my power;
'Twill make your cause the fairer.

SOMERTON AND WARBECK [*together*]

O, with all our hearts, sir.

YOUNG BANKS

[*Aside*] There's my rival taken up for hangman's meat. Tom
told me he was about a piece of villainy. Mates and morris-   65
men, you see here's no longer piping, no longer dancing.

45 'The Flowers ... May' A dance tune no longer extant
46 *against the hair* 'against the grain' (proverbial)
49 *beholding* indebted
51 s.d. *DOG ... OFFICERS* (Q places this before line 51)
54–5 *charge ... Somerton* Warbeck and Somerton are falsely arrested at Sir
    Arthur's house, while Sir Arthur, guilty of sexual abuse, remains free
63 s.d. *SOMERTON AND WARBECK* (AMBO [that is, both] Q)

This news of murder has slain the morris. You that go the
foot way, fare ye well. I am for the gallop. Come, Ningle.

Exe[unt YOUNG BANKS *and* DOG]

SAWGUT
[*Strikes his fiddle*] Ay? Nay and my fiddle be come to himself again, I care not. I think the Devil has been abroad   70
amongst us today. I'll keep thee out of thy fit now if I can.

Exe[unt SAWGUT *and* MORRIS DANCERS]

SIR ARTHUR
These things are full of horror, full of pity.
But if this time be constant to the proof,
The guilt of both these gentlemen I dare take
Upon mine own danger; yet howsoever, sir,   75
Your power must be obeyed.
WARBECK   Oh most willingly, sir.
'Tis a most sweet affliction. I could not meet
A joy in the best shape with better will.
Come, fear not, sir; nor judge, nor evidence,
Can bind him o'er, who's freed by conscience.   80
SOMERTON
Mine stands so upright to the middle zone,
It takes no shadow to't, it goes alone.

Exeunt

ACT IV, SCENE i

Enter OLD BANKS *and two or three* COUNTRYMEN

OLD BANKS
My horse this morning runs most piteously of the glanders,
whose nose yesternight was as clean as any man's here now

68 *foot* pedestrian
71 *fit* attack of lunacy
73 *constant* in keeping with
81 *Mine* my conscience
   middle zone equator, denoting balance, perpetual sunlight
82 *goes alone* goes without a shadow

1 *glanders* A contagious disease in horses causing swelling under the jaw and a
running nose; such an illness often led to accusations of witchcraft

coming from the barber's; and this I'll take my death upon't
is long of this jadish witch, Mother Sawyer.

FIRST COUNTRYMAN
    I took my wife and a servingman in our town of Edmonton,   5
thrashing in my barn together, such corn as country
wenches carry to market; and examining my polecat why
she did so, she swore in her conscience she was bewitched.
And what witch have we about us, but Mother Sawyer?

SECOND COUNTRYMAN
    Rid the town of her, else all our wives will do nothing else   10
but dance about other country maypoles.

THIRD COUNTRYMAN
    Our cattle fall, our wives fall, our daughters fall, and maid-
servants fall; and we ourselves shall not be able to stand, if
this beast be suffered to graze amongst us.

        Enter W. HAMLUC, *with thatch and a link*

HAMLUC
    Burn the witch, the witch, the witch, the witch.   15

ALL
    What hast got there?

---

3 *take* stake
4 *long* on account
5 *took* caught, found
6 *thrashing* (with sexual implications)
7 *polecat* prostitute
11 *maypoles* Brightly coloured poles, decorated with flowers, around which vil-
lagers danced on May Day; the poles were regarded as symbols of fertility
12–14 *Our ... us* Such events were the most frequent charges for witchcraft; the
lines also carry sexual implications
14 s.d. *thatch* straw or dry grass. Goodcole writes in *The Wonderfull Discouerie*: 'A
Great, and long suspicion was held of this person to be a witch, and the eye of
Mr. *Arthur Robinson*, a worthy Iustice of Peace, who dweleth at *Totnam* neere
to her, was watchfull ouer her, and her wayes, and that not without iust cause;
still hauing his former long suspicion of her, by the information of her neighbours that dwelt about her: from suspicion, to proceed to great presumptions,
seeing the death of Nurse-children and Cattell, strangely and suddenly to
happen. And to finde out who should bee the author of this mischiefe, an old
ridiculous custome was vsed, which was to plucke the Thatch of her house, and
to burne it, and it being so burned, the author of such mischiefe should presently
then come: and it was obserued and confirmed to the Court, that *Elizabeth
Sawyer* would presently frequent the house of them that burnt the thatch which
they pluckt of her house, and come without any sending for' (sigs. A4–A4v). In
Stuart England, arson was considered a felony
link torch

HAMLUC

A handful of thatch plucked off a hovel of hers. And they
say, when 'tis burning, if she be a witch, she'll come running in.

OLD BANKS

Fire it, fire it. I'll stand between thee and home for any   20
danger.

As that burns, enter the WITCH [SAWYER]

SAWYER

Diseases, plagues; the curse of an old woman
Follow and fall upon you.

ALL

Are you come, you old trot?

OLD BANKS

You hot whore, must we fetch you with fire in your tail?   25

FIRST COUNTRYMAN

This thatch is as good as a jury to prove she is a witch.

ALL

Out, witch; beat her, kick her, set fire on her.

SAWYER

Shall I be murdered by a bed of serpents? Help, help!

Enter SIR ARTHUR CLARINGTON, *and a* JUSTICE

ALL

Hang her, beat her, kill her.

JUSTICE

How now? Forbear this violence.   30

SAWYER

A crew of villains, a knot of bloody hangmen
Set to torment me I know not why.

---

17 *hovel of hers* Mother Sawyer is defending her home; like dunking in which the
accused either drowned or, if not, was condemned, this test of witchcraft cannot
fail to produce as a witch someone already considered guilty

18–19 *burning ... running* a common means both to reveal the guilty and counter
her spells simultaneously

22–3 *curse ... you* a cursing tongue was taken as a certain sign of witchcraft

24 *trot* hag, old woman

25 *hot* lusty

28 s.d. *JUSTICE* The local justice of the peace was the King's representative for all judicial
matters; he used common law which was an imprecise combination of precedent,
custom and statute. The term of service was indefinite, lasting perhaps ten years,
although some JPs in Essex held office for as long as 30 years. Goodcole identifies this
one as Arthur Robinson

JUSTICE

Alas, neighbour Banks, are you a ringleader
In mischief? Fie, to abuse an aged woman!

OLD BANKS

Woman? a she-hellcat, a witch. To prove her one, we no   35
sooner set fire on the thatch of her house, but in she came
running, as if the Devil had sent her in a barrel of gunpowder; which trick as surely proves her a witch, as the pox
in a snuffling nose is a sign a man is a whore-master.

JUSTICE

Come, come; firing her thatch? Ridiculous: 40
Take heed sirs what you do.
Unless your proofs come better armed,
Instead of turning her into a witch,
You'll prove yourselves stark fools.

ALL

Fools?   45

JUSTICE

Arrant fools.

OLD BANKS

Pray, Master Justice What-do-you-call-'um, hear me but in
one thing. This grumbling Devil owes me I know no good
will ever since I fell out with her.

SAWYER

And breakest my back with beating me.   50

OLD BANKS

I'll break it worse.

SAWYER

Wilt thou?

39 *snuffling nose* discharge from the nose was believed to indicate syphilis and
reveal that a man was a frequenter of prostitutes

40 *firing her thatch* So Goodcole: 'This triall, though it was slight and ridiculous,
yet it setled a resolution in those whom it concerned, to finde out by all meanes
they could endeauour, her long, and close carried Witchery, to explaine it to the
world; and being descried, to pay in the ende such a worker of Iniquity, her
wages, and that which shee had deserued, (namely, *shame* and *Death*) from
which the Diuell, that had so long deluded her, did not come as shee said, to
shew the least helpe of his vnto her to deliuer her: but being descried in his waies,
and workes, immediately he fled, leauing her to shift and answere for her selfe'
(sig. A4v)
Ridiculous The Justice's forthright exposure of such charges, ensuring sympathy
for Mother Sawyer, contradicts historical fact and is highly unrepresentative of
justices' opinions at the time. Such sympathy is characteristic of Dekker's
thought and playwriting

JUSTICE
You must not threaten her. 'Tis against the law.

[*To* OLD BANKS]

Go on.

OLD BANKS
So, sir, ever since, having a dun cow tied up in my backside,   55
let me go thither, or but cast mine eye at her, and if I should
be hanged, I cannot choose, though it be ten times in an
hour, but run to the cow, and taking up her tail kiss (saving
your worship's reverence) my cow behind; that the whole
town of Edmonton has been ready to bepiss themselves   60
with laughing me to scorn.

JUSTICE
And this is long of her?

OLD BANKS
Who the devil else? For is any man such an ass, to be such
a baby, if he were not bewitched?

SIR ARTHUR
Nay, if she be a witch, and the harms she does   65
End in such sports, she may 'scape burning.

JUSTICE
Go, go; pray vex her not. She is a subject,
And you must not be judges of the law
To strike her as you please.

ALL
No, no, we'll find cudgel enough to strike her.   70

OLD BANKS
Ay, no lips to kiss but my cow's —?

Exeunt [OLD BANKS *and* COUNTRYMEN]

55 *dun* brown
   backside back yard
55–69 *So . . . please* George Gifford records in *A Dialogue Concerning Witches and
   Witchcraftes* (1593), 'A third man came in, and he sayd she [a witch] was once
   angry with him, he had a dun cow which was tyed up in a house, for it was
   winter, he feared that some euill would follow, and for his life he could not come
   in where she was, but he must needes take up her tayle and kisse under it' (sig.
   I4v). The Revels editor notes, 'It is likely that Gifford is the source of Banks'
   anecdote. Certainly Sir Arthur's response and the Justice's admonishment reflect
   something of Gifford's sceptical attitude to witch belief' (p. 241)
58 *saving* apologising in advance because of
60 *bepiss* urinate on
63 *Who . . . else?* A common expression of impatience
66 *burning* In England, accused witches were hanged rather than burned at the
   stake as on the Continent
67 *subject* As a subject of the king, Mother Sawyer holds certain legal rights

SAWYER
  Rots and foul maladies eat up thee and thine.

JUSTICE
  Here's none now, Mother Sawyer,
  But this gentleman, myself, and you;
  Let us to some mild questions; have you mild answers?   75
  Tell us honestly, and with a free confession,
  (We'll do our best to wean you from it)
  Are you a witch, or no?
SAWYER   [*Angrily*] I am none.

JUSTICE
  Be not so furious.

SAWYER
  [*Somewhat calmer*] I am none. None but base curs   80
  So bark at me. I am none.
  Or would I were. If every poor old woman
  Be trod on thus by slaves, reviled, kicked, beaten,
  As I am daily, she, to be revenged,
  Had need turn witch.   85

SIR ARTHUR
  And you to be revenged have sold your soul to th' Devil.

SAWYER
  Keep thine own from him.

JUSTICE
  You are too saucy, and too bitter.

SAWYER
  Saucy? By what commission can he
  Send my soul on the Devil's errand,   90
  More than I can his? Is he
  A landlord of my soul, to thrust it
  When he list out of door?

JUSTICE
  Know whom you speak to.

SAWYER
  A man. Perhaps, no man. Men in gay clothes,   95
  Whose backs are laden with titles and honours,
  Are within far more crooked than I am;
  And if I be a witch, more witch-like.

SIR ARTHUR
  You're a base hell-hound. And now, sir,

76 *free* without duress
80 *curs* scoundrels
93 *list* choose

Let me tell you, far and near she's bruited   100
For a woman that maintains a spirit
That sucks her.
SAWYER   I defy thee.
SIR ARTHUR
   Go, go. I can, if need be, bring
An hundred voices, e'en here in Edmonton,
That shall loud proclaim thee for a secret   105
And pernicious witch.
SAWYER   Ha, ha!
JUSTICE
   Do you laugh? Why laugh you?
SAWYER
   At my name. The brave name this knight gives me – witch!
JUSTICE
   Is the name of witch so pleasing to thine ear?
SIR ARTHUR
   Pray, sir, give way, and let her tongue gallop on.   110
SAWYER
   A witch? Who is not?
Hold not that universal name in scorn then.
What are your painted things in princes' courts?
Upon whose eyelids lust sits blowing fires
To burn men's souls in sensual hot desires.   115
Upon whose naked paps a lecher's thought

---

100 *bruited* rumoured, reported
101–2 *a spirit ... her* Thus Goodcole's account: '*Question. In what places of your body did the Diuell sucke of your bloud, and whether did hee himselfe chuse the place, or did you your selfe appoint him the place? tell the truth, I charge you, as you will answere vnto the Almighty God, and tell the reason if that you can, why he would sucke your bloud. Answer.* The place where the Diuell suckt my bloud was a little aboue my fundiment, and that place chosen by himselfe; and in that place by continuall drawing, there is a thing in the forme of a Teate, at which the diuell would suck mee. And I asked the Diuell why hee would sucke my bloud, and hee sayd it was to nourish him. *Question. Whether did you pull vp your coates or no when the Deuill came to sucke you? Answer.* No I did not, but the Diuell would put his head vnder my coates, and I did willingly suffer him to doe what hee would. *Question. How long would the time bee, that the Diuell would continue sucking of you, and whether did you endure any paine, the time that hee was sucking of you? Answer.* He would be sucking of me the continuance of a quarter of an howre, and when hee suckt me, I then felt no paine at all' (sigs. C3–C3v). Cf. s.d.II.i.145
112–15 *Hold ... desires* The playwrights utilize individual psychology here for more general satire common to (and of) the period
113 *painted things* women wearing cosmetics

Acts sin in fouler shapes than can be wrought.

JUSTICE
But those work not as you do.

SAWYER   No, but far worse.
These by enchantments can whole lordships change
To trunks of rich attire, turn ploughs and teams   120
To Flanders mares and coaches; and huge trains
Of servitors, to a French butterfly.
Have you not city-witches who can turn
Their husbands' wares, whole standing shops of wares,
To sumptuous tables, gardens of stol'n sin?   125
In one year wasting, what scarce twenty win,
Are not these witches?

JUSTICE   Yes, yes, but the law
Casts not an eye on these.

SAWYER   Why then on me,
Or any lean old beldam? Reverence once
Had wont to wait on age. Now an old woman   130
Ill-favoured grown with years, if she be poor,
Must be called bawd or witch. Such so abused
Are the coarse witches. T'other are the fine,
Spun for the Devil's own wearing.

SIR ARTHUR   And so is thine.

SAWYER
She on whose tongue a whirlwind sits to blow   135
A man out of himself, from his soft pillow,
To lean his head on rocks and fighting waves,
Is not that scold a witch? The man of law
Whose honeyed hopes the credulous client draws,
(As bees by tinkling basins) to swarm to him,   140
From his own hive to work the wax in his;
He is no witch, not he.

119 *lordships* estates
121 *Flanders mares* a breed of heavy strong horses bred to draw carriages
122 *servitors* male servants
    French butterfly gaudily dressed, irresponsible person
125 *gardens* Traditionally places of sexual assignation
130 *wont* accustomed
130-2 *Now ... witch* This definition closely follows that of Reginald Scot (see note
    to II.i.3–4); that the playwrights make use of Scot and Gifford suggests their own
    scepticism concerning witchcraft beliefs and procedures
132 *bawd* procuress
140-1 *bees ... his* According to popular belief, bees could be summoned by banging
    on pots and pans; Thomas Tusser in *Five Hundred Points of Good Husbandry*
    says this was a way to claim ownership of them

SIR ARTHUR   But these men-witches
Are not in trading with hell's merchandise,
Like such as you are, that for a word, a look,
Denial of a coal of fire, kill men,   145
Children and cattle.
SAWYER   Tell them, sir, that do so.
Am I accused for such an one?
SIR ARTHUR   Yes, 'twill be sworn.
SAWYER
Dare any swear I ever tempted maiden
With golden hooks flung at her chastity,
To come and lose her honour? And being lost,   150
To pay not a denier for't? Some slaves have done it.
Men-witches can without the fangs of law,
Drawing once one drop of blood, put counterfeit pieces
Away for true gold.
SIR ARTHUR   By one thing she speaks,
I know now she's a witch, and dare no longer   155
Hold conference with the fury.
JUSTICE   Let's then away.
Old woman, mend thy life, get home and pray.

       Exeunt [SIR ARTHUR CLARINGTON *and* JUSTICE]

SAWYER
For his confusion.

       Enter DOG

       My dear Tom-boy welcome.
I am torn in pieces by a pack of curs
Clapped all upon me, and for want of thee.
Comfort me. Thou shalt have the teat anon.   160
DOG
Bow, wow. I'll have it now.
SAWYER   I am dried up
With cursing and with madness; and have yet

---

151 *denier* A French copper coin of little value
154–6 *By ... fury* Another anticipation as well as a motive for attacking Mother
    Sawyer: Sir Arthur thinks that using the witch's power to divine relationships,
    Mother Sawyer has recognised his affair with Winifred
158 *dear Tom-boy* Mother Sawyer's ready acceptance of Dog betrays the friendly
    Justice's departing caution suggesting the power of a village's condemnation of
    a woman like her
160 *Clapped* set upon forcefully
162–3 *dried ... cursing* Mother Sawyer claims a choleric temperament, both a physi-
    cal and medical condition

No blood to moisten these sweet lips of thine.
Stand on thy hind-legs up. Kiss me, my Tommy, 165
And rub away some wrinkles on my brow
By making my old ribs to shrug for joy
Of thy fine tricks. What hast thou done? Let's tickle.

[*They embrace*]

Hast thou struck the horse lame as I bid thee?
DOG
Yes, and nipped the suckling child.
SAWYER   Ho, ho, my dainty, 170
My little pearl. No lady loves her hound,
Monkey, or parakeet, as I do thee.
DOG
The maid has been churning butter nine hours;
But it shall not come.
SAWYER   Let 'em eat cheese and choke.
DOG   I had rare sport 175
Among the clowns i'th'morris.
SAWYER   I could dance
Out of my skin to hear thee. But, my curl-pate,
That jade, that foul-tongued whore, Nan Ratcliffe,

---

167 *shrug* moving the body from side to side as a sign of joy
168 *tickle* become affectionate. Again Mother Sawyer condemns herself. In the 1984
    Bristol production, Mother Sawyer tickled Dog's stomach; in the 1981 RSC pro-
    duction, the two rolled on the floor together
171 *pearl* Then a common name for a dog
173–4 *The ... come* So Reginald Scot in *The Discouerie of Witchcraft* (1584): 'They
    can also bring to passe, that chearne as long as you list, your butter will not
    come; especiallie if either the maids haue eaten vp the creame; or the goodwife
    haue sold the butter before in the market. Whereof I haue had some triall,
    although there may be true and naturall causes to hinder the common course
    thereof: as for example. Put a little sope or sugar into your chearne of creame,
    and there will neuer come anie butter, chearne as long as you list' (1.4; p. 11)
177 *curl-pate* curly-headed person (an affectionate term)
178–81 *That ... heart?* The playwrights return here to recorded history. According
    to Goodcole, 'She was also indited, for that shee the said *Elizabeth Sawyer*, by
    Diaboolicall helpe, and out of her malice afore-thought, did witch vnto death
    Agnes Ratcliffe, a neighbour of hers, dwelling in the towne of *Edmonton* where
    shee did likewise dwell, and the cause that vrged her thereunto was, because that
    Elizabeth Ratceife [sic] did strike a Sowe of hers in her sight, for licking vp a little
    Soape where shee had laide it, and for that *Elizabeth Sawyer* would be reuenged
    of her' (sigs. B1v–B2)

Who for a little soap licked by my sow,
Struck, and almost had lamed it. Did not I charge thee   180
To pinch that quean to th'heart?

DOG

Bow, wow, wow. Look here else.

Enter ANNE RATCLIFFE *mad*

RATCLIFFE

See, see, see; the Man i'th' Moon has built a new windmill,
and what running there's from all quarters of the city to
learn the art of grinding!   185

SAWYER

Ho, ho, ho! I thank thee, my sweet mongrel.

RATCLIFFE

Hoyda! A pox of the Devil's false hopper! All the golden
meal runs into the rich knaves' purses, and the poor have
nothing but bran. Hey derry down! Are you not Mother
Sawyer?   190

SAWYER

No, I am a lawyer.

RATCLIFFE

Art thou? I prithee let me scratch thy face; for thy pen has
flayed off a great many men's skins. You'll have brave
doings in the vacation; for knaves and fools are at variance
in every village. I'll sue Mother Sawyer, and her own sow   195
shall give in evidence against her.

SAWYER

[*To* DOG] Touch her.

---

181 *pinch ... th'heart?* kill her
   quean whore
185 *grinding* (1) to grind corn; (2) to pimp or extort (cf. Job 31:10)
187 *Hoyda!* a nonsense exclamation
   hopper a container through which grain passes for grinding
189 *Hey derry down!* A common refrain from songs
192 *scratch thy face* A common way to disempower a witch was to draw her blood
   (or her *maleficium*) out of her. 'A good countrey Yeoman', an 'honest man', 'per-
   swaded himselfe, by such a one she was bewitched and hee was as faithfully per-
   swaded, that if he could but have 2 or 3 good scratches, at her face, wherby he
   might draw blood of her, he should recouer presently' (*The seuerall practises of
   Iohane Harnson, and her daughter, condemned and executed at Hartford, for
   Witch craft, the 4 of August last, 1606* [1607], sigs. C3–C3v); cf. George Gifford
   in *A Dialogue Concerning Witches and Witchcraftes* (1593): 'What say you to
   the boy which healed within few daies af[ter] he had scratched the witch,
   whereas his sores were most grieuous before, and could not be cured?' (sig. H1)
194 *vacation* The period when law courts were not in session

[DOG *rubs against* ANNE RATCLIFFE]

RATCLIFFE
Oh my ribs are made of a paned hose, and they break.
There's a Lancashire hornpipe in my throat. Hark how it
tickles it, with doodle, doodle, doodle, doodle. Welcome   200
sergeants: welcome Devil. Hands, hands; hold hands, and
dance around, around, around.

> *Enter* OLD BANKS, *his son* [YOUNG BANKS] *the Clown,*
> OLD RATCLIFFE [*and*] COUNTRY-FELLOWS

OLD RATCLIFFE
She's here; alas, my poor wife is here.

OLD BANKS
Catch her fast, and have her into some close chamber. Do,
for she's as many wives are, stark mad.   205

YOUNG BANKS
The witch, Mother Sawyer, the witch, the Devil.

OLD RATCLIFFE
O, my dear wife! Help, sirs!

> [OLD RATCLIFFE *and the* COUNTRY-FELLOWS] *car*[*ry*]
> *her off*

OLD BANKS
You see your work, Mother Bumby.

---

197 *Touch her* Mother Sawyer's vicious command to harm a neighbour with whom
   she has a trifling quarrel complicates the reaction to a character who has been
   sympathetically portrayed
198–202 *Oh ... around* Anne Ratcliffe's madness draws on Bedlam scenes in
   Dekker's *Honest Whore Part I* as well as on contemporary scenes of madness in
   Senecan tragedy and the Londoner's experiences seeing Bedlamites
198 *paned hose* breeches of cloth strips of various colours
199 *Lancashire hornpipe* (1) a wind instrument similar to a clarinet; (2) a lively
   dance. In 1612 Lancashire underwent 'an epidemic' of witchcraft when 12 persons were executed
200 *doodle ... doodle* A sound imitating a hornpipe
201 *sergeants* court officers
   welcome Devil Anne Ratcliffe is bewitched
204 *close* (1) locked; (2) small; (3) confining
208 *Mother Bumby* The title character in John Lyly's comedy (1589) who was, properly speaking, a wise woman and not a witch – that is, a woman who used her
   special powers for healing others. But the term was later applied to women who
   used power for evil ends. T. I. mentions in *A World of wonders* (1595) 'I might
   heere noate the cruell deuises of mother *Bumby* the witch of *Rochester*: the tiran-
   nie of the witches of *Warboys*, and many other' (sig. E4)

SAWYER

My work? Should she and all you here run mad,
Is the work mine?   210

YOUNG BANKS

No, on my conscience, she would not hurt a Devil of two
years old.

Enter OLD RATCLIFFE *and the rest*

How, now? What's become of her?

OLD RATCLIFFE

Nothing. She's become nothing, but the miserable trunk of
a wretched woman. We were in her hands as reeds in a   215
mighty tempest. Spite of our strengths, away she brake; and
nothing in her mouth being heard, but 'the Devil, the witch,
the witch, the Devil'; she beat out her own brains, and so
died.

YOUNG BANKS

It's any man's case, be he never so wise, to die when his   220
brains go a-wool-gathering.

OLD BANKS

Masters, be ruled by me; let's all to a Justice. Hag, thou
hast done this, and thou shalt answer it.

SAWYER

Banks, I defy thee.

OLD BANKS

Get a warrant first to examine her, then ship her to   225
Newgate. Here's enough, if all her other villainies were pardoned, to burn her for a witch. You have a spirit, they say,
comes to you in the likeness of a dog; we shall see your cur
at one time or other. If we do, unless it be the Devil himself, he shall go howling to the gaol in one chain, and thou 230
in another.

211–12 *she . . . old* Cf. 'She would not harm a fly', 'There's no more harm in him than in
a devil of two years old', both proverbial

218 *beat out her own brains* T. I. in *A World of wonders* (1595) recounts the 'facts' of 'a
Witch named mother white-coate alias mother *Arnold* alias mother *Glassenbury*' of
Barking who drives the fishermen Thomas Clark and William Daulbie to attempt
suicide (sigs. E2v–E3)

219 *died* Mother Sawyer becomes indirectly responsible for Anne Ratcliffe's death in
opposition to Frank who is directly responsible for Susan's

221 *brains go a-wool-gathering* Proverbial (W582)

225 *ship* convey

226 *Newgate* A London prison for felons; Elizabeth Sawyer, incarcerated there, thus came
in contact with Henry Goodcole who was her 'continuall visitor'

230 *gaol* (goal Q)

SAWYER
  Be hanged thou in a third, and do thy worst.

YOUNG BANKS
  How, Father? You send the poor dumb thing howling to th'
  gaol? He that makes him howl, makes me roar.

OLD BANKS
  Why, foolish boy, dost thou know him?   235

YOUNG BANKS
  No matter, if I do or not. He's bailable I am sure by law.
  But if the dog's word will not be taken, mine shall.

OLD BANKS
  Thou bail for a dog?

YOUNG BANKS
  Yes, or a bitch either, being my friend. I'll lie by the heels
  myself, before Puppison shall. His dog-days are not come   240
  yet, I hope.

OLD BANKS
  What manner of dog is it? Didst ever see him?

YOUNG BANKS
  See him? Yes, and given him a bone to gnaw twenty times.
  The dog is no court-foisting hound, that fills his belly full
  by base wagging his tail; neither is it a citizen's water-   245
  spaniel, enticing his master to go a-ducking twice or thrice
  a week, whilst his wife makes ducks and drakes at home.
  This is no Paris-garden bandog neither, that keeps a bow-
  wow-wowing, to have butchers bring their curs thither, and
  when all comes to all, they run away like sheep. Neither is 250
  this the Black Dog of Newgate.

232 *in a third* quickly
233 *poor dumb thing* That is, Dog, not Mother Sawyer
239 *lie by the heels* (1) put in the stocks; (2) put in chains
240 *Puppison* An affectionate term for puppy
     dog-days days of suffering (and possibly death); see note to III.i.99
244 *court-foisting hound* The common term of contempt for a lapdog
247 *makes ducks and drakes* has illicit affairs; proverbial (D632)
248 *Paris-garden* A bear-baiting arena in Southwark near the theatres
     bandog fierce mastiff used to bait bears or bulls
251 *Black Dog of Newgate* A black dog, commonly believed an evil spirit haunting
     Newgate prison; *The Black Dog of Newgate*, a popular pamphlet by the high-
     wayman Luke Hutton published in 1596, has the dog represent not the Devil but
     the corrupt (devilish) practices of the prison guards such as false arrests and bilk-
     ing victims. In 1598 *Luke Huttons Lamentacion*, one of many ballads on the
     same theme, appeared

OLD BANKS

No, Goodman Son-fool, but the Dog of Hell-gate.

YOUNG BANKS

I say, Goodman Father-fool, it's a lie.

ALL

He's bewitched.

YOUNG BANKS

A gross lie as big as myself. The Devil in St Dunstan's will   255
as soon drink with this poor cur, as with any Temple-bar
laundress that washes and wrings lawyers.

[*Enter* DOG]

DOG

Bow, wow, wow, wow.

ALL

O the Dog's here, the Dog's here.

OLD BANKS

It was the voice of a dog.   260

YOUNG BANKS

The voice of a dog? If that voice were a dog's, what voice
had my mother? So I am a dog. Bow, wow, wow. It was I
that barked so, Father, to make coxcombs of these clowns.

OLD BANKS

However, we'll be coxcombed no longer. Away therefore to
th' Justice for a warrant; and then, Gammer Gurton, have   265
at your needle of witchcraft.

SAWYER

And prick thine own eyes out. Go, peevish fools.

Exeunt [OLD BANKS, OLD RATCLIFFE *and* COUNTRYMEN]

YOUNG BANKS

Ningle, you had like to have spoiled all with your bowings.
I was glad to put 'em off with one of my dog-tricks on a
sudden; I am bewitched, little cost-me-nought, to love thee   270

252 *Goodman* A common term of address for yeomen and farmers
      Dog of Hell-gate According to the myth, Cerberus
255 *Devil in St Dunstan's* Devil Tavern in Fleet Street near St Dunstan's Church and
      next to Temple Bar, one of the Inns of Court (named for the tavern sign in which
      St Dunstan pulls on the Devil's nose with pincers)
257 *laundress* A cant term for whore
265 *warrant* An order to commit to prison; cf. the false accusations of Warbeck and
      Somerton
      Gammer Gurton A bewitching storyteller who has the title-role in a comedy by
      W. Stevenson (1553); the farce is centred on the search for her lost needle (with
      sexual implications)

– a pox, that morris makes me spit in thy mouth. I dare not
stay. Farewell, Ningle; you whoreson dog's nose. Farewell
witch.   *Exit*

DOG
  Bow, wow, wow, wow.

SAWYER
  Mind him not, he's not worth thy worrying.   275
  Run at a fairer game. That foul-mouthed knight,
  Scurvy Sir Arthur, fly at him, my Tommy;
  And pluck out's throat.

DOG
  No, there's a dog already biting's conscience.

SAWYER
  That's a sure bloodhound. Come, let's home and play.   280
  Our black work ended, we'll make holiday.

                                                                        Exeunt

ACT IV, SCENE ii

Enter KATHERINE: *a bed thrust forth, on it* FRANK *in a
slumber*

KATHERINE
  Brother, brother! So sound asleep? That's well.

FRANK
  No, not I, sister. He that's wounded here,
  As I am; (all my other hurts are bitings
  Of a poor flea) but he that here once bleeds,
  Is maimed incurably.

KATHERINE   My good sweet brother,   5
  (For now my sister must grow up in you)
  Though her loss strikes you through, and that I feel
  The blow as deep, I pray thee be not cruel
  To kill me too, by seeing you cast away
  In your own helpless sorrow. Good love, sit up.   10
  And if you can give physic to yourself,

---

271 *spit in thy mouth* want to please you; from the common belief that dogs liked
     people who spat in their mouths
272 *whoreson dog's nose* Here a term of endearment
279 *biting's conscience* Perhaps a further reference to Dog's awareness of Sir Arthur's
     affair with Winifred

3–4 *bitings ... flea* 'It is but a flea-biting' is proverbial (F355), but cf. IV.i.279
11 *physic* medicine, treatment

515

I shall be well.

FRANK   I'll do my best.

KATHERINE   I thank you.
What do you look about for?

FRANK   Nothing, nothing.
But I was thinking, sister.

KATHERINE   Dear heart, what?

FRANK
Who but a fool would thus be bound to a bed,   15
Having this room to walk in?

KATHERINE   Why do you talk so?
Would you were fast asleep.

FRANK   No, no; I'm not idle.
But here's my meaning. Being robbed as I am,
Why should my soul, which married was to hers,
Live in divorce, and not fly after her?   20
Why should not I walk hand in hand with death
To find my love out?

KATHERINE   That were well, indeed.
Your time being come, when death is sent to call you,
No doubt you shall meet her.

FRANK   Why should not I go
Without calling?

KATHERINE   Yes, brother, so you might,   25
Were there no place to go to when you're gone,
But only this.

FRANK   Troth, sister, thou sayest true.
For when a man has been an hundred years,
Hard travelling o'er the tottering bridge of age,
He's not the thousand part upon his way.   30
All life is but a wandering to find home.
When we are gone, we are there. Happy were man
Could here his voyage end; he should not then
Answer how well or ill he steered his soul,
By heaven's or by hell's compass; how he put in   35
(Losing blessed goodness' shore) at such a sin;
Nor how life's dear provision he has spent.
Nor how far he in's navigation went
Beyond commission. This were a fine reign,
To do ill, and not hear of it again.
Yet then were man more wretched than a beast.   40
For, sister, our dead pay is sure the best.

KATHERINE
'Tis so, the best or worst. And I wish heaven

17 *idle* delirious

To pay (and so I know it will) that traitor,   45
That devil Somerton (who stood in mine eye
Once as an angel) home to his deservings.
What villain but himself, once loving me,
With Warbeck's soul would pawn his own to hell,
To be revenged on my poor sister?

FRANK   Slaves!
A pair of merciless slaves! Speak no more of them.   50

KATHERINE
I think this talking hurts you.

FRANK   Does me no good, I'm sure.
I pay for't everywhere.

KATHERINE   I have done then.
Eat, if you cannot sleep. You have these two days
Not tasted any food. Jane, is it ready?

FRANK   55
What's ready? What's ready?

[JANE *enters with a plate of chicken*]

KATHERINE
I have made ready a roasted chicken for you.
Sweet, wilt thou eat?

FRANK   A pretty stomach on a sudden – yes –
There's one in the house can play upon a lute.
Good girl, let's hear him too.

KATHERINE   You shall, dear brother.

[*Exit* JANE]

Would I were a musician, you should hear   60
How I would feast your ear.

Lute plays

                  Stay, mend your pillow,
And raise you higher.

FRANK   I am up too high.
Am I not, sister, now?

KATHERINE   No, no, 'tis well.
Fall to, fall to. A knife. Here's never a knife.
Brother, I'll look out yours. [*She searches his clothes*]

Enter DOG, *shrugging as it were for joy, and dances*

FRANK   Sister, O sister,   65
I am ill upon a sudden; and can eat nothing.

65 s.d. *joy* Dog is happy at his ability to expose Frank

517

KATHERINE
  In very deed you shall. The want of food
  Makes you so faint. [*Finds knife but does not remove it*]
    Ha! Here's none in your pocket.
  I'll go fetch a knife.
                                Exit
FRANK   Will you? 'Tis well, all's well.

  She gone, he searches first one, then the other pocket.
  Knife found. DOG *runs off. He lies on one side. The*
  SPIRIT *of* SUSAN *his second wife comes to the bed-side.*
  He stares at it, and turning to the other side, it's there
  too. In the meantime, WINIFRED *as a page comes in,*
  stands at his bed's feet sadly. He frighted, sits upright.
              The SPIRIT *vanishes.*

FRANK
  What art thou?
WINIFRED   A lost creature.
FRANK   So am I too.   70
  Win? Ah, my she-page!
WINIFRED   For your sake I put on
  A shape that's false; yet do I wear a heart
  True to you as your own.
FRANK   Would mine and thine
  Were fellows in one house. Kneel by me here.
  On this side now? How dar'st thou come to mock me   75
  On both sides of my bed?
WINIFRED   When?
FRANK   But just now.
  Outface me, stare upon me with strange postures.
  Turn my soul wild by a face in which were drawn
  A thousand ghosts leapt newly from their graves,
  To pluck me into a winding-sheet.
WINIFRED   Believe it,   80
  I came no nearer to you than yon place,
  At your bed's feet; and of the house had leave,

---

68 s.d. [*Finds knife ...*] The discovery of the knife with Susan's blood on it is a
    strong but problematic image: did Frank overlook this in his emotional state
    during the murder, deliberately hide it and then later forget about it, or keep it
    out of a sense of guilt, hoping it might later be discovered?
69 s.d. *SPIRIT of SUSAN* (1) A sign of Frank's sense of guilt projected in a ghost
    of his creation; (2) an act of the Devil, perhaps through the agency of Dog.
    Susan's ghost has not returned to accuse Frank, in all probability, since she for-
    gave him at the time of her death. Goodcole says scurrilous ballads reported
    'Spirits' attending Mother Sawyer in prison (sig. A3v)
79 *ghosts ... graves* A common belief held that ghosts announced impending deaths

Calling myself your horse-boy, in to come,
And visit my sick master.
FRANK   Then 'twas my fancy.   85
Some windmill in my brains for want of sleep.
WINIFRED
Would I might never sleep, so you could rest.
But you have plucked a thunder on your head,
Whose noise cannot cease suddenly. Why should you
Dance at the wedding of a second wife?   90
When scarce the music which you heard at mine
Had ta'en a farewell of you. O this was ill!
And they who thus can give both hands away,
In th'end shall want their best limbs.
FRANK   Winifred,
The chamber-door fast?
WINIFRED   Yes.
FRANK   Sit thee then down;   95
And when thou hast heard me speak, melt into tears.
Yet I to save those eyes of thine from weeping,
Being to write a story of us two,
Instead of ink, dipped my sad pen in blood.
When of thee I took leave, I went abroad   100
Only for pillage, as a freebooter,
What gold soe'er I got, to make it thine.
To please a father, I have Heaven displeased.
Striving to cast two wedding rings in one,
Through my bad workmanship I now have none.
I have lost her and thee.   105
WINIFRED   I know she's dead.
But you have me still.
FRANK   Nay, her this hand
Murdered; and so I lose thee too.
WINIFRED   Oh me!
FRANK
Be quiet, for thou my evidence art,
Jury and judge. Sit quiet and I'll tell all.

> *As they whisper, enter at one end of the stage* OLD
> CARTER *and* KATHERINE, DOG *at the other, pawing
> softly at* FRANK

85 *Some ... sleep* Proverbial (W455). Cf. *The Merry Devil of Edmonton*: 'what, are
     your braines alwayes water-milles? must they euer runne round?' (II.i.3–4)
100 *pillage ... freebooter* Frank is confessing his deeds metaphorically, perhaps
     unable yet to face the truth of his actions directly
     freebooter pirate
109 s.d. *DOG ... FRANK* This action shows Dog maintains his control over Frank

KATHERINE
I have run madding up and down to find you,   110
Being laden with the heaviest news that ever
Poor daughter carried.

OLD CARTER   Why? Is the boy dead?

KATHERINE
Dead, sir! O, Father, we are cozened. You are told
The murderer sings in prison, and he laughs here.
This villain killed my sister. See else, see,   115
A bloody knife in's pocket.

OLD CARTER   Bless me, patience!

FRANK
The knife, the knife, the knife!

KATHERINE
What knife?

Exit DOG

FRANK   To cut my chicken up, my chicken;
Be you my carver, Father.

OLD CARTER   That I will.

KATHERINE
[*Aside*] How the Devil steels our brows after doing ill!   120

FRANK
My stomach and my sight are taken from me;
All is not well within me.

OLD CARTER
I believe thee, boy. I that have seen so many moons clap
their horns on other men's foreheads to strike them sick, yet
mine to 'scape and be well! I that never cast away a fee   125
upon urinals, but am as sound as an honest man's conscience when he's dying, I should cry out as thou dost, 'All
is not well within me', felt I but the bag of thy

110 *madding* anxiously
113 *cozened* deceived
114 *The ... prison* Common belief (and tradition) held that a prisoner sang just
before his death
115 *See else* If you do not believe me
124 *horns* sign of a cuckold; Old Carter tells Frank he knows of his guilt (since
Katherine told him of the knife at 116)
126 *urinals* When a sick man's health was in doubt, glass vessels of urine were sent
to a medical examiner. Old Carter has no doubt of Frank's guilt and does not
wish to waste money on such tests
128 *bag* sack in the body containing poison
129 *impostumes* swellings or cysts; that is, physical (perhaps demonstrating moral)
corruption

imposthumes. Ah poor villain! Ah my wounded rascal! All
my grief is, I have now small hope of thee.   130

FRANK
Do the surgeons say, my wounds are dangerous then?

OLD CARTER
Yes, yes, and there's no way with thee but one.

FRANK
Would he were to open them.

OLD CARTER
I'll go to fetch him. I'll make an holiday to see thee as I
wish.   *Exit to fetch* OFFICERS   135

FRANK
A wondrous kind old man.

WINIFRED
[*Aside*] Your sin's the blacker, so to abuse his goodness.
[*To* FRANK] Master, how do you?
FRANK   Pretty well now, boy.
I have such odd qualms come 'cross my stomach!
I'll fall to. Boy, cut me.
WINIFRED   [*Aside*] You have cut me, I'm sure.   140
[*To* FRANK] A leg or wing, sir.
FRANK   No, no, no. A wing?
[*Aside*] Would I had wings but to soar up yon tower.
But here's a clog that hinders me.

> [*Enter*] FATHER [OLD CARTER] *with* [SUSAN's *body*] *in a*
> *coffin* [*carried by* SERVANTS]

What's that?

OLD CARTER
That? What? O, now I see her, 'tis a young wench, my
daughter, sirrah, sick to the death. And hearing thee to be   145
an excellent rascal for letting blood, she looks out at a case-
ment, and cries, 'Help, help', 'stay that man'; 'him I must
have, or none'.

FRANK
For pity's sake, remove her. See, she stares
With one broad open eye still in my face.   150

132 *there's ... one* Proverbial (W148)
137 *Your ... goodness* The line is deeply problematic. While Winifred seems to wres-
   tle with her conscience over Frank's murder – performed (as he saw it) for her
   sake – she may also be recalling that her silence over the affair with Sir Arthur
   which led to her marriage makes her complicit in the murder as well
146 *letting blood* According to popular belief, a corpse bled again when confronted
   by its killer
150 *one broad open eye* Frank suffers another attack of conscience in Susan's second
   unexpected appearance (cf. III.ii.37)

OLD CARTER

Thou puttest both hers out, like a villain as thou art; yet
see, she is willing to lend thee one again to find out the murderer, and that's thyself.

FRANK

Old man, thou liest.

OLD CARTER

So shalt thou i'th'gaol. Run for officers.   155

KATHERINE

O thou merciless slave! She was
(Though yet above ground) in her grave
To me, but thou hast torn it up again. Mine eyes
Too much drowned, now must feel more rain.

OLD CARTER

Fetch officers.   160

Exit KATHERINE

FRANK

For whom?

OLD CARTER

For thee, sirrah, sirrah. Some knives have foolish posies
upon them, but thine has a villainous one; look. Oh! it is
enamelled with the heart-blood of thy hated wife, my
beloved daughter. What sayst thou to this evidence? Is't not   165
sharp? Does't not strike home? Thou canst not answer honestly, and without a trembling heart, to this one point, this
terrible bloody point.

WINIFRED

I beseech you, sir. Strike him no more;
You see he's dead already.   170

OLD CARTER

O, sir! You held his horses, you are as arrant a rogue as he.
Up, go you too.

FRANK

As you're a man, throw not upon that woman
Your loads of tyranny, for she's innocent.

OLD CARTER

How? How? A woman? Is't grown to a fashion for women   175
in all countries to wear the breeches?

WINIFRED

I am not as my disguise speaks me, sir, his page;
But his first only wife, his lawful wife.

155 gaol (goal Q)
162 *posies* mottoes, verses

OLD CARTER
How? How? More fire i'th'bedstraw?

WINIFRED
The wrongs which singly fell upon your daughter,   180
On me are multiplied. She lost a life,
But I, an husband and myself must lose,
If you call him to a bar for what he has done.

OLD CARTER
He has done it then?

WINIFRED
Yes, 'tis confessed to me.

FRANK   Dost thou betray me?   185

WINIFRED
O, pardon me, dear heart! I am mad to lose thee,
And know not what I speak. But if thou didst,
I must arraign this father for two sins,
Adultery and murder.

Enter KATHERINE

KATHERINE   Sir, they are come.

OLD CARTER
Arraign me for what thou wilt, all Middlesex knows me   190
better for an honest man than the middle of a market-place
knows thee for an honest woman. Rise, sirrah, and don
your tacklings, rig yourself for the gallows, or I'll carry thee
thither on my back. Your trull shall to the gaol go with you;
there be as fine Newgate birds as she that can draw him in.   195
Pox on's wounds.

FRANK
I have served thee, and my wages now are paid.
Yet my worst punishment shall, I hope, be stayed.

Exeunt

179 *fire i'th' bedstraw* more hidden mischief; proverbial (F272)
188 *father* Winifred accuses Frank of her pregnancy (thus concealing her affair with Sir Arthur) but Old Carter, confused and culpable, thinks she means him in the following lines. Presumably the playwrights use this occasion to show how widespread complicity and guilt are in socially constructed victims, for Winifred is otherwise treated sympathetically
193 *tacklings* clothes
    I'll carry thee A puzzling allusion to the customary image of the Devil carrying a sinner off to Hell
194 *trull* strumpet, prostitute
    gaol (goal Q) Dekker himself was in debtors' prison from 1613 to 1619
198 *worst punishment* damnation

ACT V, SCENE i

Enter MOTHER SAWYER *alone*

SAWYER

Still wronged by every slave? And not a dog
Bark in his dame's defence? I am called witch,
Yet am myself bewitched from doing harm.
Have I given up myself to thy black lust
Thus to be scorned? Not see me in three days?   5
I'm lost without my Tomalin. Prithee come,
Revenge to me is sweeter far than life;
Thou art my raven, on whose coal-black wings
Revenge comes flying to me. O my best love!
I am on fire, (even in the midst of ice)   10
Raking my blood up, till my shrunk knees feel
Thy curled head leaning on them. Come then, my darling.
If in the air thou hover'st, fall upon me
In some dark cloud, and as I oft have seen
Dragons and serpents in the elements,   15
Appear thou now so to me. Art thou i'th'sea?
Muster up all the monsters from the deep,
And be the ugliest of them. So that my bulch
Show but his swart cheek to me, let earth cleave,
And break from hell, I care not. Could I run   20
Like a swift powder-mine beneath the world,
Up would I blow it all, to find out thee,
Though I lay ruined in it. Not yet come!
I must then fall to my old prayer.
Sanctibiceter nomen tuum.   25
Not yet come! Worrying of wolves,
Biting of mad dogs, the manges and the –

Enter DOG [*now white*]

---

6 *Tomalin* Diminutive of Tom; a sign of affection

7 *Revenge ... sweeter* Proverbial (R90)

8 *raven* As a bird of ill omen. Mother Sawyer's greater powers of understanding and speech may be inconsistent with her position but this allows the playwrights to make her more sympathetic and to underscore some issues in the play

10 *fire ... ice* Struggling for forceful language, Mother Sawyer has only outmoded Petrarchisms

18 *bulch* bulchin or bullcalf; a term of endearment

19 *swart* black

DOG
  How now! Whom art thou cursing?
SAWYER
  Thee. Ha! No, 'tis my black cur I am cursing,
  For not attending on me.
DOG   I am that cur.   30
SAWYER
  Thou liest. Hence, come not nigh me.
DOG   Bow, wow.
SAWYER
  Why dost thou thus appear to me in white,
  As if thou wert the ghost of my dear love?
DOG
  I am dogged, list not to tell thee, yet
  To torment thee. My whiteness puts thee   35
  In mind of thy winding sheet.
SAWYER   Am I near death?
DOG
  Yes, if the Dog of Hell be near thee. When
  The Devil comes to thee as a lamb,
  Have at thy throat.
SAWYER   Off, cur.
DOG   He has the back
  Of a sheep, but the belly of an otter: 40
  Devours by sea and land. Why am I in white?
  Didst thou not pray to me?
SAWYER
  Yes, thou dissembling hell-hound.
  Why now in white more than at other times?

29–75 (Q is printed in prose)

31 *nigh* near

32 *Why ... white* Goodcole writes, '*Question. In what shape would the Diuell
   come vnto you? Answere.* Always in the shape of a dogge, and of two collars,
   sometimes of blacke and sometimes of white' (sig. C2v). According to his
   account of *Daemonologie* in 1621, Edward Fairfax's daughter Helen saw supernatural agents in the forms of a black cat and a white cat

34 *dogged* perverse, cruel. Dog's trick on Mother Sawyer (by turning white) is the
   last act of victimization against her in the play

36 *winding sheet* shroud
   sheet (sweet Q)

39 *Have at* guard

41–2 *Why ... me?* So Goodcole: '*Would the Diuell come vnto you, all in one bignesse? Answ.* No; when hee came vnto mee in the blacke shape, he then was
   biggest, and in the white the least; and when that I was praying, hee then would
   come vnto me in the white colour' (sig. D1v)

DOG

Be blasted with the news; whiteness is day's foot-boy,   45
A fore-runner to light, which shows thy old rivelled face.
Villains are stripped naked, the witch must be beaten
Out of her cockpit.

SAWYER   Must she? She
Shall not; thou art a lying spirit.
Why to mine eyes art thou a flag   50
Of truce? I am at peace with none;
'Tis the black colour or none, which I fight under.
I do not like thy puritan paleness.
Glowing furnaces are far more hot
Than they which flame outright. If thou
My old dog art, go and bite   55
Such as I shall set thee on.

DOG   I will not.

SAWYER
I'll sell my self to twenty thousands fiends,
To have thee torn in pieces then.

DOG   Thou canst not.
Thou art so ripe to fall into hell, that no more   60
Of my kennel will so much as bark at him
That hangs thee.

SAWYER   I shall run mad.

DOG   Do so.
Thy time is come to curse, and rave, and die.
The glass of thy sins is full, and it must run out at gallows.

SAWYER
It cannot, ugly cuz, I'll confess nothing;   65
And not confessing, who dare come and swear
I have bewitched them? I'll not confess one mouthful.

---

45 *foot-boy* page
46 *rivelled* wrinkled
48 *cockpit* A place for cockfights, a common sport, with a pun on the Cockpit
Theatre where this play was performed in London
53 *puritan* hypocritical
59 *torn in pieces* Cf. II.i.136
64 *glass* hourglass
run out (of time)
65 *I'll confess nothing* Confessions were not taken on oath since they were self-
incriminating. This gives more point and purpose to chaplains like Henry
Goodcole for their services (and, in his case, publications)

DOG
Choose, and be hanged or burned.

SAWYER
Spite of the Devil and thee, I'll muzzle up   70
My tongue from telling tales.

DOG
Spite of thee and the Devil, thou'lt be condemned.

SAWYER
Yes, when?

DOG   And ere the executioner catch thee
Full in's claws, thou'lt confess all.

SAWYER
Out dog!

DOG   Out witch! Thy trial is at hand.
Our prey being had, the Devil does laughing stand.   75

The DOG *stands aloof. Enter* OLD BANKS, RATCLIFFE
and COUNTRYMEN

OLD BANKS
She's here; attach her. Witch, you must go with us.

SAWYER
Whither? to hell?

OLD BANKS
No, no, no, old crone; your mittimus shall be made thither,
but your own jailors shall receive you. Away with her.

[*They take hold of* MOTHER SAWYER]

SAWYER
My Tommy! My sweet Tom-boy! O thou dog!   80
Dost thou now fly to thy kennel and forsake me?
Plagues and consumptions –

Exeunt [*all except* DOG]

DOG   Ha, ha, ha, ha!
Let not the world, witches or devils condemn,

68 *hanged or burned* One popular belief was that witches who confessed would
have the lesser punishment of hanging; in fact, only witches found guilty of murdering their husbands or masters were burned

76 *attach* arrest

78 *mittimus* A warrant ordering a person to be imprisoned until trial

81 *Dost . . . me?* Thus Goodcole: 'being descried, to pay in the ende such a worker
of Iniquity, her wages, and that which shee had deserued, (namely, *shame* and
Death) from which the Diuell, that had so long deluded her, did not come as shee
said, to shew the least helpe of his vnto her to deliuer her: but being descried in
his waies, and workes, immediately he fled' (sig. A4v)

They follow us, and then we follow them.

[*Enter*] YOUNG BANKS *to the* DOG

YOUNG BANKS
I would fain meet with mine ingle once more; he has had a   85
claw amongst 'em. My rival, that loved my wench, is like to
be hanged like an innocent; a kind cur where he takes; but
where he takes not, a dogged rascal. I know the villain loves
me.

[DOG] *barks*

No! Art thou there? That's Tom's voice, but 'tis not he; this   90
is a dog of another hair. This? Bark and not speak to me?
Not Tom then. There's as much difference betwixt Tom
and this, as betwixt white and black.
DOG
Hast thou forgot me?

[DOG *barks*]

YOUNG BANKS
That's Tom again. Prithee ningle speak, is thy name Tom?   95
DOG
Whilst I served my old Dame Sawyer, 'twas. I'm gone
From her now.
YOUNG BANKS
Gone? Away with the witch then too. She'll never thrive if
thou leavest her; she knows no more how to kill a cow, or
a horse, or a sow, without thee, than she does to kill a   100
goose.
DOG
No, she has done killing now, but must be killed
For what she has done. She's shortly to be hanged.
YOUNG BANKS
Is she? In my conscience if she be, 'tis thou hast brought her
to the gallows, Tom.
                                                              105
DOG
Right. I served her to that purpose, 'twas part of my wages.

---

85 *fain* willingly, gladly
85–6 *he ... claw* Naive Young Banks has no difficulty in recognizing the work of
the Devil
87 *innocent* (1) guiltless; (2) idiot
98 prefix YOUNG BANKS (DOG Q)
101 *goose* (1) idiot; (2) prostitute. Contemporary authors were arguing that as servants of the Devil, witches made no decisions on their own
106 *DOG* (sig. H4 in Q which misnumbers p. 55 and p. 35)

YOUNG BANKS
This was no honest servant's part, by your leave Tom. This
remember, I pray you, between you and I; I entertained you
ever as a dog, not as a Devil.

DOG
True; and so I used thee doggedly,   110
Not devilishly. I have deluded thee
For sport to laugh at. The wench thou seekst
After thou never spakst with, but a spirit
In her form, habit and likeness. Ha, ha!

YOUNG BANKS
I do not then wonder at the change of your garments, if you   115
can enter into shapes of women too.

DOG
Any shape to blind such silly eyes
As thine; but chiefly those coarse creatures,
Dog or cat, hare, ferret, frog, toad.

YOUNG BANKS
Louse or flea?   120

DOG
Any poor vermin.

YOUNG BANKS
It seems you Devils have poor thin souls, that you can
bestow yourselves in such small bodies. But pray you, Tom,
one question at parting (I think I shall never see you more)
where do you borrow those bodies that are none of your   125
own? The garment-shape you may hire at broker's.

DOG
Why wouldst thou know that? Fool,
It avails thee not.

YOUNG BANKS
Only for my mind's sake, Tom, and to tell some of my
friends.   130

DOG
I'll thus much tell thee. Thou never art so distant
From an evil spirit, but that thy oaths,
Curses and blasphemies pull him to thine elbow.
Thou never tellst a lie, but that a Devil
Is within hearing it; thy evil purposes   135
Are ever haunted; but when they come to act,

---

110 *doggedly* affectionately, in contrast to Dog's low opinion of Young Banks at
lines 117–18
126 *broker's* pawnbroker's, second-hand dealer's
131–40 *Thou ... thee* Since the Devil's agent is giving conventional Puritan doctrine
here, the speech is both polemical and satirical

As thy tongue slandering, bearing false witness,
Thy hand stabbing, stealing, cosening, cheating,
He's then within thee. Thou playst, he bets upon thy part;
Although thou lose, yet he will gain by thee.   140

YOUNG BANKS

Ay? Then he comes in the shape of a rook.

DOG

The old cadaver of some self-strangled wretch
We sometimes borrow, and appear human.
The carcass of some disease-slain strumpet,
We varnish fresh, and wear as her first beauty.   145
Didst never hear? if not, it has been done.
An hot luxurious lecher in his twines,
When he has thought to clip his dalliance,
There has provided been for his embrace
A fine hot flaming Devil in her place.   150

YOUNG BANKS

Yes, I am partly a witness to this, but I never could embrace
her. I thank thee for that, Tom; well, again I thank thee,
Tom, for all this counsel; without a fee too. There's few
lawyers of thy mind now. Certainly Tom, I begin to pity
thee.   155

DOG

Pity me? For what?

YOUNG BANKS

Were it not possible for thee to become an honest dog yet?
'Tis a base life that you lead, Tom, to serve witches, to kill
innocent children, to kill harmless cattle, to 'stroy corn and
fruit, etc. 'Twere better yet to be a butcher, and kill for   160
yourself.

DOG

Why? These are all my delights, my pleasures, fool.

YOUNG BANKS

Or Tom, if you could give your mind to ducking, I know
you can swim, fetch and carry, some shop-keeper in
London would take great delight in you, and be a tender   165

---

141 *rook* (1) a black bird; (2) a swindler
147 *twines* embraces
148 *When ... dalliance* when the Devil embraces the lecher
159 *'stroy* destroy
160 *etc.* (& Q) Hoy conjectures & to be 'a sign that the actor is to go on speaking
    extemporaneously' (III, 266)
163–5 *ducking ... delight* The use of water spaniels for duck hunting was a popular
    sport

master over you. Or if you have a mind to the game, either
at bull or bear, I think I could prefer you to Moll Cutpurse.

DOG
Ha, ha! I should kill all the game, bulls, bears, dogs,
And all, not a cub to be left.

YOUNG BANKS
You could do, Tom, but you must play fair, you should be   170
staved off else. Or if your stomach did better like to serve
in some nobleman's, knight's, or gentleman's kitchen, if
you could brook the wheel, and turn the spit, your labour
could not be much; when they have roast meat, that's but
once or twice in the week at most, here you might lick your   175
own toes very well. Or if you could translate yourself into
a lady's arming puppy, there you might lick sweet lips, and
do many pretty offices; but to creep under an old witch's
coats, and suck like a great puppy, fie upon't! I have heard
beastly things of you, Tom.   180

DOG
Ha, ha! The worse thou heardst of me, the better 'tis.
Shall I serve thee, fool, at the self-same rate?

YOUNG BANKS
No, I'll see thee hanged, thou shalt be damned first; I know
thy qualities too well, I'll give no suck to such whelps;
therefore henceforth I defy thee; out and avaunt.   185

DOG
Nor will I serve for such a silly soul.
I am for greatness now, corrupted greatness;
There I'll shug in, and get a noble countenance.
Serve some Briarean footcloth-strider,

---

167 *bull or bear* the sports of bull-baiting or bear-baiting
   prefer recommend
   Moll Cutpurse Mary Frith, a well-known woman in London who dressed in
   men's clothing and had a reputation as a fighter, a bawd and a cutpurse; this may
   be a self-referential joke since Dekker had improved her reputation in his play
   about her, *The Roaring Girl* (1611), written with Thomas Middleton
171 *staved* driven or beaten; a term used for dogs in bull- and bear-baiting
173 *wheel* treadwheel (that turned a spit in roasting)
177 *arming puppy* a small dog carried in the arms
178 *offices* services
185 *out and avaunt* be off with you
186 s.d. *DOG* (sig. I1 Q; p. 57 misnumbered here as p. 41)
188 *shug* elbow, force the way, shove
   countenance patronage
189 *Briarean footcloth-strider* corrupt official; (Briareus was a giant in Greek
   mythology who had 100 hands; an ornamented footcloth indicated high rank)

That has an hundred hands to catch at bribes,　　　　190
But not a finger's nail of charity.
Such, like the dragon's tail, shall pull down hundreds
To drop and sink with him. I'll stretch myself,
And draw this bulk small as a silver wire,
Enter at the least pore tobacco fume　　　　　　　195
Can make a breach for. Hence silly fool,
I scorn to prey on such an atom soul.

YOUNG BANKS
Come out, come out, you cur; I will beat thee out of the
bounds of Edmonton, and tomorrow we go in procession,
and after thou shalt never come in again. If thou goest to 200
London, I'll make thee go about by Tyburn, stealing in by
Thieving Lane. If thou canst rub thy shoulder against a
lawyer's gown, as thou passest by Westminster Hall, do; if
not, to the stairs amongst the bandogs, take water, and the
Devil go with thee.　　　　　　　　　　　　　205

Exeunt [YOUNG] BANKS, DOG *barking*

ACT V, SCENE ii

Enter JUSTICE, SIR ARTHUR [CLARINGTON], WARBECK,
[SOMERTON, OLD] CARTER [*and*] KATHERINE

JUSTICE
Sir Arthur, though the bench hath mildly
Censured your errors, yet you have indeed

192 *dragon's tail* As a common image of punishment; see Rev. 12:3–4
197 *atom* tiny, irrelevant
199 *procession* The 'beating of the bounds', a formal periodic establishment of
boundaries reinforced through a perambulation of them
201 *Tyburn* The chief London location for public executions
202 *Thieving Lane* A short street in Westminster curving from the west side of King
Street to Broken Cross, the route thieves were taken to Gatehouse Prison; cf.
Rowley, *Match at Midnight*, I.i; sig. C2
203 *Westminster Hall* A court of justice along the Thames west of London
204 *stairs* landing-place on the Thames
bandogs mastiffs used to guard the steps
take water embark

0 s.d. *Enter ... KATHERINE* (Q does not designate new scene)
1 *bench* (1) judge; (2) court

Been the instrument that wrought all
Their misfortunes. I would wish you paid down
Your fine speedily and willingly.

SIR ARTHUR   I'll need no urging to it.   5

OLD CARTER
    If you should 'twere a shame to you; for if I should speak
    my conscience, you are worthier to be hanged of the two,
    all things considered; and now make what you can of it.
    But I am glad these gentlemen are freed.

WARBECK
    We knew our innocence.

SOMERTON   And therefore feared it not.   10

KATHERINE
    But I am glad that I have you safe.

                        Noise within

JUSTICE   How now! What noise is that?

OLD CARTER
    Young Frank is going the wrong way. Alas, poor youth! Now I
    begin to pity him.

                                            [*Exeunt*]

ACT V, SCENE iii

Enter YOUNG [FRANK] THORNEY *and Halberds. Enter
as to see the Execution,* OLD CARTER, OLD THORNEY,
KATHERINE, WINIFRED *weeping*

OLD THORNEY
    Here let our sorrows wait him. To press nearer
    The place of his sad death, some apprehensions
    May tempt our grief too much, at height already.
    Daughter, be comforted.

12 *the wrong way* to the gallows (for a misdirected life); cf. the proverb for some-
    thing going amiss (W168)

0 s.d. *Enter ... weeping* (Q does not designate new scene)
    Halberds Soldiers who carried halberds, spears with an axe-blade at the head
1 *wait him* Old Thorney suggests Frank is not on stage; perhaps the stage direc-
    tion refers to his passing over the stage, with guards
4 *Daughter* daughter-in-law

WINIFRED   Comfort and I
  Are too far separated to be joined   5
  But in eternity. I share too much
  Of him that's going thither.

OLD CARTER
  Poor woman, 'twas not thy fault. I grieve to see thee weep
  for him that hath my pity too.

WINIFRED
  My fault was lust, my punishment was shame;   10
  Yet I am happy that my soul is free
  Both from consent, foreknowledge and intent
  Of any murder. But of mine own honour,
  Restored again by a fair satisfaction,
  And since not to be wounded.

OLD THORNEY   Daughter, grieve not   15
  For what necessity forceth; rather resolve
  To conquer it with patience.
  Alas, she faints!

WINIFRED   My griefs are strong upon me.
  My weakness scarce can bear them.

[VOICES] *within*
  Away with her! Hang her, Witch!   20

    Enter [MOTHER] SAWYER *to execution,* OFFICERS *with*
      halberds, [*and*] COUNTRY-PEOPLE

OLD CARTER
  The witch, that instrument of mischief! Did not she witch
  the Devil into my son-in-law, when he killed my poor
  daughter? Do you hear, Mother Sawyer?

SAWYER
  What would you have? Cannot a poor old woman

---

13 *But* and

14 *satisfaction* repentance, atonement

15–16 *grieve ... forceth* 'Never grieve for what you cannot help' was proverbial
    (G453)

20 *Hang ... Witch!* Although witchcraft was taken seriously under King James,
    only 35 executions are recorded between 1603 and 1616 and only five between
    1616 and 1625, including Mother Sawyer's

20 s.d. *Enter ... COUNTRY-PEOPLE* 'On Saturday, being the fourteenth day of
    Aprill, Anno Dom. 1621. this *Elizabeth Sawyer* late of *Edmonton*, in the County
    of *Middlesex* Spinster, was arraigned, and indited three seuerall times at Iustice
    Hall in the Old Baily in *London*' (Goodcole, sig. B1v)

24–5 *What ... vexation?* 'Thus God did wonderfully ouertake her in her owne
    wickednesse, to make her tongue to be the meanes of her owne destruction'
    (Goodcole, sig. B1)

Have your leave to die without vexation?   25

OLD CARTER
Did you not bewitch Frank to kill his wife? He could never
have done't without the Devil.

SAWYER
Who doubts it? But is every devil mine?
Would I had one now whom I might command
To tear you all in pieces. Tom would have done't   30
Before he left me.

OLD CARTER
Thou didst bewitch Anne Ratcliffe to kill herself.

SAWYER
Churl, thou liest; I never did her hurt.
Would you were all as near your ends as I am,
That gave evidence against me for it.   35

FIRST COUNTRYMAN
I'll be sworn, Master Carter, she bewitched Gammer
Washbowl's sow, to cast her pigs a day before she would
have farrowed, yet they were sent up to London, and sold
for as good Westminster dog-pigs, at Bartholomew Fair, as
ever great-bellied ale-wife longed for.   40

SAWYER
These dogs will mad me. I was well resolved
To die in my repentance; though 'tis true,
I would live longer if I might. Yet since
I cannot, pray torment me not; my conscience

---

26 *bewitch Frank* Mother Sawyer has no involvement in Susan's death; Old Carter's
accusation is another instance of village victimization

32 *Thou ... herself* Cf. Goodcole: '*Question. Whether did you procure the death of
Agnes Ratcliefe, for which you were found guilty by the Iury? Answere.* No, I
did not by any means procure against her the least hurt' (sig. C2v)

37 *cast* give birth to

39 *dog-pigs* Male roasted pigs, a common item of sale at Bartholomew Fair in
Smithfields, London (on St Bartholomew's Day, 24 August)

40 *great-bellied ale-wife* Common belief held that pregnant women especially
craved roast pig

41 *dogs* cowards

42–5 *though ... be* Thus Goodcole: '*Quest. What moues you now to make this confession: did any vrge you to it, or bid you doe it, is it for any hope of life you doe
it? Answ.* No: I doe it to cleere my conscience, and now hauing done it, I am the
more quiet, and the better prepared, and willing thereby to suffer death; for I
haue no hope at all of my life, although I must confesse, I would liue longer if I
might' (sig. D1v)

Is settled as it shall be. All take heed   45
How they believe the Devil; at last he'll cheat you.

OLD CARTER
Thou'dst best confess all truly.

SAWYER   Yet again?
Have I scarce breath enough to say my prayers?
And would you force me to spend that in bawling?
Bear witness, I repent all former evil;   50
There is no damned conjuror like the Devil.

ALL
Away with her, away!

                [*Exeunt* MOTHER SAWYER *with* OFFICERS]

        Enter FRANK *to execution*, OFFICERS, JUSTICE, SIR
        ARTHUR [CLARINGTON], WARBECK [*and*] SOMERTON

OLD THORNEY
Here's the sad object which I yet must meet
With hope of comfort, if a repentant end
Make him more happy than misfortune would   55
Suffer him here to be.

FRANK   Good sirs, turn from me;
You will revive affliction almost killed
With my continual sorrow.

OLD THORNEY   O Frank, Frank!
Would I had sunk in mine own wants, or died
But one bare minute ere thy fault was acted.   60

FRANK
To look upon your sorrows executes me
Before my execution.

WINIFRED   Let me pray you, sir.

FRANK
Thou much wronged woman, I must sigh for thee,
As he that's only loath to leave the world,
For that he leaves thee in it unprovided,
Unfriended; and for me to beg a pity   65
From any man to thee when I am gone,
Is more than I can hope; nor to say truth,
Have I deserved it. But there is payment

45–6 *All … you* Mother Sawyer's contrition and her death as a warning to others
  anticipates Frank's death (cf. 73–90) where both deliver the play's moral message, but her early and more abrasive remarks (33–5) complicate any easy judg-
  ment of her

58 *O Frank, Frank!* (italics Q)

Belongs to goodness from the great exchequer 70
Above; it will not fail thee, Winifred;
Be that thy comfort.
OLD THORNEY   Let it be thine too,
Untimely-lost young man.
FRANK   He is not lost,
Who bears his peace within him. Had I spun 75
My web of life out at full length, and dreamed
Away my many years in lusts, in surfeits,
Murders of reputations, gallant sins
Commended or approved; then though I had
Died easily, as great and rich men do, 80
Upon my own bed, not compelled by justice,
You might have mourned for me indeed; my miseries
Had been as everlasting, as remedyless.
But now the law hath not arraigned, condemned
With greater rigour my unhappy fact, 85
Than I myself have every little sin
My memory can reckon from my childhood.
A court hath been kept here, where I am found
Guilty; the difference is, my impartial judge
Is much more gracious than my faults
Are monstrous to be named; yet they are monstrous. 90
OLD THORNEY
Here's comfort in this penitence.
WINIFRED   It speaks
How truly you are reconciled, and quickens
My dying comfort, that was near expiring
With my last breath. Now this repentance makes thee
As white as innocence; and my first sin with thee, 95
Since which I knew none like it, by my sorrow,
Is clearly cancelled. Might our souls together
Climb to the height of their eternity,
And there enjoy what earth denied us, happiness.
But since I must survive, and be the monument 100
Of thy loved memory, I will preserve it

---

70 *great exchequer* dispensation in heaven (the great exchequer is God)

77 *Murders* (sig. I2v; Q misnumbers p. 60 as p. 43)

84 *fact* crime, evil; this is a common term in contemporary pamphlets for alleged acts of witchcraft

87 *court* Presumably the quarter sessions of assizes which judged all major criminal cases bound over to it by the local court; the playwrights have collapsed the time to parallel the judgement on Mother Sawyer, which was routine and swift, with that of Frank, which would have been referred

With a religious care, and pay thy ashes
A widow's duty, calling that end best,
Which, though it stain the name, makes the soul blest.

FRANK

Give me thy hand, poor woman; do not weep.   105

[*They hold hands*]

Farewell. Thou dost forgive me?

WINIFRED   'Tis my part
To use that language.

FRANK   Oh that my example
Might teach the world hereafter what a curse
Hangs on their heads, who rather choose to marry
A goodly portion, than a dower of virtues!   110
Are you there, gentlemen? There is not one
Amongst you whom I have not wronged: you most;
I robbed you of a daughter; but she is
In heaven; and I must suffer for it willingly.

OLD CARTER

Ay, ay, she's in heaven, and I am glad to see thee so well   115
prepared to follow her. I forgive thee with all my heart; if
thou hadst not had ill counsel, thou wouldst not have done
as thou didst. The more shame for them.

SOMERTON

Spare your excuse to me, I do conceive
What you would speak. I would you could as easily   120
Make satisfaction to the law, as to my wrongs.
I am sorry for you.

WARBECK   And so am I.
And heartily forgive you.

KATHERINE   I will pray for you,
For her sake, who I am sure, did love you dearly.

SIR ARTHUR

Let us part friendly too. I am ashamed   125
Of my part in thy wrongs.

FRANK   You are all merciful,
And send me to my grave in peace. Sir Arthur,
Heavens send you a new heart. [*Turns to* OLD THORNEY]
    Lastly to you, sir;
And though I have deserved not to be called

---

115 *Ay, ay* (sig. I3; Q misnumbers p. 61 as p. 44); Q prints this speech as poetry

Your son, yet give me leave upon my knees, 130
To beg a blessing.

[FRANK *kneels*]

OLD THORNEY   Take it. Let me wet
Thy cheeks with the last tears my griefs have left me.
O Frank, Frank, Frank!
FRANK   Let me beseech you, gentlemen,
To comfort my old father, keep him with ye;
Love this distressed widow; and as often 135
As you remember what a graceless man
I was, remember likewise that these are
Both free, both worthy of a better fate,
Than such a son or husband as I have been.
All help me with your prayers. On, on, 'tis just 140
That law should purge the guilt of blood and lust.

Exit [*with* OFFICERS]

OLD CARTER
Go thy ways. I did not think to have shed one tear for thee,
but thou hast made me water my plants spite of my heart.
Master Thorney, cheer up, man; whilst I can stand by you,
you shall not want help to keep you from falling. We have 145
lost our children both on's the wrong way, but we cannot
help it. Better or worse, 'tis now as 'tis.

OLD THORNEY
I thank you sir; you are more kind than I
Have cause to hope or look for.

OLD CARTER   150
Master Somerton, is Kate yours or no?

SOMERTON
We are agreed.
KATHERINE   And, but my faith is passed,
I should fear to be married, husbands are
So cruelly unkind. Excuse me that
I am thus troubled.
SOMERTON   Thou shalt have no cause.

JUSTICE   155
Take comfort, Mistress Winifred. Sir Arthur,
For his abuse to you, and to your husband,

---

133 *O ... Frank!* (italics Q)
143 *water my plants* weep
146 *on's* of us
155–8 *Take ... marks* (Q assigns this speech to [Old] Cart[er])

539

Is by the bench enjoined to pay you down
A thousand marks.

SIR ARTHUR   Which I will soon discharge.

WINIFRED

Sir, 'tis too great a sum to be employed
Upon my funeral.   160

OLD CARTER

Come, come, if ill luck had served, Sir Arthur, and every
man had his due, somebody might have tottered ere this,
without paying fines. Like it as you list. Come to me,
Winifred, shalt be welcome. Make much of her, Kate, I
charge you. I do not think but she's a good wench, and hath   165
had wrong as well as we. So let's every man home to
Edmonton with heavy hearts, yet as merry as we can,
though not as we would.

JUSTICE

Join friends in sorrow; make of all the best.
Harms past may be lamented, not redressed.   170

Exeunt

EPILOGUE

WINIFRED

I am a widow still, and must not sort
A second choice, without a good report;

158 *marks* coins worth 13s.4d. each, or two-thirds of a pound sterling; this fine is
comparatively a very large one
soon discharge Sir Arthur's ready willingness to pay, and his ability next to
Mother Sawyer's poverty and Old Thorney's potential bankruptcy, pointedly
and ruefully displays the privilege of class and underscores Frank's mixture of
guilt (for murdering Susan) and innocence (of Sir Arthur's manipulation of him)

159 *too great a sum* Winifred's line confirms the play's concern with class distinctions as permanent as well as privileged, and as unassociated with morality and
intention

162 *tottered* swinging, as in being hanged

163 *Like ... list* whether you like it or not
Come to me Old Carter's invitation further condemns Sir Arthur

166–70 *So ... redressed* The troubling and unsettled ending of the play is not so
much a structural weakness as a fairly common convention for tragicomedy and
here a true reflection as well of the troubling and complicated characters and
social situations as yet not fully resolved

1 *sort* make

Which though some widows find, and few deserve,
Yet I dare not presume, but will not swerve
From modest hopes. All noble tongues are free; 5
The gentle may speak one kind word for me.

PHEN.

FINIS

7 *PHEN*. Ezekiel Fenn, the actor, identified by Bentley (II, 433) as a boy born in the parish of St Martin in the Fields in 1620. He played Sophonisba in Nabbes' *Hannibal and Scipio*, presented at the Cockpit in Drury Lane in 1635 by Queen Henrietta's Company, as well as Winifred in this play. Henry Glapthorne's *Poems* (1639) has a 'Prologue' written 'For *Ezekial Fen* at his first Acting a Man's Part'

NOTES ON THE TEXTS

A WOMAN KILLED WITH KINDNESS

There are two early authoritative editions of this play. One is the quarto of 1607, the other the quarto of 1617, which describes itself on the title-page as the 'third Edition'. There are good reasons for assuming that the 1607 quarto is in fact the first edition of the play, and no reasons at all for challenging the statement that the 1617 quarto is the third edition. It therefore appears that a second edition was produced sometime between 1607 and 1617, but is now no longer extant. However, this missing edition may have a bearing upon the relationship between Q1 (1607) and Q3 (1617) and their respective claims to textual authority.[1]

The First Quarto exists in a unique copy now in the British Library. The title-page reads:

> A / WOMAN / KILDE / with Kindneffe. / *Written by Tho: Heywood.* / [device: McKerrow 355] / LONDON / Printed by William Iaggard dwelling in Barbican, and / are to be fold in Paules Church-yard. / by Iohn Hodgets. 1607.

It is gathered A–H^4 [–A1] and consists of 31 unnumbered leaves, having the title on A2 recto, the Prologue on A3 recto, and the text beginning on A4 recto.

It is also certain that the copy for Q1 was authorial manuscript rather than theatrical prompt book. There are a number of reasons for this view. In the first place, the 1607 quarto reveals some uncertainty about the name of Sir Charles's sister. When she first appears she is 'Iane' (Scene III) before Heywood settles for 'Susan' (with a vestigal 'Iane' in Scene XIV). There are also the imprecise stage directions referring to '*3. or 4. seruingmen*' (Scene VIII), '*countrie Wenches, and two or three Musitians*' (Scene II), or the entry of an unspecified number of '*Seruingmen*' (twice in Scene XII). There is some confusion over the number of persons killed in the quarrel scene between Sir Charles and Sir Francis. The stage direction indicates that '*one of Sir Francis his huntsmen*' is killed, but Charles is immediately repentant and wishes to 'breathe in them new life, whom I have slain'. He is discovered by his sister 'among the dead' and taken by the Sheriff to answer for the lives 'of these dead men'. Vagueness and indecision of this kind we would expect to find only in copy very close to authorial foul papers; it would certainly not be tolerated in any

---

1   The fullest analysis of the play's printing history is given by K. M. Sturgess, 'The Early Quartos of Heywood's *A woman killed with kindness*', in *The Library* (5th series) xxv (1979), pp. 93–104.

theatrical manuscript. It is also reasonable to expect that any reprinted edition of the play would have made some attempt to eliminate the inconsistencies at least, and for this reason it seems likely that the quarto of 1607 is indeed the First Edition, even though the absence of any entry in the Stationers' Register makes the dating of the first publication less than absolutely sure.

There are, moreover, indications that the spelling and punctuation of the 1607 quarto correspond with Heywood's in the manuscript of *The Captives* and *Callisto*.[2] Sturgess suggests that we can see characters develop in Heywood's foul papers, citing the example of Spiggot, emerging from the Butler of earlier scenes as late as Scene XII. Or Sisly, who has no independent existence in the stage entry for Scene II (being merely one of the 'Wenches'), but who becomes a significant minor character as Anne's serving-maid. There is much to confirm the belief that authorial foul papers provided the copy for Q1.

The second authoritative edition extant is the quarto of 1617 which describes itself on the title-page as the 'Third edition'. The transcription is as follows:

A / WOMAN / KILDE / with Kindneſſe / *As it hath beene oftentimes Acted by / the Queenes Maiest. Seruants. / Written by* THO. HEYWOOD. / The Third Edition. / [device: McKerrow 283) / LONDON, / Printed by Iſaac Iaggard, 1617.

The book consists of 36 leaves, A–I[4], regularly signed $3, and having the title-page on A1 recto, the Prologue on A2 recto, and the Text from A3 recto to I4 recto, with an Epilogue on the verso of the final leaf. No press variants have been reported, nor have I found any. One bibliographical fact of interest to emerge, however, is that the compositor who appears single-handedly to have set this edition was almost certainly Jaggard's compositor B, whose working practices have been pretty well investigated and recorded in view of his influence upon the printing of Shakespeare's texts in particular.[3]

The central issue of Q3's relationship to Q1 turns upon the question of the copy text for the 1617 quarto. The two scholars who have hitherto given closest scrutiny to the early quartos, R. W. Van Fossen and K. M. Sturgess, reach quite different conclusions. Van Fossen frankly admitted

---

2 See K. Palmer's review of Van Fossen's edition in *M.L.R.* lvii (1962), p. 415.
3 Sturgess cites D. F. MacKenzie, 'Compositor B's role in *The Merchant of Venice*, Q2 (1619)', *SB* xii (1959), pp. 75–90. Also Alice Walker, *Textual Problems in the First Folio* (1953) and 'Compositor Determination and Other Problems in Shakespearean Texts'; *SB* vii (1955), pp. 3–15; and W. S. Kable, 'Compositor B, the Pavier quartos and copy spellings', *SB* (1968), pp. 129–61.

that he was unable to determine the relationship between the two editions, but was at least prepared to state that there were no bibliographical links between them that were capable of demonstration. He argued for the independent authority of Q3 on the grounds of a series of distinctions between the two editions, each of which has been carefully contraverted by Sturgess: (a) Q3 is (unusually for a reprint) longer than Q1. (Attributable almost entirely, says Sturgess, to a change in type-size.) (b) Q3's spellings and speech-heads do not show the influence of Q1. (Sturgess reminds us that it is precisely compositor B's marked spelling and typographical habits that identify his work.) (c) Van Fossen claims that there are marked differences in lineation between the two quartos. (Sturgess again appeals to B's known practice.) (d) There are discrepancies between the two in the marking of exits. (Sturgess explains these discrepancies as resulting from *ad hoc* editing by the compositor, accounting in this way for all but one omission in Q3.) Van Fossen's conclusion that Q1 and Q3 derive independently from manuscript or manuscripts is clearly shaken by Sturgess's explanations. The latter goes on to argue that the copy for Q3 was not a revised manuscript, but probably a copy of Q2 (in its turn derived bibliographically from Q1), which had at some stage in its descent been subject to revision.

Having disarmed Van Fossen's argument for the independence of the two extant editions, Sturgess presents his evidence for the presence of Q1-derived copy in Q3. The 'strong bibliographical link' and 'short line of descent' are supported by the following arguments: (a) An explanation of textual confusion in Scene III, lines 25–31, and a similar textual misreading in Scene VII, line 40. (b) The omission of a speech-head in both quartos at Scene III, line 57. (c) Indications that the substitution of lowercase for upper-case 'w' in Q1 led to a similar substitution in Q3. (d) The suggestion that lineation differences show B's 'characteristically cavalier treatment of copy-text', assuming his copy to have been Q1.

A number of these arguments deserve closer attention. Sturgess gives no reference for the third point and it is therefore hard to take it seriously. There are many instances of lower-case for upper-case 'w' in Q3, in italic at least. The instance that he mentions (Scene XI, line 45) is plausibly explained by the influence of Q1, through there is already some evidence of desperation on the part of the compositor to find cap. W at this stage of his setting.

Sturgess's second argument regarding the omission of the speech-heading for Susan/Iane does *not* stand up to examination. The omission of the character's name when she speaks immediately following her entry is, as he says, unique in Q1. Unfortunately, it is not so rare in Q3. Sturgess claims that there is but one other instance (an exception which he explains away as the consequence of the compositor having already a full measure). I have counted five instances in Q3 of an entry followed by a speech unsignalled by a speech-head. The arrangement is far from uncommon in Q3 when a character enters alone and immediately speaks. Its bibliographical significance is minimal (see Susan in Scene III; Shafton in Scene V; Wendoll in Scene VI; Shafton in Scene VII; and Wendoll in Scene XVI).

If we turn now to the first argument in favour of linking Q1 to Q3 bibliographically, we enter the area of textual criticism. On two occasions Q1, according to Sturgess, was responsible for misreadings which Q3 unsuccessfully attempted to correct, demonstrating its dependence by its failures. The first of these two instances occurs in the argument between Sir Francis and Sir Charles in Scene III. In Q1 two successive speeches are assigned to Sir Francis, quite erroneously. The correction proposed by Q3 gives the second speech to Charles, alters the next two speech ascriptions accordingly before suppressing one speech-head and running two speeches from Q1 together in order to restore the pattern of speakers as in the 1607 quarto. Sturgess maintains that in so doing the compositor of Q3 (or Q2) misunderstood the nature of the mistake, which was a simple omission of the speech-heading from the final line of what appears as the first of the successive speeches attributed to Sir Francis. The alternatives may be clarified as follows:

1607	1617	Sturg	Text
Fran.	*Fran.*	*Fran.*	. . . she did discomfit Some of her feathers, but she brake away!
		Char.	Come, come, your hawk is but a rifler.
Fran.	*Char.*	*Fran.*	How?
Char.	*Fran.*	*Char.*	Ay, and you dogs are trindle-tails and curs.
Fran.	*Char.*	*Fran.*	You stir my blood!
Char.		*Char.*	You keep not one good hound in all your kennel, Nor one good hawk upon your perch.

Sturgess's emendation is attractive not least because it is economical in its explanation of the original fault. It is also made apparently more plausible by the observation that the line from which Q1 dropped the speech-head ('Come, come, your hawk is but a rifler') begins a new page (B3 recto) in Q1. In effect, this means that the error of the dropped speech head occurred not once but twice, since the catchword reads 'Come,' when we would expect '*Char.*' The likelihood of the compositor making an error with a word which he had to set twice is presumably somewhat diminished. But the question also arises of the effect upon the text of any such change as Sturgess proposes. Sturgess himself allows that Sir Charles's guilt is increased by his emendation, while the changes in the 1617 text 'obscure' that guilt. The line in question is either an insulting riposte to Sir Francis's rationalisation of the match, or it is the culmination of that same defence. Of the two characters, it is Sir Francis who subsequently reveals himself as the more cruel and malicious, and (by contrast) Sir Charles who enjoys our sympathies. The rash insults directed against hawks and hounds are perhaps for that reason more likely to come from Francis. He has also in the circumstances more cause to be heated than Charles. It may also be thought doubtful that a man whose language has risen to the choler of 'rifler' and 'trindle-tails and curs' would then descend to the plainness of 'You keep not one good hound in all your kennel, / Nor one good hawk upon your perch.' In this respect it must be said that the Q3 emended text makes quite as much sense as that proposed by Sturgess, and offers no real inconsistencies, in spite of inferring rather more confusion in the papers which provided copy-text for Q1. I have therefore retained the Q3 reading in the present text.

The second instance of textual 'corruption' concerns a word in Scene VII, line 40, when Sir Charles is describing the hardship he and his sister have endured to retain their land.

> This palm you see
> Labour hath glowed within; her silver brow,
> That never tasted a rough winter's blast
> Without a mask or fan, doth with a grace
> Defy cold winter and his storms outface. (VII.39–43)

The Q1 text reads 'Labor hath gloud within', which becomes 'Labour hath glow'd within' in Q3, ignoring the possibility that Q1 intended 'gloved'. Sturgess proposes 'galled' and cites another Heywoodian portrait of Labour 'with galled hands'.[4] Heywood's handwriting was, of course, notoriously bad,[5] but once again there is nothing inconsistent about the quarto readings, and I have favoured a conservative reading of this line, adopting Q3's 'glowed'. In other words, I have not accepted that Q1 was a misreading (merely a spelling variant) nor that Q3 offers an erroneous

---

4 *Pleasant Dialogues and Dramas* (1637) contains the following lines in the story of Timon: 'O wondrous! Poverty by him fast stands / And the rough fellow Labor, with gallid hands.' (Cited by Sturgess, p. 102.)

5 See W. W. Greg's *English Literary Autographs 1550-1650* (1925) and *Dramatic Documents from the Elizabethan Playhouses* (1931), and the Malone Society reprint of *The Captives* (1953) for specimens.

emendation. Consequently, the proof of further linkage between Q1 and Q3 is not here established.

Having consistently challenged the basis of Sturgess's case for Q3's dependence on Q1, we are brought to a position which seems barely an advance upon Van Fossen's disavowal. The strength of Sturgess's confidence that Q3 depended upon the earlier printed edition seems misplaced, although he has certainly established it as something more than a possibility. The text for this edition is based upon Q1 as the only clearly authoritative edition. Very few of the variants supplied by Q3 are not attributable to compositorial intervention. Instances of revision that require more than an alert compositor would normally supply include the correction of inconsistency over Susan/Jane and at Scene XVII, line 54 the change from 'maister Frankford' to 'brother Acton'. It may be that such faults in Q1 were sufficiently serious to merit the author's attention in preparing copy for the second or third editions. The case in favour of the dependence of Q3 on Q1 remains the stronger, and can easily accommodate a theory of authorial revision in these few instances.

BRIAN SCOBIE

THE TAMER TAMED

The Tamer Tamed survives in three early texts: the versions printed in the 1647 and 1679 folio editions of the works of Fletcher and his collaborators (hereafter F and F2), and a scribal manuscript probably prepared for a private patron, now owned by the Folger Shakespeare Library (MS J.b.3, hereafter MS).[6] F and F2 include two short scenes and some shorter sections omitted in MS, while MS retains some oaths that appear to have been censored in F and eleven short sections of text that may also have been censored.[7] F includes a prologue and epilogue which are not in MS, and there are also some differences in the stage directions which may indicate performance in different venues. F2 is based on F but includes a song in II.v omitted from both MS and F; it also attempts to restore some of the missing oaths. It is usually thought that F demonstrates the effects of Herbert's censorship, and that MS was copied out at an earlier date; Livingston goes so far as to argue that it 'probably represents the play as it was performed in 1611'.[8]

The majority of editions of The Tamer Tamed have been based on F, but with the incorporation of some material from MS; Daileader and Taylor, however, base their 2006 edition on MS, but incorporate some material from F. They also attempt to recreate some of the oaths that they assume to appear in a bowdlerised form in MS – their edition is, they declare, 'more "offensive" than any previous printed text of the play' (p. 5). In this way, editors attempt to recreate a version of a lost, uncensored text as it may originally have been intended by Fletcher and/or the company that first performed it.

This is a tendency that I have tried to resist in this edition, which is based on MS. Unlike Daileader and Taylor, I have not drawn on the folio texts unless material is clearly missing from MS or MS's reading is incomprehensible; such changes are indicated and discussed in notes, where alternative folio-only readings are also provided. Spelling and punctuation have been modernised throughout; entrance directions are given precisely where they stand in MS (F's alternative placings are detailed in the notes), and changes to lineation are also indicated in the notes. I have noted some of the scribal corrections in MS, but have not attempted to be comprehensive. Longer folio-only passages are printed in full in

---

6 For detailed accounts of the texts, and a facsimile of MS, see Livingston, Woman's Prize.
7 See Livingston, Woman's Prize, p. xv, and pp. xiv–xxv for a table of the differences that may be attributable to censorship.
8 'Herbert's Censorship', 215; see also Woman's Prize, pp. xx–xi.

Appendix 1 to the present text, while F's prologue and epilogue are presented alongside later theatrical material in Appendix 2.

LUCY MUNRO

THE DUCHESS OF MALFI

This New Mermaid critical edition is based on a fresh analysis of the first quarto of 1623, the only authoritative edition; my copy-text is the British Museum copy of Q1, shelf-mark 644.f.72, collated with the principal subsequent editions. Q1 exists in one uncorrected and two corrected states, designated Q1a, Q1b and Q1c. The second corrected state is found only in sheet G, outer forme. Several press variants are clearly alterations not corrections; the indications are that the author made them and several other additions which are printed in the margins of Q1. Modernisation is according to the conventions of the New Mermaid series. The collation indicates all substantial emendations of the copy-text, variants which are not adopted but are of some interest, and changes in copy-text lineation. Where necessary there are textual notes in the Commentary. I have added stage directions (indicated by square brackets) wherever they are essential to provide a performable version of the text, and in the same spirit I have modernised punctuation, using as light a touch as possible. Single quotation marks are used for *sententiae*, as at II.iii.53–4.

Brown argued convincingly that Q1 was set by formes, not *seriatim*, and by two compositors; NCW (pp. 451–2) provide an analysis of punctuation patterns to further strengthen this hypothesis. The printers' copy, as Brown argued, was virtually certainly a scribal transcript by Ralph Crane – it has group entries for the characters at the head of each scene, very few and inadequate stage directions, and heavy punctuation. These features do not correspond to those in Q1 of Webster's *The White Devil* which almost certainly was set from Webster's manuscript, whereas they do correspond to Crane's practice as a professional scribe elsewhere. There are other characteristics in Q1 of *The Duchess of Malfi* which suggest Crane: the heavy use of parentheses and of a terminal colon especially in short dialogue lines, the habit of not beginning verse lines with a majuscule, the unusual use of the hyphen, the use of italic script for headings, songs, letters, titles and proper nouns. Crane intervened in many ways when transcribing dramatic texts, and T. H. Howard-Hill, *Ralph Crane and Some Shakespeare First Folio Comedies* (1972), concludes that Crane's habits seriously affect the authority of texts printed from his transcripts. The absence of profanities in the play, first noted by G. P. V. Akrigg, contrasts with *The White Devil* which has twenty-four uses of 'God' against *The Duchess of Malfi*'s none. A Jacobean statute (3 Jac. I) forbade profanities, so it is probable the playhouse manuscript (the copy Crane probably used in making his transcript) was censored, substituting 'Heaven' for 'God' – as at III.v.79–80.

BRIAN GIBBONS

THE WITCH OF EDMONTON

The Stationers' Register records that Edward Blackmore 'Entred for his Copie (under ye hand of Mr Thomason Warden) a booke called The Witch of Edmonton a Tragicomedy by Will: Rowley &c' on 21 May 1658, some 37 years after the source pamphlet of Henry Goodcole and the first recorded performances. The only extant edition of the play is a quarto of that year, which seems to have derived from a revival of the play in the 1630s since it includes the names of actors then belonging to Queen Henrietta Maria's Men – Theophilus Bird and Ezekiel Fenn as well as (presumably) Hamluc, Poldavis and W. Mago. Bentley (I, 251–2; II, 378; III, 271–2) conjectures a MS prompt copy of the revived production; Bowers (III, 483–6) argues for an autograph copy of 'a rather literal scribal copy preliminary to the prompt book'. But the quarto, with its irregular and often omitted stage directions, would seem at least one step removed from prompt-copy. That it is closely related to a theatrical script, however, is clear enough from the punctuation alone: unlike pointing even for its own time, the play reads phrasally and dramatically. The rather heavy pointing in places, in fact, would direct actors to slow down certain scenes, often those involving the actions with the highest dramatic pitch.

The quarto is often badly set and remains uncorrected in all the copies examined, arguing only one typesetting with no proof corrections: four pages are clearly misnumbered in Act V; act and scene divisions are inconsistent; prose and poetry are mixed (so that Mother Sawyer, for example, speaks in both); there are varying speech prefixes ('Young Banks' also appears as 'Clown'; 'Young Thorney' also appears as 'Frank'); and a number of words and even lines have become loose, with the Huntington Library copy, having the most worn type and the loosest lines, representing a late stage of the print-run.

For this edition, all eight known copies of the play were collated: British Library 644.c.17 (which was used as copy-text); British Library C.12. f.p.(5); Malone 238 at the Bodleian Library; D (Dyce) 25.C.70 at the Victoria and Albert; STR. 117/18 (Stoner Bequest) at Eton College; the copy at the Huntington Library; Harvard *14433.26.13* at the Houghton Library; and Yale 162 at the Elizabethan Club (which notes on the fly leaf, 'Extremely rare, & most interesting play'). Two other copies are actually ghosts: the copy catalogued at the Folger Shakespeare Library is a facsimile of the Huntington Library copy; the copy listed for the Furness Library at the University of Pennsylvania is a photostat of the Harvard copy. The quarto collates A^2; $B–I^4$: A1, title-page; A1v, blank; A2, actors names; A2v, distich and prologue; B1–13v, text; I4, Epilogue; I4v, blank.

Textual editing is an act of mediation; all texts are essentially provisional. For the present text, all irregular speech prefixes, stage directions and typesetting errors (noted in the text) have been regularised, and abbreviations have been spelled out. In keeping with the principles of this series, words have been modernised (including Winnifride as Winifred) and italics and capitalisations removed. The pointing, however, is another matter: unlike other modern texts of this play which punctuate by twentieth-century practices, it seems clear that this is a theatrical text in which the punctuation often controls interpretation and delivery. Thus some speeches printed as questions in other editions are here restored to declarations; speeches are more often broken into phrases. For the most part, the signs for longer pauses in Stuart England (: and .) have both been treated as (.) to distinguish their time of pausing from (,) and (;). The intention has been to bring the text as close to its original performances as extant evidence will allow. References for proverbs are to Morris Palmer Tilley, *A Dictionary of Proverbs in England in the Sixteenth and Seventeenth Centuries* (Ann Arbor, 1950).

ARTHUR KINNEY

 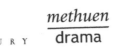